On Core Mathematics

Geometry

 HOUGHTON MIFFLIN HARCOURT

Cover photo: water droplet/leaf   Dimitri Vervitsiotis/Getty Images

Printed in the U.S.A.

ISBN 978-0-547-61724-4

 7 8 9 10 0982 20 19 18 17 16 15 14

4500468077   C D E F G

Contents

▶ Unit 6 Trigonometry

▶ Unit 7 Circles

▶ Unit 10 Three-Dimensional Figures and Volume

▶ Unit 11 Probability

Learning the Common Core State Standards

Has your state adopted the Common Core standards? If so, then students will be learning both mathematical content standards and the mathematical practice standards that underlie them. The supplementary material found in *On Core Mathematics Geometry* will help students succeed with both.

Here are some of the special features you'll find in *On Core Mathematics Geometry*.

INTERACTIVE LESSONS

Students actively participate in every aspect of a lesson. They read the mathematical concepts in an Engage, carry out an activity in an Explore, complete the solution of an Example, and demonstrate reasoning in a Proof. This interactivity promotes a deeper understanding of the mathematics.

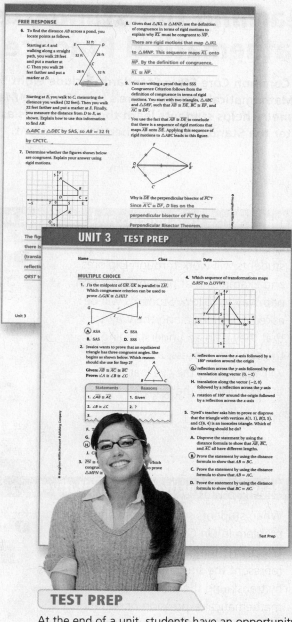

REFLECTIVE LEARNING

Students learn to be reflective thinkers through the follow-up questions after each Engage, Explore, Example, and Proof in a lesson. The Reflect questions challenge students to really think about the mathematics they have just encountered and to share their understanding with the class.

TEST PREP

At the end of a unit, students have an opportunity to practice the material in multiple choice and free response formats used on standardized tests.

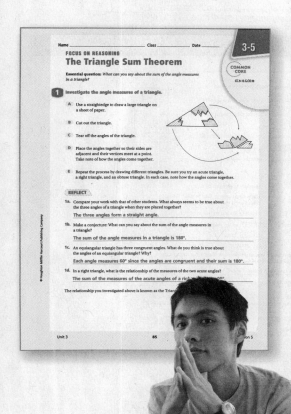

FOCUS ON REASONING

Special lessons focus on reasoning. They provide opportunities for students to explore concepts using inductive reasoning, to make conjectures, and to prove their conjectures using deductive reasoning.

Learning the Standards for Mathematical Practice

The Common Core State Standards include eight Standards for Mathematical Practice. Here's how *On Core Mathematics Geometry* helps students learn those standards as they master the Standards for Mathematical Content.

① Make sense of problems and persevere in solving them.

In *On Core Mathematics Geometry*, students will work through Explores and Examples that present a solution pathway to follow. Students will be asked questions along the way so that they gain an understanding of the solution process, and then they will apply what they've learned in the Practice for the lesson.

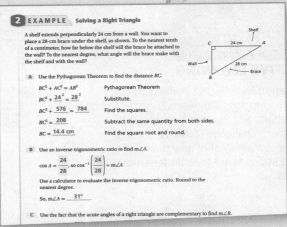

2 EXAMPLE Solving a Right Triangle

A shelf extends perpendicularly 24 cm from a wall. You want to place a 28-cm brace under the shelf, as shown. To the nearest tenth of a centimeter, how far below the shelf will the brace be attached to the wall? To the nearest degree, what angle will the brace make with the shelf and with the wall?

A Use the Pythagorean Theorem to find the distance BC.

$$BC^2 + AC^2 = AB^2$$ Pythagorean Theorem
$$BC^2 + \underline{24}^2 = \underline{28}^2$$ Substitute.
$$BC^2 + \underline{576} = \underline{784}$$ Find the squares.
$$BC^2 = \underline{208}$$ Subtract the same quantity from both sides.
$$BC \approx \underline{14.4 \text{ cm}}$$ Find the square root and round.

B Use an inverse trigonometric ratio to find m$\angle A$.

$$\cos A = \frac{24}{28}, \text{ so } \cos^{-1}\left(\frac{24}{28}\right) = m\angle A$$

Use a calculator to evaluate the inverse trigonometric ratio. Round to the nearest degree.

So, m$\angle A \approx \underline{31°}$.

C Use the fact that the acute angles of a right triangle are complementary to find m$\angle B$.

② Reason abstractly and quantitatively.

When students solve a real-world problem in *On Core Mathematics Geometry*, they will learn to represent the situation symbolically by translating the problem into a mathematical expression or equation. Students will use these mathematical models to solve the problem and then state the answer in terms of the problem context. Students will reflect on the solution process in order to check their answers for reasonableness and to draw conclusions.

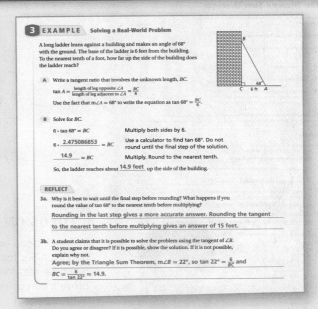

3 EXAMPLE Solving a Real-World Problem

A long ladder leans against a building and makes an angle of 68° with the ground. The base of the ladder is 6 feet from the building. To the nearest tenth of a foot, how far up the side of the building does the ladder reach?

A Write a tangent ratio that involves the unknown length, BC.

$$\tan A = \frac{\text{length of leg opposite } \angle A}{\text{length of leg adjacent to } \angle A} = \frac{BC}{6}$$

Use the fact that m$\angle A = 68°$ to write the equation as $\tan 68° = \frac{BC}{6}$.

B Solve for BC.

$$6 \cdot \tan 68° = BC$$ Multiply both sides by 6.
$$6 \cdot \underline{2.475086853} = BC$$ Use a calculator to find tan 68°. Do not round until the final step of the solution.
$$\underline{14.9} \approx BC$$ Multiply. Round to the nearest tenth.

So, the ladder reaches about $\underline{14.9 \text{ feet}}$ up the side of the building.

REFLECT

3a. Why is it best to wait until the final step before rounding? What happens if you round the value of tan 68° to the nearest tenth before multiplying?

Rounding in the last step gives a more accurate answer. Rounding the tangent

to the nearest tenth before multiplying gives an answer of 15 feet.

3b. A student claims that it is possible to solve the problem using the tangent of $\angle B$. Do you agree or disagree? If it is possible, show the solution. If it is not possible, explain why not.

Agree; by the Triangle Sum Theorem, m$\angle B = 22°$, so $\tan 22° = \frac{6}{BC}$ and

$BC = \frac{6}{\tan 22°} \approx 14.9$.

③ Construct viable arguments and critique the reasoning of others.

Throughout *On Core Mathematics Geometry*, students will be asked to make conjectures, construct mathematical arguments, explain their reasoning, and justify their conclusions. Reflect questions offer opportunities for cooperative learning and class discussion. Students will have additional opportunities to critique reasoning in Error Analysis problems.

REFLECT

2a. Given that $\triangle PQR \cong \triangle STU$, $PQ = 2.7$ ft, and $PR = 3.4$ ft, is it possible to determine the length of $\overline{TU}$? If so, find the length. If not, explain why not.

No; the side of $\triangle PQR$ that corresponds to $\overline{TU}$ is $\overline{QR}$, and the length of this side is not known.

2b. A student claims that any two congruent triangles must have the same perimeter. Do you agree or disagree? Why?

Agree; since the corresponding sides are congruent, the sum of the side lengths (perimeter) must be the same for both triangles.

---

3. **Error Analysis** A student who is 72 inches tall wants to find the height of a flagpole. He measures the length of the flagpole's shadow and the length of his own shadow at the same time of day, as shown in his sketch below. Explain the error in the student's work.

> The triangles are similar by the AA Similarity Criterion, so corresponding sides are proportional.
> $\frac{x}{72} = \frac{48}{128}$
> $x = 72 \cdot \frac{48}{128}$, so $x = 27$ in.

72 in.   48 in.   x   128 in.

The proportion is incorrect because the ratios do not compare the triangles in the same order. It should be $\frac{x}{72} = \frac{128}{48}$ and $x = 192$ in.

4. A graphic designer wants to lay out a grid system for a brochure that is 15 cm

④ Model with mathematics.

On Core Mathematics Geometry presents problems in a variety of contexts such as science, business, and everyday life. Students will use models such as equations, tables, diagrams, and graphs to represent the information in the problem and to solve the problem. Then students will interpret their results in context.

④ EXAMPLE Solving a Real-World Problem

Police want to set up a camera to identify drivers who run the red light at point *C* on Mason Street. The camera must be mounted on a fence that intersects Mason Street at a 40° angle, as shown, and the camera should ideally be 120 feet from point *C*. What points along the fence, if any, are suitable locations for the camera?

170 ft

40° Fence — Mason Street — *A* *C*

A Because the side opposite ∠*A* is shorter than $\overline{AC}$, it may be possible to form two triangles. Use the Law of Sines to find possible values for m∠*B*.

$\frac{\sin A}{a} = \frac{\sin B}{b}$	Law of Sines
$\frac{\sin 40°}{120} = \frac{\sin B}{170}$	Substitute.
$\frac{170 \sin 40°}{120} = \sin B$	Solve for sin *B*.
$0.9106 \approx \sin B$	Use a calculator. Round to 4 decimal places.

170 ft   120 ft   Mason Street
40° *B* *B* Fence   *A* *C*

There is an acute angle and an obtuse angle that have this value as their sine. To find the acute angle, use a calculator and round to the nearest tenth.

$\sin^{-1}(0.9106) \approx 65.6°$

To find the obtuse angle, note that ∠1 and ∠2 have the same sine, $\frac{y}{\sqrt{x^2+y^2}}$, and notice that these angles are supplementary. Thus, the obtuse angle is supplementary to the acute angle you found above.

$(-x, y)$ $\sqrt{x^2+y^2}$ $\sqrt{x^2+y^2}$ (x, y)
y   2   1   y

So, m∠*B* $\approx$ 65.6° or 114.4°.

REFLECT

4a. How you can check your answers?
Possible answer: Use the calculated values to check that $\frac{\sin A}{a} = \frac{\sin B}{b} = \frac{\sin C}{c}$.

4b. Suppose the camera needs to be *at most* 120 feet from point *C*. In this case, where should the camera be mounted along the fence?
The camera should be mounted more than 80.7 ft from point *A* but less than 179.8 ft from point *A*.

4c. What is the minimum distance at which the camera can be located from point *C* if it is to be mounted on the fence? Explain your answer.
About 109.3 ft. The minimum distance occurs when ∠*B* is a right angle.
In this case, $\sin 40° = \frac{CB}{170}$, so $CB \approx 109.3$.

⑤ Use appropriate tools strategically.

Students will use a variety of tools in *On Core Mathematics Geometry*, including manipulatives, paper and pencil, and technology. Students might use manipulatives to develop concepts, paper and pencil to practice skills, and technology (such as graphing calculators, spreadsheets, or geometry software) to investigate more complicated mathematical ideas.

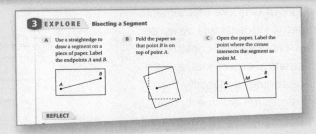

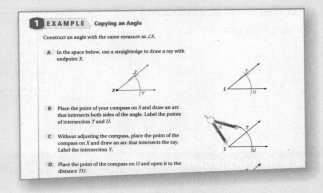

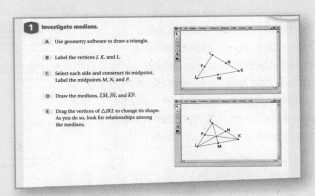

⑥ Attend to precision.

Precision refers not only to the correctness of arithmetic calculations, algebraic manipulations, and geometric reasoning but also to the proper use of mathematical language, symbols, and units to communicate mathematical ideas. Throughout *On Core Mathematics Geometry* students will demonstrate their skills in these areas when asked to calculate, describe, show, explain, prove, and predict.

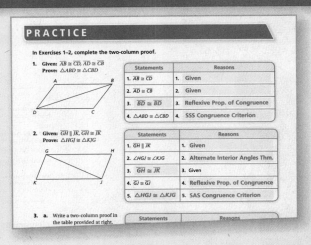

⑦ Look for and make use of structure.

In *On Core Mathematics Geometry*, students will look for patterns or regularity in mathematical structures such as expressions, equations, geometric figures, and graphs. Becoming familiar with underlying structures will help students build their understanding of more complicated mathematical ideas.

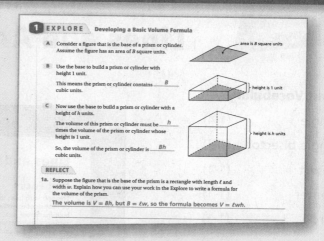

1 EXPLORE Developing a Basic Volume Formula

A. Consider a figure that is the base of a prism or cylinder. Assume the figure has an area of B square units.

area is B square units

B. Use the base to build a prism or cylinder with height 1 unit.

This means the prism or cylinder contains ____B____ cubic units.

height is 1 unit

C. Now use the base to build a prism or cylinder with a height of h units.

The volume of this prism or cylinder must be ____h____ times the volume of the prism or cylinder whose height is 1 unit.

So, the volume of the prism or cylinder is ____Bh____ cubic units.

height is h units

REFLECT

1a. Suppose the figure that is the base of the prism is a rectangle with length ℓ and width w. Explain how you can use your work in the Explore to write a formula for the volume of the prism.

The volume is $V = Bh$, but $B = \ell w$, so the formula becomes $V = \ell wh$.

⑧ Look for and express regularity in repeated reasoning.

In *On Core Mathematics Geometry*, students will have the opportunity to explore and reflect on mathematical processes in order to come up with general methods for performing calculations and solving problems.

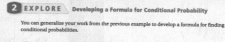

2 EXPLORE Developing a Formula for Conditional Probability

You can generalize your work from the previous example to develop a formula for finding conditional probabilities.

A. Recall how you calculated $P(B \mid A)$, the probability that a participant who took the medicine did not get a headache.

You found that $P(B \mid A) = \frac{48}{60}$.

Use the table shown here to help you write this quotient in terms of events A and B.

$P(B \mid A) = \dfrac{n(A \cap B)}{n(A)}$

		Event A		
		Took Medicine	No Medicine	TOTAL
Event B	Headache	12	15	27
	No Headache	$48 = n(A \cap B)$	25	$73 = n(B)$
	TOTAL	$60 = n(A)$	40	100

B. Now divide the numerator and denominator of the quotient by $n(S)$, the number of outcomes in the sample space. This converts the counts to probabilities.

$P(B \mid A) = \dfrac{n(A \cap B)}{n(A)} \Big/ {}_{n(S)}^{n(S)} = \dfrac{P(A \cap B)}{P(A)}$

REFLECT

2a. Write a formula for $P(A \mid B)$ in terms of $n(A \cap B)$ and $n(B)$.

$P(A \mid B) = \dfrac{n(A \cap B)}{n(B)}$

2b. Write a formula for $P(A \mid B)$ in terms of $P(A \cap B)$ and $P(B)$.

$P(A \mid B) = \dfrac{P(A \cap B)}{P(B)}$

UNIT 1

Lines and Angles

Unit Vocabulary

angle	(1-4)
angle bisector	(1-4)
bisect	(1-1)
center	(1-1)
circle	(1-1)
converse	(1-7)
distance along a line	(1-1)
endpoint	(1-1)
length	(1-1)
line	(1-1)
line segment	(1-1)
linear pair	(1-6)
midpoint	(1-1)
opposite rays	(1-6)
parallel lines	(1-5)
perpendicular bisector	(1-5)
perpendicular lines	(1-5)
plane	(1-1)
point	(1-1)
postulate	(1-6)
proof	(1-6)
radius	(1-1)
ray	(1-1)
sides	(1-4)
theorem	(1-6)
vertex	(1-4)

UNIT 1

UNIT 1

Lines and Angles

Unit Focus

This unit introduces the building blocks of geometry. You will learn how definitions of essential geometric terms, such as *line segment* and *angle*, are built from more basic terms. You will also learn to use a variety of tools and techniques to construct geometric figures. Finally, you will begin to write proofs that justify key relationships among lines and angles.

Unit at a Glance

COMMON CORE

Lesson		Standards for Mathematical Content
1-1	Basic Terms and Constructions	CC.9-12.G.CO.1, CC.9-12.G.CO.12
1-2	The Distance Formula	CC.9-12.G.GPE.4
1-3	The Midpoint Formula	CC.9-12.G.GPE.4
1-4	Angles	CC.9-12.G.CO.1, CC.9-12.G.CO.12
1-5	Parallel and Perpendicular Lines	CC.9-12.G.CO.1, CC.9-12.G.CO.12
1-6	Proofs About Line Segments and Angles	CC.9-12.G.CO.9
1-7	Proofs About Parallel and Perpendicular Lines	CC.9-12.G.CO.9
	Test Prep	

UNIT 1

© Houghton Mifflin Harcourt Publishing Company

Unpacking the Common Core State Standards

Use the table to help you understand the Standards for Mathematical Content that are taught in this unit. Refer to the lessons listed after each standard for exploration and practice.

COMMON CORE Standards for Mathematical Content	What It Means For You
CC.9-12.G.CO.1 Know precise definitions of angle, circle, perpendicular line, parallel line, and line segment, based on the undefined notions of point, line, distance along a line, and distance around a circular arc. Lessons 1-1, 1-4, 1-5	In geometry, it is important to understand the exact meaning of the terms you use. You will see how definitions of geometric terms are built upon the definitions of more basic terms and upon several terms that are understood without being formally defined.
CC.9-12.G.CO.9 Prove theorems about lines and angles. Lessons 1-6, 1-7	A proof is a logical argument that uses definitions, properties, and previously proven facts to demonstrate that a mathematical statement is true. You will learn to write proofs about relationships among angles formed by intersecting lines and among angles formed by a line that crosses parallel lines.
CC.9-12.G.CO.12 Make formal geometric constructions with a variety of tools and methods (compass and straightedge, string, reflective devices, paper folding, dynamic geometric software, etc.). Lessons 1-1, 1-4, 1-5	A construction is a method of drawing a geometric figure while adhering to certain rules. For example, using only a compass and an unmarked straightedge, you can copy and bisect segments and angles, and you can construct perpendicular and parallel lines.
CC.9-12.G.GPE.4 Use coordinates to prove simple geometric theorems algebraically. Lessons 1-2, 1-3	You will be introduced to two useful formulas in this unit: the distance formula and the midpoint formula. You will use these formulas here and in later units to write proofs about figures on a coordinate plane.

© Houghton Mifflin Harcourt Publishing Company

Unpacking the Common Core State Standards

This page lists and explains the Standards for Mathematical Content that are addressed in this unit. For information about the Standards for Mathematical Practice, which are integrated throughout the text, see Teacher Edition pages x–xiii.

Notes

_____

_____

_____

_____

_____

_____

_____

_____

_____

_____

Basic Terms and Constructions

Essential question: *What tools and methods can you use to copy a segment, bisect a segment, and construct a circle?*

COMMON CORE **Standards for Mathematical Content**

CC.9-12.G.CO.1 Know precise definitions of ... circle, ... and line segment, based on the undefined notions of point, line, distance along a line, ...

CC.9-12.G.CO.12 Make formal geometric constructions with a variety of tools and methods (compass and straightedge, string, reflective devices, paper folding, dynamic geometric software, etc.).

Vocabulary

point	midpoint
line	bisect
line segment	plane
ray	circle
endpoint	center
distance along a line	radius
length	

Prerequisites

None

Math Background

Students have worked with points, lines, angles, triangles, and other geometric figures since the elementary grades. This course revisits many ideas that may be familiar to students, but does so in a systematic way in order to build a deductive system. The first step in this process is to decide which terms will be assumed to be understood (undefined terms) and to give definitions of basic vocabulary words using these undefined terms.

INTRODUCE

You may wish to begin by having students look up an adjective in the dictionary, such as *furious*. The definition of *furious* may include the word *angry*. Have students look up the word *angry*. Its definition may include the word *enraged*. Have students look up the word *enraged*. Its definition may include the word *furious*. This sort of circular logic can help students understand that in mathematics it is not possible to define every word in terms of more basic words. Certain words must be taken as undefined terms.

TEACH

1 EXAMPLE

Questioning Strategies

- What are the endpoints of the segment? *P and Q*
- Is there a difference between $\overleftrightarrow{PQ}$ and $\overleftrightarrow{QP}$? No; they name the same line.
- Is there a difference between $\overrightarrow{PQ}$ and $\overrightarrow{QP}$? Yes; the rays have different endpoints and they continue forever in opposite directions.

EXTRA EXAMPLE

Use the figure to name each of the following in as many ways as possible.

A. a line line *RS*, line *SR*, $\overleftrightarrow{RS}$ $\overleftrightarrow{SR}$
B. a segment $\overline{RS}$, $\overline{SR}$

2 EXAMPLE

Questioning Strategies

- Does it matter if endpoint *C* is on the right side of the line segment that you construct? Why or why not? It does not matter, as long as $\overline{CD}$ has the same length as $\overline{AB}$.
- How can you check your construction with a ruler? Measure $\overline{AB}$ and $\overline{CD}$ to check that they have the same length.

EXTRA EXAMPLE

Construct a segment with the same length as $\overline{JK}$.

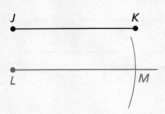

Name_____ Class_____ Date_____

1-1

Basic Terms and Constructions

COMMON CORE
CC.9-12.G.CO.1,
CC.9-12.G.CO.12

Essential question: *What tools and methods can you use to copy a segment, bisect a segment, and construct a circle?*

In geometry, the terms *point* and *line* are undefined terms. Although these terms do not have formal definitions, the table shows how mathematicians use these words.

Term	Geometric Figure	Ways to Reference the Figure
A **point** is a specific location. It has no dimension and is represented by a dot.	•P	Point P
A **line** is a connected straight path. It has no thickness and it continues forever in both directions.	A B ℓ	Line ℓ, line AB, line BA, $\overleftrightarrow{AB}$, or $\overleftrightarrow{BA}$

As shown in the following table, other terms can be defined using the above terms as building blocks.

Term	Geometric Figure	Ways to Reference the Figure
A **line segment** (or *segment*) is a portion of a line consisting of two points and all points between them.	C D	Line segment CD, line segment DC, $\overline{CD}$, or $\overline{DC}$
A **ray** is a portion of a line that starts at a point and continues forever in one direction.	G H	Ray GH or $\overrightarrow{GH}$

An **endpoint** is a point at either end of a line segment or the starting point of a ray. In the above examples, *C* and *D* are the endpoints of $\overline{CD}$, and point *G* is the endpoint of $\overrightarrow{GH}$.

1 EXAMPLE Naming Geometric Figures

Use the figure below in Parts A and B.

A One name for the line shown in the figure is $\overleftrightarrow{PQ}$.

Other names for $\overleftrightarrow{PQ}$ are line m, line PQ, line QP, and $\overleftrightarrow{QP}$.

B $\overline{PQ}$ is a line segment because it is a portion of a line consisting of two points and all the points between them.

Other names for $\overline{PQ}$ are line segment PQ, line segment QP, and $\overline{QP}$.

© Houghton Mifflin Harcourt Publishing Company

The **distance along a line** is undefined until a unit distance, such as 1 inch or 1 centimeter, is chosen. By placing a ruler alongside the line, you can associate a number from the ruler with each of two points on the line and then take the absolute value of the difference of the numbers to find the distance between the points. This distance is the **length** of the segment determined by the points.

In the figure, the length of $\overline{RS}$, written *RS*, is the distance between *R* and *S*. $RS = |4 - 1| = |3| = 3$ cm.

A *construction* is a geometric drawing that uses only a compass and a straightedge. You can construct a line segment whose length is equal to that of a given segment by using only these tools.

2 EXAMPLE Copying a Segment

Construct a segment with the same length as $\overline{AB}$.

A In the space below, draw a line segment that is longer than $\overline{AB}$. Choose an endpoint of the segment and label it *C*.

B Set the opening of your compass to the distance *AB*, as shown.

C Place the point of the compass on *C*. Make a small arc that intersects your line segment. Label the point *D* where the arc intersects the segment. $\overline{CD}$ is the required line segment.

REFLECT

2a. Why does this construction result in a line segment with the same length as $\overline{AB}$?

The compass opening matches the length of $\overline{AB}$ and reproduces this length on the new segment.

2b. What must you assume about the compass for this construction to work?

The size of the compass opening does not change when the compass is moved to a new location.

The **midpoint** of a line segment is the point that divides the segment into two segments that have the same length. The midpoint is said to **bisect** the segment. In the figure, the tick marks show that $PM = MQ$. Therefore, *M* is the midpoint of $\overline{PQ}$ and *M* bisects $\overline{PQ}$.

© Houghton Mifflin Harcourt Publishing Company

Notes

3 EXPLORE

Materials: straightedge, tracing paper (optional)

Questioning Strategies
• Why do you fold the paper so that point *B* is on top of point *A*? Matching the endpoints in this way ensures that the fold divides the segment in half.

Teaching Strategies
If possible, have students use tracing paper for this activity. This will make it easier to see the original segment once the paper is folded. Restaurant supply stores sell small squares of paper that are used to separate hamburger patties. These thin sheets of "patty paper" are inexpensive and work especially well in all paper-folding investigations.

4 EXAMPLE

Questioning Strategies
• Why do you set the opening of the compass to the distance *AB*? This ensures that the radius of the circle equals the length of the segment.

• How can you name the circle you constructed? Circle *C*

EXTRA EXAMPLE
Construct a circle with radius *MN*.

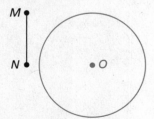

CLOSE

Essential Question
What tools and methods can you use to copy a segment, bisect a segment, and construct a circle? You can use a compass and straightedge to copy a segment, paper folding to bisect a segment, and a compass to construct a circle.

Summarize
Have students write step-by-step instructions for copying a segment, bisecting a segment, and constructing a circle with a given radius.

PRACTICE

Where skills are taught	Where skills are practiced
1 EXAMPLE	EXS. 1–3
2 EXAMPLE	EXS. 4, 7, 8
4 EXAMPLE	EX. 5

Exercise 6: Students use reasoning to consider what it would mean to construct the midpoint of a ray.

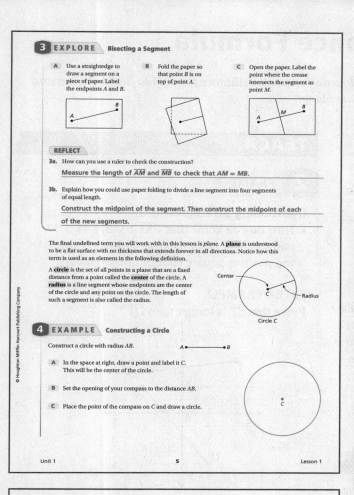

3 EXPLORE Bisecting a Segment

A Use a straightedge to draw a segment on a piece of paper. Label the endpoints *A* and *B*.

B Fold the paper so that point *B* is on top of point *A*.

C Open the paper. Label the point where the crease intersects the segment as point *M*.

REFLECT

3a. How can you use a ruler to check the construction?

Measure the length of $\overline{AM}$ and $\overline{MB}$ to check that $AM = MB$.

3b. Explain how you could use paper folding to divide a line segment into four segments of equal length.

Construct the midpoint of the segment. Then construct the midpoint of each

of the new segments.

The final undefined term you will work with in this lesson is *plane*. A **plane** is understood to be a flat surface with no thickness that extends forever in all directions. Notice how this term is used as an element in the following definition.

A **circle** is the set of all points in a plane that are a fixed distance from a point called the **center** of the circle. A **radius** is a line segment whose endpoints are the center of the circle and any point on the circle. The length of such a segment is also called the radius.

4 EXAMPLE Constructing a Circle

Construct a circle with radius *AB*.

A •————————• B

A In the space at right, draw a point and label it *C*. This will be the center of the circle.

B Set the opening of your compass to the distance *AB*.

C Place the point of the compass on *C* and draw a circle.

© Houghton Mifflin Harcourt Publishing Company

REFLECT

4a. How could you use a piece of string, a thumbtack, and a pencil to construct a circle with radius *AB*?

Tie a pencil to one end of the string. Place the string along $\overline{AB}$ so that the pencil

point is on *A*. Use a thumbtack to pin the string to the paper at *B*. Hold the string

taut and move the pencil around the thumbtack to draw a circle.

PRACTICE

Use the figure to name each of the following.

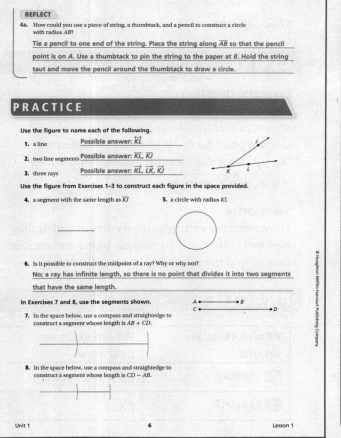

1. a line   Possible answer: $\overleftrightarrow{KL}$

2. two line segments   Possible answer: $\overline{KL}$, $\overline{KJ}$

3. three rays   Possible answer: $\overrightarrow{KL}$, $\overrightarrow{LK}$, $\overrightarrow{KJ}$

Use the figure from Exercises 1–3 to construct each figure in the space provided.

4. a segment with the same length as $\overline{KJ}$

5. a circle with radius *KL*

6. Is it possible to construct the midpoint of a ray? Why or why not?

No; a ray has infinite length, so there is no point that divides it into two segments

that have the same length.

In Exercises 7 and 8, use the segments shown.

A •———• B
C •——————• D

7. In the space below, use a compass and straightedge to construct a segment whose length is *AB* + *CD*.

8. In the space below, use a compass and straightedge to construct a segment whose length is *CD* − *AB*.

© Houghton Mifflin Harcourt Publishing Company

The Distance Formula

Essential question: *How do you use the distance formula to find distances and lengths in the coordinate plane?*

COMMON CORE Standards for Mathematical Content

CC.9-12.G.GPE.4 Use coordinates to prove simple geometric theorems algebraically.

Prerequisites

The Pythagorean Theorem, Grade 8

Math Background

The distance formula is a direct consequence of the Pythagorean Theorem. Note that the distance formula reduces to a simpler version in the case of points that lie on a horizontal or vertical line. For example, if two points lie on a vertical line, then they have the same x-coordinates and the distance between the points is $\sqrt{(x_2 - x_1)^2 + (y_2 - y_1)^2} = \sqrt{(y_2 - y_1)^2} = |y_2 - y_1|$. Similarly, the distance between two points that lie on a horizontal line is $|x_2 - x_1|$.

INTRODUCE

Begin by briefly reviewing the Pythagorean Theorem. Explain that the Pythagorean Theorem can be used to find the distance between two points in a coordinate plane.

1 EXPLORE

Questioning Strategies

• Can you apply the Pythagorean Theorem to any triangle? **No; it applies only to right triangles.**

• What does the Pythagorean Theorem say? **The sum of the squares of the lengths of the legs of a right triangle is equal to the square of the length of the hypotenuse.**

 MATHEMATICAL PRACTICE **Highlighting the Standards**

Example 2 and its follow-up question address Standard 7 (Look for and make sure of structure). In particular, as students work with the distance formula, help them to recognize that $(x_2 - x_1)^2 = (x_1 - x_2)^2$. This means that you can subtract the coordinates in either order when you use the formula.

TEACH

2 EXAMPLE

Questioning Strategies

• How do you know that $\sqrt{41} > \sqrt{37}$? **41 > 37, and the inequality is preserved when you take the positive square root of both numbers.**

EXTRA EXAMPLE

Prove that $\overline{ST}$ is longer than $\overline{UV}$.

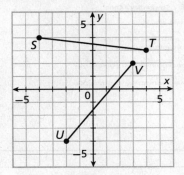

$ST = \sqrt{65}$, $UV = \sqrt{61}$ and $\sqrt{65} > \sqrt{61}$.

CLOSE

Essential Question

How do you use the distance formula to find distances and lengths in the coordinate plane?
Let one point be (x_1, y_1) and let the other be (x_2, y_2). Then the distance between the points is $\sqrt{(x_2 - x_1)^2 + (y_2 - y_1)^2}$.

Summarize

Have students write a journal entry in which they plot two points on a coordinate plane and explain how to find the distance between the points.

PRACTICE

Where skills are taught	Where skills are practiced
1 EXPLORE	EXS. 1–2
2 EXAMPLE	EX. 3

Name_____ Class_____ Date_____

1-2

COMMON CORE

CC.9-12.G.GPE.4

The Distance Formula

Essential question: *How do you use the distance formula to find distances and lengths in the coordinate plane?*

1 EXPLORE Finding a Distance in the Coordinate Plane

You can use the Pythagorean Theorem to help you find the distance between the points $A(2, 5)$ and $B(-4, -3)$.

A Plot the points A and B in the coordinate plane at right.

B Draw $\overline{AB}$.

C Draw a vertical line through point A and a horizontal line through point B to create a right triangle. Label the intersection of the vertical line and the horizontal line as point C.

D Each small grid square is 1 unit by 1 unit. Use this fact to find the lengths AC and BC.

$AC =$ ___8___ $BC =$ ___6___

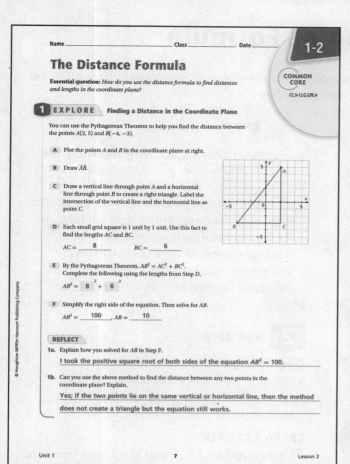

E By the Pythagorean Theorem, $AB^2 = AC^2 + BC^2$. Complete the following using the lengths from Step D.

$AB^2 = $ ___8___^{2} + ___6___^{2}

F Simplify the right side of the equation. Then solve for AB.

$AB^2 =$ ___100___ , $AB =$ ___10___

REFLECT

1a. Explain how you solved for AB in Step F.

I took the positive square root of both sides of the equation $AB^2 = 100$.

1b. Can you use the above method to find the distance between any two points in the coordinate plane? Explain.

Yes; if the two points lie on the same vertical or horizontal line, then the method does not create a triangle but the equation still works.

The process of using the Pythagorean Theorem can be generalized to give a formula for finding the distance between two points in the coordinate plane.

The Distance Formula

The distance between two points (x_1, y_1) and (x_2, y_2) in the coordinate plane is

$$\sqrt{(x_2 - x_1)^2 + (y_2 - y_1)^2}.$$

2 EXAMPLE Using the Distance Formula

Prove that $\overline{CD}$ is longer than $\overline{AB}$.

A Write the coordinates of A, B, C, and D.

$A(-2, 3)$, B ___(4, 2)___ , C ___(2, 0)___ , D ___(-3, -4)___

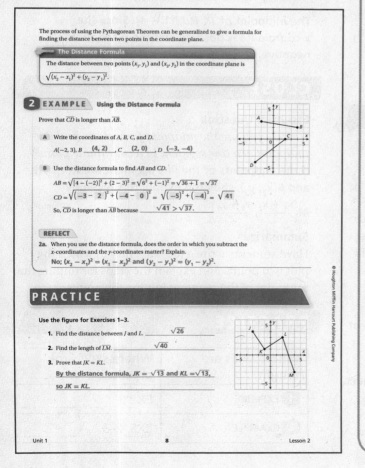

B Use the distance formula to find AB and CD.

$AB = \sqrt{[4 - (-2)]^2 + (2 - 3)^2} = \sqrt{6^2 + (-1)^2} = \sqrt{36 + 1} = \sqrt{37}$

$CD = \sqrt{(-3 - \ 2\ )^2 + (-4 - \ 0\ )^2} = \sqrt{(-5)^2 + (-4)^2} = \sqrt{41}$

So, $\overline{CD}$ is longer than $\overline{AB}$ because ___$\sqrt{41} > \sqrt{37}$___.

REFLECT

2a. When you use the distance formula, does the order in which you subtract the x-coordinates and the y-coordinates matter? Explain.

No; $(x_2 - x_1)^2 = (x_1 - x_2)^2$ and $(y_2 - y_1)^2 = (y_1 - y_2)^2$.

PRACTICE

Use the figure for Exercises 1–3.

1. Find the distance between J and L. ___$\sqrt{26}$___

2. Find the length of $\overline{LM}$. ___$\sqrt{40}$___

3. Prove that $JK = KL$.

By the distance formula, $JK = \sqrt{13}$ and $KL = \sqrt{13}$, so $JK = KL$.

The Midpoint Formula

Essential question: *How do you use the midpoint formula to find the midpoint of a line segment in a coordinate plane?*

COMMON CORE **Standards for Mathematical Content**

CC.9-12.G.GPE.4 Use coordinates to prove simple geometric theorems algebraically.

Prerequisites
None

Math Background
Along with the distance formula, the midpoint formula is one of the key tools of coordinate geometry. Students will write coordinate proofs later in this course and they will find that these two formulas, along with facts about the slopes of parallel and perpendicular lines (see Lessons 8-4 and 8-5), are enough to prove a wide range of theorems.

INTRODUCE

Remind students that they have already worked with midpoints in Lesson 1-1. In particular, students learned to use paper folding to find the midpoint of a segment. Explain that in this lesson, students will harness the power of coordinate geometry to find the exact coordinates of the midpoint of a given line segment.

TEACH

1 EXPLORE

Materials: ruler

Questioning Strategies
- In Step A, what would happen if you measured to the nearest centimeter instead of the nearest millimeter? **The location of the midpoint would not be as accurate.**

- How could you use paper folding to check the locations of the midpoints? **For each segment, fold the page so that the endpoints lie on top of each other. The crease intersects the segment at the midpoint.**

- How could you use the distance formula to check the locations of the midpoints? **Check that the distance from one endpoint to the midpoint equals the distance from the other endpoint to the midpoint.**

MATHEMATICAL PRACTICE — Highlighting the Standards

Standard 8 (Look for and express regularity in repeated reasoning) encourages students to look for general methods and shortcuts. The Explore gives students a chance to find midpoints by measuring, then discover the "shortcut" known as the midpoint formula.

2 EXAMPLE

Questioning Strategies
- What do you know about points that lie in Quadrant III? **The *x*- and *y*-coordinates are both negative.**

EXTRA EXAMPLE
$\overline{JK}$ has endpoints $J(5, 1)$ and $K(-3, -3)$. Prove that the midpoint M of $\overline{JK}$ lies in Quadrant IV.

The midpoint of $\overline{JK}$ is $M(1, -1)$. Since the *x*-coordinate is positive and the *y*-coordinate is negative, *M* lies in Quadrant IV.

CLOSE

Essential Question
How do you use the midpoint formula to find the midpoint of a line segment in a coordinate plane?
If the endpoints of the line segment are $A(x_1, y_1)$ and $B(x_2, y_2)$, then the midpoint is given by $M\left(\dfrac{x_1 + x_2}{2}, \dfrac{y_1 + y_2}{2}\right)$.

Summarize
Have students write a journal entry in which they plot two points and explain the steps for finding the midpoint of the segment joining the points.

PRACTICE

Where skills are taught	Where skills are practiced
1 EXPLORE	EX. 1
2 EXAMPLE	EXS. 2–3

Name_____ Class_____ Date_____

The Midpoint Formula

Essential question: *How do you use the midpoint formula to find the midpoint of a line segment in a coordinate plane?*

COMMON CORE
CC.9-12.G.GPE.4

1 EXPLORE Finding Midpoints of Line Segments

Follow the steps below for each of the given line segments.

A Use a ruler to measure the length of the line segment to the nearest millimeter.

B Find half the length of the segment. Measure this distance from one endpoint to locate the midpoint of the segment. Plot a point at the midpoint.

C Record the coordinates of the segment's endpoints and the coordinates of the segment's midpoint in the table below.

D In each row of the table, compare the *x*-coordinates of the endpoints to the *x*-coordinate of the midpoint. Then compare the *y*-coordinates of the endpoints to the *y*-coordinate of the midpoint. Look for patterns.

Endpoint	Endpoint Coordinates	Endpoint	Endpoint Coordinates	Midpoint Coordinates
A	(4, 4)	B	(2, 0)	(3, 2)
C	(3, 5)	D	(−5, 1)	(−1, 3)
E	(−2, −2)	F	(4, −4)	(1, −3)

REFLECT

1a. Make a conjecture: If you know the coordinates of the endpoints of a line segment, how can you find the coordinates of the midpoint?

The *x*-coordinate of the midpoint is the mean of the *x*-coordinates of the endpoints;

the *y*-coordinate of the midpoint is the mean of the *y*-coordinates of the endpoints.

1b. What are the coordinates of the midpoint of a line segment with endpoints at the origin and at the point (a, b)?

$\left(\frac{a}{2}, \frac{b}{2}\right)$

© Houghton Mifflin Harcourt Publishing Company

The patterns you observed can be generalized to give a formula for the coordinates of the midpoint of any line segment in the coordinate plane.

> **The Midpoint Formula**
>
> The midpoint M of $\overline{AB}$ with endpoints $A(x_1, y_1)$ and $B(x_2, y_2)$ is given by
>
> $M\left(\frac{x_1 + x_2}{2}, \frac{y_1 + y_2}{2}\right)$.

2 EXAMPLE Using the Midpoint Formula

$\overline{PQ}$ has endpoints $P(-4, 1)$ and $Q(2, -3)$. Prove that the midpoint M of $\overline{PQ}$ lies in Quadrant III.

A Use the given endpoints to identify x_1, x_2, y_1, and y_2.

$x_1 = -4, x_2 = 2, y_1 = \underline{\quad 1 \quad}, y_2 = \underline{\quad -3 \quad}$

B By the midpoint formula, the *x*-coordinate of M is $\frac{x_1 + x_2}{2} = \frac{-4 + 2}{2} = \frac{-2}{2} = -1$.

The *y*-coordinate of M is $\frac{y_1 + y_2}{2} = \frac{1 + -3}{2} = \frac{-2}{2} = -1$.

M lies in Quadrant III because its *x*- and *y*-coordinates are both negative.

REFLECT

2a. What must be true about PM and QM? Show that this is the case.

$PM = PQ$; by the distance formula $PM = PQ = \sqrt{13}$.

PRACTICE

1. Find the coordinates of the midpoint of $\overline{AB}$ with endpoints $A(-10, 3)$ and $B(2, -2)$. $\left(\frac{-10 + 2}{2}, \frac{3 + (-2)}{2}\right) = \left(-4, \frac{1}{2}\right)$

2. $\overline{RS}$ has endpoints $R(3, 5)$ and $S(-3, -1)$. Prove that the midpoint M of $\overline{RS}$ lies on the *y*-axis.

By the midpoint formula, M has coordinates (0, 2). M lies on the *y*-axis because its

x-coordinate is 0.

3. $\overline{CD}$ has endpoints $C(1, 4)$ and $D(5, 0)$. $\overline{EF}$ has endpoints $E(4, 5)$ and $F(2, -1)$. Prove that the segments have the same midpoint.

The midpoint of $\overline{CD}$ is (3, 2). The midpoint of $\overline{EF}$ is (3, 2). So, the midpoints of the

segments are the same point.

© Houghton Mifflin Harcourt Publishing Company

Angles

1-4

Essential question: *What tools and methods can you use to copy an angle and bisect an angle?*

COMMON CORE Standards for Mathematical Content

CC.9-12.G.CO.1 Know precise definitions of angle, ...

CC.9-12.G.CO.12 Make formal geometric constructions with a variety of tools and methods (compass and straightedge, string, reflective devices, paper folding, dynamic geometric software, etc.).

Vocabulary
angle
vertex
sides
angle bisector

Prerequisites
Basic Terms and Constructions, Lesson 1-1

Math Background
Compass and straightedge constructions date to ancient Greece. In fact, one of the classic problems of ancient Greek mathematics was the trisection of the angle. That is, using a compass and straightedge is it possible to construct an angle whose measure is one-third that of an arbitrary given angle? It was not until 1837 that this construction was proven to be impossible. On the other hand, it is straightforward to bisect any angle, and students learn this fundamental construction in this lesson.

INTRODUCE

You may want to start with a brief brainstorming session in which students share their prior knowledge about angles. List students' ideas on the board, perhaps in the form of an idea web or other graphic organizer. Prior knowledge may include vocabulary related to angles and/or facts about angles in geometric figures. Tell the class that this lesson introduces two constructions related to angles.

TEACH

 EXAMPLE

Questioning Strategies
- Do the rays of the angle you construct need to be the same length as the rays of the given angle? Why or why not? No; the measure of the angle is determined only by the size of the opening between the rays, not by the lengths of the rays.

- When you draw the initial arc that intersects the sides of ∠S, does it matter how wide you open the compass? No, as long as the arc intersects both sides of the angle.

EXTRA EXAMPLE
Construct an angle with the same measure as ∠A.

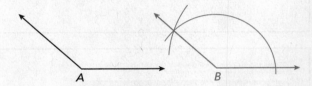

Differentiated Instruction
Some students may have difficulty visualizing two angles that have the same measure, especially if the sides of the angles are shown with rays of different lengths. You want to have students construct their copy of ∠S on a piece of tracing paper. Then students can place the copy on the top of the original angle to check that the measures are the same.

Angles

Essential question: *What tools and methods can you use to copy an angle and bisect an angle?*

COMMON CORE

CC9-12.G.CO.1,
CC9-12.G.CO.12

An **angle** is a figure formed by two rays with the same endpoint. The common endpoint is the **vertex** of the angle. The rays are the **sides** of the angle.

Angles may be measured in degrees (°). There are 360° in a circle, so an angle that measures 1° is $\frac{1}{360}$ of a circle. You write m∠A for the measure of ∠A.

Angles may be classified by their measures.

Acute Angle	Right Angle	Obtuse Angle	Straight Angle
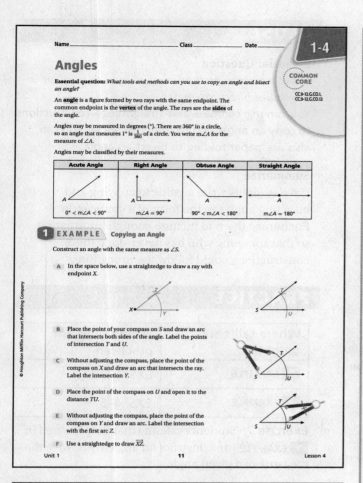			
0° < m∠A < 90°	m∠A = 90°	90° < m∠A < 180°	m∠A = 180°

1 EXAMPLE   Copying an Angle

Construct an angle with the same measure as ∠S.

A In the space below, use a straightedge to draw a ray with endpoint X.

B Place the point of your compass on S and draw an arc that intersects both sides of the angle. Label the points of intersection T and U.

C Without adjusting the compass, place the point of the compass on X and draw an arc that intersects the ray. Label the intersection Y.

D Place the point of the compass on U and open it to the distance TU.

E Without adjusting the compass, place the point of the compass on Y and draw an arc. Label the intersection with the first arc Z.

F Use a straightedge to draw $\overrightarrow{XZ}$.

REFLECT

1a. How can you use a protractor to check your construction?

Check that m∠S = m∠X.

1b. If you draw ∠X so that its sides appear to be longer than the sides shown for ∠S, can the two angles have the same measure? Explain.

Yes; the measure of an angle depends only upon the portion of a circle that the angle encompasses, not upon the apparent length of its sides.

An **angle bisector** is a ray that divides an angle into two angles that both have the same measure. In the figure, $\overrightarrow{BD}$ bisects ∠ABC, so m∠ABD = m∠DBC. The arcs in the figure show equal angle measures.

The following example shows how you can use a compass and straightedge to bisect an angle.

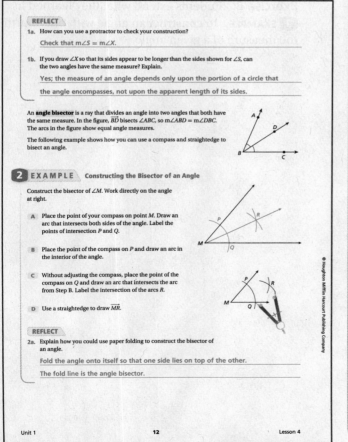

2 EXAMPLE   Constructing the Bisector of an Angle

Construct the bisector of ∠M. Work directly on the angle at right.

A Place the point of your compass on point M. Draw an arc that intersects both sides of the angle. Label the points of intersection P and Q.

B Place the point of the compass on P and draw an arc in the interior of the angle.

C Without adjusting the compass, place the point of the compass on Q and draw an arc that intersects the arc from Step B. Label the intersection of the arcs R.

D Use a straightedge to draw $\overrightarrow{MR}$.

REFLECT

2a. Explain how you could use paper folding to construct the bisector of an angle.

Fold the angle onto itself so that one side lies on top of the other.

The fold line is the angle bisector.

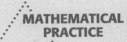

MATHEMATICAL PRACTICE | Highlighting the Standards

Discuss Standard 5 (Use appropriate tools strategically) as students work on Example 2. In particular, ask students whether they think a compass and straightedge create an angle bisector more or less accurately than paper folding or measuring with a protractor. Have students justify their responses and state any assumptions they may be making about these tools.

2 EXAMPLE

Questioning Strategies

• How can you use a protractor to check your construction? **Measure each of the smaller angles created by the bisector. Their measure should be half that of the original angle.**

• How is the bisector of an angle similar to the bisector of a line segment? **The bisector of an angle divides it into two angles with the same measure; the bisector of a line segment divides it into two line segments with the same length.**

EXTRA EXAMPLE
Construct the bisector of ∠J.

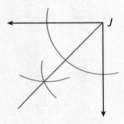

Avoid Common Errors
Remind students not to change the compass setting when they draw the intersecting arcs from points *P* and *Q*. In order to help students see why this is important, you may want to have them do a construction in which they change the compass setting between arcs. Students will see that the resulting ray does not bisect the angle.

CLOSE

Essential Question
What tools and methods can you use to copy an angle and bisect an angle?
You can use compass-and-straightedge constructions to copy an angle and to bisect an angle. You can also use paper folding to bisect an angle.

Summarize
Have students write a guide to copying and bisecting angles in the form of a comic strip. Encourage them to include enough information so that someone who has never done these constructions could follow the procedure.

PRACTICE

Where skills are taught	Where skills are practiced
1 EXAMPLE	EXS. 1–3
2 EXAMPLE	EXS. 4–6

Exercise 7: Students extend what they learned in 1 EXAMPLE to construct an angle with twice the measure of a given angle.

Exercise 8: Students extend what they learned in 2 EXAMPLE to construct an angle with one-fourth the measure of a given angle.

PRACTICE

Construct an angle with the same measure as the given angle.

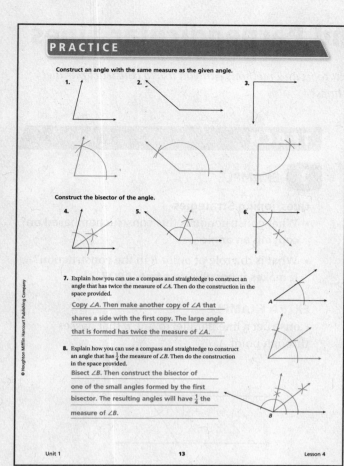

1.

2.

3.

Construct the bisector of the angle.

4.

5.

6.

7. Explain how you can use a compass and straightedge to construct an angle that has twice the measure of ∠A. Then do the construction in the space provided.

   Copy ∠A. Then make another copy of ∠A that

   shares a side with the first copy. The large angle

   that is formed has twice the measure of ∠A.

   A

8. Explain how you can use a compass and straightedge to construct an angle that has $\frac{1}{4}$ the measure of ∠B. Then do the construction in the space provided.

   Bisect ∠B. Then construct the bisector of

   one of the small angles formed by the first

   bisector. The resulting angles will have $\frac{1}{4}$ the

   measure of ∠B.

   B

Parallel and Perpendicular Lines

Essential question: *What tools and methods can you use to construct parallel lines and perpendicular lines?*

Standards for Mathematical Content

CC.9-12.G.CO.1 Know precise definitions of ... perpendicular line, parallel line ...

CC.9-12.G.CO.12 Make formal geometric constructions with a variety of tools and methods (compass and straightedge, string, reflective devices, paper folding, dynamic geometric software, etc.).

Vocabulary

parallel lines

perpendicular lines

perpendicular bisector

Prerequisites

Angles, Lesson 1-4

Math Background

Perpendicular bisectors play an important role in geometry. In this lesson, students learn to construct the perpendicular bisector of a line segment. In Lesson 2-4, students learn that points on the perpendicular bisector of a segment are exactly those points that are equidistant from the endpoints of the segment. In Lesson 3-3, students use this property as they prove congruence criteria for triangles. Having students trace this thread throughout the course is a good way to help them see the underlying structure of geometry.

INTRODUCE

Ask students to give examples of parallel lines in everyday situations. Students might mention railroad tracks or the stripes on a shirt. Then ask them to give examples of perpendicular lines. Students might suggest the corner of a window frame or the lines in a plus sign. Tell students they will learn formal definitions of these terms in this lesson.

TEACH

1 EXAMPLE

Questioning Strategies

- What construction is this construction based on? **copying an angle**

- What is the role of point *R* in the construction? **It makes it possible to name ∠PQR.**

EXTRA EXAMPLE

Construct a line parallel to line *n* that passes through point *A*.

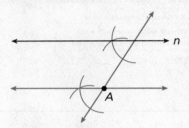

2 EXAMPLE

Questioning Strategies

- Why do you have to use a compass setting that is greater than half the length of $\overline{AB}$ when you draw the initial arc? **This ensures that the two arcs centered at points A and B will intersect.**

- In addition to the perpendicular bisector, what does this construction allow you to find? **the midpoint of the given segment**

EXTRA EXAMPLE

Construct the perpendicular bisector of $\overline{JK}$.

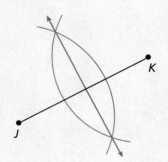

Parallel and Perpendicular Lines

1-5

COMMON CORE

CC9-12.G.CO.1,
CC9-12.G.CO.12

Essential question: *What tools and methods can you use to construct parallel lines and perpendicular lines?*

Parallel lines lie in the same plane and do not intersect. In the figure, line ℓ is parallel to line m and you write $\ell \parallel m$. The arrows on the lines also indicate that the lines are parallel.

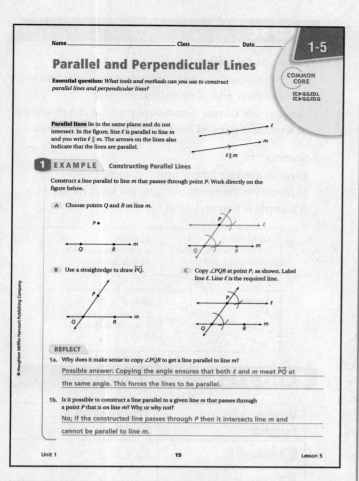

1 EXAMPLE Constructing Parallel Lines

Construct a line parallel to line m that passes through point P. Work directly on the figure below.

A. Choose points Q and R on line m.

B. Use a straightedge to draw $\overrightarrow{PQ}$.

C. Copy $\angle PQR$ at point P, as shown. Label line ℓ. Line ℓ is the required line.

REFLECT

1a. Why does it make sense to copy $\angle PQR$ to get a line parallel to line m?

Possible answer: Copying the angle ensures that both ℓ and m meet $\overrightarrow{PQ}$ at the same angle. This forces the lines to be parallel.

1b. Is it possible to construct a line parallel to a given line m that passes through a point P that is *on* line m? Why or why not?

No; if the constructed line passes through P then it intersects line m and cannot be parallel to line m.

Perpendicular lines are lines that intersect at right angles. In the figure, line ℓ is perpendicular to line m and you write $\ell \perp m$. The right angle mark in the figure indicates that the lines are perpendicular.

The **perpendicular bisector** of a line segment is a line perpendicular to the segment at the segment's midpoint.

2 EXAMPLE Constructing a Perpendicular Bisector

Construct the perpendicular bisector of $\overline{AB}$. Work directly on the figure below.

A. Place the point of your compass at A. Using a compass setting that is greater than half the length of $\overline{AB}$, draw an arc.

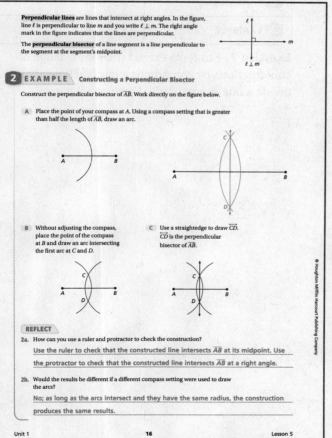

B. Without adjusting the compass, place the point of the compass at B and draw an arc intersecting the first arc at C and D.

C. Use a straightedge to draw $\overleftrightarrow{CD}$. $\overleftrightarrow{CD}$ is the perpendicular bisector of $\overline{AB}$.

REFLECT

2a. How can you use a ruler and protractor to check the construction?

Use the ruler to check that the constructed line intersects $\overline{AB}$ at its midpoint. Use the protractor to check that the constructed line intersects $\overline{AB}$ at a right angle.

2b. Would the results be different if a different compass setting were used to draw the arcs?

No; as long as the arcs intersect and they have the same radius, the construction produces the same results.

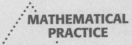

MATHEMATICAL PRACTICE — Highlighting the Standards

In Example 2, students use a compass and straightedge to construct the perpendicular bisector of a segment. Be sure to ask them if the resulting perpendicular bisector would be different if they started the construction with a different compass setting. Although students may not be able to give a complete justification for the fact that the results would be the same, posing such questions prompts students to think deeply about mathematical structure (Standard 7).

3 EXAMPLE

Questioning Strategies

• When you draw the arc in Step A, does the size of the compass opening matter? **No, as long as it is large enough so that the arc intersects line *m* in two points.**

• How can you use a protractor to check the construction? **Measure the angle formed by the perpendicular to make sure it measures 90°.**

EXTRA EXAMPLE

Construct a line perpendicular to line *n* that passes through point *Q*.

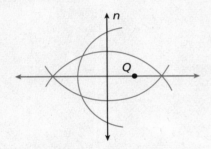

Differentiated Instruction

Kinesthetic learners may benefit from constructing the perpendicular to a given line, through a given point by paper folding. Have students fold the given line upon itself so that the fold passes through the given point. When the paper is unfolded, the crease will be perpendicular to line *n*, passing through point *Q*.

Essential Question

What tools and methods can you use to construct parallel lines and perpendicular lines?

You can use compass-and-straightedge constructions to construct parallel lines and perpendicular lines.

Summarize

Have students make graphic organizers to summarize the vocabulary terms from this lesson. A sample is shown below.

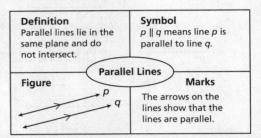

PRACTICE

Where skills are taught	Where skills are practiced
1 EXAMPLE	EXS. 1–2
2 EXAMPLE	EXS. 3–4
3 EXAMPLE	EXS. 5–6

Exercise 7: Students extend their knowledge of constructions by constructing parallel lines that divide a line segment into three equal parts.

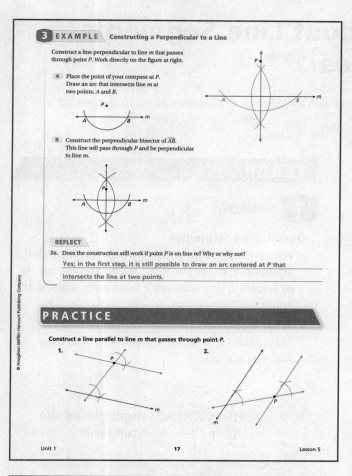

3 EXAMPLE   Constructing a Perpendicular to a Line

Construct a line perpendicular to line *m* that passes through point *P*. Work directly on the figure at right.

A   Place the point of your compass at *P*. Draw an arc that intersects line *m* at two points, *A* and *B*.

B   Construct the perpendicular bisector of $\overline{AB}$. This line will pass through *P* and be perpendicular to line *m*.

REFLECT

3a. Does the construction still work if point *P* is on line *m*? Why or why not?

Yes; in the first step, it is still possible to draw an arc centered at *P* that intersects the line at two points.

PRACTICE

Construct a line parallel to line *m* that passes through point *P*.

1.

2.

Unit 1   17   Lesson 5

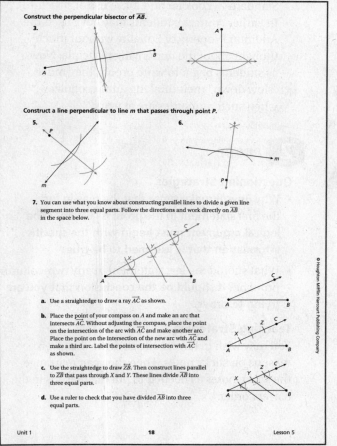

Construct the perpendicular bisector of $\overline{AB}$.

3.

4.

Construct a line perpendicular to line *m* that passes through point *P*.

5.

6.

7. You can use what you know about constructing parallel lines to divide a given line segment into three equal parts. Follow the directions and work directly on $\overline{AB}$ in the space below.

   a. Use a straightedge to draw a ray $\overrightarrow{AC}$ as shown.

   b. Place the point of your compass on *A* and make an arc that intersects $\overline{AC}$. Without adjusting the compass, place the point on the intersection of the arc with $\overline{AC}$ and make another arc. Place the point on the intersection of the new arc with $\overline{AC}$ and make a third arc. Label the points of intersection with $\overline{AC}$ as shown.

   c. Use the straightedge to draw $\overline{ZB}$. Then construct lines parallel to $\overline{ZB}$ that pass through *X* and *Y*. These lines divide $\overline{AB}$ into three equal parts.

   d. Use a ruler to check that you have divided $\overline{AB}$ into three equal parts.

Unit 1   18   Lesson 5

© Houghton Mifflin Harcourt Publishing Company

Notes

Proofs About Line Segments and Angles

Essential question: *How do you prove basic theorems about line segments and angles?*

COMMON CORE **Standards for Mathematical Content**

CC.9-12.G.CO.9 Prove theorems about lines and angles.

Vocabulary
proof
theorem
postulate
opposite rays
linear pair

Prerequisites
Basic Terms and Constructions, Lesson 1-1
Properties of Equality, Algebra 1

Math Background
Proof is a central focus of geometry. It takes time for students to understand the difference between a proof, a convincing argument, and an "off-the-cuff" explanation. In this lesson, students are introduced to proofs and the two-column format for writing proofs. In later lessons, students will write flow proofs and paragraph proofs. At this early stage, however, two-column proofs are usually best because they emphasize the fact that every statement must be justified with a supporting reason.

INTRODUCE

Ask students what it means to prove something. Have students give examples from everyday life or from literature and movies. For example, students may be familiar with mystery novels in which a detective proves that a suspect is guilty or innocent of a crime. Be sure students understand that a key aspect of such novels is a logical sequence of ideas (alibis, clues, etc.) that leads to a conclusion. In the same way, a proof in geometry is a logical sequence of statements and reasons that demonstrates the truth of a theorem.

TEACH

1 ENGAGE

Questioning Strategies
- Which property do you use when you solve the equation $x + 2 = 16$? Why? **Subtraction Property of Equality; you subtract 2 from both sides of the equation.**
- What is an example of the Transitive Property of Equality? **If $3 + 1 = 4$ and $4 = 6 - 2$, then $3 + 1 = 6 - 2$.**

 MATHEMATICAL PRACTICE **Highlighting the Standards**

This lesson is an ideal opportunity to discuss Standard 7 (Look for and make use of structure). In earlier courses, students may have used the Addition Property of Equality without much thought about the underlying principle. Now, as students begin to write proofs, they must "slow down" their thinking and recognize when such properties are at work.

2 PROOF

Questioning Strategies
- Why does it make sense that the reason for the first statement in the proof is "Given"? **The logical argument must begin with the specific information that is assumed to be true.**
- What should the last statement in any two-column proof be? **It should be the conclusion that you are trying to prove.**

Teaching Strategies
You may wish to have students write the given reasons on sticky notes. Then they can rearrange the sticky notes as needed to put the reasons in the correct order.

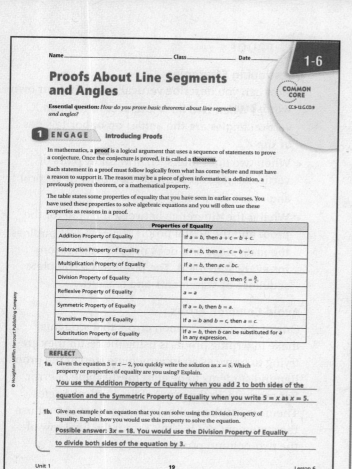

Name _____ Class _____ Date _____

Proofs About Line Segments and Angles

1-6

COMMON CORE
CC.9-12.G.CO.9

Essential question: *How do you prove basic theorems about line segments and angles?*

1 ENGAGE   **Introducing Proofs**

In mathematics, a **proof** is a logical argument that uses a sequence of statements to prove a conjecture. Once the conjecture is proved, it is called a **theorem**.

Each statement in a proof must follow logically from what has come before and must have a reason to support it. The reason may be a piece of given information, a definition, a previously proven theorem, or a mathematical property.

The table states some properties of equality that you have seen in earlier courses. You have used these properties to solve algebraic equations and you will often use these properties as reasons in a proof.

Properties of Equality	
Addition Property of Equality	If $a = b$, then $a + c = b + c$.
Subtraction Property of Equality	If $a = b$, then $a - c = b - c$.
Multiplication Property of Equality	If $a = b$, then $ac = bc$.
Division Property of Equality	If $a = b$ and $c \neq 0$, then $\frac{a}{c} = \frac{b}{c}$.
Reflexive Property of Equality	$a = a$
Symmetric Property of Equality	If $a = b$, then $b = a$.
Transitive Property of Equality	If $a = b$ and $b = c$, then $a = c$.
Substitution Property of Equality	If $a = b$, then b can be substituted for a in any expression.

REFLECT

1a. Given the equation $3 = x - 2$, you quickly write the solution as $x = 5$. Which property or properties of equality are you using? Explain.

> You use the Addition Property of Equality when you add 2 to both sides of the equation and the Symmetric Property of Equality when you write 5 = x as x = 5.

1b. Give an example of an equation that you can solve using the Division Property of Equality. Explain how you would use this property to solve the equation.

> Possible answer: 3x = 18. You would use the Division Property of Equality to divide both sides of the equation by 3.

© Houghton Mifflin Harcourt Publishing Company

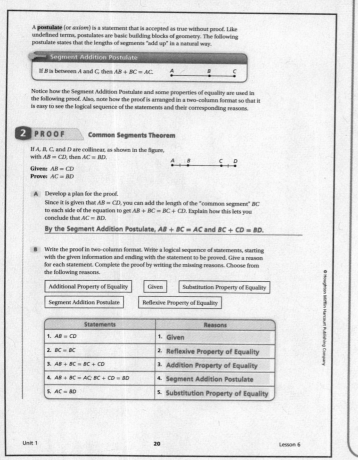

A **postulate** (or *axiom*) is a statement that is accepted as true without proof. Like undefined terms, postulates are basic building blocks of geometry. The following postulate states that the lengths of segments "add up" in a natural way.

Segment Addition Postulate

If B is between A and C, then $AB + BC = AC$.

Notice how the Segment Addition Postulate and some properties of equality are used in the following proof. Also, note how the proof is arranged in a two-column format so that it is easy to see the logical sequence of the statements and their corresponding reasons.

2 PROOF   **Common Segments Theorem**

If A, B, C, and D are collinear, as shown in the figure, with $AB = CD$, then $AC = BD$.

Given: $AB = CD$
Prove: $AC = BD$

A   Develop a plan for the proof.
Since it is given that $AB = CD$, you can add the length of the "common segment" BC to each side of the equation to get $AB + BC = BC + CD$. Explain how this lets you conclude that $AC = BD$.

> By the Segment Addition Postulate, AB + BC = AC and BC + CD = BD.

B   Write the proof in two-column format. Write a logical sequence of statements, starting with the given information and ending with the statement to be proved. Give a reason for each statement. Complete the proof by writing the missing reasons. Choose from the following reasons.

Additional Property of Equality	Given	Substitution Property of Equality

Segment Addition Postulate	Reflexive Property of Equality

Statements	Reasons
1. $AB = CD$	1. Given
2. $BC = BC$	2. Reflexive Property of Equality
3. $AB + BC = BC + CD$	3. Addition Property of Equality
4. $AB + BC = AC$; $BC + CD = BD$	4. Segment Addition Postulate
5. $AC = BD$	5. Substitution Property of Equality

© Houghton Mifflin Harcourt Publishing Company

Notes

3 PROOF

Questioning Strategies

- What does it mean for two angles to be a linear pair? The angles are adjacent angles whose noncommon sides are opposite rays.
- What do you need to do in order to show that two angles are supplementary? You must show that the sum of the angle measures is 180°.
- What must be true about opposite rays? The rays form a straight angle.
- What can you conclude about a straight angle? Its measure is 180°.

Technology

Although the Linear Pair Theorem is straightforward, you may want to have students explore the theorem using geometry software. To do so, have them construct a linear pair of angles, determine the measure of each angle, and use the software's Calculate tool to find the sum of the measures. Students can change the size of the angles and see that the measures change while their sum remains constant. The advantage to using geometry software for a simple result like this is that it gives students a chance to practice using the software before they tackle more complex relationships in later lessons.

Differentiated Instruction

If students have difficulty supplying the missing reasons in the proof, give them the four reasons in random order and ask them to write the correct reason in the appropriate line of the proof. This type of scaffolding can also be helpful for English language learners until they become more comfortable with the vocabulary of deductive reasoning.

4 PROOF

Questioning Strategies

- How can you describe vertical angles in your own words? When two lines intersect to form an X, vertical angles are the angles on opposite sides of the X.
- When two lines intersect, how many pairs of vertical angles are formed? Two pairs of vertical angles are formed.
- What is the difference between the plan for the proof and the actual proof? The plan just outlines the main steps and does not provide reasons for every statement. The proof has a complete sequence of statements and reasons.

Avoid Common Errors

One of the most common errors that students make in writing proofs is using the result they are trying to prove as an intermediate step in the proof. Remind students to be alert for this type of error. For example, in the proof of the Vertical Angles Theorem, students should be sure they do not use the statement $m\angle 1 = m\angle 3$ until the final row of the two-column proof.

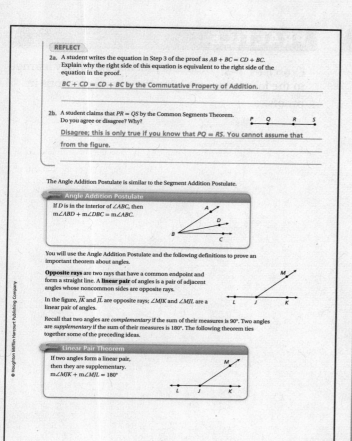

REFLECT

2a. A student writes the equation in Step 3 of the proof as $AB + BC = CD + BC$. Explain why the right side of this equation is equivalent to the right side of the equation in the proof.

$BC + CD = CD + BC$ by the Commutative Property of Addition.

2b. A student claims that $PR = QS$ by the Common Segments Theorem. Do you agree or disagree? Why?

Disagree; this is only true if you know that $PQ = RS$. You cannot assume that from the figure.

The Angle Addition Postulate is similar to the Segment Addition Postulate.

Angle Addition Postulate

If D is in the interior of $\angle ABC$, then $m\angle ABD + m\angle DBC = m\angle ABC$.

You will use the Angle Addition Postulate and the following definitions to prove an important theorem about angles.

Opposite rays are two rays that have a common endpoint and form a straight line. A **linear pair** of angles is a pair of adjacent angles whose noncommon sides are opposite rays.

In the figure, $\vec{JK}$ and $\vec{JL}$ are opposite rays; $\angle MJK$ and $\angle MJL$ are a linear pair of angles.

Recall that two angles are *complementary* if the sum of their measures is 90°. Two angles are *supplementary* if the sum of their measures is 180°. The following theorem ties together some of the preceding ideas.

Linear Pair Theorem

If two angles form a linear pair, then they are supplementary.
$m\angle MJK + m\angle MJL = 180°$

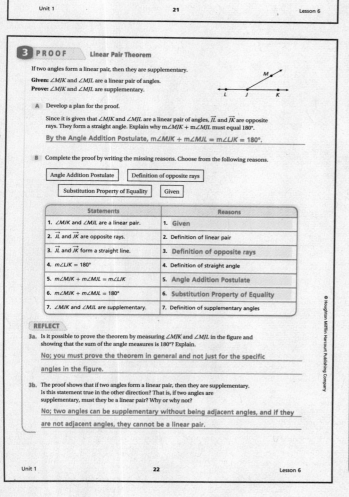

3 PROOF   Linear Pair Theorem

If two angles form a linear pair, then they are supplementary.

Given: $\angle MJK$ and $\angle MJL$ are a linear pair of angles.
Prove: $\angle MJK$ and $\angle MJL$ are supplementary.

A Develop a plan for the proof.

Since it is given that $\angle MJK$ and $\angle MJL$ are a linear pair of angles, $\vec{JL}$ and $\vec{JK}$ are opposite rays. They form a straight angle. Explain why $m\angle MJK + m\angle MJL$ must equal 180°.

By the Angle Addition Postulate, $m\angle MJK + m\angle MJL = m\angle LJK = 180°$.

B Complete the proof by writing the missing reasons. Choose from the following reasons.

| Angle Addition Postulate | Definition of opposite rays |
| Substitution Property of Equality | Given |

Statements	Reasons
1. $\angle MJK$ and $\angle MJL$ are a linear pair.	1. Given
2. $\vec{JL}$ and $\vec{JK}$ are opposite rays.	2. Definition of linear pair
3. $\vec{JL}$ and $\vec{JK}$ form a straight line.	3. Definition of opposite rays
4. $m\angle LJK = 180°$	4. Definition of straight angle
5. $m\angle MJK + m\angle MJL = m\angle LJK$	5. Angle Addition Postulate
6. $m\angle MJK + m\angle MJL = 180°$	6. Substitution Property of Equality
7. $\angle MJK$ and $\angle MJL$ are supplementary.	7. Definition of supplementary angles

REFLECT

3a. Is it possible to prove the theorem by measuring $\angle MJK$ and $\angle MJL$ in the figure and showing that the sum of the angle measures is 180°? Explain.

No; you must prove the theorem in general and not just for the specific angles in the figure.

3b. The proof shows that if two angles form a linear pair, then they are supplementary. Is this statement true in the other direction? That is, if two angles are supplementary, must they be a linear pair? Why or why not?

No; two angles can be supplementary without being adjacent angles, and if they are not adjacent angles, they cannot be a linear pair.

Essential Question

How do you prove basic theorems about line segments and angles?

To prove basic theorems, you write logical arguments based on properties of equality and fundamental geometry postulates.

Summarize

Have students make a graphic organizer to show how some of the properties, postulates, and theorems in this lesson build upon one another. A sample is shown below.

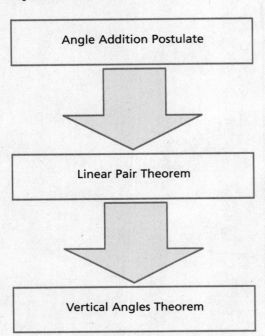

Exercises 1–3: Students practice what they learned in the lesson by supplying the missing reasons in proofs.

Recall that two angles are *vertical angles* if their sides form two pairs of opposite rays. In the figure below, ∠1 and ∠3 are vertical angles, as are ∠2 and ∠4.

4 PROOF   **Vertical Angles Theorem**

If two angles are vertical angles, then they have equal measures.

Given: ∠1 and ∠3 are vertical angles.
Prove: m∠1 = m∠3

A   Develop a plan for the proof.

Since ∠1 and ∠2 are a linear pair, and ∠2 and ∠3 are a linear pair, these pairs of angles are supplementary. This means m∠1 + m∠2 = 180° and m∠2 + m∠3 = 180°. By substitution, m∠1 + m∠2 = m∠2 + m∠3. What is the final step in the plan?

Subtract m∠2 from both sides to conclude m∠1 = m∠3.

B   Complete the proof by writing the missing reasons. Choose from the following reasons.

| Definition of supplementary angles | Subtraction Property of Equality |
| Substitution Property of Equality | Linear Pair Theorem | Given |

Statements	Reasons
1. ∠1 and ∠3 are vertical angles.	1. **Given**
2. ∠1 and ∠2 are a linear pair; ∠2 and ∠3 are a linear pair.	2. **Definition of linear pair**
3. ∠1 and ∠2 are supplementary; ∠2 and ∠3 are supplementary.	3. **Linear Pair Theorem**
4. m∠1 + m∠2 = 180°; m∠2 + m∠3 = 180°	4. **Definition of supplementary angles**
5. m∠1 + m∠2 = m∠2 + m∠3	5. **Substitution Property of Equality**
6. m∠1 = m∠3	6. **Subtraction Property of Equality**

REFLECT

4a. Explain how to find m∠1, m∠2, and m∠3 in the figure.

∠1 forms a linear pair with the 128° angle. Therefore, these angles are supplementary, so m∠1 = 52°. Similarly, m∠3 = 52°. By the Vertical Angles Theorem, m∠2 = 128°.

© Houghton Mifflin Harcourt Publishing Company

PRACTICE

In Exercises 1–2, complete each proof by writing the missing statements or reasons.

1. If A, B, C, and D are collinear, as shown in the figure, with AC = BD, then AB = CD.

A   B   C   D

Given: AC = BD
Prove: AB = CD

Statements	Reasons
1. AC = BD	1. **Given**
2. AC = AB + BC; BD = BC + CD	2. **Segment Addition Postulate**
3. AB + BC = BC + CD	3. Substitution Property of Equality
4. AB = CD	4. **Subtraction Property of Equality**

2. Given: $\overrightarrow{KM}$ bisects ∠JKL.
Prove: m∠2 = m∠3

Statements	Reasons
1. $\overrightarrow{KM}$ bisects ∠JKL.	1. **Given**
2. m∠1 = m∠2	2. **Definition of angle bisector**
3. ∠1 and ∠3 form two pairs of opposite rays.	3. **Given**
4. ∠1 and ∠3 are vertical angles.	4. **Definition of vertical angles**
5. m∠1 = m∠3	5. **Vertical Angles Theorem**
6. m∠2 = m∠3	6. **Substitution Property of Equality**

3. In the figure, X is the midpoint of $\overline{WY}$, and Y is the midpoint of $\overline{XZ}$. Explain how to prove WX = YZ.

W   X   Y   Z

By the definition of midpoint, WX = XY and XY = YZ. By the Substitution Property of Equality, WX = YZ.

© Houghton Mifflin Harcourt Publishing Company

Proofs About Parallel and Perpendicular Lines

Essential question: *How do you prove theorems about parallel and perpendicular lines?*

⋯COMMON⋯ Standards for
⋮ CORE ⋮ Mathematical Content
⋯⋯⋯⋯⋯

CC.9-12.G.CO.9 Prove theorems about lines and angles.

Vocabulary

converse

Prerequisites

Proofs About Line Segments and Angles, Lesson 1-6

Math Background

When two parallel lines are cut by a transversal, alternate interior angles have the same measure, corresponding angles have the same measure, and same-side interior angles are supplementary. One of these three facts must be taken as a postulate and then the other two may be proved. In this book, the statement about same-side interior angles is taken as the postulate. This is closely related to one of the postulates stated in Euclid's *Elements*: "If a straight line falling on two straight lines make the interior angles on the same side less than two right angles, the two straight lines, if produced indefinitely, meet on that side on which are the angles less than the two right angles."

INTRODUCE

Draw a pair of parallel lines on the board and then draw a transversal that intersects them. Ask students which of the angles in the figure appear to have the same measure. Ask them if they think the relationships hold only for this figure or if they hold for any pair of parallel lines that are cut by a transversal. Have students draw their own sets of parallel lines that are cut by a transversal so they can test their conjectures. Tell them they will investigate and prove some of these conjectures in this lesson.

TEACH

1 ENGAGE

Questioning Strategies

- When two lines are cut by a transversal, how many pairs of corresponding angles are formed? 4
- When two lines are cut by a transversal, how many pairs of same-side interior angles are formed? 2
- In the figure where $p \parallel q$, what does the Same-Side Interior Angles Postulate tell you about m∠3 and m∠6? The sum of these measures is 180°.

Differentiated Instruction

Have visual learners use highlighters to color-code the different angle pairs. For example, students can use a yellow highlighter to highlight the term *corresponding angles* and then use the same highlighter to mark ∠1 and ∠5.

2 PROOF

Questioning Strategies

- Do you have to write separate proof for every pair of alternate interior angles in the figure? Why or why not? No; you can write the proof for any pair of alternate interior angles. The same reasoning applies to all the pairs.
- For the second statement in the proof, could you use "∠4 and ∠5 are supplementary" rather than "∠3 and ∠6 are supplementary"? Explain. Yes, but then you would need to rewrite the subsequent steps accordingly to arrive at the conclusion that m∠3 = m∠5.

Name_____ Class_____ Date_____

Proofs About Parallel and Perpendicular Lines

COMMON CORE
CC.9-12.G.CO.9

Essential question: *How do you prove theorems about parallel and perpendicular lines?*

1 ENGAGE   Introducing Transversals

Recall that a *transversal* is a line that intersects two coplanar lines at two different points. In the figure, line *t* is a transversal. The table summarizes the names of angle pairs formed by a transversal.

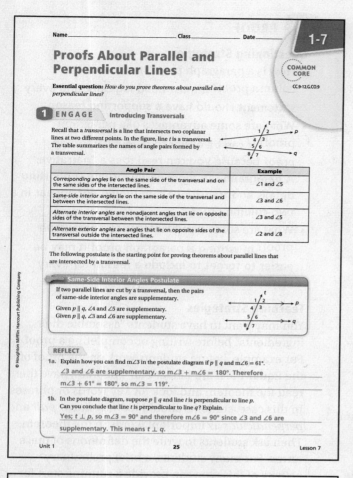

Angle Pair	Example
Corresponding angles lie on the same side of the transversal and on the same sides of the intersected lines.	∠1 and ∠5
Same-side interior angles lie on the same side of the transversal and between the intersected lines.	∠3 and ∠6
Alternate interior angles are nonadjacent angles that lie on opposite sides of the transversal between the intersected lines.	∠3 and ∠5
Alternate exterior angles are angles that lie on opposite sides of the transversal outside the intersected lines.	∠2 and ∠8

The following postulate is the starting point for proving theorems about parallel lines that are intersected by a transversal.

> **Same-Side Interior Angles Postulate**
>
> If two parallel lines are cut by a transversal, then the pairs of same-side interior angles are supplementary.
>
> Given $p \parallel q$, ∠4 and ∠5 are supplementary.
> Given $p \parallel q$, ∠3 and ∠6 are supplementary.

REFLECT

1a. Explain how you can find m∠3 in the postulate diagram if $p \parallel q$ and m∠6 = 61°.

∠3 and ∠6 are supplementary, so m∠3 + m∠6 = 180°. Therefore

m∠3 + 61° = 180°, so m∠3 = 119°.

1b. In the postulate diagram, suppose $p \parallel q$ and line *t* is perpendicular to line *p*. Can you conclude that line *t* is perpendicular to line *q*? Explain.

Yes; $t \perp p$, so m∠3 = 90° and therefore m∠6 = 90° since ∠3 and ∠6 are

supplementary. This means $t \perp q$.

---

2 PROOF   Alternate Interior Angles Theorem

If two parallel lines are cut by a transversal, then the pairs of alternate interior angles have the same measure.

Given: $p \parallel q$
Prove: m∠3 = m∠5

Complete the proof by writing the missing reasons. Choose from the following reasons. You may use a reason more than once.

Same-Side Interior Angles Postulate	Given	Definition of supplementary angles
Subtraction Property of Equality	Substitution Property of Equality	Linear Pair Theorem

Statements	Reasons
1. $p \parallel q$	1. Given
2. ∠3 and ∠6 are supplementary.	2. Same-Side Interior Angles Postulate
3. m∠3 + m∠6 = 180°	3. Definition of supplementary angles
4. ∠5 and ∠6 are a linear pair.	4. Given
5. ∠5 and ∠6 are supplementary.	5. Linear Pair Theorem
6. m∠5 + m∠6 = 180°	6. Definition of supplementary angles
7. m∠3 + m∠6 = m∠5 + m∠6	7. Substitution Property of Equality
8. m∠3 = m∠5	8. Subtraction Property of Equality

REFLECT

2a. Suppose m∠4 = 57° in the above figure. Describe two different ways to determine m∠6.

By the Alt. Int. Angles Theorem, m∠6 = 57°. Also, ∠4 and ∠5 are supplementary,

so m∠5 = 123°. Since ∠5 and ∠6 are supplementary, m∠6 = 57°.

2b. In the above figure, explain why ∠1, ∠3, ∠5, and ∠7 all have the same measure.

m∠1 = m∠3 (Vert. Angles Theorem), m∠3 = m∠5 (Alt. Int. Angles Theorem),

m∠5 = m∠7 (Vert. Angles Theorem); use the Transitive Property of Equality to

show that any of the 4 angles has the same measure as any of the others.

2c. In the above figure, is it possible for all eight angles to have the same measure? If so, what is that measure?

Yes; if m∠1 = m∠2 = 90°, then all eight angles have measure 90°.

This happens if line *t* is perpendicular to lines *p* and *q*.

© Houghton Mifflin Harcourt Publishing Company

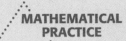

MATHEMATICAL PRACTICE

Highlighting the Standards

Standard 3 (Construct viable arguments and critique the reasoning of others) is at the heart of this proof-based lesson. You may wish to have students pair up with a "proof buddy." Students can exchange their work with this partner and check that their partner's logical arguments make sense. This is a good way to get students in the habit of constructively critiquing other students' reasoning.

 3 PROOF

Questioning Strategies

- What can you use as reasons in a proof?

  Given information, properties, postulates, previously-proven theorems

- How can you check that the first and last statements in a two-column proof are correct?

  The first statement should match the "Given" and the last statement should match the "Prove."

Teaching Strategy

Before introducing the converses of the Same-Side Interior Angles Postulate, the Alternate Interior Angles Theorem, and the Corresponding Angles Theorem, you may want to spend a few minutes talking about statements and their converses. Have students give the converse for statements based on everyday situations such as, "If you live in Cleveland, then you live in Ohio." Forming the converses of such statements can help students see that the converse of a true statement may or may not be true.

4 PROOF

Questioning Strategies

- How is a paragraph proof similar to a two-column proof? It must build logically, and every statement should have a supporting reason.

- What are some advantages of a paragraph proof? It can be easier to read a paragraph proof because you can read it as a "narrative." A paragraph can more easily include supporting details and transitions that would not appear in a two-column proof.

- What are some disadvantages of a paragraph proof? In writing a paragraph proof it may be easier to forget to include a reason for every statement.

Teaching Strategies

You may want to have students "assemble their ingredients" before writing or completing a proof. For example, before students work on the proof of the Equal-Measure Linear Pair Theorem, have them read the theorem and look for key words or phrases. In this case, students should identify *linear pair* and *perpendicular* as important words in the theorem. Then ask students to write the definitions of these terms. For many students, a brief preliminary activity of this type can provide a running start for their work on the proof itself.

3 PROOF Corresponding Angles Theorem

If two parallel lines are cut by a transversal, then the
pairs of corresponding angles have the same measure.

Given: $p \parallel q$
Prove: $m\angle 1 = m\angle 5$

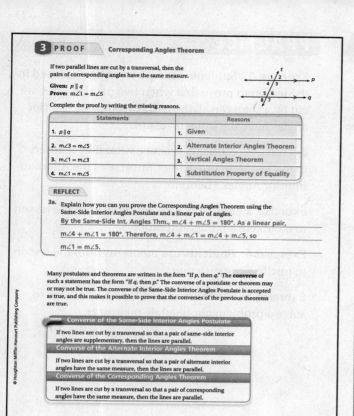

Complete the proof by writing the missing reasons.

Statements	Reasons
1. $p \parallel q$	1. Given
2. $m\angle 3 = m\angle 5$	2. Alternate Interior Angles Theorem
3. $m\angle 1 = m\angle 3$	3. Vertical Angles Theorem
4. $m\angle 1 = m\angle 5$	4. Substitution Property of Equality

REFLECT

3a. Explain how you can you prove the Corresponding Angles Theorem using the
Same-Side Interior Angles Postulate and a linear pair of angles.

By the Same-Side Int. Angles Thm., $m\angle 4 + m\angle 5 = 180°$. As a linear pair,

$m\angle 4 + m\angle 1 = 180°$. Therefore, $m\angle 4 + m\angle 1 = m\angle 4 + m\angle 5$, so

$m\angle 1 = m\angle 5$.

Many postulates and theorems are written in the form "If p, then q." The **converse** of
such a statement has the form "If q, then p." The converse of a postulate or theorem may
or may not be true. The converse of the Same-Side Interior Angles Postulate is accepted
as true, and this makes it possible to prove that the converses of the previous theorems
are true.

Converse of the Same-Side Interior Angles Postulate

If two lines are cut by a transversal so that a pair of same-side interior
angles are supplementary, then the lines are parallel.

Converse of the Alternate Interior Angles Theorem

If two lines are cut by a transversal so that a pair of alternate interior
angles have the same measure, then the lines are parallel.

Converse of the Corresponding Angles Theorem

If two lines are cut by a transversal so that a pair of corresponding
angles have the same measure, then the lines are parallel.

A *paragraph proof* is another way of presenting a mathematical argument. As in a
two-column proof, the argument must flow logically and every statement should
have a reason. The following example shows a paragraph proof.

4 PROOF Equal-Measure Linear Pair Theorem

If two intersecting lines form a linear pair of angles
with equal measures, then the lines are perpendicular.

Given: $m\angle 1 = m\angle 2$
Prove: $\ell \perp m$

Complete the following paragraph proof.

It is given that $\angle 1$ and $\angle 2$ form a linear pair. Therefore, $\angle 1$ and $\angle 2$ are supplementary
by the ___Linear Pair Theorem___ . By the definition of supplementary angles,
$m\angle 1 + m\angle 2 = 180°$. It is also given that $m\angle 1 = m\angle 2$. So, $m\angle 1 + m\angle 1 = 180°$ by the
___Substitution Property of Equality___ . Simplifying gives $2m\angle 1 = 180°$ and $m\angle 1 = 90°$
by the Division Property of Equality. Therefore, $\angle 1$ is a right angle and $\ell \perp m$ by the
___definition of perpendicular___

REFLECT

4a. State the converse of the Equal-Measure Linear Pair Theorem shown above.
Is the converse true?

If two intersecting lines are perpendicular, then they form a linear pair of angles

with equal measures; yes.

PRACTICE

In Exercises 1–2, complete each proof by writing the missing statements or reasons.

1. If two parallel lines are cut by a transversal, then the
pairs of alternate exterior angles have the same measure.

Given: $p \parallel q$
Prove: $m\angle 1 = m\angle 7$

Statements	Reasons
1. $p \parallel q$	1. Given
2. $m\angle 1 = m\angle 5$	2. Corresponding Angles Theorem
3. $m\angle 5 = m\angle 7$	3. Vertical Angles Theorem
4. $m\angle 1 = m\angle 7$	4. Substitution Property of Equality

© Houghton Mifflin Harcourt Publishing Company

CLOSE

Essential Question
How do you prove theorems about parallel and perpendicular lines?
You prove theorems about parallel lines by starting with the Same-Side Interior Angles Postulate.
You also use the Linear Pair Theorem, the Vertical Angles Theorem, the definition of supplementary angles, and properties of equality. You prove theorems about perpendicular lines by citing definitions, the Linear Pair Theorem, and properties of equality.

Summarize
Have students write a journal entry in which they summarize the key postulates and theorems of this lesson. Encourage them to include a labeled figure with each posulate or theorem.

PRACTICE

Exercise 1: Students practice what they learned in the lesson to prove that when two parallel lines are cut by a transversal, the pairs of alternate exterior angles have the same measure.

Exercise 2: Students practice what they learned in the lesson to prove the Converse of the Alternate Interior Angles Theorem.

Exercise 3: Students use theorems from the lesson to complete a paragraph proof.

Exercise 4: Students use theorems from the lesson to justify a construction.

Exercise 5: Students extend their knowledge to solve a problem about angle measures.

2. Prove the Converse of the Alternate Interior Angles Theorem.

Given: m∠3 = m∠5
Prove: p ∥ q

Statements	Reasons
1. m∠3 = m∠5	1. Given
2. ∠5 and ∠6 are a linear pair.	2. Definition of linear pair
3. ∠5 and ∠6 are supplementary.	3. Linear Pair Theorem
4. m∠5 + m∠6 = 180°	4. Definition of supplementary angles
5. m∠3 + m∠6 = 180°	5. Substitution Property of Equality
6. ∠3 and ∠6 are supplementary.	6. Definition of supplementary angles
7. p ∥ q	7. Conv. of Same-Side Int. Angles Post.

3. Complete the paragraph proof.

Given: ℓ ∥ m and p ∥ q
Prove: m∠1 = m∠2

It is given that p ∥ q, so m∠1 = m∠3 by the <u>Corresponding Angles Theorem</u>.
It is also given that ℓ ∥ m, so m∠3 = m∠2 by the <u>Alt. Int. Angles Theorem</u>.
Therefore, m∠1 = m∠2 by the <u>Transitive Property of Equality</u>.

4. The figure shows a given line *m*, a given point *P*, and the construction of a line ℓ that is parallel to line *m*. Explain why line ℓ is parallel to line *m*.

The construction creates a pair of corresponding angles with the same measure, so the lines are parallel by the Converse of the Corresponding Angles Theorem.

5. Can you use the information in the figure to conclude that p ∥ q? Why or why not?

Yes; m∠3 = 71° (Vert. Angles Thm.) and 71° + 109° = 180°, so same-side interior angles are supplementary, and by the Converse of the Same-Side Interior Angles Postulate, p ∥ q.

Standards	Item
CC.9-12.G.CO.1	1, 6
CC.9-12.G.CO.9	2, 7
CC.9-12.G.CO.12	3, 5, 8, 9
CC.9-12.GPE.4	4, 10

TEST PREP DOCTOR ✚

Multiple Choice: Item 2

- Students who answered **F** may have incorrectly assumed that any statement that uses the term *supplementary* must have *Definition of supplementary angles* as its reason.
- Students who answered **G** or **H** may think that the Vertical Angles Theorem says that vertical angles are supplementary.

Multiple Choice: Item 4

- Students who answered **F** or **H** may have use the "taxicab" distance to find *AB* and *CD* (that is, they may have counted the total number of horizontal units and vertical units it is necessary to travel in order to move from one endpoint to the other).
- Students who answered **J** may have forgotten to apply the square root in the distance formula.

Multiple Choice: Item 7

- Students who answered **A** may have incorrectly assumed that any statement that uses the term *supplementary* must have *Definition of supplementary angles* as its reason.
- Students who answered **C** may not understand that $\angle 4$ and $\angle 5$ are not a linear pair.
- Students who answered **D** may not understand the definition of vertical angles.

Free Response: Item 9

- Students who failed to draw any perpendicular bisector may have had trouble because they drew arcs from points *J* and *K* that did not intersect. Remind students to set their compass opening to more than half the length of $\overline{JK}$.
- Students who drew a perpendicular that does not intersect $\overline{JK}$ at its midpoint may have changed the compass setting after drawing the arc from one of the endpoints.

Name _____ Class _____ Date _____

MULTIPLE CHOICE

1. Which term has the following definition?

It is a portion of a line consisting of two points and all points between them.

A. angle   C. line segment

B. endpoint   D. ray

2. Alberto is proving that vertical angles have the same measure. He begins as shown below. Which reason should he use for Step 3?

Given: $\angle 1$ and $\angle 2$ are vertical angles.
Prove: $m\angle 1 = m\angle 2$

Statements	Reasons
1. $\angle 1$ and $\angle 2$ are vertical angles.	1. Given
2. $\angle 1$ and $\angle 3$ are a linear pair.	2. Definition of linear pair
3. $\angle 1$ and $\angle 3$ are supplementary.	3. ?

F. Definition of supplementary angles

G. Definition of vertical angles

H. Vertical Angles Theorem

J. Linear Pair Theorem

3. Lisa wants to use a compass and straightedge to copy $\overline{XY}$. She uses the straightedge to draw a line segment, and she labels one endpoint Q. What should she do next?

A. Open the compass to distance XY.

B. Open the compass to distance XQ.

C. Use a ruler to measure $\overline{XY}$.

D. Use the straightedge to draw $\overline{XQ}$.

4. You want to prove that $\overline{AB}$ is longer than $\overline{CD}$. To do so, you use the distance formula to find the lengths of the segments. Which of the following are the correct lengths?

F. $AB = 7, CD = 8$

G. $AB = \sqrt{37}, CD = \sqrt{34}$

H. $AB = \sqrt{49}, CD = \sqrt{64}$

J. $AB = 37, CD = 34$

5. Kendrick is using a compass and straightedge to copy $\angle Q$. The figure shows the portion of the construction that he has already completed. Where should Kendrick place the point of the compass to do the next step of the construction?

A. point Q

B. point R

C. point X

D. point Y

6. Which of the following is the correct phrase to complete the definition of an angle?

An angle is a figure formed by two rays _____.

F. that intersect

G. with one point in common

H. that do not overlap

J. with the same endpoint

7. Keiko is writing the proof shown below. Which reason should she use for Step 2?

Given: $\ell \parallel m$
Prove: $m\angle 4 = m\angle 6$

Statements	Reasons
1. $\ell \parallel m$	1. Given
2. $\angle 4$ and $\angle 5$ are supplementary.	2. ?

A. Definition of supplementary angles

B. Same-Side Interior Angles Postulate

C. Linear Pair Theorem

D. Vertical Angles Theorem

8. Which compass-and-straightedge construction do you use when you construct a line parallel to a given line through a point not on the line?

F. copying an angle

G. copying a segment

H. bisecting an angle

J. bisecting a segment

FREE RESPONSE

9. Work directly on the figure below to construct the perpendicular bisector of $\overline{JK}$.

10. $\overline{GH}$ has endpoints $G(1, 3)$ and $H(-5, -1)$. Prove that the midpoint of $\overline{GH}$ lies in Quadrant II.

Let the midpoint be M. By the midpoint formula, the x-coordinate of M is $\frac{x_1 + x_2}{2} = \frac{1 + (-5)}{2} = \frac{-4}{2} = -2$. The y-coordinate of M is $\frac{y_1 + y_2}{2} = \frac{3 + (-1)}{2} = \frac{2}{2} = 1$. The coordinates of M are $(-2, 1)$, which is a point in Quadrant II, since the x-coordinate is negative and the y-coordinate is positive.

© Houghton Mifflin Harcourt Publishing Company

UNIT 2

Transformations

Unit Vocabulary

angle of rotation	(2-6)
center of rotation	(2-6)
component form	(2-5)
image	(2-1)
indirect proof	(2-3)
initial point	(2-5)
pre-image	(2-1)
reflection	(2-2)
rigid motion	(2-1)
rotation	(2-6)
terminal point	(2-5)
transformation	(2-1)
translation	(2-5)
vector	(2-5)

UNIT 2

Transformations

Unit Focus

A transformation is a function that changes the position, shape, and/or size of a figure. In this unit, you will work with a variety of transformations, but you will focus on transformations that are rigid motions. Rigid motions preserve the size and shape of a figure. As you will see, reflections (flips), translations (slides), and rotations (turns) are all rigid motions. As you work with these transformations, you will learn to draw transformed figures and apply the transformations to help you write proofs.

Unit at a Glance

COMMON CORE

Lesson		Standards for Mathematical Content
2-1	Transformations and Rigid Motions	CC.9-12.G.CO.2
2-2	Reflections	CC.9-12.G.CO.2, CC.9-12.G.CO.4, CC.9-12.G.CO.5, CC.9-12.G.CO.6
2-3	Angle Bisectors	CC.9-12.G.CO.2, CC.9-12.G.CO.9
2-4	Perpendicular Bisectors	CC.9-12.G.CO.2, CC.9-12.G.CO.9
2-5	Translations	CC.9-12.G.CO.2, CC.9-12.G.CO.4, CC.9-12.G.CO.5, CC.9-12.G.CO.6
2-6	Rotations	CC.9-12.G.CO.2, CC.9-12.G.CO.4, CC.9-12.G.CO.5, CC.9-12.G.CO.6
	Test Prep	

© Houghton Mifflin Harcourt Publishing Company

UNIT 2

Unit 2   33   Transformations

Unpacking the Common Core State Standards

Use the table to help you understand the Standards for Mathematical Content that are taught in this unit. Refer to the lessons listed after each standard for exploration and practice.

COMMON CORE Standards for Mathematical Content	What It Means For You
CC.9-12.G.CO.2 Represent transformations in the plane using, e.g., transparencies and geometry software; describe transformations as functions that take points in the plane as inputs and give other points as outputs. Compare transformations that preserve distance and angle to those that do not (e.g., translation versus horizontal stretch). Lessons 2-1, 2-2, 2-3, 2-4, 2-5, 2-6	You will explore several different transformations and compare their properties. You will also learn to use function notation to describe transformations.
CC.9-12.G.CO.4 Develop definitions of rotations, reflections, and translations in terms of angles, circles, perpendicular lines, parallel lines, and line segments. Lessons 2-2, 2-5, 2-6	You are already familiar with reflections, translations, and rotations as flips, slides, and turns, respectively. Now you will develop more rigorous mathematical definitions for these transformations.
CC.9-12.G.CO.5 Given a geometric figure and a rotation, reflection, or translation, draw the transformed figure using, e.g., graph paper, tracing paper, or geometry software. Specify a sequence of transformations that will carry a given figure onto another. Lessons 2-2, 2-5, 2-6	In this unit, you will use a variety of tools to show the effect of a transformation upon a figure.
CC.9-12.G.CO.6 Use geometric descriptions of rigid motions to transform figures and to predict the effect of a given rigid motion on a given figure; given two figures, use the definition of congruence in terms of rigid motions to decide if they are congruent. Lessons 2-2, 2-5, 2-6	The result of a transformation can sometimes be surprising. With experience, you will learn to predict the effect of a transformation upon a given figure.
CC.9-12.G.CO.9 Prove theorems about lines and angles. Lessons 2-3, 2-4	You can use what you know about transformations to help you prove theorems about basic geometric figures, such as bisectors of angles and perpendicular bisectors of segments.

UNIT 2

© Houghton Mifflin Harcourt Publishing Company

Unpacking the Common Core State Standards

This page lists and explains the Standards for Mathematical Content that are addressed in this unit. For information about the Standards for Mathematical Practice, which are integrated throughout the text, see Teacher Edition pages x–xiii.

UNIT 2

Notes

_____

_____

_____

_____

_____

_____

_____

_____

_____

_____

_____

_____

Transformations and Rigid Motions

Essential question: *How do you identify transformations that are rigid motions?*

⋯COMMON⋯ **Standards for**
CORE **Mathematical Content**

CC.9-12.G.CO.2 ... Compare transformations that preserve distance and angle to those that do not (e.g., translation versus horizontal stretch).

Vocabulary

transformation

pre-image

image

rigid motion (isometry)

Prerequisites

None

Math Background

This book takes a transformations-based approach to much of geometry. For example, in Lesson 3-1, congruence will be defined in terms of transformations. In Lesson 5-3, similarity will also be defined in terms of transformations. Because transformations play such a central role in the course, this introductory lesson is especially important. In addition to providing definitions of key terms, the lesson introduces transformations as functions and gives students a chance to explore a wide range of transformations before focusing on specific transformations in upcoming lessons.

INTRODUCE

Students have seen transformations in earlier grades, but in a more informal way. Begin this lesson by asking them to define *transformation* in their own words. Then have students give examples of transformations. If no one suggests it, remind students that they have already worked with flips, turns, and slides in earlier grades. Tell students that they will greatly enhance their knowledge of these transformations in this course.

TEACH

1 ENGAGE

Questioning Strategies

• How is the notation $T(A) = A'$ similar to the more familiar function notation $y = f(x)$? **The object inside the parentheses is the input. The object on the other side of the equal sign is the output. The letter in front of the parentheses gives the name of the function or transformation.**

• What does the "prime" symbol mean in A'? **It tells you that the point A' is the image of point A.**

• In the coordinate notation $(x, y) \rightarrow (x + 2, y - 3)$, what does the arrow tell you? **It tells you that the point (x, y) is mapped to the point $(x + 2, y + 3)$.**

Teaching Strategies

You may want to give students verbal descriptions of a variety of transformations. For example, the simplest transformation is the transformation that maps every point to itself. This is known as the identity transformation. Another transformation is the transformation that maps every point to the origin. Giving students examples of these "extreme" transformations will help them realize that not every transformation is a flip, turn, or slide.

2 EXPLORE

Questioning Strategies

• What do all of the transformations have in common? **They all map a right triangle to a right triangle.**

• Which of these transformations would you use if you wanted to make an enlargement of the given triangle? **D**

2-1

Transformations and Rigid Motions

Essential question: *How do you identify transformations that are rigid motions?*

COMMON
CORE

CC.9-12.G.CO.2

1 ENGAGE · Introducing Transformations

A **transformation** is a function that changes the position, shape, and/or size of a figure. The inputs for the function are points in the plane; the outputs are other points in the plane. A figure that is used as the input of a transformation is the **pre-image**. The output is the **image**.

For example, the transformation T moves point A to point A'. Point A is the pre-image, and A' is the image. You can use function notation to write $T(A) = A'$. Note that a transformation is sometimes called a *mapping*. Transformation T maps point A to point A'.

Coordinate notation is one way to write a rule for a transformation on a coordinate plane. The notation uses an arrow to show how the transformation changes the coordinates of a general point, (x, y).

For example, the notation $(x, y) \rightarrow (x + 2, y - 3)$ means that the transformation adds 2 to the x-coordinate of a point and subtracts 3 from its y-coordinate. Thus, this transformation maps the point $(6, 5)$ to the point $(8, 2)$.

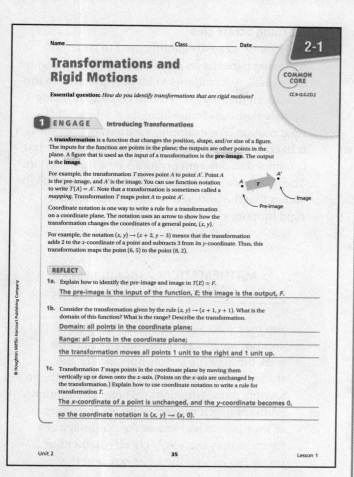

REFLECT

1a. Explain how to identify the pre-image and image in $T(E) = F$.

The pre-image is the input of the function, E; the image is the output, F.

1b. Consider the transformation given by the rule $(x, y) \rightarrow (x + 1, y + 1)$. What is the domain of this function? What is the range? Describe the transformation.

Domain: all points in the coordinate plane;

Range: all points in the coordinate plane;

the transformation moves all points 1 unit to the right and 1 unit up.

1c. Transformation T maps points in the coordinate plane by moving them vertically up or down onto the x-axis. (Points on the x-axis are unchanged by the transformation.) Explain how to use coordinate notation to write a rule for transformation T.

The x-coordinate of a point is unchanged, and the y-coordinate becomes 0,

so the coordinate notation is $(x, y) \rightarrow (x, 0)$.

© Houghton Mifflin Harcourt Publishing Company

2 EXPLORE · Classifying Transformations

Investigate the effects of various transformations on the given right triangle.

* Use coordinate notation to help you find the image of each vertex of the triangle.
* Plot the images of the vertices.
* Connect the images of the vertices to draw the image of the triangle.

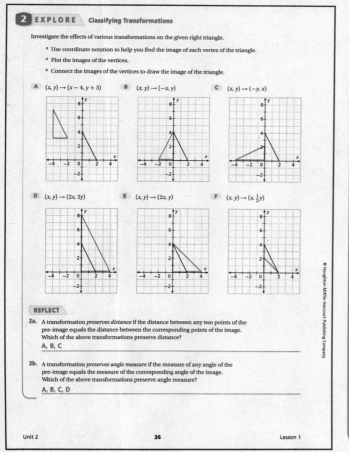

A $(x, y) \rightarrow (x - 4, y + 3)$

B $(x, y) \rightarrow (-x, y)$

C $(x, y) \rightarrow (-y, x)$

D $(x, y) \rightarrow (2x, 2y)$

E $(x, y) \rightarrow (2x, y)$

F $(x, y) \rightarrow (x, \frac{1}{2}y)$

© Houghton Mifflin Harcourt Publishing Company

REFLECT

2a. A transformation *preserves distance* if the distance between any two points of the pre-image equals the distance between the corresponding points of the image. Which of the above transformations preserve distance?

A, B, C

2b. A transformation *preserves angle measure* if the measure of any angle of the pre-image equals the measure of the corresponding angle of the image. Which of the above transformations preserve angle measure?

A, B, C, D

3 EXAMPLE

Questioning Strategies

- How can you describe a rigid motion in your own words? **A rigid motion moves a figure without changing its size or shape.**

- What must be true about the pre-image and image under a rigid motion? **They have the same size and shape.**

EXTRA EXAMPLE

The figures show the pre-image ($\triangle MNP$) and image ($\triangle M'N'P'$) under a transformation. Determine whether the transformation appears to be a rigid motion. Explain.

A.

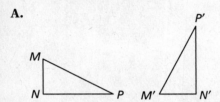

Rigid motion; the transformation does not change the size or shape of the figure.

B.

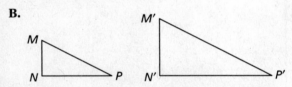

Not a rigid motion; the transformation changes the size of the figure.

C.

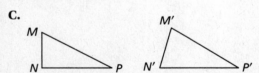

Not a rigid motion; the transformation changes the shape of the figure.

Teaching Strategies

Rigid motions are frequently used to generate repeating patterns on clothing, in architecture, and in artwork. Ask students to identify patterns in the classroom that may have been created by taking a single figure and transforming it repeatedly by a rigid motion. For example, a pattern of floor tiles is likely to consist of a single shape (a square) that is mapped to different positions by a rigid motion. The fact that all of the tiles are same size and shape shows that the underlying transformation is a rigid motion.

MATHEMATICAL PRACTICE — **Highlighting the Standards**

You may wish to address Standard 5 (Use appropriate tools strategically) as students work through the lesson. Specifically, ask students what tools they can use to help them identify transformations that are rigid motions. Students might suggest using tracing paper or transparencies to trace the pre-image of a figure so they can easily check whether the image has exactly the same size and shape.

A **rigid motion** (or *isometry*) is a transformation that changes the position of a figure without changing the size or shape of the figure.

3 EXAMPLE   Identifying Rigid Motions

The figures show the pre-image ($\triangle ABC$) and image ($\triangle A'B'C'$) under a transformation. Determine whether the transformation appears to be a rigid motion. Explain.

A

The transformation does not change the size or shape of the figure

Therefore, the transformation appears to be a rigid motion.

B

The transformation changes the shape of the figure.

Therefore, the transformation does not appear to be a rigid motion.

C

The transformation changes the size of the figure. Therefore, the

transformation does not appear to be a rigid motion.

REFLECT

3a. How could you use tracing paper or a transparency to help you identify rigid motions?

Trace the pre-image. Move the tracing to see if it perfectly matches the image.

If so, the transformation is a rigid motion.

3b. Which of the transformations on the previous page appear to be rigid motions?

A, B, C

Rigid motions have some important properties. These are summarized below.

Properties of Rigid Motions (isometries)
* Rigid motions preserve distance.
* Rigid motions preserve angle measure.
* Rigid motions preserve betweenness.
* Rigid motions preserve collinearity.

The above properties ensure that if a figure is determined by certain points, then its image after a rigid motion is also determined by those points. For example, $\triangle ABC$ is determined by its vertices, points A, B, and C. The image of $\triangle ABC$ after a rigid motion is the triangle determined by A', B', and C'.

PRACTICE

Draw the image of the triangle under the given transformation. Then tell whether the transformation appears to be a rigid motion.

1. $(x, y) \rightarrow (x + 3, y)$

rigid motion

2. $(x, y) \rightarrow (3x, 3y)$

not a rigid motion

3. $(x, y) \rightarrow (x, -y)$

rigid motion

4. $(x, y) \rightarrow (-x, -y)$

rigid motion

5. $(x, y) \rightarrow (x, 3y)$

not a rigid motion

6. $(x, y) \rightarrow (x - 4, y - 4)$

rigid motion

Notes

Essential Question

How do you identify transformations that are rigid motions?

Rigid motions are those transformations that change the position of a figure without changing the figure's size or shape.

Summarize

Have students make a graphic organizer to summarize what they know so far about transformations and rigid motions. An example is shown below.

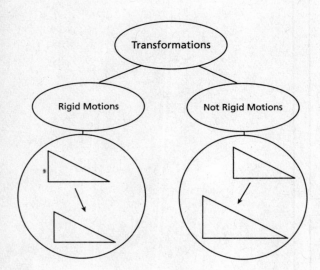

Where skills are taught	Where skills are practiced
2 EXPLORE	EXS. 1–6
3 EXAMPLE	EXS. 7–10

Exercises 11–14: Students extend what they learned about transformations and transformation notation.

Exercise 15: Students use reasoning to solve a problem about properties of rigid motions.

The figures show the pre-image (*ABCD*) and image (*A'B'C'D*) under a transformation. Determine whether the transformation appears to be a rigid motion. Explain.

7.

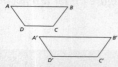

No; the transformation changes the shape of the figure.

8.

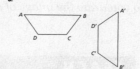

Yes; the transformation does not change the shape or size of the figure.

9.

Yes; the transformation does not change the shape or size of the figure.

10.

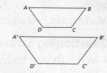

No; the transformation changes the size of the figure.

In Exercises 11–14, consider a transformation *T* that maps $\triangle XYZ$ to $\triangle X'Y'Z'$.

11. What is the image of $\overline{XY}$? _____ $\overline{X'Y'}$

12. What is $T(Z)$? _____ Z'

13. What is the pre-image of $\angle Y'$? _____ $\angle Y$

14. Can you conclude that $XY = X'Y'$? Why or why not?

No; you do not know if the transformation is a rigid motion.

15. Point *M* is the midpoint of $\overline{AB}$. After a rigid motion, can you conclude that *M'* is the midpoint of $\overline{A'B'}$? Why or why not?

Yes; a rigid motion preserves distance, betweenness, and collinearity, so *M'* will be equidistant from *A'* and *B'* and also on $\overline{A'B'}$, so it is the midpoint of $\overline{A'B'}$.

Reflections

Essential question: *How do you draw the image of a figure under a reflection?*

COMMON CORE Standards for Mathematical Content

CC.9-12.G.CO.2 ... describe transformations as functions that take points in the plane as inputs and give other points as outputs. ...

CC.9-12.G.CO.4 Develop definitions of ... reflections ... in terms of ... perpendicular lines ... and line segments

CC.9-12.G.CO.5 Given a geometric figure and a ... reflection ... draw the transformed figure using, e.g., graph paper, tracing paper, or geometry software.

CC.9-12.G.CO.6 Use geometric descriptions of rigid motions to transform figures and to predict the effect of a given rigid motion on a given figure; ...

Vocabulary

reflection

Prerequisites

Transformations and Rigid Motions, Lesson 2-1

Math Background

Reflections are one of the three rigid motions that students will study. (Translations are covered in Lesson 2-5 and rotations are covered in Lesson 2-6). Reflections may be considered the most basic of the rigid motions because the other two rigid motions can be expressed in terms of reflections. In particular, every translation is a composition of reflections across parallel lines. Every rotation is a composition of reflections across intersecting lines.

INTRODUCE

Ask students to describe everyday examples of reflections. Students might mention mirrors or the reflection of a mountain in a lake. Ask students to describe characteristics of these reflections. Be sure students realize that in every case the reflected object is the same size and shape as the original object.

TEACH

1 EXPLORE

Materials: straightedge, tracing paper

Questioning Strategies

- Why do you have to flip the tracing paper over and move it so that line ℓ lies on top of itself? **This makes line ℓ the line of reflection.**

- Once you've drawn the reflection image, how can you use paper folding to check your work? **Fold the page on the line of reflection. The pre-image and image should match up perfectly.**

- What is the image of the line of reflection? **The line of reflection is its own image.**

Technology

You may wish to have students carry out the Explore using geometry software. To do so, first have students construct a figure similar to the given pre-image. Then have them construct a line and mark it as the line of reflection by choosing Mark Mirror from the Transform menu. Finally, have students select the pre-image and choose Reflect from the Transform menu.

MATHEMATICAL PRACTICE Highlighting the Standards

Making conjectures is an essential part of mathematics and an important aspect of Standard 3 (Construct viable arguments and critique the reasoning of others). This standard states that students should "reasoning inductively" and the Explore gives students an excellent opportunity to do so. In particular, students should look back at their work and make a conjecture about the reflection image of a point that lies on the line of reflection.

Reflections

2-2

COMMON CORE

CC 9-12.G.CO.2,
CC 9-12.G.CO.4,
CC 9-12.G.CO.5,
CC 9-12.G.CO.6

Essential question: *How do you draw the image of a figure under a reflection?*

One type of rigid motion is a reflection.
A *reflection* is a transformation that moves points by flipping them over a line called the *line of reflection*.
The figure shows the reflection of quadrilateral *ABCD* across line *ℓ*.
Notice that the pre-image and image are mirror images of each other.

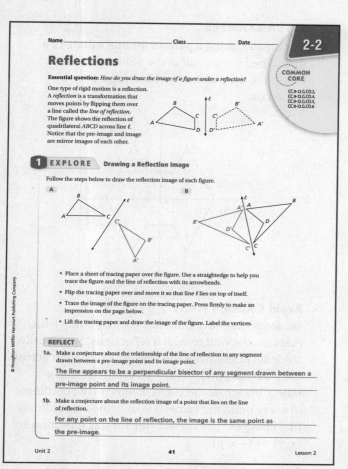

1 EXPLORE   Drawing a Reflection Image

Follow the steps below to draw the reflection image of each figure.

- Place a sheet of tracing paper over the figure. Use a straightedge to help you trace the figure and the line of reflection with its arrowheads.
- Flip the tracing paper over and move it so that line *ℓ* lies on top of itself.
- Trace the image of the figure on the tracing paper. Press firmly to make an impression on the page below.
- Lift the tracing paper and draw the image of the figure. Label the vertices.

REFLECT

1a. Make a conjecture about the relationship of the line of reflection to any segment drawn between a pre-image point and its image point.

The line appears to be a perpendicular bisector of any segment drawn between a pre-image point and its image point.

1b. Make a conjecture about the reflection image of a point that lies on the line of reflection.

For any point on the line of reflection, the image is the same point as the pre-image.

© Houghton Mifflin Harcourt Publishing Company

Your work may help you understand the formal definition of a reflection.

A **reflection** across line *ℓ* maps a point *P* to its image *P′* as follows.

- If *P* is not on line *ℓ*, then *ℓ* is the perpendicular bisector of $\overline{PP'}$.
- If *P* is on line *ℓ*, then *P = P′*.

The notation $r_\ell(P) = P'$ says that the image of point *P* after a reflection across line *ℓ* is *P′*.

2 EXAMPLE   Constructing a Reflection Image

Work directly on the figure below and follow the given steps to construct the image of △*ABC* after a reflection across line *m*.

A Start with point *A*. Construct a perpendicular to line *m* that passes through point *A*.

B Label the intersection of the perpendicular and line *m* as point *X*.

C Place the point of your compass on point *X* and open the compass to the distance *XA*. Make an arc to mark this distance on the perpendicular on the other side of line *m*.

D Label the point where the arc intersects the perpendicular as point *A′*.

E Repeat the steps for the other vertices of △*ABC*.
(*Hint:* It may be helpful to extend line *m* in order to construct perpendiculars from points *B* and *C*.)

REFLECT

2a. Reflections have all the properties of rigid motions. For example, reflections preserve distance and angle measure. Explain how you could use a ruler and protractor to check this in your construction.

Check that *AB = A′B′*, *BC = B′C′*, *AC = A′C′*, *m∠A = m∠A′*, *m∠B = m∠B′*, and *m∠C = m∠C′*.

© Houghton Mifflin Harcourt Publishing Company

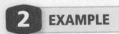

2 EXAMPLE

Questioning Strategies

- How many perpendiculars to line m will you have to construct in order to construct the reflection image of $\triangle ABC$? Why? **Three; you construct one perpendicular for each vertex of the triangle.**

- How can you check that you constructed the image correctly? **Fold the page on line m and check that the image and pre-image match up perfectly.**

EXTRA EXAMPLE

Construct the image of $\triangle DEF$ after a reflection across line m.

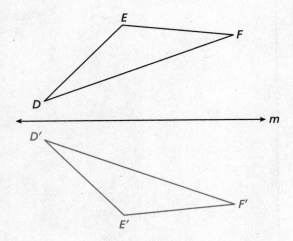

3 EXAMPLE

Questioning Strategies

- How will the right half of the logo compare to the left half? **It will be the same size and shape as the left half, but it will be a mirror image of the left half.**

- What does the rule $(x, y) \rightarrow (-x, y)$ mean? **To reflect a point across the y-axis, use the opposite of the x-coordinate and keep the y-coordinate the same.**

EXTRA EXAMPLE

You are designing a pattern for one square of a quilt. The bottom half of the pattern is shown. Complete the pattern by reflecting it across the x-axis.

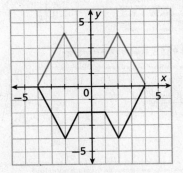

Avoid Common Errors

Students may have difficulty remembering which rules correspond to which reflections. Specifically, students might write the rule for a reflection across the y-axis as $(x, y) \rightarrow (x, -y)$. Point out that a reflection across the y-axis, keeps the y-coordinate of every point the same; it is only the x-coordinate that changes. The correct rule for this reflection is $(x, y) \rightarrow (-x, y)$.

The table provides coordinate notation for reflections in a coordinate plane.

Rules for Reflections in a Coordinate Plane	
Reflection across the x-axis	$(x, y) \rightarrow (x, -y)$
Reflection across the y-axis	$(x, y) \rightarrow (-x, y)$
Reflection across the line $y = x$	$(x, y) \rightarrow (y, x)$

3 EXAMPLE   Drawing a Reflection in a Coordinate Plane

You are designing a logo for a bank. The left half of the logo is shown. You will complete the logo by reflecting this figure across the y-axis.

A   In the space below, sketch your prediction of what the completed logo will look like.

B   In the table at right, list the vertices of the left half of the logo. Then use the rule for a reflection across the y-axis to write the vertices of the right half of the logo.

C   Plot the vertices of the right half of the logo. Then connect the vertices to complete the logo. Compare the completed logo to your prediction.

Left Half (x, y)	Right Half (−x, y)
(0, 4)	(0, 4)
(−3, 2)	(3, 2)
(−2, 0)	(2, 0)
(−3, −3)	(3, −3)
(0, −2)	(0, −2)

REFLECT

3a.   Explain how your prediction compares to the completed logo.

Answers will vary.

3b.   How can you use paper folding to check that you completed the logo correctly?

Fold along the line of reflection and check that the two halves lie on top

of each other.

PRACTICE

Use tracing paper to help you draw the reflection image of each figure across line *m*. Label the vertices of the image using prime notation.

1.
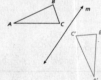

2.
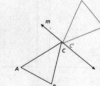

3.

4.

5.

6.

Essential Question

How do you draw the image of a figure under a reflection?

You can draw the image of a figure under a reflection by using tracing paper or by doing a compass-and-straightedge construction.

Summarize

Have students make a graphic organizer that summarizes reflections in a coordinate plane. A sample is shown below.

Where skills are taught	Where skills are practiced
1 EXPLORE	EXS. 1–6
2 EXAMPLE	EXS. 7–8
3 EXAMPLE	EXS. 9–15

Exercise 16: Students extend what they learned in **3** EXAMPLE to solve a reasoning problem.

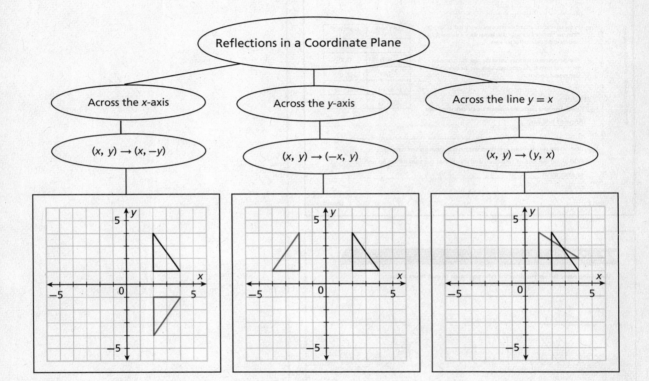

Use a compass and straightedge to construct the reflection image of each figure across line *m*. Label the vertices of the image using prime notation.

7.

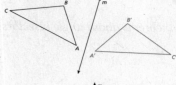

8.

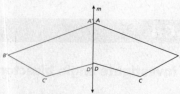

Give the image of each point after a reflection across the given line.

9. (3, 1); *x*-axis

(3, −1)

10. (−6, −3); *y*-axis

(6, −3)

11. (0, −2); *y* = *x*

(−2, 0)

12. (−4, 3); *y*-axis

(4, 3)

13. (5, 5); *y* = *x*

(5, 5)

14. (−7, 0); *x*-axis

(−7, 0)

15. As the first step in designing a logo, you draw the figure shown in the first quadrant of the coordinate plane. Then you reflect the figure across the *x*-axis. You complete the design by reflecting the original figure and its image across the *y*-axis. Draw the completed design.

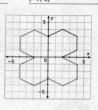

16. When point *P* is reflected across the *y*-axis, its image lies in Quadrant IV. When point *P* is reflected across the line *y* = *x*, its position does not change. What can you say about the coordinates of point *P*?

Both coordinates are negative, and the *x*- and *y*-coordinates are equal.

2-3

FOCUS ON REASONING
Angle Bisectors

Essential question: *What are the key theorems about angle bisectors?*

COMMON CORE **Standards for Mathematical Content**

CC.9-12.G.CO.2 ... describe transformations as functions that take points in the plane as inputs and give other points as outputs. ...

CC.9-12.G.CO.9 Prove theorems about lines and angles.

Vocabulary
indirect proof

Prerequisites
Angles, Lesson 1-4

Proofs about Lines and Angles, Lesson 1-6

Reflections, Lesson 2-2

Math Background
This is one of several related lessons that build the deductive framework for addressing Common Core Standard CC.9-12.G.CO.8 (Explain how the criteria for triangle congruence (ASA, SAS, and SSS) follow from the definition of congruence in terms of rigid motions). This lesson covers basic theorems about angle bisectors. Lesson 2-4 addresses theorems about perpendicular bisectors. The theorems from these lessons serve as the raw materials for proving, in Lesson 3-3, that triangle congruence criteria follow from the transformation-based definition of congruence.

INTRODUCE

Begin by discussing indirect proofs. You may want to give students some examples based on everyday situations. For instance, ask students how they would prove that they were not in Paris yesterday. Students are likely to give an indirect proof ("If I had been in Paris, I couldn't have this receipt from the local grocery store with yesterday's date on it.") Be sure to emphasize that the first step in an indirect proof is assuming that what you are trying to prove is false.

TEACH

1 Investigate angle bisectors.

Questioning Strategies
- Is the angle bisector unique? Why? Yes, it is the line that divides the angle exactly in half.
- What do you use as the line of reflection in the investigation? the angle bisector
- Why do you think that the angle bisector is the line of reflection for each side of the angle is the image of each other? It divides the angle exactly in half so each part of the angle is exactly like the other.

2 Prove the Angle Bisection Theorem.

Questioning Strategies
- What are you trying to prove? The image of $\overrightarrow{BA}$ under a reflection across line m is $\overrightarrow{BC}$.
- How can you write a statement that says that this is false? The image of $\overrightarrow{BA}$ under a reflection across line m is not $\overrightarrow{BC}$.
- The proof shows that the image of $\overrightarrow{BA}$ under a reflection across line m is $\overrightarrow{BC}$. Do you also need to prove that the image of $\overrightarrow{BC}$ under a reflection across line m is $\overrightarrow{BA}$? Why or why not? No; the names of the rays are arbitrary, so the same argument shows that the image of $\overrightarrow{BC}$ under a reflection across line m is $\overrightarrow{BA}$.

Name _____ Class _____ Date _____

FOCUS ON REASONING
Angle Bisectors

Essential question: *What are the key theorems about angle bisectors?*

1 Investigate angle bisectors.

A Follow these steps to explore reflections across an angle bisector.

- Use a straightedge to draw a large angle on a sheet of paper.
- Use a protractor to help you draw the bisector of the angle.
- Fold the paper along the angle bisector and note the result.
- Compare your observations with those of other students.

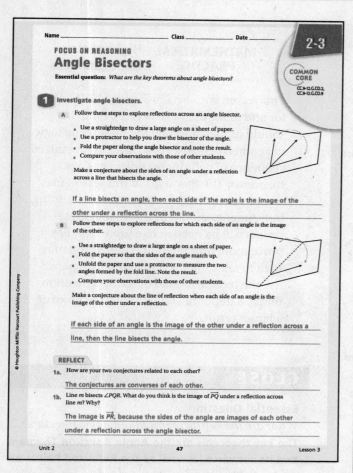

Make a conjecture about the sides of an angle under a reflection across a line that bisects the angle.

If a line bisects an angle, then each side of the angle is the image of the
other under a reflection across the line.

B Follow these steps to explore reflections for which each side of an angle is the image of the other.

- Use a straightedge to draw a large angle on a sheet of paper.
- Fold the paper so that the sides of the angle match up.
- Unfold the paper and use a protractor to measure the two angles formed by the fold line. Note the result.
- Compare your observations with those of other students.

Make a conjecture about the line of reflection when each side of an angle is the image of the other under a reflection.

If each side of an angle is the image of the other under a reflection across a
line, then the line bisects the angle.

REFLECT

1a. How are your two conjectures related to each other?

The conjectures are converses of each other.

1b. Line *m* bisects ∠PQR. What do you think is the image of $\overrightarrow{PQ}$ under a reflection across line *m*? Why?

The image is $\overrightarrow{PR}$, because the sides of the angle are images of each other

under a reflection across the angle bisector.

You can use reflections and their properties to prove theorems about angle bisectors. These theorems will be very useful in proofs later on.

The first proof is an **indirect proof** (or a *proof by contradiction*). To write such a proof, you assume that what you are trying to prove is false and you show that this assumption leads to a contradiction.

2 Prove the Angle Bisection Theorem.

If a line bisects an angle, then each side of the angle is the image of the other under a reflection across the line.

Given: Line *m* is the bisector of ∠ABC.

Prove: The image of $\overrightarrow{BA}$ under a reflection across line *m* is $\overrightarrow{BC}$.

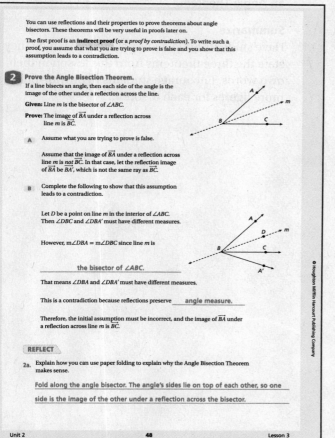

A Assume what you are trying to prove is false.

Assume that the image of $\overrightarrow{BA}$ under a reflection across line *m* is *not* $\overrightarrow{BC}$. In that case, let the reflection image of $\overrightarrow{BA}$ be $\overrightarrow{BA'}$, which is not the same ray as $\overrightarrow{BC}$.

B Complete the following to show that this assumption leads to a contradiction.

Let *D* be a point on line *m* in the interior of ∠ABC. Then ∠DBC and ∠DBA' must have different measures.

However, m∠DBA = m∠DBC since line *m* is

_____the bisector of ∠ABC._____

That means ∠DBA and ∠DBA' must have different measures.

This is a contradiction because reflections preserve ____angle measure.____

Therefore, the initial assumption must be incorrect, and the image of $\overrightarrow{BA}$ under a reflection across line *m* is $\overrightarrow{BC}$.

REFLECT

2a. Explain how you can use paper folding to explain why the Angle Bisection Theorem makes sense.

Fold along the angle bisector. The angle's sides lie on top of each other, so one

side is the image of the other under a reflection across the bisector.

Notes

© Houghton Mifflin Harcourt Publishing Company

3 Prove the Converse of the Angle Bisection Theorem.

Questioning Strategies

- Is this proof also an indirect proof? Why or why not? **No; this proof does not begin by assuming that what you are trying to prove is false.**

- How do you know that point *B* lies on line *m*? **Point *B* is fixed under the reflection across line *m* and the only fixed points under a reflection are the points on the line of reflection.**

- In the last line of the proof, what reason could you give for the statement "Therefore, line *m* bisects $\angle ABC$"? **This follows from the definition of an angle bisector.**

4 Prove the Reflected Points on an Angle Theorem.

Questioning Strategies

- What does $r_m(A) = A'$ mean? **Point *A'* is the image of point *A* under a reflection across line *m*.**

- Why do you think the Reflected Points on an Angle Theorem is the last of the three theorems presented in this lesson? **The proof of this theorem depends upon the Angle Bisection Theorem, so that theorem must be proved first.**

Differentiated Instruction

Some students may have difficulty visualizing the Reflected Points on an Angle Theorem. You may want to have students do a brief hands-on activity to explore the theorem. To do so, have students draw an angle on a sheet of tracing paper. Then have them use a ruler to plot points on each side of the angle that are the same distance from the vertex. Students can fold the paper to find the angle bisector and note that the two points they plotted are images of each other under the reflection across the bisector.

This lesson connects to Standard 7 (Look for and make use of structure). Students should understand that the underlying logic of geometry consists of a carefully-organized sequence of definitions, postulates, and theorems. The theorems in this lesson may not seem especially important or interesting, but students should be aware that these results will be needed later on when they prove more prominent theorems. You may wish to tell students that mathematicians use the term *lemma* to describe a theorem that is a stepping-stone toward the proof of a larger result.

CLOSE

Essential Question

What are the key theorems about angle bisectors? **The key theorems are the Angle Bisection Theorem and its converse, as well as the Reflected Points on an Angle Theorem.**

Summarize

Have students write a journal entry in which they state the three theorems from this lesson in their own words. Encourage students to provide one or more figures for each theorem.

3 Prove the Converse of the Angle Bisection Theorem.

If each side of an angle is the image of the other under
a reflection across a line, then the line bisects the angle.

Given: ∠ABC and line *m* such that the image of $\overrightarrow{BA}$ under
a reflection across line *m* is $\overrightarrow{BC}$.

Prove: Line *m* bisects ∠ABC.

Complete the following proof.

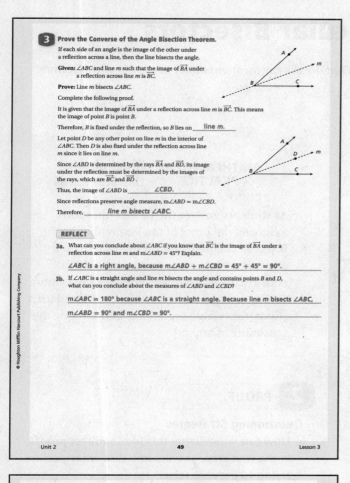

It is given that the image of $\overrightarrow{BA}$ under a reflection across line *m* is $\overrightarrow{BC}$. This means
the image of point *B* is point *B*.

Therefore, *B* is fixed under the reflection, so *B* lies on _____line *m.*_____

Let point *D* be any other point on line *m* in the interior of
∠ABC. Then *D* is also fixed under the reflection across line
m since it lies on line *m*.

Since ∠ABD is determined by the rays $\overrightarrow{BA}$ and $\overrightarrow{BD}$, its image
under the reflection must be determined by the images of
the rays, which are $\overrightarrow{BC}$ and $\overrightarrow{BD}$.

Thus, the image of ∠ABD is _____∠CBD._____

Since reflections preserve angle measure, m∠ABD = m∠CBD.

Therefore, _____line *m* bisects ∠ABC._____

REFLECT

3a. What can you conclude about ∠ABC if you know that $\overrightarrow{BC}$ is the image of $\overrightarrow{BA}$ under a
reflection across line *m* and m∠ABD = 45°? Explain.

∠ABC is a right angle, because m∠ABD + m∠CBD = 45° + 45° = 90°.

3b. If ∠ABC is a straight angle and line *m* bisects the angle and contains points *B* and *D*,
what can you conclude about the measures of ∠ABD and ∠CBD?

m∠ABC = 180° because ∠ABC is a straight angle. Because line *m* bisects ∠ABC,

m∠ABD = 90° and m∠CBD = 90°.

© Houghton Mifflin Harcourt Publishing Company

---

4 Prove the Reflected Points on an Angle Theorem.

If two points of an angle are located the same distance from the vertex but on different
sides of the angle, then the points are images of each other under a reflection across
the line that bisects the angle.

Given: Line *m* is the bisector of ∠ABC and BA = BC.

Prove: $r_m(A) = C$ and $r_m(C) = A$.

Complete the following proof.

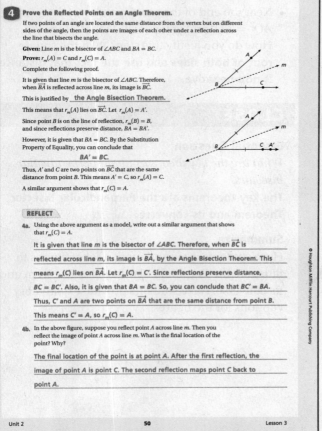

It is given that line *m* is the bisector of ∠ABC. Therefore,
when $\overrightarrow{BA}$ is reflected across line *m*, its image is $\overrightarrow{BC}$.

This is justified by ___the Angle Bisection Theorem.___

This means that $r_m(A)$ lies on $\overrightarrow{BC}$. Let $r_m(A) = A'$.

Since point *B* is on the line of reflection, $r_m(B) = B$,
and since reflections preserve distance, BA = BA'.

However, it is given that BA = BC. By the Substitution
Property of Equality, you can conclude that

_____BA' = BC._____

Thus, A' and C are two points on $\overrightarrow{BC}$ that are the same
distance from point *B*. This means A' = C, so $r_m(A) = C$.
A similar argument shows that $r_m(C) = A$.

REFLECT

4a. Using the above argument as a model, write out a similar argument that shows
that $r_m(C) = A$.

It is given that line *m* is the bisector of ∠ABC. Therefore, when $\overrightarrow{BC}$ is

reflected across line *m*, its image is $\overrightarrow{BA}$, by the Angle Bisection Theorem. This

means $r_m(C)$ lies on $\overrightarrow{BA}$. Let $r_m(C) = C'$. Since reflections preserve distance,

BC = BC'. Also, it is given that BA = BC. So, you can conclude that BC' = BA.

Thus, C' and A are two points on $\overrightarrow{BA}$ that are the same distance from point *B*.

This means C' = A, so $r_m(C) = A$.

4b. In the above figure, suppose you reflect point *A* across line *m*. Then you
reflect the image of point *A* across line *m*. What is the final location of the
point? Why?

The final location of the point is at point *A*. After the first reflection, the

image of point *A* is point *C*. The second reflection maps point *C* back to

point *A*.

© Houghton Mifflin Harcourt Publishing Company

Notes

Perpendicular Bisectors

Essential question: *What are the key theorems about perpendicular bisectors?*

COMMON **Standards for**
CORE **Mathematical Content**

CC.9-12.G.CO.2 ... describe transformations as functions that take points in the plane as inputs and give other points as outputs. ...

CC.9-12.G.CO.9 Prove theorems about lines and angles.

Prerequisites

Parallel and Perpendicular Lines, Lesson 1-5

Reflections, Lesson 2-2

The Pythagorean Theorem, Grade 8

Math Background

This is one of several related lessons that build the deductive framework for addressing Common Core Standard CC.9-12.G.CO.8 (Explain how the criteria for triangle congruence (ASA, SAS, and SSS) follow from the definition of congruence in terms of rigid motions). Lesson 2-3 presented basic theorems about angle bisectors. This lesson addresses theorems about perpendicular bisectors. The theorems from these lessons serve as the raw materials for proving, in Lesson 3-3, that triangle congruence criteria follow from the transformation-based definition of congruence.

INTRODUCE

A point is on the perpendicular bisector of a line segment *if and only if* the point is equidistant from the segment's endpoints. Because this statement is a biconditional, there are two parts to the proof. The two parts are presented separately in this lesson as the Perpendicular Bisector Theorem and its converse.

TEACH

1 PROOF

Questioning Strategies

• Suppose you construct the perpendicular bisector of $\overline{CD}$ and then choose any point Q on the perpendicular bisector. If you measure the distance from Q to each endpoint of the segment, what do you expect to find? **QC = QD**

MATHEMATICAL PRACTICE — Highlighting the Standards

As students answer the Reflect questions following the proof of the Perpendicular Bisector Theorem, ask them to share their answers with classmates and have them constructively critique each other's reasoning. Doing so addresses a key aspect of Standard 3 (Construct viable arguments and critique the reasoning of others).

2 PROOF

Questioning Strategies

• How can you tell that this is an indirect proof? **In the first step, you assume that what you are trying to prove is false.**

• Near the end of the proof, you know that $AQ^2 = BQ^2$ and you conclude that $AQ = BQ$. How do you justify this step? **Take the square root of both sides and use the fact that distance is non-negative.**

CLOSE

Essential Question

What are the key theorems about perpendicular bisectors?

The key theorems are the Perpendicular Bisector Theorem and its converse.

Summarize

Have students draw and mark a set of figures to illustrate the Perpendicular Bisector Theorem and its converse. Have students provide explanatory captions for the figures.

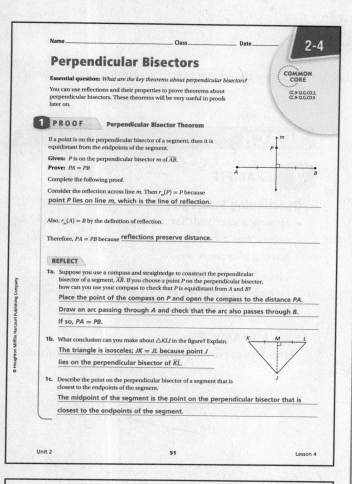

Name_____ Class_____ Date_____

2-4

Perpendicular Bisectors

COMMON CORE

CC.9-12.G.CO.2,
CC.9-12.G.CO.9

Essential question: *What are the key theorems about perpendicular bisectors?*

You can use reflections and their properties to prove theorems about perpendicular bisectors. These theorems will be very useful in proofs later on.

1 PROOF Perpendicular Bisector Theorem

If a point is on the perpendicular bisector of a segment, then it is equidistant from the endpoints of the segment.

Given: P is on the perpendicular bisector m of $\overline{AB}$.

Prove: $PA = PB$

Complete the following proof.

Consider the reflection across line m. Then $r_m(P) = P$ because

point P lies on line m, which is the line of reflection.

Also, $r_m(A) = B$ by the definition of reflection.

Therefore, $PA = PB$ because reflections preserve distance.

REFLECT

1a. Suppose you use a compass and straightedge to construct the perpendicular bisector of a segment, $\overline{AB}$. If you choose a point P on the perpendicular bisector, how can you use your compass to check that P is equidistant from A and B?

Place the point of the compass on P and open the compass to the distance PA.

Draw an arc passing through A and check that the arc also passes through B.

If so, $PA = PB$.

1b. What conclusion can you make about $\triangle KLJ$ in the figure? Explain.

The triangle is isosceles; $JK = JL$ because point J

lies on the perpendicular bisector of $\overline{KL}$.

1c. Describe the point on the perpendicular bisector of a segment that is closest to the endpoints of the segment.

The midpoint of the segment is the point on the perpendicular bisector that is

closest to the endpoints of the segment.

© Houghton Mifflin Harcourt Publishing Company

The converse of the Perpendicular Bisector Theorem is also true. In order to prove the converse, you will use an indirect proof and the Pythagorean Theorem.

Recall that the Pythagorean Theorem states that in a right triangle with legs of length a and b and hypotenuse of length c, $a^2 + b^2 = c^2$.

$$a^2 + b^2 = c^2$$

2 PROOF Converse of the Perpendicular Bisector Theorem

If a point is equidistant from the endpoints of a segment, then it lies on the perpendicular bisector of the segment.

Given: $PA = PB$

Prove: P is on the perpendicular bisector m of $\overline{AB}$.

A Assume what you are trying to prove is false.

Assume that point P is *not* on the perpendicular bisector m of $\overline{AB}$. Then when you draw a perpendicular from P to the line containing A and B, the perpendicular intersects this line at a point Q, which is not the midpoint of $\overline{AB}$.

B Complete the following to show that this assumption leads to a contradiction.

$\overline{PQ}$ forms two right triangles, $\triangle AQP$ and $\triangle BQP$.

$AQ^2 + QP^2 = PA^2$ and $BQ^2 + QP^2 = PB^2$ by the Pythagorean Theorem.

Subtract these equations:

$$\begin{array}{r} AQ^2 + QP^2 = PA^2 \\ BQ^2 + QP^2 = PB^2 \\ \hline AQ^2 - BQ^2 = PA^2 - PB^2 \end{array}$$

However, $PA^2 - PB^2 = 0$ because $PA = PB.$

Therefore, $AQ^2 - BQ^2 = 0$. This means $AQ^2 = BQ^2$ and $AQ = BQ$. This contradicts the fact that Q is not the midpoint of $\overline{AB}$. Thus, the initial assumption must be incorrect, and P must lie on the perpendicular bisector of $\overline{AB}$.

REFLECT

2a. In the proof, once you know $AQ^2 = BQ^2$, why can you conclude $AQ = BQ$?

Take the square root of both sides. Since distances are nonnegative, $AQ = BQ$.

2b. Explain how the converse of the Perpendicular Bisector Theorem justifies the compass-and-straightedge construction of the perpendicular bisector of a segment.

The construction involves making two arcs that intersect in two points. Each of

these two intersection points is equidistant from the endpoints of the segment,

because the arcs use the same radius. So, both of the intersection points are on

the perpendicular bisector of the segment.

© Houghton Mifflin Harcourt Publishing Company

2-5 Translations

Essential question: How do you draw the image of a figure under a translation?

COMMON CORE Standards for Mathematical Content

CC.9-12.G.CO.2 ... describe transformations as functions that take points in the plane as inputs and give other points as outputs. ...

CC.9-12.G.CO.4 Develop definitions of ... translations ... in terms of ... parallel lines ... and line segments.

CC.9-12.G.CO.5 Given a geometric figure and a ... translation ... draw the transformed figure using, e.g., graph paper, tracing paper, or geometry software.

CC.9-12.G.CO.6 Use geometric descriptions of rigid motions to transform figures and to predict the effect of a given rigid motion on a given figure; ...

Vocabulary

vector
initial point
terminal point
component form
translation

Prerequisites

Parallel and Perpendicular Lines, Lesson 1-5
Transformations and Rigid Motions, Lesson 2-1

Math Background

Translations are the second of the three rigid motions that students will study in this course (reflections were covered in Lesson 2-2 and rotations will be covered in Lesson 2-6). It is easy to understand a translation informally by thinking of it as a slide in a given direction by a given distance. Providing a mathematical definition of translations requires a bit more groundwork. In fact, it is most efficient to define translations in terms of vectors.

INTRODUCE

Ask students to give everyday examples of slides or translations. If no one suggests it, you might describe an object moving along a straight conveyor belt in a factory. This is an example of a translation because the object slides along a straight path from a starting point to an ending point. Tell the class they will learn more about translations and will see how to define translations in terms of vectors.

TEACH

1 EXAMPLE

Questioning Strategies

- How is a vector different from a line segment? **A vector has a direction; a line segment does not have a direction.**
- How is ⟨5, 3⟩ different from (5, 3)? **⟨5, 3⟩ represents a vector in a coordinate plane, whereas (5, 3) is a point.**

EXTRA EXAMPLE

Name the vector and write it in component form.

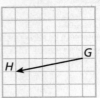

$\overrightarrow{GH}$; ⟨−5, −1⟩

2 EXAMPLE

Questioning Strategies

- Before constructing the translation image, where do you predict the image will lie? Why? **It will lie about 5 cm to the right and a bit above the pre-image. This is the distance and direction given by the translation vector.**
- What can you say about the length AA'? **It is equal to the magnitude of $\vec{v}$.**
- Why do the figures that accompany the steps of the example show the construction marks for copying an angle? **This is the method for constructing a line through A that is parallel to $\vec{v}$.**

EXTRA EXAMPLE

Construct the image of $\triangle DEF$ after a translation along $\vec{v}$.

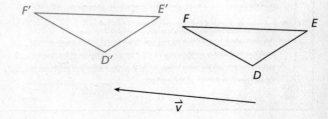

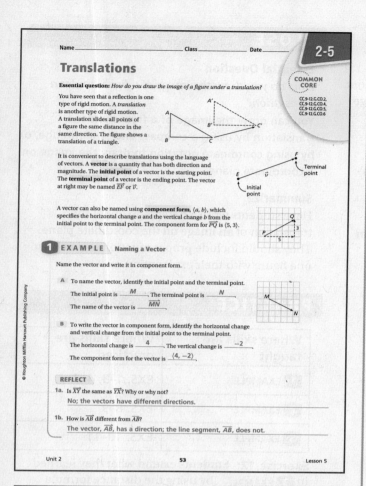

Name _____ Class _____ Date _____

2-5

Translations

Essential question: *How do you draw the image of a figure under a translation?*

You have seen that a reflection is one type of rigid motion. A *translation* is another type of rigid motion. A translation slides all points of a figure the same distance in the same direction. The figure shows a translation of a triangle.

COMMON CORE

CC.9-12.G.CO.2,
CC.9-12.G.CO.4,
CC.9-12.G.CO.5,
CC.9-12.G.CO.6

It is convenient to describe translations using the language of vectors. A **vector** is a quantity that has both direction and magnitude. The **initial point** of a vector is the starting point. The **terminal point** of a vector is the ending point. The vector at right may be named $\overrightarrow{EF}$ or $\vec{v}$.

A vector can also be named using **component form**, $\langle a, b \rangle$, which specifies the horizontal change a and the vertical change b from the initial point to the terminal point. The component form for $\overrightarrow{PQ}$ is $\langle 5, 3 \rangle$.

1 EXAMPLE Naming a Vector

Name the vector and write it in component form.

A To name the vector, identify the initial point and the terminal point.

The initial point is ___*M*___ The terminal point is ___*N*___

The name of the vector is ___$\overrightarrow{MN}$___

B To write the vector in component form, identify the horizontal change and vertical change from the initial point to the terminal point.

The horizontal change is ___4___ The vertical change is ___−2___

The component form for the vector is ___$\langle 4, -2 \rangle$___

REFLECT

1a. Is $\overrightarrow{XY}$ the same as $\overrightarrow{YX}$? Why or why not?

No; the vectors have different directions.

1b. How is $\overrightarrow{AB}$ different from $\overline{AB}$?

The vector, $\overrightarrow{AB}$, has a direction; the line segment, $\overline{AB}$, does not.

Unit 2   53   Lesson 5

You can use vectors to give a formal definition of *translation*.

A **translation** is a transformation along a vector such that the segment joining a point and its image has the same length as the vector and is parallel to the vector.

The notation $T_{\vec{v}}(P) = P'$ says that the image of point P after a translation along vector $\vec{v}$ is P'.

2 EXAMPLE Constructing a Translation Image

Work directly on the figure below and follow the given steps to construct the image of $\triangle ABC$ after a translation along $\vec{v}$.

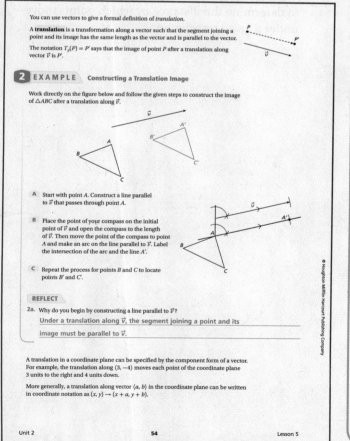

A Start with point A. Construct a line parallel to $\vec{v}$ that passes through point A.

B Place the point of your compass on the initial point of $\vec{v}$ and open the compass to the length of $\vec{v}$. Then move the point of the compass to point A and make an arc on the line parallel to $\vec{v}$. Label the intersection of the arc and the line A'.

C Repeat the process for points B and C to locate points B' and C'.

REFLECT

2a. Why do you begin by constructing a line parallel to $\vec{v}$?

Under a translation along $\vec{v}$, the segment joining a point and its image must be parallel to $\vec{v}$.

A translation in a coordinate plane can be specified by the component form of a vector. For example, the translation along $\langle 3, -4 \rangle$ moves each point of the coordinate plane 3 units to the right and 4 units down.

More generally, a translation along vector $\langle a, b \rangle$ in the coordinate plane can be written in coordinate notation as $(x, y) \rightarrow (x + a, y + b)$.

Unit 2   54   Lesson 5

Questioning Strategies

- Suppose you transform a figure with a translation along $\langle -8, 0 \rangle$. How will the location of the image compare to the location of the pre-image? **The image will be 8 units directly to the left of the pre-image.**

- How can you write the translation along $\langle -8, 0 \rangle$ in coordinate notation? $(x, y) \rightarrow (x - 8, y)$

EXTRA EXAMPLE

Draw the image of the triangle under a translation along $\langle 5, -3 \rangle$.

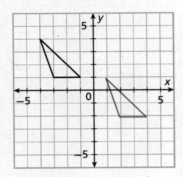

MATHEMATICAL PRACTICE — Highlighting the Standards

Standard 2 (Reason abstractly and quantitatively) can be addressed in the follow-up discussion to Example 3. In particular, the Reflect questions include some "what-if" scenarios. Such questions present an excellent opportunity for students to stretch their reasoning abilities. You might have students pose their own "what-if" questions related to Example 3. Then have them answer the questions posed by classmates.

Essential Question

How do you draw the image of a figure under a translation?

You can draw the image of a figure under a translation by using a compass and straightedge, or by using coordinate notation to draw the image on a coordinate plane.

Summarize

Have students write a paragraph about the translation of an image on the coordinate plane. They should include proper notation and at least one figure with their explanation.

PRACTICE

Where skills are taught	Where skills are practiced
1 EXAMPLE	EXS. 1–3, 4–7
2 EXAMPLE	EXS. 8–9
3 EXAMPLE	EXS. 10–11

Exercise 12: Students extend what they learned in **3** EXAMPLE by using the distance formula to determine the distance by which points move under a given translation.

3 EXAMPLE Drawing a Translation in a Coordinate Plane

Draw the image of the triangle under a translation along ⟨−3, 2⟩.

A Before drawing the image, predict the quadrant in which the image will lie.

Possible answer: Quadrant II

B In the table below, list the vertices of the triangle. Then use the rule for the translation to write the vertices of the image.

Pre-Image (x, y)	Image (x − 3, y + 2)
(0, 3)	(−3, 5)
(1, −1)	(−2, 1)
(−1, −1)	(−4, 1)

C Plot the vertices of the image. Then connect the vertices to complete the image. Compare the completed image to your prediction.

REFLECT

3a. Give an example of a translation that would move the original triangle into Quadrant IV.

Possible answer: translation along ⟨2, −5⟩

3b. Suppose you translate the original triangle along ⟨−10, −10⟩ and then reflect the image across the y-axis. In which quadrant would the final image lie? Explain.

Quadrant IV; the translation image lies in Quadrant III. After a reflection across

the y-axis, all points in Quadrant III are mapped to Quadrant IV.

PRACTICE

Name the vector and write it in component form.

1.

GH; ⟨5, 4⟩

2.

JD; ⟨0, −4⟩

3.

VS; ⟨−2, 3⟩

Draw and label a vector with the given name and component form.

4. MP; ⟨3, −1⟩

5. CB; ⟨−3, 0⟩

6. HK; ⟨−5, 4⟩
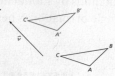

7. A vector has initial point (−2, 2) and terminal point (2, −1). Write the vector in component form. Then find the magnitude of the vector by using the distance formula.

⟨4, −3⟩; 5

Use a compass and straightedge to construct the image of each triangle after a translation along v̄. Label the vertices of the image.

8.

9.

Draw the image of the figure under the given translation.

10. ⟨3, −2⟩

11. ⟨−4, 4⟩

12. a. Use coordinate notation to name the translation that maps △ABC to △A′B′C′.

(x, y) → (x − 1, y − 5)

b. What distance does each point move under this translation?

√26 units

Rotations

Essential question: How do you draw the image of a figure under a rotation?

COMMON CORE Standards for Mathematical Content

CC.9-12.G.CO.2 ... describe transformations as functions that take points in the plane as inputs and give other points as outputs. ...

CC.9-12.G.CO.4 Develop definitions of rotations ... in terms of angles, circles, ...

CC.9-12.G.CO.5 Given a geometric figure and a rotation ... draw the transformed figure using, e.g., graph paper, tracing paper, or geometry software.

CC.9-12.G.CO.6 Use geometric descriptions of rigid motions to transform figures and to predict the effect of a given rigid motion on a given figure; ...

Vocabulary

center of rotation

angle of rotation

rotation

Prerequisites

Angles, Lesson 1-4

Transformations and Rigid Motions, Lesson 2-1

Math Background

Rotations are the last of the three rigid motions that students will study in this course (reflections were covered in Lesson 2-2 and translations were covered in Lesson 2-5). Rotations are presented last because they are somewhat more difficult to draw than the other rigid motions and because predicting the effect of a rotation may be more difficult for some students than predicting the effect of a reflection or translation. For these reasons, rotations lend themselves well to investigations that use geometry software.

INTRODUCE

Ask students to describe familiar examples of turns or rotations. Students might mention the motion of a DVD in a DVD player, the motion of the wheel of a car, or the motion of a doorknob. Ask students what these motions have in common. Help them see that they all involve moving points around a fixed point.

TEACH

1 EXPLORE

Materials: geometry software

Questioning Strategies

- When you use the software's default setting of a 90° rotation about the center, do you get a clockwise or counterclockwise rotation? How do you know? **Counterclockwise; the pre-image rotates 90° (a quarter turn) in the counterclockwise direction.**

- What would you do to get a 90° clockwise rotation? **Enter 270° for the angle of rotation.**

- Which points, if any, do not move under the rotation? **Point *P***

Technology

If time permits, be sure to have students use the software to experiment with different angles of rotation. In particular, ask students to investigate what happens when the angle of rotation is 360°. Students should find that this rotation moves points back to their starting point; as such, this rotation is equivalent to the identity transformation. You might also have students explore the effect of rotations that have angles of rotation greater than 360°. In this case, students may discover that they can find equivalent rotations by subtracting multiples of 360° until the angle of rotation is between 0° and 360°.

MATHEMATICAL PRACTICE Highlighting the Standards

As students work through the Explore, address Standard 5 (Use appropriate tools strategically) by asking students to discuss the pros and cons of using geometry software to investigate properties of rotations. Be sure students recognize that such software has the advantage of making it easy to change parameters (such as the angle of rotation) so that they can observe the effects of the changes.

Rotations

2-6

COMMON CORE

CC.9-12.G.CO.2,
CC.9-12.G.CO.4,
CC.9-12.G.CO.5,
CC.9-12.G.CO.6

Name_____ Class_____ Date_____

Essential question: *How do you draw the image of a figure under a rotation?*

You have seen that reflections and translations are two types of rigid motions. The final rigid motion you will consider is a *rotation*. A rotation turns all points of the plane around a point called the **center of rotation**. The **angle of rotation** tells you the number of degrees through which points rotate around the center of rotation.

The figure shows a 120° counterclockwise rotation around point *P*. When no direction is specified, you can assume the rotation is in the counterclockwise direction.

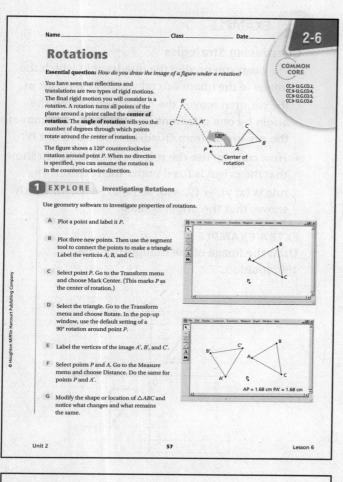

1 EXPLORE   Investigating Rotations

Use geometry software to investigate properties of rotations.

A   Plot a point and label it *P*.

B   Plot three new points. Then use the segment tool to connect the points to make a triangle. Label the vertices *A*, *B*, and *C*.

C   Select point *P*. Go to the Transform menu and choose Mark Center. (This marks *P* as the center of rotation.)

D   Select the triangle. Go to the Transform menu and choose Rotate. In the pop-up window, use the default setting of a 90° rotation around point *P*.

E   Label the vertices of the image *A′*, *B′*, and *C′*.

F   Select points *P* and *A*. Go to the Measure menu and choose Distance. Do the same for points *P* and *A′*.

G   Modify the shape or location of △*ABC* and notice what changes and what remains the same.

AP = 1.68 cm   PA′ = 1.68 cm

REFLECT

1a. Make a conjecture about the distance of a point and its image from the center of rotation.

Every point and its image are the same distance from the center of rotation.

1b. What are the advantages of using geometry software rather than tracing paper or a compass and straightedge to investigate rotations?

Possible answer: Geometry software makes it easy to observe the effect of changing the shape or location of the pre-image.

A **rotation** is a transformation about a point *P* such that (1) every point and its image are the same distance from *P* and (2) all angles with vertex *P* formed by a point and its image have the same measure.

The notation $R_{P, m°}(A) = A'$ says that the image of point *A* after a rotation of *m*° about point *P* is *A′*.

2 EXAMPLE   Drawing a Rotation Image

Work directly on the figure below and follow the given steps to draw the image of △*ABC* after a 150° rotation about point *P*.

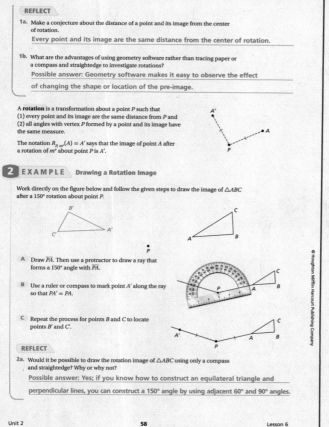

A   Draw $\overline{PA}$. Then use a protractor to draw a ray that forms a 150° angle with $\overline{PA}$.

B   Use a ruler or compass to mark point *A′* along the ray so that *PA′ = PA*.

C   Repeat the process for points *B* and *C* to locate points *B′* and *C′*.

REFLECT

2a. Would it be possible to draw the rotation image of △*ABC* using only a compass and straightedge? Why or why not?

Possible answer: Yes; if you know how to construct an equilateral triangle and perpendicular lines, you can construct a 150° angle by using adjacent 60° and 90° angles.

Questioning Strategies

- What is m∠CPC'? **150°**

- What segment has the same length as $\overline{BP}$? $\overline{B'P}$

- How can you use tracing paper to check your construction? **Trace △ABC. Place the point of the pencil on P and rotate the paper 150° counterclockwise. The traced version of △ABC should lie on top of △A'B'C'.**

EXTRA EXAMPLE
Draw the image of △JKL after a 70° rotation about point P.

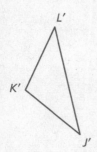

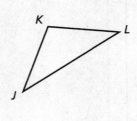

Teaching Strategies

Take a moment to discuss the tools that are used for this construction. Students should realize that they are using a protractor and ruler because they do not have a way to use a compass and straightedge to construct a 150° angle. Although it is theoretically possible to use a compass and straightedge to construct a 150° angle, students do not yet have the necessary background for this. Also, students should be aware that it is generally not possible to construct an angle with an arbitrary given measure. For example, in order to draw the rotation image of a figure under a 13° rotation, a protractor and ruler are the only feasible tools.

Questioning Strategies

- How can you predict the quadrant in which the image of the quadrilateral will lie? **Every 90° of the rotation moves the pre-image around the origin by one quadrant, so a 270° rotation moves the pre-image from Quadrant I to Quadrant IV.**

- How can you use the rule for the rotation to show that the origin is fixed under the rotation? **The rule is (x, y) → (y, −x), so (0, 0) → (0, 0), which shows that the origin is fixed.**

EXTRA EXAMPLE
Draw the image of the triangle under a 180° rotation.

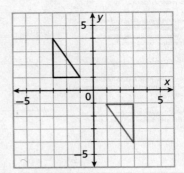

The table provides coordinate notation for rotations in a coordinate plane. You can assume that all rotations in a coordinate plane are rotations about the origin. Also, note that a 270° rotation is equivalent to turning $\frac{3}{4}$ of a complete circle.

Rules for Rotations in a Coordinate Plane	
Rotation of 90°	$(x, y) \rightarrow (-y, x)$
Rotation of 180°	$(x, y) \rightarrow (-x, -y)$
Rotation of 270°	$(x, y) \rightarrow (y, -x)$

3 EXAMPLE Drawing a Rotation in a Coordinate Plane

Draw the image of the quadrilateral under a 270° rotation.

A Before drawing the image, predict the quadrant in which the image will lie.

Possible answer: Quadrant IV

B In the table below, list the vertices of the quadrilateral. Then use the rule for the rotation to write the vertices of the image.

Pre-Image (x, y)	Image (y, −x)
(3, 1)	(1, −3)
(4, 2)	(2, −4)
(1, 4)	(4, −1)
(0, 2)	(2, 0)

C Plot the vertices of the image. Then connect the vertices to complete the image. Compare the completed image to your prediction.

REFLECT

3a. What would happen if you rotated the image of the quadrilateral an additional 90° about the origin? Why does this make sense?

The final image would coincide with the original figure. The total amount

of the rotation would be 360°, which is a full circle.

3b. Suppose you rotate the original quadrilateral by 810°. In which quadrant will the image lie? Explain.

Quadrant II; subtracting 720° (2 × 360°) from 810° shows that this rotation is

equivalent to a 90° rotation, which moves the quadrilateral in Quadrant II.

PRACTICE

Use a ruler and protractor to draw the image of each figure after a rotation about point P by the given number of degrees. Label the vertices of the image.

1. 50°

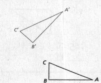

2. 80°

3. 160°

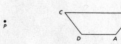

4. a. Use coordinate notation to write a rule for the rotation that maps △ABC to △A′B′C′.

$(x, y) \rightarrow (-y, x)$

b. What is the angle of rotation?

90°

Notes

Essential Question

How do you draw the image of a figure under a rotation?

You can draw the image of a figure under a rotation by using geometry software or by using protractor and ruler.

Summarize

Have students make a graphic organizer to summarize what they know about rotations in a coordinate plane. A sample is shown below.

Where skills are taught	Where skills are practiced
2 EXAMPLE	EXS. 1–3
3 EXAMPLE	EXS. 4–9

Exercise 10: Students extend what they learned in 3 EXAMPLE by writing a transformation that involves a rotation followed by a translation.

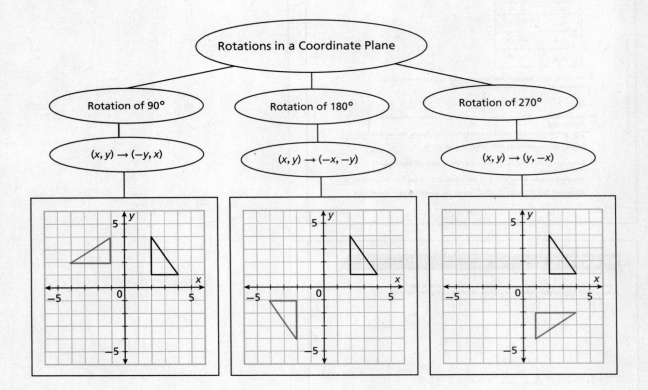

Draw the image of the figure after the given rotation.

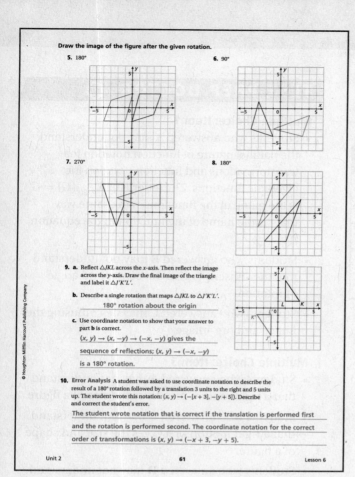

5. 180°

6. 90°

7. 270°

8. 180°

9. a. Reflect △JKL across the x-axis. Then reflect the image across the y-axis. Draw the final image of the triangle and label it △J′K′L′.

   b. Describe a single rotation that maps △JKL to △J′K′L′.

   180° rotation about the origin

   c. Use coordinate notation to show that your answer to part **b** is correct.

   (x, y) → (x, −y) → (−x, −y) gives the

   sequence of reflections; (x, y) → (−x, −y)

   is a 180° rotation.

10. Error Analysis A student was asked to use coordinate notation to describe the result of a 180° rotation followed by a translation 3 units to the right and 5 units up. The student wrote this notation: (x, y) → (−[x + 3], −[y + 5]). Describe and correct the student's error.

The student wrote notation that is correct if the translation is performed first

and the rotation is performed second. The coordinate notation for the correct

order of transformations is (x, y) → (−x + 3, −y + 5).

Notes

UNIT 2 TEST PREP

COMMON CORE CORRELATION

Standards	Items
CC.9-12.G.CO.2	1, 3, 9
CC.9-12.G.CO.4	4, 7
CC.9-12.G.CO.5	5, 8
CC.9-12.G.CO.6	2, 6, 9
CC.9-12.G.CO.9	10

TEST PREP DOCTOR ⊕

Multiple Choice: Item 1

- Students who answered **A** may not understand the parallel nature of function notation for transformations and function notation for algebraic functions. The letter R in $R_{P,\,60°}(G) = G'$ is the name of the function, in the same way that f is the name of the function in the equation $f(x) = y$.

- Students who answered **B** may not understand that the subscripts give the center and angle of rotation.

- Students who answered **C** may be confusing the image and pre-image.

Multiple Choice: Item 3

- Students who answered **A** may not understand that a rigid motion preserves the size of a figure.

- Students who answered **B** may not understand that a rigid motion preserves the size and shape of a figure.

- Students who answered **D** may not understand that a rigid motion preserves the shape of a figure.

Free Response: Item 8

- Students who drew $\triangle A'B'C'$ so that it has the same size and shape as $\triangle ABC$, but drew it in the wrong location, may have had trouble using their compass to mark distances equal to the magnitude of $\vec{\nu}$.

- Students who drew $\triangle A'B'C'$ in such a way that it does not have the same size and shape as $\triangle ABC$ may have had difficulty constructing a line that is parallel to a given line and that passes through a given point.

Name _____ Class _____ Date _____

MULTIPLE CHOICE

1. The function notation $R_{P,90°}(G) = G'$ describes the effect of a rotation. Which point is the image under this rotation?

A. point R C. point G

B. point P **D.** point G'

2. What is the image of the point $(4, -1)$ after a reflection across the line $y = x$?

F. $(-4, 1)$ **H.** $(-1, 4)$

G. $(4, 1)$ J. $(1, -4)$

3. Each figure shows the pre-image ($\triangle JKL$) and image ($\triangle J'K'L'$) under a transformation. Which transformation appears to be a rigid motion?

A.

B.
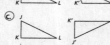

C.
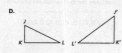

D.

4. Which transformation is defined as a transformation along a vector such that the segment joining a point and its image has the same length as the vector and is parallel to the vector?

F. reflection

G. rigid motion

H. rotation

J. translation

5. Keisha wants to use a compass and straightedge to draw the image of $\triangle XYZ$ after a reflection across line m. What should she do first?

A. Construct a perpendicular to line m that passes through point X.

B. Construct a line parallel to line m that passes through point X.

C. Copy $\angle X$ on the opposite side of line m.

D. Copy $\overline{XZ}$ on the opposite side of line m.

6. You transform a figure on the coordinate plane using the rigid motion $(x, y) \rightarrow (-y, x)$. What effect does this transformation have on the figure?

F. 90° rotation about the origin

G. 180° rotation about the origin

H. reflection across the x-axis

J. reflection across the y-axis

---

7. Which transformation has a definition that is based on perpendicular bisectors?

A. reflection

B. rigid motion

C. rotation

D. translation

FREE RESPONSE

8. Work directly on the figure below to construct the image of $\triangle ABC$ after a translation along $\vec{v}$. Label the image $\triangle A'B'C'$.

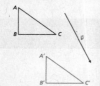

9. $\triangle RST$ has vertices $R(1, -3)$, $S(3, -1)$, and $T(4, -3)$. Give the coordinate notation for a transformation that rotates $\triangle RST$ 180° about the origin. Then give the coordinates of the image of $\triangle RST$ under this transformation.

$(x, y) \rightarrow (-x, -y)$; the image of $\triangle RST$

has vertices $R'(-1, 3)$, $S'(-3, 1)$, and

$T'(-4, 3)$.

10. The Reflected Points on an Angle Theorem states that if two points of an angle are located the same distance from the vertex but on different sides of the angle, then the points are images of each other under a reflection across the line that bisects the angle.

To prove the theorem, you set up the figure shown below, in which line m is the bisector of $\angle ABC$ and $BA = BC$. You want to prove that $r_m(A) = C$.

a. You first state that when $\overrightarrow{BA}$ is reflected across line m, its image is $\overrightarrow{BC}$. What postulate or theorem justifies this?

Angle Bisection Theorem

b. You conclude that $r_m(A)$ must lie on $\overrightarrow{BC}$, and you let $r_m(A) = A'$. You also state that $r_m(B) = B$ since B is on the line of reflection. Then you conclude that $BA = BA'$. What reason do you give?

Reflections preserve distance.

c. It is given that $BA = BC$, so you use the Substitution Property of Equality to conclude that $BA' = BC$. How do you complete the proof?

A' and C are two points on $\overrightarrow{BC}$

that are the same distance from B,

so A' = C and $r_m(A) = C$.

Congruence and Triangles

Unit Vocabulary

base	(3-6)
base angles	(3-6)
centroid	(3-9)
concurrent	(3-9)
congruent	(3-1)
corollary	(3-5)
corresponding parts	(3-2)
exterior angle	(3-5)
interior angle	(3-5)
legs	(3-6)
median	(3-9)
midsegment	(3-8)
point of concurrency	(3-9)
remote interior angle	(3-5)
vertex angle	(3-6)

UNIT 3

UNIT 3

Congruence and Triangles

Unit Focus

You have already learned that rigid motions preserve the size and shape of a figure. In this unit, you will learn that two figures are congruent (have the same size and shape) if and only if one figure can be mapped to the other by a sequence of rigid motions. You will also learn that there are some shortcuts for showing that triangles are congruent. Once you know these shortcuts, which are called congruence criteria, you will use them to prove facts about triangles. Along the way, you will also learn to write coordinate proofs.

Unit at a Glance

COMMON CORE

Lesson		Standards for Mathematical Content
3-1	Congruence	CC.9-12.G.CO.5, CC.9-12.G.CO.6
3-2	Congruence and Triangles	CC.9-12.G.CO.7
3-3	Developing Congruence Criteria	CC.9-12.G.CO.7, CC.9-12.G.CO.8
3-4	Using Congruence Criteria	CC.9-12.G.SRT.5
3-5	The Triangle Sum Theorem	CC.9-12.G.CO.10
3-6	The Isosceles Triangle Theorem	CC.9-12.G.CO.10
3-7	Coordinate Proofs	CC.9-12.G.CO.10, CC.9-12.G.GPE.4
3-8	Midsegments of a Triangle	CC.9-12.G.CO.10, CC.9-12.G.GPE.4
3-9	Medians of a Triangle	CC.9-12.G.CO.10, CC.9-12.G.GPE.4
	Test Prep	

UNIT 3

Unpacking the Common Core State Standards

Use the table to help you understand the Standards for Mathematical Content that are taught in this unit. Refer to the lessons listed after each standard for exploration and practice.

COMMON CORE Standards for Mathematical Content	What It Means For You
CC.9-12.G.CO.5 Given a geometric figure and a rotation, reflection, or translation, draw the transformed figure using, e.g., graph paper, tracing paper, or geometry software. **Specify a sequence of transformations that will carry a given figure onto another.** Lesson 3-1	Given two figures with the same size and shape, you will find a sequence of reflections, translations, and/or rotations that moves one figure onto the other.
CC.9-12.G.CO.6 Use geometric descriptions of rigid motions to transform figures and to predict the effect of a given rigid motion on a given figure; **given two figures, use the definition of congruence in terms of rigid motions to decide if they are congruent.** Lesson 3-1	You will learn that two figures are congruent if and only if there is a sequence of reflections, translations, and/or rotations that maps one figure onto the other. You will use this definition to decide if figures are congruent.
CC.9-12.G.CO.7 Use the definition of congruence in terms of rigid motions to show that two triangles are congruent if and only if corresponding pairs of sides and corresponding pairs of angles are congruent. Lessons 3-2, 3-3	You will use the definition of congruence to develop a method of determining whether two triangles are congruent. The method is based on comparing corresponding parts of the triangles.
CC.9-12.G.CO.8 Explain how the criteria for triangle congruence (ASA, SAS, and SSS) follow from the definition of congruence in terms of rigid motions. Lesson 3-3	You will use the definition of congruence to develop several shortcuts for proving that two triangles are congruent.
CC.9-12.G.CO.10 Prove theorems about triangles. Lessons 3-5, 3-6, 3-7, 3-8, 3-9	You will explore and prove theorems about the interior and exterior angles of triangles, base angles of isosceles triangles, properties of midsegments of triangles, and the concurrency of medians of a triangle.
CC.9-12.G.SRT.5 Use congruence and similarity criteria for triangles to solve problems and to prove relationships in geometric figures. Lesson 3-4	Once you know how to prove that two triangles are congruent, you will use triangle congruence to solve real-world and mathematical problems.
CC.9-12.G.GPE.4 Use coordinates to prove simple geometric theorems algebraically. Lessons 3-7, 3-8, 3-9	You have already seen a wide range of purely geometric proofs. These proofs used postulates and theorems to build logical arguments. Now you will learn how to write coordinate proofs. These proofs also use logic, but they apply ideas from algebra to help demonstrate geometric relationships.

UNIT 3

Unpacking the Common Core State Standards

This page lists and explains the Standards for Mathematical Content that are addressed in this unit. For information about the Standards for Mathematical Practice, which are integrated throughout the text, see Teacher Edition pages x–xiii.

UNIT 3

Notes

3-1 Congruence

Essential question: *What does it mean for two figures to be congruent?*

COMMON CORE **Standards for Mathematical Content**

CC.9-12.G.CO.5 ... Specify a sequence of transformations that will carry a given figure onto another.

CC.9-12.G.CO.6 ... given two figures, use the definition of congruence in terms of rigid motions to decide if they are congruent.

Vocabulary
congruent

Prerequisites
Transformations and Rigid Motions, Lesson 2-1

Math Background
The definition of congruence given in this book is different from the definition that is presented in many traditional geometry texts. In those texts, two figures are defined to be congruent if they have the same size and shape. Here, two figures are defined to be congruent if there is a sequence of rigid motions that maps one to the other. From this definition it follows that the two figures have the same size and shape. Over the next few lessons, this transformations-based definition will be used to develop the standard congruence criteria for triangles (SSS, SAS, and ASA).

INTRODUCE

Define *congruence*. Ask students to give examples of congruent figures in the classroom. Students might mention floor tiles that have the same size and shape, or desktops that are all rectangles with the same size and shape. Tell students that "the same size and shape" is an informal way of deciding whether two figures may be congruent, but that a more formal mathematical definition of congruence is based on rigid motions.

TEACH

1 EXAMPLE

Questioning Strategies
- Do the triangles in part A appear to be congruent? Why or why not? No; they do not have the same size.
- Do the quadrilaterals in part B appear to be congruent? Why or why not? Yes; they have the same size and shape.

EXTRA EXAMPLE
Use the definition of congruence in terms of rigid motions to determine whether the two figures are congruent and explain your answer.

A.

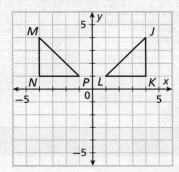

Congruent; a rigid motion (reflection across the *y*-axis) maps △*JKL* to △*MNP*.

B.

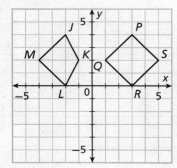

Not congruent; there is no sequence of rigid motions that maps *JKLM* to *PQRS*.

Name_____ Class_____ Date_____

3-1

COMMON CORE

CC.9-12.G.CO.5,
CC.9-12.G.CO.6

Congruence

Essential question: *What does it mean for two figures to be congruent?*

Two figures are *congruent* if they have the same size and shape. A more formal mathematical definition of congruence depends on the notion of rigid motions.

Two plane figures are **congruent** if and only if one can be obtained from the other by rigid motions (that is, by a sequence of reflections, translations, and/or rotations.)

1 EXAMPLE   Determining If Figures are Congruent

Use the definition of congruence in terms of rigid motions to determine whether the two figures are congruent and explain your answer.

A △ABC and △DEF have different sizes.

Since rigid motions preserve distance, there is no sequence of rigid motions that will map △ABC to △DEF.

Therefore, the figures are not congruent.

B You can map *JKLM* to *PQRS* by the translation that has the following coordinate notation:

$(x, y) \rightarrow (x + 5, y + 3)$

A translation is a rigid motion.

Therefore, the figures are congruent.

REFLECT

1a. Why does the fact that △ABC and △DEF have different sizes lead to the conclusion that there is no sequence of rigid motions that maps △ABC to △DEF?

Since rigid motions preserve distance, any sequence of rigid motions would map $\overline{AB}$ to a segment of the same length. Since △DEF has no such segment, there can be no sequence of rigid motions that maps △ABC to △DEF.

© Houghton Mifflin Harcourt Publishing Company

The definition of congruence tells you that when two figures are known to be congruent, there must be some sequence of rigid motions that maps one to the other. You will investigate this idea in the next example.

2 EXAMPLE   Finding a Sequence of Rigid Motions

For each pair of congruent figures, find a sequence of rigid motions that maps one figure to the other.   Possible answers are given.

A You can map △ABC to △RST by a reflection followed by a translation. Provide the coordinate notation for each.

Reflection: $(x, y) \rightarrow (-x, y)$

Followed by...

Translation: $(x, y) \rightarrow (x, y - 5)$

B You can map △DFG to △HJK by a rotation followed by a translation. Provide the coordinate notation for each.

Rotation: $(x, y) \rightarrow (-y, x)$

Followed by...

Translation: $(x, y) \rightarrow (x, y + 1)$

REFLECT

2a. Explain how you could use tracing paper to help you find a sequence of rigid motions that maps one figure to another congruent figure.

Trace one of the figures. Slide, flip, and/or turn the paper so that the traced figure fits perfectly on top of the other figure. The slides (translations), flips (reflections), and turns (rotations) form the required sequence.

2b. Given two congruent figures, is there a *unique* sequence of rigid motions that maps one figure to the other? Use one or more of the above examples to explain your answer.

The sequence is not unique. For example, you can map △ABC to △RST by the translation $(x, y) \rightarrow (x, y - 5)$ followed by the reflection $(x, y) \rightarrow (-x, y)$.

© Houghton Mifflin Harcourt Publishing Company

Questioning Strategies

• For each pair of figures, how do you know that a sequence of rigid motions that maps one figure to the other must exist? **The figures are known to be congruent. By definition, there is a sequence of rigid motions that maps one to the other.**

EXTRA EXAMPLE

For each pair of congruent figures, find a sequence of rigid motions that maps one figure to the other.

A.

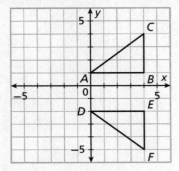

Reflection across the x-axis, $(x, y) \rightarrow (x, -y)$, followed by the translation $(x, y) \rightarrow (x, y - 1)$.

B.

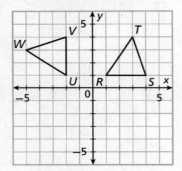

Rotation of 90°, $(x, y) \rightarrow (-y, x)$, followed by the translation $(x, y) \rightarrow (x - 1, y)$.

3 EXPLORE

Materials: ruler, protractor

Questioning Strategies

• If there is a sequence of flips, slides, and/or turns that maps one figure to another, what can you conclude? Why? **The figures are congruent by the definition of congruence.**

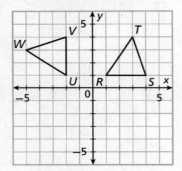

MATHEMATICAL PRACTICE · **Highlighting the Standards**

The Explore in this lesson gives students a chance to make conjectures about congruent line segments and congruent angles. Making and justifying conjectures is a key part of Standard 3 (Construct viable arguments and critique the reasoning of others). Be sure students understand that the type of reasoning used in the Explore is called inductive reasoning. Have students describe other instances in which they used inductive reasoning to develop a conjecture.

CLOSE

Essential Question

What does it mean for two figures to be congruent?
Two plane figures are congruent if and only if one can be obtained from the other by a sequence of reflections, translations, and/or rotations.

Summarize

Have students write a journal entry in which they summarize what they know so far about congruence. Prompt students to include examples and non-examples of congruent figures.

PRACTICE

Where skills are taught	Where skills are practiced
1 EXAMPLE	EXS. 1–3
2 EXAMPLE	EXS. 4–6

Exercise 7: Students apply what they have learned to decide whether congruence is transitive.

3 EXPLORE Investigating Congruent Segments and Angles

A Use a straightedge to trace $\overline{AB}$ on a piece of tracing paper. Then slide, flip, and/or turn the tracing paper to determine if there is a sequence of rigid motions that maps $\overline{AB}$ to one of the other line segments.

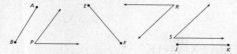

B Repeat the process with the other line segments and the angles in order to determine which pairs of line segments and which pairs of angles, if any, are congruent.

Congruent line segments: $\overline{EF}$ and $\overline{JK}$

Congruent angles: $\angle R$ and $\angle S$

C Use a ruler to measure the congruent line segments. Use a protractor to measure the congruent angles.

REFLECT

3a. Make a conjecture about congruent line segments.

Congruent line segments have the same length.

3b. Make a conjecture about congruent angles.

Congruent angles have the same measure.

The symbol of congruence is ≅. You read the statement $\overline{UV} \cong \overline{XY}$ as "Line segment UV is congruent to line segment XY."

Congruent line segments have the same length, so $\overline{UV} \cong \overline{XY}$ implies $UV = XY$ and vice versa. Congruent angles have the same measure, so $\angle C \cong \angle D$ implies m$\angle C$ = m$\angle D$ and vice versa. Because of this, there are properties of congruence that resemble the properties of equality, and you can use these properties as reasons in proofs.

Properties of Congruence	
Reflexive Property of Congruence	$\overline{AB} \cong \overline{AB}$
Symmetric Property of Congruence	If $\overline{AB} \cong \overline{CD}$, then $\overline{CD} \cong \overline{AB}$.
Transitive Property of Congruence	If $\overline{AB} \cong \overline{CD}$ and $\overline{CD} \cong \overline{EF}$, then $\overline{AB} \cong \overline{EF}$.

PRACTICE

Use the definition of congruence in terms of rigid motions to determine whether the two figures are congruent and explain your answer.

1.

Congruent; a rigid motion (reflection across y-axis) maps △ABC to △DEF.

2.

Not congruent; there is no sequence of rigid motions that maps JKLM to PQRS.

3.

Congruent; a rigid motion (rotation by 180°) maps △TUV to △XYZ.

For each pair of congruent figures, find a sequence of rigid motions that maps one figure to the other. Give coordinate notation for the transformations you use.

Possible answers are given.

4.

Reflect △CDE across x-axis, $(x, y) \rightarrow (x, -y)$, then use the translation $(x, y) \rightarrow (x + 5, y)$.

5.

Rotate JKLM 180°, $(x, y) \rightarrow (-x, -y)$, then use the translation $(x, y) \rightarrow (x - 1, y + 1)$.

6.

Reflect △ABC across y-axis, $(x, y) \rightarrow (-x, y)$, then use the translation $(x, y) \rightarrow (x, y - 2)$.

7. △ABC ≅ △DEF and △DEF ≅ △GHJ. Can you conclude △ABC ≅ △GHJ? Explain.

Yes; extend the sequence of rigid motions that maps △ABC to △DEF by the sequence that maps △DEF to △GHJ to make a sequence that maps △ABC to △GHJ.

Congruence and Triangles

Essential question: What can you conclude about two triangles that are congruent?

COMMON CORE Standards for Mathematical Content

CC.9-12.G.CO.7 Use the definition of congruence in terms of rigid motions to show that two triangles are congruent if and only if corresponding pairs of sides and corresponding pairs of angles are congruent.

Vocabulary

corresponding parts

Prerequisites

Congruence, Lesson 3-1

Math Background

In this lesson, students learn that if two triangles are congruent then corresponding pairs of sides and corresponding pairs of angles are congruent. This follows readily from the rigid-motion definition of congruence. In the next lesson, students prove the converse. That is, they will show that if corresponding pairs of sides and corresponding pairs of angles are congruent, then the triangles are congruent.

INTRODUCE

Ask students to imagine two cars that are congruent. That is, have them consider two cars that have exactly the same size and shape. Ask students what they can conclude about specific parts of the cars. For example, students might mention that the cars' steering wheels must also be congruent (same size and same shape). Similarly, the cars' dashboards must be congruent (same size and same shape). These types of observations should seem natural in the familiar context of identical cars. Tell students that in this lesson they will apply this type of reasoning to congruent triangles.

TEACH

1 EXAMPLE

Questioning Strategies

- What is the pre-image of $\overline{DE}$? $\overline{AB}$

- What is the image of $\angle B$? $\angle E$

EXTRA EXAMPLE

$\triangle RST \cong \triangle UVW$. Find UW and $m\angle S$. Explain your reasoning.

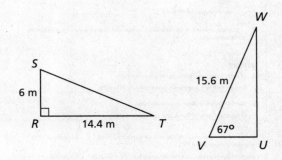

$UW = 14.4$ m since $\overline{UW} \cong \overline{RT}$; $m\angle S = 67°$ since $\angle S \cong \angle V$.

2 EXAMPLE

Questioning Strategies

- When you are given two congruent triangles, how many pairs of corresponding angles are there? How many pairs of corresponding sides are there? There are three pairs of corresponding angles and three pairs of corresponding sides.

- What is another way to write $\triangle RGK \cong \triangle MQB$? Possible answer: $\triangle GKR \cong \triangle QBM$

EXTRA EXAMPLE

$\triangle TWH \cong \triangle KPL$. Write six congruence statements about corresponding parts.

$\overline{TW} \cong \overline{KP}$; $\overline{WH} \cong \overline{PL}$; $\overline{TH} \cong \overline{KL}$; $\angle T \cong \angle K$; $\angle W \cong \angle P$; $\angle H \cong \angle L$

Teaching Strategy

Be sure students understand that they can identify corresponding angles by choosing pairs of letters in corresponding positions in a congruence statement. For example, in $\triangle RGK \cong \triangle MQB$, the letters K and B both appear in the third position in the name of their respective triangles. This means $\angle K \cong \angle B$. In a similar way, pairs of letters that are in corresponding positions yield pairs of corresponding sides.

Name_____ Class_____ Date_____

Congruence and Triangles

Essential question: *What can you conclude about two triangles that are congruent?*

When you know that two triangles are congruent, you can make conclusions about the sides and angles of the triangles.

COMMON CORE

CC.9-12.G.CO.7

1 EXAMPLE Finding an Unknown Dimension

$\triangle ABC \cong \triangle DEF$. Find DE and m$\angle B$. Explain your reasoning.

A Complete the following to find DE.

Because $\triangle ABC \cong \triangle DEF$, there is a sequence of rigid motions that maps $\triangle ABC$ to $\triangle DEF$.

This same sequence of rigid motions maps $\overline{AB}$ to ___$\overline{DE}$___.

This means $\overline{AB} \cong$ ___$\overline{DE}$___.

Congruent segments have the same length, so $AB =$ ___DE___.

$AB = $ ___2.6 cm___, so $DE = $ ___2.6 cm___.

B To find m$\angle B$, use similar reasoning to show that $\angle B \cong$ ___$\angle E$___.

So, m$\angle B = $ ___65°___.

REFLECT

1a. If you know $\triangle ABC \cong \triangle DEF$, what six congruence statements about segments and angles can you write? Why?

$\overline{AB} \cong \overline{DE}$, $\overline{BC} \cong \overline{EF}$, $\overline{AC} \cong \overline{DF}$, $\angle A \cong \angle D$, $\angle B \cong \angle E$, $\angle C \cong \angle F$. The rigid motions that

map $\triangle ABC$ to $\triangle DEF$ also map the sides and angles of $\triangle ABC$ to the sides and

angles of $\triangle DEF$, which establishes the congruencies.

When two triangles are congruent, the **corresponding parts** are the sides and angles that are images of each other. You write a congruence statement for two figures by matching the corresponding parts. In other words, the statement $\triangle ABC \cong \triangle DEF$ contains the information that $\overline{AB}$ corresponds to $\overline{DE}$ (and $\overline{AB} \cong \overline{DE}$), $\angle A$ corresponds to $\angle D$ (and $\angle A \cong \angle D$), and so on.

© Houghton Mifflin Harcourt Publishing Company

The following theorem is often abbreviated CPCTC. The proof of the theorem is similar to the argument presented in the previous example.

Corresponding Parts of Congruent Triangles are Congruent Theorem (CPCTC)

If two triangles are congruent, then corresponding sides are congruent and corresponding angles are congruent.

The converse of CPCTC is also true. That is, if you are given two triangles and you know that the six pairs of corresponding sides and corresponding angles are congruent, then you can conclude that the triangles are congruent. In the next lesson, you will see that you need only three pairs of congruent corresponding parts in order to conclude that the triangles are congruent, provided they are chosen in the right way.

2 EXAMPLE Using CPCTC

$\triangle RGK \cong \triangle MQB$. Write six congruence statements about corresponding parts.

A Identify corresponding sides.

$$\triangle RGK \cong \triangle MQB$$

Corresponding sides

Corresponding sides are named using pairs of letters in the same position on either side of the congruence statement.

$\overline{RG} \cong \overline{MQ}$; $\overline{GK} \cong$ ___$\overline{QB}$___ ; ___$\overline{RK}$___ $\cong$ ___$\overline{MB}$___

B Identify corresponding angles.

$$\triangle RGK \cong \triangle MQB$$

Corresponding angles

Corresponding angles are named using letters in the same position on either side of the congruence statement.

$\angle R \cong \angle M$; $\angle G \cong$ ___$\angle Q$___ ; ___$\angle K$___ $\cong$ ___$\angle B$___

REFLECT

2a. Given that $\triangle PQR \cong \triangle STU$, $PQ = 2.7$ ft, and $PR = 3.4$ ft, is it possible to determine the length of $\overline{TU}$? If so, find the length. If not, explain why not.

No; the side of $\triangle PQR$ that corresponds to $\overline{TU}$ is $\overline{QR}$, and the length of this

side is not known.

2b. A student claims that any two congruent triangles must have the same perimeter. Do you agree or disagree? Why?

Agree; since the corresponding sides are congruent, the sum of the side

lengths (perimeter) must be the same for both triangles.

© Houghton Mifflin Harcourt Publishing Company

Highlighting the Standards

This lesson provides an interesting connection to Standard 6 (Attend to precision). Specifically, students must be careful when they write congruence statements. A statement like $\triangle ABC \cong \triangle DEF$ contains the information that the triangles are congruent, as well as information about the corresponding sides and angles. In other words, students should recognize that the above congruence statement contains the same information as $\triangle BCA \cong \triangle EFD$, but different information from the statement $\triangle ABC \cong \triangle DFE$.

CLOSE

Essential Question

What can you conclude about two triangles that are congruent?

If two triangles are congruent, then corresponding sides and corresponding angles are congruent.

Summarize

Have students write a journal entry in which they state the Corresponding Parts of Congruent Triangles are Congruent Theorem in their own words. Encourage them to include one or more labeled figures as part of the journal entry.

PRACTICE

Where skills are taught	Where skills are practiced
1 EXAMPLE	EXS. 1–4
2 EXAMPLE	EXS. 5–7

Exercise 8: Students extend what they learned in **1** EXAMPLE and **2** EXAMPLE to solve a real-world problem.

PRACTICE

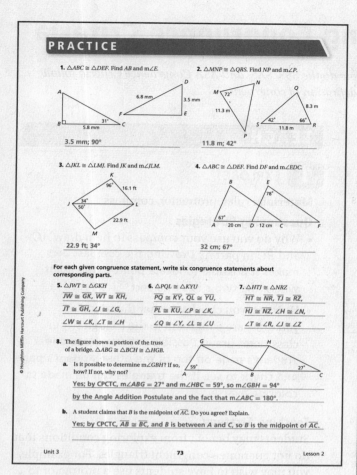

1. △ABC ≅ △DEF. Find AB and m∠E.

3.5 mm; 90°

2. △MNP ≅ △QRS. Find NP and m∠P.

11.8 m; 42°

3. △JKL ≅ △LMJ. Find JK and m∠JLM.

22.9 ft; 34°

4. △ABC ≅ △DEF. Find DF and m∠EDC.

32 cm; 67°

For each given congruence statement, write six congruence statements about corresponding parts.

5. △JWT ≅ △GKH

$\overline{JW} \cong \overline{GK}$, $\overline{WT} \cong \overline{KH}$,

$\overline{JT} \cong \overline{GH}$, ∠J ≅ ∠G,

∠W ≅ ∠K, ∠T ≅ ∠H

6. △PQL ≅ △KYU

$\overline{PQ} \cong \overline{KY}$, $\overline{QL} \cong \overline{YU}$,

$\overline{PL} \cong \overline{KU}$, ∠P ≅ ∠K,

∠Q ≅ ∠Y, ∠L ≅ ∠U

7. △HTJ ≅ △NRZ

$\overline{HT} \cong \overline{NR}$, $\overline{TJ} \cong \overline{RZ}$,

$\overline{HJ} \cong \overline{NZ}$, ∠H ≅ ∠N,

∠T ≅ ∠R, ∠J ≅ ∠Z

8. The figure shows a portion of the truss of a bridge. △ABG ≅ △BCH ≅ △HGB.

a. Is it possible to determine m∠GBH? If so, how? If not, why not?

Yes; by CPCTC, m∠ABG = 27° and m∠HBC = 59°, so m∠GBH = 94°

by the Angle Addition Postulate and the fact that m∠ABC = 180°.

b. A student claims that B is the midpoint of $\overline{AC}$. Do you agree? Explain.

Yes; by CPCTC, $\overline{AB} \cong \overline{BC}$, and B is between A and C, so B is the midpoint of $\overline{AC}$.

Notes

3-3 Developing Congruence Criteria

Essential question: *How do the SSS, SAS, and ASA Congruence Criteria follow from the rigid-motion definition of congruence?*

COMMON CORE Standards for Mathematical Content

CC.9-12.G.CO.7 Use the definition of congruence in terms of rigid motions to show that two triangles are congruent if and only if corresponding pairs of sides and corresponding pairs of angles are congruent.

CC.9-12.G.CO.8 Explain how the criteria for triangle congruence (ASA, SAS, and SSS) follow from the definition of congruence in terms of rigid motions.

Prerequisites

Congruence and Triangles, Lesson 3-2

Math Background

In this lesson, students prove the converse of the CPCTC Theorem. That is, if you are given two triangles and you know that the six pairs of corresponding sides and corresponding angles are congruent, then you can conclude that the triangles are congruent. In fact, it is not even necessary to know that all six pairs of corresponding parts are congruent. As students will see, there are conditions involving just three pairs of congruent corresponding parts that allow you to conclude that the triangles are congruent.

INTRODUCE

Introduce the word *criterion* and its plural, *criteria*. Ask students if they can define *criterion* and give an example of its use. If no one suggests it, you might discuss a college's criteria for deciding which students they will accept (a completed application, a minimum grade-point average, a minimum SAT score, and so on.) Tell students that they will develop criteria for determining when two triangles are congruent. Once they have a pair of triangles that satisfy any of these criteria, they will be able to conclude that the triangles are congruent.

TEACH

 EXPLORE

Materials: ruler, protractor, compass

Questioning Strategies

- Why do you use your compass to help draw $\overline{AC}$ and $\overline{BC}$ in part A? **Drawing the compass arcs makes it possible to locate point C, the point where the two sides intersect.**

- How can you check whether the triangles you draw are congruent to the triangles your classmates draw? **Possible answer: Place one student's page on top of the other student's page and check to see if the triangles can be made to coincide exactly.**

Teaching Strategy

Students may benefit from exploring conditions that do not guarantee congruent triangles. For example, you may wish to have students use a protractor to draw triangles with angles that measure 35°, 50°, and 95°. Then have students compare their triangles with those of classmates. Students will see that all of these triangles have the same shape, but not necessarily the same size. Since the triangles are not all congruent, the activity shows that there is no AAA Congruence Criterion.

MATHEMATICAL PRACTICE | **Highlighting the Standards**

As students jot down their findings from the Explore, address Standard 3 (Construct viable arguments and critique the reasoning of others) by asking students to communicate their results to the class. As students share their findings, ask if anyone found different results. Promoting this type of dialog in the classroom is an essential aspect the standard.

Name_____ Class_____ Date_____

3-3

Developing Congruence Criteria

Essential question: *How do the SSS, SAS, and ASA Congruence Criteria follow from the rigid-motion definition of congruence?*

COMMON CORE

CC-9-12.G.CO.7,
CC-9-12.G.CO.8

1 EXPLORE Investigating Triangle Congruence

Use the given instructions to help you identify which of the following conditions result in unique triangles. In each case, compare the triangle you draw to the triangles made by classmates. Are your triangles congruent?

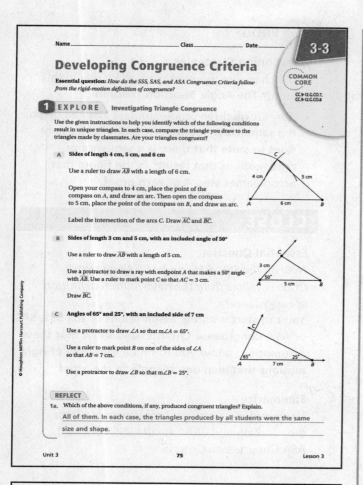

A Sides of length 4 cm, 5 cm, and 6 cm

Use a ruler to draw $\overline{AB}$ with a length of 6 cm.

Open your compass to 4 cm, place the point of the compass on *A*, and draw an arc. Then open your compass to 5 cm, place the point of the compass on *B*, and draw an arc.

Label the intersection of the arcs *C*. Draw $\overline{AC}$ and $\overline{BC}$.

B Sides of length 3 cm and 5 cm, with an included angle of 50°

Use a ruler to draw $\overline{AB}$ with a length of 5 cm.

Use a protractor to draw a ray with endpoint *A* that makes a 50° angle with $\overline{AB}$. Use a ruler to mark point *C* so that $AC = 3$ cm.

Draw $\overline{BC}$.

C Angles of 65° and 25°, with an included side of 7 cm

Use a protractor to draw $\angle A$ so that $m\angle A = 65°$.

Use a ruler to mark point *B* on one of the sides of $\angle A$ so that $AB = 7$ cm.

Use a protractor to draw $\angle B$ so that $m\angle B = 25°$.

REFLECT

1a. Which of the above conditions, if any, produced congruent triangles? Explain.

All of them. In each case, the triangles produced by all students were the same

size and shape.

You have seen that when two triangles are congruent, the corresponding sides and corresponding angles are congruent. Conversely, if all six pairs of corresponding sides and corresponding angles of two triangles are congruent, then the triangles are congruent.

Each of the following proofs serves as a proof of this converse. In each case, the proof demonstrates a "shortcut," in which only three pairs of congruent corresponding parts are needed in order to conclude that the triangles are congruent.

2 PROOF SSS Congruence Criterion

If three sides of one triangle are congruent to three sides of another triangle, then the triangles are congruent.

Given: $\overline{AB} \cong \overline{DE}$, $\overline{BC} \cong \overline{EF}$, and $\overline{AC} \cong \overline{DF}$.

Prove: $\triangle ABC \cong \triangle DEF$

To prove the triangles are congruent, you will find a sequence of rigid motions that maps $\triangle ABC$ to $\triangle DEF$. Complete the following steps of the proof.

A Since $\overline{AB} \cong \overline{DE}$, there is a sequence of rigid motions that maps $\overline{AB}$ to $\underline{\overline{DE}}$.

Apply this sequence of rigid motions to $\triangle ABC$ to get $\triangle A'B'C'$, which shares a side with $\triangle DEF$.

If C' lies on the same side of $\overline{DE}$ as *F*, reflect $\triangle A'B'C'$ across $\overline{DE}$. This results in the figure at right.

B $\overline{A'C'} \cong \overline{AC}$ because $\underline{\text{rigid motions preserve distance}}$.

It is also given that $\overline{AC} \cong \overline{DF}$.

Therefore, $\overline{A'C'} \cong \overline{DF}$ because of the $\underline{\text{Transitive}}$ Property of Congruence.

By a similar argument, $\overline{B'C'} \cong \underline{\overline{EF}}$.

C Because $\overline{A'C'} \cong \overline{DF}$, *D* lies on the perpendicular bisector of $\overline{FC'}$, by the Converse of the Perpendicular Bisector Theorem. Similarly, because $\overline{B'C'} \cong \overline{EF}$, *E* lies on the perpendicular bisector of $\overline{FC'}$. So, $\overline{DE}$ is the perpendicular bisector of $\overline{FC'}$.

By the definition of reflection, the reflection across $\overline{DE}$ maps C' to $\underline{F}$.

The proof shows that there is a sequence of rigid motions that maps $\triangle ABC$ to $\triangle DEF$. Therefore, $\triangle ABC \cong \triangle DEF$.

PROOF

Questioning Strategies

- What do you need to do in order to prove that two triangles are congruent? **You must show that there is a sequence of rigid motions that maps one triangle to the other.**

- What is the sequence of rigid motions that maps $\triangle ABC$ to $\triangle DEF$? **It is the initial sequence of rigid motions that maps $\overline{AB}$ to $\overline{DE}$ as in Step A, followed by the reflection across $\overline{DE}$.**

Differentiated Instruction

Some students may have difficulty following the reasoning behind this proof. These students may profit from a brief hands-on investigation of the proof. Have the students trace the triangles in the figure that accompanies the "given" and "prove" statements. Then have them cut out the triangles. Ask students to find a sequence of rigid motions that maps one triangle onto the other. Students should keep track of the flips, turns, and slides they use. Tell students that the proof is a more formal written description of this sequence of rigid motions.

3 **PROOF**

Questioning Strategies

- How is this proof similar to the proof of the SSS Congruence Criterion? **Both proofs show that there is a sequence of rigid motions that maps one triangle to the other.**

- How are the proofs different? **The proof of the SSS Congruence Criterion requires the Perpendicular Bisector Theorem. The proof of the SAS Congruence Criterion requires the Reflected Points on an Angle Theorem.**

4 **PROOF**

Questioning Strategies

- Which earlier theorem plays a key role in this proof? **The Angle Bisection Theorem**

- How are all three proofs similar? **They all begin the same way: You use the pair of congruent sides to state that there is a sequence of rigid motions that results in the figure that accompanies step A of each proof.**

CLOSE

Essential Question

How do the SSS, SAS, and ASA Congruence Criteria follow from the rigid-motion definition of congruence?
You can start with the assumptions of the SSS, SAS, or ASA Congruence Criterion and show that these assumptions allow you to find a sequence of rigid motions that map one triangle to the other.

Summarize

Have students write a journal entry in which they explain and illustrate the SSS, SAS, and ASA Congruence Criteria.

REFLECT

2a. The proof uses the fact that congruence is transitive. That is, if you know figure $A \cong$ figure B, and figure $B \cong$ figure C, you can conclude that figure $A \cong$ figure C. Why is this true?

You can extend the sequence of rigid motions that maps figure A to figure B

by the sequence that maps figure B to figure C to make a sequence that maps

figure A to figure C. This shows that figure $A \cong$ figure C.

3 PROOF   SAS Congruence Criterion

If two sides and the included angle of one triangle are congruent to two sides and the included angle of another triangle, then the triangles are congruent.

Given: $\overline{AB} \cong \overline{DE}$, $\angle B \cong \angle E$, and $\overline{BC} \cong \overline{EF}$.

Prove: $\triangle ABC \cong \triangle DEF$

To prove the triangles are congruent, you will find a sequence of rigid motions that maps $\triangle ABC$ to $\triangle DEF$. Complete the following steps of the proof.

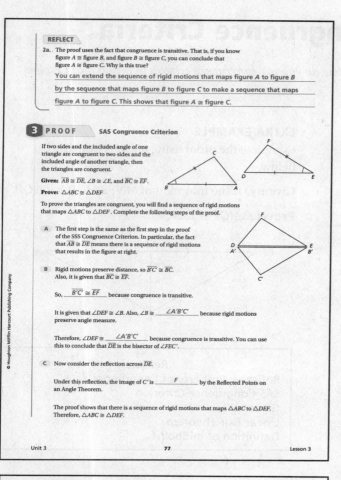

A The first step is the same as the first step in the proof of the SSS Congruence Criterion. In particular, the fact that $\overline{AB} \cong \overline{DE}$ means there is a sequence of rigid motions that results in the figure at right.

B Rigid motions preserve distance, so $\overline{B'C'} \cong \overline{BC}$. Also, it is given that $\overline{BC} \cong \overline{EF}$.

So, $\overline{B'C'} \cong \overline{EF}$ because congruence is transitive.

It is given that $\angle DEF \cong \angle B$. Also, $\angle B \cong \underline{\angle A'B'C'}$ because rigid motions preserve angle measure.

Therefore, $\angle DEF \cong \underline{\angle A'B'C'}$ because congruence is transitive. You can use this to conclude that $\overline{DE}$ is the bisector of $\angle FEC'$.

C Now consider the reflection across $\overline{DE}$.

Under this reflection, the image of C' is $\underline{F}$ by the Reflected Points on an Angle Theorem.

The proof shows that there is a sequence of rigid motions that maps $\triangle ABC$ to $\triangle DEF$. Therefore, $\triangle ABC \cong \triangle DEF$.

REFLECT

3a. Explain how the Reflected Points on an Angle Theorem lets you conclude that the image of C' under a reflection across $\overline{DE}$ is F.

C' and F are the same distance from the vertex of $\angle FEC'$ but on different rays,

so they are images of each other under a reflection across the angle bisector.

4 PROOF   ASA Congruence Criterion

If two angles and the included side of one triangle are congruent to two angles and the included side of another triangle, then the triangles are congruent.

Given: $\overline{AB} \cong \overline{DE}$, $\angle A \cong \angle D$, and $\angle B \cong \angle E$.

Prove: $\triangle ABC \cong \triangle DEF$

To prove the triangles are congruent, you will find a sequence of rigid motions that maps $\triangle ABC$ to $\triangle DEF$. Complete the following steps of the proof.

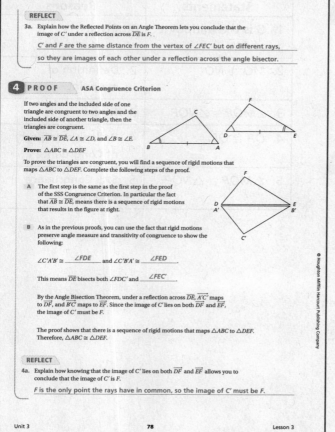

A The first step is the same as the first step in the proof of the SSS Congruence Criterion. In particular the fact that $\overline{AB} \cong \overline{DE}$, means there is a sequence of rigid motions that results in the figure at right.

B As in the previous proofs, you can use the fact that rigid motions preserve angle measure and transitivity of congruence to show the following:

$\angle C'A'B' \cong \underline{\angle FDE}$ and $\angle C'B'A' \cong \underline{\angle FED}$

This means $\overline{DE}$ bisects both $\angle FDC'$ and $\underline{\angle FEC'}$.

By the Angle Bisection Theorem, under a reflection across $\overline{DE}$, $\overrightarrow{A'C'}$ maps to $\overrightarrow{DF}$, and $\overrightarrow{B'C'}$ maps to $\overrightarrow{EF}$. Since the image of C' lies on both $\overrightarrow{DF}$ and $\overrightarrow{EF}$, the image of C' must be F.

The proof shows that there is a sequence of rigid motions that maps $\triangle ABC$ to $\triangle DEF$. Therefore, $\triangle ABC \cong \triangle DEF$.

REFLECT

4a. Explain how knowing that the image of C' lies on both $\overrightarrow{DF}$ and $\overrightarrow{EF}$ allows you to conclude that the image of C' is F.

F is the only point the rays have in common, so the image of C' must be F.

Using Congruence Criteria

Essential question: *How do you use congruence criteria in proofs and to solve problems?*

COMMON **Standards for**
CORE **Mathematical Content**

CC.9-12.G.SRT.5 Use congruence ... criteria for triangles to solve problems and to prove relationships in geometric figures.

Prerequisites
Developing Congruence Criteria, Lesson 3-3

Math Background
In the last lesson, students learned that there are some shortcuts for proving triangles congruent. Rather than showing that there is a sequence of rigid motions that maps one triangle to the other, students can now use the SSS, SAS, or ASA Congruence Criterion. These criteria may be used to prove that two triangles are congruent (as in Examples 1 and 2), or they may be used as one step in the solution of a larger mathematical or real-world problem (Example 3).

INTRODUCE

Begin by briefly reviewing the SSS, SAS, and ASA Congruence Criteria. Explain to the class that one aspect of proving triangles congruent is knowing which of the criteria to use. Tell students they will gain this type of experience in this lesson and in the ones that follow.

TEACH

 **EXAMPLE**

Questioning Strategies
• What does the Reflexive Property of Congruence say? **Every line segment is congruent to itself; every angle is congruent to itself.**

• How do you know that $\angle ABD \cong \angle CBD$? **It is given that $\overrightarrow{BD}$ bisects $\angle ABC$, and the bisector creates a pair of congruent angles in the interior of $\angle ABC$.**

EXTRA EXAMPLE
Complete the proof using reasons from the list below.

Given: Q is the midpoint of $\overline{MN}$; $\angle MQP \cong \angle NQP$.

Prove: $\triangle MQP \cong \triangle NQP$

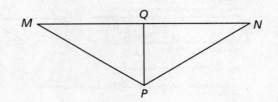

Reasons
Reflexive Property of Congruence
SAS Congruence Criterion
Given
Linear Pair Theorem
Definition of midpoint

Statements	Reasons
1. Q is the midpoint of $\overline{MN}$.	1. Given
2. $\overline{MQ} \cong \overline{NQ}$	2. Definition of midpoint
3. $\angle MQP \cong \angle NQP$	3. Given
4. $\overline{QP} \cong \overline{QP}$	4. Reflexive Property of Congruence
5. $\triangle MQP \cong \triangle NQP$	5. SAS Congruence Criterion

Name_____ Class_____ Date_____

Using Congruence Criteria

Essential question: *How do you use congruence criteria in proofs and to solve problems?*

You have seen that it is possible to prove that two triangles are congruent without using the definition of congruence. Instead, you can use the theorems known as the SSS, SAS, and ASA Congruence Criteria.

1 EXAMPLE   Using the SAS Congruence Criterion

Complete the proof.

Given: $\overline{BD}$ bisects $\angle ABC$ and $\overline{AB} \cong \overline{BC}$.

Prove: $\triangle ABD \cong \triangle CBD$

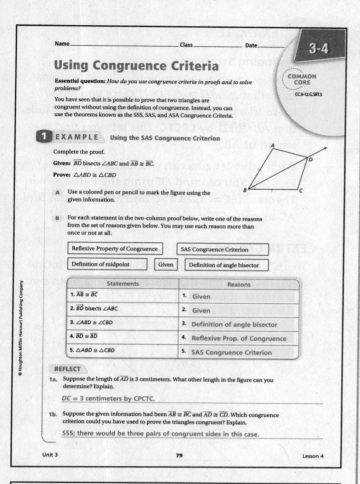

A Use a colored pen or pencil to mark the figure using the given information.

B For each statement in the two-column proof below, write one of the reasons from the set of reasons given below. You may use each reason more than once or not at all.

Reflexive Property of Congruence		SAS Congruence Criterion
Definition of midpoint	Given	Definition of angle bisector

Statements	Reasons
1. $\overline{AB} \cong \overline{BC}$	1. Given
2. $\overline{BD}$ bisects $\angle ABC$.	2. Given
3. $\angle ABD \cong \angle CBD$	3. Definition of angle bisector
4. $\overline{BD} \cong \overline{BD}$	4. Reflexive Prop. of Congruence
5. $\triangle ABD \cong \triangle CBD$	5. SAS Congruence Criterion

REFLECT

1a. Suppose the length of $\overline{AD}$ is 3 centimeters. What other length in the figure can you determine? Explain.

DC = 3 centimeters by CPCTC.

1b. Suppose the given information had been $\overline{AB} \cong \overline{BC}$ and $\overline{AD} \cong \overline{CD}$. Which congruence criterion could you have used to prove the triangles congruent? Explain.

SSS; there would be three pairs of congruent sides in this case.

A **flow proof** makes it possible to see how the steps of the proof are logically connected to each other. The next example shows how to develop a flow proof.

2 EXAMPLE   Using the SSS Congruence Criterion

Complete the flow proof.

Given: M is the midpoint of $\overline{RT}$; $\overline{SR} \cong \overline{ST}$

Prove: $\triangle RSM \cong \triangle TSM$

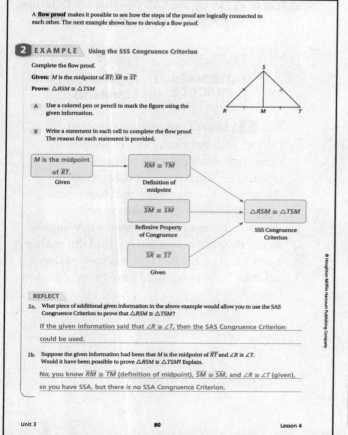

A Use a colored pen or pencil to mark the figure using the given information.

B Write a statement in each cell to complete the flow proof. The reason for each statement is provided.

M is the midpoint of $\overline{RT}$. Given	→	$\overline{RM} \cong \overline{TM}$ Definition of midpoint	
		$\overline{SM} \cong \overline{SM}$ Reflexive Property of Congruence	$\triangle RSM \cong \triangle TSM$ SSS Congruence Criterion
		$\overline{SR} \cong \overline{ST}$ Given	

REFLECT

2a. What piece of additional given information in the above example would allow you to use the SAS Congruence Criterion to prove that $\triangle RSM \cong \triangle TSM$?

If the given information said that $\angle R \cong \angle T$, then the SAS Congruence Criterion could be used.

2b. Suppose the given information had been that M is the midpoint of $\overline{RT}$ and $\angle R \cong \angle T$. Would it have been possible to prove $\triangle RSM \cong \triangle TSM$? Explain.

No; you know $\overline{RM} \cong \overline{TM}$ (definition of midpoint), $\overline{SM} \cong \overline{SM}$, and $\angle R \cong \angle T$ (given), so you have SSA, but there is no SSA Congruence Criterion.

2 EXAMPLE

Questioning Strategies

- What are some advantages of a flow proof? **The flow proof makes it easy to see how one statement of a proof leads to another.**

- Would it be possible to write this proof in two-column format? Explain. **Yes; each statement in the flow proof has a reason, so it would be possible to reorganize the proof into a two-column table.**

- Why does it make sense that there are three arrows pointing to the last cell of the proof? **It takes three pieces of information to use the SSS Congruence Criterion.**

EXTRA EXAMPLE

Complete the flow proof.

Given: D is the midpoint of $\overline{EF}$; $\overline{EC} \cong \overline{FC}$

Prove: $\triangle EDC \cong \triangle FDC$

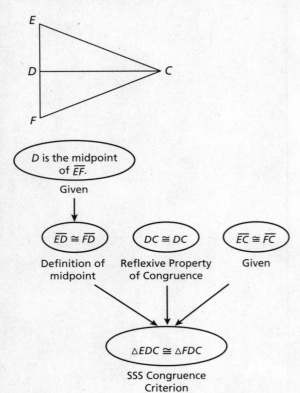

Avoid Common Errors

Remind students that they should not assume information from a figure unless it is marked or stated in the given information. For example, some students may assume that $\angle RSM \cong \angle TSM$ because these angles appear to be congruent in the figure. Although these angles can be proven to be congruent using CPCTC, students should not assume this in proving that $\triangle RSM \cong \triangle TSM$.

3 EXAMPLE

Questioning Strategies

- In order to solve the problem, why do you first show that $\triangle ABC \cong \triangle EDC$? Once you know these triangles are congruent, you can conclude that $\overline{AB} \cong \overline{ED}$ by CPCTC. This lets you find the length of $\overline{AB}$.

- What other lengths can you find in the figure? Explain. **You can find EC using the Pythagorean Theorem ($EC \approx 1328.8$ ft) and then you can find AC using CPCTC.**

EXTRA EXAMPLE

To find the distance PQ across a pond, you locate points as shown in the figure. Explain how to use this information to find PQ.

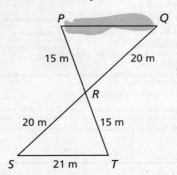

$\triangle PQR \cong \triangle TSR$ by the SAS Congruence Criterion. $\overline{TS} \cong \overline{PQ}$ by CPCTC, so $PQ = 21$ m.

MATHEMATICAL PRACTICE   **Highlighting the Standards**

Use **3 EXAMPLE** to discuss Standard 4 (Model with mathematics). In particular, encourage students to develop the habit of mind in which they ask themselves if the answer to a modeling problem seems reasonable. Prompt students to understand that an answer of 875 feet seems reasonable as the distance across a river. Had the answer been 3 feet or 125,000 feet, a review of the solution for errors would have been indicated.

Once you have shown that two triangles are congruent, you can use the fact that corresponding parts of congruent triangles are congruent (CPCTC) to draw conclusions about side lengths and angle measures.

3 EXAMPLE Solving a Problem Using CPCTC

Solve the following problem.

You want to find the distance across a river. In order to find the distance *AB*, you locate points as described below. Explain how to use this information and the figure to find *AB*.

1. Identify a landmark, such as a tree, at *A*. Place a marker (*B*) directly across the river from *A*.

2. At *B*, turn 90° away from *A* and walk 1000 feet in a straight line. Place a marker (*C*) at this location.

3. Continue walking another 1000 feet. Place a marker (*D*) at this location.

4. Turn 90° away from the river and walk until the marker *C* aligns with *A*. Place a marker (*E*) at this location. Measure $\overline{DE}$.

A Show △*ABC* ≅ △*EDC*.

- Based on the information marked in the figure, which pairs of sides or pairs of angles do you know to be congruent?

  ∠*B* ≅ ∠*D*, $\overline{BC}$ ≅ $\overline{DC}$

- What additional pair of sides or pair of angles do you know to be congruent? Why?

  ∠*BCA* ≅ ∠*DCE* by the Vertical Angles Theorem.

- How can you conclude that △*ABC* ≅ △*EDC*?

  ASA Congruence Criterion

B Use corresponding parts of congruent triangles.

- Which side of △*EDC* corresponds to $\overline{AB}$? _____ $\overline{ED}$

- What is the length of $\overline{AB}$? Why?

  875 feet; $\overline{AB}$ ≅ $\overline{ED}$ by CPCTC

REFLECT

3a. Suppose you had walked 500 feet from *B* to *C* and then walked another 500 feet from *C* to *D*. Would that have changed the distance *ED*? Explain.

No; you would still have *ED* = *AB* by CPCTC. Since the distance across the river does not change, *ED* does not change.

PRACTICE

In Exercises 1–2, complete the two-column proof.

1. Given: $\overline{AB}$ ≅ $\overline{CD}$, $\overline{AD}$ ≅ $\overline{CB}$
   Prove: △*ABD* ≅ △*CBD*

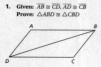

Statements	Reasons
1. $\overline{AB}$ ≅ $\overline{CD}$	1. Given
2. $\overline{AD}$ ≅ $\overline{CB}$	2. Given
3. $\overline{BD}$ ≅ $\overline{BD}$	3. Reflexive Prop. of Congruence
4. △*ABD* ≅ △*CBD*	4. SSS Congruence Criterion

2. Given: $\overline{GH}$ ∥ $\overline{JK}$, $\overline{GH}$ ≅ $\overline{JK}$
   Prove: △*HGJ* ≅ △*KJG*

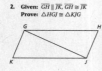

Statements	Reasons
1. $\overline{GH}$ ∥ $\overline{JK}$	1. Given
2. ∠*HGJ* ≅ ∠*KJG*	2. Alternate Interior Angles Thm.
3. $\overline{GH}$ ≅ $\overline{JK}$	3. Given
4. $\overline{GJ}$ ≅ $\overline{GJ}$	4. Reflexive Prop. of Congruence
5. △*HGJ* ≅ △*KJG*	5. SAS Congruence Criterion

3. **a.** Write a two-column proof in the table provided at right. You may not need to use all the rows of the table for your proof.
   Given: ∠*MQP* ≅ ∠*NPQ*, ∠*MPQ* ≅ ∠*NQP*
   Prove: △*MQP* ≅ △*NPQ*

Statements	Reasons
1. ∠*MQP* ≅ ∠*NPQ*	1. Given
2. ∠*MPQ* ≅ ∠*NQP*	2. Given
3. $\overline{QP}$ ≅ $\overline{QP}$	3. Reflexive Prop. of Congruence
4. △*MQP* ≅ △*NPQ*	4. ASA Congruence Criterion
5.	5.
6.	6.

b. What additional congruence statements can you write using CPCTC?

$\overline{MQ}$ ≅ $\overline{NP}$, $\overline{QP}$ ≅ $\overline{PQ}$, $\overline{MP}$ ≅ $\overline{NQ}$, ∠*M* ≅ ∠*N*

Notes

Essential Question

How do you use congruence criteria in proofs and to solve problems?

You use the SSS, SAS, and ASA criteria to show that triangles are congruent, which then makes it possible to find unknown lengths by using CPCTC.

Summarize

Have students write a journal entry in which they summarize the steps for determining an unknown length from a given figure, as in Example 3. You may want to challenge students to write their own problem that uses a method similar to the one in Example 3.

PRACTICE

Where skills are taught	Where skills are practiced
1 EXAMPLE	EXS. 1–3
2 EXAMPLE	EX. 4
3 EXAMPLE	EXS. 5–6

Exercise 7: Students extend what they learned in the lesson and use algebra to solve a problem.

Exercise 8: Students use what they learned in the lesson to solve an open-ended problem.

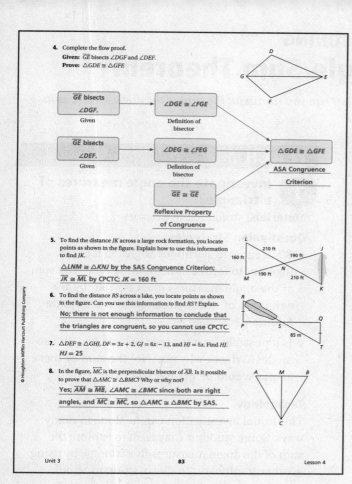

4. Complete the flow proof.
   Given: $\overline{GE}$ bisects $\angle DGF$ and $\angle DEF$.
   Prove: $\triangle GDE \cong \triangle GFE$

| $\overline{GE}$ bisects $\angle DGF$. | → | $\angle DGE \cong \angle FGE$ |
| Given | | Definition of bisector |

| $\overline{GE}$ bisects $\angle DEF$. | → | $\angle DEG \cong \angle FEG$ |
| Given | | Definition of bisector |

$\overline{GE} \cong \overline{GE}$
Reflexive Property of Congruence

$\triangle GDE \cong \triangle GFE$
ASA Congruence Criterion

5. To find the distance JK across a large rock formation, you locate points as shown in the figure. Explain how to use this information to find JK.

   $\triangle LNM \cong \triangle KNJ$ by the SAS Congruence Criterion; $\overline{JK} \cong \overline{ML}$ by CPCTC; $JK = 160$ ft

6. To find the distance RS across a lake, you locate points as shown in the figure. Can you use this information to find RS? Explain.

   No; there is not enough information to conclude that the triangles are congruent, so you cannot use CPCTC.

7. $\triangle DEF \cong \triangle GHJ$, $DF = 3x + 2$, $GJ = 6x - 13$, and $HJ = 5x$. Find HJ.
   $HJ = 25$

8. In the figure, $\overleftrightarrow{MC}$ is the perpendicular bisector of $\overline{AB}$. Is it possible to prove that $\triangle AMC \cong \triangle BMC$? Why or why not?
   Yes; $\overline{AM} \cong \overline{MB}$, $\angle AMC \cong \angle BMC$ since both are right angles, and $\overline{MC} \cong \overline{MC}$, so $\triangle AMC \cong \triangle BMC$ by SAS.

© Houghton Mifflin Harcourt Publishing Company

FOCUS ON REASONING
The Triangle Sum Theorem

Essential question: *What can you say about the sum of the angle measures in a triangle?*

COMMON CORE Standards for Mathematical Content

CC.9-12.G.CO.10 Prove theorems about triangles.

Vocabulary
corollary

interior angle

exterior angle

remote interior angle

Prerequisites
Proofs about Parallel and Perpendicular Lines, Lesson 1-7

Math Background
This is the first of several Focus on Reasoning lessons in this book. These lessons all include a hands-on investigation that gives students a chance to use inductive reasoning to make a conjecture. This is followed by a proof in which students use deductive reasoning to justify their conjecture. Although the inductive/deductive format is the central organizing feature of Focus on Reasoning lessons, these lessons may also include examples, real-world applications, and/or additional proofs.

INTRODUCE

Begin by asking students to state properties that hold for every triangle. Students might mention that every triangle has three sides or that every triangle has three angles. Tell students that they will be learning some additional properties that can be added to the list. You may want to record the properties on a large sheet of paper and add to the list as students learn new properties.

TEACH

1 **Investigate the angle measures of a triangle.**

Materials: straightedge, scissors

Questioning Strategies
- What can you say about angles that come together to form a straight line? Why? The sum of the angle measures must be 180° by the definition of a straight angle and the Angle Addition Postulate.

- Is it possible for a triangle to have two obtuse angles? Why or why not? No; the sum of these angles would be greater than 180°.

Technology
This initial investigation can be done in many ways. Some students may wish to explore the sum of the angle measures in a triangle by using geometry software. To do so, students should construct a triangle, measure the three angles, and use the Calculate tool (under the Measure menu) to find the sum of the angle measures. As students drag the vertices of the triangle to change its shape, the individual angle measures will change, but the sum of the measures will remain 180°.

MATHEMATICAL PRACTICE — Highlighting the Standards

Standard 3 (Construct viable arguments and critique the reasoning of others) includes the idea of counterexamples. You may wish to discuss counterexamples in the context of the Triangle Sum Theorem. For example, present the following statement to the class: "Every triangle has an obtuse angle." Give students a chance to refute this statement by asking them to provide a specific counterexample, such as a triangle whose angle measures are 40°, 60°, and 80°.

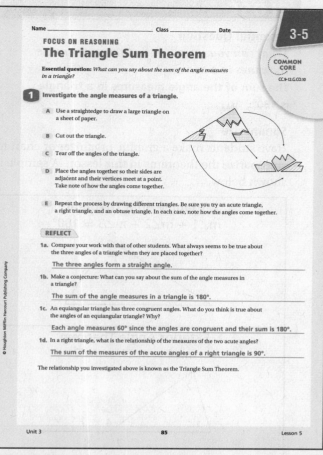

FOCUS ON REASONING
The Triangle Sum Theorem

Name _____ Class _____ Date _____

Essential question: *What can you say about the sum of the angle measures in a triangle?*

1 Investigate the angle measures of a triangle.

A Use a straightedge to draw a large triangle on a sheet of paper.

B Cut out the triangle.

C Tear off the angles of the triangle.

D Place the angles together so their sides are adjacent and their vertices meet at a point. Take note of how the angles come together.

E Repeat the process by drawing different triangles. Be sure you try an acute triangle, a right triangle, and an obtuse triangle. In each case, note how the angles come together.

REFLECT

1a. Compare your work with that of other students. What always seems to be true about the three angles of a triangle when they are placed together?

The three angles form a straight angle.

1b. Make a conjecture: What can you say about the sum of the angle measures in a triangle?

The sum of the angle measures in a triangle is 180°.

1c. An equiangular triangle has three congruent angles. What do you think is true about the angles of an equiangular triangle? Why?

Each angle measures 60° since the angles are congruent and their sum is 180°.

1d. In a right triangle, what is the relationship of the measures of the two acute angles?

The sum of the measures of the acute angles of a right triangle is 90°.

The relationship you investigated above is known as the Triangle Sum Theorem.

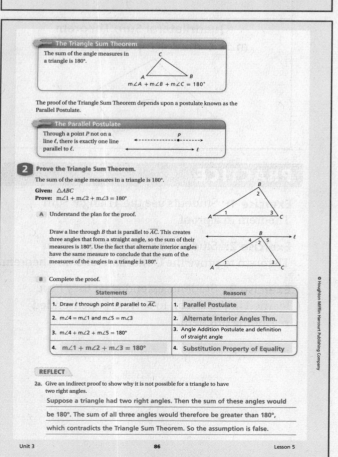

The Triangle Sum Theorem

The sum of the angle measures in a triangle is 180°.

$$m\angle A + m\angle B + m\angle C = 180°$$

The proof of the Triangle Sum Theorem depends upon a postulate known as the Parallel Postulate.

The Parallel Postulate

Through a point P not on a line ℓ, there is exactly one line parallel to ℓ.

2 Prove the Triangle Sum Theorem.

The sum of the angle measures in a triangle is 180°.

Given: $\triangle ABC$
Prove: $m\angle 1 + m\angle 2 + m\angle 3 = 180°$

A Understand the plan for the proof.

Draw a line through B that is parallel to $\overline{AC}$. This creates three angles that form a straight angle, so the sum of their measures is 180°. Use the fact that alternate interior angles have the same measure to conclude that the sum of the measures of the angles in a triangle is 180°.

B Complete the proof.

Statements	Reasons
1. Draw ℓ through point B parallel to $\overline{AC}$.	1. **Parallel Postulate**
2. $m\angle 4 = m\angle 1$ and $m\angle 5 = m\angle 3$	2. **Alternate Interior Angles Thm.**
3. $m\angle 4 + m\angle 2 + m\angle 5 = 180°$	3. Angle Addition Postulate and definition of straight angle
4. $m\angle 1 + m\angle 2 + m\angle 3 = 180°$	4. **Substitution Property of Equality**

REFLECT

2a. Give an indirect proof to show why it is not possible for a triangle to have two right angles.

Suppose a triangle had two right angles. Then the sum of these angles would

be 180°. The sum of all three angles would therefore be greater than 180°,

which contradicts the Triangle Sum Theorem. So the assumption is false.

2 Prove the Triangle Sum Theorem.

Questioning Strategies

- What type of reasoning did you use to make your conjecture? **inductive reasoning**

- What type of reasoning are you using in this proof? **deductive reasoning**

- Is it possible to draw more than one line through point *B* that is parallel to $\overline{AC}$? Explain. **No; according to the Parallel Postulate, there is exactly one such line.**

3 Prove the Exterior Angle Theorem.

Questioning Strategies

- Why is the Exterior Angle Theorem sometimes called a corollary of the Triangle Sum Theorem? **The Exterior Angle Theorem can be proved easily once you know the Triangle Sum Theorem.**

- In the figure, if ∠4 is a right angle, what can you say about ∠1 and ∠2? **∠1 and ∠2 are complementary.**

Essential Question

What can you say about the sum of the angle measures in a triangle?

The sum of the angle measures in a triangle is 180°.

Summarize

Have students make a graphic organizer or chart to summarize the theorems in this lesson. A sample is shown below.

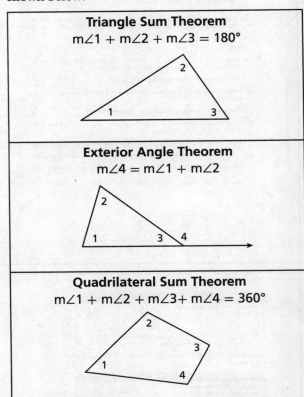

Triangle Sum Theorem
m∠1 + m∠2 + m∠3 = 180°

Exterior Angle Theorem
m∠4 = m∠1 + m∠2

Quadrilateral Sum Theorem
m∠1 + m∠2 + m∠3 + m∠4 = 360°

Exercise 1: Students use the Triangle Sum Theorem in a proof.

Exercise 2: Students use the Triangle Sum Theorem to prove the Quadrilateral Sum Theorem.

Exercise 3: Students extend what they have learned in the lesson to solve an open-ended reasoning problem.

A **corollary** to a theorem is a statement that can be proved easily by using the theorem. A useful corollary to the Triangle Sum Theorem involves exterior angles of a triangle.

When you extend the sides of a polygon, the original angles may be called **interior angles** and the angles that form linear pairs with the interior angles are the **exterior angles**.

Each exterior angle of a triangle has two remote interior angles. A **remote interior angle** is an interior angle that is not adjacent to the exterior angle.

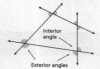

Interior angle

Exterior angles

Remote interior angles

Exterior angle

3 Prove the Exterior Angle Theorem.

The measure of an exterior angle of a triangle is equal to the sum of the measures of its remote interior angles.

Given: $\triangle ABC$
Prove: $m\angle 4 = m\angle 1 + m\angle 2$

Complete the proof.

Statements	Reasons
1. $\angle 3$ and $\angle 4$ are supplementary.	1. Linear Pair Theorem
2. $m\angle 3 + m\angle 4 = 180°$	2. Definition of supplementary angles
3. $m\angle 1 + m\angle 2 + m\angle 3 = 180°$	3. Triangle Sum Theorem
4. $m\angle 3 + m\angle 4 = m\angle 1 + m\angle 2 + m\angle 3$	4. Substitution Property of Equality
5. $m\angle 4 = m\angle 1 + m\angle 2$	5. Subtraction Property of Equality

REFLECT

3a. Explain how you could verify the Exterior Angle Theorem using a method similar to that of the Explore.

Tear off the remote interior angles. The two angles together will fit perfectly in the exterior angle.

Another important corollary of the Triangle Sum Theorem is the Quadrilateral Sum Theorem. You will prove the theorem as an exercise.

Quadrilateral Sum Theorem

The sum of the angle measures in a quadrilateral is 360°.

PRACTICE

1. Complete the proof that the acute angles of a right triangle are complementary.

Given: $\triangle ABC$ with $\angle C$ a right angle
Prove: $\angle A$ and $\angle B$ are complementary.

Statements	Reasons
1. $\angle C$ is a right angle.	1. Given
2. $m\angle C = 90°$	2. Definition of right angle
3. $m\angle A + m\angle B + m\angle C = 180°$	3. Triangle Sum Theorem
4. $m\angle A + m\angle B + 90° = 180°$	4. Substitution Property of Equality
5. $m\angle A + m\angle B = 90°$	5. Subtraction Property of Equality
6. $\angle A$ and $\angle B$ are complementary.	6. Definition of complementary angles

2. Write a paragraph proof of the Quadrilateral Sum Theorem.

Given: Quadrilateral $ABCD$
Prove: $m\angle A + m\angle B + m\angle C + m\angle D = 360°$
(*Hint:* Draw diagonal $\overline{AC}$ and number the angles formed.)

Draw $\overline{AC}$ to form two triangles, as shown. Then $m\angle A + m\angle B + m\angle C + m\angle D =$

$(m\angle 1 + m\angle 6) + m\angle 2 + (m\angle 3 + m\angle 4) + m\angle 5 =$

$(m\angle 1 + m\angle 2 + m\angle 3) + (m\angle 4 + m\angle 5 + m\angle 6).$

By the Triangle Sum Theorem, this equals $180° + 180° = 360°$.

3. If two angles of one triangle are congruent to two angles of another triangle, must the third angles of the triangles also be congruent? Why or why not?

Yes; given $\triangle ABC$ and $\triangle DEF$ with $m\angle A = m\angle D$ and $m\angle B = m\angle E$, then

$m\angle A + m\angle B + m\angle C = 180°$ and $m\angle D + m\angle E + m\angle F = 180°,$

so $m\angle A + m\angle B + m\angle C = m\angle D + m\angle E + m\angle F.$

Then $m\angle C = m\angle F$ by the Subtraction Property of Equality.

Notes

FOCUS ON REASONING
The Isosceles Triangle Theorem

Essential question: *What can you say about the base angles of an isosceles triangle?*

Standards for Mathematical Content

CC.9-12.G.CO.10 Prove theorems about triangles.

Vocabulary

legs

vertex angle

base

base angles

Prerequisites

Angle Bisectors, Lesson 2-3

Using Congruence Criteria, Lesson 3-4

The Triangle Sum Theorem, Lesson 3-5

Math Background

This Focus on Reasoning lesson gives students the opportunity to investigate the Isosceles Triangle Theorem from both an inductive and deductive perspective. In particular, the opening activity leads students to make a conjecture about the measures of the base angles of an isosceles triangle. Students prove their conjecture and its converse in the remainder of the lesson.

INTRODUCE

Students should already be familiar with isosceles triangles from earlier grades. Ask a volunteer to define *isosceles triangle* and have students give real-world examples of isosceles triangles. If possible, you might display a photo of the Transamerica Pyramid in San Francisco, whose faces are isosceles triangles, or show the class a football pennant or other flag in the shape of an isosceles triangle. Tell students they will be investigating properties of isosceles triangles in this lesson.

TEACH

1 Investigate isosceles triangles.

Questioning Strategies

- What must be true about the triangles you construct in order for them to be isosceles triangles? They must have at least two congruent sides.

- How could you draw isosceles triangles without using a compass? Possible answer: Draw $\angle A$ and plot point B on one side of $\angle A$. Then use a ruler to measure $\overline{AB}$ and plot point C on the other side of $\angle A$ so that $AC = AB$.

2 Prove the Isosceles Triangle Theorem.

Questioning Strategies

- What can you say about an isosceles triangle, $\triangle ABC$, with base angles $\angle B$ and $\angle C$, if you know that $m\angle A = 100°$? Explain. By the Isosceles Triangle Theorem, $\angle B \cong \angle C$, and $m\angle B + m\angle C = 80°$ by the Triangle Sum Theorem, so $m\angle B = m\angle C = 40°$.

- What can you say about the angles of an isosceles right triangle? The angles of the triangle measure 90°, 45°, and 45°.

Differentiated Instruction

You may want to challenge advanced students by asking them to come up with a proof of the Isosceles Triangle Theorem that is different from the two proofs that are presented on the student page. For example, students might draw the bisector of $\angle A$ and then use the SAS Congruence Criterion to show that the two triangles formed by the bisector are congruent. Such a proof would conclude by showing that $\angle B \cong \angle C$ by CPCTC.

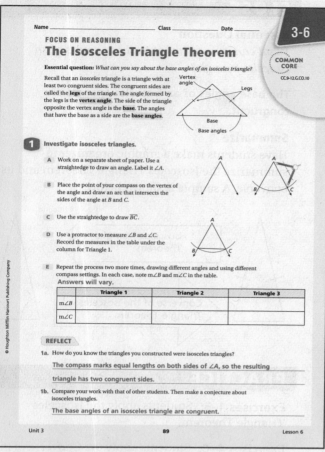

Name _____ Class _____ Date _____

FOCUS ON REASONING
The Isosceles Triangle Theorem

COMMON CORE
CC.9-12.G.CO.10

Essential question: *What can you say about the base angles of an isosceles triangle?*

Recall that an *isosceles* triangle is a triangle with at least two congruent sides. The congruent sides are called the **legs** of the triangle. The angle formed by the legs is the **vertex angle**. The side of the triangle opposite the vertex angle is the **base**. The angles that have the base as a side are the **base angles**.

1 Investigate isosceles triangles.

A Work on a separate sheet of paper. Use a straightedge to draw an angle. Label it ∠A.

B Place the point of your compass on the vertex of the angle and draw an arc that intersects the sides of the angle at B and C.

C Use the straightedge to draw $\overline{BC}$.

D Use a protractor to measure ∠B and ∠C. Record the measures in the table under the column for Triangle 1.

E Repeat the process two more times, drawing different angles and using different compass settings. In each case, note m∠B and m∠C in the table. **Answers will vary.**

	Triangle 1	Triangle 2	Triangle 3
m∠B			
m∠C			

REFLECT

1a. How do you know the triangles you constructed were isosceles triangles?

The compass marks equal lengths on both sides of ∠A, so the resulting

triangle has two congruent sides.

1b. Compare your work with that of other students. Then make a conjecture about isosceles triangles.

The base angles of an isosceles triangle are congruent.

Unit 3   89   Lesson 6

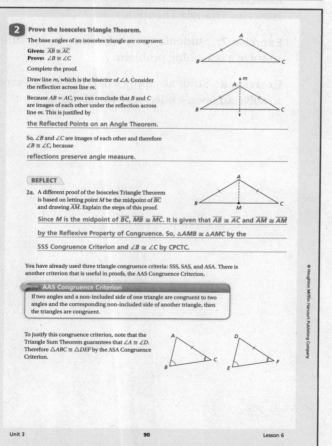

2 Prove the Isosceles Triangle Theorem.

The base angles of an isosceles triangle are congruent.

Given: $\overline{AB} \cong \overline{AC}$
Prove: ∠B ≅ ∠C

Complete the proof.

Draw line *m*, which is the bisector of ∠A. Consider the reflection across line *m*.

Because AB = AC, you can conclude that B and C are images of each other under the reflection across line *m*. This is justified by

the Reflected Points on an Angle Theorem.

So, ∠B and ∠C are images of each other and therefore ∠B ≅ ∠C, because

reflections preserve angle measure.

REFLECT

2a. A different proof of the Isosceles Triangle Theorem is based on letting point M be the midpoint of $\overline{BC}$ and drawing $\overline{AM}$. Explain the steps of this proof.

Since M is the midpoint of $\overline{BC}$, $\overline{MB} \cong \overline{MC}$. It is given that $\overline{AB} \cong \overline{AC}$ and $\overline{AM} \cong \overline{AM}$

by the Reflexive Property of Congruence. So, △AMB ≅ △AMC by the

SSS Congruence Criterion and ∠B ≅ ∠C by CPCTC.

You have already used three triangle congruence criteria: SSS, SAS, and ASA. There is another criterion that is useful in proofs, the AAS Congruence Criterion.

AAS Congruence Criterion

If two angles and a non-included side of one triangle are congruent to two angles and the corresponding non-included side of another triangle, then the triangles are congruent.

To justify this congruence criterion, note that the Triangle Sum Theorem guarantees that ∠A ≅ ∠D. Therefore △ABC ≅ △DEF by the ASA Congruence Criterion.

Unit 3   90   Lesson 6

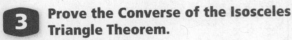

3 Prove the Converse of the Isosceles Triangle Theorem.

Questioning Strategies

- Is it possible to prove that $\triangle BAX \cong \triangle CAX$ by the ASA Congruence Criterion? Why or why not? **No; you do not yet know that $\overline{AB} \cong \overline{AC}$. This is what you are trying to prove, so you cannot assume it is true in the proof.**

Avoid Common Errors

In this lesson, students learn a fourth congruence criterion, the AAS Congruence Criterion. Having seen this new congruence criterion, students may assume that there is an SSA Congruence Criterion. Be sure students understand that SSA conditions do not guarantee a unique triangle, and tell them they will learn more about this in Lesson 6-6 when they study the Law of Sines.

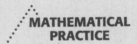

MATHEMATICAL PRACTICE   Highlighting the Standards

Exercise 8 offers an opportunity to address Standard 1 (Make sense of problems and persevere in solving them). Specifically, students will need to look for entry points in order to get started solving the problem. Encourage students to identify information that is needed to solve part (a) of the problem, and suggest that they highlight or underline this information. Later, students can reread the problem to identify additional information that is needed for part (b).

CLOSE

Essential Question

What can you say about the base angles of an isosceles triangle?

The base angles of an isosceles triangle are congruent.

Summarize

Have students make a graphic organizer to summarize the Isosceles Triangle Theorem and its converse. A sample is shown below.

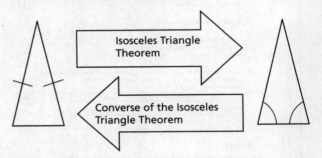

PRACTICE

Exercises 1–3: Students apply the Isosceles Triangle Theorem.

Exercises 4–6: Students apply the Converse of the Isosceles Triangle Theorem.

Exercise 7: Students apply what they have learned to solve a reasoning problem.

Exercise 8: Students apply what they have learned to solve an open-ended real-world problem.

3 Prove the Converse of the Isosceles Triangle Theorem.

If two angles of a triangle are congruent, then the sides opposite them are congruent.

Given: $\angle B \cong \angle C$
Prove: $\overline{AB} \cong \overline{AC}$

Complete the proof.

Draw line m, which is the bisector of $\angle A$. Let point X be the point where line m intersects $\overline{BC}$.

Then, by the definition of angle bisector,

$\angle BAX \cong \angle CAX$.

Also, $\overline{AX} \cong \overline{AX}$ by the Reflexive Property of Congruence. Therefore, $\triangle BAX \cong \triangle CAX$ by the AAS Congruence Criterion.

So, $\overline{AB} \cong \overline{AC}$ by __CPCTC.__

REFLECT

3a. An equiangular triangle has three congruent angles. An equilateral triangle has three congruent sides. Use the figure to help you explain why an equiangular triangle must also be an equilateral triangle.

It is given that $\angle K \cong \angle L$, so $\overline{JK} \cong \overline{JL}$ by the Converse of the Isosceles Triangle

Theorem. Similarly, $\angle K \cong \angle J$, so $\overline{JL} \cong \overline{KL}$. Therefore, $\overline{JK} \cong \overline{JL} \cong \overline{KL}$ and

$\triangle JKL$ is equilateral.

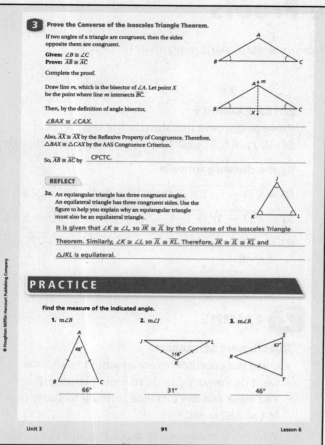

PRACTICE

Find the measure of the indicated angle.

1. $m\angle B$

48°
66°

__66°__

2. $m\angle J$

118°

__31°__

3. $m\angle R$

67°

__46°__

Find the length of the indicated side.

4. $\overline{DF}$

$4x + 2$　$5x - 2$

__18__

5. $\overline{LM}$

$7y - 6$
$2y + 9$

__15__

6. $\overline{RS}$

$5z - 8$　$4z - 2$
$3z + 12$

__30__

7. **Error Analysis** Two students are asked to find the angle measures of $\triangle XYZ$, given that $\triangle XYZ$ is isosceles. Their work is shown below. Is either answer incorrect? Explain.

Lee's Answer	Skyler's Answer
$m\angle Z = 70°$. Since an isosceles triangle has two congruent angles, $m\angle X = m\angle Y = 55°$.	$m\angle Z = 70°$. Since base angles are congruent, $m\angle Y = 70°$ also. This leaves 40° for $m\angle X$.

110°

Either answer could be correct, because the students were not told which

angles are the base angles.

8. A boat travels at a constant speed parallel to a coastline that is approximately a straight line. An observer on the coast at point P uses radar to find the distance to the boat when the boat makes an angle of 35° with the coastline. Then, 5 seconds later, the observer finds the distance to the boat when it makes an angle of 70° with the coastline. The observer wants to know if it is possible to calculate the speed of the boat.

215 ft　352 ft
70°
35°

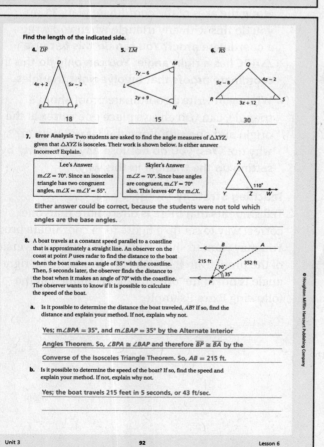

a. Is it possible to determine the distance the boat traveled, AB? If so, find the distance and explain your method. If not, explain why not.

Yes; $m\angle BPA = 35°$, and $m\angle BAP = 35°$ by the Alternate Interior

Angles Theorem. So, $\angle BPA \cong \angle BAP$ and therefore $\overline{BP} \cong \overline{BA}$ by the

Converse of the Isosceles Triangle Theorem. So, $AB = 215$ ft.

b. Is it possible to determine the speed of the boat? If so, find the speed and explain your method. If not, explain why not.

Yes; the boat travels 215 feet in 5 seconds, or 43 ft/sec.

3-7 Coordinate Proofs

Essential question: *How do you write a coordinate proof?*

COMMON CORE — Standards for Mathematical Content

CC.9-12.G.CO.10 Prove theorems about triangles.
CC.9-12.G.GPE.4 Use coordinates to prove simple geometric theorems algebraically.

Prerequisites

The Distance Formula, Lesson 1-2
The Midpoint Formula, Lesson 1-3

Math Background

Analytic geometry is the study of geometry using a coordinate system. Although certain aspects of the subject date to ancient times, the French mathematician René Descartes (1596–1650) is traditionally considered the father of analytic geometry. The strength of analytic geometry lies in its use of tools from algebra to solve geometry problems. In particular, this lesson shows how it is possible to use a Cartesian coordinate system, the distance formula, and the midpoint formula to prove results about geometric figures.

INTRODUCE

Begin with a brief review of the distance formula and the midpoint formula. Explain to students that they will be using these tools, as well as other ideas from algebra, to prove geometry theorems. Emphasize that coordinate proofs, like all other proofs that students have written up until now, require a logical sequence of ideas and supporting reasons for each statement in the proof.

TEACH

 1 EXAMPLE

Questioning Strategies

- What must you do in order to show that the triangle is or is not isosceles? **You must show that there are (or are not) two congruent sides.**

- Do you need to plot the vertices and draw the triangle in order to write the proof? **No; drawing the triangle makes the proof clearer, but the proof does not depend upon the drawing.**

EXTRA EXAMPLE

Prove or disprove that the triangle with vertices $R(-3, 1)$, $S(1, 5)$, and $T(3, -1)$ is an isosceles triangle.

By the distance formula,

$$RS = \sqrt{(1-(-3))^2 + (5-1)^2} = \sqrt{4^2 + 4^2} = \sqrt{32},$$

$$ST = \sqrt{(3-1)^2 + (-1-5)^2} = \sqrt{2^2 + (-6)^2} = \sqrt{40},$$

$$RT = \sqrt{(3-(-3))^2 + (-1-1)^2} = \sqrt{6^2 + (-2)^2} = \sqrt{40}.$$

Since $\overline{ST} \cong \overline{RT}$, the triangle is isosceles.

2 EXAMPLE

Questioning Strategies

- Once the coordinates are assigned as shown, what do you need to do to write the proof? **You must use the distance formula to show that $MA = MB = MC$.**

- Why are you allowed to place two sides of $\triangle ABC$ along the axes of the coordinate plane? Can you do this with any triangle when you write a coordinate proof? **You can do this because $\triangle ABC$ has a right angle. You can only do this in coordinate proofs that involve right triangles.**

- When you write a coordinate proof about a triangle, can you always place one vertex at the origin and one side along the x-axis? Why or why not? **Yes; you do not lose any generality by setting up the triangle in this way.**

Teaching Strategy

Tell students that there is often more than one correct way to set up a figure for a coordinate proof. You may want to show students an alternate version of the proof from **2 EXAMPLE** in which the right angle is not at the origin. This is outlined in the following Extra Example.

Name _____ **Class** _____ **Date** _____

Coordinate Proofs

3-7

COMMON CORE
CC.9-12.G.CO.10,
CC.9-12.G.GPE.4

Essential question: *How do you write a coordinate proof?*

You have already seen a wide range of purely geometric proofs. These proofs used postulates and theorems to build logical arguments. Now you will learn how to write coordinate proofs. These proofs also use logic, but they apply ideas from algebra to help demonstrate geometric relationships.

1 EXAMPLE Proving or Disproving a Statement

Prove or disprove that the triangle with vertices $A(4, 2)$, $B(-1, 4)$, and $C(2, -3)$ is an isosceles triangle.

A Plot the vertices and draw the triangle.

B Use the distance formula to find the length of each side of $\triangle ABC$.

$AB = \sqrt{(-1-4)^2 + (4-2)^2} = \sqrt{(-5)^2 + 2^2} = \sqrt{29}$

$BC = \sqrt{[2-(-1)]^2 + (-3-4)^2} = \sqrt{3^2 + (-7)^2} = \sqrt{58}$

$AC = \sqrt{(2-4)^2 + (-3-2)^2} = \sqrt{(-2)^2 + (-5)^2} = \sqrt{29}$

C Draw a conclusion based on your results. State whether or not the triangle is isosceles and why.

The triangle is isosceles because $\overline{AB} \cong \overline{AC}$.

REFLECT

1a. What other conclusion(s) can you make about the sides or angles of $\triangle ABC$? Explain.

$\angle B \cong \angle C$ by the Converse of the Isosceles Triangle Theorem.

1b. Suppose you map $\triangle ABC$ to $\triangle A'B'C'$ by the translation $(x, y) \rightarrow (x - 3, y - 2)$. Is $\triangle A'B'C'$ an isosceles triangle? Why or why not?

Yes; any translation is a rigid motion, so it preserves distance. Therefore,

$\overline{A'B'} \cong \overline{A'C'}$ and $\triangle A'B'C'$ is isosceles.

© Houghton Mifflin Harcourt Publishing Company

Unit 3   93   Lesson 7

You can write a coordinate proof to prove general facts about geometric figures. The first step in such a proof is using variables to assign general coordinates to a figure using only what is known about the figure.

2 EXAMPLE Writing a Coordinate Proof

Prove that in a right triangle, the midpoint of the hypotenuse is equidistant from all three vertices.

A Assign coordinates to the figure.

Let the triangle be $\triangle ABC$. Since the triangle is a right triangle, assume $\angle B$ is a right angle. Place $\angle B$ at the origin and place the legs along the positive x- and y-axes.

Since the proof involves a midpoint, use multiples of 2 in assigning coordinates to A and C, as shown.

B Let M be the midpoint of the hypotenuse, $\overline{AC}$. Use the midpoint formula to find the coordinates of M.

$M\left(\dfrac{2a + 0}{2}, \dfrac{0 + 2c}{2}\right) = M\left(\boxed{a}, \boxed{c}\right)$

C Use the distance formula to find MA, MB, and MC.

$MA = \sqrt{\left(2a - \boxed{a}\right)^2 + \left(0 - \boxed{c}\right)^2} = \sqrt{\boxed{a}^2 + \boxed{c}^2}$

$MB = \sqrt{\left(\boxed{a} - 0\right)^2 + \left(\boxed{c} - 0\right)^2} = \sqrt{\boxed{a}^2 + \boxed{c}^2}$

$MB = \sqrt{\left(\boxed{a} - 0\right)^2 + \left(\boxed{c} - 2c\right)^2} = \sqrt{\boxed{a}^2 + \boxed{c}^2}$

So, the midpoint of the hypotenuse is equidistant from all three vertices because

$MA = MB = MC$.

REFLECT

2a. Explain why it is more convenient to assign the coordinates as $A(2a, 0)$ and $C(0, 2c)$ rather than $A(a, 0)$ and $C(0, c)$.

This choice eliminates the need for fractions in the coordinates of M.

2b. Can you write the proof by assigning the coordinates as $A(2n, 0)$ and $C(0, 2n)$?

No; this would assume the triangle is isosceles. The statement to be

proved applies to all right triangles, not just isosceles right triangles.

© Houghton Mifflin Harcourt Publishing Company

Unit 3   94   Lesson 7

Unit 3   **94**   Lesson 7

EXTRA EXAMPLE

Use the coordinates shown below to prove that in a right triangle, the midpoint of the hypotenuse is equidistant from all three vertices.

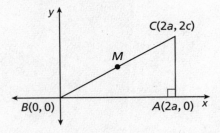

Let M be the midpoint of the hypotenuse, $\overline{BC}$. Then by the midpoint formula, the coordinates of M are $M(a, c)$.

By the distance formula,

$$MA = \sqrt{(2a - a)^2 + (0 - c)^2} = \sqrt{a^2 + c^2},$$

$$MB = \sqrt{(a - 0)^2 + (c - 0)^2} = \sqrt{a^2 + c^2},$$

$$MC = \sqrt{(2a - a)^2 + (2c - c)^2} = \sqrt{a^2 + c^2}.$$

So the midpoint of the hypotenuse is equidistant from all three vertices because $MA = MB = MC$.

⋰ **MATHEMATICAL PRACTICE**　**Highlighting the Standards**

Exercise 4 gives students experience critiquing the work of another student. This is an important element of Standard 3 (Construct viable arguments and critique the reasoning of others). In this exercise, students must pinpoint the aspect of the student's proof that is incorrect. Students should recognize that some parts of an argument may be correct (i.e., a correct calculation using the distance formula) while other parts of the argument may be incorrect (i.e., an incorrect assignment of coordinates for the figure).

CLOSE

Essential Question

How do you write a coordinate proof?

To write a coordinate proof, you use variables to assign general coordinates to a figure and then use the distance formula, the midpoint formula, and/or other algebraic facts to construct a logical argument.

Summarize

Have students write a journal entry in which they explain how to assign coordinates to a figure in a coordinate proof. Encourage them to discuss general triangles as well as right triangles, and ask students to include examples of triangles that have been assigned coordinates.

PRACTICE

Where skills are taught	Where skills are practiced
1 EXAMPLE	EXS. 1–2
2 EXAMPLE	EX. 3

Exercise 4: Students use reasoning to critique an incorrect coordinate proof.

1. Prove or disprove that the triangle with vertices $R(-2, -2)$, $S(1, 4)$, and $T(4, -5)$ is an equilateral triangle.

   By the distance formula, $RS = \sqrt{45}$, $RT = \sqrt{45}$, and $ST = \sqrt{90}$. Since the three sides do not all have the same length, the triangle is not equilateral.

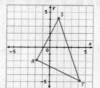

2. $\triangle ABC$ has vertices $A(-4, 1)$, $B(-3, 4)$, and $C(-1, 1)$. $\triangle DEF$ has vertices $D(2, -3)$, $E(5, -2)$, and $F(2, 0)$. Prove or disprove that the triangles are congruent.

   By the distance formula, $AC = DF = 3$, $AB = DE = \sqrt{10}$, and $BC = EF = \sqrt{13}$. Therefore, $\triangle ABC \cong \triangle DEF$ by the SSS Congruence Criterion.

3. Write a coordinate proof to prove that the diagonals of a rectangle are congruent. Use the space at right to show how to assign coordinates. Then write the proof below.

   Assign coordinates as shown. By the distance formula, $BD = \sqrt{a^2 + c^2}$ and $AC = \sqrt{a^2 + c^2}$. Therefore $\overline{BD} \cong \overline{AC}$, so the diagonals are congruent.

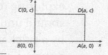

4. **Error Analysis** A student proves that every right triangle is isosceles by assigning coordinates as shown at right and by using the distance formula to show that $PQ = a$ and $RQ = a$. Explain the error in the student's proof.

   The proof is not correct because the assigned coordinates do not result in a general right triangle. The coordinates of R should be (a, b).

FOCUS ON REASONING
Midsegments of a Triangle

Essential question: *What must be true about the segment that connects the midpoints of two sides of a triangle?*

COMMON
CORE
Standards for Mathematical Content

CC.9-12.G.CO.10 Prove theorems about triangles.

CC.9-12.G.GPE.4 Use coordinates to prove simple geometric theorems algebraically.

Vocabulary

midsegment

Prerequisites

The Distance Formula, Lesson 1-2

The Midpoint Formula, Lesson 1-3

Coordinate Proofs, Lesson 3-7

Slope of Parallel Lines, Algebra 1

Math Background

A major goal of geometry is understanding properties that are true for every triangle. Students have already seen the Triangle Sum Theorem in Lesson 3-5 and they will investigate the concurrency of the medians of a triangle in Lesson 3-9. This lesson focuses on facts about triangle midsegments. Note that the results are proved here using coordinate methods. They can also be proved using the SAS Similarity Criterion (see Lesson 5-4).

INTRODUCE

Define *midsegment*. Make a sketch on the board showing students how to draw a midsegment, and point out that every triangle has three midsegments. Explain that in this lesson, students will primarily work with one midsegment at a time.

TEACH

Investigate midsegments.

Questioning Strategies

• What is the name for the angle pair consisting of ∠*ADE* and ∠*ABC*? **corresponding angles**

• What theorems do you know about this type of angle pair? **If two lines are cut by a transversal so that a pair of corresponding angles have the same measure, then the lines are parallel.**

MATHEMATICAL PRACTICE **Highlighting the Standards**

To address Standard 5 (Use appropriate tools strategically), ask students why geometry software is an especially effective tool for exploring midsegment properties. Students should understand that measurements made by a ruler and protractor would not be as accurate as those made by the geometry software. Also, the software makes it easy to change the shape of the figure and observe the relevant relationships in a wide variety of triangles.

2 **Prove the Midsegment Theorem.**

Questioning Strategies

• Once you assign vertex *B* the coordinates (0, 0) and vertex *C* the coordinates (2*p*, 0), why do you use the new variables *q* and *r* to assign coordinates to vertex *A*, rather than writing its coordinates in terms of the variable *p*? **This ensures that A is a general point whose location does not depend upon the other points.**

• What are some ways you can prove that two line segments are parallel? Which of these methods may work best in a coordinate proof? **Show corresponding angles have the same measure, show the lines have the same slope, etc. In a coordinate proof, it may be easiest to show that the lines have the same slope.**

CLOSE

Essential Question

What must be true about the segment that connects the midpoints of two sides of a triangle?

The segment is parallel to the third side of the triangle and half as long as the third side.

Summarize

Have students write a journal entry stating the Midsegment Theorem in their own words.

Name _____ Class _____ Date _____

3-8

FOCUS ON REASONING

Midsegments of a Triangle

COMMON CORE

CC.9-12.G.CO.10,
CC.9-12.G.GPE.4

Essential question: *What must be true about the segment that connects the midpoints of two sides of a triangle?*

A **midsegment** of a triangle is a line segment that connects the midpoints of two sides of the triangle.

1 Investigate midsegments.

A   Use geometry software to draw a triangle.

B   Label the vertices *A*, *B*, and *C*.

C   Select $\overline{AB}$ and construct its midpoint.
Select $\overline{AC}$ and construct its midpoint.
Label the midpoints *D* and *E*.

D   Draw the midsegment, $\overline{DE}$.

E   Measure the lengths of $\overline{DE}$ and $\overline{BC}$.

F   Measure $\angle ADE$ and $\angle ABC$.

G   Drag the vertices of $\triangle ABC$ to change
its shape. As you do so, look for
relationships in the measurements.

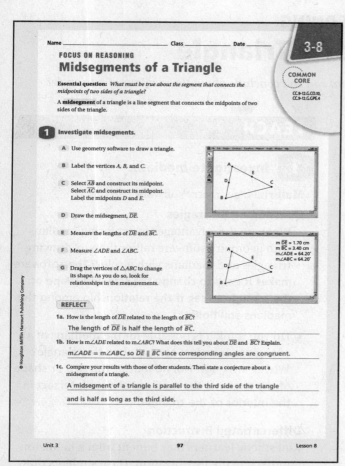

m $\overline{DE}$ = 1.70 cm
m $\overline{BC}$ = 3.40 cm
m∠ADE = 64.20°
m∠ABC = 64.20°

REFLECT

1a.   How is the length of $\overline{DE}$ related to the length of $\overline{BC}$?

The length of $\overline{DE}$ is half the length of $\overline{BC}$.

1b.   How is m∠ADE related to m∠ABC? What does this tell you about $\overline{DE}$ and $\overline{BC}$? Explain.

m∠ADE = m∠ABC, so $\overline{DE} \parallel \overline{BC}$ since corresponding angles are congruent.

1c.   Compare your results with those of other students. Then state a conjecture about a
midsegment of a triangle.

A midsegment of a triangle is parallel to the third side of the triangle

and is half as long as the third side.

---

2 Prove the Midsegment Theorem.

A midsegment of a triangle is parallel to the third side
of the triangle and is half as long as the third side.

Given: $\overline{DE}$ is a midsegment of $\triangle ABC$.
Prove: $\overline{DE} \parallel \overline{BC}$ and $DE = \frac{1}{2} BC$.

A   Use a coordinate proof. Place $\triangle ABC$ on a
coordinate plane so that one vertex is at the origin
and one side lies on the *x*-axis, as shown. For
convenience, assign vertex *C* the coordinates
$(2p, 0)$ and assign vertex *A* the coordinates $(2q, 2r)$.

B   Use the midpoint formula to find the coordinates of
D and *E*. Complete the calculations.

$D\left(\frac{2q + 0}{2}, \frac{2r + 0}{2}\right) = D(q, r)$ $E\left(\frac{2q + 2p}{2}, \frac{2r + 0}{2}\right) = E\left(\boxed{q + p}, \boxed{r}\right)$

C   To prove that $\overline{DE} \parallel \overline{BC}$, first find the slopes of $\overline{DE}$ and $\overline{BC}$.

Slope of $\overline{DE} = \dfrac{\boxed{r} - \boxed{r}}{q + p - \boxed{q}} = 0$

Slope of $\overline{BC} = \dfrac{0 - 0}{2p - 0} = 0$

What conclusion can you make based on the slopes? Why?

$\overline{DE} \parallel \overline{BC}$ since the slopes of the segments are equal.

D   Show how to use the distance formula to prove that $DE = \frac{1}{2} BC$.

$DE = \sqrt{(q + p - q)^2 + (r - r)^2} = \sqrt{p^2} = p;$
$BC = \sqrt{(2p - 0)^2 + (0 - 0)^2} = \sqrt{(2p)^2} = 2p.$ So $DE = \frac{1}{2} BC.$

REFLECT

2a.   Explain why it is more convenient to assign the coordinates as $C(2p, 0)$ and
$A(2q, 2r)$ rather than $C(p, 0)$ and $A(q, r)$.

This choice eliminates the need for fractions in the coordinates of *D* and *E*.

2b.   Explain how the perimeter of $\triangle JKL$ compares to that of $\triangle MNP$.

The perimeter of $\triangle JKL$ is twice the perimeter of $\triangle MNP$.

© Houghton Mifflin Harcourt Publishing Company

© Houghton Mifflin Harcourt Publishing Company

FOCUS ON REASONING
Medians of a Triangle

Essential question: *What can you conclude about the medians of a triangle?*

COMMON CORE Standards for Mathematical Content

CC.9-12.G.CO.10 Prove theorems about triangles.

CC.9-12.G.GPE.4 Use coordinates to prove simple geometric theorems algebraically.

Vocabulary

median

concurrent

point of concurrency

centroid

Prerequisites

The Midpoint Formula, Lesson 1-3

Coordinate Proofs, Lesson 3-7

The Equation of a Line, Algebra 1

Math Background

In this Focus on Reasoning lesson, students use geometry software to explore the medians of a triangle. They use inductive reasoning to make the conjecture that the medians of a triangle are concurrent and then they use deductive reasoning to complete a coordinate proof of this fact.

INTRODUCE

Discuss the use of the word *median* in mathematics and in everyday situations. Students should already be familiar with medians from their study of data and statistics in earlier grades. Explain that there is another use of the term *median* in mathematics. Then define the median of a triangle. Make a sketch on the board showing students how to draw a median, and point out that every triangle has three medians. Tell students they will use geometry software and inductive reasoning to make a conjecture about medians.

TEACH

 Investigate medians.

Materials: geometry software

Questioning Strategies

- What are the advantages to exploring medians with geometry software rather than by drawing triangles and medians with a ruler? **The software makes it easy to change the size and shape of the triangle to see if the relationship among the medians still holds.**

- Do you think it is possible for the medians of a triangle to intersect at a point on the triangle? Why or why not? **No; no matter the size or shape of the triangle, the medians always intersect in the interior of the triangle.**

Differentiated Instruction

Kinesthetic learners may benefit from a hands-on approach to the investigation. Have students draw a large triangle on a sheet of paper and cut it out. Then have them use a ruler to find the midpoint of each side of the triangle. Students can then fold the triangle along the line through each vertex and the midpoint of the opposite side. The three creases represent the medians of the triangle and students should find that the creases intersect at a common point.

Name _____ Class _____ Date _____

FOCUS ON REASONING

Medians of a Triangle

3-9

COMMON CORE
CC.9-12.G.CO.10,
CC.9-12.G.GPE.4

Essential question: *What can you conclude about the medians of a triangle?*

A **median** of a triangle is a line segment whose endpoints are a vertex of the triangle and the midpoint of the opposite side. Every triangle has three medians. In the figure, $\overline{LM}$ is a median of $\triangle JKL$.

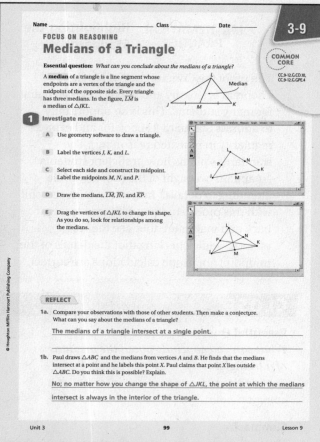

1 Investigate medians.

A   Use geometry software to draw a triangle.

B   Label the vertices *J*, *K*, and *L*.

C   Select each side and construct its midpoint. Label the midpoints *M*, *N*, and *P*.

D   Draw the medians, $\overline{LM}$, $\overline{JN}$, and $\overline{KP}$.

E   Drag the vertices of $\triangle JKL$ to change its shape. As you do so, look for relationships among the medians.

REFLECT

1a.   Compare your observations with those of other students. Then make a conjecture. What can you say about the medians of a triangle?

The medians of a triangle intersect at a single point.

1b.   Paul draws $\triangle ABC$ and the medians from vertices *A* and *B*. He finds that the medians intersect at a point and he labels this point *X*. Paul claims that point *X* lies outside $\triangle ABC$. Do you think this is possible? Explain.

No; no matter how you change the shape of $\triangle JKL$, the point at which the medians

intersect is always in the interior of the triangle.

Three or more lines are said to be **concurrent** when they intersect at a point. The point is called the **point of concurrency**. You have seen that the medians of a triangle are concurrent. The point of concurrency of the medians of a triangle is called the **centroid** of the triangle.

Concurrency of Medians Theorem

The medians of a triangle are concurrent.

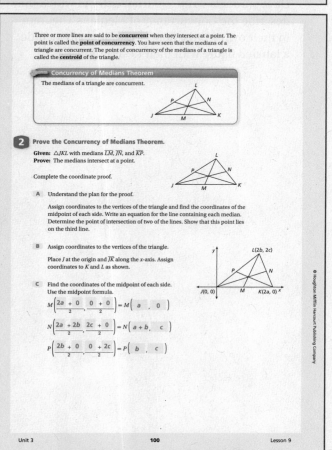

2 Prove the Concurrency of Medians Theorem.

Given: $\triangle JKL$ with medians $\overline{LM}$, $\overline{JN}$, and $\overline{KP}$.
Prove: The medians intersect at a point.

Complete the coordinate proof.

A   Understand the plan for the proof.

Assign coordinates to the vertices of the triangle and find the coordinates of the midpoint of each side. Write an equation for the line containing each median. Determine the point of intersection of two of the lines. Show that this point lies on the third line.

B   Assign coordinates to the vertices of the triangle.

Place *J* at the origin and $\overline{JK}$ along the *x*-axis. Assign coordinates to *K* and *L* as shown.

C   Find the coordinates of the midpoint of each side. Use the midpoint formula.

$$M\left(\frac{2a + 0}{2}, \frac{0 + 0}{2}\right) = M\left(\boxed{a}, \boxed{0}\right)$$

$$N\left(\frac{2a + 2b}{2}, \frac{2c + 0}{2}\right) = N\left(\boxed{a + b}, \boxed{c}\right)$$

$$P\left(\frac{2b + 0}{2}, \frac{0 + 2c}{2}\right) = P\left(\boxed{b}, \boxed{c}\right)$$

© Houghton Mifflin Harcourt Publishing Company

2 Prove the Concurrency of Medians Theorem.

Questioning Strategies

- What type of proof is used to prove the Concurrency of Medians Theorem? **It is a coordinate proof.**
- In the proof, why do you write equations for the lines containing the medians? **This allows you to determine the point of intersection of two of the lines. Then you can show that this intersection point lies on the third line.**

Avoid Common Errors

Students may get lost in the algebra that is required to complete the proof and lose track of the overall structure of the proof. To help students stay on track, you may want to have students write the main steps of the proof and then check off the steps as they complete them.

1. Assign coordinates to the vertices.
2. Find the coordinates of the midpoint of each side.
3. Write equations for the lines containing the medians.
4. Find the point of intersection of two of the lines.
5. Show that the point of intersection lies on the third line.

MATHEMATICAL PRACTICE **Highlighting the Standards**

The proof the Concurrency of Medians Theorem is lengthy and it may be challenging for many students. This is an opportunity to address Standard 8 (Look for and express regularity in repeated reasoning). The standard explains how proficient students "maintain oversight of the process, while attending to details." In order to be successful with this proof, students will need to step back and make sure they see the "big picture," while checking that the details of the midpoint and slope calculations are correct.

CLOSE

Essential Question

What can you conclude about the medians of a triangle?

The medians of a triangle all intersect at a common point.

Summarize

Have students write a journal entry in which they describe the Concurrency of Medians Theorem in their own words. Remind students to include a labeled figure with their description.

D Write the equation for the line containing $\overleftrightarrow{JN}$. To do so, use the *point-slope form* of the equation of a line: If a line has slope m and passes through (x_0, y_0), then the line's equation is $y - y_0 = m(x - x_0)$.

Slope of $\overleftrightarrow{JN} = \dfrac{c - 0}{a + b - 0} = \dfrac{c}{a + b}$

To write the equation of $\overleftrightarrow{JN}$, use the fact that the line passes through $(0, 0)$.

Equation of $\overleftrightarrow{JN}$: $y - 0 = \dfrac{c}{a + b}(x - 0)$ or $y = \dfrac{c}{a + b} x$

E Write the equations for the lines containing $\overleftrightarrow{LM}$ and $\overleftrightarrow{PK}$.

Slope of $\overleftrightarrow{LM} = \dfrac{2c - 0}{2b - a} = \dfrac{2c}{2b - a}$

Equation of $\overleftrightarrow{LM}$: $y - 0 = \dfrac{2c}{2b - a}(x - a)$ or $y = \dfrac{2c}{2b - a}(x - a)$

Slope of $\overleftrightarrow{PK} = \dfrac{c - 0}{b - 2a} = \dfrac{c}{b - 2a}$

Equation of $\overleftrightarrow{PK}$: $y - 0 = \dfrac{c}{b - 2a}(x - 2a)$ or $y = \dfrac{c}{b - 2a}(x - 2a)$

F Find the point of intersection of $\overleftrightarrow{JN}$ and $\overleftrightarrow{LM}$. To do so, set the right side of the equation for $\overleftrightarrow{JN}$ equal to the right side of the equation for $\overleftrightarrow{LM}$. Then solve for x, to find the x-coordinate of the point of intersection.

$\dfrac{c}{a + b} x = \dfrac{2c}{2b - a}(x - a)$	Write the equation for x.
$cx(2b - a) = 2c(x - a)(a + b)$	Multiply both sides by $(a + b)(2b - a)$.
$2bcx - acx = (2cx - 2ac)(a + b)$	Multiply.
$2bcx - acx = 2acx - 2a^2c + 2bcx - 2abc$	Multiply on right side of equation.
$-acx = 2acx - 2a^2c - 2abc$	Subtract $2bcx$ from both sides.
$-3acx = -2a^2c - 2abc$	Subtract $2acx$ from both sides.
$-3x = -2a - 2b$	Factor out ac; divide both sides by ac.
$x = \dfrac{2a + 2b}{3}$	Divide both sides by -3.

To find the y-coordinate of the point of intersection, substitute this value of x into the equation for $\overleftrightarrow{JN}$ and solve for y.

$$y = \frac{c}{a + b} x = \frac{c}{a + b} \cdot \frac{2a + 2b}{3} = \frac{2c}{3}$$

The coordinates of the point of intersection of $\overleftrightarrow{JN}$ and $\overleftrightarrow{LM}$ are $\left(\dfrac{2a + 2b}{3}, \dfrac{2c}{3} \right)$.

G Now show that the point you found in Step F lies on $\overleftrightarrow{PK}$. To do so, substitute the x-coordinate of the point into the equation for $\overleftrightarrow{PK}$. Then simplify to show that the corresponding y-value is the same as the y-coordinate you calculated in Step F.

$y = \dfrac{c}{b - 2a}(x - 2a)$	Write the equation for $\overleftrightarrow{PK}$.
$y = \dfrac{c}{b - 2a}\left(\dfrac{2a + 2b}{3} - 2a\right)$	Substitute the x-coordinate of the point.
$y = \dfrac{c}{b - 2a}\left(\dfrac{2b - 4a}{3}\right)$	Subtract inside the parentheses.
$y = \dfrac{c}{b - 2a}\left(\dfrac{2(b - 2a)}{3}\right)$	Factor the numerator inside the parentheses.
$y = \dfrac{c}{1}\left(\dfrac{2}{3}\right)$	Divide to remove common factors.
$y = \dfrac{2c}{3}$	Simplify.

Because this y-value is the same as the y-coordinate of the point of intersection from Step F, the point also lies on $\overleftrightarrow{PK}$. This shows that the medians are concurrent.

REFLECT

2a. Explain how you can find the coordinates of the centroid of a triangle with vertices $R(0, 0)$, $S(6, 0)$, and $T(3, 9)$.

Comparing to the generic coordinates shows that $2a = 6$, $2b = 3$, and $2c = 9$, so

substitute the values $a = 3$, $b = \frac{3}{2}$, and $c = \frac{9}{2}$ in the expressions for the coordinates

of the point of intersection. The centroid is $(3, 3)$.

2b. A student proves the Concurrency of Medians Theorem by first assigning coordinates to the vertices of $\triangle JKL$ as $J(0, 0)$, $K(2a, 0)$, and $L(2a, 2c)$. The students says that this choice of coordinates makes the algebra in the proof a bit easier. Do you agree with the student's choice of coordinates? Explain.

No; these coordinates result in a triangle that is a right triangle, so the proof

would not hold for triangles in general.

2c. A student claims that the averages of the x-coordinates and of the y-coordinates of the vertices of a triangle are the x- and y-coordinates of the centroid. Does the coordinate proof of the Concurrency of Medians Theorem support the claim? Explain.

Yes. The x-coordinates of the vertices are 0, $2a$, and $2b$; their average is $\frac{(2a + 2b)}{3}$.

The y-coordinates of the vertices are 0, 0, and $2c$; their average is $\frac{2c}{3}$. This agrees

with the expressions for the coordinates of the centroid.

COMMON CORE CORRELATION

Standard	Item
CC.9-12.G.CO.5	4
CC.9-12.G.CO.6	7
CC.9-12.G.CO.7	8
CC.9-12.G.CO.8	9
CC.9-12.G.CO.10	2
CC.9-12.G.SRT.5	1, 3, 6
CC.9-12.G.GPE.4	5

TEST PREP DOCTOR ⊕

Multiple Choice: Item 4

- Students who answered **F** may have incorrectly visualized the effect of a 180° rotation around the origin.

- Students who answered **H** may have mistaken the given vector, $\langle -2, 0 \rangle$, for the vector $\langle 0, -2 \rangle$, which produces the correct result.

- Students who answered **J** may have incorrectly visualized the effect of a reflection across the x-axis.

Free Response: Item 7

- Students who answered that the figures are congruent because corresponding sides are congruent and corresponding angles are congruent may not have read the problem carefully. (Students are asked to explain the congruence of the figures in terms of *rigid motions*.)

- Students who answered that the figures are not congruent may not understand the meaning of the term *congruent*.

Free Response: Item 9

- Students who assert that $\triangle A'B'C'$ and $\triangle DEF$ are congruent by SSS as part of their explanation of why $\overline{DE}$ is the perpendicular bisector of $\overline{FC'}$ do not understand the point of the proof. The proof is supposed to *establish* the SSS Congruence Criterion, so applying SSS to the figure is not allowed. (You can't treat what you're trying to prove as a given.)

- Students who establish either that D is on the perpendicular bisector of $\overline{FC'}$ or that E is on the perpendicular bisector of $\overline{FC'}$, but not both, are forgetting that two points are needed to determine a unique line. For instance, the perpendicular bisector of $\overline{FC'}$ might pass through D but not E, in which case $\overline{DE}$ is not the perpendicular bisector of $\overline{FC'}$.

UNIT 3 TEST PREP

Name _____ Class _____ Date _____

MULTIPLE CHOICE

1. J is the midpoint of $\overline{GH}$. $\overline{GK}$ is parallel to $\overline{LH}$. Which congruence criterion can be used to prove $\triangle GJK \cong \triangle HJL$?

(A.) ASA   C. SSA

B. SAS   D. SSS

2. Jessica wants to prove that an equilateral triangle has three congruent angles. She begins as shown below. Which reason should she use for Step 2?

Given: $\overline{AB} \cong \overline{AC} \cong \overline{BC}$
Prove: $\angle A \cong \angle B \cong \angle C$

Statements	Reasons
1. $\angle AB \cong \overline{AC}$	1. Given
2. $\angle B \cong \angle C$	2. ?
3.	3.

F. Triangle Sum Theorem

G. ASA Congruence Criterion

(H.) Isosceles Triangle Theorem

J. CPCTC

3. $\overline{PN} \cong \overline{QN}$, and $\overline{MN}$ bisects $\angle PNQ$. Which congruence criterion can be used to prove $\triangle MPN \cong \triangle MQN$?

A. ASA   C. SSA

(B.) SAS   D. SSS

4. Which sequence of transformations maps $\triangle RST$ to $\triangle UVW$?

F. reflection across the x-axis followed by a 180° rotation around the origin

(G.) reflection across the y-axis followed by the translation along vector $\langle 0, -2 \rangle$

H. translation along the vector $\langle -2, 0 \rangle$ followed by a reflection across the y-axis

J. rotation of 180° around the origin followed by a reflection across the x-axis

5. Tyrell's teacher asks him to prove or disprove that the triangle with vertices $A(1, 1)$, $B(2, 5)$, and $C(6, 4)$ is an isosceles triangle. Which of the following should he do?

A. Disprove the statement by using the distance formula to show that $\overline{AB}, \overline{BC}$, and $\overline{AC}$ all have different lengths.

(B.) Prove the statement by using the distance formula to show that $AB = BC$.

C. Prove the statement by using the distance formula to show that $AB = AC$.

D. Prove the statement by using the distance formula to show that $BC = AC$.

FREE RESPONSE

6. To find the distance AB across a pond, you locate points as follows.

Starting at A and walking along a straight path, you walk 28 feet and put a marker at C. Then you walk 28 feet farther and put a marker at D.

Starting at B, you walk to C, measuring the distance you walked (32 feet). Then you walk 32 feet farther and put a marker at E. Finally, you measure the distance from D to E, as shown. Explain how to use this information to find AB.

$\triangle ABC \cong \triangle DEC$ by SAS, so $AB = 32$ ft

by CPCTC.

7. Determine whether the figures shown below are congruent. Explain your answer using rigid motions.

The figures are congruent because

there is a sequence of rigid motions

(translation along $\langle 2, 0 \rangle$, then

reflection across the x-axis) that maps

$QRST$ to $ABCD$.

8. Given that $\triangle JKL \cong \triangle MNP$, use the definition of congruence in terms of rigid motions to explain why $\overline{KL}$ must be congruent to $\overline{NP}$.

There are rigid motions that map $\triangle JKL$

to $\triangle MNP$. This sequence maps $\overline{KL}$ onto

$\overline{NP}$. By the definition of congruence,

$\overline{KL} \cong \overline{NP}$.

9. You are writing a proof that the SSS Congruence Criterion follows from the definition of congruence in terms of rigid motions. You start with two triangles, $\triangle ABC$ and $\triangle DEF$, such that $\overline{AB} \cong \overline{DE}$, $\overline{BC} \cong \overline{EF}$, and $\overline{AC} \cong \overline{DF}$.

You use the fact that $\overline{AB} \cong \overline{DE}$ to conclude that there is a sequence of rigid motions that maps $\overline{AB}$ onto $\overline{DE}$. Applying this sequence of rigid motions to $\triangle ABC$ leads to this figure.

Why is $\overline{DE}$ the perpendicular bisector of $\overline{FC'}$?

Since $\overline{A'C'} \cong \overline{DF}$, D lies on the

perpendicular bisector of $\overline{FC'}$ by the

Perpendicular Bisector Theorem.

Similarly, $\overline{B'C'} \cong \overline{EF}$, so E lies on

the perpendicular bisector of $\overline{FC'}$.

Therefore, $\overline{DE}$ is the perpendicular

bisector of $\overline{FC'}$.

UNIT 4

Quadrilaterals and Polygons

Unit Vocabulary

angle of rotational
symmetry   (4-1)

diagonal   (4-3)

line of
symmetry   (4-1)

line symmetry   (4-1)

rectangle   (4-5)

rhombus   (4-5)

rotational
symmetry   (4-1)

symmetry   (4-1)

UNIT 4

Quadrilaterals and Polygons

Unit Focus

At the beginning of this unit, you will apply what you know about reflections and rotations to investigate the concept of symmetry. You will also study parallelograms and explore the properties of these quadrilaterals. Your knowledge of triangle congruence criteria will be useful in proving properties of parallelograms. You will also develop criteria that can be used to show that a quadrilateral is a parallelogram and you will investigate special parallelograms, including rectangles and rhombuses.

Unit at a Glance

COMMON CORE

Lesson		Standards for Mathematical Content
4-1	Symmetry	CC.9-12.G.CO.3
4-2	Sides and Angles of Parallelograms	CC.9-12.G.CO.11, CC.9-12.G.SRT.5
4-3	Diagonals of Parallelograms	CC.9-12.G.CO.11, CC.9-12.G.SRT.5
4-4	Criteria for Parallelograms	CC.9-12.G.CO.11, CC.9-12.G.SRT.5
4-5	Special Parallelograms	CC.9-12.G.CO.11, CC.9-12.G.SRT.5
	Test Prep	

Unpacking the Common Core State Standards

Use the table to help you understand the Standards for Mathematical Content that are taught in this unit. Refer to the lessons listed after each standard for exploration and practice.

COMMON CORE Standards for Mathematical Content	What It Means For You
CC.9-12.G.CO.3 Given a rectangle, parallelogram, trapezoid, or regular polygon, describe the rotations and reflections that carry it onto itself. Lesson 4-1	You are already familiar with shapes that have symmetry. In this lesson, you will learn to discuss symmetry in terms of reflections and rotations.
CC.9-12.G.CO.11 Prove theorems about parallelograms. Lessons 4-2, 4-3, 4-4, 4-5	A parallelogram is a quadrilateral with two pairs of parallel sides. You will investigate and prove properties involving the sides, angles, and diagonals of parallelograms, and you will develop criteria that can be used to show that a quadrilateral is a parallelogram.
CC.9-12.G.SRT.5 Use congruence and similarity criteria for triangles to solve problems and to prove relationships in geometric figures. Lessons 4-2, 4-3, 4-4, 4-5	The congruence criteria for triangles that you studied in Unit 3 are useful elements in proofs about parallelograms and other quadrilaterals. You will learn how to use triangle congruence criteria in a wide range of proofs about quadrilaterals.

Unit 4   106   Quadrilaterals and Polygons

Unpacking the Common Core State Standards

This page lists and explains the Standards for Mathematical Content that are addressed in this unit. For information about the Standards for Mathematical Practice, which are integrated throughout the text, see Teacher Edition pages x–xiii.

Notes

Symmetry

Essential question: *How do you determine whether a figure has line symmetry or rotational symmetry?*

COMMON CORE Standards for Mathematical Content

CC.9-12.G.CO.3 Given a rectangle, parallelogram, trapezoid, or regular polygon, describe the rotations and reflections that carry it onto itself.

Vocabulary

symmetry

line symmetry

line of symmetry

rotational symmetry

angle of rotational symmetry

Prerequisites

Reflections, Lesson 2-2

Rotations, Lesson 2-6

Math Background

Symmetry is a familiar concept from everyday situations. The goal of this lesson is to define symmetry in mathematical terms. Students may be surprised to learn that there are two types of symmetry: line (or reflection) symmetry and rotational symmetry. In fact, it is also possible to define a symmetry based on translations. A pattern has *translation symmetry* if it can be translated along a vector so that the image coincides with the pre-image. The pattern of hexagons shown below has translation symmetry (assuming the pattern continues indefinitely in all directions).

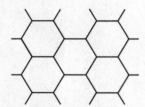

INTRODUCE

Ask students if they can give examples of objects that have symmetry. Students might mention a cat's face, a butterfly's wings, or a valentine heart. Tell students they will learn how to use mathematical language to identify and describe symmetry.

TEACH

1 EXAMPLE

Questioning Strategies

- How could you use a mirror to check a figure for line symmetry? **If you stand the mirror on edge along a line of symmetry, the part of the figure that is visible and its reflection will together form the whole figure.**

- How many lines of symmetry does an equilateral triangle have? What are the lines of symmetry? **Three; they are the three angle bisectors.**

EXTRA EXAMPLE

Determine whether each figure has line symmetry. If so, draw all lines of symmetry

A.

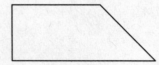

no line symmetry

B.

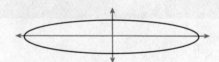

line symmetry

C.

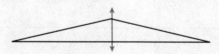

line symmetry

D.

line symmetry

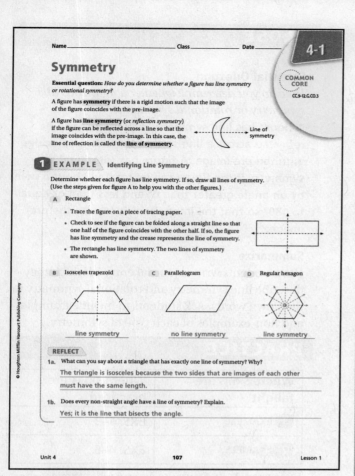

Symmetry

Name_____ Class_____ Date_____

4-1

COMMON CORE
CC.9-12.G.CO.3

Essential question: *How do you determine whether a figure has line symmetry or rotational symmetry?*

A figure has **symmetry** if there is a rigid motion such that the image of the figure coincides with the pre-image.

A figure has **line symmetry** (or *reflection symmetry*) if the figure can be reflected across a line so that the image coincides with the pre-image. In this case, the line of reflection is called the **line of symmetry**.

Line of symmetry

1 EXAMPLE Identifying Line Symmetry

Determine whether each figure has line symmetry. If so, draw all lines of symmetry. (Use the steps given for figure A to help you with the other figures.)

A Rectangle

- Trace the figure on a piece of tracing paper.
- Check to see if the figure can be folded along a straight line so that one half of the figure coincides with the other half. If so, the figure has line symmetry and the crease represents the line of symmetry.
- The rectangle has line symmetry. The two lines of symmetry are shown.

B Isosceles trapezoid   **C** Parallelogram   **D** Regular hexagon

line symmetry   no line symmetry   line symmetry

REFLECT

1a. What can you say about a triangle that has exactly one line of symmetry? Why?

The triangle is isosceles because the two sides that are images of each other must have the same length.

1b. Does every non-straight angle have a line of symmetry? Explain.

Yes; it is the line that bisects the angle.

Unit 4   107   Lesson 1

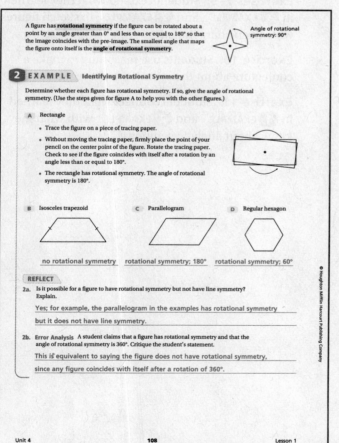

A figure has **rotational symmetry** if the figure can be rotated about a point by an angle greater than 0° and less than or equal to 180° so that the image coincides with the pre-image. The smallest angle that maps the figure onto itself is the **angle of rotational symmetry**.

Angle of rotational symmetry: 90°

2 EXAMPLE Identifying Rotational Symmetry

Determine whether each figure has rotational symmetry. If so, give the angle of rotational symmetry. (Use the steps given for figure A to help you with the other figures.)

A Rectangle

- Trace the figure on a piece of tracing paper.
- Without moving the tracing paper, firmly place the point of your pencil on the center point of the figure. Rotate the tracing paper. Check to see if the figure coincides with itself after a rotation by an angle less than or equal to 180°.
- The rectangle has rotational symmetry. The angle of rotational symmetry is 180°.

B Isosceles trapezoid   **C** Parallelogram   **D** Regular hexagon

no rotational symmetry   rotational symmetry; 180°   rotational symmetry; 60°

REFLECT

2a. Is it possible for a figure to have rotational symmetry but not have line symmetry? Explain.

Yes; for example, the parallelogram in the examples has rotational symmetry but it does not have line symmetry.

2b. Error Analysis A student claims that a figure has rotational symmetry and that the angle of rotational symmetry is 360°. Critique the student's statement.

This is equivalent to saying the figure does not have rotational symmetry, since any figure coincides with itself after a rotation of 360°.

Unit 4   108   Lesson 1

Questioning Strategies
• How do you know that the angle of rotational symmetry for the rectangle is not 90°? When you rotate the rectangle by 90°, the image does not coincide with the pre-image.

EXTRA EXAMPLE
Determine whether each figure has rotational symmetry. If so, give the angle of rotational symmetry.

A.

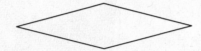

rotational symmetry; 180°

B.

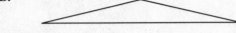

no rotational symmetry

C.

rotational symmetry; 72°

D.

rotational symmetry; 180°

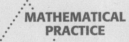

MATHEMATICAL PRACTICE — Highlighting the Standards

Exercise 10 gives students a chance to use inductive reasoning to make a conjecture. This is an important part of Standard 3 (Construct viable arguments and critique the reasoning of others). Have students describe the process they used to make their conjectures and ask them what they could do to check that their conjectures are correct.

CLOSE

Essential Question
How do you determine whether a figure has line symmetry or rotational symmetry?
A figure has line symmetry if the figure can be reflected across a line so that the image coincides with the pre-image. A figure has rotational symmetry if the figure can be rotated about a point by an angle greater than 0° and less than or equal to 180° so that the image coincides with the pre-image.

Summarize
Have students write a journal entry in which they describe line symmetry and rotational symmetry in their own words. Ask students to include examples and non-examples of each type of symmetry.

PRACTICE

Where skills are taught	Where skills are practiced
1 EXAMPLE	EXS. 1–3
2 EXAMPLE	EXS. 4–6

Exercises 7–9: Students extend what they learned in **1** EXAMPLE and **2** EXAMPLE to sketch figures with given characteristics.

Exercise 10: Students use reasoning to make a conjecture about the symmetry of a regular *n*-gon.

Exercise 11: Students connect what they learned in **1** EXAMPLE and **2** EXAMPLE with what they know about analytic geometry.

PRACTICE

Determine whether each figure has line symmetry. If so, draw all lines of symmetry.

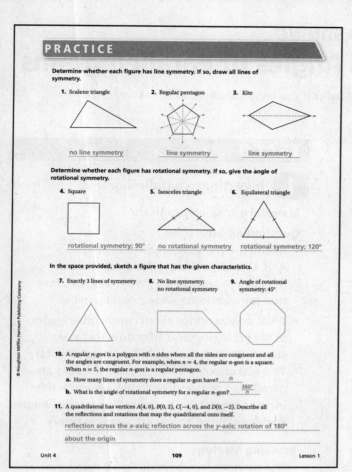

1. Scalene triangle

no line symmetry

2. Regular pentagon

line symmetry

3. Kite

line symmetry

Determine whether each figure has rotational symmetry. If so, give the angle of rotational symmetry.

4. Square

rotational symmetry; 90°

5. Isosceles triangle

no rotational symmetry

6. Equilateral triangle

rotational symmetry; 120°

In the space provided, sketch a figure that has the given characteristics.

7. Exactly 3 lines of symmetry

8. No line symmetry; no rotational symmetry

9. Angle of rotational symmetry: 45°

10. A *regular n-gon* is a polygon with n sides where all the sides are congruent and all the angles are congruent. For example, when $n = 4$, the regular n-gon is a square. When $n = 5$, the regular n-gon is a regular pentagon.

   a. How many lines of symmetry does a regular n-gon have? ___n___

   b. What is the angle of rotational symmetry for a regular n-gon? ___$\frac{360°}{n}$___

11. A quadrilateral has vertices $A(4, 0)$, $B(0, 2)$, $C(-4, 0)$, and $D(0, -2)$. Describe all the reflections and rotations that map the quadrilateral onto itself.

   reflection across the x-axis; reflection across the y-axis; rotation of 180°

   about the origin

© Houghton Mifflin Harcourt Publishing Company

Unit 4   109   Lesson 1

Notes

FOCUS ON REASONING
Sides and Angles of Parallelograms

Essential question: *What can you conclude about the sides and angles of a parallelogram?*

COMMON CORE
Standards for Mathematical Content

CC.9-12.G.CO.11 Prove theorems about parallelograms.

CC.9-12.G.SRT.5 Use congruence ... criteria for triangles to solve problems and to prove relationships in geometric figures.

***

Prerequisites

Proofs About Parallel and Perpendicular Lines, Lesson 1-7

Using Congruence Criteria, Lesson 3-4

Math Background

This Focus on Reasoning lesson is the first of several lessons about quadrilaterals. In these lessons, students extend their work with triangles from Unit 3 by using triangle congruence criteria and triangle properties to prove facts about parallelograms and other four-sided polygons. This lesson gives students a chance to use inductive and deductive reasoning to investigate properties of the sides and angles of parallelograms.

INTRODUCE

Students have encountered parallelograms in earlier grades. Ask a volunteer to define *parallelogram*. Students may have only an informal idea of what a parallelogram is (e.g., "a slanted rectangle"), so be sure they understand that the mathematical definition of a parallelogram is a quadrilateral with two pairs of parallel sides. You may want to show students how they can make a parallelogram by drawing lines on either side of a ruler, changing the position of the ruler, and drawing another pair of lines. Ask students to explain why this method creates a parallelogram.

TEACH

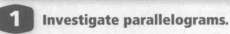

1 Investigate parallelograms.

Materials: geometry software

Questioning Strategies

- As you use the software to drag points *A*, *B*, *C*, and/or *D*, does the quadrilateral remain a parallelogram? Why? **Yes; the lines that form opposite sides remain parallel.**

- What do you notice about consecutive angles in the parallelogram? Why does this make sense? **Consecutive angles are supplementary. This makes sense because opposite sides are parallel, so consecutive angles are same-side interior angles. By the Same-Side Interior Angles Postulate, these angles are supplementary.**

Teaching Strategy

Some students may have difficulty with terms like *opposite sides* or *consecutive angles*. Remind students that opposite sides of a quadrilateral do not share a vertex (that is, they do not intersect). Consecutive sides of a quadrilateral do share a vertex (that is, they intersect). Opposite angles of a quadrilateral do not share a side. Consecutive angles of a quadrilateral do share a side. You may want to help students draw and label a quadrilateral for reference.

2 Prove that opposite sides of a parallelogram are congruent.

Questioning Strategies

- Why do you think the proof is based on drawing the diagonal $\overline{DB}$? **Drawing the diagonal creates two triangles; then you can use triangle congruence criteria and CPCTC.**

Name _____ Class _____ Date _____

4-2

FOCUS ON REASONING

Sides and Angles of Parallelograms

COMMON CORE

CC.9-12.G.CO.11,
CC.9-12.G.SRT.5

Essential question: *What can you conclude about the sides and angles of a parallelogram?*

Recall that a *parallelogram* is a quadrilateral that has two pairs of parallel sides. You use the symbol $\square$ to name a parallelogram. For example, the figure shows $\square ABCD$.

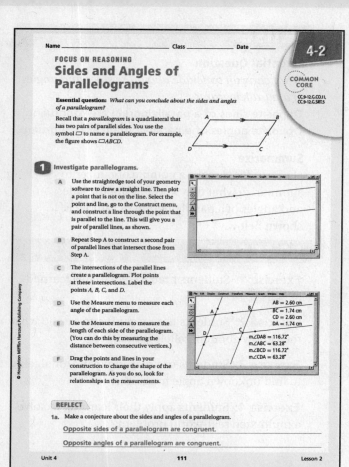

1 Investigate parallelograms.

A   Use the straightedge tool of your geometry software to draw a straight line. Then plot a point that is not on the line. Select the point and line, go to the Construct menu, and construct a line through the point that is parallel to the line. This will give you a pair of parallel lines, as shown.

B   Repeat Step A to construct a second pair of parallel lines that intersect those from Step A.

C   The intersections of the parallel lines create a parallelogram. Plot points at these intersections. Label the points *A*, *B*, *C*, and *D*.

D   Use the Measure menu to measure each angle of the parallelogram.

E   Use the Measure menu to measure the length of each side of the parallelogram. (You can do this by measuring the distance between consecutive vertices.)

F   Drag the points and lines in your construction to change the shape of the parallelogram. As you do so, look for relationships in the measurements.

```
AB = 2.60 cm
BC = 1.74 cm
CD = 2.60 cm
DA = 1.74 cm

m∠DAB = 116.72°
m∠ABC = 63.28°
m∠BCD = 116.72°
m∠CDA = 63.28°
```

REFLECT

1a. Make a conjecture about the sides and angles of a parallelogram.

Opposite sides of a parallelogram are congruent.

Opposite angles of a parallelogram are congruent.

© Houghton Mifflin Harcourt Publishing Company

You may have discovered the following theorem about parallelograms.

> **Theorem**
>
> If a quadrilateral is a parallelogram, then opposite sides are congruent.

2 Prove that opposite sides of a parallelogram are congruent.

Complete the proof.

Given: *ABCD* is a parallelogram.

Prove: $\overline{AB} \cong \overline{CD}$ and $\overline{AD} \cong \overline{BC}$

Statements	Reasons
1. *ABCD* is a parallelogram.	1. Given
2. Draw $\overline{DB}$.	2. Through any two points there exists exactly one line.
3. $\overline{AB} \parallel \overline{DC}$; $\overline{AD} \parallel \overline{BC}$	3. Definition of parallelogram
4. ∠*ADB* ≅ ∠*CBD*; ∠*ABD* ≅ ∠*CDB*	4. Alternate Interior Angles Theorem
5. $\overline{DB} \cong \overline{DB}$	5. Reflexive Property of Congruence
6. △*ABD* ≅ △*CDB*	6. ASA Congruence Criterion
7. *AB* ≅ *CD*; *AD* ≅ *BC*	7. CPCTC

REFLECT

2a. Explain how you can use the rotational symmetry of a parallelogram to give an argument that supports the above theorem.

Under a 180° rotation about the center of the parallelogram, each side is mapped

to its opposite side. Since rotations preserve distance, this shows that opposite

sides are congruent.

2b. One side of a parallelogram is twice as long as another side. The perimeter of the parallelogram is 24 inches. Is it possible to find all the side lengths of the parallelogram? If so, find the lengths. If not, explain why not.

Yes; consecutive sides have lengths *x*, 2*x*, *x*, and 2*x*, so *x* + 2*x* + *x* + 2*x* = 24, or

6*x* = 24. Therefore *x* = 4 and the side lengths are 4 in., 8 in., 4 in., and 8 in.

© Houghton Mifflin Harcourt Publishing Company

Teaching Strategy

The lesson concludes with the theorem that states that opposite angles of a parallelogram are congruent. The proof of this theorem is left as an exercise (Exercise 1). Be sure students recognize that the proof of this theorem is similar to the proof that opposite sides of a parallelogram are congruent. Noticing such similarities is an important problem-solving skill.

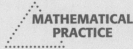

MATHEMATICAL PRACTICE   **Highlighting the Standards**

Exercise 4 is a multi-part exercise that includes opportunities for mathematical modeling, reasoning, and communication. It is a good opportunity to address Standard 4 (Model with mathematics). Draw students' attention to the way they interpret their mathematical results in the context of the real-world situation. Specifically, ask students to explain what their mathematical findings tell them about the appearance and layout of the park.

CLOSE

Essential Question

What can you conclude about the sides and angles of a parallelogram?

Opposite sides of a parallelogram are congruent.
Opposite angles of a parallelogram are congruent.

Summarize

Have students make a graphic organizer to summarize what they know about the sides and angles of a parallelogram. A sample is shown below.

PRACTICE

Exercise 1: Students practice what they learned in **2** EXAMPLE .

Exercise 2: Students use reasoning to extend what they know about parallelograms.

Exercise 3: Students use reasoning and/or algebra to find unknown angle measures.

Exercise 4: Students apply their learning to solve a multi-step real-world problem.

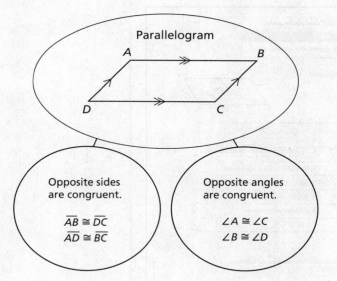

The angles of a parallelogram also have an important property. It is stated in the following theorem, which you will prove as an exercise.

> **Theorem**
>
> If a quadrilateral is a parallelogram, then opposite angles are congruent.

PRACTICE

1. Prove the above theorem about opposite angles of a parallelogram.

Given: *ABCD* is a parallelogram.
Prove: $\angle A \cong \angle C$ and $\angle B \cong \angle D$

(*Hint:* You only need to prove that $\angle A \cong \angle C$. A similar argument can be used to prove that $\angle B \cong \angle D$. Also, you may or may not need to use all the rows of the table in your proof.)

Statements	Reasons
1. *ABCD* is a parallelogram.	1. Given
2. Draw $\overline{DB}$.	2. Through any two points there exists exactly one line.
3. $\overline{AB} \parallel \overline{DC}$; $\overline{AD} \parallel \overline{BC}$	3. Definition of parallelogram
4. $\angle ADB \cong \angle CBD$; $\angle ABD \cong \angle CDB$	4. Alternate Interior Angles Theorem
5. $\overline{DB} \cong \overline{DB}$	5. Reflexive Property of Congruence
6. $\triangle ABD \cong \triangle CDB$	6. ASA Congruence Criterion
7. $\angle A \cong \angle C$	7. CPCTC

2. Explain why consecutive angles of a parallelogram are supplementary.

Consecutive angles of a parallelogram are same-side interior angles for a

pair of parallel lines (the opposite sides of the parallelogram), so the angles

are supplementary by the Same-Side Interior Angles Postulate.

3. In the figure, *JKLM* is a parallelogram. Find the measure of each of the numbered angles.

$m\angle 1 = 19°$; $m\angle 2 = 43°$; $m\angle 3 = 118°$;

$m\angle 4 = 118°$; $m\angle 5 = 19°$

---

4. A city planner is designing a park in the shape of a parallelogram. As shown in the figure, there will be two straight paths through which visitors may enter the park. The paths are bisectors of consecutive angles of the parallelogram, and the paths intersect at point *P*.

a. Work directly on the parallelograms below and use a compass and straightedge to construct the bisectors of $\angle A$ and $\angle B$. Then use a protractor to measure $\angle APB$ in each case.

Make a conjecture about $\angle APB$.

$\angle APB$ is a right angle.

b. Write a paragraph proof to show that your conjecture is always true. (*Hint:* Suppose $m\angle BAP = x°$, $m\angle ABP = y°$, and $m\angle APB = z°$. What do you know about $x + y + z$? What do you know about $2x + 2y$?)

By the Triangle Sum Theorem, $x + y + z = 180$. Also, $m\angle DAB = (2x)°$ and

$m\angle ABC = (2y)°$. By the Same-Side Interior Angles Postulate $m\angle DAB +$

$m\angle ABC = 180°$. So $2x + 2y = 180$ and $x + y = 90$. Substituting this in the

first equation gives $90 + z = 180$ and $z = 90$.

c. When the city planner takes into account the dimensions of the park, she finds that point *P* lies on $\overline{DC}$, as shown. Explain why it must be the case that $DC = 2AD$. (*Hint:* Use congruent base angles to show that $\triangle DAP$ and $\triangle CPB$ are isosceles.)

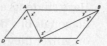

$\angle DAP \cong \angle BAP$ since $\overline{AP}$ is an angle bisector. Also, $\angle DPA \cong \angle BAP$ by the

Alternate Interior Angles Theorem. Therefore, $\angle DAP \cong \angle DPA$. This means

$\triangle DAP$ is isosceles, with $\overline{AD} \cong \overline{DP}$. Similarly, $\overline{BC} \cong \overline{PC}$. Also, $\overline{BC} \cong \overline{AD}$ as

opposite sides of a parallelogram. So, $DC = DP + PC = AD + BC = AD +$

$AD = 2AD$.

FOCUS ON REASONING
Diagonals of Parallelograms

Essential question: What can you conclude about the diagonals of a parallelogram?

COMMON CORE Standards for Mathematical Content

CC.9-12.G.CO.11 Prove theorems about parallelograms.

CC.9-12.G.SRT.5 Use congruence ... criteria for triangles to solve problems and to prove relationships in geometric figures.

Vocabulary
diagonal

Prerequisites
Proofs About Parallel and Perpendicular Lines, Lesson 1-7

Using Congruence Criteria, Lesson 3-4

Math Background
This is the second of two lessons that highlight the properties of parallelograms. As in all Focus on Reasoning lessons, students begin by taking an inductive approach to the topic as they make a conjecture about the diagonals of a parallelogram. Then they use inductive reasoning to prove that their conjecture is true.

INTRODUCE

Define *diagonal*. Draw a polygon on the board and draw the diagonals with dashed lines. Tell students they will explore the diagonals of a parallelogram.

TEACH

1 Investigate diagonals of parallelograms.

Materials: geometry software

Questioning Strategies
- How many diagonals does a parallelogram have? Is this true for every quadrilateral? **Two; yes**

- If a quadrilateral is named *PQRS*, what are the diagonals? $\overline{PR}$ **and** $\overline{QS}$

- Are the diagonals of a parallelogram ever congruent? If so, when does this appear to happen? **Yes; when the parallelogram is a rectangle**

2 Prove diagonals of a parallelogram bisect each other.

Questioning Strategies
- Why do you think this theorem was introduced after the theorems about the sides and angles of a parallelogram? **The proof of this theorem depends upon the fact that opposite sides of a parallelogram are congruent.**

  MATHEMATICAL PRACTICE   **Highlighting the Standards**

As students work on the proof in this lesson, ask them to think about how the format of the proof makes it easier to understand the underlying structure of the argument. This addresses elements of Standard 3 (Construct viable arguments and critique the reasoning of others). Students should recognize that a flow proof shows how one statement connects to the next. This may not be as apparent in a two-column format. You may want to have students rewrite the proof in a two-column format as a way of exploring this further.

CLOSE

Essential Question
What can you conclude about the diagonals of a parallelogram?
The diagonals of a parallelogram bisect each other.

Summarize
Have students add what they know about the diagonals of a parallelogram to the graphic organizer they made at the end of Lesson 4-2. This will give them a single graphic organizer that summarizes all the key properties of parallelograms.

Name _____ Class _____ Date _____

FOCUS ON REASONING
Diagonals of Parallelograms

Essential question: *What can you conclude about the diagonals of a parallelogram?*

COMMON
CORE

CC.9-12.G.CO.11,
CC.9-12.G.SRT.5

A segment that connects any two nonconsecutive vertices of a polygon is a **diagonal**. A parallelogram has two diagonals. In the figure, $\overline{AC}$ and $\overline{BD}$ are diagonals of $\square ABCD$.

1 **Investigate diagonals of parallelograms.**

A   Use geometry software to construct a parallelogram. (See Lesson 4-2 for detailed instructions.) Label the vertices of the parallelogram *A*, *B*, *C*, and *D*.

B   Use the segment tool to construct the diagonals, $\overline{AC}$ and $\overline{BD}$.

C   Plot a point at the intersection of the diagonals. Label this point *E*.

D   Use the Measure menu to measure the length of $\overline{AE}$, $\overline{BE}$, $\overline{CE}$, and $\overline{DE}$. (You can do this by measuring the distance between the relevant endpoints.)

E   Drag the points and lines in your construction to change the shape of the parallelogram. As you do so, look for relationships in the measurements.

AE = 1.52 cm
BE = 2.60 cm
CE = 1.52 cm
DE = 2.60 cm

REFLECT

1a. Make a conjecture about the diagonals of a parallelogram.

The diagonals of a parallelogram bisect each other.

1b. A student claims that the perimeter of $\triangle AEB$ is always equal to the perimeter of $\triangle CED$. Without doing any further measurements in your construction, explain whether or not you agree with the student's statement.

Agree; AE = CE, BE = DE, and AB = DC since opposite sides of a parallelogram

are congruent. So, AE + BE + AB = CE + DE + DC.

You may have discovered the following theorem about parallelograms.

Theorem

If a quadrilateral is a parallelogram, then the diagonals bisect each other.

2 **Prove diagonals of a parallelogram bisect each other.**

Complete the proof.

Given: ABCD is a parallelogram.

Prove: $\overline{AE} \cong \overline{CE}$ and $\overline{BE} \cong \overline{DE}$.

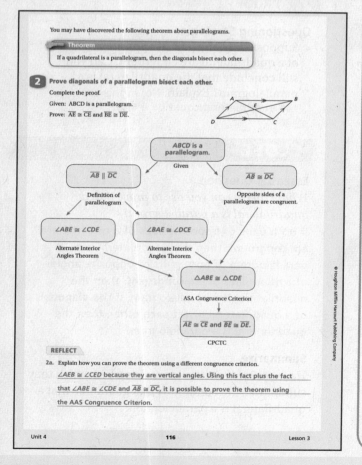

ABCD is a parallelogram.

Given

$\overline{AB} \parallel \overline{DC}$

Definition of parallelogram

$\overline{AB} \cong \overline{DC}$

Opposite sides of a parallelogram are congruent.

$\angle ABE \cong \angle CDE$

Alternate Interior Angles Theorem

$\angle BAE \cong \angle DCE$

Alternate Interior Angles Theorem

$\triangle ABE \cong \triangle CDE$

ASA Congruence Criterion

$\overline{AE} \cong \overline{CE}$ and $\overline{BE} \cong \overline{DE}$.

CPCTC

REFLECT

2a. Explain how you can prove the theorem using a different congruence criterion.

$\angle AEB \cong \angle CED$ because they are vertical angles. Using this fact plus the fact

that $\angle ABE \cong \angle CDE$ and $\overline{AB} \cong \overline{DC}$, it is possible to prove the theorem using

the AAS Congruence Criterion.

Criteria for Parallelograms

Essential question: *What criteria can you use to prove that a quadrilateral is a parallelogram?*

COMMON CORE Standards for Mathematical Content

CC.9-12.G.CO.11 Prove theorems about parallelograms.

CC.9-12.G.SRT.5 Use congruence ... criteria for triangles to solve problems and to prove relationships in geometric figures.

Prerequisites

Proofs About Parallel and Perpendicular Lines, Lesson 1-7

Using Congruence Criteria, Lesson 3-4

Math Background

In Lessons 4-2 and 4-3, students learned about three properties of parallelograms: opposite sides are congruent, opposite angles are congruent, and the diagonals bisect each other. As students will see in this lesson, each of these conditions is sufficient to conclude that a quadrilateral is a parallelogram.

INTRODUCE

Remind students of the criteria they know for determining when two triangles are congruent (SSS, SAS, ASA, and AAS). Explain that there are also criteria for determining when a quadrilateral is a parallelogram. One of these is based on the definition of a parallelogram. That is, if opposite sides of a quadrilateral are parallel, then the quadrilateral is a parallelogram. Other criteria are based on the converses of the theorems in Lessons 4-2 and 4-3.

TEACH

 PROOF

Questioning Strategies

• What must you do in order to prove that *ABCD* is a parallelogram? Show that the opposite sides are parallel.

MATHEMATICAL PRACTICE **Highlighting the Standards**

The follow-up question for the proof of the Opposite Sides Criterion provides a connection to Standard 6 (Attend to precision). Students may read the question quickly and decide that there is enough information to conclude that the quadrilateral is a parallelogram. Further reflection should convince them that this is not the case because it is not known whether the congruent sides are opposite each other. Remind students that it is important to slow down and pay close attention to the details that are given (or not given) in any mathematics problem.

2 PROOF

Questioning Strategies

• Suppose only one pair of opposite angles of a quadrilateral are congruent. Can you still conclude that the quadrilateral is a parallelogram? Explain. No; in this case, the quadrilateral could be a kite.

CLOSE

Essential Question

What criteria can you use to prove that a quadrilateral is a parallelogram?
If both pairs of opposite sides of a quadrilateral are congruent, then the quadrilateral is a parallelogram. If both pairs of opposite angles of a quadrilateral are congruent, then the quadrilateral is a parallelogram. If the diagonals of a quadrilateral bisect each other, then the quadrilateral is a parallelogram.

Summarize

Have students write a journal entry in which they summarize the conditions that guarantee that a quadrilateral is a parallelogram.

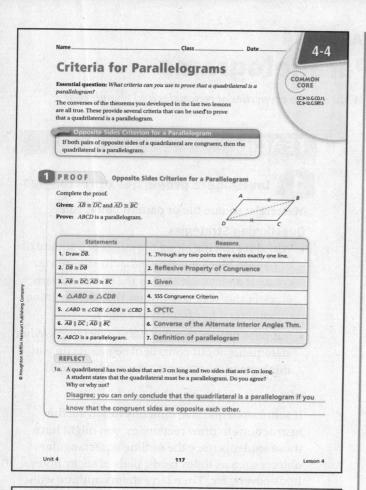

Name _____ **Class** _____ **Date** _____

Criteria for Parallelograms

COMMON CORE

CC-9-12.G.CO.11,
CC-9-12.G.SRT.5

Essential question: *What criteria can you use to prove that a quadrilateral is a parallelogram?*

The converses of the theorems you developed in the last two lessons are all true. These provide several criteria that can be used to prove that a quadrilateral is a parallelogram.

> ### Opposite Sides Criterion for a Parallelogram
> If both pairs of opposite sides of a quadrilateral are congruent, then the quadrilateral is a parallelogram.

1 PROOF   Opposite Sides Criterion for a Parallelogram

Complete the proof.

Given: $\overline{AB} \cong \overline{DC}$ and $\overline{AD} \cong \overline{BC}$

Prove: *ABCD* is a parallelogram.

Statements	Reasons
1. Draw $\overline{DB}$.	1. Through any two points there exists exactly one line.
2. $\overline{DB} \cong \overline{DB}$	2. Reflexive Property of Congruence
3. $\overline{AB} \cong \overline{DC}$; $\overline{AD} \cong \overline{BC}$	3. Given
4. $\triangle ABD \cong \triangle CDB$	4. SSS Congruence Criterion
5. $\angle ABD \cong \angle CDB$; $\angle ADB \cong \angle CBD$	5. CPCTC
6. $\overline{AB} \parallel \overline{DC}$; $\overline{AD} \parallel \overline{BC}$	6. Converse of the Alternate Interior Angles Thm.
7. *ABCD* is a parallelogram.	7. Definition of parallelogram

REFLECT

1a. A quadrilateral has two sides that are 3 cm long and two sides that are 5 cm long. A student states that the quadrilateral must be a parallelogram. Do you agree? Why or why not?

Disagree; you can only conclude that the quadrilateral is a parallelogram if you

know that the congruent sides are opposite each other.

> ### Opposite Angles Criterion for a Parallelogram
> If both pairs of opposite angles of a quadrilateral are congruent, then the quadrilateral is a parallelogram.

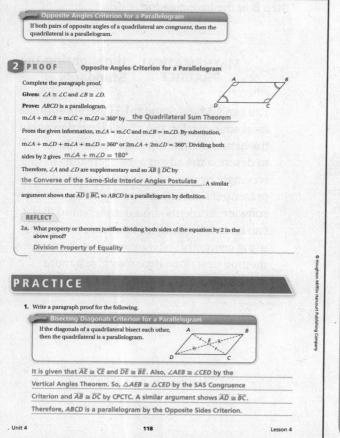

2 PROOF   Opposite Angles Criterion for a Parallelogram

Complete the paragraph proof.

Given: $\angle A \cong \angle C$ and $\angle B \cong \angle D$.

Prove: *ABCD* is a parallelogram.

$m\angle A + m\angle B + m\angle C + m\angle D = 360°$ by   the Quadrilateral Sum Theorem

From the given information, $m\angle A = m\angle C$ and $m\angle B = m\angle D$. By substitution,

$m\angle A + m\angle D + m\angle A + m\angle D = 360°$ or $2m\angle A + 2m\angle D = 360°$. Dividing both

sides by 2 gives $m\angle A + m\angle D = 180°$

Therefore, $\angle A$ and $\angle D$ are supplementary and so $\overline{AB} \parallel \overline{DC}$ by

the Converse of the Same-Side Interior Angles Postulate   . A similar

argument shows that $\overline{AD} \parallel \overline{BC}$, so *ABCD* is a parallelogram by definition.

REFLECT

2a. What property or theorem justifies dividing both sides of the equation by 2 in the above proof?

Division Property of Equality

PRACTICE

1. Write a paragraph proof for the following.

> ### Bisecting Diagonals Criterion for a Parallelogram
> If the diagonals of a quadrilateral bisect each other, then the quadrilateral is a parallelogram.

It is given that $\overline{AE} \cong \overline{CE}$ and $\overline{DE} \cong \overline{BE}$. Also, $\angle AEB \cong \angle CED$ by the

Vertical Angles Theorem. So, $\triangle AEB \cong \triangle CED$ by the SAS Congruence

Criterion and $\overline{AB} \cong \overline{DC}$ by CPCTC. A similar argument shows $\overline{AD} \cong \overline{BC}$.

Therefore, *ABCD* is a parallelogram by the Opposite Sides Criterion.

FOCUS ON REASONING
Special Parallelograms

Essential question: *What are the properties of rectangles and rhombuses?*

4-5

COMMON CORE Standards for Mathematical Content

CC.9-12.G.CO.11 Prove theorems about parallelograms.

CC.9-12.G.SRT.5 Use congruence ... criteria for triangles to solve problems and to prove relationships in geometric figures.

Vocabulary
rectangle

rhombus

Prerequisites
Using Congruence Criteria, Lesson 3-4

Sides and Angles of Parallelograms, Lesson 4-2

Diagonals of Parallelograms, Lesson 4-3

Criteria for Parallelograms, Lesson 4-4

Math Background
A rectangle is a quadrilateral with four right angles (or, equivalently, four congruent angles). A rhombus is a quadrilateral with four congruent sides. As students learn in this lesson, both types of quadrilaterals are parallelograms. Note that a square is a quadrilateral with four right angles and four congruent sides. This means a square is both a rectangle and a rhombus, as well as a parallelogram.

INTRODUCE

Ask students to point out examples of rectangles in the classroom (windows, desktops, textbook covers, and so forth). Then ask students if they can define *rectangle*. Students may have the misconception that rectangles are defined to be parallelograms with four right angles. Explain that the definition states that a rectangle is a quadrilateral with four right angles. The fact that a rectangle is a parallelogram is something that must be proved.

TEACH

1 Investigate properties of rectangles.

Materials: square tile or pattern block, ruler

Questioning Strategies
- Why does tracing along the edges of a square tile or pattern block guarantee that the figure you create is a rectangle? Using the tile or pattern block in this way guarantees that the resulting quadrilateral has four right angles.

- Suppose quadrilateral *PQRS* is a rectangle. What statements about congruent segments do you think are true? $\overline{PQ} \cong \overline{RS}$, $\overline{PS} \cong \overline{QR}$, $\overline{PR} \cong \overline{QS}$

Differentiated Instruction
If some students have difficulty following the instructions to draw rectangles, you might have these students trace the outline of rectangular objects such as index cards, pads of sticky notes, book covers, etc. Then have them continue with Step B of the investigation.

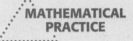

MATHEMATICAL PRACTICE   **Highlighting the Standards**

You can address Standard 5 (Use appropriate tools strategically) in a class discussion about the hands-on investigation. Ask students to describe the advantages of creating a rectangle by using the drawing method presented here rather than by using geometry software. Students should understand that it can be cumbersome to construct rectangles using geometry software and that the drawing method described here may give a more immediate entry point into the investigation.

Name _____ Class _____ Date _____

4-5

FOCUS ON REASONING
Special Parallelograms

COMMON CORE

CC-9-12.G.CO.11,
CC-9-12.G.SRT.5

Essential question: *What are the properties of rectangles and rhombuses?*

A **rectangle** is a quadrilateral with four right angles. The figure shows rectangle *ABCD*.

1 Investigate properties of rectangles.

A   Use a tile or pattern block and the following method to draw three different rectangles on a separate sheet of paper.

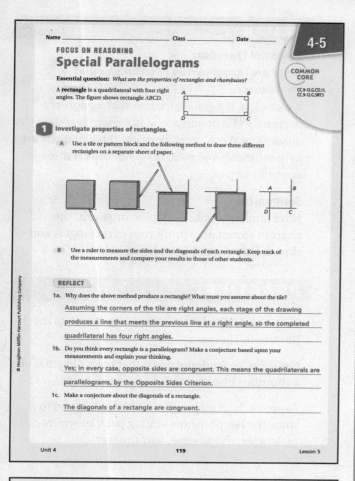

B   Use a ruler to measure the sides and the diagonals of each rectangle. Keep track of the measurements and compare your results to those of other students.

REFLECT

1a. Why does the above method produce a rectangle? What must you assume about the tile?

Assuming the corners of the tile are right angles, each stage of the drawing

produces a line that meets the previous line at a right angle, so the completed

quadrilateral has four right angles.

1b. Do you think every rectangle is a parallelogram? Make a conjecture based upon your measurements and explain your thinking.

Yes; in every case, opposite sides are congruent. This means the quadrilaterals are

parallelograms, by the Opposite Sides Criterion.

1c. Make a conjecture about the diagonals of a rectangle.

The diagonals of a rectangle are congruent.

You may have discovered the following theorem about rectangles.

Rectangle Theorem

A rectangle is a parallelogram with congruent diagonals.

In order to prove the above theorem, it is convenient to use a theorem that states that all right angles are congruent. The proof of this theorem is straightforward: If ∠X and ∠Y are right angles, then m∠X = 90° and m∠Y = 90° so m∠X = m∠Y and ∠X ≅ ∠Y.

2 Prove the Rectangle Theorem.

Complete the proof.

Given: *ABCD* is a rectangle.
Prove: *ABCD* is a parallelogram; $\overline{AC} \cong \overline{BD}$.

A   First prove that *ABCD* is a parallelogram. Since *ABCD* is a rectangle, ∠A and

∠C are right angles. So, ∠A ≅ ∠C because all right angles are congruent .

By similar reasoning, ∠B ≅ ∠D. Therefore, *ABCD* is a parallelogram by

the Opposite Angles Criterion for a Parallelogram

B   Now prove that the diagonals are congruent. Since *ABCD* is a parallelogram,

$\overline{AD} \cong \overline{BC}$ because opposite sides of a parallelogram are congruent .

Also, $\overline{DC} \cong \overline{DC}$ by the reflexive property of congruence. By the definition

of a rectangle, ∠D and ∠C are right angles, and so ∠D ≅ ∠C because

all right angles are congruent.

Therefore, △ADC ≅ △BCD by   the SAS Congruence Criterion

and $\overline{AC} \cong \overline{BD}$ by   CPCTC   .

REFLECT

2a. Error Analysis A student says you can also prove the diagonals are congruent by using the SSS Congruence Criterion to show that △ADC ≅ △BCD. Do you agree? Explain.

No; in order to use the SSS Congruence Criterion, you would have to know

that $\overline{AC} \cong \overline{BD}$, which is what you are trying to prove.

2 Prove the Rectangle Theorem.

Questioning Strategies

- What two things do you have to prove in order to prove the theorem? Prove *ABCD* is a parallelogram; prove the diagonals of *ABCD* are congruent.

Avoid Common Errors

Students may try to prove that a rectangle is a parallelogram by stating that $\overline{AB} \cong \overline{DC}$ and $\overline{AD} \cong \overline{BC}$, so *ABCD* is a parallelogram by the Opposite Sides Criterion for a Parallelogram. However, the given information states only that *ABCD* is a rectangle (that is, *ABCD* has four right angles). The fact that a rectangle has opposite sides that are congruent is a consequence of the fact that a rectangle is a parallelogram. In order to avoid circular reasoning, congruent opposite sides cannot be used as part of this proof.

 Prove diagonals of a rhombus are perpendicular.

Questioning Strategies

- Why do the diagonals of a rhombus bisect each other? Since a rhombus is a parallelogram, the diagonals bisect each other.

- To prove that $\overline{JL} \perp \overline{MK}$, do you need to show that all four of the angles formed by the intersecting diagonals are right angles? Why or why not? No; you only need to show that one angle is a right angle. If one angle is a right angle, it's easy to see that the others must also be right angles by the Vertical Angles Theorem and the Linear Pair Theorem.

CLOSE

Essential Question

What are the properties of rectangles and rhombuses?

A rectangle is a parallelogram with congruent diagonals. If a quadrilateral is a rhombus, then the quadrilateral is a parallelogram, the diagonals are perpendicular, and each diagonal bisects a pair of opposite angles.

Summarize

Have students make a graphic organizer or chart to summarize properties of rectangles and rhombuses. A sample is shown below.

PRACTICE

Exercise 1: Students prove the converse of the Rectangle Theorem.

Exercise 2: Students prove that each diagonal of a rhombus bisects a pair of opposite angles.

Exercise 3: Students draw a Venn diagram to show the relationships among parallelograms, rectangles, rhombuses, and squares.

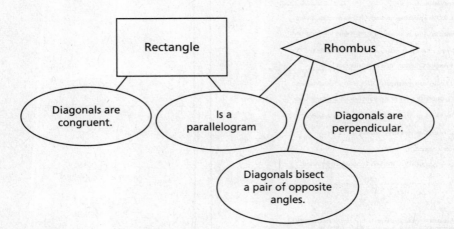

A **rhombus** is a quadrilateral with four congruent sides. The figure shows rhombus *JKLM*.

The following is a summary of some properties of rhombuses. You will prove these properties below and in the exercises.

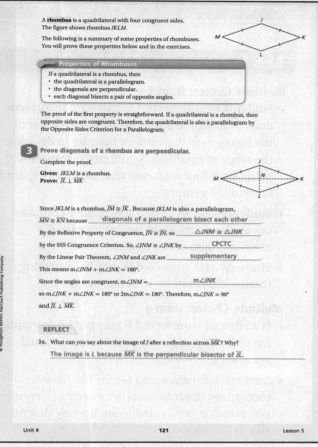

> **Properties of Rhombuses**
>
> If a quadrilateral is a rhombus, then
> * the quadrilateral is a parallelogram.
> * the diagonals are perpendicular.
> * each diagonal bisects a pair of opposite angles.

The proof of the first property is straightforward. If a quadrilateral is a rhombus, then opposite sides are congruent. Therefore, the quadrilateral is also a parallelogram by the Opposite Sides Criterion for a Parallelogram.

3 **Prove diagonals of a rhombus are perpendicular.**

Complete the proof.

Given: *JKLM* is a rhombus.
Prove: $\overline{JL} \perp \overline{MK}$

Since *JKLM* is a rhombus, $\overline{JM} \cong \overline{JK}$. Because *JKLM* is also a parallelogram,

$\overline{MN} \cong \overline{KN}$ because ___diagonals of a parallelogram bisect each other___.

By the Reflexive Property of Congruence, $\overline{JN} \cong \overline{JN}$, so ___$\triangle JNM \cong \triangle JNK$___

by the SSS Congruence Criterion. So, $\angle JNM \cong \angle JNK$ by ___CPCTC___.

By the Linear Pair Theorem, $\angle JNM$ and $\angle JNK$ are ___supplementary___.

This means m$\angle JNM$ + m$\angle JNK$ = 180°.

Since the angles are congruent, m$\angle JNM$ = ___m$\angle JNK$___

so m$\angle JNK$ + m$\angle JNK$ = 180° or 2m$\angle JNK$ = 180°. Therefore, m$\angle JNK$ = 90°

and $\overline{JL} \perp \overline{MK}$.

REFLECT

3a. What can you say about the image of *J* after a reflection across $\overline{MK}$? Why?

___The image is *L* because $\overline{MK}$ is the perpendicular bisector of $\overline{JL}$.___

PRACTICE

1. Prove the converse of the Rectangle Theorem. That is, if a parallelogram has congruent diagonals, then the parallelogram is a rectangle.

   Given: *ABCD* is a parallelogram; $\overline{AC} \cong \overline{BD}$.
   Prove: *ABCD* is a rectangle.

   Because opposite sides of a parallelogram are congruent, $\overline{AB} \cong \overline{DC}$. It is

   given that $\overline{AC} \cong \overline{BD}$, and $\overline{AD} \cong \overline{AD}$ by the Reflexive Property of Congruence.

   So, $\triangle ABD \cong \triangle DCA$ by the SSS Congruence Criterion, and $\angle BAD \cong \angle CDA$ by

   CPCTC. But these angles are supplementary since $\overline{AB} \parallel \overline{DC}$. Therefore,

   m$\angle BAD$ + m$\angle CDA$ = 180°. So m$\angle BAD$ + m$\angle BAD$ = 180° by substitution,

   2m$\angle BAD$ = 180°, and m$\angle BAD$ = 90°. A similar argument shows the other

   angles of *ABCD* are right angles, so *ABCD* is a rectangle.

2. Prove that if a quadrilateral is a rhombus, then each diagonal bisects a pair of opposite angles.

   Given: *JKLM* is a rhombus.
   Prove: $\overline{MK}$ bisects $\angle JML$ and $\angle JKL$;
   $\overline{JL}$ bisects $\angle MJK$ and $\angle MLK$.

   Since *JKLM* is a rhombus, $\overline{JM} \cong \overline{LM}$ and $\overline{JK} \cong \overline{LK}$. $\overline{MK} \cong \overline{MK}$ by the

   Reflexive Property of Congruence. So, $\triangle MJK \cong \triangle MLK$ by the SSS

   Congruence Criterion. Thus, $\angle JMK \cong \angle LMK$ and $\angle JKM \cong \angle LMK$ by

   CPCTC, and so $\overline{MK}$ bisects $\angle JML$ and $\angle JKL$. A similar argument shows

   that $\overline{JL}$ bisects $\angle MJK$ and $\angle MLK$.

3. A *square* is a quadrilateral with four right angles and four congruent sides. In the space at right, draw a Venn diagram to show how squares, rectangles, rhombuses, and parallelograms are related to each other.

   Parallelogram ▱

   Rectangle ▭   Square ■   Rhombus ◇

COMMON CORE CORRELATION

Standard	Items
CC.9–12.G.CO.3	1, 4, 5, 6
CC.9–12.G.CO.11	2, 3, 7
CC.9–12.G.SRT.5	3, 7, 8

TEST PREP DOCTOR ⊕

Multiple Choice: Item 1

- Students who answered **A** may have incorrectly drawn radial line segments from the center of the hexagon to the vertices in order to determine the angle of rotational symmetry. There should be six such line segments that are evenly spaced around the center.

- Students who answered **B** may have confused the angle of rotational symmetry with the interior angles of the figure.

- Students who answered **D** may be confusing rotational symmetry with line symmetry.

Multiple Choice: Item 4

- Students who answered **F** may not understand the definition of line symmetry or rotational symmetry.

- Students who answered **G** may not have recognized the rotational symmetry of a regular polygon that is oriented in such a way that no side is horizontal.

- Students who answered **H** may only be looking for line symmetry that is determined by a vertical line of symmetry.

Free Response: Item 5

- Students who drew an isosceles trapezoid may not recognize that an isosceles trapezoid has one line of symmetry. The trapezoid must be non-isosceles in order to have no lines of symmetry.

- Students who did not draw a trapezoid may not understand the definition of *trapezoid*. Remind them that a trapezoid is a quadrilateral with exactly one pair of parallel opposite sides.

Name _____ Class _____ Date _____

MULTIPLE CHOICE

1. Which of the following figures has an angle of rotational symmetry of 90°?

   A.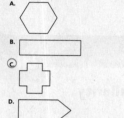

   B.

   C.

   D.

2. Ming is proving that opposite sides of a parallelogram are congruent. He begins as shown. Which reason should he use for Step 3?

   Given: $PQRS$ is a parallelogram
   Prove: $\overline{PQ} \cong \overline{RS}$; $\overline{PS} \cong \overline{QR}$

Statements	Reasons
1. $PQRS$ is a parallelogram	1. Given
2. Draw $\overline{SQ}$.	2. Through 2 pts. there is exactly one line.
3. $\overline{PQ} \parallel \overline{RS}$; $\overline{PS} \parallel \overline{QR}$	3. ?

   F. Definition of parallelogram
   G. Alternate Interior Angles Theorem
   H. Reflexive Property of Congruence
   J. CPCTC

3. $DEFG$ is a rhombus. You want to prove the property that a diagonal of a rhombus bisects a pair of opposite angles. To prove that $\overline{DF}$ bisects $\angle GDE$, you first show that $\triangle GDF \cong \triangle EDF$ using the definition of rhombus, the Reflexive Property of Congruence, and the SSS Congruence Criterion. What other reasons are needed to complete the proof?

   A. Isosceles Triangle Theorem; SAS Congruence Criterion
   B. Definition of perpendicular; Triangle Sum Theorem
   C. If a quadrilateral is a parallelogram, then opposite angles are congruent; definition of angle bisector
   D. Congruent Parts of Congruent Triangles are Congruent; definition of angle bisector

4. Which is the best description of the symmetry of this regular pentagon?

   F. has neither line symmetry nor rotational symmetry
   G. has line symmetry but not rotational symmetry
   H. has rotational symmetry but not line symmetry
   J. has both line symmetry and rotational symmetry

FREE RESPONSE

5. In the space below, draw an example of a trapezoid that does *not* have line symmetry.

6. In the space below, draw an example of a parallelogram that has exactly two lines of symmetry. Draw the lines of symmetry. Then give the most specific name for the parallelogram you drew.

   rhombus

7. Rosa is using the figure below to prove that the diagonals of a parallelogram bisect each other. She starts by stating that $\overline{LM} \cong \overline{PN}$ since opposite sides of a parallelogram are congruent. What should she do next in order to show that $\triangle LQM \cong \triangle NQP$? What congruence criterion will she use?

   $\angle MLQ \cong \angle PNQ$ and $\angle LMQ \cong \angle NPQ$

   by the Alternate Interior Angles

   Theorem. Then $\triangle LQM \cong \triangle NQP$ by

   the ASA Congruence Criterion.

8. Prove the following. You may not need all the rows of the table in your proof.

   Given: $ABCD$ is a rectangle. $\overline{AE} \cong \overline{FB}$
   Prove: $\triangle DAF \cong \triangle CBE$

Statements	Reasons
1. $\overline{AE} \cong \overline{FB}$	1. Given
2. $\overline{AF} \cong \overline{EB}$	2. Common Segments Theorem
3. $ABCD$ is a rectangle.	3. Given
4. $ABCD$ is a parallelogram.	4. Rectangle Theorem
5. $\overline{AD} \cong \overline{BC}$	5. Opposite sides of a parallelogram are congruent.
6. $\angle A$ and $\angle B$ are right angles.	6. Definition of rectangle
7. $\angle A \cong \angle B$	7. All right angles are congruent.
8. $\triangle DAF \cong \triangle CBE$	8. SAS Congruence Criterion

UNIT 5

Transformations and Similarity

Unit Vocabulary

center of dilation	(5-1)
dilation	(5-1)
scale factor	(5-1)
similar	(5-3)
similarity transformation	(5-3)

UNIT 5

Transformations and Similarity

Unit Focus

Informally speaking, two figures are similar if they have the same shape, but not necessarily the same size. In this unit, you will put this idea into mathematical terms. To do so, you will first study a new transformation, the dilation. Then you will see how to define similarity in terms of transformations. As you did with congruence, you will develop criteria that can be used to show that two triangles are similar. Then you will apply similarity to a wide range of real-world problems and mathematical theorems.

Unit at a Glance

COMMON CORE

Lesson		Standards for Mathematical Content
5-1	Properties of Dilations	CC.9-12.G.SRT.1, CC.9-12.G.CO.2
5-2	Drawing Dilations	CC.9-12.G.CO.2
5-3	Similarity	CC.9-12.G.SRT.2, CC.9-12.G.C.1
5-4	Similarity and Triangles	CC.9-12.G.SRT.2, CC.9-12.G.SRT.3
5-5	Solving Problems Using Similarity	CC.9-12.G.SRT.5, CC.9-12.G.MG.3*
5-6	The Triangle Proportionality Theorem	CC.9-12.G.SRT.4, CC.9-12.G.SRT.5
5-7	Proving the Pythagorean Theorem	CC.9-12.G.SRT.4, CC.9-12.G.SRT.5
	Test Prep	

UNIT 5

Unit 5 125 Transformations and Similarity

UNIT 5

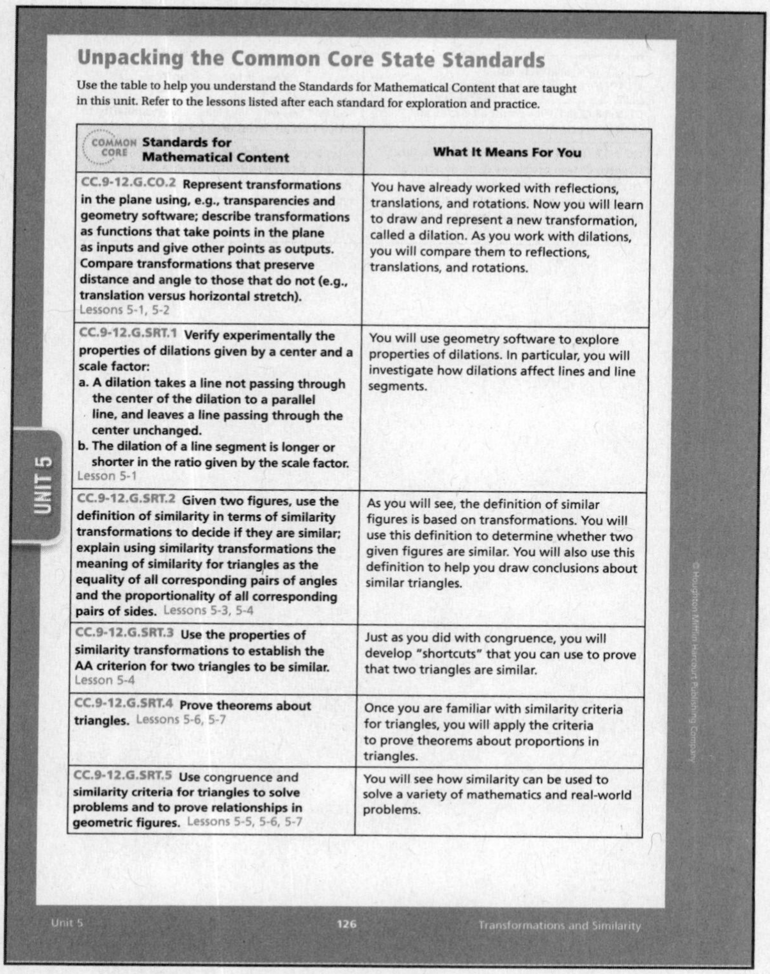

Unpacking the Common Core State Standards

Use the table to help you understand the Standards for Mathematical Content that are taught in this unit. Refer to the lessons listed after each standard for exploration and practice.

COMMON CORE Standards for Mathematical Content	What It Means For You
CC.9-12.G.CO.2 Represent transformations in the plane using, e.g., transparencies and geometry software; describe transformations as functions that take points in the plane as inputs and give other points as outputs. Compare transformations that preserve distance and angle to those that do not (e.g., translation versus horizontal stretch). Lessons 5-1, 5-2	You have already worked with reflections, translations, and rotations. Now you will learn to draw and represent a new transformation, called a dilation. As you work with dilations, you will compare them to reflections, translations, and rotations.
CC.9-12.G.SRT.1 Verify experimentally the properties of dilations given by a center and a scale factor: a. A dilation takes a line not passing through the center of the dilation to a parallel line, and leaves a line passing through the center unchanged. b. The dilation of a line segment is longer or shorter in the ratio given by the scale factor. Lesson 5-1	You will use geometry software to explore properties of dilations. In particular, you will investigate how dilations affect lines and line segments.
CC.9-12.G.SRT.2 Given two figures, use the definition of similarity in terms of similarity transformations to decide if they are similar; explain using similarity transformations the meaning of similarity for triangles as the equality of all corresponding pairs of angles and the proportionality of all corresponding pairs of sides. Lessons 5-3, 5-4	As you will see, the definition of similar figures is based on transformations. You will use this definition to determine whether two given figures are similar. You will also use this definition to help you draw conclusions about similar triangles.
CC.9-12.G.SRT.3 Use the properties of similarity transformations to establish the AA criterion for two triangles to be similar. Lesson 5-4	Just as you did with congruence, you will develop "shortcuts" that you can use to prove that two triangles are similar.
CC.9-12.G.SRT.4 Prove theorems about triangles. Lessons 5-6, 5-7	Once you are familiar with similarity criteria for triangles, you will apply the criteria to prove theorems about proportions in triangles.
CC.9-12.G.SRT.5 Use congruence and similarity criteria for triangles to solve problems and to prove relationships in geometric figures. Lessons 5-5, 5-6, 5-7	You will see how similarity can be used to solve a variety of mathematics and real-world problems.

UNIT 5

Unpacking the Common Core State Standards

This page lists and explains the Standards for Mathematical Content that are addressed in this unit. For information about the Standards for Mathematical Practice, which are integrated throughout the text, see Teacher Edition pages x–xiii.

UNIT 5

Notes

COMMON CORE Standards for Mathematical Content	What It Means For You
CC.9-12.G.C.1 Prove that all circles are similar. Lesson 5-3	You will use what you learn about similarity to prove that all circles are similar.
CC.9-12.G.MG.3 Apply geometric methods to solve design problems (e.g., designing an object or structure to satisfy physical constraints or minimize cost; **working with typographic grid systems based on ratios).*** Lesson 5-5	A typographic grid system is a tool that graphic designers use to prepare page layouts. You can apply similarity to help create a typographic grid system.

Notes

_____

_____

_____

_____

_____

_____

_____

_____

_____

_____

Notes

Properties of Dilations

Essential question: *What are the key properties of dilations?*

CC.9-12.G.CO.2 ... Compare transformations that preserve distance and angle to those that do not. (e.g., translation versus horizontal stretch).

CC.9-12.G.SRT.1 Verify experimentally the properties of dilations given by a center and a scale factor:

a. A dilation takes a line not passing through the center of the dilation to a parallel line, and leaves a line passing through the center unchanged.

b. The dilation of a line segment is longer or shorter in the ratio given by the scale factor.

Vocabulary

dilation

center of dilation

scale factor

Prerequisites

Transformations and Rigid Motions, Lesson 2-1

Math Background

Dilations are the last of the major transformations that students will study in this course. Unlike earlier transformations (reflections, translations, and rotations), dilations are not rigid motions. That is, they do not preserve *both* the shape and the size of a figure. However, dilations do preserve the shape of a figure. Thus, every dilation is either an enlargement or a reduction.

INTRODUCE

Begin by discussing how the terms *dilate* and *dilation* are used in everyday situations. The word *dilate* means "make larger or cause to expand." Students who have visited an optometrist may be familiar with eye drops that dilate, or widen, the pupil of an eye. Tell students they will now learn about a transformation called a dilation.

TEACH

1 EXPLORE

Materials: geometry software

Questioning Strategies

- Do dilations appear to preserve angle measure? Why or why not? Yes; $m\angle P' = m\angle P$, $m\angle Q' = m\angle Q$, and $m\angle R' = m\angle R$.

- Do dilations appear to preserve distance? Why or why not? No; $P'Q' \neq PQ$ (unless the scale factor is 1).

- What happens when you dilate with a scale factor of 1? The image and pre-image coincide (i.e., the figure is unchanged).

2 EXPLORE

Materials: geometry software

Questioning Strategies

- As you increase the scale factor of the dilation, what happens to the image of line *m*? The image moves farther from the center of dilation and from line *m*.

- As you decrease the scale factor of the dilation, what happens to the image of line *m*? The image moves closer to the center of dilation.

- Is it ever possible for the image of line *m* to coincide exactly with line *m*? Explain. Yes; when the scale factor is 1 or when line *m* passes through the center of dilation.

Technology

When students use geometry software to explore dilations, they should be careful that only one point (point *O*) is selected before they go to the Transform menu to mark the point as the center of dilation. Students should also make sure all of the triangle is selected (i.e., all three vertices and all three sides) before they apply the Dilate tool.

5-1

Properties of Dilations

Essential question: *What are the key properties of dilations?*

You have already worked extensively with three transformations: reflections, translations, and rotations. Now you will focus on a fourth type of transformation: dilations. Dilations are defined as follows.

COMMON
CORE

CC.9-12.G.SRT.1,
CC.9-12.G.CO.2

Let O be a point and let k be a positive real number. For any point P, let $D(P) = P'$, where P' is the point on $\overrightarrow{OP}$ such that $OP' = k \cdot OP$. Then D is the **dilation** with **center of dilation** O and **scale factor** k. If necessary, the center of dilation and scale factor can be included in the function notation by writing $D_{O,k}(P) = P'$.

The figure shows a dilation with scale factor 2 because $OP' = 2OP$ and $OQ' = 2OQ$.

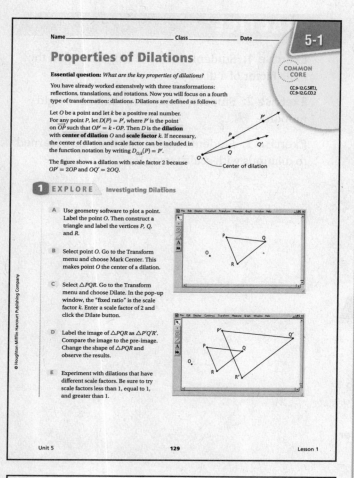

Center of dilation

1 EXPLORE   Investigating Dilations

A   Use geometry software to plot a point. Label the point O. Then construct a triangle and label the vertices P, Q, and R.

B   Select point O. Go to the Transform menu and choose Mark Center. This makes point O the center of a dilation.

C   Select $\triangle PQR$. Go to the Transform menu and choose Dilate. In the pop-up window, the "fixed ratio" is the scale factor k. Enter a scale factor of 2 and click the Dilate button.

D   Label the image of $\triangle PQR$ as $\triangle P'Q'R'$. Compare the image to the pre-image. Change the shape of $\triangle PQR$ and observe the results.

E   Experiment with dilations that have different scale factors. Be sure to try scale factors less than 1, equal to 1, and greater than 1.

© Houghton Mifflin Harcourt Publishing Company

REFLECT

1a. In general, how does a dilation transform a figure?

A dilation changes the size of a figure (unless the scale factor is 1) without changing its shape.

1b. Do you think dilations are rigid motions? Why or why not?

No; dilations change the size of a figure, so they are not rigid motions (unless the scale factor is 1).

1c. How does the value of k affect a dilation? What can you say about a dilation when $0 < k < 1$? when $k > 1$?

When $0 < k < 1$, the dilation reduces the figure. When $k > 1$, the dilation enlarges the figure.

2 EXPLORE   Investigating Properties of Dilations

A   Use geometry software to plot a point. Label the point O. Then construct a straight line and label it m.

B   Construct the image of line m under a dilation with center O and scale factor 2.

C   Try dilations with different scale factors and try dragging the line to new positions. Notice what happens when the line passes through O.

D   Delete the line and its image. Construct a segment, $\overline{AB}$.

E   Construct the image of $\overline{AB}$ under a dilation with center O and scale factor 2. Label the image $\overline{A'B'}$.

F   Measure the length of $\overline{AB}$ and $\overline{A'B'}$.

G   Try dilations with different scale factors. In each case, compare the lengths of $\overline{AB}$ and $\overline{A'B'}$.

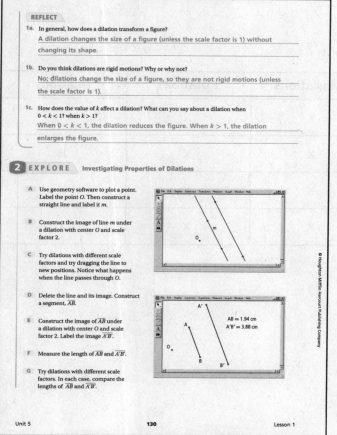

AB = 1.94 cm
A'B' = 3.88 cm

© Houghton Mifflin Harcourt Publishing Company

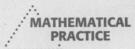

MATHEMATICAL PRACTICE   Highlighting the Standards

The Explores in this lesson offer opportunities for inductive reasoning, which is one aspect of Standard 3 (Construct viable arguments and critique the reasoning of others). For example, in Explore 1, students are asked to make a conjecture about the effect that the scale factor k has on a dilation. Students should base their conjectures upon their observations from working with geometry software. Encourage students to share their thinking with the class. Ask them to compare and, if necessary, refine their conjectures.

PRACTICE

Exercise 1: Students measure a figure to find the scale factor of a dilation.

Exercise 2: Students compare dilations to rigid motions.

Exercise 3: Students apply what they have learned to dilations with scale factor 1.

CLOSE

Essential Question
What are the key properties of dilations?
Dilations preserve angle measure, betweenness, and collinearity. A dilation maps a line not passing through the center of dilation to a parallel line and leaves a line passing through the center unchanged. The dilation of a line segment is longer or shorter in the ratio given by the scale factor.

Summarize
Have students make a graphic organizer or table to compare properties of reflections, translations, rotations, and dilations. A sample is shown below.

	Reflections	Translations	Rotations	Dilations
Preserves distance	X	X	X	
Preserves angle measure	X	X	X	X
Preserves betweenness	X	X	X	X
Preserves collinearity	X	X	X	X

REFLECT

2a. What can you say about the image of a straight line under a dilation? Does your answer depend upon the location of the line? Explain.

The image of a straight line *m* is a line parallel to line *m*. The only exception

is when line *m* passes through the center of dilation. In that case, the dilation

leaves the line unchanged.

2b. How is the length of a line segment related to the length of its image under a dilation with scale factor *k*?

The image of the line segment is longer or shorter in the ratio given by the scale

factor. That is, $A'B' = k \cdot AB$.

You may have discovered that dilations preserve the shape, but not the size, of figures. The following summary describes the key properties of dilations.

Properties of Dilations

- Dilations preserve angle measure.
- Dilations preserve betweenness.
- Dilations preserve collinearity.
- A dilation maps a line not passing through the center of dilation to a parallel line and leaves a line passing through the center unchanged.
- The dilation of a line segment is longer or shorter in the ratio given by the scale factor.

PRACTICE

1. The figure shows the image *A'* of point *A* under a dilation with center *O*. Explain how you can use a ruler to find the scale factor of the dilation. Then find the scale factor.

Measure *OA'* and *OA*. Find the ratio $\frac{OA'}{OA}$. In this case,

the scale factor is $\frac{1}{3}$.

2. Compare dilations to rigid motions. How are they similar? How are they different?

Dilations have the same properties as rigid motions, except for

preserving distance.

3. Describe the effect of a dilation with scale factor 1.

This dilation leaves every figure unchanged.

Drawing Dilations

Essential question: *How do you draw the image of a figure under a dilation?*

COMMON Standards for
CORE   Mathematical Content

CC.9-12.G.CO.2 Represent transformations in the plane using, e.g., transparencies and geometry software; describe transformations as functions that take points in the plane as inputs and give other points as outputs. ...

Prerequisites
Properties of Dilations, Lesson 5-1

Math Background
In this lesson, students extend their work with dilations by learning how to draw the dilation image of a given figure. Students use a compass and straightedge to draw dilations. Then, they perform dilations on a coordinate plane. Lesson 5-1 and this lesson serve as a foundation for upcoming lessons that will define similarity in terms of transformations.

INTRODUCE

Briefly remind students of the definition of *dilation*. Tell students they will be using a compass and straightedge to draw the dilation image of a figure. To that end, you may want to spend a few minutes reviewing the compass-and-straightedge construction for copying a line segment, as the steps for constructing a dilation image are based on that.

TEACH

1 EXAMPLE

Questioning Strategies
- How do you know $OA' = 3OA$? You add two copies of $\overline{OA}$ onto the end of $\overline{OA}$, so the total length is $3OA$.

- What would you do differently if the scale factor of the dilation were 4? I would add one more copy of $\overline{OA}$ onto the end of $\overline{OA}$ to locate A', and repeat for B' and C'.

EXTRA EXAMPLE
Construct the image of $\triangle DEF$ after a dilation with center of dilation O and scale factor 2.

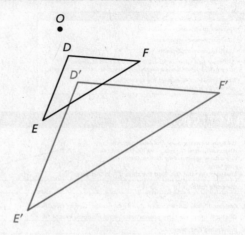

2 EXAMPLE

Questioning Strategies
- Do you expect the image of *ABCDE* to be an enlargement or a reduction of the pre-image? Why? Enlargement; the scale factor is greater than 1.

- In which quadrant or quadrants will the image lie? Explain. The pre-image lies in all four quadrants, so the image will also lie in all four quadrants.

EXTRA EXAMPLE
Draw the image of the pentagon after a dilation with scale factor $\frac{1}{2}$.

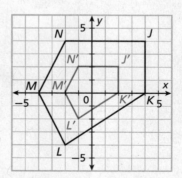

Drawing Dilations

5-2

COMMON CORE

CC.9-12.G.CO.2

Essential question: *How do you draw the image of a figure under a dilation?*

You have already used geometry software to draw the image of a figure under a dilation. The following example shows how to construct the image using a compass and straightedge.

1 EXAMPLE Constructing a Dilation Image

Work directly on the figure below and follow the given steps to construct the image of △ABC after a dilation with center of dilation O and scale factor 3.

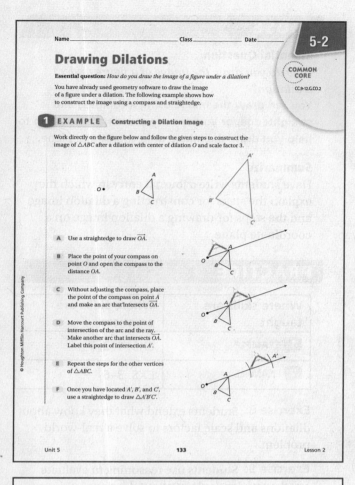

A Use a straightedge to draw $\overrightarrow{OA}$.

B Place the point of your compass on point O and open the compass to the distance OA.

C Without adjusting the compass, place the point of the compass on point A and make an arc that intersects $\overrightarrow{OA}$.

D Move the compass to the point of intersection of the arc and the ray. Make another arc that intersects $\overrightarrow{OA}$. Label this point of intersection A'.

E Repeat the steps for the other vertices of △ABC.

F Once you have located A', B', and C', use a straightedge to draw △A'B'C'.

REFLECT

1a. Explain how you can you use a ruler to check your construction.

Measure the sides of the triangle and its image to check that OA' = 3OA,

OB' = 3OB, and OC' = 3OC.

1b. Without using a protractor, how does m∠OAB compare to m∠OA'B'? Why?

m∠OAB = m∠OA'B' since $\overline{AB} \parallel \overline{A'B'}$ and these are corresponding angles.

1c. How can you change the construction to draw the image of △ABC after a dilation with center of dilation O and scale factor $\frac{1}{2}$?

Construct the bisectors of $\overline{OA}$, $\overline{OB}$, and $\overline{OC}$ to find the midpoints of these

segments. Use the straightedge to connect the midpoints to form △A'B'C'.

When you work with dilations in the coordinate plane, you can assume the center of dilation is the origin. To find the image of a point after a dilation with scale factor k, multiply each coordinate of the point by k. Using coordinate notation, a dilation with scale factor k is written as follows: $(x, y) \rightarrow (kx, ky)$.

2 EXAMPLE Drawing a Dilation in a Coordinate Plane

Draw the image of the pentagon after a dilation with scale factor $\frac{3}{2}$.

A In the table below, list the vertices of the pentagon. Then use the rule for the dilation to write the vertices of the image.

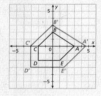

Pre-Image (x, y)	Image $\left(\frac{3}{2}x, \frac{3}{2}y\right)$
A(3, 0)	A'(4$\frac{1}{2}$, 0)
B(0, 2)	B'(0, 3)
C(−2, 0)	C'(−3, 0)
D(−2, −2)	D'(−3, −3)
E(1, −2)	E'(1$\frac{1}{2}$, −3)

B Plot the vertices of the image. Connect the vertices to complete the image.

Differentiated Instruction

Students may wonder how to construct the dilation image of a figure when the scale factor is not a whole number. While it is not possible to use a compass and straightedge to construct the image for every scale factor, certain scale factors are possible using a combination of the construction for copying a segment, the construction of a segment bisector, and the construction for dividing a segment into a given ratio. You may want to challenge students to use some combination of these constructions to draw the image of $\triangle ABC$ after a dilation with center of dilation O and scale factor $1\frac{3}{4}$.

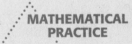
MATHEMATICAL PRACTICE | **Highlighting the Standards**

Exercise 9 addresses Standard 3 (Construct viable arguments and critique the reasoning of others). The exercise presents a claim about dilations. Students must evaluate the claim to decide whether or not it is correct. In this case, the claim is likely to sound plausible to students, so they will need to think deeply about the situation to recognize that the claim is incorrect. Remind students that they should explain the flaw in the given statement and give a corrected version of the statement.

Essential Question

How do you draw the image of a figure under a dilation?

You can draw the image using a compass and straightedge, or you can use coordinate notation to help you draw the image on a coordinate plane.

Summarize

Have students write a journal entry in which they explain the steps for constructing a dilation image and the steps for drawing a dilation image on a coordinate plane.

PRACTICE

Where skills are taught	Where skills are practiced
1 EXAMPLE	EXS. 1–2, 7
2 EXAMPLE	EXS. 3–6

Exercise 8: Students extend what they know about dilations and scale factors to solve a real-world problem.

Exercise 9: Students use reasoning to evaluate another student's claim about dilations.

REFLECT

2a. Explain how to use the distance formula to check that $\overline{B'C'}$ is the correct length.

By the distance formula, $BC = \sqrt{(0-(-2))^2 + (2-0)^2} = \sqrt{8} = 2\sqrt{2}$ and

$B'C' = \sqrt{(0-(-3))^2 + (3-0)^2} = \sqrt{18} = 3\sqrt{2}$. So $B'C' = \frac{3}{2} BC$, which is correct.

2b. A student claims that under a dilation centered at the origin with scale factor k, a point and its image always lie in the same quadrant. Do you agree or disagree? Explain.

Agree; for example, if the point lies in Quadrant II, then its x-coordinate is negative

and its y-coordinate is positive. Multiplying both coordinates by k does not change

their signs, so the image also lies in Quadrant II.

PRACTICE

Use a compass and straightedge to construct the image of the figure after a dilation with center O and the given scale factor. Label the vertices of the image.

1. scale factor: 4

2. scale factor: $\frac{1}{2}$

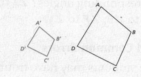

Draw the image of the figure after a dilation with the given scale factor.

3. scale factor: 2

4. scale factor: $\frac{1}{4}$

5. scale factor: $\frac{2}{3}$

6. scale factor: 3

7. $\triangle A'B'C'$ is the image of $\triangle ABC$ under a dilation. Explain how you can use a straightedge to find the center of dilation. Then use your method to draw a dot at the center of dilation.

Draw $\overleftrightarrow{AA'}$ and $\overleftrightarrow{BB'}$. The point where the lines

intersect is the center of dilation.

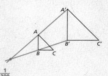

8. Each centimeter on a scale drawing of a park represents three meters of actual distance. What is the scale factor of the dilation that maps the park to the scale drawing? $\frac{1}{300}$

9. Error Analysis A student claims that a dilation with scale factor m and center of dilation O that is followed by a dilation with scale factor n and center of dilation O is equivalent to a single dilation with scale factor $m + n$ and center of dilation O. Do you agree or disagree? Explain.

Disagree; the first dilation multiplies lengths by m and the second dilation

multiplies lengths by n, so the overall effect is to multiply lengths by mn,

rather than $m + n$. The equivalent dilation has scale factor mn.

Notes

5-3 Similarity

Essential question: *What does it mean for two figures to be similar?*

COMMON CORE Standards for Mathematical Content

CC.9-12.G.SRT.2 Given two figures, use the definition of similarity in terms of similarity transformations to decide if they are similar; ...
CC.9-12.G.C.1 Prove that all circles are similar.

Vocabulary
similarity transformation
similar

Prerequisites
Transformations and Rigid Motions, Lesson 2-1
Properties of Dilations, Lesson 5-1
Drawing Dilations, Lesson 5-2

Math Background
Just as congruence was defined in terms of rigid motions in Unit 3, so will similarity now be defined in terms of similarity transformations. Similarity transformations preserve the shape of a figure. In Lesson 5-4, it will be shown that the familiar AA Similarity Criterion follows from this definition of similarity.

INTRODUCE

Begin by telling the class that two figures are similar if they have the same shape but not necessarily the same size. You may wish to have students give examples of similar figures. Possibilities include a photograph and its enlargement or a garden plot and its reduction on a scale drawing. Tell students that the formal mathematical definition of similarity, like the definition of congruence, is based on transformations.

TEACH

1 ENGAGE

Questioning Strategies
- If two figures are congruent are they also similar? Why or why not? **Yes; if figures are congruent, then there is a sequence of rigid motions that maps one to the other, but rigid motions are also similarity transformations, so the figures must also be similar.**

- In the statement $\triangle JTF \sim \triangle PBW$, what are the corresponding angles? **$\angle J$ corresponds to $\angle P$; $\angle T$ to $\angle B$; $\angle F$ to $\angle W$.**

Avoid Common Errors
Some students may have trouble determining scale factors. In particular, they may have difficulty distinguishing a dilation with a scale factor of k from a dilation with a scale factor of $\frac{1}{k}$. Remind students that they should always compare the image to the pre-image. For instance, in the figure on the student page, $\overline{A'B'}$ is twice as long as $\overline{AB}$. Therefore, $\frac{A'B'}{AB} = 2$, and the scale factor of the dilation is 2. Also, remind students that if the image is an enlargement of the pre-image, then the scale factor must be greater than 1.

2 EXAMPLE

Questioning Strategies
- How can you tell which pairs of figures are likely to be similar? **Figures that appear to have the same shape are likely to be similar.**

Name_____ Class_____ Date_____

Similarity

Essential question: *What does it mean for two figures to be similar?*

COMMON
CORE

CC.9-12.G.SRT.2,
CC.9-12.G.C.1

1 ENGAGE   Introducing Similarity

A **similarity transformation** is a transformation in which the image has the same shape as the pre-image. Specifically, the similarity transformations are the rigid motions (reflections, translations, and rotations) as well as dilations.

Two plane figures are **similar** if and only if one can be obtained from the other by similarity transformations (that is, by a sequence of reflections, translations, rotations, and/or dilations).

The symbol for similar is ~. As with congruence, it is customary to write a similarity statement so that corresponding vertices of the figures are listed in the same order. In the figure below, $\triangle A'B'C'$ is the image of $\triangle ABC$ after a dilation with center O and scale factor 2. Since a dilation is a similarity transformation, the two triangles are similar and you write $\triangle ABC \sim \triangle A'B'C'$.

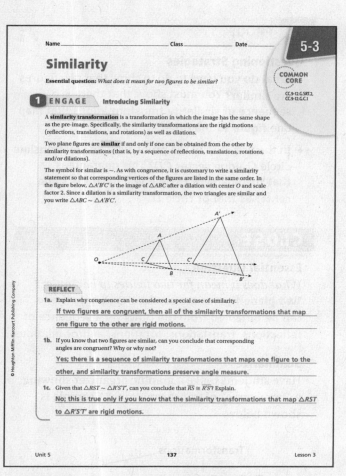

REFLECT

1a. Explain why congruence can be considered a special case of similarity.

If two figures are congruent, then all of the similarity transformations that map
one figure to the other are rigid motions.

1b. If you know that two figures are similar, can you conclude that corresponding angles are congruent? Why or why not?

Yes; there is a sequence of similarity transformations that maps one figure to the
other, and similarity transformations preserve angle measure.

1c. Given that $\triangle RST \sim \triangle R'S'T'$, can you conclude that $\overline{RS} \cong \overline{R'S'}$? Explain.

No; this is true only if you know that the similarity transformations that map $\triangle RST$
to $\triangle R'S'T'$ are rigid motions.

© Houghton Mifflin Harcourt Publishing Company

2 EXAMPLE   Determining If Figures Are Similar

Use the definition of similarity in terms of similarity transformations to determine whether the two figures are similar. Explain your answer.

A $\triangle JKL$ and $\triangle MNP$ have different angle measures.

Since similarity transformations preserve angle measure, there is no sequence of similarity transformations that will map $\triangle JKL$ to $\triangle MNP$.

Therefore, the figures are not similar

B You can map $\triangle RST$ to $\triangle XYZ$ by the dilation that has the coordinate notation

$(x, y) \rightarrow (3x, 3y)$

A dilation is a similarity transformation.

Therefore, the figures are similar

C You can map $ABCD$ to $EFGH$ by the dilation that has the coordinate notation

$(x, y) \rightarrow (2x, 2y)$

followed by the reflection that has the coordinate notation

$(x, y) \rightarrow (x, -y)$

Dilations and reflections are similarity transformations.

Therefore, the figures are similar

REFLECT

2a. In Part B above, how can you show that the triangles are similar using a different similarity transformation?

Map $\triangle XYZ$ to $\triangle RST$ using the dilation $(x, y) \rightarrow \left(\frac{1}{3}x, \frac{1}{3}y\right)$.

2b. In Part C above, does the order in which you perform the similarity transformations matter? Explain.

No; you can do the dilation followed by the reflection or vice versa. In either case,
the similarity transformations map $ABCD$ to $EFGH$.

© Houghton Mifflin Harcourt Publishing Company

Use the definition of similarity in terms of similarity transformations to determine whether the two figures are similar. Explain your answer.

A.

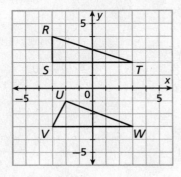

Not similar; there is no sequence of similarity transformations that maps △RST to △UVW.

B.

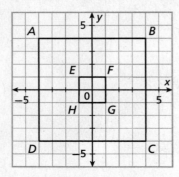

Similar; the dilation $(x, y) \longrightarrow \left(\frac{1}{4}x, \frac{1}{4}y\right)$ maps *ABCD* to *EFGH*.

C.

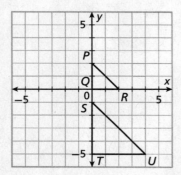

Similar; the dilation $(x, y) \longrightarrow (2x, 2y)$ followed by the translation $(x, y) \longrightarrow (x, y - 5)$ maps △PQR to △STU.

3 PROOF

Questioning Strategies

- What do you have to do to show that two figures are similar? You must show that there is a sequence of similarity transformations that map one figure to the other.

- In the first step of the proof, why do you translate circle *C* along vector $\overrightarrow{CD}$? This guarantees that the image of circle *C* will have the same center as that of circle *D*.

CLOSE

Essential Question

What does it mean for two figures to be similar? Two plane figures are similar if and only if one can be obtained from the other by a sequence of reflections, translations, rotations, and/or dilations.

Summarize

Have students make a graphic organizer showing a "family tree" of transformations. A sample is shown below.

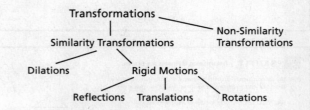

PRACTICE

Where skills are taught	Where skills are practiced
2 EXAMPLE	EXS. 1–6

Exercise 7: Students use reasoning skills to analyze a similarity statement.

You can use the definition of similarity to prove theorems about figures.

> **Theorem**
> All circles are similar.

3 PROOF   All Circles Are Similar

Complete the proof.

Given: Circle C with center C and radius r;
circle D with center D and radius s.

Prove: Circle C is similar to circle D.

To prove similarity, show that there is a sequence of similarity transformations that maps circle C to circle D.

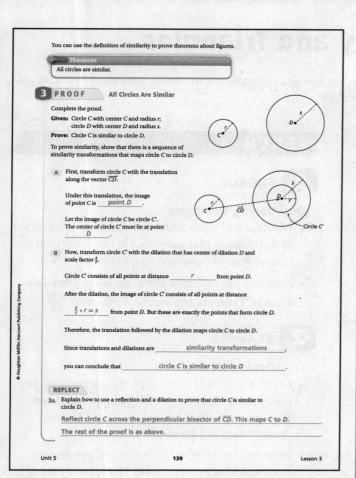

A First, transform circle C with the translation along the vector $\overrightarrow{CD}$.

Under this translation, the image of point C is ___point D___

Let the image of circle C be circle C'. The center of circle C' must lie at point ___D___.

B Now, transform circle C' with the dilation that has center of dilation D and scale factor $\frac{s}{r}$.

Circle C' consists of all points at distance ___r___ from point D.

After the dilation, the image of circle C' consists of all points at distance

$\frac{s}{r} \cdot r = s$ from point D. But these are exactly the points that form circle D.

Therefore, the translation followed by the dilation maps circle C to circle D.

Since translations and dilations are ___similarity transformations___,

you can conclude that ___circle C is similar to circle D___.

REFLECT

3a. Explain how to use a reflection and a dilation to prove that circle C is similar to circle D.

___Reflect circle C across the perpendicular bisector of $\overline{CD}$. This maps C to D.___
___The rest of the proof is as above.___

© Houghton Mifflin Harcourt Publishing Company

PRACTICE

Use the definition of similarity in terms of similarity transformations to determine whether the two figures are similar. Explain your answer.

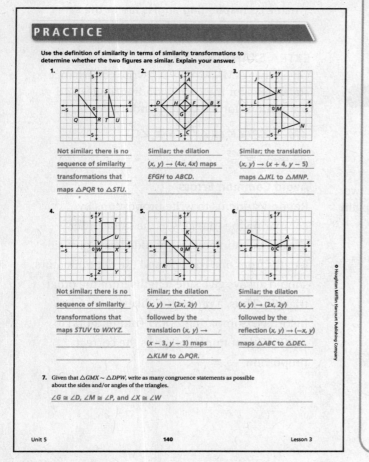

1. Not similar; there is no sequence of similarity transformations that maps △PQR to △STU.

2. Similar; the dilation $(x, y) \rightarrow (4x, 4x)$ maps EFGH to ABCD.

3. Similar; the translation $(x, y) \rightarrow (x + 4, y - 5)$ maps △JKL to △MNP.

4. Not similar; there is no sequence of similarity transformations that maps STUV to WXYZ.

5. Similar; the dilation $(x, y) \rightarrow (2x, 2y)$ followed by the translation $(x, y) \rightarrow (x - 3, y - 3)$ maps △KLM to △PQR.

6. Similar; the dilation $(x, y) \rightarrow (2x, 2y)$ followed by the reflection $(x, y) \rightarrow (-x, y)$ maps △ABC to △DEC.

7. Given that △GMX ~ △DPW, write as many congruence statements as possible about the sides and/or angles of the triangles.

$\angle G \cong \angle D$, $\angle M \cong \angle P$, and $\angle X \cong \angle W$

© Houghton Mifflin Harcourt Publishing Company

Similarity and Triangles

Essential question: *What can you conclude about similar triangles? How can you prove triangles are similar?*

COMMON **Standards for**
CORE **Mathematical Content**

CC.9-12.G.SRT.2 ... explain using similarity transformations the meaning of similarity for triangles as the equality of all corresponding pairs of angles and the proportionality of all corresponding pairs of sides.

CC.9-12.G.SRT.3 Use the properties of similarity transformations to establish the AA criterion for two triangles to be similar.

Prerequisites
Similarity, Lesson 5-3

Math Background
In this lesson, students study similar triangles. First, they learn that when two triangles are similar, the corresponding angles are congruent and the corresponding sides are proportional. This is the equivalent of the CPCTC theorem, but with the necessary changes for similarity rather than congruence. Then, students prove that the AA Similarity Criterion follows from the transformation-based definition of similarity.

INTRODUCE

Remind students that when they studied congruence, they first learned the definition of congruence in terms of rigid motions and then applied congruence to triangles. Specifically, students learned some shortcuts for proving that two triangles are congruent (SSS, SAS, ASA, AAS). Explain that in the same way, students will now consider what it means for two triangles to be similar. Tell students they will learn about some shortcuts for proving that two triangles are similar.

TEACH

1 ENGAGE

Questioning Strategies
- What do you think is the approximate scale factor of the dilation that maps $\triangle ABC$ to $\triangle A'B'C'$ in the figure? **Possible answer: approximately 1.5**
- How did you estimate the scale factor? **Possible answer: Estimate the value of the ratio $\frac{A'B'}{AB}$.**

2 EXAMPLE

Questioning Strategies
- Given a similarity statement about triangles, how many pairs of corresponding angles are there? How many pairs of corresponding sides are there? **There are three pairs of each.**
- How do you determine corresponding angles from a similarity statement? **The letters that name corresponding angles are in the same position in each triangle name.**

EXTRA EXAMPLE
Given that $\triangle MKS \sim \triangle PYC$, write congruence statements for the corresponding angles and proportions for the corresponding sides.

$\angle M \cong \angle P, \angle K \cong \angle Y, \angle S \cong \angle C,$

$\frac{MK}{PY} = \frac{KS}{YC} = \frac{MS}{PC}$

Avoid Common Errors
Remind students to write proportions by comparing the triangles in the same order. That is, the numerators should always give side lengths from one triangle and the denominators should always give side lengths from the other triangle. Thus, a proportion like $\frac{RS}{UV} = \frac{VW}{ST}$ is incorrect. Comparing $\triangle RST$ (numerators) to $\triangle UVW$ (denominators) gives the correct proportion, $\frac{RS}{UV} = \frac{ST}{VW}$.

Similarity and Triangles

Essential question: *What can you conclude about similar triangles and how can you prove triangles are similar?*

Name_____ Class_____ Date_____

1 ENGAGE Applying Similarity to Triangles

Recall that when two figures are similar, there is a sequence of similarity transformations that maps one figure to the other. In particular, given $\triangle ABC \sim \triangle DEF$, you can first apply a dilation to $\triangle ABC$ to make both triangles the same size. Then you can apply a sequence of rigid motions to the dilated image of $\triangle ABC$ to map it to $\triangle DEF$.

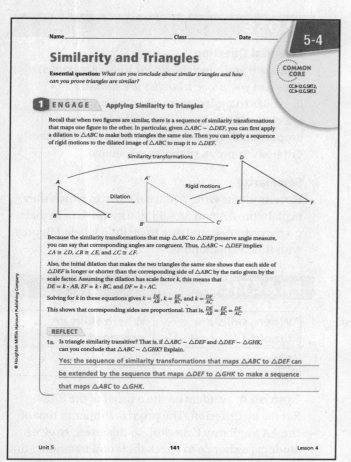

Because the similarity transformations that map $\triangle ABC$ to $\triangle DEF$ preserve angle measure, you can say that corresponding angles are congruent. Thus, $\triangle ABC \sim \triangle DEF$ implies $\angle A \cong \angle D$, $\angle B \cong \angle E$, and $\angle C \cong \angle F$.

Also, the initial dilation that makes the two triangles the same size shows that each side of $\triangle DEF$ is longer or shorter than the corresponding side of $\triangle ABC$ by the ratio given by the scale factor. Assuming the dilation has scale factor k, this means that $DE = k \cdot AB$, $EF = k \cdot BC$, and $DF = k \cdot AC$.

Solving for k in these equations gives $k = \frac{DE}{AB}$, $k = \frac{EF}{BC}$, and $k = \frac{DF}{AC}$.

This shows that corresponding sides are proportional. That is, $\frac{DE}{AB} = \frac{EF}{BC} = \frac{DF}{AC}$.

REFLECT

1a. Is triangle similarity transitive? That is, if $\triangle ABC \sim \triangle DEF$ and $\triangle DEF \sim \triangle GHK$, can you conclude that $\triangle ABC \sim \triangle GHK$? Explain.

Yes; the sequence of similarity transformations that maps $\triangle ABC$ to $\triangle DEF$ can

be extended by the sequence that maps $\triangle DEF$ to $\triangle GHK$ to make a sequence

that maps $\triangle ABC$ to $\triangle GHK$.

---

2 EXAMPLE Identifying Congruent Angles and Proportional Sides

Given that $\triangle RST \sim \triangle UVW$, write congruence statements for the corresponding angles and proportions for the corresponding sides.

A Corresponding angles are listed in the same position in each triangle name.

$\angle R \cong \angle U$, $\angle S \cong \angle V$, $\angle T \cong \angle W$

B Corresponding sides are named by pairs of letters in the same position in each triangle name.

$\frac{UV}{RS} = \frac{VW}{ST} = \frac{UW}{RT}$

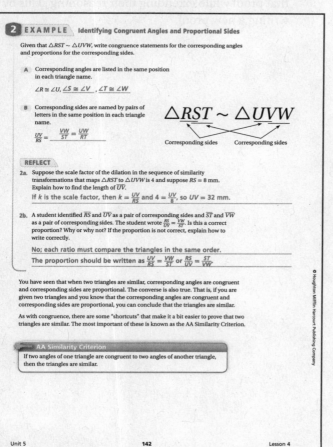

$$\triangle RST \sim \triangle UVW$$

Corresponding sides   Corresponding sides

REFLECT

2a. Suppose the scale factor of the dilation in the sequence of similarity transformations that maps $\triangle RST$ to $\triangle UVW$ is 4 and suppose $RS = 8$ mm. Explain how to find the length of $\overline{UV}$.

If k is the scale factor, then $k = \frac{UV}{RS}$ and $4 = \frac{UV}{8}$, so $UV = 32$ mm.

2b. A student identified $\overline{RS}$ and $\overline{UV}$ as a pair of corresponding sides and $\overline{ST}$ and $\overline{VW}$ as a pair of corresponding sides. The student wrote $\frac{RS}{UV} = \frac{VW}{ST}$. Is this a correct proportion? Why or why not? If the proportion is not correct, explain how to write correctly.

No; each ratio must compare the triangles in the same order.

The proportion should be written as $\frac{UV}{RS} = \frac{VW}{ST}$ or $\frac{RS}{UV} = \frac{ST}{VW}$.

You have seen that when two triangles are similar, corresponding angles are congruent and corresponding sides are proportional. The converse is also true. That is, if you are given two triangles and you know that the corresponding angles are congruent and corresponding sides are proportional, you can conclude that the triangles are similar.

As with congruence, there are some "shortcuts" that make it a bit easier to prove that two triangles are similar. The most important of these is known as the AA Similarity Criterion.

AA Similarity Criterion

If two angles of one triangle are congruent to two angles of another triangle, then the triangles are similar.

Questioning Strategies

- How do you use the AA Similarity Criterion to show two triangles are similar? **Show that two angles of one triangle are congruent to two angles of the other triangle. This lets you conclude that the two triangles are similar.**

- How is this proof similar to those of the SSS, SAS, and ASA Congruence Criteria? **You show that there is an appropriate sequence of transformations that maps one triangle to the other.**

Teaching Strategies

Students will have practice using the AA Similarity Criterion in Lesson 5-5. However, you may want to give students a quick example of how the criterion can be used. Draw the following figure on the board. Ask students whether the triangles are similar and why or why not. If necessary, help students understand that by the Triangle Sum Theorem, $m\angle C = 37°$ so the triangles are similar by the AA Similarity Criterion.

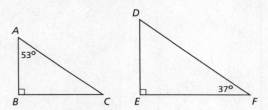

Exercise 4 requires students to write a complete proof. This is an opportunity to address Standard 6 (Attend to precision). In particular, every proof depends upon careful attention to mathematical definitions. Ask students to point out the definitions that are used in the proof. Have them explain how the definitions serve as elements of the overall deductive argument.

CLOSE

Essential Question

What can you conclude about similar triangles? How can you prove triangles are similar?
In similar triangles, corresponding angles are congruent, and corresponding sides are proportional. You can use the AA or SAS Similarity Criterion to prove triangles are similar.

Summarize

Have students write a journal entry in which they explain the AA and SAS Similarity Criteria in their own words. Ask students to include labeled figures with their explanations.

PRACTICE

Where skills are taught	Where skills are practiced
2 EXAMPLE	EXS. 1–3

Exercise 4: Students write a proof of the SAS Similarity Criterion. The proof is similar to that of the AA Similarity Criterion, so this exercise gives students a chance to check their understanding of that proof while extending their reasoning skills by writing a new proof.

3 PROOF   AA Similarity Criterion

Given: $\angle A \cong \angle X$ and $\angle B \cong \angle Y$
Prove: $\triangle ABC \sim \triangle XYZ$

To prove the triangles are similar, you will find a sequence of similarity transformations that maps $\triangle ABC$ to $\triangle XYZ$. Complete the following steps of the proof.

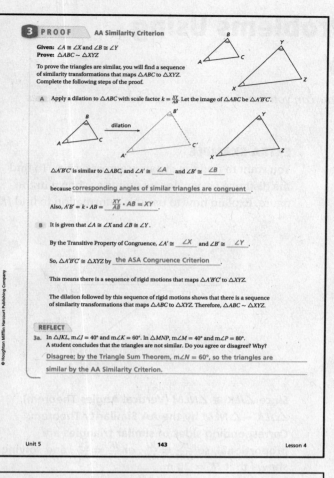

A   Apply a dilation to $\triangle ABC$ with scale factor $k = \frac{XY}{AB}$. Let the image of $\triangle ABC$ be $\triangle A'B'C'$.

$\triangle A'B'C'$ is similar to $\triangle ABC$, and $\angle A' \cong$ ___$\angle A$___ and $\angle B' \cong$ ___$\angle B$___

because ___corresponding angles of similar triangles are congruent___.

Also, $A'B' = k \cdot AB =$ ___$\frac{XY}{AB} \cdot AB = XY$___.

B   It is given that $\angle A \cong \angle X$ and $\angle B \cong \angle Y$.

By the Transitive Property of Congruence, $\angle A' \cong$ ___$\angle X$___ and $\angle B' \cong$ ___$\angle Y$___.

So, $\triangle A'B'C' \cong \triangle XYZ$ by ___the ASA Congruence Criterion___.

This means there is a sequence of rigid motions that maps $\triangle A'B'C'$ to $\triangle XYZ$.

The dilation followed by this sequence of rigid motions shows that there is a sequence of similarity transformations that maps $\triangle ABC$ to $\triangle XYZ$. Therefore, $\triangle ABC \sim \triangle XYZ$.

REFLECT

3a. In $\triangle JKL$, $m\angle J = 40°$ and $m\angle K = 60°$. In $\triangle MNP$, $m\angle M = 40°$ and $m\angle P = 80°$. A student concludes that the triangles are not similar. Do you agree or disagree? Why?

___Disagree; by the Triangle Sum Theorem, $m\angle N = 60°$, so the triangles are___
___similar by the AA Similarity Criterion.___

Unit 5   143   Lesson 4

There is another criterion that can be used to show that two triangles are similar. You will prove this criterion as an exercise.

SAS Similarity Criterion

If two sides of one triangle are proportional to two sides of another triangle and their included angles are congruent, then the triangles are similar.

PRACTICE

For each similarity statement, write congruence statements for the corresponding angles and proportions for the corresponding sides.

1. $\triangle GHJ \sim \triangle PQR$

$\angle G \cong \angle P$, $\angle H \cong \angle Q$,

$\angle J \cong \angle R$,

$\frac{PQ}{GH} = \frac{QR}{HJ} = \frac{PR}{GJ}$

2. $\triangle TWR \sim \triangle YSP$

$\angle T \cong \angle Y$, $\angle W \cong \angle S$,

$\angle R \cong \angle P$,

$\frac{YS}{TW} = \frac{SP}{WR} = \frac{YP}{TR}$

3. $\triangle PJL \sim \triangle WDM$

$\angle P \cong \angle W$, $\angle J \cong \angle D$,

$\angle L \cong \angle M$,

$\frac{WD}{PJ} = \frac{DM}{JL} = \frac{WM}{PL}$

4. Prove the SAS Similarity Criterion.

Given: $\frac{XY}{AB} = \frac{XZ}{AC}$ and $\angle A \cong \angle X$
Prove: $\triangle ABC \sim \triangle XYZ$
(*Hint:* The main steps of the proof are similar to those of the proof of the AA Similarity Criterion.)

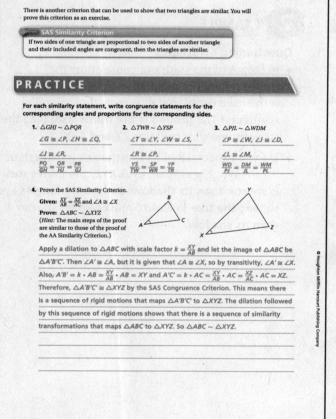

Apply a dilation to $\triangle ABC$ with scale factor $k = \frac{XY}{AB}$ and let the image of $\triangle ABC$ be

$\triangle A'B'C'$. Then $\angle A' \cong \angle A$, but it is given that $\angle A \cong \angle X$, so by transitivity, $\angle A' \cong \angle X$.

Also, $A'B' = k \cdot AB = \frac{XY}{AB} \cdot AB = XY$ and $A'C' = k \cdot AC = \frac{XY}{AB} \cdot AC = \frac{XZ}{AC} \cdot AC = XZ$.

Therefore, $\triangle A'B'C' \cong \triangle XYZ$ by the SAS Congruence Criterion. This means there

is a sequence of rigid motions that maps $\triangle A'B'C'$ to $\triangle XYZ$. The dilation followed

by this sequence of rigid motions shows that there is a sequence of similarity

transformations that maps $\triangle ABC$ to $\triangle XYZ$. So $\triangle ABC \sim \triangle XYZ$.

Unit 5   144   Lesson 4

Solving Problems Using Similarity

Essential question: *How can you use similar triangles and similar rectangles to solve problems?*

COMMON **Standards for**
CORE **Mathematical Content**

CC.9-12.G.SRT.5 Use ... similarity criteria for triangles to solve problems and to prove relationships in geometric figures.

CC.9-12.G.MG.3 Apply geometric methods to solve design problems (e.g., ... working with typographic grid systems based on ratios).*

Prerequisites

Similarity and Triangles, Lesson 5-4

Math Background

In this lesson, students use similarity to solve a variety of real-world problems. The general process is the same for every problem: First, show that two figures are similar; then, use the fact that corresponding sides are proportional to find an unknown side length.

INTRODUCE

Remind students that they have already used congruence to solve real-world problems. For example, to find the distance across a pond, students showed that two triangles were congruent and then used CPCTC to find an unknown side length that corresponded to the distance across the pond. Tell students that this lesson presents similar problems (i.e., problems in which unknown lengths must be determined), but in this case students will use similarity and the proportionality of corresponding sides to find the unknown length.

TEACH

1 EXAMPLE

Questioning Strategies

• Do you expect *XY* to be less than or greater than 327 feet? Why? **Less than; the side lengths of △XYZ are all less than the corresponding side lengths in △VWZ.**

EXTRA EXAMPLE

You want to find the distance across a river. To find the distance *JK*, you locate points as shown in the figure. Explain how to use this information to find *JK*.

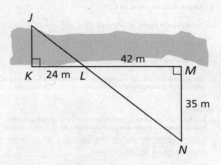

Since $\angle JLK \cong \angle NLM$ (Vertical Angles Theorem), $\triangle JLK \sim \triangle NLM$ by the AA Similarity Theorem. Corresponding sides of similar triangles are proportional, so $\frac{JK}{NM} = \frac{KL}{ML}$, or $\frac{JK}{35} = \frac{24}{42}$, and solving shows that $JK = 20$ m.

2 EXAMPLE

Questioning Strategies

• In Step A of the solution, you assume the sun's rays are parallel so that $\overline{ZX} \parallel \overline{CA}$. What is the transversal that intersects these parallel segments? **The ground is the transversal (i.e., the straight line that contains $\overline{ZY}$ and $\overline{CB}$).**

• Do you expect *AB* to be less than or greater than 7.2 m? Why? **Less than; in △XYZ, the meter stick is shorter than its shadow. Since the triangles are similar, the tree in △ABC must also be shorter than its shadow.**

Name_____ Class_____ Date_____

5-5

Solving Problems Using Similarity

COMMON CORE

CC.9-12.G.SRT.5, CC.9-12.G.MG.3*

Essential question: *How can you use similar triangles and similar rectangles to solve problems?*

When you know that two polygons are similar, you can often use the proportionality of corresponding sides to find unknown side lengths.

1 EXAMPLE   Finding an Unknown Distance

You want to find the distance across a canyon. In order to find the distance *XY*, you locate points as described below. Explain how to use this information and the figure to find *XY*.

1. Identify a landmark, such as a tree, at *X*. Place a marker (*Y*) directly across the canyon from *X*.

2. At *Y*, turn 90° away from *X* and walk 400 feet in a straight line. Place a marker (*Z*) at this location.

3. Continue walking another 600 feet. Place a marker (*W*) at this location.

4. Turn 90° away from the canyon and walk until the marker *Z* aligns with *X*. Place a marker (*V*) at this location. Measure $\overline{WV}$.

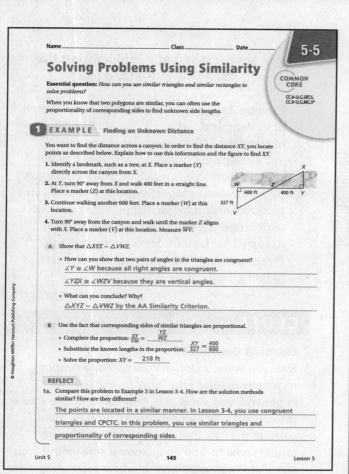

A   Show that $\triangle XYZ \sim \triangle VWZ$.

• How can you show that two pairs of angles in the triangles are congruent?

$\angle Y \cong \angle W$ because all right angles are congruent.

$\angle YZX \cong \angle WZV$ because they are vertical angles.

• What can you conclude? Why?

$\triangle XYZ \sim \triangle VWZ$ by the AA Similarity Criterion.

B   Use the fact that corresponding sides of similar triangles are proportional.

• Complete the proportion: $\frac{XY}{VW} = \frac{YZ}{WZ}$

• Substitute the known lengths in the proportion: $\frac{XY}{327} = \frac{400}{600}$

• Solve the proportion: $XY = $ 218 ft

REFLECT

1a.   Compare this problem to Example 3 in Lesson 3-4. How are the solution methods similar? How are they different?

The points are located in a similar manner. In Lesson 3-4, you use congruent

triangles and CPCTC. In this problem, you use similar triangles and

proportionality of corresponding sides.

© Houghton Mifflin Harcourt Publishing Company

2 EXAMPLE   Finding an Unknown Height

In order to find the height of a palm tree, you measure the tree's shadow and, at the same time of day, you measure the shadow cast by a meter stick that you hold at a right angle to the ground. The measurements are shown in the figure. Find the height of the tree.

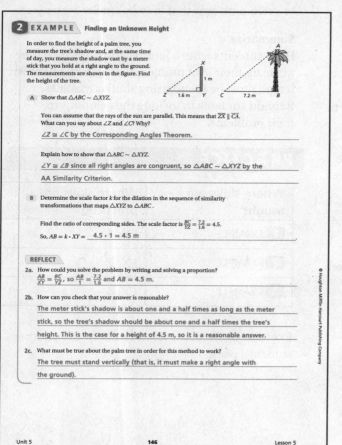

A   Show that $\triangle ABC \sim \triangle XYZ$.

You can assume that the rays of the sun are parallel. This means that $\overline{ZX} \parallel \overline{CA}$. What can you say about $\angle Z$ and $\angle C$? Why?

$\angle Z \cong \angle C$ by the Corresponding Angles Theorem.

Explain how to show that $\triangle ABC \sim \triangle XYZ$.

$\angle Y \cong \angle B$ since all right angles are congruent, so $\triangle ABC \sim \triangle XYZ$ by the

AA Similarity Criterion.

B   Determine the scale factor *k* for the dilation in the sequence of similarity transformations that maps $\triangle XYZ$ to $\triangle ABC$.

Find the ratio of corresponding sides. The scale factor is $\frac{BC}{YZ} = \frac{7.2}{1.6} = 4.5$.

So, $AB = k \cdot XY = $ 4.5 · 1 = 4.5 m   .

REFLECT

2a.   How could you solve the problem by writing and solving a proportion?

$\frac{AB}{XY} = \frac{BC}{YZ}$, so $\frac{AB}{1} = \frac{7.2}{1.6}$ and $AB = 4.5$ m.

2b.   How can you check that your answer is reasonable?

The meter stick's shadow is about one and a half times as long as the meter

stick, so the tree's shadow should be about one and a half times the tree's

height. This is the case for a height of 4.5 m, so it is a reasonable answer.

2c.   What must be true about the palm tree in order for this method to work?

The tree must stand vertically (that is, it must make a right angle with

the ground).

© Houghton Mifflin Harcourt Publishing Company

EXTRA EXAMPLE

To find the height of a building, you measure the building's shadow and, at the same time of day, you measure the shadow cast by a friend who is 6 feet tall. The measurements are shown in the figure. Find the height of the building.

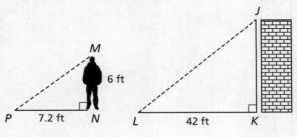

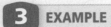

$JK = 35$ feet

3 EXAMPLE

Questioning Strategies

• How do you know when two rectangles are similar? **They are similar if corresponding sides are proportional (or if they have the same ratio of length to width).**

• Why is the number of horizontal 2-centimeter bands one more than the number of rows of rectangles? **There is a band above each row of rectangles as well as an extra 2-cm band at the bottom of the poster.**

EXTRA EXAMPLE

A designer wants to lay out a grid system for a poster that is 80 cm tall by 120 cm long. The grid must have margins of 5 cm along all edges and 5 cm between each horizontal row of rectangles. There must be 5 rows of rectangles, and each rectangle must be similar to the postcard itself. What are the dimensions of the rectangles? How many rectangles should appear in each row? How much space should be between the columns of rectangles?

10 cm tall and 15 cm long; 7 rectangles per row; 0.8$\overline{3}$ cm between columns (or 10 cm tall and 6.$\overline{6}$ cm long; 16 rectangles per row; 0.$\overline{2}$ cm between columns).

CLOSE

Essential Question

How can you use similar triangles and similar rectangles to solve problems?
In general, you show that two triangles are similar using the AA or SAS Similarity Criterion. Then, you use the fact that corresponding sides are proportional to find an unknown side length. You can also use proportionality of corresponding sides to solve problems that involve similar rectangles.

Summarize

Have students write a journal entry in which they make up their own problem in which an unknown length must be found using similar triangles. Remind students to include the solutions to their problems.

PRACTICE

Where skills are taught	Where skills are practiced
1 EXAMPLE	EX. 1
2 EXAMPLE	EX. 2
3 EXAMPLE	EX. 4

Exercise 3: Students identify an error in another student's work.

Notes

3 EXAMPLE Solving a Problem About Similar Rectangles

A typographic grid system is a set of horizontal and vertical lines that determine the placement of type on a page. The lines create an array of identical rectangles.

A graphic designer wants to lay out a new grid system for a poster that is 54 cm wide by 72 cm tall. The grid must have margins of 2 cm along all edges and 2 cm between each horizontal row of rectangles. There must be 5 rows of rectangles and each rectangle must be similar to the poster itself.

What are the dimensions of the rectangles? How many rectangles should appear in each row? How much space should be between the columns of rectangles?

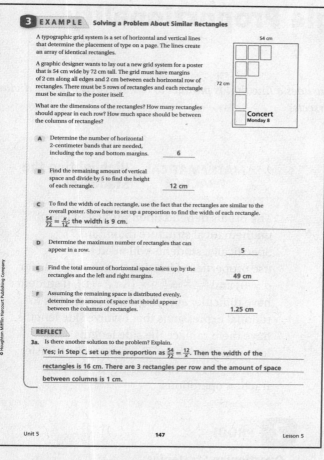

A Determine the number of horizontal 2-centimeter bands that are needed, including the top and bottom margins. **6**

B Find the remaining amount of vertical space and divide by 5 to find the height of each rectangle. **12 cm**

C To find the width of each rectangle, use the fact that the rectangles are similar to the overall poster. Show how to set up a proportion to find the width of each rectangle.
$\frac{54}{72} = \frac{x}{12}$; the width is 9 cm.

D Determine the maximum number of rectangles that can appear in a row. **5**

E Find the total amount of horizontal space taken up by the rectangles and the left and right margins. **49 cm**

F Assuming the remaining space is distributed evenly, determine the amount of space that should appear between the columns of rectangles. **1.25 cm**

REFLECT

3a. Is there another solution to the problem? Explain.

Yes; in Step C, set up the proportion as $\frac{54}{72} = \frac{12}{x}$. Then the width of the rectangles is 16 cm. There are 3 rectangles per row and the amount of space between columns is 1 cm.

© Houghton Mifflin Harcourt Publishing Company

Unit 5 · 147 · Lesson 5

PRACTICE

1. To find the distance XY across a lake, you locate points as shown in the figure. Explain how to use this information to find XY.

$\triangle XYZ \sim \triangle VUZ$ by the SAS Similarity Criterion,
so $\frac{XY}{VU} = \frac{XZ}{VZ}$. Then $\frac{XY}{500} = \frac{800}{400}$, so $XY = 1000$ ft.

2. In order to find the height of a cliff, you stand at the bottom of the cliff, walk 60 ft from the base, and place a mirror on the ground. Then you face the cliff and step back 5 feet so that you can see the top of the cliff in the mirror. Assuming your eyes are 6 feet above ground, explain how to use this information to find the height of the cliff. (*Hint:* When light strikes a mirror, the angle of incidence is congruent to the angle of reflection, as marked in the figure.)

$\triangle JKM \sim \triangle PQM$ by the AA Similarity Criterion,
so $\frac{JK}{PQ} = \frac{MK}{MQ}$. Then $\frac{JK}{6} = \frac{60}{5}$, so $JK = 72$ ft.

3. Error Analysis A student who is 72 inches tall wants to find the height of a flagpole. He measures the length of the flagpole's shadow and the length of his own shadow at the same time of day, as shown in his sketch below. Explain the error in the student's work.

> The triangles are similar by the AA Similarity Criterion, so corresponding sides are proportional.
> $\frac{x}{72} = \frac{48}{128}$
> $x = 72 \cdot \frac{48}{128}$, so $x = 27$ in.

The proportion is incorrect because the ratios do not compare the triangles in the same order. It should be $\frac{x}{72} = \frac{128}{48}$ and $x = 192$ in.

4. A graphic designer wants to lay out a grid system for a brochure that is 15 cm wide by 20 cm tall. The grid must have margins of 1 cm along all edges and 1 cm between each horizontal row of rectangles. There must be 4 rows of rectangles and each rectangle must be similar to the brochure itself. What are the dimensions of the rectangles? How many rectangles should appear in each row? How much space should be between the columns of rectangles? Give two different solutions.

3.75 cm tall by 2.8125 cm wide; 4 rectangles per row; ≈ 0.583 cm between.

3.75 cm tall by 5 cm wide; 2 rectangles per row; 3 cm between

© Houghton Mifflin Harcourt Publishing Company

Unit 5 · 148 · Lesson 5

Unit 5 — **148** — Lesson 5

The Triangle Proportionality Theorem

Essential question: How does a line that is parallel to one side of a triangle divide the two sides that it intersects?

COMMON CORE Standards for Mathematical Content

CC.9-12.G.SRT.4 Prove theorems about triangles.

CC.9-12.G.SRT.5 Use ... similarity criteria for triangles to solve problems and to prove relationships in geometric figures.

Prerequisites
Similarity and Triangles, Lesson 5-4

Math Background
The Triangle Proportionality Theorem and its converse may be stated as a single biconditional: A line that intersects two sides of a triangle is parallel to the third side of the triangle *if and only if* it divides the intersected sides proportionally.

MATHEMATICAL PRACTICE — Highlighting the Standards

The proofs depend upon proficient use of mathematical structure (Standard 7). Specifically, students will need to use properties of fractions, such as $\frac{a}{a} = 1$ (for $a \neq 0$) and $\frac{a+b}{c} = \frac{a}{c} + \frac{b}{c}$ (for $c \neq 0$). If students have difficulty applying these properties to rational expressions that involve side lengths, have them replace the side lengths with lowercase variables. This may make it easier for students to recognize the underlying fraction operations.

INTRODUCE

Have students use a straightedge to draw $\triangle ABC$. Then, have them construct a line, $\overleftrightarrow{EF}$, parallel to $\overleftrightarrow{BC}$, as shown in the figure on the student page. Have students measure the required segments to calculate the ratios $\frac{AE}{EB}$ and $\frac{AF}{FC}$. Ask students what they notice, and check that all students got similar results. Tell students that the relationship they discovered is known as the Triangle Proportionality Theorem.

TEACH

1 PROOF

Questioning Strategies

- In the third line of Step B, where does the 1 on each side of the equation come from?
  On the left side of the equation and similarly, on the right side, it comes from writing
  $$\frac{AE + EB}{AE} = \frac{AE}{AE} + \frac{EB}{AE}$$ and using the fact that
  $$\frac{AE}{AE} = 1.$$

2 PROOF

Questioning Strategies

- What are the main steps of the proof? **First, show that the two triangles, $\triangle AEF$ and $\triangle ABC$, are similar by the SAS Similarity Criterion. Then, use congruent corresponding angles to show that $\overleftrightarrow{EF}$ is parallel to $\overline{BC}$.**

- How is this proof similar to that of the Triangle Proportionality Theorem? **Both proofs use properties of fractions and the Segment Addition Postulate to work with proportions. Both proofs also use the fact that you can take the reciprocal of both sides of a proportion.**

CLOSE

Essential Question
How does a line that is parallel to one side of a triangle divide the two sides that it intersects?
If a line parallel to one side of a triangle intersects the other two sides, then it divides those sides proportionally.

Summarize
Have students write a journal entry in which they explain the Triangle Proportionality Theorem and its converse in their own words. Ask students to include figures with their explanation.

Name_____ Class_____ Date_____

The Triangle Proportionality Theorem

COMMON CORE

CC.9-12.G.SRT.4,
CC.9-12.G.SRT.5

Essential question: *How does a line that is parallel to one side of a triangle divide the two sides that it intersects?*

The following theorem is sometimes known as the Side-Splitting Theorem. It describes what happens when a line that is parallel to one side of a triangle "splits" the other two sides.

> **Triangle Proportionality Theorem**
>
> If a line parallel to one side of a triangle intersects the other two sides, then it divides those sides proportionally.

1 PROOF Triangle Proportionality Theorem

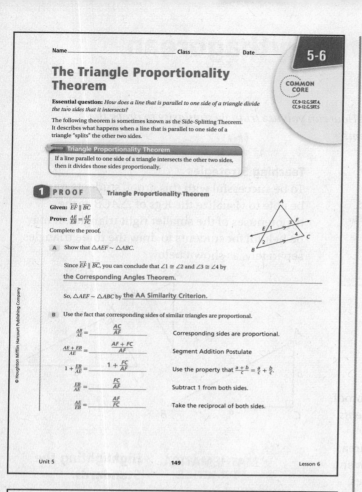

Given: $\overline{EF} \parallel \overline{BC}$

Prove: $\dfrac{AE}{EB} = \dfrac{AF}{FC}$

Complete the proof.

A Show that $\triangle AEF \sim \triangle ABC$.

Since $\overline{EF} \parallel \overline{BC}$, you can conclude that $\angle 1 \cong \angle 2$ and $\angle 3 \cong \angle 4$ by the Corresponding Angles Theorem.

So, $\triangle AEF \sim \triangle ABC$ by the AA Similarity Criterion.

B Use the fact that corresponding sides of similar triangles are proportional.

$\dfrac{AB}{AE} = \dfrac{AC}{AF}$	Corresponding sides are proportional.
$\dfrac{AE + EB}{AE} = \dfrac{AF + FC}{AF}$	Segment Addition Postulate
$1 + \dfrac{EB}{AE} = 1 + \dfrac{FC}{AF}$	Use the property that $\dfrac{a+b}{c} = \dfrac{a}{c} + \dfrac{b}{c}$.
$\dfrac{EB}{AE} = \dfrac{FC}{AF}$	Subtract 1 from both sides.
$\dfrac{AE}{EB} = \dfrac{AF}{FC}$	Take the reciprocal of both sides.

REFLECT

1a. Explain how you can conclude $\triangle AEF \sim \triangle ABC$ without using $\angle 3$ and $\angle 4$.

$\angle A \cong \angle A$ by the Reflexive Property of Congruence, and $\angle 1 \cong \angle 2$ since they are corresponding angles; $\triangle AEF \sim \triangle ABC$ by the AA Similarity Criterion.

> **Converse of the Triangle Proportionality Theorem**
>
> If a line divides two sides of a triangle proportionally, then it is parallel to the third side.

2 PROOF Converse of the Triangle Proportionality Theorem

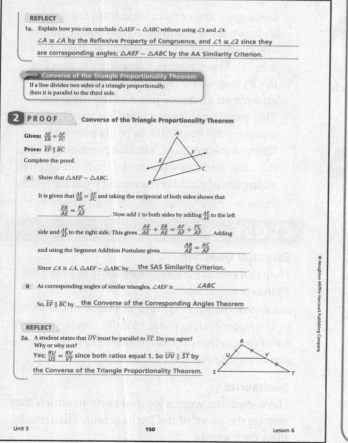

Given: $\dfrac{AE}{EB} = \dfrac{AF}{FC}$

Prove: $\overline{EF} \parallel \overline{BC}$

Complete the proof.

A Show that $\triangle AEF \sim \triangle ABC$.

It is given that $\dfrac{AE}{EB} = \dfrac{AF}{FC}$ and taking the reciprocal of both sides shows that

$\dfrac{EB}{AE} = \dfrac{FC}{AF}$. Now add 1 to both sides by adding $\dfrac{AE}{AE}$ to the left

side and $\dfrac{AF}{AF}$ to the right side. This gives $\dfrac{AE}{AE} + \dfrac{EB}{AE} = \dfrac{AF}{AF} + \dfrac{FC}{AF}$. Adding

and using the Segment Addition Postulate gives $\dfrac{AB}{AE} = \dfrac{AC}{AF}$.

Since $\angle A \cong \angle A$, $\triangle AEF \sim \triangle ABC$ by the SAS Similarity Criterion.

B As corresponding angles of similar triangles, $\angle AEF \cong \underline{\quad \angle ABC \quad}$

So, $\overline{EF} \parallel \overline{BC}$ by the Converse of the Corresponding Angles Theorem

REFLECT

2a. A student states that $\overline{UV}$ must be parallel to $\overline{ST}$. Do you agree? Why or why not?

Yes; $\dfrac{RU}{US} = \dfrac{RV}{VT}$ since both ratios equal 1. So $\overline{UV} \parallel \overline{ST}$ by the Converse of the Triangle Proportionality Theorem.

Proving the Pythagorean Theorem

Essential question: How can you use triangle similarity to prove the Pythagorean Theorem?

Standards for Mathematical Content

CC.9-12.G.SRT.4 Prove theorems about triangles.

CC.9-12.G.SRT.5 Use ... similarity criteria for triangles to solve problems and to prove relationships in geometric figures.

Prerequisites
Similarity and Triangles, Lesson 5-4

Math Background
The Pythagorean Theorem was known in many ancient civilizations, including those of Egypt, India, and China. The oldest known axiomatic proof of the theorem, however, dates to Euclid's *Elements* (circa 300 BCE). Since then, hundreds of proofs have been given, including proofs that rely on area, proofs that use calculus, and the proof that is given in this lesson, which is based on similar triangles.

INTRODUCE

Review the Pythagorean Theorem, emphasizing that the theorem applies only to right triangles. You may want to show students a simple example, such as a 3-4-5 right triangle, in which it is easy to see that $3^2 + 4^2 = 5^2$.

TEACH

PROOF

Questioning Strategies
- The perpendicular from C to the hypotenuse creates two new triangles, $\triangle AXC$ and $\triangle CXB$. What can you say about these triangles and the original triangle? All three triangles are similar to one another.
- What is the hypotenuse of $\triangle AXC$? of $\triangle CXB$? $\overline{AC}$; $\overline{CB}$

Teaching Strategies
To be successful with this proof, students must be able to visualize the legs of $\triangle ACB$ as the hypotenuses of the smaller right triangles. It may be helpful for students to draw the three triangles separately, as shown below.

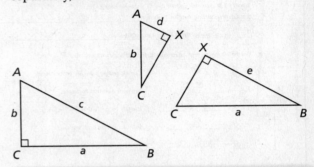

Highlighting the Standards

Distinguishing correct logic from flawed logic is part of Standard 3 (Construct viable arguments and critique the reasoning of others). The question following the proof of the Pythagorean Theorem asks students to analyze an alternate proof of the theorem. This proof uses flawed logic because it assumes the result that is being proved. Discuss the perils of "circular reasoning" with the class and ask students to share additional examples of circular reasoning from daily life.

CLOSE

Essential Question
How can you use triangle similarity to prove the Pythagorean Theorem?
Draw a perpendicular from the right-angle vertex to the hypotenuse. Then, identify similar triangles, write proportions for corresponding sides, and use algebra to derive the Pythagorean Theorem.

Summarize
Have students write a journal entry in which they rewrite the proof of the Pythagorean Theorem in their own words.

5-7

Proving the Pythagorean Theorem

COMMON CORE

CC.9-12.G.SRT.4,
CC.9-12.G.SRT.5

Essential question: *How can you use triangle similarity to prove the Pythagorean Theorem?*

You have already used the Pythagorean Theorem in earlier courses and in earlier lessons of this book. There are many proofs of this familiar theorem. The proof in this lesson is based on using what you know about similar triangles.

> **The Pythagorean Theorem**
> In a right triangle, the sum of the squares of the lengths of the legs is equal to the square of the length of the hypotenuse.

1 PROOF   The Pythagorean Theorem

Given: $\triangle ABC$ is a right triangle with legs of length a and b and hypotenuse of length c.

Prove: $a^2 + b^2 = c^2$

Complete the proof.

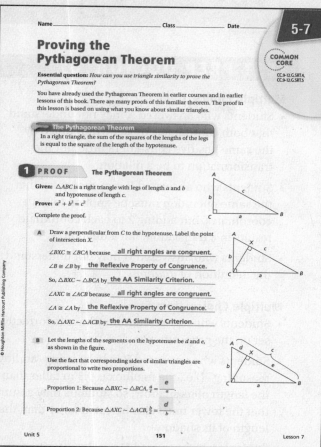

A   Draw a perpendicular from C to the hypotenuse. Label the point of intersection X.

$\angle BXC \cong \angle BCA$ because __all right angles are congruent.__

$\angle B \cong \angle B$ by __the Reflexive Property of Congruence.__

So, $\triangle BXC \sim \triangle BCA$ by __the AA Similarity Criterion.__

$\angle AXC \cong \angle ACB$ because __all right angles are congruent.__

$\angle A \cong \angle A$ by __the Reflexive Property of Congruence.__

So, $\triangle AXC \sim \triangle ACB$ by __the AA Similarity Criterion.__

B   Let the lengths of the segments on the hypotenuse be d and e, as shown in the figure.

Use the fact that corresponding sides of similar triangles are proportional to write two proportions.

Proportion 1: Because $\triangle BXC \sim \triangle BCA$, $\dfrac{a}{c} = \dfrac{e}{a}$.

Proportion 2: Because $\triangle AXC \sim \triangle ACB$, $\dfrac{b}{c} = \dfrac{d}{b}$.

C   Now perform some algebra to complete the proof as follows.

Multiply both sides of Proportion 1 by ac. Write the resulting equation.

$a^2 = ce$

Multiply both sides of Proportion 2 by bc. Write the resulting equation.

$b^2 = cd$

Adding the above equations gives this: $a^2 + b^2 = ce + cd$

Factor the right side of the equation: $a^2 + b^2 = c(e + d)$

Finally, use the fact that $e + d = $ ___c___ by the Segment Addition

Postulate to rewrite the equation as $a^2 + b^2 = c^2$

REFLECT

1a. **Error Analysis** A student wrote a proof of the Pythagorean Theorem, as shown below.

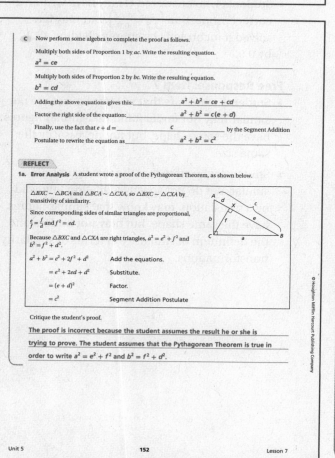

> $\triangle BXC \sim \triangle BCA$ and $\triangle BCA \sim \triangle CXA$, so $\triangle BXC \sim \triangle CXA$ by transitivity of similarity.
>
> Since corresponding sides of similar triangles are proportional, $\dfrac{e}{f} = \dfrac{f}{d}$ and $f^2 = ed$.
>
> Because $\triangle BXC$ and $\triangle CXA$ are right triangles, $a^2 = e^2 + f^2$ and $b^2 = f^2 + d^2$.
>
> $a^2 + b^2 = e^2 + 2f^2 + d^2$ Add the equations.
>
> $= e^2 + 2ed + d^2$ Substitute.
>
> $= (e + d)^2$ Factor.
>
> $= c^2$ Segment Addition Postulate

Critique the student's proof.

__The proof is incorrect because the student assumes the result he or she is__

__trying to prove. The student assumes that the Pythagorean Theorem is true in__

__order to write $a^2 = e^2 + f^2$ and $b^2 = f^2 + d^2$.__

Standard	Items
CC.9-12.G.CO.2	1, 6
CC.9-12.G.SRT.1	3
CC.9-12.G.SRT.2	7
CC.9-12.G.SRT.3	8
CC.9-12.G.SRT.4	2
CC.9-12.G.SRT.5	5
CC.9-12.G.C.1	9
CC.9-12.G.MG.3*	4

TEST PREP DOCTOR ⊕

Multiple Choice: Item 1

- Students who answered **A** may not understand that both coordinates must be multiplied by the same positive constant in order for the transformation to be a dilation.

- Students who answered **B** may recognize that the same operation must be applied to both coordinates, but adding 2 to each coordinate results in a translation, not a dilation.

- Students who answered **D** may not understand the definition of *dilation*.

Multiple Choice: Item 5

- Students who answered **A** may have incorrectly set up the proportion as $\frac{x}{0.9} = \frac{40.2}{1.2}$.

- Students who answered **B** may be using "additive reasoning" (i.e., the mailbox is 0.3 m taller than the length of its shadow, so students may assume that the tower must also be 0.3 m taller than the length of its shadow).

- Students who answered **C** may have written a correct proportion $\left(\frac{x}{1.2} = \frac{40.2}{0.9}\right)$, but may have solved it incorrectly by simply dividing 40.2 by 0.9.

Free Response: Item 7

- Students who state that the two figures are not similar may not understand that similar figures have the same shape, but not necessarily the same size.

- Students who state that the two figures are similar, but do not specify a dilation followed by a translation, may know that similar figures have the same shape, but may not understand the definition of similarity in terms of similarity transformations.

Name _____ Class _____ Date _____

MULTIPLE CHOICE

1. Which of the following transformations is a dilation?

A. $(x, y) \rightarrow (2x, y)$

B. $(x, y) \rightarrow (x + 2, y + 2)$

C. $(x, y) \rightarrow (2x, 2y)$

D. $(x, y) \rightarrow (x, y - 2)$

2. Juan is proving the Triangle Proportionality Theorem. Which reason should he use for Step 3?

Given: $\overline{XY} \parallel \overline{BC}$

Prove: $\frac{AX}{XB} = \frac{AY}{YC}$

Statements	Reasons
1. $\overline{XY} \parallel \overline{BC}$	1. Given
2. $\angle 1 \cong \angle 2$; $\angle 3 \cong \angle 4$	2. Corresponding Angles Theorem
3. $\triangle AXY \sim \triangle ABC$	3. ?

F. ASA Congruence Criterion

G. Definition of corresponding angles

H. Definition of similarity

J. AA Similarity Criterion

3. Katie uses geometry software to draw a line ℓ and a point O that is not on line ℓ. Then she constructs the image of line ℓ under a dilation with center O and scale factor 4. Which of the following *best* describes the image of line ℓ?

A. a line parallel to line ℓ

B. a line perpendicular to line ℓ

C. a line passing through point O

D. a line that coincides with line ℓ

4. A graphic designer wants to lay out a grid system for a book cover that is 12 cm wide by 15 cm tall. The grid will have an array of identical rectangles, margins of 1 cm along all edges, and 1 cm between each horizontal row of rectangles. There must be 4 rows of rectangles and each rectangle must be similar to the cover itself. Which of the following are possible dimensions of the rectangles?

F. 2.5 cm tall by 2 cm wide

G. 2.75 cm tall by 2.2 cm wide

H. 3 cm tall by 2.4 cm wide

J. 3.25 cm tall by 2.6 cm wide

5. In order to find the height of a radio tower, you measure the tower's shadow and, at the same time of day, you measure the shadow cast by a mailbox that is 1.2 meters tall. The measurements are shown in the figure. What is the height of the tower?

A. 30.15 m   C. 44.67 m

B. 40.5 m   D. 53.6 m

6. Which of the following is *not* preserved under a dilation?

F. angle measure

G. betweenness

H. collinearity

J. distance

© Houghton Mifflin Harcourt Publishing Company

FREE RESPONSE

7. Use the definition of similarity in terms of similarity transformations to determine whether the two figures are similar. Explain your answer.

Similar; the dilation $(x, y) \rightarrow \left(\frac{1}{4}x, \frac{1}{4}y\right)$

followed by the translation $(x, y) \rightarrow$

$(x + 1, y - 2)$ maps $\triangle ABC$ to $\triangle DEF$.

8. You are proving that the AA Similarity Criterion follows from the definition of similarity in terms of similarity transformations.

Given: $\angle R \cong \angle U$ and $\angle S \cong \angle V$

Prove: $\triangle RST \sim \triangle UVW$

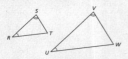

You begin by applying a dilation to $\triangle RST$. What is the scale factor k of the dilation? Why do you choose this scale factor?

$k = \frac{UV}{RS}$; this ensures that the image of

$\triangle RST$ is congruent to $\triangle UVW$ by the

ASA Congruence Criterion.

9. You are proving that all circles are similar. You start with the two circles shown below.

a. First you perform a transformation on circle A so that the image of point A is point B. Describe the transformation you use.

Translation along the vector $\overline{AB}$

b. The image of circle A is circle A', as shown.

Circle A'

What transformation do you apply to circle A' in order to complete the proof? Why?

Dilation with center of dilation B

and scale factor $\frac{b}{a}$. The image of

circle A' will consist of all points at a

distance $\frac{b}{a} \cdot a = b$ from point B, and

these are the points that form circle B.

So this shows that there is a sequence

of similarity transformations

(translation followed by dilation) that

maps circle A to circle B.

© Houghton Mifflin Harcourt Publishing Company

UNIT 6

Trigonometry

Unit Vocabulary

adjacent	(6-1)
cosine	(6-2)
inverse trigonometric ratio	(6-4)
opposite	(6-1)
sine	(6-2)
tangent	(6-1)
trigonometric ratio	(6-2)

Trigonometry

Unit Focus

In this unit, you will work with trigonometric ratios. Trigonometric ratios are based on right triangles and similarity. As you will see, these ratios are useful in solving a variety of mathematical and real-world problems. As you study trigonometry, you will learn about two special right triangles, and you will learn how to find unknown side lengths and unknown angle measures in right and non-right triangles.

Unit at a Glance

COMMON CORE

Lesson		Standards for Mathematical Content
6-1	The Tangent Ratio	CC.9-12.G.SRT.6
6-2	The Sine and Cosine Ratios	CC.9-12.G.SRT.6, CC.9-12.G.SRT.7
6-3	Special Right Triangles	CC.9-12.G.SRT.6, CC.9-12.G.SRT.7
6-4	Solving Right Triangles	CC.9-12.G.SRT.8
6-5	Trigonometric Ratios of Obtuse Angles	CC.9-12.G.SRT.9(+)
6-6	The Law of Sines	CC.9-12.G.SRT.10(+), CC.9-12.G.SRT.11(+)
6-7	The Law of Cosines	CC.9-12.G.SRT.10(+), CC.9-12.G.SRT.11(+)
	Test Prep	

Unpacking the Common Core State Standards

Use the table to help you understand the Standards for Mathematical Content that are taught in this unit. Refer to the lessons listed after each standard for exploration and practice.

COMMON CORE Standards for Mathematical Content	What It Means For You
CC.9-12.G.SRT.6 Understand that by similarity, side ratios in right triangles are properties of the angles in the triangle, leading to definitions of trigonometric ratios for acute angles. Lessons 6-1, 6-2, 6-3	Given an acute angle, all right triangles that contain this angle must be similar to each other. You will see how to use this idea to define the tangent, sine, and cosine ratios.
CC.9-12.G.SRT.7 Explain and use the relationship between the sine and cosine of complementary angles. Lessons 6-2, 6-3	The acute angles in a right triangle are complementary. This leads to a useful relationship between the sine and cosine of complementary angles.
CC.9-12.G.SRT.8 Use trigonometric ratios and the Pythagorean Theorem to solve right triangles in applied problems. Lesson 6-4	Trigonometric ratios are powerful tools for solving real-world problems. You will see how to use trigonometric ratios to find unknown heights, distances, and angle measures in a wide range of problems.
CC.9-12.G.SRT.9(+) Derive the formula $A = \frac{1}{2}ab \sin(C)$ for the area of a triangle by drawing an auxiliary line from a vertex perpendicular to the opposite side. Lesson 6-5	You already know the formula $A = \frac{1}{2}bh$ for the area of a triangle. Now you will derive a new formula for the area of a triangle that does not depend upon knowing the altitude of the triangle.
CC.9-12.G.SRT.10(+) Prove the Laws of Sines and Cosines and use them to solve problems. Lessons 6-6, 6-7	The Law of Sines and the Law of Cosines describe relationships among the sides and angles of a triangle. You will see how the definitions of trigonometric ratios can be used to prove these relationships.
CC.9-12.G.SRT.11(+) Understand and apply the Law of Sines and the Law of Cosines to find unknown measurements in right and non-right triangles (e.g., surveying problems, resultant forces). Lessons 6-6, 6-7	You will use the Law of Sines and the Law of Cosines to find unknown distances and/or angle measures in real-world problems.

Unpacking the Common Core State Standards

This page lists and explains the Standards for Mathematical Content that are addressed in this unit. For information about the Standards for Mathematical Practice, which are integrated throughout the text, see Teacher Edition pages x–xiii.

Notes

The Tangent Ratio

Essential question: *How do you find the tangent ratio for an acute angle of a right triangle?*

COMMON CORE
Standards for Mathematical Content

CC.9-12.G.SRT.6 Understand that by similarity, side ratios in right triangles are properties of the angles in the triangle, leading to definitions of trigonometric ratios for acute angles.

Vocabulary
adjacent

opposite

tangent

Prerequisites
Similarity and Triangles, Lesson 5-4

Math Background
Students work with three trigonometric ratios in this course: tangent, sine, and cosine. The tangent is treated separately for two reasons. First, working with a single ratio gives students a chance to focus on the conceptual underpinnings of trigonometry. That is, right triangles with a given acute angle, $\angle A$, are all similar, so the ratio of the length of the leg opposite $\angle A$ to the length of the leg adjacent to $\angle A$ is constant for all such triangles. Second, students sometimes have difficulty deciding which trigonometric ratio to use when solving a problem. By working with tangents first, students can instead focus on the general process for solving a problem via trigonometry.

INTRODUCE

Draw a right triangle on the board and point out the hypotenuse and the two legs. Label an acute angle as $\angle A$ and show students the leg opposite $\angle A$ and the leg adjacent to $\angle A$. Draw right triangles in different orientations and have students identify the leg opposite $\angle A$ and the leg adjacent to $\angle A$.

TEACH

1 EXPLORE

Materials: geometry software

Questioning Strategies
- What is m$\angle A$? Why? **30°; the angle is formed by a 30° rotation about point A.**
- In $\triangle ABC$, which side is the hypotenuse? How do you know? **$\overline{AB}$ is the hypotenuse because it is opposite the right angle, $\angle C$.**

> **MATHEMATICAL PRACTICE**   **Highlighting the Standards**
>
> Standard 3 (Construct viable arguments and critique the reasoning of others) includes communicating results to others. The Explore offers an opportunity for students to formulate and describe a conjecture. As students share their findings, ask questions to help them refine their statements. For example, students may state their conjecture as, "The ratios are equal." Prompt students to be more specific ("What ratios?"). Coaching students so they communicate their findings clearly and precisely will help them meet this standard for mathematical practice.

Teaching Strategies
Students can use their calculators to find tangent ratios of acute angles. (Remind students to check that their calculators are in Degree mode.) Students may wonder where these values come from. Tell them that they can find approximate tangent ratios themselves. For example, to find 53°, use a protractor and straightedge to draw any right triangle that has a 53° angle. Then use a ruler to measure the length of the side opposite the 53° angle and the length of the side adjacent to the 53° angle. The ratio of these lengths gives an estimate for tan 53°.

The Tangent Ratio

Essential question: *How do you find the tangent ratio for an acute angle of a right triangle?*

COMMON CORE
CC.9-12.G.SRT.6

In this unit, you will be working extensively with right triangles, so some new vocabulary will be helpful. Given a right triangle, $\triangle ABC$, with a right angle at vertex C, the leg **adjacent** to $\angle A$ is the leg that forms one side of $\angle A$. The leg **opposite** $\angle A$ is the leg that does not form a side of $\angle A$.

1 EXPLORE Investigating a Ratio in a Right Triangle

A Use geometry software to draw a horizontal segment. Label one endpoint of the segment A.

B Select point A, go to the Transform menu, and choose Mark Center.

C Select the segment, go to the Transform menu, and choose Rotate. Enter 30° for the angle of rotation. Label the endpoint of the rotation image B.

D Select point B and the original line segment. Use the Construct menu to construct a perpendicular from B to the segment. Plot a point at the point of intersection and label the point C.

E Use the Measure menu to measure $\overline{BC}$ and $\overline{AC}$. Then use the Calculate tool to calculate the ratio $\frac{BC}{AC}$.

F Drag the points and lines to change the size and location of the triangle. Notice what happens to the measurements.

G Repeat the above steps using a different angle of rotation.

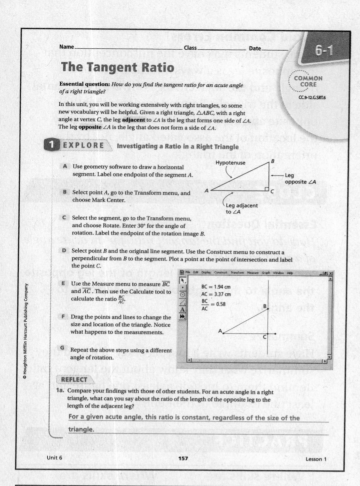

REFLECT

1a. Compare your findings with those of other students. For an acute angle in a right triangle, what can you say about the ratio of the length of the opposite leg to the length of the adjacent leg?

For a given acute angle, this ratio is constant, regardless of the size of the

triangle.

You may have discovered that in a right triangle the ratio of the length of the leg opposite an acute angle to the length of the leg adjacent to the angle is constant. You can use what you know about similarity to see why this is true.

Consider the right triangles $\triangle ABC$ and $\triangle DEF$, in which $\angle A \cong \angle D$, as shown. By the AA Similarity Criterion, $\triangle ABC \sim \triangle DEF$. This means the lengths of the sides of $\triangle DEF$ are each k times the lengths of the corresponding sides of $\triangle ABC$.

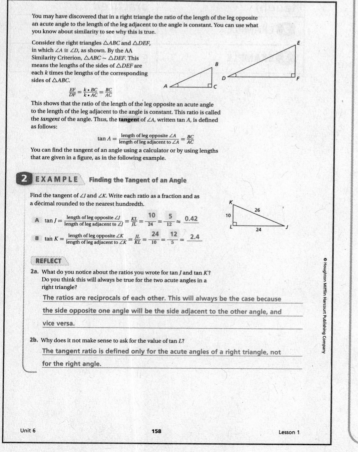

$$\frac{EF}{DF} = \frac{k \cdot BC}{k \cdot AC} = \frac{BC}{AC}$$

This shows that the ratio of the length of the leg opposite an acute angle to the length of the leg adjacent to the angle is constant. This ratio is called the *tangent* of the angle. Thus, the **tangent** of $\angle A$, written tan A, is defined as follows:

$$\tan A = \frac{\text{length of leg opposite to } \angle A}{\text{length of leg adjacent to } \angle A} = \frac{BC}{AC}$$

You can find the tangent of an angle using a calculator or by using lengths that are given in a figure, as in the following example.

2 EXAMPLE Finding the Tangent of an Angle

Find the tangent of $\angle J$ and $\angle K$. Write each ratio as a fraction and as a decimal rounded to the nearest hundredth.

A $\tan J = \frac{\text{length of leg opposite } \angle J}{\text{length of leg adjacent to } \angle J} = \frac{KL}{JL} = \frac{10}{24} = \frac{5}{12} \approx \underline{0.42}$

B $\tan K = \frac{\text{length of leg opposite } \angle K}{\text{length of leg adjacent to } \angle K} = \frac{JL}{KL} = \frac{24}{10} = \frac{12}{5} = \underline{2.4}$

REFLECT

2a. What do you notice about the ratios you wrote for tan J and tan K? Do you think this will always be true for the two acute angles in a right triangle?

The ratios are reciprocals of each other. This will always be the case because

the side opposite one angle will be the side adjacent to the other angle, and

vice versa.

2b. Why does it not make sense to ask for the value of tan L?

The tangent ratio is defined only for the acute angles of a right triangle, not

for the right angle.

2 EXAMPLE

Questioning Strategies

- How do you identify the leg opposite ∠*J*? **It is the leg that does not form a side of ∠*J*.**

- How do you identify the leg adjacent to ∠*J*? **It is the leg that forms a side of ∠*J*.**

EXTRA EXAMPLE

Find the tangent of ∠*M* and ∠*N*. Write each ratio as a fraction and as a decimal rounded to the nearest hundredth.

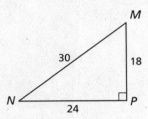

$\tan M = \frac{4}{3} \approx 1.33$; $\tan N = \frac{3}{4} = 0.75$

3 EXAMPLE

Questioning Strategies

- Is 14.9 feet a reasonable answer? Why or why not? **It is reasonable because $\overline{BC}$ appears to be about twice as long as $\overline{AC}$, and AC = 6 ft.**

EXTRA EXAMPLE

To help remove debris from the roof of a 30-foot building, workers use a straight chute, as shown in the figure. To the nearest tenth of a foot, how far from the base of the building does the chute touch the sidewalk? **12.7 ft**

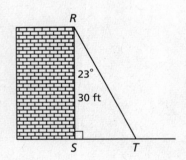

Avoid Common Errors

Some students may have the misconception that the opposite leg is always a vertical side of the triangle and the adjacent leg is always a horizontal side of the triangle. Remind students that the opposite and adjacent sides are determined by the location of the associated angle, not by the orientation of the triangle.

CLOSE

Essential Question

How do you find the tangent ratio for an acute angle of a right triangle?

You find the ratio of the length of the leg opposite the angle to the length of the leg adjacent to the angle.

Summarize

Have students write a journal entry in which they summarize what they know about the tangent ratio. Remind them to include at least one figure and at least one example in their entry.

PRACTICE

Where skills are taught	Where skills are practiced
2 EXAMPLE	EXS. 1–3
3 EXAMPLE	EXS. 4–8

When you know the length of a leg of a right triangle and the measure of one of the acute angles, you can use the tangent to find the length of the other leg. This is especially useful in real-world problems.

3 EXAMPLE Solving a Real-World Problem

A long ladder leans against a building and makes an angle of 68° with the ground. The base of the ladder is 6 feet from the building. To the nearest tenth of a foot, how far up the side of the building does the ladder reach?

A Write a tangent ratio that involves the unknown length, *BC*.

$$\tan A = \frac{\text{length of leg opposite } \angle A}{\text{length of leg adjacent to } \angle A} = \frac{BC}{6}$$

Use the fact that $m\angle A = 68°$ to write the equation as $\tan 68° = \frac{BC}{6}$.

B Solve for *BC*.

$6 \cdot \tan 68° = BC$ ⟶ Multiply both sides by 6.

$6 \cdot \underline{2.475086853} = BC$ ⟶ Use a calculator to find tan 68°. Do not round until the final step of the solution.

$\underline{14.9} \approx BC$ ⟶ Multiply. Round to the nearest tenth.

So, the ladder reaches about __14.9 feet__ up the side of the building.

REFLECT

3a. Why is it best to wait until the final step before rounding? What happens if you round the value of tan 68° to the nearest tenth before multiplying?

__Rounding in the last step gives a more accurate answer. Rounding the tangent__

__to the nearest tenth before multiplying gives an answer of 15 feet.__

3b. A student claims that it is possible to solve the problem using the tangent of ∠*B*. Do you agree or disagree? If it is possible, show the solution. If it is not possible, explain why not.

__Agree; by the Triangle Sum Theorem, m∠B = 22°, so tan 22° = $\frac{6}{BC}$ and__

__$BC = \frac{6}{\tan 22°} \approx 14.9$.__

© Houghton Mifflin Harcourt Publishing Company

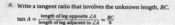

PRACTICE

Find the tangent of ∠*A* and ∠*B*. Write each ratio as a fraction and as a decimal rounded to the nearest hundredth.

1.

$\tan A = \frac{3}{4} = 0.75;$
$\tan B = \frac{4}{3} \approx 1.33$

2.

$\tan A = \frac{8}{15} \approx 0.53;$
$\tan B = \frac{15}{8} \approx 1.88$

3.

$\tan A = \frac{35}{12} \approx 2.92;$
$\tan B = \frac{12}{35} \approx 0.34$

Find the value of *x* to the nearest tenth.

4.

__8.7__

5.

__5.5__

6.

__289.0__

7. A hiker whose eyes are 5.5 feet above ground stands 25 feet from the base of a redwood tree. She looks up at an angle of 71° to see the top of the tree. To the nearest tenth of a foot, what is the height of the tree?

__78.1 ft__

8. Error Analysis To find the distance *XY* across a large rock formation, a student stands facing one endpoint of the formation, backs away from it at a right angle for 20 meters, and then turns 55° to look at the other endpoint of the formation. The student's calculations are shown. Critique the student's work.

__The student set up the tangent ratio incorrectly.__

__It should be $\tan 55° = \frac{XY}{20}$, which gives $XY \approx 28.6$.__

$\tan 55° = \frac{20}{XY}$

$XY \cdot \tan 55° = 20$

$XY = \frac{20}{\tan 55°} \approx 14.0 \text{ m}$

© Houghton Mifflin Harcourt Publishing Company

The Sine and Cosine Ratios

Essential question: *How do you find the sine and cosine ratios for an acute angle of a right triangle?*

COMMON **Standards for**
CORE **Mathematical Content**

CC.9-12.G.SRT.6 Understand that by similarity, side ratios in right triangles are properties of the angles in the triangle, leading to definitions of trigonometric ratios for acute angles.

CC.9-12.G.SRT.7 Explain and use the relationship between the sine and cosine of complementary angles.

Vocabulary

trigonometric ratio

sine

cosine

Prerequisites

The Tangent Ratio, Lesson 6-1

Math Background

In this lesson, students are introduced to the two remaining trigonometric ratios that will be treated in this course, the sine and the cosine. Be sure students understand that these ratios, like the tangent, are well defined because all right triangles with a given acute angle, $\angle A$, are similar. Therefore, the ratio of the length of the leg opposite $\angle A$ to the length of the hypotenuse (the sine) and the ratio of the length of the leg adjacent to $\angle A$ to the length of the hypotenuse (the cosine) are constant.

INTRODUCE

Define *sine* and *cosine*. Draw a triangle, $\triangle ABC$, on the board so that $\angle C$ is a right angle. Work with students to write sin A, cos A, and tan A in terms of the triangle's side lengths.

$$\sin A = \frac{BC}{AB} \qquad \cos A = \frac{AC}{AB} \qquad \tan A = \frac{BC}{AC}$$

TEACH

1 EXAMPLE

Questioning Strategies

• How do you determine the leg opposite $\angle R$? Look for the leg of the triangle that does not form a side of $\angle R$.

• Do you think it is possible for the value of a sine or cosine to be greater than 1? Why or why not? It is not possible; since the hypotenuse is the longest side of a right triangle, any ratio that has the length of the hypotenuse as the denominator will be less than 1.

EXTRA EXAMPLE

Write each trigonometric ratio as a fraction and as a decimal rounded to the nearest hundredth.

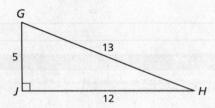

A. $\sin G \; \frac{12}{13} \approx 0.92$ **B.** $\sin H \; \frac{5}{13} \approx 0.38$

C. $\cos G \; \frac{5}{13} \approx 0.38$ **D.** $\cos H \; \frac{12}{13} \approx 0.92$

2 EXAMPLE

Questioning Strategies

• What does it mean for two angles to be complementary? The sum of their measures is 90°.

• How can you check your answer? Use a calculator to check that cos 33° ≈ 0.839.

EXTRA EXAMPLE

Given that cos 14° ≈ 0.970, write the sine of a complementary angle.

sin 76° ≈ 0.970

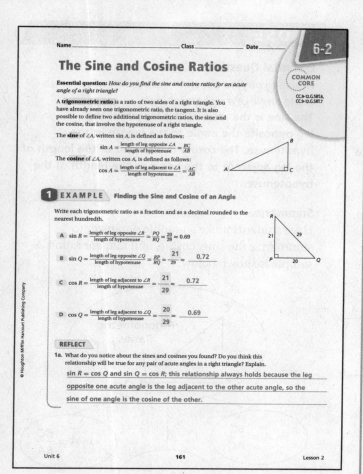

Name_____ Class_____ Date_____

The Sine and Cosine Ratios

6-2

COMMON CORE

CC.9-12.G.SRT.6, CC.9-12.G.SRT.7

Essential question: *How do you find the sine and cosine ratios for an acute angle of a right triangle?*

A **trigonometric ratio** is a ratio of two sides of a right triangle. You have already seen one trigonometric ratio, the tangent. It is also possible to define two additional trigonometric ratios, the sine and the cosine, that involve the hypotenuse of a right triangle.

The **sine** of $\angle A$, written sin A, is defined as follows:

$$\sin A = \frac{\text{length of leg opposite } \angle A}{\text{length of hypotenuse}} = \frac{BC}{AB}$$

The **cosine** of $\angle A$, written cos A, is defined as follows:

$$\cos A = \frac{\text{length of leg adjacent to } \angle A}{\text{length of hypotenuse}} = \frac{AC}{AB}$$

1 EXAMPLE Finding the Sine and Cosine of an Angle

Write each trigonometric ratio as a fraction and as a decimal rounded to the nearest hundredth.

A $\sin R = \dfrac{\text{length of leg opposite } \angle R}{\text{length of hypotenuse}} = \dfrac{PQ}{RQ} = \dfrac{20}{29} \approx 0.69$

B $\sin Q = \dfrac{\text{length of leg opposite } \angle Q}{\text{length of hypotenuse}} = \dfrac{RP}{RQ} = \dfrac{21}{29} \approx \underline{0.72}$

C $\cos R = \dfrac{\text{length of leg adjacent to } \angle R}{\text{length of hypotenuse}} = \dfrac{21}{29} \approx \underline{0.72}$

D $\cos Q = \dfrac{\text{length of leg adjacent to } \angle Q}{\text{length of hypotenuse}} = \dfrac{20}{29} \approx \underline{0.69}$

REFLECT

1a. What do you notice about the sines and cosines you found? Do you think this relationship will be true for any pair of acute angles in a right triangle? Explain.

sin R = cos Q and sin Q = cos R; this relationship always holds because the leg

opposite one acute angle is the leg adjacent to the other acute angle, so the

sine of one angle is the cosine of the other.

© Houghton Mifflin Harcourt Publishing Company

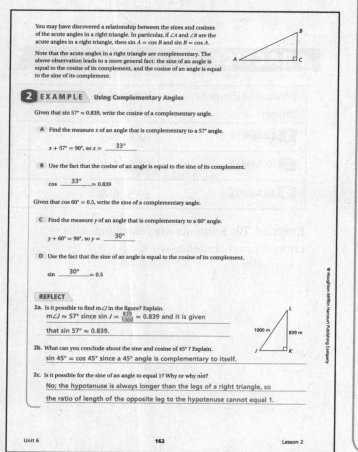

You may have discovered a relationship between the sines and cosines of the acute angles in a right triangle. In particular, if $\angle A$ and $\angle B$ are the acute angles in a right triangle, then sin A = cos B and sin B = cos A.

Note that the acute angles in a right triangle are complementary. The above observation leads to a more general fact: the sine of an angle is equal to the cosine of its complement, and the cosine of an angle is equal to the sine of its complement.

2 EXAMPLE Using Complementary Angles

Given that sin 57° ≈ 0.839, write the cosine of a complementary angle.

A Find the measure x of an angle that is complementary to a 57° angle.

$x + 57° = 90°$, so $x = \underline{\quad 33° \quad}$

B Use the fact that the cosine of an angle is equal to the sine of its complement.

cos $\underline{\quad 33° \quad} \approx 0.839$

Given that cos 60° = 0.5, write the sine of a complementary angle.

C Find the measure y of an angle that is complementary to a 60° angle.

$y + 60° = 90°$, so $y = \underline{\quad 30° \quad}$

D Use the fact that the sine of an angle is equal to the cosine of its complement.

sin $\underline{\quad 30° \quad} = 0.5$

REFLECT

2a. Is it possible to find m$\angle J$ in the figure? Explain.

m$\angle J \approx 57°$ since sin $J = \frac{839}{1000} = 0.839$ and it is given

that sin 57° ≈ 0.839.

2b. What can you conclude about the sine and cosine of 45° ? Explain.

sin 45° = cos 45° since a 45° angle is complementary to itself.

2c. Is it possible for the sine of an angle to equal 1? Why or why not?

No; the hypotenuse is always longer than the legs of a right triangle, so

the ratio of length of the opposite leg to the hypotenuse cannot equal 1.

© Houghton Mifflin Harcourt Publishing Company

Questioning Strategies

- Can you use either the sine or cosine ratio to find x? Explain. **Yes; you can solve $\sin 8° = \frac{x}{16}$ or you can solve $\cos 82° = \frac{x}{16}$.**

- Once you know that x is approximately 2.2 feet, how can you use the tangent ratio to find y? **Solve $\tan 8° = \frac{2.2}{y}$.**

EXTRA EXAMPLE

A 10-foot access ramp leads to the top of a platform, as shown in the figure. The ramp makes an angle of 6° with the ground. To the nearest tenth of a foot, what is the height of the platform? How far does the ramp extend in front of the platform?

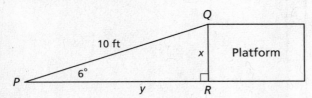

1.0 ft; 9.9 ft

MATHEMATICAL PRACTICE   **Highlighting the Standards**

You can address Standard 6 (Attend to precision) as you discuss Example 3. Ask students how their results would have been different if they had evaluated 16 sin 8° by evaluating sin 8°, rounding the result, and then multiplying by 16. Remind students that they will get the most accurate result by rounding *only* in the final step of the solution. This means they should evaluate an expression like 16 sin 8° by entering the entire expression into their calculator and then rounding the result.

CLOSE

Essential Question

How do you find the sine and cosine ratios for an acute angle of a right triangle?
The sine is the ratio of the length of the leg opposite the angle to the length of the hypotenuse. The cosine is the ratio of the length of the leg adjacent to the angle to the length of the hypotenuse.

Summarize

Have students make a graphic organizer to summarize the sine, cosine, and tangent ratios. A sample is shown below.

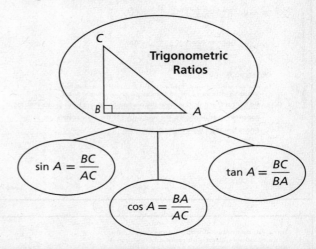

PRACTICE

Where skills are taught	Where skills are practiced
1 EXAMPLE	EXS. 1–3
2 EXAMPLE	EXS. 4–5
3 EXAMPLE	EXS. 6–9

Exercise 10: Students use reasoning skills to critique other students' work.

3 EXAMPLE Solving a Real-World Problem

A loading dock at a factory has a 16-foot ramp in front of it, as shown in the figure. The ramp makes an angle of 8° with the ground. To the nearest tenth of a foot, what is the height of the loading dock? How far does the ramp extend in front of the loading dock? (The figure is not drawn to scale, so you cannot measure it to solve the problem.)

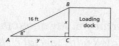

A Find the height x of the loading dock.

$\sin A = \frac{\text{length of leg opposite } \angle A}{\text{length of hypotenuse}} = \frac{x}{16}$, so $\sin 8° = \frac{x}{16}$.

Solve the equation for x.

$x = 16 \sin 8°$

Use a calculator to evaluate the expression, then round.

$x \approx$ ___2.2___

So, the height of the loading dock is about ___2.2 ft___

B Find the distance y that the ramp extends in front of the loading dock.

$\cos A = \frac{\text{length of leg adjacent to } \angle A}{\text{length of hypotenuse}} = \frac{y}{16}$, so $\cos$ __8°__ $= \frac{y}{16}$.

Solve the equation for y.

$y = 16 \cos 8°$

Use a calculator to evaluate the expression, then round.

$y \approx$ ___15.8___

So, the distance the ramp extends in front of the loading dock is about ___15.8 ft___

REFLECT

3a. A student claimed that she found the height of the loading dock by using the cosine. Explain her thinking.

Since $\angle A$ and $\angle B$ are complementary, m$\angle B$ = 82°. Then cos 82° = $\frac{x}{16}$ and

x = 16 cos 82° ≈ 2.2.

3b. Suppose the owner of the factory decides to build a new ramp for the loading dock so that the new ramp makes an angle of 5° with the ground. How far will this ramp extend from the loading dock? Explain.

Approximately 25.1 ft; in this case, tan 5° = $\frac{2.2}{y}$, so $y = \frac{2.2}{\tan 5°}$.

Evaluating the expression shows that y ≈ 25.1.

PRACTICE

Find the given trigonometric ratios. Write each ratio as a fraction and as a decimal rounded to the nearest hundredth.

1. sin R, cos R

sin R = $\frac{30}{34}$ ≈ 0.88;

cos R = $\frac{16}{34}$ ≈ 0.47

2. cos D, cos E

cos D = $\frac{65}{97}$ ≈ 0.67;

cos E = $\frac{72}{97}$ ≈ 0.74

3. sin M, sin N

sin M = $\frac{9}{15}$ = 0.6;

sin N = $\frac{12}{15}$ = 0.8

4. Given that sin 15° ≈ 0.259, write the cosine of a complementary angle.   cos 75° ≈ 0.259

5. Given that cos 62° ≈ 0.469, write the sine of a complementary angle.   sin 28° ≈ 0.469

Find the value of x to the nearest tenth.

6.

9.8

7.

24.5

8.

11.7

9. You are building a skateboard ramp from a piece of wood that is 3.1 meters long. You want the ramp to make an angle of 25° with the ground. To the nearest tenth of a meter, what is the length of the ramp's base? What is its height?

Length of base: 2.8 m; height: 1.3 m

10. **Error Analysis** Three students were asked to find the value of x in the figure. The equations they used are shown at right. Which students, if any, used a correct equation? Explain the other students' errors and then find the value of x.

Jamila's equation is correct. Lee should have

written sin 57° = $\frac{15}{x}$. Tyler's equation has two errors;

he should have written cos 33° = $\frac{15}{x}$.

x ≈ 17.9

Lee's equation: sin 57° = $\frac{x}{15}$

Jamila's equation: cos 33° = $\frac{15}{x}$

Tyler's equation: sin 33° = $\frac{x}{15}$

© Houghton Mifflin Harcourt Publishing Company

6-3

Special Right Triangles

Essential question: *What can you say about the side lengths and the trigonometric ratios associated with special right triangles?*

COMMON Standards for
CORE   Mathematical Content

CC.9-12.G.SRT.6 Understand that by similarity, side ratios in right triangles are properties of the angles in the triangle, leading to definitions of trigonometric ratios for acute angles.

CC.9-12.G.SRT.7 Explain and use the relationship between the sine and cosine of complementary angles.

Prerequisites

The Tangent Ratio, Lesson 6-1

The Sine and Cosine Ratios, Lesson 6-2

Math Background

This lesson consists of three investigations in which students explore 45°-45°-90° and 30°-60°-90° triangles. These special right triangles occur so often in mathematical and real-world problems, that it is well worth spending some time understanding the relationships among the sides of these triangles. You may also want to have students use these triangles to help them memorize the sine, cosine, and tangent of 30°, 45°, and 60°. Knowing these values by heart will serve students well in Algebra 2 and beyond.

INTRODUCE

Ask students to use a protractor, ruler, and/or compass to help them draw an isosceles right triangle. Then, ask students what appears to be true about the angles of the triangle. Students should find that both acute angles of the triangle measure 45°.

TEACH

1 EXPLORE

Questioning Strategies

- How can you find the length of the hypotenuse of an isosceles right triangle if you know the length of one of the legs? **Multiply the length of the leg by $\sqrt{2}$.**

- How can you find the length of the legs of an isosceles right triangle if you know the length of the hypotenuse? **Divide the length of the hypotenuse by $\sqrt{2}$.**

Differentiated Instruction

Kinesthetic learners may benefit from verifying the results of the Explore via a simple paper folding activity. Have students take a square piece of paper and fold it in half diagonally. This creates an isosceles right triangle. Then ask students to measure one leg of the triangle to the nearest millimeter, and have them use this information and the results of the Explore to predict the length of the hypotenuse. Finally, have students measure the length of the hypotenuse to check their predictions.

2 EXPLORE

Questioning Strategies

- What can you say about the angles of an equilateral triangle? **All three angles measure 60°.**

- How can you find the length of the hypotenuse of a 30°-60°-90° triangle if you know the length of the shorter leg? **Multiply the length of the shorter leg by 2.**

- What is the ratio of the length of the hypotenuse to the length of the shorter leg in any 30°-60°-90° triangle? **The ratio is 2 to 1.**

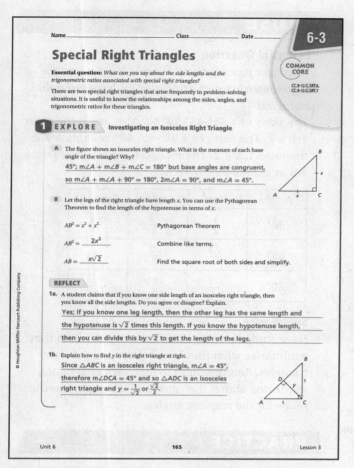

Name_____ Class_____ Date_____

6-3

Special Right Triangles

Essential question: *What can you say about the side lengths and the trigonometric ratios associated with special right triangles?*

COMMON CORE
CC.9-12.G.SRT.6,
CC.9-12.G.SRT.7

There are two special right triangles that arise frequently in problem-solving situations. It is useful to know the relationships among the sides, angles, and trigonometric ratios for these triangles.

1 EXPLORE Investigating an Isosceles Right Triangle

A The figure shows an isosceles right triangle. What is the measure of each base angle of the triangle? Why?

45°; $m\angle A + m\angle B + m\angle C = 180°$ but base angles are congruent,

so $m\angle A + m\angle A + 90° = 180°$, $2m\angle A = 90°$, and $m\angle A = 45°$.

B Let the legs of the right triangle have length x. You can use the Pythagorean Theorem to find the length of the hypotenuse in terms of x.

$AB^2 = x^2 + x^2$ Pythagorean Theorem

$AB^2 = \underline{2x^2}$ Combine like terms.

$AB = \underline{x\sqrt{2}}$ Find the square root of both sides and simplify.

REFLECT

1a. A student claims that if you know one side length of an isosceles right triangle, then you know all the side lengths. Do you agree or disagree? Explain.

Yes; if you know one leg length, then the other leg has the same length and

the hypotenuse is $\sqrt{2}$ times this length. If you know the hypotenuse length,

then you can divide this by $\sqrt{2}$ to get the length of the legs.

1b. Explain how to find y in the right triangle at right.

Since $\triangle ABC$ is an isosceles right triangle, $m\angle A = 45°$,

therefore $m\angle DCA = 45°$ and so $\triangle ADC$ is an isosceles

right triangle and $y = \frac{1}{\sqrt{2}}$ or $\frac{\sqrt{2}}{2}$.

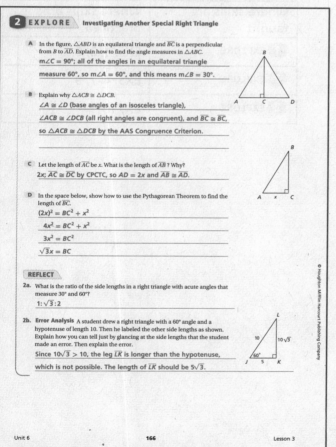

2 EXPLORE Investigating Another Special Right Triangle

A In the figure, $\triangle ABD$ is an equilateral triangle and $\overline{BC}$ is a perpendicular from B to $\overline{AD}$. Explain how to find the angle measures in $\triangle ABC$.

$m\angle C = 90°$; all of the angles in an equilateral triangle

measure 60°, so $m\angle A = 60°$, and this means $m\angle B = 30°$.

B Explain why $\triangle ACB \cong \triangle DCB$.

$\angle A \cong \angle D$ (base angles of an isosceles triangle),

$\angle ACB \cong \angle DCB$ (all right angles are congruent), and $\overline{BC} \cong \overline{BC}$,

so $\triangle ACB \cong \triangle DCB$ by the AAS Congruence Criterion.

C Let the length of $\overline{AC}$ be x. What is the length of $\overline{AB}$? Why?

$2x$; $\overline{AC} \cong \overline{DC}$ by CPCTC, so $AD = 2x$ and $\overline{AB} \cong \overline{AD}$.

D In the space below, show how to use the Pythagorean Theorem to find the length of $\overline{BC}$.

$(2x)^2 = BC^2 + x^2$

$4x^2 = BC^2 + x^2$

$3x^2 = BC^2$

$\sqrt{3}x = BC$

REFLECT

2a. What is the ratio of the side lengths in a right triangle with acute angles that measure 30° and 60°?

$1 : \sqrt{3} : 2$

2b. **Error Analysis** A student drew a right triangle with a 60° angle and a hypotenuse of length 10. Then he labeled the other side lengths as shown. Explain how you can tell just by glancing at the side lengths that the student made an error. Then explain the error.

Since $10\sqrt{3} > 10$, the leg $\overline{LK}$ is longer than the hypotenuse,

which is not possible. The length of $\overline{LK}$ should be $5\sqrt{3}$.

MATHEMATICAL PRACTICE
Highlighting the Standards

You can address Standard 7 (Look for and make use of structure) as you teach this lesson. Emphasize to students that some geometric figures have inherent properties or relationships that are useful in solving problems. For example, in order to find the height x of a 6-foot skateboard ramp that makes a 30° angle with the ground, students could set up and solve the equation $\sin 30° = \frac{x}{6}$. However, recognizing the 30°-60°-90° triangle in this problem means that a quicker solution is available. That is, the length of the shorter leg of a 30°-60°-90° triangle is half the length of the hypotenuse, so the height is 3 feet.

3 EXPLORE

Questioning Strategies

- How do you use the triangles to find sin 30°? **Look at the 30°-60°-90° triangle and find the ratio of the length of the leg opposite the 30° angle to the length of the hypotenuse; the ratio is $\frac{1}{2}$.**

- Why does it make sense that tan 45° = 1? **The tangent is the ratio of the length of the leg opposite the 45° angle to the length of the leg adjacent to the 45° angle. Since both legs have the same length, this ratio must be 1.**

CLOSE

Essential Question

What can you say about the side lengths and the trigonometric ratios associated with special right triangles?

The sides of a 45°-45°-90° triangle are in the ratio 1:1: $\sqrt{2}$. The sides of a 30°-60°-90° triangle are in the ratio 1: $\sqrt{3}$:2. The related trigonometric ratios are as shown below.

Angle	Sine	Cosine	Tangent
30°	$\frac{1}{2}$	$\frac{\sqrt{3}}{2}$	$\frac{\sqrt{3}}{3}$
45°	$\frac{\sqrt{2}}{2}$	$\frac{\sqrt{2}}{2}$	1
60°	$\frac{\sqrt{3}}{2}$	$\frac{1}{2}$	$\sqrt{3}$

Summarize

Have students write a journal entry in which they summarize what they know about special right triangles. Remind them to include a chart, such as the one above, that summarizes trigonometric ratios for the relevant angles.

PRACTICE

Where skills are taught	Where skills are practiced
1 EXPLORE	EXS. 1–3, 8
2 EXPLORE	EXS. 4–7, 9
3 EXPLORE	EX. 10

The right triangles you investigated are sometimes called 45°-45°-90° and 30°-60°-90° right triangles. The side-length relationships that you discovered are all you need to determine the exact values of the sine, cosine, and tangent of 30°, 45°, and 60°.

3 EXPLORE Determining Trigonometric Ratios

A Use your previous work to fill in the missing side lengths.

B Use the above triangles to help you complete the chart. Write each trigonometric ratio as a simplified fraction.

Angle	Sine	Cosine	Tangent
30°	$\frac{1}{2}$	$\frac{\sqrt{3}}{2}$	$\frac{\sqrt{3}}{3}$
45°	$\frac{\sqrt{2}}{2}$	$\frac{\sqrt{2}}{2}$	1
60°	$\frac{\sqrt{3}}{2}$	$\frac{1}{2}$	$\sqrt{3}$

REFLECT

3a. What patterns or relationships do you see in the sine and cosine columns? Why do these patterns or relationships make sense?

sin 30° = cos 60°, sin 60° = cos 30°, and sin 45° = cos 45°; these

relationships make sense because the sine of an angle equals the

cosine of its complement.

3b. For which angles is the tangent ratio less than 1? equal to 1? greater than 1?

The tangent is less than 1 for angle measures less than 45°,

equal to 1 for 45°, and greater than 1 for acute angle measures

greater than 45°.

PRACTICE

Find the value of *x*. Give your answer in simplest radical form.

1.

$3\sqrt{2}$

2.

$7\sqrt{2}$

3.

2

4.

$\frac{1}{2}$

5.

$5\sqrt{3}$

6.

$6\sqrt{3}$

7.

14

8.

$\frac{15}{2}\sqrt{2}$

9.

12

10. Error Analysis Two students were asked to find the value of *x* in the figure at right. Which student's work is correct? Explain the other student's error.

Roberto's Work	Aaron's Work
sin 60° = $\frac{\sqrt{3}}{2}$, but from the figure, sin 60° = $\frac{x}{8}$, so $\frac{\sqrt{3}}{2} = \frac{x}{8}$. Multiplying both sides by 8 gives $8 \cdot \frac{\sqrt{3}}{2} = x$, so $x = 4\sqrt{3}$.	In a 30°-60°-90° triangle, the side lengths are in a ratio of 1: $\sqrt{3}$:2, so *x* must be $\sqrt{3}$ times the length of $\overline{AB}$. Therefore, $x = 8\sqrt{3}$.

Roberto's work is correct. Aaron had the correct ratios for the

side lengths, but applied them incorrectly to the given triangle. AC = 8, so

BC = 4 and AC = $\sqrt{3} \cdot BC = 4\sqrt{3}$.

Solving Right Triangles

Essential question: *How do you find an unknown angle measure in a right triangle?*

COMMON Standards for
CORE Mathematical Content

CC.9-12.G.SRT.8 Use trigonometric ratios and the Pythagorean Theorem to solve right triangles in applied problems.

Vocabulary

inverse trigonometric ratio

Prerequisites

Translations (material on vectors), Lesson 2-5

The Tangent Ratio, Lesson 6-1

The Sine and Cosine Ratios, Lesson 6-2

Math Background

Solving a right triangle means finding the measures of all its angles and finding the lengths of all its sides. It is possible to solve a right triangle if you know two side lengths. In this case, you can use the Pythagorean Theorem to find the remaining side length. Then you can use an inverse trigonometric ratio to find the measure of one acute angle. The fact that the acute angles of a right triangle are complementary makes it possible to find the remaining angle measure. It is also possible to solve a right triangle if you know one side length and an acute angle measure. In this case, you can use trigonometric ratios to find the other side lengths and use the fact that the acute angles of a right triangle are complementary to find the remaining angle measure.

INTRODUCE

Begin by introducing the idea of an inverse trigonometric ratio. You may wish to point out to students that they have already worked with inverses when they learned about squares and square roots. For example, if you know that the square of 8 and -8 is 64, then you can say that the "inverse square" (or square root) of 64 is 8 or -8. In a similar way, inverse trigonometric ratios let you find an angle measure if you know the value of the angle's sine, cosine, or tangent.

TEACH

1 EXAMPLE

Questioning Strategies

- Is it possible to find m∠K before finding m∠J? If so, how? yes; m∠K = $\tan^{-1}\left(\frac{35}{12}\right)$.

EXTRA EXAMPLE

Find m∠A. Round to the nearest degree.

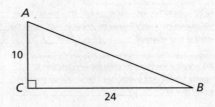

67°

Avoid Common Errors

Be sure students understand that the "-1" in the expression $\tan^{-1}\left(\frac{12}{35}\right)$ represents an inverse function. It does *not* represent the reciprocal $\frac{1}{\tan\left(\frac{12}{35}\right)}$. It should generally be clear from context whether the "-1" is an inverse function or a negative exponent.

2 EXAMPLE

Questioning Strategies

- What side lengths and angles do you need to find? *BC*, m∠A, and m∠B

- Can you find these in any order? Explain. **Yes; you can use an inverse trigonometric ratio to first find either angle measure and then find the other using the fact that the acute angles of a right triangle are complementary. You can find *BC* at any point by using the Pythagorean Theorem.**

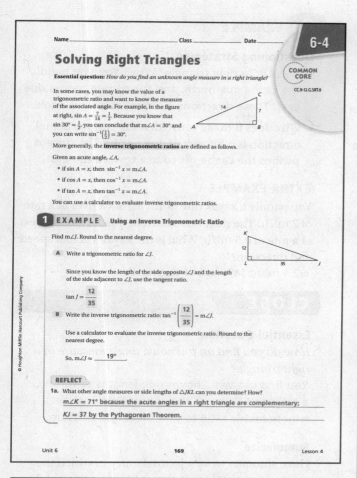

Name_____ Class_____ Date_____

Solving Right Triangles

6-4

COMMON CORE

CC.9-12.G.SRT.8

Essential question: *How do you find an unknown angle measure in a right triangle?*

In some cases, you may know the value of a
trigonometric ratio and want to know the measure
of the associated angle. For example, in the figure
at right, $\sin A = \frac{7}{14} = \frac{1}{2}$. Because you know that
$\sin 30° = \frac{1}{2}$, you can conclude that $m\angle A = 30°$ and
you can write $\sin^{-1}\left(\frac{1}{2}\right) = 30°$.

More generally, the **inverse trigonometric ratios** are defined as follows.

Given an acute angle, $\angle A$,

* if $\sin A = x$, then $\sin^{-1} x = m\angle A$.
* if $\cos A = x$, then $\cos^{-1} x = m\angle A$.
* if $\tan A = x$, then $\tan^{-1} x = m\angle A$.

You can use a calculator to evaluate inverse trigonometric ratios.

1 EXAMPLE Using an Inverse Trigonometric Ratio

Find $m\angle J$. Round to the nearest degree.

A Write a trigonometric ratio for $\angle J$.

Since you know the length of the side opposite $\angle J$ and the length
of the side adjacent to $\angle J$, use the tangent ratio.

$$\tan J = \frac{12}{35}$$

B Write the inverse trigonometric ratio: $\tan^{-1}\left(\frac{12}{35}\right) = m\angle J$.

Use a calculator to evaluate the inverse trigonometric ratio. Round to the
nearest degree.

So, $m\angle J \approx \underline{\quad 19° \quad}$.

REFLECT

1a. What other angle measures or side lengths of $\triangle JKL$ can you determine? How?

$m\angle K = 71°$ because the acute angles in a right triangle are complementary;

$KJ = 37$ by the Pythagorean Theorem.

© Houghton Mifflin Harcourt Publishing Company

Unit 6   169   Lesson 4

Solving a right triangle means finding the lengths of all its sides and the measures of all its
angles. To solve a right triangle you need to know two side lengths or one side length and
an acute angle measure.

2 EXAMPLE Solving a Right Triangle

A shelf extends perpendicularly 24 cm from a wall. You want to
place a 28-cm brace under the shelf, as shown. To the nearest tenth
of a centimeter, how far below the shelf will the brace be attached to
the wall? To the nearest degree, what angle will the brace make with
the shelf and with the wall?

A Use the Pythagorean Theorem to find the distance BC.

$BC^2 + AC^2 = AB^2$ Pythagorean Theorem

$BC^2 + \underline{24}^2 = \underline{28}^2$ Substitute.

$BC^2 + \underline{576} = \underline{784}$ Find the squares.

$BC^2 = \underline{208}$ Subtract the same quantity from both sides.

$BC \approx \underline{14.4 \text{ cm}}$ Find the square root and round.

B Use an inverse trigonometric ratio to find $m\angle A$.

$\cos A = \dfrac{24}{28}$, so $\cos^{-1}\left(\dfrac{24}{28}\right) = m\angle A$

Use a calculator to evaluate the inverse trigonometric ratio. Round to the
nearest degree.

So, $m\angle A \approx \underline{\quad 31° \quad}$.

C Use the fact that the acute angles of a right triangle are complementary to find $m\angle B$.

So, $m\angle B \approx \underline{\quad 59° \quad}$.

REFLECT

2a. Is it possible to find $m\angle B$ before you find $m\angle A$? If so, how?

Yes; use the inverse sine ratio; $\sin B = \frac{24}{28}$, and $\sin^{-1}\left(\frac{24}{28}\right) \approx 59°$.

© Houghton Mifflin Harcourt Publishing Company

Unit 6   170   Lesson 4

Notes

EXTRA EXAMPLE

Rasheed is building a shelf that folds down from the wall. When it is lowered, the shelf will extend 14 inches from the wall and will be supported by a 17-inch-long chain. To the nearest tenth of an inch, how far above the shelf should the chain be attached to the wall? To the nearest degree, what angle will the chain make with the shelf and the wall when the shelf is folded down?

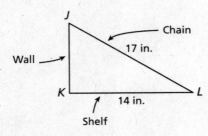

9.6 in.; 35°; 55°

3 EXAMPLE

Questioning Strategies

- Is $\triangle ABC$ a right triangle? Why? **Yes; you paddle the canoe due north, and the current moves due east. These directions intersect at a right angle.**

- Why does it make sense that the canoe's actual direction is a bit east of due north? **The current pushes the canoe off course toward the east.**

EXTRA EXAMPLE

You paddle a kayak due north across a river at a rate of 2 mi/h. The river has a current that flows due west at a rate of 0.5 mi/h. What is the kayak's actual speed and direction?
≈2.1 mi/h; 14° west of due north

CLOSE

Essential Question

How do you find an unknown angle measure in a right triangle?
You first use two known side lengths to form a ratio and then use the appropriate inverse trigonometric ratio to find the angle measure.

Summarize

Have students write a journal entry in which they create an example that shows how to solve a right triangle. Students should specify the known side lengths or angle measures and explain how to find the unknown side lengths and angle measures.

PRACTICE

Where skills are taught	Where skills are practiced
1 EXAMPLE	EXS. 1–6
2 EXAMPLE	EXS. 7–8
3 EXAMPLE	EX. 9

Exercise 10: Students critique the work of another student.

You learned about vectors in Lesson 2-5. As you will see, vectors are useful for modeling real-world situations. To do so, it is helpful to know how to add vectors.

To add two vectors, $\vec{u}$ and $\vec{v}$, place the initial point of $\vec{v}$ on the terminal point of $\vec{u}$. The *resultant* is the vector that joins the initial point of $\vec{u}$ with the terminal point of $\vec{v}$.

3 EXAMPLE   Modeling a Situation with Vectors

You paddle a canoe due north across a river at a rate of 3 mi/h. The river has a 1 mi/h current that flows due east. What is your canoe's actual speed and direction?

A   Model the situation with vectors. Use vectors to represent the motion of the canoe ($\overline{AB}$) and the current ($\overline{BC}$). The magnitude of vectors represents the speeds. The resultant ($\overline{AC}$) represents the actual speed and direction of the canoe.

B   Use the Pythagorean Theorem to find the magnitude of $\overline{AC}$.

$AC^2 = \underline{3}^2 + \underline{1}^2$ Pythagorean Theorem

$AC^2 = \underline{10}$ Square the terms and add.

$AC \approx \underline{3.2}$ Take the square root of both sides. Round to the nearest tenth.

So, the actual speed of the canoe is about $\underline{3.2}$ mi/h

C   Use an inverse trigonometric ratio to find m∠A.

$\tan A = \dfrac{1}{3}$, so $\tan^{-1}\left(\dfrac{1}{3}\right) = m\angle A$

Use a calculator to evaluate the inverse trigonometric ratio. Round to the nearest degree.

$m\angle A \approx \underline{18°}$

So, the canoe's actual direction is about $\underline{18°}$ east of due north.

REFLECT

3a.   Why does it make sense that the canoe's actual speed is greater than both the speed at which you paddle and the speed of the current?

The speed is represented by the hypotenuse of a right triangle, which must

be longer than either of the legs.

PRACTICE

Find m∠A. Round to the nearest degree.

1.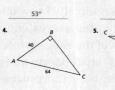

   $53°$

2.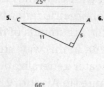

   $25°$

3.

   $37°$

4.
   $51°$

5.
   $66°$

6.
   $43°$

7. A ladder leans against a wall and reaches a point 15 feet up the wall. The base of the ladder is 3.9 feet from the wall. To the nearest tenth of a foot, what is the length of the ladder? To the nearest degree, what angle does the ladder make with the wall and with the ground?

   Length of ladder: 15.5 ft; angle with wall: 15°; angle with ground: 75°

8. A 7.2-meter guy wire goes from the top of a utility pole to a point on the ground that is 3 meters from the base of the pole. To the nearest tenth of a meter, how tall is the utility pole? To the nearest degree, what angle does the guy wire make with the pole and with the ground?

   Height of pole: 6.5 m; angle with pole: 25°; angle with ground: 65°

9. A plane flies due north at 500 mi/h. There is a crosswind blowing due east at 60 mi/h. What is the plane's actual speed to the nearest tenth? What is the plane's actual direction to the nearest degree?

   Actual speed: 503.6 mi/h; actual direction: 7° east of due north

10. **Error Analysis**   A student found m∠P as shown. Critique the student's work.

    This method does not work,

    because the triangle is not a right

    triangle.

    $\sin P = \dfrac{18}{25}$, so

    $m\angle P = \sin^{-1}\left(\dfrac{18}{25}\right) \approx 46°$

© Houghton Mifflin Harcourt Publishing Company

Trigonometric Ratios of Obtuse Angles

Essential question: How can you use the sine ratio to find a formula for the area of a triangle?

COMMON Standards for
CORE Mathematical Content

CC.9-12.G.SRT.9(+) Derive the formula $A = \frac{1}{2} ab \sin(C)$ for the area of a triangle by drawing an auxiliary line from a vertex perpendicular to the opposite side.

Prerequisites

The Tangent Ratio, Lesson 6-1

The Sine and Cosine Ratios, Lesson 6-2

Math Background

The ultimate goal of this lesson is to develop and apply the formula $A = \frac{1}{2} ab \sin C$ for the area of a triangle. In the formula, a and b are two side lengths, and $\angle C$ is the included angle. Because the formula works for any triangle, $\angle C$ may be acute, right, or obtuse. Therefore, it is necessary to extend our definitions of the trigonometric ratios to include all angle measures between 0° and 180°. In Algebra 2, students will learn how to define trigonometric ratios for *any* angle measure by using the unit circle. In this lesson, the approach will be similar, but it will be restricted to angles whose terminal side lies in quadrants I and II.

INTRODUCE

Remind students that so far in this unit they have worked exclusively with right triangles. Explain that the remaining lessons of the unit deal with general triangles. However, to use trigonometric ratios with general triangles, it is first necessary to extend the definition of the sine, cosine, and tangent ratios to all angle measures between 0° and 180°.

TEACH

1 EXPLORE

Questioning Strategies

- In Step A, suppose $m\angle A = 45°$. Do the formulas for sin A, cos A, and tan A give the expected values? Explain. **Yes; In this case, $x = y = 1$, and the formulas give $\sin A = \frac{1}{\sqrt{2}}$, $\cos A = \frac{1}{\sqrt{2}}$, and tan A = 1, all of which are correct.**

- For angles whose measure is greater than 90° but less than 180°, why are the cosine and tangent negative? **For these angles, x is negative in the formulas for cosine and tangent. This makes the value of the cosine and tangent negative.**

MATHEMATICAL PRACTICE

Highlighting the Standards

This lesson addresses Standard 8 (Look for and express regularity in repeated reasoning). As students extend the definitions of the sine, cosine, and tangent ratios, they use reasoning to develop formulas that are not only consistent with what they already know about these trigonometric ratios but also extend the possible arguments of the sine, cosine, and tangent. In this way, students are moving toward greater generalization. This process will continue (in Algebra 2) when students learn how to turn the trigonometric ratios into full-fledged trigonometric functions.

Teaching Strategies

It is convenient for students to know the sine, cosine, and tangent of 90°. In the figure on the student page that accompanies Step C, the coordinates of point B may be taken to be $(0, 1)$ when $\angle A$ is a right angle. Using the formulas for the trigonometric ratios with $x = 0$ and $y = 1$ shows that sin 90° = 1, cos 90° = 0, and tan 90° is undefined, since division by 0 is undefined.

Name_____ Class_____ Date_____

Trigonometric Ratios of Obtuse Angles

COMMON CORE
CC.9-12.G.SRT.9(+)

Essential question: *How can you use the sine ratio to the find a formula for the area of a triangle?*

So far, you have used trigonometric ratios with acute angles in right triangles. You can also use trigonometric ratios with the angles in non-right triangles, but you will first need to extend the definitions of the trigonometric ratios as shown below.

1 EXPLORE   Extending the Trigonometric Ratios

A First, extend the trigonometric ratios to right triangles on a coordinate plane.

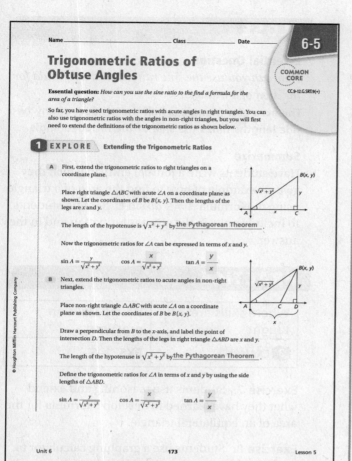

Place right triangle $\triangle ABC$ with acute $\angle A$ on a coordinate plane as shown. Let the coordinates of B be $B(x, y)$. Then the lengths of the legs are x and y.

The length of the hypotenuse is $\sqrt{x^2 + y^2}$ by the Pythagorean Theorem.

Now the trigonometric ratios for $\angle A$ can be expressed in terms of x and y.

$$\sin A = \frac{y}{\sqrt{x^2 + y^2}} \qquad \cos A = \frac{x}{\sqrt{x^2 + y^2}} \qquad \tan A = \frac{y}{x}$$

B Next, extend the trigonometric ratios to acute angles in non-right triangles.

Place non-right triangle $\triangle ABC$ with acute $\angle A$ on a coordinate plane as shown. Let the coordinates of B be $B(x, y)$.

Draw a perpendicular from B to the x-axis, and label the point of intersection D. Then the lengths of the legs in right triangle $\triangle ABD$ are x and y.

The length of the hypotenuse is $\sqrt{x^2 + y^2}$ by the Pythagorean Theorem.

Define the trigonometric ratios for $\angle A$ in terms of x and y by using the side lengths of $\triangle ABD$.

$$\sin A = \frac{y}{\sqrt{x^2 + y^2}} \qquad \cos A = \frac{x}{\sqrt{x^2 + y^2}} \qquad \tan A = \frac{y}{x}$$

C Finally, extend the trigonometric ratios to obtuse angles in non-right triangles.

Place non-right triangle $\triangle ABC$ with obtuse $\angle A$ on a coordinate plane as shown. Let the coordinates of B be $B(x, y)$.

Draw a perpendicular from B to the x-axis, and label the point of intersection D. Then let the "lengths" of the legs in right triangle $\triangle ABD$ be x and y, where it is understood that $x < 0$.

The length of the hypotenuse, $\overline{AB}$, is _____$\sqrt{x^2 + y^2}$_____ .

Define the trigonometric ratios for $\angle A$ in terms of x and y by using the sides of $\triangle ABD$.

$$\sin A = \frac{y}{\sqrt{x^2 + y^2}} \qquad \cos A = \frac{x}{\sqrt{x^2 + y^2}} \qquad \tan A = \frac{y}{x}$$

D You can use a calculator to find trigonometric ratios for obtuse angles. Use a calculator to complete the table below. Round to the nearest hundredth.

Angle	Sine	Cosine	Tangent
97°	0.99	−0.12	−8.14
122°	0.85	−0.53	−1.60
165°	0.26	−0.97	−0.27

REFLECT

1a. Look for patterns in your table. Make a conjecture about the trigonometric ratios of obtuse angles.

For an obtuse angle, the sine is positive; the cosine and tangent are negative.

1b. Suppose $\angle A$ is obtuse. How do the definitions of the sine, cosine, and tangent for obtuse angles in Part C above explain why some of these trigonometric ratios are positive and some are negative?

In the definitions, $x < 0$, $y > 0$, and $\sqrt{x^2 + y^2} > 0$, so $\sin A = \frac{y}{\sqrt{x^2 + y^2}} > 0$,

but $\cos A = \frac{x}{\sqrt{x^2 + y^2}} < 0$ and $\tan A = \frac{y}{x} < 0$.

Questioning Strategies
- What formula do you already know for the area of a triangle? $A = \frac{1}{2}bh$

- What do the variables stand for in this formula? *b* is the length of the triangle's base; *h* is the triangle's height.

3 **EXAMPLE**

Questioning Strategies
- What units will you use for your answer? How do you know? **Square centimeters; the lengths are given in centimeters, so the area should be expressed in square centimeters.**

- Suppose you are told that sin 114° is close to 1. How can you use this information to estimate the triangle's area? **In this case, the area is approximately $\frac{1}{2} \cdot 13 \cdot 11 \cdot 1 = 71.5$ cm².**

EXTRA EXAMPLE
Find the area of the triangle to the nearest tenth.

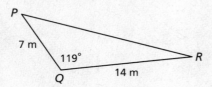

42.9 m²

CLOSE

Essential Question
How can you use the sine ratio to find a formula for the area of a triangle?
The area of a triangle is half the product of any two side lengths times the sine of the included angle.

Summarize
Have students write a journal entry in which they give an example of how to find the area of a triangle using the formula $A = \frac{1}{2}ab \sin C$. Remind students to include units in the given information and in the answer.

PRACTICE

Where skills are taught	Where skills are practiced
3 EXAMPLE	EXS. 1–6

Exercise 7: Students use reasoning and extend what they have learned to develop a formula for the area of an equilateral triangle.

Exercise 8: Students use a graphing calculator to explore a function that gives the area of an isosceles triangle for different measures of the vertex angle. Students make a conjecture about the vertex angle that results in the greatest area.

Now you can derive a formula for the area of a triangle that works for any triangle as long as you know two side lengths and the measure of the included angle.

2 EXPLORE   Deriving an Area Formula

A   Let △ABC be a triangle with side lengths a, b, and c, as shown.

Draw an altitude from A to side $\overline{BC}$. Let h be the length of the altitude.

Then $\sin C = \dfrac{h}{b}$.

Solving for h shows that h = <u>b sin C</u>.

B   The standard formula for the area of a triangle is Area = $\frac{1}{2}$ (base)(height).

In △ABC, the length of the base is <u>a</u> and the height is <u>h</u>.

Area = <u>$\frac{1}{2}ah$</u>

Now substitute the expression for h from Part A.

Area = <u>$\frac{1}{2}ab \sin C$</u>

REFLECT

2a. How can you state in words the formula you derived above?

<u>The area of a triangle is half the product of any two side lengths times the</u>
<u>sine of the included angle.</u>

2b. Does the area formula work if angle C is a right angle? Explain.

<u>Yes; if angle C is a right angle, then sin C = sin 90° = 1, and the area formula</u>
<u>simplifies to $\frac{1}{2}$ ab, as expected.</u>

3 EXAMPLE   Using the Area Formula

Find the area of the triangle at right to the nearest tenth.

Let the known side lengths be a and b.

Then a = <u>13</u> and b = <u>11</u>.

Let the known angle be C, so m∠C = <u>114°</u>.

Then Area = $\frac{1}{2}$ ab sin C = $\frac{1}{2}$<u>13</u> • <u>11</u> • sin(<u>114°</u>).

Use a calculator to evaluate the expression. Then round.

So, the area of the triangle is <u>65.3 cm²</u>.

REFLECT

3a. Suppose you double each of the given side lengths in the triangle but keep the measure of the included angle the same. How does the area change? Explain.

<u>The area is multiplied by 4, because $\frac{1}{2}$(2 • 13)(2 • 11) sin 114° =</u>
<u>(2 • 2) $\frac{1}{2}$(13)(11) sin 114°.</u>

PRACTICE

Find the area of each triangle to the nearest tenth.

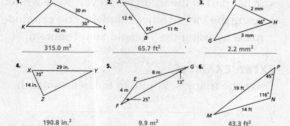

1. <u>315.0 m²</u>

2. <u>65.7 ft²</u>

3. <u>2.2 mm²</u>

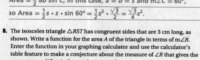

4. <u>190.8 in.²</u>

5. <u>9.9 m²</u>

6. <u>43.3 ft²</u>

7. Explain how you can derive a formula for the area of an equilateral triangle with side length s. (*Hint:* Use the area formula from this lesson and what you know about the angle measures of an equilateral triangle.)

<u>Area = $\frac{1}{2}$ ab sin C; in this case, a = b = s and m∠C = 60°,</u>
<u>so Area = $\frac{1}{2}$ s • s • sin 60° = $\frac{1}{2}$ s² • $\frac{\sqrt{3}}{2}$ = $\frac{\sqrt{3}}{4}$ s².</u>

8. The isosceles triangle △RST has congruent sides that are 3 cm long, as shown. Write a function for the area A of the triangle in terms of m∠R. Enter the function in your graphing calculator and use the calculator's table feature to make a conjecture about the measure of ∠R that gives the greatest area. What is the maximum area?

<u>A = $\frac{9}{2}$ sin R; the maximum area occurs when m∠R = 90°,</u>
<u>and the maximum area is 4.5 cm².</u>

The Law of Sines

Essential question: What is the Law of Sines and how do you use it to solve problems?

COMMON CORE Standards for Mathematical Content

CC.9-12.G.SRT.10(+) Prove the Law of Sines ... and use [it] to solve problems.

CC.9-12.G.SRT.11(+) Understand and apply the Law of Sines ... to find unknown measurements in right and non-right triangles (e.g., surveying problems, resultant forces).

Prerequisites

Trigonometric Ratios of Obtuse Angles, Lesson 6-5

Math Background

In Unit 3, students learned various conditions that determine a unique triangle. For example, if you know the measure of two angles and the length of the included side (ASA), then the triangle is uniquely determined. That is, all triangles that satisfy these conditions will be congruent. This means it should be possible to calculate the remaining angle measure and the remaining side lengths. As students will learn in this lesson and the next, the Law of Sines and the Law of Cosines make it possible to solve triangles when you are given three pieces of information that determine a unique triangle.

INTRODUCE

Draw the following triangle on the board.

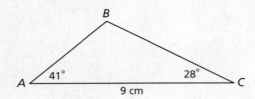

Ask students whether all triangles with these angle measures and included side length are congruent, and why. **Yes; ASA Congruence Criterion**

Explain that the goal of this lesson is to find a way to determine the remaining side lengths and angle measure.

TEACH

1 PROOF

Questioning Strategies

- In Step A of the proof, how do you solve the two equations for h? **Multiply both sides of $\sin A = \frac{h}{b}$ by b. Multiply both sides of $\sin B = \frac{h}{a}$ by a.**

- How can you state the Law of Sines in your own words? **Possible answer: The ratio of the sine of an angle to the length of the opposite side is constant for all three angles of a triangle.**

Differentiated Instruction

Some students may find it easier to understand the following proof of the Law of Sines. By the area formula from Lesson 6-5, the area of the triangle is $\frac{1}{2} ab \sin C = \frac{1}{2} ac \sin B = \frac{1}{2} bc \sin A$. Dividing through by $\frac{1}{2} abc$ shows that $\frac{\sin C}{c} = \frac{\sin B}{b} = \frac{\sin A}{a}$.

2 EXAMPLE

Questioning Strategies

- Does the Law of Sines apply to this problem? How do you know? **Yes; you are given ASA information, so you can use the Law of Sines to solve the triangle.**

- What part of the triangle can you solve without using the Law of Sines? Explain. **You can find $m\angle G$ by using the Triangle Sum Theorem.**

EXTRA EXAMPLE

Solve the triangle. Round to the nearest tenth.

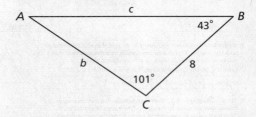

$m\angle A = 36°; b = 9.3; c = 13.4$

Name_____ Class_____ Date_____

The Law of Sines

Essential question: *What is the Law of Sines and how do you use it to solve problems?*

6-6

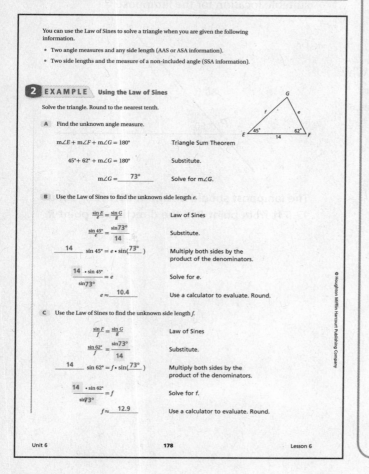

COMMON
CORE

CC.9-12.G.SRT.10(+),
CC.9-12.G.SRT.11(+)

You can use sines and cosines to solve problems that involve non-right triangles. One example is the Law of Sines, which is a relationship that holds for any triangle.

Law of Sines

For $\triangle ABC$, $\dfrac{\sin A}{a} = \dfrac{\sin B}{b} = \dfrac{\sin C}{c}$.

1 PROOF   The Law of Sines

Complete the proof.

Given: $\triangle ABC$
Prove: $\dfrac{\sin A}{a} = \dfrac{\sin B}{b} = \dfrac{\sin C}{c}$

A Draw an altitude from C to side $\overline{AB}$. Let h be the length of the altitude.

Then $\sin A = \dfrac{h}{b}$ and $\sin B = \dfrac{h}{a}$.

Solve the two equations for h.

$h = \underline{\quad b \sin A \quad}$ and $h = \underline{\quad a \sin B \quad}$

B Write a new equation by setting the right sides of the above equations equal to each other.

$\underline{\quad b \sin A \quad} = \underline{\quad a \sin B \quad}$ Substitute.

$\underline{\quad \dfrac{\sin A}{a} \quad} = \underline{\quad \dfrac{\sin B}{b} \quad}$ Divide both sides by ab.

Similar reasoning shows that $\dfrac{\sin A}{a} = \dfrac{\sin C}{c}$ and $\dfrac{\sin B}{b} = \dfrac{\sin C}{c}$.

REFLECT

1a. Write an alternate form of the Law of Sines in which the side lengths are the numerators of the ratios. Explain why it is valid to rewrite the Law of Sines in this way.

$\dfrac{a}{\sin A} = \dfrac{b}{\sin B} = \dfrac{c}{\sin C}$; this is valid because you can multiply both sides of the proportion $\dfrac{m}{n} = \dfrac{p}{q}$ by nq and then divide both sides by mp to show that $\dfrac{n}{m} = \dfrac{q}{p}$.

You can use the Law of Sines to solve a triangle when you are given the following information.

- Two angle measures and any side length (AAS or ASA information).
- Two side lengths and the measure of a non-included angle (SSA information).

2 EXAMPLE   Using the Law of Sines

Solve the triangle. Round to the nearest tenth.

A Find the unknown angle measure.

$m\angle E + m\angle F + m\angle G = 180°$ Triangle Sum Theorem

$45° + 62° + m\angle G = 180°$ Substitute.

$m\angle G = \underline{\quad 73° \quad}$ Solve for $m\angle G$.

B Use the Law of Sines to find the unknown side length e.

$\dfrac{\sin E}{e} = \dfrac{\sin G}{g}$ Law of Sines

$\dfrac{\sin 45°}{e} = \dfrac{\sin 73°}{14}$ Substitute.

$\underline{\quad 14 \quad} \sin 45° = e \cdot \sin(\underline{73°})$ Multiply both sides by the product of the denominators.

$\dfrac{14 \cdot \sin 45°}{\sin 73°} = e$ Solve for e.

$e \approx \underline{\quad 10.4 \quad}$ Use a calculator to evaluate. Round.

C Use the Law of Sines to find the unknown side length f.

$\dfrac{\sin F}{f} = \dfrac{\sin G}{g}$ Law of Sines

$\dfrac{\sin 62°}{f} = \dfrac{\sin 73°}{14}$ Substitute.

$\underline{\quad 14 \quad} \sin 62° = f \cdot \sin(\underline{73°})$ Multiply both sides by the product of the denominators.

$\dfrac{14 \cdot \sin 62°}{\sin 73°} = f$ Solve for f.

$f \approx \underline{\quad 12.9 \quad}$ Use a calculator to evaluate. Round.

© Houghton Mifflin Harcourt Publishing Company

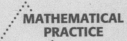

MATHEMATICAL PRACTICE — Highlighting the Standards

This lesson offers an ideal opportunity to address Standard 4 (Model with mathematics) as students solve problems using the Law of Sines. Part of the standard stresses that students "routinely interpret their mathematical results in the context of the situation and reflect on whether the results make sense." Students can hone these skills by solving the real-world problem in Example 4.

Avoid Common Errors

If students are getting incorrect results when they use the Law of Sines, have them check that their calculator is set to Degree Mode. To do so, press the MODE key and make sure that Degree (not Radian) is highlighted.

 3 EXPLORE

Materials: straightedge, protractor, compass

Questioning Strategies

* What type of triangle is formed when $a = 2$?
  30°-60°-90° triangle
* What type of triangle is formed when $a = 4$?
  isosceles triangle
* How many triangles are formed when $a = 3$? Why does this happen? Two; the compass makes an arc that intersects the side of $\angle A$ in two places.

4 EXAMPLE

Questioning Strategies

* Is SSA information given in this problem? Explain. Yes; you know an angle measure (40°), the length of an adjacent side (170 ft), and the length of the side opposite the known angle (120 ft).
* What are the main steps in solving the problem? Use the Law of Sines to find all possible values for m∠B. For each value, use the Triangle Sum Theorem to find m∠C. Then use the Law of Sines to find c.

Teaching Strategies

If students have difficulty getting started, point out there is only one possible first step. Given the information in the problem, m∠B must be found before m∠C or c can be determined.

EXTRA EXAMPLE

A city park has two straight paths that intersect at a 50° angle, as shown in the figure. There is a lamppost at points P, Q, and R. City planners want to put another lamppost in the park on path $\overleftrightarrow{PR}$ and they want the new lampost to be 70 feet from the one at point Q. What point or points along $\overleftrightarrow{PR}$ is a suitable location for the lamppost?

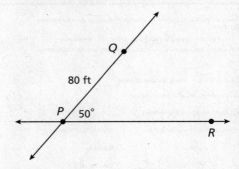

The lamppost should be about 85.3 ft or about 17.6 ft from point P in the direction of point R.

REFLECT

2a. In Part C, why is it better to write the Law of Sines as $\frac{\sin F}{f} = \frac{\sin G}{g}$ and use the known values of m∠G and g rather than write the Law of Sines as $\frac{\sin F}{f} = \frac{\sin E}{e}$ and use the known value of m∠E and the calculated value of e?

It is better to use the values of g and m∠G since these are known exactly.

The calculated value of e is an approximation, so it would lead to a value

of f that is less accurate.

The Law of Sines may be used to solve a triangle when you are given SSA information. However, you have seen that there is no SSA Congruence Criterion. Therefore, this type of given information may not lead to a unique triangle. This is known as the *ambiguous case* of the Law of Sines.

3 EXPLORE Investigating the Ambiguous Case

You will investigate triangles for which you are given SSA information. In particular, you will be given m∠A and the side lengths a and b. You will then determine how many triangles, if any, may be formed.

A Use a straightedge and protractor to draw ∠A such that m∠A = 30°.

B Use a ruler to mark a point C on one side of the angle so that b = 4 cm.

C Now open your compass to a length a that is given in the table below. Place the point of the compass at point C and draw an arc that intersects the other side of ∠A. The point or points of intersection are possible locations for vertex B.

For example, when a = 1, there are no points of intersection, so no triangle is formed.

Repeat Step C for each given value of a and complete the table.

Length a (cm)	1	2	2.5	3	3.5	4	5
Number of Triangles Formed	0	1	2	2	2	1	1

REFLECT

3a. Compare your work with that of other students. Then make a conjecture: For what values of a are no triangles formed? For what values of a is exactly one triangle formed? For what values of a are two triangles formed?

No triangle is formed when a < 2. Exactly one triangle is formed when

a = 2 or when a ≥ 4. Two triangles are formed when 2 < a < 4.

When you are given SSA information and the side opposite the angle whose measure is known is shorter than the other known side, it may sometimes be possible to form two triangles. The following example illustrates this.

4 EXAMPLE Solving a Real-World Problem

Police want to set up a camera to identify drivers who run the red light at point C on Mason Street. The camera must be mounted on a fence that intersects Mason Street at a 40° angle, as shown, and the camera should ideally be 120 feet from point C. What points along the fence, if any, are suitable locations for the camera?

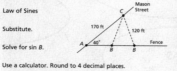

A Because the side opposite ∠A is shorter than $\overline{AC}$, it may be possible to form two triangles. Use the Law of Sines to find possible values for m∠B.

$\frac{\sin A}{a} = \frac{\sin B}{b}$ Law of Sines

$\frac{\sin 40°}{120} = \frac{\sin B}{170}$ Substitute.

$\frac{170 \sin 40°}{120} = \sin B$ Solve for sin B.

$0.9106 \approx \sin B$ Use a calculator. Round to 4 decimal places.

There is an acute angle and an obtuse angle that have this value as their sine. To find the acute angle, use a calculator and round to the nearest tenth.

$\sin^{-1}(0.9106) \approx 65.6°$

To find the obtuse angle, note that ∠1 and ∠2 have the same sine, $\frac{y}{\sqrt{x^2+y^2}}$, and notice that these angles are supplementary. Thus, the obtuse angle is supplementary to the acute angle you found above.

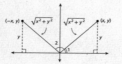

So, m∠B ≈ 65.6° or 114.4°.

MATHEMATICAL PRACTICE — Highlighting the Standards

Standard 1 (Make sense of problems and persevere in solving them) includes the idea of planning a "solution pathway." You may want to encourage students to plan a solution pathway before they tackle Exercises 7 and 8. To do so, students should outline the steps they will use to solve the problem. (These can be based on the steps in Example 4). As students move through the solution process, they can check off the steps as they complete them. This will help students stay on track and maintain oversight of the solution process.

Where skills are taught	Where skills are practiced
2 EXAMPLE	EXS. 1–6
4 EXAMPLE	EXS. 7–8

CLOSE

Essential Question

What is the Law of Sines and how do you use it to solve problems?

For $\triangle ABC$, the Law of Sines states that $\frac{\sin A}{a} = \frac{\sin B}{b} = \frac{\sin C}{c}$. You use the Law of Sines to solve a triangle when you know ASA, AAS, or SSA information.

Summarize

Have students make a graphic organizer to summarize the Law of Sines and to show when it may be used to solve a triangle. A sample is shown below.

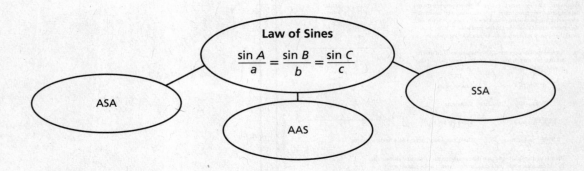

B For each possible measure of ∠B, find the corresponding measure of ∠C and then find c.

Case 1: ∠B is acute.

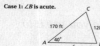

m∠A + m∠B + m∠C = 180°

40° + __65.6°__ + m∠C = 180°

So, m∠C = __74.4°__ .

Use the Law of Sines to find c.

$\frac{\sin A}{a} = \frac{\sin C}{c}$

$\frac{\sin 40°}{120} = \frac{\sin 74.4°}{c}$

$c = \frac{120 \sin 74.4°}{\sin 40°} \approx$ __179.8 ft__

Case 2: ∠B is obtuse.

m∠A + m∠B + m∠C = 180°

40° + __114.4°__ + m∠C = 180°

So, m∠C = __25.6°__ .

Use the Law of Sines to find c.

$\frac{\sin A}{a} = \frac{\sin C}{c}$

$\frac{\sin 40°}{120} = \frac{\sin 25.6°}{c}$

$c = \frac{120 \sin 25.6°}{\sin 40°} \approx$ __80.7 ft__

So, the camera should be mounted on the fence about __179.8__ ft or __80.7__ ft from point A.

REFLECT

4a. How you can check your answers?

Possible answer: Use the calculated values to check that $\frac{\sin A}{a} = \frac{\sin B}{b} = \frac{\sin C}{c}$.

4b. Suppose the camera needs to be *at most* 120 feet from point C. In this case, where should the camera be mounted along the fence?

The camera should be mounted more than 80.7 ft from point A but less

than 179.8 ft from point A.

4c. What is the minimum distance at which the camera can be located from point C if it is to be mounted on the fence? Explain your answer.

About 109.3 ft. The minimum distance occurs when ∠B is a right angle.

In this case, sin 40° = $\frac{CB}{170}$, so CB ≈ 109.3.

PRACTICE

Solve each triangle. Round to the nearest tenth.

1.

m∠B = 57°, a = 22.8,

c = 36.8

2.

m∠S = 72°, s = 18.1,

t = 17.8

3.

m∠M = 23°, m = 3.7,

p = 9.3

4.

m∠E = 28°, d = 22.6,

f = 30.6

5.

m∠M = 42°, k = 29.6,

m = 19.8

6.

m∠C = 124°, a = 2.1,

b = 3.5

7. A stone wall makes an angle of 51° with the side of a barn that is 12 m long. You want to make a goat pen by using 10 m of fencing to enclose a triangular region, as shown. At what distance from point C should the fencing be attached to the stone wall? Is there more than one possibility?

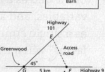

There are two possible locations: about 11.2 m from

point C or 3.9 m from point C.

8. Two straight highways intersect in the town of Greenwood, as shown. City planners want to build a straight access road from Fernville to Highway 101, and they want the access road to be no more than 4 miles long. Describe the possible locations at which the new access road could meet Highway 101. Where should it meet Highway 101 for the shortest possible access road?

The access road should intersect Highway 101 at a point that is between

approximately 1.7 km and 5.4 km from point G. For the shortest road, it should

intersect about 3.5 km from point G.

The Law of Cosines

Essential question: *What is the Law of Cosines and how do you use it to solve problems?*

COMMON CORE · Standards for Mathematical Content

CC.9-12.G.SRT.10(+) Prove the Law of ... Cosines and use [it] to solve problems.

CC.9-12.G.SRT.11(+) Understand and apply the ... Law of Cosines to find unknown measurements in right and non-right triangles (e.g., surveying problems, resultant forces).

Prerequisites

Trigonometric Ratios of Obtuse Angles, Lesson 6-5
The Law of Sines, Lesson 6-6

Math Background

In Lesson 6-6, students learned to use the Law of Sines to solve a triangle when given ASA, AAS, or SSA information about the triangle. When given SSS or SAS information, a different tool is needed in order to solve the triangle. In this lesson, students learn that the required tool is the Law of Cosines.

INTRODUCE

Draw the following triangle on the board. Ask students whether they can solve the triangle using the Law of Sines.

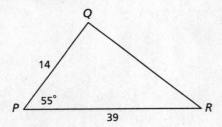

Give students a chance to use the Law of Sines. They will discover that it is not possible to solve the triangle in this way. Explain that students will learn a new technique for solving triangles in this lesson.

TEACH

1 PROOF

Questioning Strategies

- What type of triangle is $\triangle ADC$? **right triangle**
- What are the legs in $\triangle ADC$? What is the hypotenuse? **The legs are $\overline{CD}$ and $\overline{AD}$; the hypotenuse is $\overline{AC}$.**
- What type of triangle is $\triangle CDB$? **right triangle**
- What are the legs in $\triangle CDB$? What is the hypotenuse? **The legs are $\overline{CD}$ and $\overline{DB}$; the hypotenuse is $\overline{CB}$.**

MATHEMATICAL PRACTICE · **Highlighting the Standards**

You can address Standard 7 (Look for and make use of structure) while teaching students about the Law of Cosines. First have students compare the Law of Cosines to the Pythagorean Theorem. Students may notice that the Law of Cosines resembles the Pythagorean Theorem. In fact, the right side of the equation looks like the Pythagorean Theorem ($b^2 + c^2$) with a "correction factor" ($-2bc \cos A$). Furthermore, when $\angle A$ is a right angle, $\cos A = \cos 90° = 0$, and the Law of Cosines becomes the Pythagorean Theorem.

This discussion offers a perfect example of what the standard refers to as the ability to "see complicated things, such as some algebraic expressions, as single objects or as composed of several objects." That is, $-2bc \cos A$ may be viewed as a product of a number, two variables, and a cosine, or it may be viewed as a single entity that serves as a "correction factor" when $\angle A$ is not a right angle.

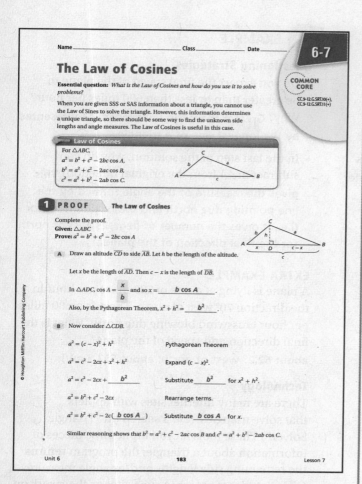

The Law of Cosines

6-7

COMMON CORE

CC.9-12.G.SRT.10(+),
CC.9-12.G.SRT.11(+)

Essential question: *What is the Law of Cosines and how do you use it to solve problems?*

When you are given SSS or SAS information about a triangle, you cannot use the Law of Sines to solve the triangle. However, this information determines a unique triangle, so there should be some way to find the unknown side lengths and angle measures. The Law of Cosines is useful in this case.

Law of Cosines

For $\triangle ABC$,

$a^2 = b^2 + c^2 - 2bc \cos A$,
$b^2 = a^2 + c^2 - 2ac \cos B$,
$c^2 = a^2 + b^2 - 2ab \cos C$.

1 PROOF The Law of Cosines

Complete the proof.

Given: $\triangle ABC$
Prove: $a^2 = b^2 + c^2 - 2bc \cos A$

A Draw an altitude $\overline{CD}$ to side $\overline{AB}$. Let h be the length of the altitude.

Let x be the length of $\overline{AD}$. Then $c - x$ is the length of $\overline{DB}$.

In $\triangle ADC$, $\cos A = \dfrac{x}{b}$ and so $x = \underline{\ b \cos A\ }$.

Also, by the Pythagorean Theorem, $x^2 + h^2 = \underline{\ b^2\ }$.

B Now consider $\triangle CDB$.

$a^2 = (c - x)^2 + h^2$	Pythagorean Theorem
$a^2 = c^2 - 2cx + x^2 + h^2$	Expand $(c - x)^2$.
$a^2 = c^2 - 2cx + \underline{\ b^2\ }$	Substitute $\underline{\ b^2\ }$ for $x^2 + h^2$.
$a^2 = b^2 + c^2 - 2cx$	Rearrange terms.
$a^2 = b^2 + c^2 - 2c(\underline{\ b \cos A\ })$	Substitute $\underline{\ b \cos A\ }$ for x.

Similar reasoning shows that $b^2 = a^2 + c^2 - 2ac \cos B$ and $c^2 = a^2 + b^2 - 2ab \cos C$.

REFLECT

1a. Explain why the Law of Cosines may be considered a generalization of the Pythagorean Theorem. (*Hint:* When $\angle A$ is a right angle, what happens to the formula $a^2 = b^2 + c^2 - 2bc \cos A$?)

When $\angle A$ is a right angle, $\cos A = \cos 90° = 0$, and the formula becomes

$a^2 = b^2 + c^2$, which is the Pythagorean Theorem.

2 EXAMPLE Using the Law of Cosines

Solve the triangle. Round to the nearest tenth.

A Find the measure of the obtuse angle first.

$b^2 = a^2 + c^2 - 2ac \cos B$	Law of Cosines
$18^2 = 10^2 + 13^2 - 2(10)(13)\cos B$	Substitute.
$\cos B = \dfrac{18^2 - 10^2 - 13^2}{-2(10)(13)}$	Solve for $\cos B$.
$\cos B \approx \underline{\ -0.2115\ }$	Simplify. Round to four decimal places.
$m\angle B \approx \cos^{-1}(\underline{\ -0.2115\ }) \approx \underline{\ 102.2°\ }$	Solve for $m\angle B$.

B Use the Law of Sines to find $m\angle C$.

$\dfrac{\sin C}{c} = \dfrac{\sin B}{b}$	Law of Sines
$\dfrac{\sin C}{13} = \dfrac{\sin 102.2°}{18}$	Substitute.
$\sin C = \dfrac{13 \sin 102.2°}{18} \approx \underline{\ 0.7059\ }$	Multiply both sides by 13, and then simplify.
$m\angle C \approx \sin^{-1}(\underline{\ 0.7059\ }) \approx \underline{\ 44.9°\ }$	Solve for $m\angle C$.

C Use the Triangle Sum Theorem to find the remaining angle measure.

$m\angle A \approx 180° - \underline{\ 102.2°\ } - \underline{\ 44.9°\ } = \underline{\ 32.9°\ }$

Notes

Questioning Strategies

• Given SSS information, how can you tell which angle of the triangle has the greatest measure? **The angle opposite the longest side has the greatest measure.**

• When you find that $\cos B \approx -0.2115$, what does this tell you about $\angle B$? **This means $m\angle B$ is greater than 90° and less than 180°.**

EXTRA EXAMPLE

Solve the triangle. Round to the nearest tenth.

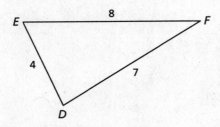

$m\angle D \approx 89.0°$; $m\angle E \approx 61.0°$; $m\angle F \approx 30.0°$

Differentiated Instruction

Some students may have difficulty solving the equation $18^2 = 10^2 + 13^2 - 2(10)(13)\cos B$ for $\cos B$. You might suggest that these students do some simplification before solving for $\cos B$. For example, evaluating the squared terms gives $324 = 100 + 169 - 2(10)(13)\cos B$, and a further round of simplifying gives an equation that looks even more manageable: $324 = 269 - 260\cos B$. Encourage students to continue in this way, as needed, until they are able to solve for $\cos B$.

Questioning Strategies

• Do you expect the final speed of the plane to be greater than or less than 600 miles per hour? Why? **Greater than; the final speed is represented by the longest side of a triangle.**

• In the last step of the solution, why do you subtract $m\angle A$ from the original direction? **This gives the measure of the angle formed by the line pointing due north and the resultant vector (i.e., it gives the number of degrees east of north for the final direction of the plane).**

EXTRA EXAMPLE

A plane is flying at a rate of 520 miles per hour in the direction 70° west of north. There is an 80 miles per hour crosswind blowing due north. What is the final direction and speed of the plane? **about 62.2° west of north; about 552.5 mi/h**

Technology

There are many Internet sites with applets that solve triangles. (Do a search on "Triangle Solver.") These tools let you input three pieces of information about a triangle; the program returns the remaining side lengths and/or angle measures. Giving students access to such sites as they work on problems involving the Law of Sines and the Law of Cosines can help boost their confidence if they use the sites *only* to check their work once they have gone through the steps to solve a problem.

REFLECT

2a. Why is it best to find the measure of the obtuse angle first and then find another angle measure using the Law of Sines?

There can be at most one obtuse angle in a triangle. By finding the measure of this angle first, you don't have to worry about the ambiguous case when using the Law of Sines.

2b. In Part B, is it possible to find m∠C without using the Law of Sines? Explain.

Yes; you can use the Law of Cosines again.

In the previous example, you were given SSS information about a triangle. In the following example about vectors, you will be given SAS information.

3 EXAMPLE   Solving a Vector Problem

A plane is flying at a rate of 600 mi/h in the direction 60° east of north. There is a 50 mi/h crosswind blowing due north. What is the final direction and speed of the plane?

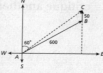

A   Represent the situation with vectors. The plane's velocity is represented by $\overrightarrow{AB}$ and the wind's velocity is represented by $\overrightarrow{BC}$.

Explain how to find m∠ABC.

m∠ABC = 120°; $\overrightarrow{CB}$ is parallel to the north-south line and same-side interior angles are supplementary; 180° − 60° = 120°.

B   Use the Law of Cosines to find b, the magnitude of $\overrightarrow{AC}$.

$b^2 = a^2 + c^2 - 2ac \cos ABC$ Law of Cosines

$b^2 = 50^2 + 600^2 - 2(50)(600) \cos 120°$ Substitute.

$b^2 = $ ___392,500___   Simplify.

$b \approx $ ___626.5___   Take the square root. Round to the nearest tenth.

C   Use the Law of Sines to find m∠A.

$\dfrac{\sin A}{a} = \dfrac{\sin B}{b}$ Law of Sines

$\dfrac{\sin BAC}{50} = \dfrac{\sin 120°}{626.5}$ Substitute.

$\sin A = \dfrac{50 \sin 120°}{626.5} \approx$ ___0.0691___   Multiply both sides by 50, and then simplify.

$m\angle A \approx \sin^{-1}($ ___0.0691___ $) \approx$ ___4.0°___   Solve for m∠A.

D   Subtract m∠A from the original direction of the plane to find its final direction.

So, the final direction of the plane is ___56°___ east of north.

The plane's final speed is ___626.5 mi/h___ .

REFLECT

3a. Does your answer seem reasonable? Why?

The answer is reasonable because the plane's final speed should be a bit greater than its original speed and its final direction should be a bit closer to due north.

3b. A student claimed that he solved the problem using only the Law of Sines. Explain his method or explain why he must have made an error.

He must have made an error. The problem provides SAS information, but the Law of Sines can be used only with ASA, AAS, or SSA information.

PRACTICE

Solve each triangle. Round to the nearest tenth.

1.

2.

3.

m∠A = 44.4°, m∠B = 34.1°,   m∠D = 97.4°, m∠E = 54.8°,   m∠J = 79.9°, m∠K = 46.8°,
m∠C = 101.5°   m∠C = 27.8°   m∠L = 53.3°

Essential Question

What is the Law of Cosines and how do you use it to solve problems?

For any triangle, $\triangle ABC$, the Law of Cosines states

$$a^2 = b^2 + c^2 - 2bc \cos A,$$

$$b^2 = a^2 + c^2 - 2ac \cos B, \text{ and}$$

$$c^2 = a^2 + b^2 - 2ab \cos C.$$

You use the Law of Cosines to solve a triangle when you are given SSS or SAS information.

Summarize

Have students make a graphic organizer to summarize the Law of Sines, the Law of Cosines, and when each of the laws may be used. Students might add information to the graphic organizer they made for Lesson 6-6. A sample is shown below.

Where skills are taught	Where skills are practiced
2 EXAMPLE	EXS. 1–6
4 EXAMPLE	EXS. 7–9

Exercise 10: Students use what they learned to critique another student's work.

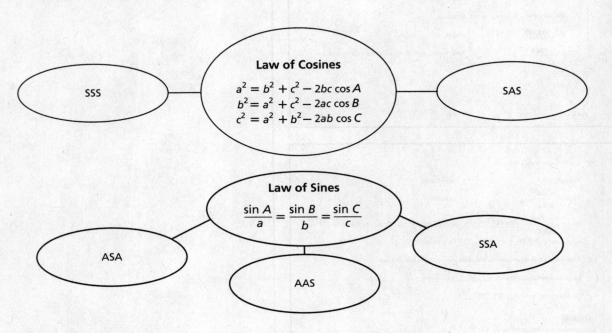

Solve each triangle. Round to the nearest tenth.

4.

5.

6.

$a = 20.7$, $m\angle B = 59.7°$, $m = 12.7$, $m\angle M = 41.1°$, $e = 13.3$, $m\angle D = 16.7°$,

$m\angle C = 69.3°$ $m\angle P = 70.9°$ $m\angle F = 113.3°$

7. A sailboat sets out from shore, sailing due north at 10 mi/h. There is a crosswind blowing 5 mi/h in the direction 45° east of north. What is the final direction and speed of the sailboat?

14.6° east of north at 14.0 mi/h

8. A plane is flying at a rate of 550 mi/h in the direction 40° east of north. There is a 30 mi/h crosswind blowing due south. What is the final direction and speed of the plane?

42.1° east of north at 527.4 mi/h

9. A surveyor at point *S* locates a rock formation 530 meters away at point *P*. The surveyor turns clockwise 102° and locates a rock formation 410 meters away at point *R*. To the nearest tenth of a meter, what is the distance between the rock formations?

734.4 m

10. **Error Analysis** A student was asked to find m∠*A* in the triangle shown below. The student's work is shown. Determine whether the student made an error and, if so, correct the error.

$$a^2 = b^2 + c^2 - 2bc \cos A$$
$$8^2 = 12^2 + 15^2 - 2(12)(15)\cos A$$
$$\cos A = \frac{8^2 - 12^2 - 15^2}{2(12)(15)} \approx -0.8472$$
$$m\angle A \approx \cos^{-1}(-0.8472) \approx 147.9°$$

The student made an error in writing the ratio for cos *A*; the denominator should be negative; the correct value for m∠*A* is about 32.1°.

COMMON CORE CORRELATION

Standards	Item
CC.9-12.G.SRT.6	5
CC.9-12.G.SRT.7	1
CC.9-12.G.SRT.8	4, 7
CC.9-12.G.SRT.9(+)	6
CC.9-12.G.SRT.10(+)	2, 3, 8, 9
CC.9-12.G.SRT.11(+)	3, 9

TEST PREP DOCTOR ✛

Multiple Choice: Item 4

- Students who answered **G** used the sine to solve the problem, but may have done so incorrectly by writing $\sin 28° = \frac{2}{b}$ $\left(\text{rather than } \sin 28° = \frac{b}{2}\right)$ and solving for b.

- Students who answered **H** incorrectly used the cosine and solved $\cos 28° = \frac{b}{2}$ for b when they should have used the sine $\left(\sin 28° = \frac{b}{2}\right)$.

- Students who answered **J** incorrectly used the cosine and solved $\cos 28° = \frac{2}{b}$ for b, when they should have used the sine $\left(\sin 28° = \frac{b}{2}\right)$.

Multiple Choice: Item 5

- Students who answered **A** may think that the cosine is the ratio of the length of the leg opposite the angle to the length of the hypotenuse.

- Students who answered **B** may not understand that trigonometric ratios are defined for the acute angles of a right triangle.

- Students who answered **D** may think that the tangent is the ratio of the length of the leg opposite the angle to the length of the hypotenuse.

Free Response: Item 9

- Students who try to set up a trigonometric ratio without using the Law of Sines or the Law of Cosines may not understand that trigonometric ratios are generally used to find unknown side lengths only in right triangles.

- Students who try to use the Law of Sines may not understand that the Law of Sines does not apply when given SAS information.

- Students who use the Law of Cosines but find an incorrect distance between the landmarks may have made an error in solving the equation $p^2 = 190^2 + 241^2 - 2(190)(241)\cos 78°$ for p.

Notes

Name _____ Class _____ Date _____

MULTIPLE CHOICE

1. Given that $x°$ is the measure of an acute angle, which of the following is equal to $\sin x°$?

   A. $\cos x°$

   B. $\cos(90 - x)°$

   C. $\sin(90 - x)°$

   D. $\tan x°$

2. Shauntay is proving the Law of Sines. She draws the figure below.

Then she writes $\sin A = \frac{h}{b}$ and $\sin B = \frac{h}{a}$. From this, she concludes that $h = b \sin A$ and $h = a \sin B$. What should she do next?

   F. Draw an altitude from B to side $\overline{AC}$.

   G. Add the equations to get $2h = b \sin A + a \sin B$.

   H. Use the Pythagorean Theorem to write $c^2 + h^2 = a^2$.

   J. Write $b \sin A = a \sin B$ and then divide both sides by ab.

3. Which is closest to $m\angle S$?

   A. 41°

   B. 64°

   C. 75°

   D. 81°

4. Connor is building a skateboard ramp with the dimensions shown. Which expression can he use to find the height b of the ramp?

   F. $2 \sin 28°$

   G. $\frac{2}{\sin 28°}$

   H. $2 \cos 28°$

   J. $\frac{2}{\cos 28°}$

5. In the right triangles shown below, $\angle M \cong \angle Q$. This leads to the observation that $\triangle MNP \sim \triangle QRS$ by the AA Similarity Criterion. Therefore, corresponding sides are proportional, so $\frac{RS}{NP} = \frac{QR}{MN}$ and algebra shows that $\frac{RS}{QR} = \frac{NP}{MN}$. This last proportion is the basis for defining which of the following?

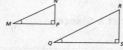

   A. the cosine of $\angle M$

   B. the cosine of $\angle P$

   C. the sine of $\angle M$

   D. the tangent of $\angle M$

FREE RESPONSE

6. You are using the figure below to derive a formula for the area of a triangle that involves the sine ratio.

First you note that $\sin C = \frac{h}{b}$ and, therefore, $h = b \sin C$. How do you complete the derivation of the formula?

The area of the triangle is Area $= \frac{1}{2}ah$.

So, by substitution, Area $= \frac{1}{2}ab \sin C$.

7. You paddle a kayak due north at the rate of 2.5 mi/h. The river has a 2 mi/h current that flows due east. You want to find the kayak's actual speed and direction.

a. In the space below, sketch and label vectors that represent the situation.

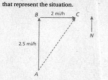

b. Find the kayak's actual speed and direction.

Actual speed: ≈ 3.2 mi/h

Actual direction: 38.7° east

of due north

8. To prove the Law of Cosines, you first draw the following figure.

Then you note that $\cos A = \frac{x}{b}$ so $x = b \cos A$ and you note that $x^2 + h^2 = b^2$ by the Pythagorean Theorem. How do you complete the proof that $a^2 = b^2 + c^2 - 2bc \cos A$?

In $\triangle CDB$, $a^2 = (c - x)^2 + h^2$ by the

Pythagorean Theorem. Expanding

gives $a^2 = c^2 - 2cx + x^2 + h^2$.

By substitution, $a^2 = c^2 - 2cx + b^2$

or $a^2 = b^2 + c^2 - 2cx$. So,

$a^2 = b^2 + c^2 - 2cb \cos A$ by

substitution.

9. A surveyor at point P locates two landmarks, A and B, as shown in the figure. Explain how the surveyor can find the distance between the landmarks to the nearest meter.

By the Law of Cosines,

$p^2 = a^2 + b^2 - 2ab \cos P$, so

$p^2 = 190^2 + 241^2 - 2(190)(241)\cos 78°$.

Simplifying gives $p^2 = 75,140.4$ and

$p \approx 274.1$. So, the distance between

the landmarks is about 274 m.

UNIT 7

Circles

Unit Vocabulary

arc	(7-1)
central angle	(7-1)
chord	(7-1)
circumcenter	(7-2)
circumcircle	(7-2)
circumscribe	(7-2)
circumscribed angle	(7-5)
incenter	(7-6)
incircle	(7-6)
inscribed	(7-3)
inscribed angle	(7-1)
major arc	(7-1)
minor arc	(7-1)
point of tangency	(7-5)
semicircle	(7-1)
tangent	(7-5)

UNIT 7

Circles

Unit Focus

In this unit, you will work with circles and explore their connection to other familiar geometric figures. First, you will learn some vocabulary associated with circles and investigate central and inscribed angles. You will also learn how to do constructions to inscribe polygons in circles and to inscribe circles in polygons. Along the way, you will study properties of tangent lines.

Unit at a Glance

COMMON CORE

Lesson		Standards for Mathematical Content
7-1	Central Angles and Inscribed Angles	CC.9-12.G.C.2
7-2	Constructing Circumscribed Circles	CC.9-12.G.C.3
7-3	Constructing Inscribed Polygons	CC.9-12.G.CO.13
7-4	Inscribed Quadrilaterals	CC.9-12.G.C.3
7-5	Tangent Lines	CC.9-12.G.C.2, G.C.4(+)
7-6	Constructing Inscribed Circles	CC.9-12.G.C.3
	Test Prep	

© Houghton Mifflin Harcourt Publishing Company

UNIT 7

Unpacking the Common Core State Standards

Use the table to help you understand the Standards for Mathematical Content that are taught in this unit. Refer to the lessons listed after each standard for exploration and practice.

COMMON CORE Standards for Mathematical Content	What It Means For You
CC.9-12.G.CO.13 Construct an equilateral triangle, a square, and a regular hexagon inscribed in a circle. Lesson 7-3	You will learn how to use a compass and straightedge to construct regular polygons in a given circle.
CC.9-12.G.C.2 Identify and describe relationships among inscribed angles, radii, and chords. Lessons 7-1, 7-5	After learning the key vocabulary associated with circles, you will explore relationships among the angles and arcs in a circle.
CC.9-12.G.C.3 Construct the inscribed and circumscribed circles of a triangle, and prove properties of angles for a quadrilateral inscribed in a circle. Lessons 7-2, 7-4, 7-6	Given a triangle, it is possible to construct a circle that passes through all three vertices. It is also possible to construct a circle such that each side of the triangle is tangent to the circle. You will see how to use a compass and straightedge to do both of these constructions.
CC.9-12.G.C.4(+) Construct a tangent line from a point outside a given circle to the circle. Lesson 7-5	From a point outside a circle, there are two lines that are tangent to the circle. You will learn how to construct these lines.

Unpacking the Common Core State Standards

This page lists and explains the Standards for Mathematical Content that are addressed in this unit. For information about the Standards for Mathematical Practice, which are integrated throughout the text, see Teacher Edition pages x–xiii.

Notes

Central Angles and Inscribed Angles

Essential question: *What is the relationship between central angles and inscribed angles in a circle?*

COMMON CORE

Standards for Mathematical Content

CC.9-12.G.C.2 Identify and describe relationships among inscribed angles, radii, and chords.

Vocabulary
chord
central angle
inscribed angle
arc
minor arc
major arc
semicircle

Prerequisites
Basic Terms and Constructions, Lesson 1-1

Math Background
In Unit 7, students turn their attention to circles. This first lesson introduces key vocabulary and the idea of the measure of an arc. Note that the measure of an arc is connected to the measure of its central angle. Students will also learn that the measure of an inscribed angle is half the measure of the intercepted arc (and, therefore, half the measure of the associated central angle when the arc is a minor arc). Later theorems build upon these ideas. Thus, the connection between central angles and arcs may be seen as the foundation for much of students' future work with circles. It is worth spending extra time to ensure that students are comfortable with the vocabulary and measurement ideas related to central angles and arcs.

INTRODUCE

Ask a volunteer to remind the class of the definition of a circle. Then, have students brainstorm facts about circles that they already know. Students might mention the relationship between the diameter of a circle and the radius. Tell students they will learn new vocabulary and theorems in this unit.

TEACH

1 ENGAGE

Questioning Strategies
- How can you tell whether an angle in a circle is a central angle or an inscribed angle? **A central angle has its vertex at the origin. An inscribed angle has its vertex on the circle.**
- How can you tell whether an arc is a minor arc or a major arc? **A minor arc is less than a semicircle; a major arc is more than a semicircle.**
- What does the prefix *semi-* mean in the word *semicircle*? **half**

MATHEMATICAL PRACTICE

Highlighting the Standards

You can address Standard 7 (Look for and make use of structure) as you discuss the Arc Addition Postulate. The standard states that "Mathematically proficient students look closely to discern a pattern or structure." Students may already have experience seeking patterns in algebraic functions, and they are likely to be familiar with geometric patterns such as tessellations. Point out that there are also underlying patterns and structures in the properties and postulates that they study in this course. For example, students may note the similarities among the Segment Addition Postulate, the Angle Addition Postulate, and the Arc Addition Postulate.

2 EXPLORE

Materials: compass, straightedge, protractor

Questioning Strategies
- Is it possible for multiple inscribed angles to have the same associated central angle? **yes**
- What is true about the inscribed angles in this case? **They all have the same measure.**

Central Angles and Inscribed Angles

7-1

COMMON CORE

CC.9-12.G.C.2

Essential question: *What is the relationship between central angles and inscribed angles in a circle?*

1 ENGAGE   Introducing Angles and Arcs

In order to begin working with circles, it is helpful to introduce some vocabulary.

A **chord** is a segment whose endpoints lie on a circle. A **central angle** is an angle whose vertex is the center of a circle. An **inscribed angle** is an angle whose vertex lies on a circle and whose sides contain chords of the circle.

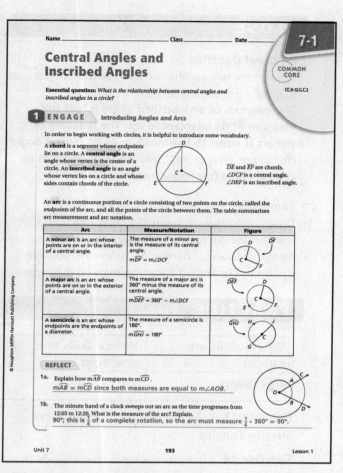

$\overline{DE}$ and $\overline{EF}$ are chords.
$\angle DCF$ is a central angle.
$\angle DEF$ is an inscribed angle.

An **arc** is a continuous portion of a circle consisting of two points on the circle, called the *endpoints* of the arc, and all the points of the circle between them. The table summarizes arc measurement and arc notation.

Arc	Measure/Notation	Figure
A **minor arc** is an arc whose points are on or in the interior of a central angle.	The measure of a minor arc is the measure of its central angle. $m\overparen{DF} = m\angle DCF$	
A **major arc** is an arc whose points are on or in the exterior of a central angle.	The measure of a major arc is 360° minus the measure of its central angle. $m\overparen{DEF} = 360° - m\angle DCF$	
A **semicircle** is an arc whose endpoints are the endpoints of a diameter.	The measure of a semicircle is 180°. $m\overparen{GHJ} = 180°$	

REFLECT

1a. Explain how $m\overparen{AB}$ compares to $m\overparen{CD}$.

$m\overparen{AB} = m\overparen{CD}$ since both measures are equal to $m\angle AOB$.

1b. The minute hand of a clock sweeps out an arc as the time progresses from 12:05 to 12:20. What is the measure of the arc? Explain.

90°; this is $\frac{1}{4}$ of a complete rotation, so the arc must measure $\frac{1}{4} \cdot 360° = 90°$.

Two arcs of a circle are *adjacent arcs* if they share an endpoint. The following postulate states that you can add the measures of adjacent arcs.

Arc Addition Postulate

The measure of an arc formed by two adjacent arcs is the sum of the measures of the two arcs.

$m\overparen{ABC} = m\overparen{AB} + m\overparen{BC}$

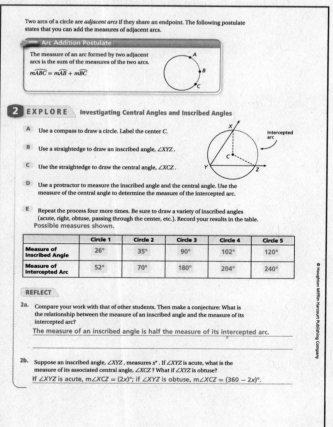

2 EXPLORE   Investigating Central Angles and Inscribed Angles

A   Use a compass to draw a circle. Label the center C.

B   Use a straightedge to draw an inscribed angle, $\angle XYZ$.

C   Use the straightedge to draw the central angle, $\angle XCZ$.

D   Use a protractor to measure the inscribed angle and the central angle. Use the measure of the central angle to determine the measure of the intercepted arc.

E   Repeat the process four more times. Be sure to draw a variety of inscribed angles (acute, right, obtuse, passing through the center, etc.). Record your results in the table. Possible measures shown.

	Circle 1	Circle 2	Circle 3	Circle 4	Circle 5
Measure of Inscribed Angle	26°	35°	90°	102°	120°
Measure of Intercepted Arc	52°	70°	180°	204°	240°

REFLECT

2a. Compare your work with that of other students. Then make a conjecture: What is the relationship between the measure of an inscribed angle and the measure of its intercepted arc?

The measure of an inscribed angle is half the measure of its intercepted arc.

2b. Suppose an inscribed angle, $\angle XYZ$, measures $x°$. If $\angle XYZ$ is acute, what is the measure of its associated central angle, $\angle XCZ$? What if $\angle XYZ$ is obtuse?

If $\angle XYZ$ is acute, $m\angle XCZ = (2x)°$; if $\angle XYZ$ is obtuse, $m\angle XCZ = (360 - 2x)°$.

Technology

The **Explore** lends itself well to geometry software. Have students construct a circle with center C and then have them plot three points, X, Y, and Z on the circle. Student can construct $\angle XYZ$ and $\angle XCZ$. By selecting the circle and points X and Z, students can also construct $\overset{\frown}{XZ}$. Have students use the Measure menu to find and compare these angle and arc measures.

 EXAMPLE

Questioning Strategies

- Can you find the four required measures in any order, or are there certain measures you must find first? **Find m$\overset{\frown}{BC}$ or m$\angle ABC$ (you need m$\overset{\frown}{BC}$ in order to find m$\overset{\frown}{BD}$).**

EXTRA EXAMPLE

Find m $\overset{\frown}{FG}$, m $\overset{\frown}{FGH}$, m$\angle HJF$, and m$\angle JFG$.

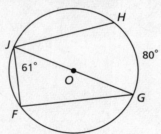

m$\overset{\frown}{FG}$ = 122°; m$\overset{\frown}{FGH}$ = 202°; m$\angle HJF$ = 101°; m$\angle JFG$ = 90°

Teaching Strategies

Whenever students solve a problem like the one in the example, encourage them to do a "consistency check" as the final step. To do so, students should label the figure with all of the measures they found and make sure that the sum of the angle measures in any triangle is 180°, that the sum of any arc measures that make a full circle is 360°, and that the measure of any inscribed angle is half the measure of its intercepted arc.

CLOSE

Essential Question

What is the relationship between central angles and inscribed angles in a circle?
The measure of an inscribed angle is half the measure of its intercepted arc. The measure of the arc is equal to the measure of its central angle (for minor arcs) or 360° minus the measure of its central angle (for major arcs).

Summarize

Have students write a journal entry in which they summarize the main vocabulary and theorems from this lesson. Encourage students to include figures to illustrate the vocabulary and theorems.

PRACTICE

Where skills are taught	Where skills are practiced
EXAMPLE	EXS. 1–12

Exercise 13: Students prove a theorem about inscribed angles.

Exercise 14: Students use what they learned in this lesson to solve a real-world problem.

You may have discovered the following relationship between an inscribed angle and its intercepted arc.

Inscribed Angle Theorem

The measure of an inscribed angle is half the measure of its intercepted arc.

$m\angle ADB = \frac{1}{2}m\widehat{AB}$

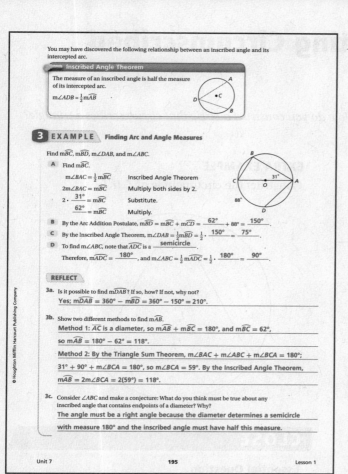

3 EXAMPLE   Finding Arc and Angle Measures

Find $m\widehat{BC}$, $m\widehat{BD}$, $m\angle DAB$, and $m\angle ABC$.

A   Find $m\widehat{BC}$.

$m\angle BAC = \frac{1}{2}m\widehat{BC}$ Inscribed Angle Theorem

$2m\angle BAC = m\widehat{BC}$ Multiply both sides by 2.

$2 \cdot \underline{31°} = m\widehat{BC}$ Substitute.

$\underline{62°} = m\widehat{BC}$ Multiply.

B   By the Arc Addition Postulate, $m\widehat{BD} = m\widehat{BC} + m\widehat{CD} = \underline{62°} + 88° = \underline{150°}$.

C   By the Inscribed Angle Theorem, $m\angle DAB = \frac{1}{2}m\widehat{BD} = \frac{1}{2} \cdot \underline{150°} = \underline{75°}$.

D   To find $m\angle ABC$, note that $\widehat{ADC}$ is a __semicircle__.

Therefore, $m\widehat{ADC} = \underline{180°}$, and $m\angle ABC = \frac{1}{2}m\widehat{ADC} = \frac{1}{2} \cdot \underline{180°} = \underline{90°}$.

REFLECT

3a. Is it possible to find $m\widehat{DAB}$? If so, how? If not, why not?

Yes; $m\widehat{DAB} = 360° - m\widehat{BD} = 360° - 150° = 210°$.

3b. Show two different methods to find $m\widehat{AB}$.

Method 1: $\overline{AC}$ is a diameter, so $m\widehat{AB} + m\widehat{BC} = 180°$, and $m\widehat{BC} = 62°$,

so $m\widehat{AB} = 180° - 62° = 118°$.

Method 2: By the Triangle Sum Theorem, $m\angle BAC + m\angle ABC + m\angle BCA = 180°$;

$31° + 90° + m\angle BCA = 180°$, so $m\angle BCA = 59°$. By the Inscribed Angle Theorem,

$m\widehat{AB} = 2m\angle BCA = 2(59°) = 118°$.

3c. Consider $\angle ABC$ and make a conjecture: What do you think must be true about any inscribed angle that contains endpoints of a diameter? Why?

The angle must be a right angle because the diameter determines a semicircle

with measure 180° and the inscribed angle must have half this measure.

The following theorem describes a key relationship between inscribed angles and diameters.

Theorem

The endpoints of a diameter lie on an inscribed angle if and only if the inscribed angle is a right angle.

PRACTICE

Use the figure to find each of the following.

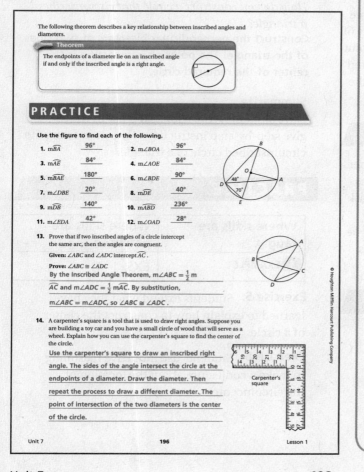

1. $m\widehat{BA}$ __96°__
2. $m\angle BOA$ __96°__
3. $m\widehat{AE}$ __84°__
4. $m\angle AOE$ __84°__
5. $m\widehat{BAE}$ __180°__
6. $m\angle BDE$ __90°__
7. $m\angle DBE$ __20°__
8. $m\widehat{DE}$ __40°__
9. $m\widehat{DB}$ __140°__
10. $m\widehat{ABD}$ __236°__
11. $m\angle EDA$ __42°__
12. $m\angle OAD$ __28°__

13. Prove that if two inscribed angles of a circle intercept the same arc, then the angles are congruent.

Given: $\angle ABC$ and $\angle ADC$ intercept $\widehat{AC}$.

Prove: $\angle ABC \cong \angle ADC$

By the Inscribed Angle Theorem, $m\angle ABC = \frac{1}{2}$ m

$\widehat{AC}$ and $m\angle ADC = \frac{1}{2}m\widehat{AC}$. By substitution,

$m\angle ABC = m\angle ADC$, so $\angle ABC \cong \angle ADC$.

14. A carpenter's square is a tool that is used to draw right angles. Suppose you are building a toy car and you have a small circle of wood that will serve as a wheel. Explain how you can use the carpenter's square to find the center of the circle.

Use the carpenter's square to draw an inscribed right

angle. The sides of the angle intersect the circle at the

endpoints of a diameter. Draw the diameter. Then

repeat the process to draw a different diameter. The

point of intersection of the two diameters is the center

of the circle.

Carpenter's square

Constructing Circumscribed Circles

Essential question: *How do you construct a circle that circumscribes a triangle?*

⊙ **COMMON** **Standards for**
CORE **Mathematical Content**

CC.9-12.G.C.3 Construct the ... circumscribed circle of a triangle ...

Vocabulary

circumscribe

circumcircle

circumcenter

Prerequisites

Parallel and Perpendicular Lines, Lesson 1-5

Perpendicular Bisectors, Lesson 2-4

Math Background

For any triangle, the perpendicular bisectors of the sides are concurrent at a point called the circumcenter of the triangle. This is one of four concurrency points of a triangle. The others are the centroid (the point of concurrency of the three medians), the incenter (the point of concurrency of the angle bisectors), and the orthocenter (the point of concurrency of the altitudes). Students explored the centroid in Lesson 3-9 and will learn about the incenter in Lesson 7-6.

INTRODUCE

Draw a triangle on the board. Ask students whether they think it is possible to draw a circle that passes through all three of the triangle's vertices. Then, ask students whether they think it is possible to draw such a circle for *any* given triangle. Students may be surprised to learn that every triangle, whatever its shape, may be circumscribed by a circle.

TEACH

1 EXAMPLE

Questioning Strategies

• What do you have to do to construct a circumcircle of △*PQR*? **Find a point that is equidistant from *P*, *Q*, and *R*. This point is the center of the required circle.**

EXTRA EXAMPLE

Construct the circumcircle of △*JKL*.

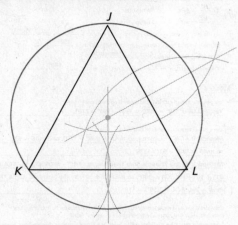

CLOSE

Essential Question

How do you construct a circle that circumscribes a triangle?
Construct the perpendicular bisectors of two sides of the triangle. The point of intersection is the center of the required circle.

Summarize

Have students write a journal entry in which they give step-by-step instructions for constructing the circumscribed circle of a triangle.

PRACTICE

Where skills are taught	Where skills are practiced
1 EXAMPLE	EXS. 1–4

Exercise 5: Students extend what they have learned to explain how to construct the center of a circle.

Exercise 6: Students use inductive reasoning to make a conjecture about the location of the circumcenter.

7-2

COMMON CORE
CC.9-12.G.C.3

Constructing Circumscribed Circles

Essential question: *How do you construct a circle that circumscribes a triangle?*

A circle is said to **circumscribe** a polygon if the circle passes through all of the polygon's vertices. In the figure, circle *C* circumscribes △*XYZ* and this circle is called the **circumcircle** of △*XYZ*.

In order to construct the circumcircle of a triangle, you need to find the center of the circle. The following example will guide you through the reasoning process to do this.

1 EXAMPLE Constructing a Circumscribed Circle

Work directly on the figure to construct the circumcircle of △*PQR*.

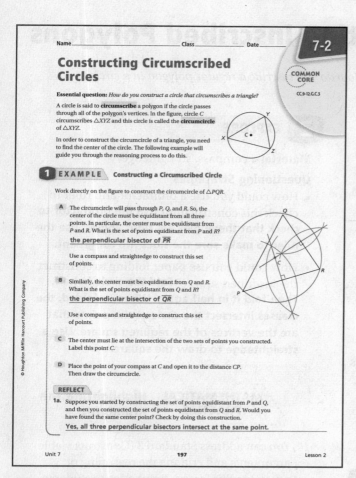

A The circumcircle will pass through *P*, *Q*, and *R*. So, the center of the circle must be equidistant from all three points. In particular, the center must be equidistant from *P* and *R*. What is the set of points equidistant from *P* and *R*?

the perpendicular bisector of $\overline{PR}$

Use a compass and straightedge to construct this set of points.

B Similarly, the center must be equidistant from *Q* and *R*. What is the set of points equidistant from *Q* and *R*?

the perpendicular bisector of $\overline{QR}$

Use a compass and straightedge to construct this set of points.

C The center must lie at the intersection of the two sets of points you constructed. Label this point *C*.

D Place the point of your compass at *C* and open it to the distance *CP*. Then draw the circumcircle.

REFLECT

1a. Suppose you started by constructing the set of points equidistant from *P* and *Q*, and then you constructed the set of points equidistant from *Q* and *R*. Would you have found the same center point? Check by doing this construction.

Yes, all three perpendicular bisectors intersect at the same point.

You may have discovered that the perpendicular bisectors of a triangle intersect at a common point. This point is called the **circumcenter** of the triangle. You will further investigate circumcenters in the exercises.

PRACTICE

Construct the circumcircle of each triangle.

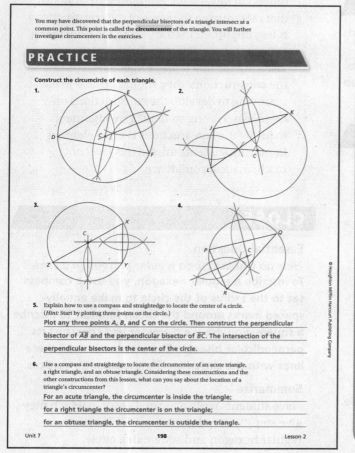

1.

2.

3.

4.

5. Explain how to use a compass and straightedge to locate the center of a circle. *(Hint: Start by plotting three points on the circle.)*

Plot any three points *A*, *B*, and *C* on the circle. Then construct the perpendicular

bisector of $\overline{AB}$ and the perpendicular bisector of $\overline{BC}$. The intersection of the

perpendicular bisectors is the center of the circle.

6. Use a compass and straightedge to locate the circumcenter of an acute triangle, a right triangle, and an obtuse triangle. Considering these constructions and the other constructions from this lesson, what can you say about the location of a triangle's circumcenter?

For an acute triangle, the circumcenter is inside the triangle;

for a right triangle the circumcenter is on the triangle;

for an obtuse triangle, the circumcenter is outside the triangle.

Constructing Inscribed Polygons

Essential question: *How do you inscribe a regular polygon in a circle?*

COMMON CORE Standards for Mathematical Content

CC.9-12.G.CO.13 Construct an equilateral triangle, a square, and a regular hexagon inscribed in a circle.

Vocabulary
inscribed

Prerequisites
Parallel and Perpendicular Lines, Lesson 1-5

Math Background
In the previous lesson, students learned to circumscribe a circle about a given triangle. In this lesson, the process is reversed. Now, the circle is the starting point, and students must construct a specified inscribed polygon. As you discuss the constructions in this lesson, highlight the dual nature of inscribing and circumscribing.

INTRODUCE

Explain what it means for a polygon to be inscribed in a figure. You may wish to draw some examples and non-examples on the board to be sure students understand that all vertices of the inscribed polygon must lie on the circle.

TEACH

1 EXPLORE

Materials: compass, straightedge

Questioning Strategies

- How many points do you need to locate on the circle to draw the hexagon? **6**

- What must be true about the points for the hexagon to be a regular hexagon? **The points must be equally spaced around the circle.**

- If *A* and *B* are two vertices of the hexagon and *O* is the center of the circle, what do you know about m∠*AOB*? Why? **This angle measures 60° because it is one of 6 congruent angles that surround the center and completely fill the circle.**

2 EXPLORE

Materials: compass, straightedge

Questioning Strategies

- How could you use a protractor and ruler to check this construction? **Use the protractor to check that the angles are right angles; use the ruler to make sure the sides are congruent.**

- How could you use paper folding to construct the inscribed square? **Fold the circle in half. Then fold it in half again. When unfolded, the creases intersect the circle at the points that are the vertices of the required square. Use a straightedge to draw the square.**

MATHEMATICAL PRACTICE **Highlighting the Standards**

You can address Standard 3 (Construct viable arguments and critique the reasoning of others) in this lesson. Emphasize to students that memorizing the steps of the constructions is less important than knowing the underlying logic that shows why the constructions work. Tell students that if they forget the steps of the constructions, they should be able to use reasoning to develop the constructions on their own. Having students give arguments to justify the constructions is a key element in moving students toward this level of mathematical confidence.

CLOSE

Essential Question
How do you inscribe a regular polygon in a circle?
To inscribe a regular hexagon, you use a compass set to the radius of the circle to make equally-spaced marks around the circumference. To inscribe a square, you draw a diameter and construct its perpendicular bisector. The intersections of these lines with the circle identify the square's vertices.

Summarize
Have students write a journal entry in which they give step-by-step instructions for inscribing a regular hexagon and square in a circle.

Constructing Inscribed Polygons

7-3

COMMON CORE

CC.9-12.G.CO.13

Essential question: *How do you inscribe a regular polygon in a circle?*

A polygon is said to be **inscribed** in a circle if all of the polygon's vertices lie on the circle. In the figure, △XYZ is inscribed in circle C. You can also say that circle C circumscribes △XYZ.

In this lesson, you will use a compass and straightedge to inscribe regular polygons in a circle.

1 EXPLORE Inscribing a Regular Hexagon

Use the space at right to inscribe a regular hexagon in a circle.

A Use your compass to draw a circle O. Label a point A on the circle.

B Without adjusting the compass, place the point of the compass at A and draw an arc that intersects the circle. Label the point of intersection B.

C Without adjusting the compass, place the point of the compass at B and draw an arc that intersects the circle. Label the point of intersection C.

D Continue in this way until you have located six points, A, B, C, D, E, and F. Then use your straightedge to draw $\overline{AB}$, $\overline{BC}$, $\overline{CD}$, $\overline{DE}$, $\overline{EF}$, and $\overline{FA}$.

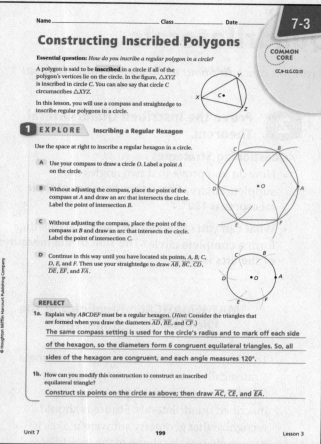

REFLECT

1a. Explain why ABCDEF must be a regular hexagon. (*Hint:* Consider the triangles that are formed when you draw the diameters $\overline{AD}$, $\overline{BE}$, and $\overline{CF}$.)

The same compass setting is used for the circle's radius and to mark off each side

of the hexagon, so the diameters form 6 congruent equilateral triangles. So, all

sides of the hexagon are congruent, and each angle measures 120°.

1b. How can you modify this construction to construct an inscribed equilateral triangle?

Construct six points on the circle as above; then draw $\overline{AC}$, $\overline{CE}$, and $\overline{EA}$.

---

2 EXPLORE Inscribing a Square

Use the space at right to inscribe a square in a circle.

A Use your compass to draw a circle O.

B Use your straightedge to draw a diameter $\overline{AB}$.

C Use the compass and straightedge to construct the perpendicular bisector of $\overline{AB}$.

D Label the points where the perpendicular bisector intersects the circle as C and D.

E Use the straightedge to draw $\overline{AD}$, $\overline{DB}$, $\overline{BC}$, and $\overline{CA}$.

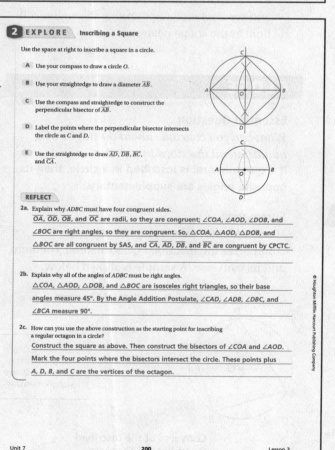

REFLECT

2a. Explain why ADBC must have four congruent sides.

$\overline{OA}$, $\overline{OD}$, $\overline{OB}$, and $\overline{OC}$ are radii, so they are congruent; ∠COA, ∠AOD, ∠DOB, and

∠BOC are right angles, so they are congruent. So, △COA, △AOD, △DOB, and

△BOC are all congruent by SAS, and $\overline{CA}$, $\overline{AD}$, $\overline{DB}$, and $\overline{BC}$ are congruent by CPCTC.

2b. Explain why all of the angles of ADBC must be right angles.

△COA, △AOD, △DOB, and △BOC are isosceles right triangles, so their base

angles measure 45°. By the Angle Addition Postulate, ∠CAD, ∠ADB, ∠DBC, and

∠BCA measure 90°.

2c. How can you use the above construction as the starting point for inscribing a regular octagon in a circle?

Construct the square as above. Then construct the bisectors of ∠COA and ∠AOD.

Mark the four points where the bisectors intersect the circle. These points plus

A, D, B, and C are the vertices of the octagon.

© Houghton Mifflin Harcourt Publishing Company

FOCUS ON REASONING
Inscribed Quadrilaterals

Essential question: *What can you conclude about the angles of a quadrilateral inscribed in a circle?*

○ **COMMON** Standards for
: **CORE** Mathematical Content

CC.9-12.G.C.3 ... prove properties of angles for a quadrilateral inscribed in a circle.

Prerequisites
Central Angles and Inscribed Angles, Lesson 7-1

Math Background
In Lesson 7-2, students learned that a circle can be circumscribed about any triangle. For quadrilaterals, the situation is a bit more complex. A circle can be circumscribed about a quadrilateral *if and only if* the opposite angles of the quadrilateral are supplementary. Equivalently, a quadrilateral can be inscribed in a circle *if and only if* its opposite angles are supplementary.

INTRODUCE

Draw a circle on the board and then draw a quadrilateral that is inscribed in the circle. Ask students whether they notice anything in particular about the inscribed quadrilateral. Students are unlikely to notice any special relationships among the angles at this point, and the subsequent investigation may help them realize that some geometric relationships are easy to identify at a glance (e.g., when parallel lines are cut by a transversal, corresponding angles are congruent), while others are less obvious.

TEACH

1 Investigate inscribed quadrilaterals.

Materials: geometry software

Questioning Strategies
- Does it matter whether the center of the circle lies inside, outside, or on the quadrilateral? No; in all of these cases, the opposite angles of the quadrilateral are supplementary.

- Is it possible to draw any conclusions about consecutive angles of the quadrilateral, such as ∠A and ∠B? No; any angle measures are possible for these angles.

2 Prove the Inscribed Quadrilateral Theorem.

Questioning Strategies
- How do you prove that two angles are supplementary? Show that the sum of their measures is 180°.

- What can you say about two arcs that together form a complete circle? The sum of the measures of the arcs is 360°.

⋯ **MATHEMATICAL PRACTICE**   **Highlighting the Standards**

To address Standard 5 (Use appropriate tools strategically), ask students why geometry software is a good tool for investigating inscribed quadrilaterals. Students should recognize that geometry software makes it easy to change the shape of the quadrilateral and see if relationships among the angles still hold as the shape changes.

CLOSE

Essential Question
What can you conclude about the angles of a quadrilateral inscribed in a circle?
If a quadrilateral is inscribed in a circle, then its opposite angles are supplementary.

Summarize
Have students make a graphic organizer to summarize the Inscribed Quadrilateral Theorem and its converse. A sample is shown below.

Inscribed Quadrilateral Theorem

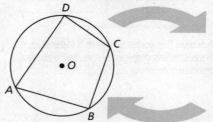

∠A and ∠C are supplementary.
∠B and ∠D are supplementary.

Converse of the Inscribed Quadrilateral Theorem

Name _____ Class _____ Date _____

FOCUS ON REASONING
Inscribed Quadrilaterals

COMMON
CORE

CC9-12.G.C.3

Essential question: *What can you conclude about the angles of a quadrilateral inscribed in a circle?*

1 Investigate inscribed quadrilaterals.

Use geometry software to inscribe a quadrilateral in a circle and explore its angle measures.

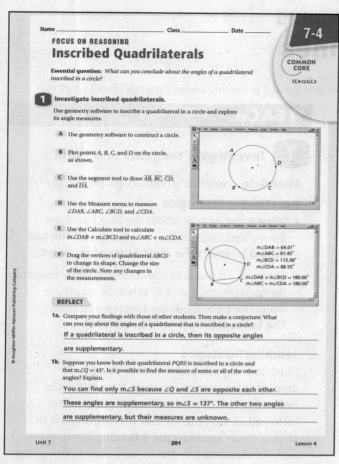

A Use geometry software to construct a circle.

B Plot points *A*, *B*, *C*, and *D* on the circle, as shown.

C Use the segment tool to draw $\overline{AB}$, $\overline{BC}$, $\overline{CD}$, and $\overline{DA}$.

D Use the Measure menu to measure ∠*DAB*, ∠*ABC*, ∠*BCD*, and ∠*CDA*.

E Use the Calculate tool to calculate m∠*DAB* + m∠*BCD* and m∠*ABC* + m∠*CDA*.

F Drag the vertices of quadrilateral *ABCD* to change its shape. Change the size of the circle. Note any changes in the measurements.

REFLECT

1a. Compare your findings with those of other students. Then make a conjecture: What can you say about the angles of a quadrilateral that is inscribed in a circle?

If a quadrilateral is inscribed in a circle, then its opposite angles
are supplementary.

1b. Suppose you know both that quadrilateral *PQRS* is inscribed in a circle and that m∠*Q* = 43°. Is it possible to find the measure of some or all of the other angles? Explain.

You can find only m∠S because ∠Q and ∠S are opposite each other.
These angles are supplementary, so m∠S = 137°. The other two angles
are supplementary, but their measures are unknown.

Inscribed Quadrilateral Theorem

If a quadrilateral is inscribed in a circle, then its opposite angles are supplementary.

The converse of the Inscribed Quadrilateral Theorem is also true. Taken together, the theorem and its converse tell you that a quadrilateral can be inscribed in a circle *if and only if* its opposite angles are supplementary.

2 Prove the Inscribed Quadrilateral Theorem.

Given: Quadrilateral *ABCD* is inscribed in circle *O*.

Prove: ∠*A* and ∠*C* are supplementary;
∠*B* and ∠*D* are supplementary.

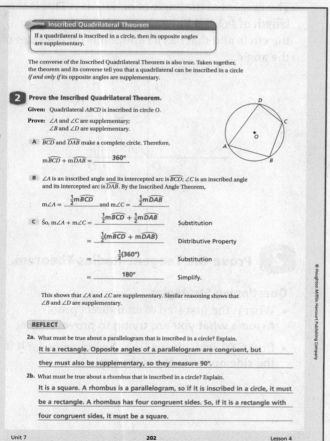

A $\overarc{BCD}$ and $\overarc{DAB}$ make a complete circle. Therefore,

$$m\overarc{BCD} + m\overarc{DAB} = \underline{\quad 360° \quad}$$

B ∠*A* is an inscribed angle and its intercepted arc is $\overarc{BCD}$; ∠*C* is an inscribed angle and its intercepted arc is $\overarc{DAB}$. By the Inscribed Angle Theorem,

$$m\angle A = \underline{\tfrac{1}{2}m\overarc{BCD}} \quad \text{and } m\angle C = \underline{\tfrac{1}{2}m\overarc{DAB}}$$

C So, $m\angle A + m\angle C = \underline{\dfrac{\tfrac{1}{2}m\overarc{BCD} + \tfrac{1}{2}m\overarc{DAB}}{}}$ Substitution

$$= \underline{\dfrac{\tfrac{1}{2}(m\overarc{BCD} + m\overarc{DAB})}{}} \quad \text{Distributive Property}$$

$$= \underline{\dfrac{\tfrac{1}{2}(360°)}{}} \quad \text{Substitution}$$

$$= \underline{\quad 180° \quad} \quad \text{Simplify.}$$

This shows that ∠*A* and ∠*C* are supplementary. Similar reasoning shows that ∠*B* and ∠*D* are supplementary.

REFLECT

2a. What must be true about a parallelogram that is inscribed in a circle? Explain.

It is a rectangle. Opposite angles of a parallelogram are congruent, but
they must also be supplementary, so they measure 90°.

2b. What must be true about a rhombus that is inscribed in a circle? Explain.

It is a square. A rhombus is a parallelogram, so if it is inscribed in a circle, it must
be a rectangle. A rhombus has four congruent sides. So, if it is a rectangle with
four congruent sides, it must be a square.

© Houghton Mifflin Harcourt Publishing Company

FOCUS ON REASONING
Tangent Lines

Essential question: What are the key theorems about tangent lines to a circle?

COMMON CORE — Standards for Mathematical Content

CC.9-12.G.C.2 Identify and describe relationships among inscribed angles, radii, and chords.

CC.9-12.G.C.4(+) Construct a tangent line from a point outside a given circle to the circle.

Vocabulary
tangent
point of tangency
circumscribed angle

Prerequisites
Central Angles and Inscribed Angles, Lesson 7-1

Math Background
In this Focus on Reasoning lesson, students investigate the relationship between a tangent line to a circle and the radius to the point of tangency. As in all Focus on Reasoning lessons, the approach is inductive at first, followed by a deductive proof. In addition to the Tangent-Radius Theorem and its converse, students learn to construct a tangent to a circle from a given point outside the circle. The justification for this construction depends upon the Converse of the Tangent-Radius Theorem. Finally, students prove the Circumscribed Angle Theorem, which depends upon the Tangent-Radius Theorem and the Quadrilateral Sum Theorem.

INTRODUCE

Define *tangent*. Tell students that the term comes from a Latin word, *tangere*, which means "to touch." Then, draw sketches to help students see that for every point on a circle, there is one and only one tangent to the circle at that point.

TEACH

1 **Investigate tangents and radii.**

Materials: compass, straightedge, protractor

Questioning Strategies
- What must be true about the line you draw through point *P* for it to be a tangent? **The line should intersect the circle at no other point.**

- Suppose $\overline{AB}$ is a diameter and you draw tangents through points *A* and *B*. What do you think would be true about the two tangent lines? **The tangent lines would be parallel.**

Teaching Strategies
Students may wonder whether there is a connection between the term *tangent* as it is defined in this lesson and the trigonometric ratio called the tangent that was introduced in Unit 6. Show students the following figure in which a circle of radius 1 is drawn on a coordinate plane. The tangent of the angle of $m°$ is $\frac{y}{1}$ or *y*. This is the length of $\overline{PQ}$, the line segment that is *tangent* to the circle and that has its endpoints on the sides of the angle.

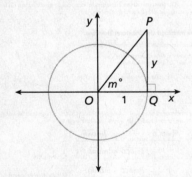

2 **Prove the Tangent-Radius Theorem.**

Questioning Strategies
- What is the first step of an indirect proof? **Assume what you are trying to prove is false.**

- In $\triangle CXP$, why must $\overline{CP}$ be the hypotenuse? **It is the side opposite the right angle.**

7-5

FOCUS ON REASONING
Tangent Lines

COMMON CORE
CC.9-12.G.C.2,
CC.9-12.G.C.4(+)

Essential question: *What are the key theorems about tangent lines to a circle?*

A **tangent** is a line in the same plane as a circle that intersects the circle in exactly one point. The point where a tangent and a circle intersect is the **point of tangency**. In the figure, line *m* is a tangent to circle *C*, and point *P* is the point of tangency.

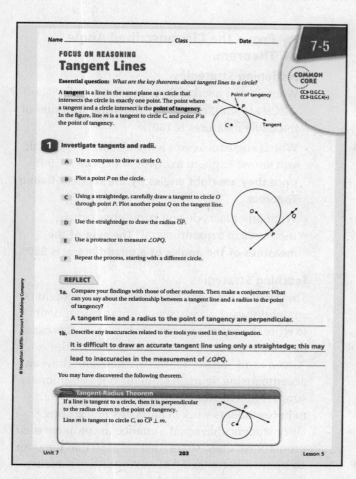

1 Investigate tangents and radii.

A Use a compass to draw a circle *O*.

B Plot a point *P* on the circle.

C Using a straightedge, carefully draw a tangent to circle *O* through point *P*. Plot another point *Q* on the tangent line.

D Use the straightedge to draw the radius $\overline{OP}$.

E Use a protractor to measure ∠*OPQ*.

F Repeat the process, starting with a different circle.

REFLECT

1a. Compare your findings with those of other students. Then make a conjecture: What can you say about the relationship between a tangent line and a radius to the point of tangency?

A tangent line and a radius to the point of tangency are perpendicular.

1b. Describe any inaccuracies related to the tools you used in the investigation.

It is difficult to draw an accurate tangent line using only a straightedge; this may

lead to inaccuracies in the measurement of ∠*OPQ*.

You may have discovered the following theorem.

> **Tangent-Radius Theorem**
> If a line is tangent to a circle, then it is perpendicular to the radius drawn to the point of tangency.
> Line *m* is tangent to circle *C*, so $\overline{CP} \perp m$.

---

2 Prove the Tangent-Radius Theorem.

Given: Line *m* is tangent to circle *C* at point *P*.

Prove: $\overline{CP} \perp m$

Complete the proof.

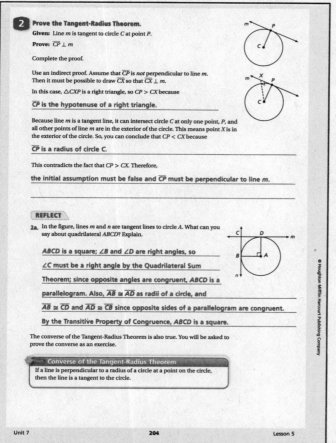

Use an indirect proof. Assume that $\overline{CP}$ is *not* perpendicular to line *m*. Then it must be possible to draw $\overline{CX}$ so that $\overline{CX} \perp m$.

In this case, △*CXP* is a right triangle, so *CP* > *CX* because

$\overline{CP}$ is the hypotenuse of a right triangle.

Because line *m* is a tangent line, it can intersect circle *C* at only one point, *P*, and all other points of line *m* are in the exterior of the circle. This means point *X* is in the exterior of the circle. So, you can conclude that *CP* < *CX* because

$\overline{CP}$ is a radius of circle *C*.

This contradicts the fact that *CP* > *CX*. Therefore,

the initial assumption must be false and $\overline{CP}$ must be perpendicular to line *m*.

REFLECT

2a. In the figure, lines *m* and *n* are tangent lines to circle *A*. What can you say about quadrilateral *ABCD*? Explain.

ABCD is a square; ∠*B* and ∠*D* are right angles, so

∠*C* must be a right angle by the Quadrilateral Sum

Theorem; since opposite angles are congruent, *ABCD* is a

parallelogram. Also, $\overline{AB} \cong \overline{AD}$ as radii of a circle, and

$\overline{AB} \cong \overline{CD}$ and $\overline{AD} \cong \overline{CB}$ since opposite sides of a parallelogram are congruent.

By the Transitive Property of Congruence, *ABCD* is a square.

The converse of the Tangent-Radius Theorem is also true. You will be asked to prove the converse as an exercise.

> **Converse of the Tangent-Radius Theorem**
> If a line is perpendicular to a radius of a circle at a point on the circle, then the line is a tangent to the circle.

3 Construct a tangent to a circle.

Questioning Strategies

- How do you construct the midpoint of $\overline{CP}$?
  Construct the perpendicular bisector of the segment by drawing arcs with the same radius from each endpoint. The line through the points of intersection of the arcs is the perpendicular bisector.

- What type of angle is $\angle CXP$? Why? It is a right angle because it is an inscribed angle in circle M and the endpoints of diameter $\overline{CP}$ lie on the angle.

Technology

You may wish to have students use geometry software to explore tangent lines. In particular, it is instructive to have students replicate the construction of a tangent line from an exterior point using geometry software. Starting with a circle, C, and a point, P, students will first need to draw the segment $\overline{CP}$, then construct the midpoint of the segment, M, and then construct the circle with center M that passes through C. Next, students must plot points at the intersections of the two circles, and, finally, draw the lines that are tangent to circle C. The final construction is shown below. Once students have done the construction, encourage them to move point P to see what elements of the construction change and what elements remain the same.

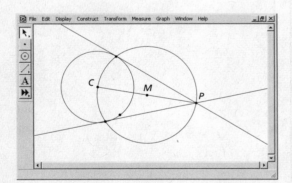

4 Prove the Circumscribed Angle Theorem.

Questioning Strategies

- What do you need to do to prove that $\angle PQR$ and $\angle PCR$ are supplementary? Show that the sum of the angle measures is 180°.

- Which angle measures in quadrilateral $QPCR$ do you know? Explain. $m\angle QPC = m\angle QRC = 90°$ since they are right angles by the Tangent-Radius Theorem.

- What other facts do you know about angle measures in a quadrilateral? The sum of the measures of the angles of a quadrilateral is 360°.

Teaching Strategies

The proof of the Circumscribed Angle Theorem is straightforward, so you may want to ask students to write the entire proof on their own. In this case, have students close their books and write the "Given" and "Prove" for the theorem and draw an accompanying figure. If students need additional support to write the proof itself, you might want to have students work in pairs or small groups. Once students have had a chance to complete their proofs, have them share their work so that they can compare different ways of writing and organizing the proof.

3 **Construct a tangent to a circle.**

Construct a tangent line from point P to circle C.

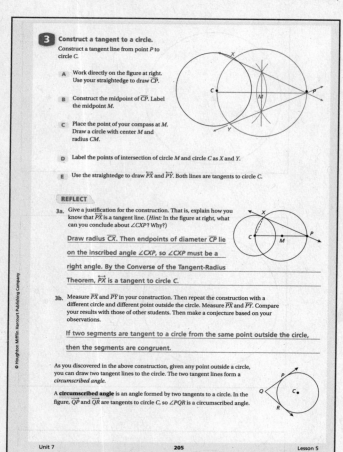

A. Work directly on the figure at right. Use your straightedge to draw $\overline{CP}$.

B. Construct the midpoint of $\overline{CP}$. Label the midpoint M.

C. Place the point of your compass at M. Draw a circle with center M and radius CM.

D. Label the points of intersection of circle M and circle C as X and Y.

E. Use the straightedge to draw $\overrightarrow{PX}$ and $\overrightarrow{PY}$. Both lines are tangents to circle C.

REFLECT

3a. Give a justification for the construction. That is, explain how you know that $\overrightarrow{PX}$ is a tangent line. (*Hint:* In the figure at right, what can you conclude about $\angle CXP$? Why?)

Draw radius $\overline{CX}$. Then endpoints of diameter $\overline{CP}$ lie

on the inscribed angle $\angle CXP$, so $\angle CXP$ must be a

right angle. By the Converse of the Tangent-Radius

Theorem, $\overrightarrow{PX}$ is a tangent to circle C.

3b. Measure $\overline{PX}$ and $\overline{PY}$ in your construction. Then repeat the construction with a different circle and different point outside the circle. Measure $\overline{PX}$ and $\overline{PY}$. Compare your results with those of other students. Then make a conjecture based on your observations.

If two segments are tangent to a circle from the same point outside the circle,

then the segments are congruent.

As you discovered in the above construction, given any point outside a circle, you can draw two tangent lines to the circle. The two tangent lines form a *circumscribed angle*.

A **circumscribed angle** is an angle formed by two tangents to a circle. In the figure, $\overrightarrow{QP}$ and $\overrightarrow{QR}$ are tangents to circle C, so $\angle PQR$ is a circumscribed angle.

> **Circumscribed Angle Theorem**
> A circumscribed angle of a circle and its associated central angle are supplementary.

4 **Prove the Circumscribed Angle Theorem.**

Given: $\angle PQR$ is a circumscribed angle.

Prove: $\angle PQR$ and $\angle PCR$ are supplementary.

Complete the proof.

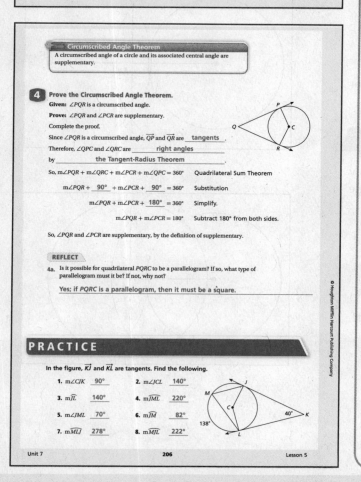

Since $\angle PQR$ is a circumscribed angle, $\overline{QP}$ and $\overline{QR}$ are ___tangents___ .

Therefore, $\angle QPC$ and $\angle QRC$ are ___right angles___

by ___the Tangent-Radius Theorem___ .

So, $m\angle PQR + m\angle QRC + m\angle PCR + m\angle QPC = 360°$ Quadrilateral Sum Theorem

$\quad m\angle PQR + \underline{90°} + m\angle PCR + \underline{90°} = 360°$ Substitution

$\quad\quad m\angle PQR + m\angle PCR + \underline{180°} = 360°$ Simplify.

$\quad\quad\quad m\angle PQR + m\angle PCR = 180°$ Subtract 180° from both sides.

So, $\angle PQR$ and $\angle PCR$ are supplementary, by the definition of supplementary.

REFLECT

4a. Is it possible for quadrilateral $PQRC$ to be a parallelogram? If so, what type of parallelogram must it be? If not, why not?

Yes; if $PQRC$ is a parallelogram, then it must be a square.

PRACTICE

In the figure, $\overrightarrow{KJ}$ and $\overrightarrow{KL}$ are tangents. Find the following.

1. $m\angle CJK$ ___90°___
2. $m\angle JCL$ ___140°___
3. $m\widehat{JL}$ ___140°___
4. $m\widehat{JML}$ ___220°___
5. $m\angle JML$ ___70°___
6. $m\widehat{JM}$ ___82°___
7. $m\widehat{MLJ}$ ___278°___
8. $m\widehat{MJL}$ ___222°___

© Houghton Mifflin Harcourt Publishing Company

Notes

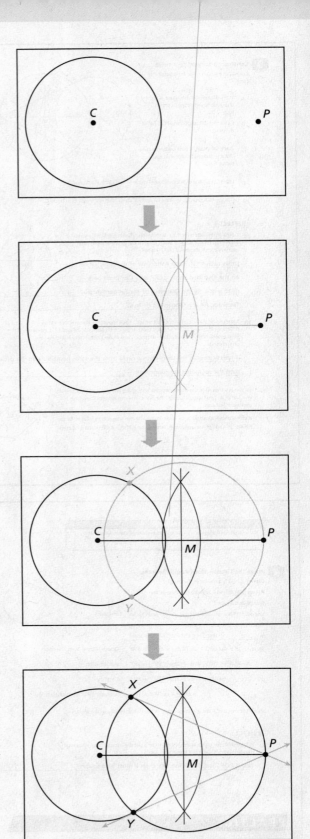

MATHEMATICAL PRACTICE — Highlighting the Standards

Standard 3 (Construct viable arguments and critique the reasoning of others) emphasizes that students should be able to recognize errors in logical arguments. Exercise 11 gives students an opportunity to hone this skill as they evaluate another student's work. Note that the error in this problem is a common one—the student assumed that two angles were congruent because they appeared to be congruent in a figure.

CLOSE

Essential Question

What are the key theorems about tangent lines to a circle?

If a line is tangent to a circle, then it is perpendicular to the radius drawn to the point of tangency. Conversely, if a line is perpendicular to a radius of a circle at a point on the circle, then the line is a tangent to the circle.

Summarize

Have students make a graphic organizer or illustrated guide that shows the steps for constructing a tangent line to a circle from a point outside the circle. A sample is shown at right.

PRACTICE

Exercises 1–8: Students use reasoning and apply the theorems of this lesson to find unknown angle measures and arc measures in a figure.

Exercise 9: Students prove the Converse of the Tangent-Radius Theorem.

Exercise 10: Students practice constructing a tangent to a circle from a point outside the circle.

Exercise 11: Students look closely at the work of another student to identify an error.

9. Prove the Converse of the Tangent-Radius Theorem.

Given: $\overline{CP} \perp m$

Prove: Line m is tangent to circle C.

(*Hint:* Let Q be any point on m other than P. Show that $CQ > CP$.)

Let Q be any point on m other than P. Then $\triangle CPQ$ is a right triangle with

hypotenuse $\overline{CQ}$. Therefore, $CQ > CP$ since the hypotenuse is the longest side

of a right triangle. Since $\overline{CP}$ is a radius, point Q must be in the exterior of circle

C. So, P is the only point of line m on circle C. Since line m intersects circle C at

exactly one point, it is a tangent.

10. Construct two tangents from point A to circle O.

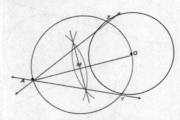

11. Error Analysis In the given figure, $\overline{QP}$ and $\overline{QR}$ are tangents. A student was asked to find m∠PSR. Critique the student's work and correct any errors.

Since ∠PQR is a circumscribed angle,
∠PQR and ∠PCR are supplementary,
so m∠PCR = 110°. Since ∠PSR ≅ ∠PCR,
you can conclude that m∠PSR = 110°.

The student made an error in assuming ∠PSR ≅ ∠PCR.

The student should have found that m$\overset{\frown}{PR}$ = 110°, so m$\overset{\frown}{PTR}$ = 250°.

Then m∠PSR = $\frac{1}{2}$m$\overset{\frown}{PTR}$ = $\frac{1}{2}$ · 250° = 125° by the Inscribed Angle Theorem.

Constructing Inscribed Circles

Essential question: How do you inscribe a circle in a triangle?

Standards for Mathematical Content

CC.9-12.G.C.3 Construct the inscribed ... circle of a triangle ...

Vocabulary
inscribed

incenter

incircle

Prerequisites
Angles, Lesson 1-4

Math Background
For any triangle, the bisectors of the angles are concurrent at a point called the incenter of the triangle. This is one of four concurrency points of a triangle. The others are the centroid (the point of concurrency of the three medians), the circumcenter (the point of concurrency of the perpendicular bisectors of the sides), and the orthocenter (the point of concurrency of the altitudes). Students explored the centroid in Lesson 3-9 and the circumcenter in Lesson 7-2.

INTRODUCE

Draw a triangle on the board. Ask students what it would mean for a circle to be inscribed in the triangle. Tell students that when a circle is inscribed, each side of the triangle is a tangent to the circle. Ask students if they think it is possible to inscribe a circle in any triangle, regardless of its shape or size. Explain to students that they will learn a technique for locating the center of the inscribed circle that works for any triangle.

TEACH

1 EXAMPLE

Questioning Strategies
• How many angle bisectors does a triangle have? **3**
• What is true about the points on the bisector of an angle? **The points are all equidistant from the sides of the angle.**

EXTRA EXAMPLE
Construct the inscribed circle for the triangle.

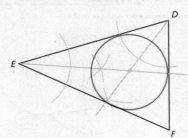

Highlighting the Standards

Standard 3 (Construct viable arguments and critique the reasoning of others) includes making conjectures. Now that students are familiar with the incenter, median, and circumcenter of a triangle, students can use geometry software to help them make a conjecture about the types of triangles in which these three points coincide. (The three points coincide in equilateral triangles.)

CLOSE

Essential Question
How do you inscribe a circle in a triangle?

Construct the bisectors of two of the triangle's angles. The point of intersection is the center of the required circle.

Summarize
Have students write a journal entry that summarizes the steps for constructing the incircle of a triangle.

PRACTICE

Where skills are taught	Where skills are practiced
1 EXAMPLE	EXS. 1–4

Exercises 5–6: Students use reasoning to extend what they learned about inscribed circles.

Name_____ Class_____ Date_____

7-6

Constructing Inscribed Circles

Essential question: *How do you inscribe a circle in a triangle?*

COMMON CORE
CC.9-12.G.C.3

A circle is **inscribed** in a polygon if each side of the polygon is tangent to the circle. In the figure, circle C is inscribed in quadrilateral WXYZ.

The following example will guide you through the reasoning process for constructing an inscribed circle in a triangle.

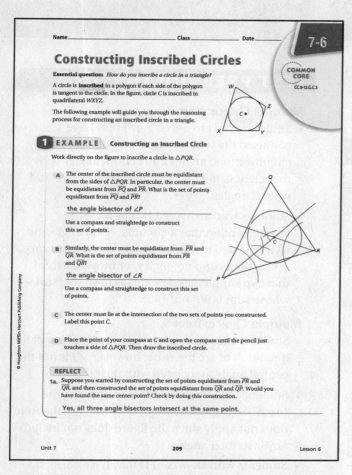

1 EXAMPLE Constructing an Inscribed Circle

Work directly on the figure to inscribe a circle in △PQR.

A The center of the inscribed circle must be equidistant from the sides of △PQR. In particular, the center must be equidistant from $\overline{PQ}$ and $\overline{PR}$. What is the set of points equidistant from $\overline{PQ}$ and $\overline{PR}$?

the angle bisector of ∠P

Use a compass and straightedge to construct this set of points.

B Similarly, the center must be equidistant from $\overline{PR}$ and $\overline{QR}$. What is the set of points equidistant from $\overline{PR}$ and $\overline{QR}$?

the angle bisector of ∠R

Use a compass and straightedge to construct this set of points.

C The center must lie at the intersection of the two sets of points you constructed. Label this point C.

D Place the point of your compass at C and open the compass until the pencil just touches a side of △PQR. Then draw the inscribed circle.

REFLECT

1a. Suppose you started by constructing the set of points equidistant from $\overline{PR}$ and $\overline{QR}$, and then constructed the set of points equidistant from $\overline{QR}$ and $\overline{QP}$. Would you have found the same center point? Check by doing this construction.

Yes, all three angle bisectors intersect at the same point.

You may have discovered that the angle bisectors of a triangle intersect at a common point. This point is called the **incenter** of the triangle. A circle that is inscribed in a triangle has its center at the incenter and is sometimes called the triangle's **incircle**.

PRACTICE

Construct the inscribed circle for each triangle.

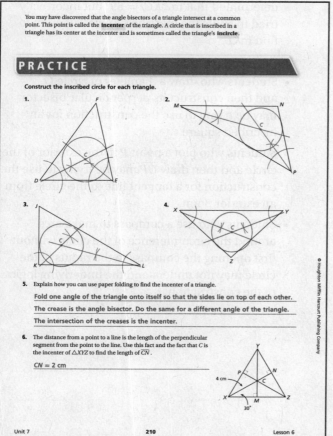

1.

2.

3.

4.

5. Explain how you can use paper folding to find the incenter of a triangle.

Fold one angle of the triangle onto itself so that the sides lie on top of each other.

The crease is the angle bisector. Do the same for a different angle of the triangle.

The intersection of the creases is the incenter.

6. The distance from a point to a line is the length of the perpendicular segment from the point to the line. Use this fact and the fact that C is the incenter of △XYZ to find the length of $\overline{CN}$.

CN = 2 cm

4 cm

30°

© Houghton Mifflin Harcourt Publishing Company

COMMON CORE CORRELATION

Standard	Items
CC.9-12.G.CO.13	8, 9
CC.9-12.G.C.2	1, 2, 3, 5, 7
CC.9-12.G.C.3	4, 10
CC.9-12.G.C.4(+)	6

TEST PREP DOCTOR ✚

Multiple Choice: Item 2

- Students who answered **F** or **J** may have confused the relationship between circumscribed angles and central angles with the relationship between inscribed angles and central angles.

- Students who answered **H** may have the misconception that a circumscribed angle and its associated central angle are complementary rather than supplementary, or they may think that two supplementary angles have measures whose sum is 90° not 180°.

Multiple Choice: Item 5

- Students who answered **A** may be thinking of the definition of arc measure; however, $\angle J$ is not the central angle associated with the arc.

- Students who answered **B** may be using the Inscribed Angle Theorem; however, the theorem does not apply since the figure does not include any inscribed angles.

- Students who answered **D** may have correctly determined that $m\angle KCJ = 65°$ but incorrectly tried to apply the Inscribed Angle Theorem to find $m\overparen{KL}$.

Free Response: Item 8

- Students who draw a diameter of circle O and then construct its perpendicular bisector may be trying to use the construction for an inscribed square.

- Students who plot a point P in the exterior of the circle and then draw $\overline{OP}$ may be trying to use the construction for a tangent line to the circle from an exterior point.

- Students who use a compass to make arcs around the circumference of the circle without first opening the compass to the radius of the circle may not understand the underlying logic of the construction.

Notes

Name _____ Class _____ Date _____

MULTIPLE CHOICE

1. Which statement describes the relationship between $\angle XYZ$ and $\angle XCZ$?

   A. $\angle XYZ \cong \angle XCZ$

   B. $m\angle XYZ = 2m\angle XCZ$

   C. $m\angle XYZ = \frac{1}{2}m\angle XCZ$

   D. $\angle XYZ$ and $\angle XCZ$ are supplementary.

2. $\overline{PR}$ and $\overline{QR}$ are tangents to circle C. Which expression represents $m\angle C$?

   F. $(2y)°$ H. $(90-y)°$

   G. $(180-y)°$ J. $\left(\frac{1}{2}y\right)°$

3. In circle O, $\angle ABC$ is an inscribed angle and $\overline{AC}$ is a diameter. Which of the following must be true?

   A. $\angle ABC$ is an acute angle.

   B. $\angle ABC$ is a right angle.

   C. $\overline{AB}$ is a radius.

   D. $\overline{AC} \perp \overline{BC}$

4. Jessica is using a compass and straightedge to construct the inscribed circle for $\triangle PQR$. Which of the following should be her first step?

   F. Construct the bisector of $\angle Q$

   G. Construct the perpendicular bisector of $\overline{QR}$

   H. Construct the perpendicular from P to $\overline{QR}$

   J. Construct the midpoint of $\overline{PR}$

5. $\overline{JK}$ is a tangent to circle C. What is $m\widehat{KL}$?

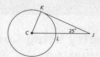

   A. 25°   C. 65°

   B. 50°   D. 130°

6. Noah is constructing a tangent from P to circle C. The figure shows what he has done so far. What should he do next?

   F. Construct a perpendicular at point P.

   G. Construct a perpendicular at point C.

   H. Construct a circle whose center is at the intersection of $\overline{CP}$ and circle C.

   J. Construct the midpoint of $\overline{CP}$.

---

7. What is $m\angle GCJ$?

   A. 39°   C. 102°

   B. 78°   D. 156°

FREE RESPONSE

8. Use a compass and straightedge to construct a regular hexagon that is inscribed in circle O.

9. Explain how you can modify your construction in Item 8 to inscribe an equilateral triangle in circle O.

   After completing the construction, use a straightedge to draw $\overline{AC}$, $\overline{CE}$, and $\overline{EA}$. $\triangle ACE$ is an equilateral triangle.

10. Quadrilateral $WXYZ$ is inscribed in circle O. Complete the following proof to show that opposite angles are supplementary.

   a. $\widehat{YZW}$ and $\widehat{WXY}$ make a complete circle.
   Therefore, $m\widehat{YZW} + m\widehat{WXY} =$ ___360°___.

   b. By the Inscribed Angle Theorem,
   $m\angle X = \frac{1}{2}m\widehat{YZW}$ and $m\angle Z = \frac{1}{2}m\widehat{WXY}$

   c. Complete the proof by showing that the sum of $m\angle X$ and $m\angle Z$ is 180°.

   $m\angle X + m\angle Z = \frac{1}{2}m\widehat{YZW} + \frac{1}{2}m\widehat{WXY}$

   $= \frac{1}{2}\left(m\widehat{YZW} + m\widehat{WXY}\right)$

   $= \frac{1}{2} \cdot 360°$

   $= 180°$

   Similar reasoning can be used to show angles W and Y are supplementary.

Geometry Using Coordinates and Equations

Unit Vocabulary

directrix   (8-2)

focus   (8-2)

parabola   (8-2)

UNIT 8

Geometry Using Coordinates and Equations

Unit Focus

In this unit, you will explore analytic geometry, which is the study of geometry using a coordinate system. First you will learn how to use the distance formula to write the equation of a circle and the equation of a parabola. Then you will see how you can use slope to partition a segment into a given ratio and to determine when lines are parallel or perpendicular. You will also write coordinate proofs using slope and solve systems of equations.

Unit at a Glance

COMMON CORE

Lesson		Standards for Mathematical Content
8-1	The Equation of a Circle	CC.9-12.G.GPE.1, CC.9-12.G.GPE.4
8-2	The Equation of a Parabola	CC.9-12.G.GPE.2
8-3	Partitioning a Segment	CC.9-12.G.GPE.6
8-4	Slope and Parallel Lines	CC.9-12.G.GPE.5
8-5	Slope and Perpendicular Lines	CC.9-12.G.GPE.5
8-6	Coordinate Proofs Using Slope	CC.9-12.G.GPE.4
8-7	Systems of Equations	CC.9-12.A.REI.7
	Test Prep	

© Houghton Mifflin Harcourt Publishing Company

UNIT 8

Unit 8   213   Geometry Using Coordinates and Equations

Unpacking the Common Core State Standards

Use the table to help you understand the Standards for Mathematical Content that are taught in this unit. Refer to the lessons listed after each standard for exploration and practice.

COMMON CORE Standards for Mathematical Content	What It Means For You
CC.9-12.A.REI.7 Solve a simple system consisting of a linear equation and a quadratic equation in two variables algebraically and graphically. Lesson 8-7	You learned how to solve systems of linear equations in Algebra. Now you will extend what you know to solve systems that involve a line and a circle or a line and a parabola.
CC.9-12.G.GPE.1 Derive the equation of a circle of given center and radius using the Pythagorean Theorem; complete the square to find the center and radius of a circle given by an equation. Lesson 8-1	Given the radius and center of a circle, you will write an equation for the circle. Conversely, given an equation of a circle, you will learn how to determine the radius and center.
CC.9-12.G.GPE.2 Derive the equation of a parabola given a focus and directrix. Lesson 8-2	You will see that the points that form a parabola can be defined in terms of their distance from a fixed point and a given line. You will use this idea and the distance formula to derive the equation of a parabola.
CC.9-12.G.GPE.4 Use coordinates to prove simple geometric theorems algebraically. Lessons 8-1, 8-6	As you will see, coordinates are useful for proving a wide range of geometry theorems. You will use what you learn about equations of circles and slopes of sides of quadrilaterals to help you write coordinate proofs.
CC.9-12.G.GPE.5 Prove the slope criteria for parallel and perpendicular lines and use them to solve geometric problems (e.g., find the equation of a line parallel or perpendicular to a given line that passes through a given point). Lessons 8-4, 8-5	You can determine whether two lines are parallel or perpendicular if you know the slopes of the lines. You will see how to use this idea to write equations of lines and to write coordinate proofs.
CC.9-12.G.GPE.6 Find the point on a directed line segment between two given points that partitions the segment in a given ratio. Lesson 8-3	You will learn how to find a point along a line segment that divides the segment in a particular way.

Unpacking the Common Core State Standards

This page lists and explains the Standards for Mathematical Content that are addressed in this unit. For information about the Standards for Mathematical Practice, which are integrated throughout the text, see Teacher Edition pages x–xiii.

Notes

_____

_____

_____

_____

_____

_____

_____

_____

_____

_____

_____

The Equation of a Circle

Essential question: *How do you write the equation of a circle if you know its radius and the coordinates of its center?*

COMMON CORE Standards for Mathematical Content

CC.9-12.G.GPE.1 Derive the equation of a circle of given center and radius using the Pythagorean Theorem; complete the square to find the center and radius of a circle given by an equation.

CC.9-12.G.GPE.4 Use coordinates to prove simple geometric theorems algebraically.

Prerequisites
Completing the Square, Algebra 1

Math Background
In Algebra 2, students study the equations of the four major conic sections: circles, ellipses, hyperbolas, and parabolas. In this unit, students get a preview of these ideas by using the Pythagorean Theorem and the distance formula to derive equations for circles and parabolas. In Lesson 8-1, students connect the geometric definition of a circle (the set of points that are a fixed distance from a given point) with the algebraic representation of it (the equation of a circle with center (h, k) and radius r is $(x - h)^2 + (y - k)^2 = r^2$).

INTRODUCE

Remind students of the definition of a circle. Then, ask students to draw a circle that has center $(3, -1)$ and radius 2 on a coordinate plane. Be sure students understand that they should plot the center first and then count 2 units up from the center, 2 units down from the center, 2 units left from the center, and 2 units right from the center to plot four points that lie on the circle. Then, students can use a compass to help draw the rest of the circle.

TEACH

1 EXPLORE

Questioning Strategies
- In $\triangle CAP$, which side is the hypotenuse? What is its length? $\overline{CP}$; r
- How do you find the length of a horizontal segment like $\overline{CA}$? Take the absolute value of the difference of the x-coordinates.
- Why do you take the absolute value? Distance cannot be negative.

2 EXAMPLE

Questioning Strategies
- What three values do you need to find? the x- and y-coordinates of the center, and the length of the radius
- How do you complete the square? Add half the coefficient of the x-term squared and add half the coefficient of the y-term squared. Add the same quantities to the other side of the equation. Now, the equation will contain two perfect squares, one involving the variable x and one involving the variable y.

EXTRA EXAMPLE
Find the center and radius of the circle whose equation is $x^2 - 2x + y^2 + 4y = 4$. Then, graph the circle.

center: (1, −2); radius: 3

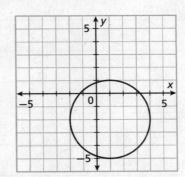

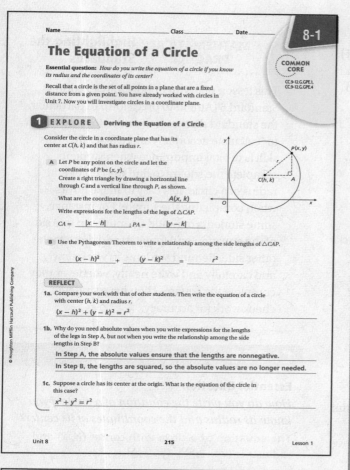

Name_____ Class_____ Date_____

The Equation of a Circle

8-1

COMMON CORE
CC.9-12.G.GPE.1,
CC.9-12.G.GPE.4

Essential question: *How do you write the equation of a circle if you know its radius and the coordinates of its center?*

Recall that a circle is the set of all points in a plane that are a fixed distance from a given point. You have already worked with circles in Unit 7. Now you will investigate circles in a coordinate plane.

1 EXPLORE   Deriving the Equation of a Circle

Consider the circle in a coordinate plane that has its center at $C(h, k)$ and that has radius r.

A Let P be any point on the circle and let the coordinates of P be (x, y).

Create a right triangle by drawing a horizontal line through C and a vertical line through P, as shown.

What are the coordinates of point A? ___$A(x, k)$___

Write expressions for the lengths of the legs of $\triangle CAP$.

$CA =$ ___$|x - h|$___ ; $PA =$ ___$|y - k|$___

B Use the Pythagorean Theorem to write a relationship among the side lengths of $\triangle CAP$.

___$(x - h)^2$___ + ___$(y - k)^2$___ = ___r^2___

REFLECT

1a. Compare your work with that of other students. Then write the equation of a circle with center (h, k) and radius r.

$(x - h)^2 + (y - k)^2 = r^2$

1b. Why do you need absolute values when you write expressions for the lengths of the legs in Step A, but not when you write the relationship among the side lengths in Step B?

In Step A, the absolute values ensure that the lengths are nonnegative.

In Step B, the lengths are squared, so the absolute values are no longer needed.

1c. Suppose a circle has its center at the origin. What is the equation of the circle in this case?

$x^2 + y^2 = r^2$

© Houghton Mifflin Harcourt Publishing Company

Equation of a Circle

The equation of a circle with center (h, k) and radius r is $(x - h)^2 + (y - k)^2 = r^2$.

2 EXAMPLE   Finding the Center and Radius of a Circle

Find the center and radius of the circle whose equation is $x^2 - 4x + y^2 + 2y = 4$. Then graph the circle.

A Complete the square to write the equation in the form $(x - h)^2 + (y - k)^2 = r^2$.

$x^2 - 4x + \boxed{} + y^2 + 2y + \boxed{} = 4 + \boxed{}$ Set up to complete the square.

$x^2 - 4x + \left(\frac{-4}{2}\right)^2 + y^2 + 2y + \left(\frac{2}{2}\right)^2 = 4 + \left(\frac{-4}{2}\right)^2 + \left(\frac{2}{2}\right)^2$ Add $\left(\frac{-4}{2}\right)^2$ and $\left(\frac{2}{2}\right)^2$ to both sides.

$x^2 - 4x + \underline{4} + y^2 + 2y + \underline{1} = 4 + \underline{5}$ Simplify.

$(x - \underline{2})^2 + (y + \underline{1})^2 = \underline{9}$ Factor.

B Identify h, k, and r to determine the center and radius.

$h = \underline{2}$ $k = \underline{-1}$ $r = \underline{3}$

So, the center is ($\underline{2}$, $\underline{-1}$) and the radius is $\underline{3}$.

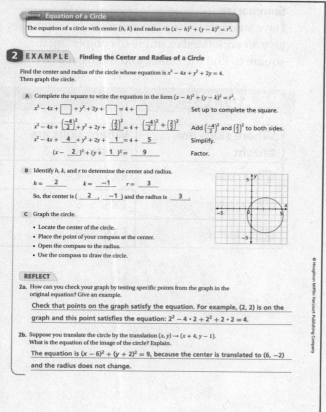

C Graph the circle.

- Locate the center of the circle.
- Place the point of your compass at the center.
- Open the compass to the radius.
- Use the compass to draw the circle.

REFLECT

2a. How can you check your graph by testing specific points from the graph in the original equation? Give an example.

Check that points on the graph satisfy the equation. For example, (2, 2) is on the graph and this point satisfies the equation: $2^2 - 4 \cdot 2 + 2^2 + 2 \cdot 2 = 4$.

2b. Suppose you translate the circle by the translation $(x, y) \rightarrow (x + 4, y - 1)$. What is the equation of the image of the circle? Explain.

The equation is $(x - 6)^2 + (y + 2)^2 = 9$, because the center is translated to (6, −2) and the radius does not change.

© Houghton Mifflin Harcourt Publishing Company

Avoid Common Errors

Some students may say that the circle with equation $(x - 2)^2 + (y + 1)^2 = 9$ has center $(-2, 1)$. It may help these students to rewrite the equation as $(x - 2)^2 + (y - (-1))^2 = 9$ and compare this to the general equation, $(x - h)^2 + (y - k)^2 = r^2$, which has center (h, k). This may help them see that the correct center is $(2, -1)$.

3 EXAMPLE

Questioning Strategies

• What steps can you use to write this proof?

First, write the equation of the circle. Then, check to see whether the given point is a solution of the equation. If so, the point lies on the circle.

• How do you determine the radius of the circle?

Count units on the coordinate grid, moving horizontally or vertically from the center to the circle.

EXTRA EXAMPLE

Prove or disprove that the point $(3, 4)$ lies on the circle that is centered at the origin and contains the point $(-5, 0)$.

The radius of the circle is 5. The equation of the circle is $x^2 + y^2 = 25$. Substituting the x- and y-coordinates of the given point into the left side of the equation gives $3^2 + 4^2$. Since this is equal to 25, the point is a solution of the equation, so it lies on the circle.

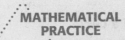

MATHEMATICAL PRACTICE · **Highlighting the Standards**

This lesson offers an opportunity to address Standard 6 (Attend to precision). In particular, the standard discusses the need for students to "calculate accurately and efficiently." This skill is of vital importance when students complete the square to find the center and radius of a circle. It is easy to make errors when completing the square. For instance, some students may add quantities to one side of the equation and forget to add them to the other side. Remind students to work slowly and carefully and write neatly, whenever they complete the square. Then have students check work for accuracy.

CLOSE

Essential Question

How do you write the equation of a circle if you know its radius and the coordinates of its center?

The equation of a circle with center (h, k) and radius r is $(x - h)^2 + (y - k)^2 = r^2$.

Summarize

Have students write a journal entry in which they give an annotated example of completing the square to find the center and radius of a circle.

PRACTICE

Where skills are taught	Where skills are practiced
1 EXPLORE	EXS. 1–4
2 EXAMPLE	EXS. 5–6
3 EXAMPLE	EXS. 7–9

3 EXAMPLE Writing a Coordinate Proof

Prove or disprove that the point $(1, \sqrt{15})$ lies on the circle that is centered at the origin and contains the point $(0, 4)$.

A Plot a point at the origin and at $(0, 4)$. Use these to help you draw the circle centered at the origin that contains $(0, 4)$.

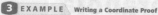

B Determine the radius: $r =$ _____4_____

C Use the radius and the coordinates of the center to write the equation of the circle.

$$x^2 + y^2 = 16$$

D Substitute the x- and y-coordinates of the point $(1, \sqrt{15})$ in the equation of the circle to check whether they satisfy the equation.

$$\underline{\quad 1 \quad}^2 + \underline{\quad \sqrt{15} \quad}^2 \stackrel{?}{=} 16 \quad \text{Substitute.}$$

$$\underline{\quad 1 \quad} + \underline{\quad 15 \quad} = 16 \quad \text{Simplify.}$$

E So, the point $(1, \sqrt{15})$ lies on the circle because

the point's x- and y-coordinates satisfy the equation of the circle.

REFLECT

3a. Explain how to determine the radius of the circle.

Possible answer: Start at the origin and move horizontally or vertically in a straight line, counting the number of units until you reach the circle.

3b. Name another point with noninteger coordinates that lies on the circle. Explain.

Possible answer: $(3, \sqrt{7})$, because $3^2 + (\sqrt{7})^2 = 16$.

3c. Explain how you can prove that the point $(2, \sqrt{5})$ does *not* lie on the circle.

The point's x- and y-coordinates do not satisfy the equation of the circle:
$2^2 + (\sqrt{5})^2 \neq 16$.

PRACTICE

Write the equation of the circle with the given center and radius.

1. center: $(0, 2)$; radius 5
    $$x^2 + (y - 2)^2 = 25$$

2. center: $(-1, 3)$; radius 8
    $$(x + 1)^2 + (y - 3)^2 = 64$$

3. center: $(-4, -5)$; radius $\sqrt{2}$
    $$(x + 4)^2 + (y + 5)^2 = 2$$

4. center: $(9, 0)$; radius $\sqrt{3}$
    $$(x - 9)^2 + y^2 = 3$$

Find the center and radius of the circle with the given equation. Then graph the circle.

5. $x^2 - 2x + y^2 = 15$
    center: $(1, 0)$; radius: 4

6. $x^2 + 4x + y^2 - 6y = -9$
    center: $(-2, 3)$; radius: 2

7. Prove or disprove that the point $(1, \sqrt{3})$ lies on the circle that is centered at the origin and contains the point $(0, 2)$.

    The radius of the circle is 2, so its equation is $x^2 + y^2 = 4$. The point $(1, \sqrt{3})$
    does lie on the circle, because its x- and y-coordinates satisfy the equation:
    $1^2 + (\sqrt{3})^2 = 1 + 3 = 4.$

8. Prove or disprove that the point $(2, \sqrt{3})$ lies on the circle that is centered at the origin and contains the point $(-3, 0)$.

    The radius of the circle is 3, so its equation is $x^2 + y^2 = 9$. The point $(2, \sqrt{3})$
    does not lie on the circle, because its x- and y-coordinates do not satisfy the
    equation: $2^2 + (\sqrt{3})^2 \neq 9.$

9. Prove or disprove that the circle with equation $x^2 - 4x + y^2 = -3$ intersects the y-axis.

    Points on the y-axis have x-coordinate 0. Substituting $x = 0$ in the equation gives
    $y^2 = -3$. This equation has no real solutions, so there are no points of the
    form $(0, y)$ on the circle. Therefore, the circle does not intersect the y-axis.

<table>
<tr><td>8-2</td><td></td></tr>
</table>

The Equation of a Parabola

Essential question: *How do you write the equation of a parabola given its focus and directrix?*

COMMON CORE Standards for Mathematical Content

CC.9-12.G.GPE.2 Derive the equation of a parabola given a focus and directrix.

Vocabulary
parabola

focus

directrix

Prerequisites
The Distance Formula, Lesson 1-2

Math Background
A *locus* is a collection of points that share a property or satisfy a given condition. In Lesson 8-1, students worked with circles. A circle may be defined as the locus of points in a plane that are a fixed distance from a given point. In this lesson, students explore parabolas. A parabola is the locus of points in a plane that are equidistant from a given point and a given line.

INTRODUCE

Begin by discussing the idea of the distance from a point to a line. Draw a point, *P,* and a line, *m,* on the board and ask students how they would define the distance between point *P* and line *m*. Students may mention that the distance should be the length of a line segment from *P* to line *m*. Explain that there are infinitely many such line segments, some of which are shown in the figure. Tell students that the distance is defined to be the length of the *shortest* segment from *P* to line *m*. This is the perpendicular segment from *P* to line *m*.

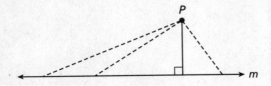

TEACH

1 EXPLORE

Materials: compass, straightedge

Questioning Strategies

- Will everyone in the class construct the same point in this investigation? Why or why not?
  No; there are infinitely many points that are equidistant from point *P* to line ℓ.
- What happens as your teacher plots more and more points? The points begin to fill in a curve that has the shape of a parabola.

Teaching Strategy

The following are a few tips for getting the best result from this Explore.

- In Step A, encourage students in different parts of the classroom to plot points on different parts of line ℓ. For example, you might have students on the right side of the room choose points to the right of the *y*-axis while students on the left side of the room choose points on the left side of the *y*-axis. The more spread out the choice of points along line ℓ, the better the resulting parabola will look.
- Encourage students to do their constructions accurately and slowly. You might have them use a ruler to check that $PX = PQ$ before they report their coordinates for point *X*.
- Plot the points that students report on a large coordinate plane in front of the class.

┊ **MATHEMATICAL** **Highlighting the**
┊ **PRACTICE** **Standards**
┊┄┄┄┄┄┄┄┄

You may wish to discuss Standard 6 (Attend to precision) as the class completes this Explore. In particular, the standard states that students should "express numerical answers with a degree of precision appropriate for the problem context." To that end, ask students whether it would make sense for a student to report the approximate coordinates of his or her point *x* as (1, 0.793). Then discuss levels of precision that do make sense for this activity.

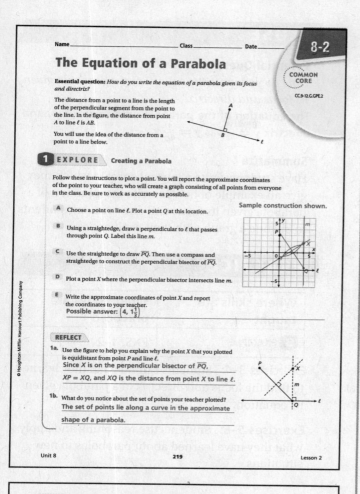

Name_____ Class_____ Date_____

The Equation of a Parabola

8-2

COMMON CORE

CC.9-12.G.GPE.2

Essential question: *How do you write the equation of a parabola given its focus and directrix?*

The distance from a point to a line is the length of the perpendicular segment from the point to the line. In the figure, the distance from point A to line ℓ is AB.

You will use the idea of the distance from a point to a line below.

1 EXPLORE Creating a Parabola

Follow these instructions to plot a point. You will report the approximate coordinates of the point to your teacher, who will create a graph consisting of all points from everyone in the class. Be sure to work as accurately as possible.

A Choose a point on line ℓ. Plot a point Q at this location.

B Using a straightedge, draw a perpendicular to ℓ that passes through point Q. Label this line m.

C Use the straightedge to draw $\overline{PQ}$. Then use a compass and straightedge to construct the perpendicular bisector of $\overline{PQ}$.

D Plot a point X where the perpendicular bisector intersects line m.

E Write the approximate coordinates of point X and report the coordinates to your teacher.
Possible answer: $\left(4, 1\frac{1}{3}\right)$

Sample construction shown.

REFLECT

1a. Use the figure to help you explain why the point X that you plotted is equidistant from point P and line ℓ.
Since X is on the perpendicular bisector of $\overline{PQ}$,

XP = XQ, and XQ is the distance from point X to line ℓ.

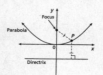

1b. What do you notice about the set of points your teacher plotted?
The set of points lie along a curve in the approximate

shape of a parabola.

© Houghton Mifflin Harcourt Publishing Company

Unit 8   219   Lesson 2

A **parabola** is the set of all points P in a plane that are equidistant from a given point, called the **focus**, and a given line, called the **directrix**.

To derive the general equation of a parabola, you can use the above definition, the distance formula, and the idea that the distance from a point to a line is the length of the perpendicular segment from the point to the line.

2 EXPLORE Deriving the Equation of a Parabola

A Let the focus of the parabola be F(0, p) and let the directrix be the line y = −p. Let P be a point on the parabola with coordinates (x, y).

B Let Q be the point of intersection of the perpendicular from P and the directrix. Then the coordinates of Q are (x, −p).

C By the definition of a parabola, FP = QP.

By the distance formula,
$FP = \sqrt{(x-0)^2 + (y-p)^2} = \sqrt{x^2 + (y-p)^2}$
and $QP = \sqrt{(x-x)^2 + (y-(-p))^2} = \sqrt{0 + (y+p)^2} = |y+p|$.

$\sqrt{x^2 + (y-p)^2}$ =	$|y+p|$	Set FP equal to QP.
$x^2 + (y-p)^2$ =	$|y+p|^2$	Square both sides.
$x^2 + y^2 - 2py + p^2$ =	$y^2 + 2py + p^2$	Expand the squared terms.
$x^2 - 2py$ =	$2py$	Subtract y^2 and p^2 from both sides.
x^2 =	$4py$	Add 2py to both sides.
$\frac{1}{4p}x^2$ =	y	Solve for y.

REFLECT

2a. Explain how the value of p determines whether the parabola opens up or down.
When p is positive, the focus is on the positive y-axis and the directrix is a

horizontal line below the x-axis, so the parabola opens up; when p is negative,

the focus is on the negative y-axis and the directrix is a horizontal line above

the x-axis, so the parabola opens down.

2b. Explain why the origin (0, 0) is always a point on a parabola with focus F(0, p) and directrix y = −p.
The distance from (0, 0) to (0, p) is |p|, and the distance from (0, 0) to the directrix

is also |p|, so (0, 0) is on the parabola by definition.

© Houghton Mifflin Harcourt Publishing Company

Unit 8   220   Lesson 2

2 EXPLORE

Questioning Strategies

• **How can you find the distance QP without using the distance formula?** Because $\overline{QP}$ is vertical, you can find the length of the segment by subtracting the y-coordinates of Q and P and taking the absolute value of the result.

• **How do you know that the origin is a point on this parabola?** Its distance from the focus, $(0, p)$ is $|p|$ and its distance from the directrix, $y = -p$, is also $|p|$, so it is equidistant from the focus and the directrix.

3 EXAMPLE

Questioning Strategies

• **What does the value of p tell you about the parabola?** Because p is negative, the parabola will open down.

• **What is the domain and range for the function described by this parabola?** The domain is all real numbers; the range is all real numbers less than or equal to zero.

EXTRA EXAMPLE

Write the equation of the parabola with focus $(0, -1)$ and directrix $y = 1$. Then, graph the parabola.
$y = -\frac{1}{4}x^2$

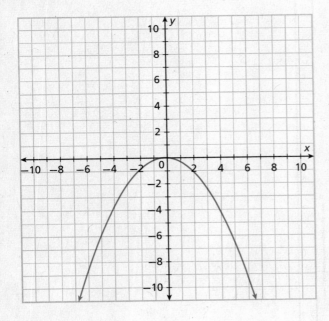

CLOSE

Essential Question

How do you write the equation of a parabola given its focus and directrix?

The equation of the parabola with focus $(0, p)$ and directrix $y = -p$ is $y = \frac{1}{4p}x^2$.

Summarize

Have students write a journal entry in which they give an example of how to write the equation of a parabola given its focus and directrix. Ask students to include a graph with their explanation.

PRACTICE

Where skills are taught	Where skills are practiced
3 EXAMPLE	EXS. 1–2

Exercises 3–4: Students extend what they learned to find the focus and directrix of a parabola given its equation.

Exercises 5–6: Students use reasoning and apply what they have learned about parabolas to new situations.

3 EXAMPLE Writing the Equation of a Parabola

Write the equation of the parabola with focus $(0, -4)$ and directrix $y = 4$.
Then graph the parabola.

A The focus of the parabola is $(0, p)$, so $p = $ ___-4___

The general equation of a parabola is $y = \frac{1}{4p}x^2$.

So, the equation of this parabola is $y = -\frac{1}{16}x^2$

B To graph the parabola, complete the table of
values. Then plot points and draw the curve.

x	y
-8	-4
-4	-1
0	0
4	-1
8	-4

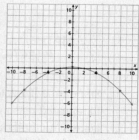

REFLECT

3a. The *vertex* of a parabola is the midpoint of the perpendicular segment from the
focus to the directrix. What is the vertex of the parabola you graphed?

$(0, 0)$

3b. Does your graph lie above or below the *x*-axis? Why does this make sense based on
the parabola's equation?

Below; x^2 is always greater than or equal to 0, so $-\frac{1}{16}x^2$ is always less than or
equal to 0. Therefore, the function's *y*-values are always less than or equal to 0.

3c. Describe any symmetry your graph has. Why does this make sense based on the
parabola's equation?

The parabola has reflection symmetry, with the *y*-axis as the line of symmetry.

This makes sense because every value of *x* and its opposite have the same *y*-value:

$-\frac{1}{16}x^2 = -\frac{1}{16}(-x)^2$.

© Houghton Mifflin Harcourt Publishing Company

PRACTICE

Write the equation of the parabola with the given focus and directrix. Then
graph the parabola.

1. focus: $(0, 2)$; directrix: $y = -2$

$y = \frac{1}{8}x^2$

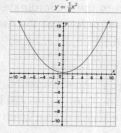

2. focus: $(0, -5)$; directrix: $y = 5$

$y = -\frac{1}{20}x^2$

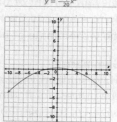

Find the focus and directrix of the parabola with the given equation.

3. $y = -\frac{1}{24}x^2$

focus: $(0, -6)$; directrix: $y = 6$

4. $y = 2x^2$

focus: $\left(0, \frac{1}{8}\right)$; directrix: $y = -\frac{1}{8}$

5. Complete the table by writing the equation of each parabola. Then use a
calculator to graph the equations in the same window to help you make a
conjecture: What happens to the graph of a parabola as the focus and directrix
move apart?

Focus	(0, 1)	(0, 2)	(0, 3)	(0, 4)
Directrix	$y = -1$	$y = -2$	$y = -3$	$y = -4$
Equation	$y = \frac{1}{4}x^2$	$y = \frac{1}{8}x^2$	$y = \frac{1}{12}x^2$	$y = \frac{1}{16}x^2$

As the focus and directrix move apart, the parabola is vertically compressed.

6. Find the length of the line segment that is parallel to the directrix
of a parabola, that passes through the focus, and that has endpoints
on the parabola.

$|4p|$, because the endpoints are $(-2p, p)$ and $(2p, p)$.

© Houghton Mifflin Harcourt Publishing Company

8-3 Partitioning a Segment

Essential question: *How do you find the point on a directed line segment that partitions the segment in a given ratio?*

COMMON CORE Standards for Mathematical Content

CC.9-12.G.GPE.6 Find the point on a directed line segment between two given points that partitions the segment in a given ratio.

Prerequisites
Slope, Algebra 1

Math Background
This is the first of three lessons based on slope. Students studied slope in Algebra 1 and learned to find the slope of a line. They also used slope to write the equation of a line, either in slope-intercept form ($y = mx + b$) or in point-slope form ($y - y_1 = m(x - x_1)$). In this lesson, students use the definition of slope (i.e., the ratio of the rise to the run) to help them find a point that divides a given line segment in a given ratio.

INTRODUCE

Draw the figure shown below on the board. Tell students that point P divides $\overline{AB}$ in the ratio 3 to 1. Ask students to explain what this means. Encourage students to give as many equivalent explanations as possible. For example, AP is 3 times PB; $\overline{AP}$ is 3 units long, while $\overline{PB}$ is 1 unit long; $\frac{AP}{BP} = 3$; and so on.

TEACH

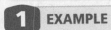

Questioning Strategies
• Do you expect point P to be closer to A or closer to B? Why? **Closer to B; P is located 60% of the way from A to B and 60% is greater than 50%.**
• How does the slope of $\overline{AP}$ compare with the slope of $\overline{AB}$? Why? **The slopes are the same since P is on $\overline{AB}$.**

EXTRA EXAMPLE
Find the coordinates of the point P that lies along the directed line segment from $A(1, 1)$ to $B(7, 3)$ and partitions the segment in the ratio 1 to 4. **(2.2, 1.4)**

MATHEMATICAL PRACTICE — Highlighting the Standards

Standard 8 (Look for and express regularity in repeated reasoning) includes looking for general methods and shortcuts. After students have solved several problems like the example, ask them to share any shortcuts they may have discovered. For instance, with practice, students may find that they can quickly determine the relevant rise and run by plotting the given points and counting units on the coordinate plane. Students may find other ways to "routinize" the process.

CLOSE

Essential Question
How do you find the point on a directed line segment that partitions the segment in a given ratio?
Find the percent of the distance from point A to point B at which the required point is located. Find the run and rise for the given segment. Add the relevant percent of the run to the x-coordinate of point A and add the relevant percent of the rise to the y-coordinate of point A.

Summarize
Have students write a journal entry to summarize the process for finding the point on a directed line segment that partitions the segment in a given ratio.

PRACTICE

Where skills are taught	Where skills are practiced
1 EXAMPLE	EXS. 1–4

Exercise 5: Students use what they learned in the example to solve a real-world problem.

Exercise 6: Students extend what they learned to solve a more challenging problem.

Name_____ Class_____ Date_____

Partitioning a Segment

Essential question: *How do you find the point on a directed line segment that partitions the segment in a given ratio?*

Recall that the *slope* of a straight line in a coordinate plane is the ratio of the *rise* to the *run*.

In the figure, the slope of $\overline{AB}$ is $\frac{rise}{run} = \frac{4}{8} = \frac{1}{2}$.

In the next several lessons, you will see how to use slope to solve geometry problems and to prove geometry theorems.

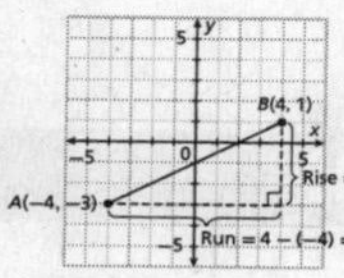

B(4, 1)
Rise = 1 − (−3) = 4
A(−4, −3)
Run = 4 − (−4) = 8

The following example also uses the idea of a *directed line segment*. This means the line segment has a direction associated with it, usually specified by moving from one endpoint to the other.

1 EXAMPLE Partitioning a Segment

Find the coordinates of the point *P* that lies along the directed line segment from *A*(3, 4) to *B*(6, 10) and partitions the segment in the ratio 3 to 2.

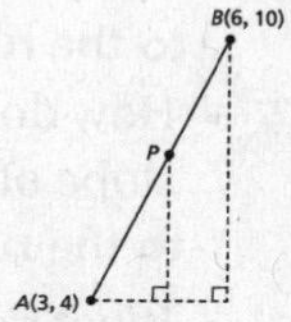

A Convert the ratio to a percent.

Point *P* is $\frac{3}{3+2} = \frac{3}{5}$ of the distance from *A* to *B*.

This is __60__% of the distance from *A* to *B*.

B Find the rise and run for $\overline{AB}$.

Rise = 10 − 4 = 6   Run = __6 − 3 = 3__

C The slope of $\overline{AP}$ must be the same as the slope of $\overline{AB}$.

So, to find the coordinates of *P*, add __60__% of the run to the *x*-coordinate of *A* and add __60__% of the rise to the *y*-coordinate of *A*.

x-coordinate of *P* = 3 + __0.6__ · 3 = __4.8__

y-coordinate of *P* = 4 + __0.6__ · __6__ = __7.6__

So, the coordinates of *P* are __(4.8, 7.6)__.

B(6, 10)
P
A(3, 4)

REFLECT

1a. Explain how you can check that the slope of $\overline{AP}$ equals the slope of $\overline{AB}$.

Slope of $\overline{AP} = \frac{rise}{run} = \frac{7.6 - 4}{4.8 - 3} = \frac{3.6}{1.8} = 2$; slope of $\overline{AB} = \frac{rise}{run} = \frac{10 - 4}{6 - 3} = \frac{6}{3} = 2$

1b. Explain how you can use the distance formula to check that *P* partitions $\overline{AB}$ in the ratio 3 to 2.

By the distance formula *AP* ≈ 4.025 and *PB* ≈ 2.683, and $\frac{AP}{PB}$ ≈ 1.5, which is 3 to 2.

PRACTICE

1. Find the coordinates of the point *P* that lies along the directed segment from *C*(−3, −2) to *D*(6, 1) and partitions the segment in the ratio 2 to 1.
(3, 0)

2. Find the coordinates of the point *P* that lies along the directed segment from *R*(−3, −4) to *S*(5, 0) and partitions the segment in the ratio 2 to 3.
(0.2, −2.4)

3. Find the coordinates of the point *P* that lies along the directed segment from *J*(−2, 5) to *K*(2, −3) and partitions the segment in the ratio 4 to 1.
(1.2, −1.4)

4. Find the coordinates of the point *P* that lies along the directed segment from *M*(5, −2) to *N*(−5, 3) and partitions the segment in the ratio 1 to 3.
(2.5, −0.75)

5. The map shows a straight highway between two towns. Highway planners want to build two new rest stops between the towns so that the two rest stops divide the highway into three equal parts. Find the coordinates of the points at which the rest stops should be built.
$\left(-1, -\frac{2}{3}\right)$ and $\left(1, 1\frac{1}{3}\right)$

Bedford
Ashton

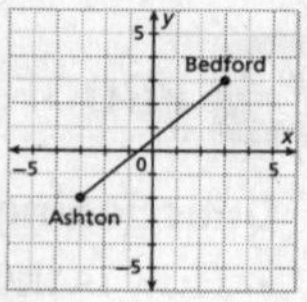

6. $\overleftrightarrow{RS}$ passes through *R*(−3, 1) and *S*(4, 3). Find a point *P* on $\overleftrightarrow{RS}$ such that the ratio of *RP* to *SP* is 5 to 4. Is there more than one possibility? Explain.

There is one point between *R* and *S*, which has coordinates $P\left(\frac{8}{9}, 2\frac{1}{9}\right)$. There is also a point beyond point *S*, which has coordinates *P*(32, 11).

Slope and Parallel Lines

Essential question: *What is the connection between slope and parallel lines?*

COMMON **Standards for**
CORE **Mathematical Content**

CC.9-12.G.GPE.5 Prove the slope criteria for parallel … lines and use [it] to solve geometric problems (e.g., find the equation of a line parallel … to a given line that passes through a given point).

Prerequisites

Proofs About Parallel and Perpendicular Lines, Lesson 1-7

Slope, Algebra 1

Linear Equations, Algebra 1

Math Background

In this lesson, students prove the slope criterion for parallel lines and use it to solve problems. Note that the proofs given here assume that the lines are neither vertical nor horizontal. It the lines are vertical, the criterion does not apply, since slope is not defined for vertical lines. If the lines are horizontal, both lines have a slope of zero and the proof is trivial.

INTRODUCE

Introduce the Slope Criterion for Parallel Lines. You may want to spend a moment discussing the biconditional nature of the criterion. Because it is an *if and only if* statement, the criterion can be used in either direction. That is, if you know that two lines are parallel, you can conclude that they have the same slope. Conversely, if you know that two lines have the same slope, you can conclude that they are parallel. You can draw a simple graphic organizer on the board to illustrate this.

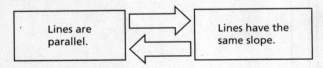

Be sure students understand that each direction of the criterion has its own proof.

TEACH

1 PROOF

Questioning Strategies

- What is a "slope triangle"? It is a right triangle that you can use to calculate the ratio of the rise to the run for a straight line.
- How do you use the slope triangle to find the slope of line m? The slope is the ratio of the rise to the run, or $\frac{BC}{AC}$.
- What ratios do you need to show are equal to prove that lines m and n have the same slope? Show that $\frac{BC}{AC} = \frac{EF}{DF}$.

 MATHEMATICAL PRACTICE **Highlighting the Standards**

You can address Standard 6 (Attend to precision) by discussing some of the finer points of the proof with students. For example, the proof that parallel lines have the same slope begins by drawing a "slope triangle" for line m and extending the horizontal side $\overline{AC}$ to intersect line n. Ask students how they know this horizontal line must eventually intersect line n. Help students understand that line n continues in both directions and, assuming that line n is not itself horizontal, it must therefore intersect any horizontal line. (If it did not intersect the horizontal line, it would be parallel to the horizontal line, meaning line n is also horizontal, which is a contradiction.)

2 PROOF

Questioning Strategies

- How is this proof similar to the proof that parallel lines have the same slope? In both proofs, you start by drawing slope triangles.
- When you extend $\overline{AC}$, why do you do it in such a way that $DF = AC$? Doing so eventually lets you conclude that $\triangle BAC \cong \triangle EDF$.

Slope and Parallel Lines

Essential question: *What is the connection between slope and parallel lines?*

Slope is useful for determining whether two lines are parallel.

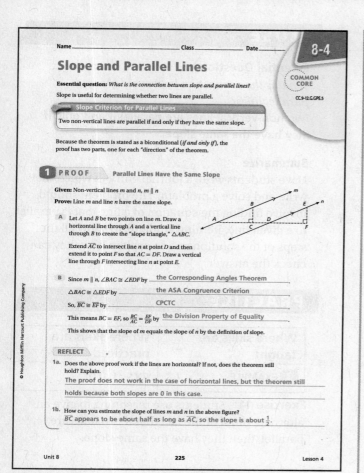

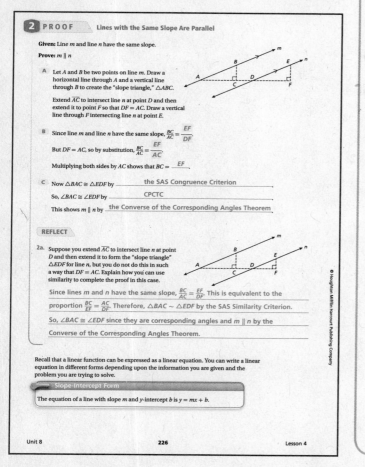

COMMON CORE
CC.9-12.G.GPE.5

Slope Criterion for Parallel Lines

Two non-vertical lines are parallel if and only if they have the same slope.

Because the theorem is stated as a biconditional (*if and only if*), the proof has two parts, one for each "direction" of the theorem.

1 PROOF — Parallel Lines Have the Same Slope

Given: Non-vertical lines m and n, $m \parallel n$

Prove: Line m and line n have the same slope.

A Let A and B be two points on line m. Draw a horizontal line through A and a vertical line through B to create the "slope triangle," $\triangle ABC$.

Extend $\overline{AC}$ to intersect line n at point D and then extend it to point F so that $AC = DF$. Draw a vertical line through F intersecting line n at point E.

B Since $m \parallel n$, $\angle BAC \cong \angle EDF$ by ___the Corresponding Angles Theorem___

$\triangle BAC \cong \triangle EDF$ by ___the ASA Congruence Criterion___

So, $\overline{BC} \cong \overline{EF}$ by ___CPCTC___

This means $BC = EF$, so $\dfrac{BC}{AC} = \dfrac{EF}{DF}$ by ___the Division Property of Equality___

This shows that the slope of m equals the slope of n by the definition of slope.

REFLECT

1a. Does the above proof work if the lines are horizontal? If not, does the theorem still hold? Explain.

The proof does not work in the case of horizontal lines, but the theorem still holds because both slopes are 0 in this case.

1b. How can you estimate the slope of lines m and n in the above figure?

$\overline{BC}$ appears to be about half as long as $\overline{AC}$, so the slope is about $\frac{1}{2}$.

2 PROOF — Lines with the Same Slope Are Parallel

Given: Line m and line n have the same slope.

Prove: $m \parallel n$

A Let A and B be two points on line m. Draw a horizontal line through A and a vertical line through B to create the "slope triangle," $\triangle ABC$.

Extend $\overline{AC}$ to intersect line n at point D and then extend it to point F so that $DF = AC$. Draw a vertical line through F intersecting line n at point E.

B Since line m and line n have the same slope, $\dfrac{BC}{AC} = \dfrac{EF}{DF}$.

But $DF = AC$, so by substitution, $\dfrac{BC}{AC} = \dfrac{EF}{AC}$.

Multiplying both sides by AC shows that $BC =$ ___EF___

C Now $\triangle BAC \cong \triangle EDF$ by ___the SAS Congruence Criterion___

So, $\angle BAC \cong \angle EDF$ by ___CPCTC___

This shows $m \parallel n$ by ___the Converse of the Corresponding Angles Theorem___

REFLECT

2a. Suppose you extend $\overline{AC}$ to intersect line n at point D and then extend it to form the "slope triangle" $\triangle EDF$ for line n, but you do not do this in such a way that $DF = AC$. Explain how you can use similarity to complete the proof in this case.

Since lines m and n have the same slope, $\dfrac{BC}{AC} = \dfrac{EF}{DF}$. This is equivalent to the proportion $\dfrac{BC}{EF} = \dfrac{AC}{DF}$. Therefore, $\triangle BAC \sim \triangle EDF$ by the SAS Similarity Criterion.

So, $\angle BAC \cong \angle EDF$ since they are corresponding angles and $m \parallel n$ by the Converse of the Corresponding Angles Theorem.

Recall that a linear function can be expressed as a linear equation. You can write a linear equation in different forms depending upon the information you are given and the problem you are trying to solve.

Slope-Intercept Form

The equation of a line with slope m and y-intercept b is $y = mx + b$.

Questioning Strategies

- In Part A, how do you know that the given line is in slope-intercept form? **It is in the form $y = mx + b$.**

- In Part A, the given line has a negative slope. What does this tell you about the given line and the required line? **Both lines slope downward as you move from left to right.**

- How can you use graphing to check your answer in Part A? **Graph the given line and the line you find as your answer. The two lines should be parallel, and the line you find as your answer should pass through the point (1, −4).**

EXTRA EXAMPLE

Write the equation of each line in slope-intercept form.

A. a line that is parallel to $y = -x - 3$ and passes through $(-1, 3)$

$y = -x + 2$

B. The line that passes through $(4, 2)$ and is parallel to the line through $(1, 5)$ and $(-3, -3)$

$y = 2x - 6$

Avoid Common Errors

Remind students that the x-coefficient gives the slope of a line only when the equation of the line is written in slope-intercept form. For example, some students might say that the slope of the line represented by the equation $y - 2x = 4$ is -2. However, the equation is not in slope-intercept form. Rewriting the equation in this form gives $y = 2x + 4$, which shows that the correct slope is 2.

CLOSE

Essential Question

What is the connection between slope and parallel lines?
Two non-vertical lines are parallel if and only if they have the same slope.

Summarize

Have students write a journal entry in which they write and solve a problem. The problem should involve finding the equation of a line that is parallel to a given line. Remind students to show all the steps of the solution and to explain how they can check the answer.

PRACTICE

Where skills are taught	Where skills are practiced
3 EXAMPLE	EXS. 1–10

Exercise 11: Students use reasoning to give an alternate proof of the fact that if two lines are parallel, then they have the same slope.

> **Point-Slope Form**
>
> The equation of a line with slope m that passes through the point (x_1, y_1)
> is $y - y_1 = m(x - x_1)$.

3 EXAMPLE Writing Equations of Parallel Lines

Write the equation of each line in slope-intercept form.

A The line parallel to $y = -2x + 3$ that passes through $(1, -4)$

The given line is in slope-intercept form and its slope is ___-2___.

The required line has slope ___-2___ because parallel lines have the same slope.

$y - y_1 = m(x - x_1)$ Use point-slope form.

$y - \underline{(-4)} = \underline{-2}(x - \underline{1})$ Substitute for m, x_1, and y_1.

$y + \underline{4} = \underline{-2x + 2}$ Simplify each side of the equation.

$y = \underline{-2x - 2}$ Write the equation in slope-intercept form.

B The line that passes through $(2, 3)$ and is parallel to the line through $(1, -2)$ and $(7, 1)$

The slope of the line through $(1, -2)$ and $(7, 1)$ is

$m = \dfrac{y_2 - y_1}{x_2 - x_1} = \dfrac{1 - \underline{-2}}{7 - \underline{1}} = \dfrac{3}{6} = \dfrac{1}{2}$.

So, the required line has slope $\dfrac{1}{2}$.

$y - y_1 = m(x - x_1)$ Use point-slope form.

$y - \underline{3} = \underline{\dfrac{1}{2}}(x - \underline{2})$ Substitute for m, x_1, and y_1.

$y = \underline{\dfrac{1}{2}x + 2}$ Simplify and write slope-intercept form.

REFLECT

3a. In Part A, how can you check that you wrote the correct equation?

The line with equation $y = -2x - 2$ has slope -2 and it passes through $(1, -4)$

because $-4 = -2(1) - 2$, so the equation is correct.

3b. In Part A, once you know the slope of the required line, how can you finish solving the problem using the slope-intercept form of a linear equation?

Since the slope is -2, the equation must be $y = -2x + b$. Substituting the x- and

y-values of the point on the line gives $-4 = -2(1) + b$, and solving for b shows

that $b = -2$.

Unit 8   227   Lesson 4

© Houghton Mifflin Harcourt Publishing Company

PRACTICE

Write the equation of each line in slope-intercept form.

1. The line with slope 3 that passes through $(0, 6)$

   $y = 3x + 6$

2. The line with slope -4 that passes through $(0, -5)$

   $y = -4x - 5$

3. The line with slope -1 that passes through $(3, 5)$

   $y = -x + 8$

4. The line with slope 5 that passes through $(2, -5)$

   $y = 5x - 15$

5. The line parallel to $y = 5x + 1$ that passes through $(3, 8)$

   $y = 5x - 7$

6. The line parallel to $y = -3x - 2$ that passes through $(-2, 7)$

   $y = -3x + 1$

7. The line that passes through $(-1, 0)$ and is parallel to the line through $(0, 1)$ and $(2, -3)$

   $y = -2x - 2$

8. The line that passes through $(3, 5)$ and is parallel to the line through $(3, 3)$ and $(-3, -1)$

   $y = \dfrac{2}{3}x + 3$

9. The line parallel to $x - 3y = -12$ that passes through $(-3, 4)$

   $y = \dfrac{1}{3}x + 5$

10. The line parallel to $3x + y = 8$ that passes through $(0, -4)$

    $y = -3x - 4$

11. Use the slope-intercept form of a linear equation to prove that if two lines are parallel then they have the same slope. (*Hint:* Use an indirect proof. Assume the lines have different slopes, m_1 and m_2. Write the equations of the lines and show that there must be a point of intersection.)

Assume the lines have different slopes, m_1 and m_2. Then the equations of the lines

are $y = m_1 x + b_1$ and $y = m_2 x + b_2$. By substitution, $m_1 x + b_1 = m_2 x + b_2$ and

solving for x shows that $x = \dfrac{b_2 - b_1}{m_1 - m_2}$, so the lines intersect at this x-value, but this

is a contradiction since the lines are parallel. So, $m_1 = m_2$.

© Houghton Mifflin Harcourt Publishing Company

Unit 8   228   Lesson 4

Slope and Perpendicular Lines

Essential question: *What is the connection between slope and perpendicular lines?*

COMMON CORE Standards for Mathematical Content

CC.9-12.G.GPE.5 Prove the slope criteria for ... perpendicular lines and use [it] to solve geometric problems (e.g., find the equation of a line ... perpendicular to a given line that passes through a given point).

Prerequisites

Slope, Algebra 1

Linear Equations, Algebra 1

Math Background

This lesson has a structure similar to that of the previous lesson. As in that lesson, a slope criterion is introduced, it is proved in two parts, and then students complete an example of its use. Note that the Slope Criterion for Perpendicular Lines is stated as follows: *Two non-vertical lines are perpendicular if and only if the product of their slopes is −1.* In some books, the criterion is stated equivalently as *two non-vertical lines are perpendicular if and only if their slopes are opposite reciprocals of each other.*

INTRODUCE

Introduce the Slope Criterion for Perpendicular Lines. As in Lesson 8-4, you may want to briefly discuss the biconditional nature of the criterion and represent it with a graphic organizer as shown below.

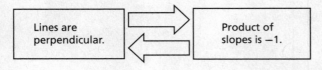

Be sure students understand that each direction of the criterion has its own proof.

TEACH

1 PROOF

Questioning Strategies

- Can either of the lines be horizontal? Why or why not? **No; it is specified that neither line is vertical. Since the lines are perpendicular, if one line were horizontal, the other would be vertical.**

- How do you find the slope of line m? **The slope is the ratio of the rise to the run in the slope triangle, $\triangle PQR$. This ratio is $\frac{QR}{PR}$, or $\frac{a}{b}$.**

MATHEMATICAL PRACTICE **Highlighting the Standards**

You can address Standard 7 (Look for and make use of structure) by discussing what it means for two numbers to have a product of −1. For example, if the product of a and b is −1, then $ab = -1$, and solving for a shows that $a = -\frac{1}{b}$. This is equivalent to saying that a and b are opposite reciprocals of each other. You may want to have students give examples of pairs of numbers that are opposite reciprocals of each other. Possibilities include 1 and −1, $\frac{2}{3}$ and $-\frac{3}{2}$, and $\frac{1}{7}$ and −7. Students can check that the product of the numbers in each pair is −1.

---

2 PROOF

Questioning Strategies

- How do you know one line has a positive slope and one line has a negative slope? **The product of the slopes is −1, so one slope must be positive and one must be negative.**

- In Step C, how do you know $\angle 2$ and $\angle 3$ are complementary? **They are adjacent angles that form a right angle.**

Name_____ Class_____ Date_____

8-5

Slope and Perpendicular Lines

COMMON CORE
CC.9-12.G.GPE.5

Essential question: *What is the connection between slope and perpendicular lines?*

Slope is useful for determining whether two lines are perpendicular.

Slope Criterion for Perpendicular Lines

Two non-vertical lines are perpendicular if and only if the product of their slopes is −1.

Like the Slope Criterion for Parallel Lines, the theorem is stated as a biconditional. Therefore, the proof has two parts, one for each "direction" of the theorem.

1 PROOF Perpendicular Lines Have Slopes Whose Product Is −1

Given: Non-vertical lines m and n, $m \perp n$.

Prove: The product of the slope of line m and the slope of line n is −1.

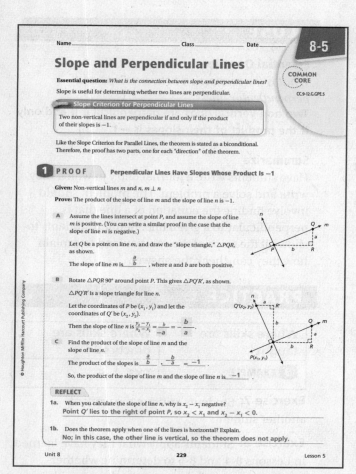

A Assume the lines intersect at point P, and assume the slope of line m is positive. (You can write a similar proof in the case that the slope of line m is negative.)

Let Q be a point on line m, and draw the "slope triangle," $\triangle PQR$, as shown.

The slope of line m is $\dfrac{a}{b}$, where a and b are both positive.

B Rotate $\triangle PQR$ 90° around point P. This gives $\triangle PQ'R'$, as shown.

$\triangle PQ'R'$ is a slope triangle for line n.

Let the coordinates of P be (x_1, y_1) and let the coordinates of Q' be (x_2, y_2).

Then the slope of line n is $\dfrac{y_2 - y_1}{x_2 - x_1} = \dfrac{b}{-a} = -\dfrac{b}{a}$.

C Find the product of the slope of line m and the slope of line n.

The product of the slopes is $\dfrac{a}{b} \cdot -\dfrac{b}{a} = \underline{-1}$.

So, the product of the slope of line m and the slope of line n is $\underline{-1}$.

REFLECT

1a. When you calculate the slope of line n, why is $x_2 - x_1$ negative?
Point Q' lies to the right of point P, so $x_2 < x_1$ and $x_2 - x_1 < 0$.

1b. Does the theorem apply when one of the lines is horizontal? Explain.
No; in this case, the other line is vertical, so the theorem does not apply.

Unit 8   229   Lesson 5

© Houghton Mifflin Harcourt Publishing Company

2 PROOF Lines with Slopes Whose Product Is −1 Are Perpendicular

Given: The product of the slope of line m and the slope of line n is −1.

Prove: $m \perp n$

A Let line m have positive slope $\dfrac{a}{b}$, where a and b are both positive.

Let line n have slope z. It is given that $z \cdot \dfrac{a}{b} = -1$.

Solving for z shows that the slope of line n is $\underline{-\dfrac{b}{a}}$.

B Assume the lines intersect at point P. Set up slope triangles for lines m and n as shown.

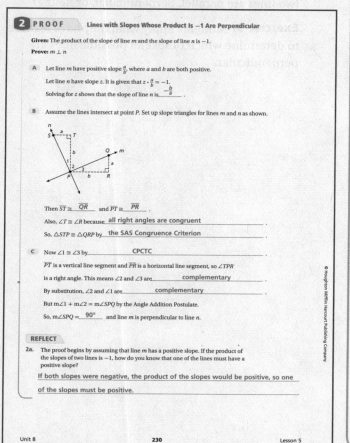

Then $\overline{ST} \cong \underline{\overline{QR}}$ and $\overline{PT} \cong \underline{\overline{PR}}$.

Also, $\angle T \cong \angle R$ because $\underline{\text{all right angles are congruent}}$.

So, $\triangle STP \cong \triangle QRP$ by $\underline{\text{the SAS Congruence Criterion}}$.

C Now $\angle 1 \cong \angle 3$ by $\underline{\text{CPCTC}}$.

$\overline{PT}$ is a vertical line segment and $\overline{PR}$ is a horizontal line segment, so $\angle TPR$

is a right angle. This means $\angle 2$ and $\angle 3$ are $\underline{\text{complementary}}$.

By substitution, $\angle 2$ and $\angle 1$ are $\underline{\text{complementary}}$.

But $m\angle 1 + m\angle 2 = m\angle SPQ$ by the Angle Addition Postulate.

So, $m\angle SPQ = \underline{90°}$ and line m is perpendicular to line n.

REFLECT

2a. The proof begins by assuming that line m has a positive slope. If the product of the slopes of two lines is −1, how do you know that one of the lines must have a positive slope?

If both slopes were negative, the product of the slopes would be positive, so one

of the slopes must be positive.

Unit 8   230   Lesson 5

© Houghton Mifflin Harcourt Publishing Company

Questioning Strategies

- What is the y-intercept of the given line? How do you know? **The equation is in slope-intercept form, so the y-intercept must be −8.**

- The given line has a positive slope. What does this tell you about the required line? Why? **It must have a negative slope because the product of the slopes is −1.**

- How can you check your answer? **Check that the product of the slopes is −1 ($-\frac{1}{3} \cdot 3 = -1$) and that (3, 1) is a solution of the equation of the required line, ($1 = -\frac{1}{3}(3) + 2$).**

EXTRA EXAMPLE
Write the equation of the line perpendicular to $y = 2x + 1$ that passes through (5, 1). Write the equation in slope-intercept form.

$$y = -\frac{1}{2}x + \frac{7}{2}$$

Technology
Students can use their graphing calculators to check that two equations represent perpendicular lines. However, students should be aware that perpendicular lines may or may not appear to be perpendicular on a graphing calculator, depending upon the viewing window that is used. To ensure that perpendicular lines appear to be perpendicular, students should go to the ZOOM menu and choose **5:ZSquare**.

CLOSE

Essential Question
What is the connection between slope and perpendicular lines?
Two non-vertical lines are perpendicular if and only if the product of their slopes is −1.

Summarize
Have students write a journal entry in which they write and solve a problem. The problem should involve finding the equation of a line that is perpendicular to a given line. Remind students to show all the steps of the solution and to explain how they can check the answer.

PRACTICE

Where skills are taught	Where skills are practiced
3 EXAMPLE	EXS. 1–6

Exercise 7: Students critique the work of another student.

Exercise 8: Students apply what they have learned in Lessons 8-4 and 8-5 to determine whether two lines are parallel, perpendicular, or neither.

Exercise 9: Students apply what they have learned to determine which of several possible lines are perpendicular.

3 **EXAMPLE**   Writing Equations of Perpendicular Lines

Write the equation of the line perpendicular to $y = 3x - 8$ that passes through $(3, 1)$.
Write the equation in slope-intercept form.

A   First find the slope of the required line.

The given line is in slope-intercept form and its slope is ____3____ .

Let the required line have slope m. Since the lines are perpendicular, the product of their slopes is -1.

So, __3__ $\cdot m = -1$, and therefore, $m = $ ___$-\frac{1}{3}$___ .

B   Now use point-slope form to find the equation of the required line.

$y - y_1 = m(x - x_1)$ Use point-slope form.

$y - \underline{1} = \dfrac{-\frac{1}{3}}{}(x - \underline{3})$ Substitute for m, x_1, and y_1.

$y - \underline{1} = \underline{-\frac{1}{3}x + 1}$ Distributive Property

$y = \underline{-\frac{1}{3}x + 2}$ Write the equation in slope-intercept form.

REFLECT

3a.   How do you find the slope of the given line?

Compare its equation to slope-intercept form $(y = mx + b)$. This shows that the

line's slope is 3.

3b.   How can you use graphing to check your answer?

Graph $y = 3x - 8$ and $y = -\frac{1}{3}x + 2$. Check that the lines are perpendicular

and that $y = -\frac{1}{3}x + 2$ passes through $(3, 1)$.

3c.   Confirm your answer by graphing on the grid below.

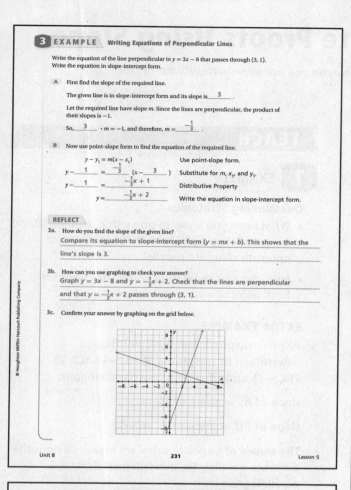

PRACTICE

Write the equation of each line in slope-intercept form.

1. The line perpendicular to $y = \frac{1}{2}x + 1$ that passes through $(1, 4)$.

$y = -2x + 6$

2. The line perpendicular to $y = -x + 2$ that passes through $(-1, -7)$.

$y = x - 6$

3. The line that passes through $(1, 2)$ and is perpendicular to the line through $(3, -2)$ and $(-3, 0)$.

$y = 3x - 1$

4. The line that passes through $(-2, 3)$ and is perpendicular to the line through $(0, 1)$ and $(-3, -1)$.

$y = -\frac{3}{2}x$

5. The line perpendicular to $2y = x + 5$ that passes through $(2, 1)$.

$y = -2x + 5$

6. The line perpendicular to $3x + y = 8$ that passes through $(0, -2)$.

$y = \frac{1}{3}x - 2$

7. Error Analysis   A student was asked to find the equation of the line perpendicular to $y - 2x = 1$ that passes through the point $(4, 3)$. The student's work is shown at right. Explain the error and give the correct equation.

The given equation is not in slope-

intercept form. The slope of the

given line is 2, so the required line

has slope $-\frac{1}{2}$. The required line's

equation is $y = -\frac{1}{2}x + 5$.

The given line has slope -2, so the required line has slope $\frac{1}{2}$.
$y - y_1 = m(x - x_1)$ *Use point-slope form.*
$y - 3 = \frac{1}{2}(x - 4)$ *Substitute for m, x_1, y_1.*
$y - 3 = \frac{1}{2}x - 2$ *Distributive Property*
$y = \frac{1}{2}x + 1$ *Add 3 to both sides.*

8. Are the lines given by the equations $-4x + y = 5$ and $-x + 4y = 12$ parallel, perpendicular, or neither? Why?

Neither; the slopes are 4 and $\frac{1}{4}$. Since the slopes are not equal and their product is

not -1, the lines are neither parallel nor perpendicular.

9. Consider the points $A(-7, 10)$, $B(12, 7)$, $C(10, -24)$, and $D(-8, -3)$. Which two lines determined by these points are perpendicular? Explain.

$\overleftrightarrow{AC} \perp \overleftrightarrow{BD}$ since the slope of $\overleftrightarrow{AC}$ is -2, the slope of $\overleftrightarrow{BD}$ is $\frac{1}{2}$, and the product of the

slopes is -1.

8-6 Coordinate Proofs Using Slope

Essential question: *How can you use slope in coordinate proofs?*

Standards for Mathematical Content

CC.9-12.G.GPE.4 Use coordinates to prove simple geometric theorems algebraically.

Prerequisites

Coordinate Proofs, Lesson 3-7

Slope and Parallel Lines, Lesson 8-4

Slope and Perpendicular Lines, Lesson 8-5

Math Background

Students have already written coordinate proofs in Lesson 3-7 and in other lessons throughout this course. Now, they have a new tool that they can use in coordinate proofs. Slope makes it possible to give a straightforward proof that a quadrilateral determined by four points is (or is not) a parallelogram. Although it is possible to prove that a quadrilateral is a parallelogram using the distance formula, this can be cumbersome, and the proof depends upon the theorem that says that if both pairs of opposite sides of a quadrilateral are congruent, then the quadrilateral is a parallelogram. Using slope, only the definition of a parallelogram is necessary.

INTRODUCE

Remind students of the slope criteria for parallel lines and for perpendicular lines. Explain that these criteria are often helpful in coordinate proofs. Explain that the criteria are especially useful when the proof requires showing that sides of a polygon are parallel or perpendicular.

TEACH

1 EXAMPLE

Questioning Strategies

- What must you show to prove that a quadrilateral is a parallelogram? Show that both pairs of opposite sides are parallel.

- How can you show this? Show that slopes of both pairs of opposite sides are equal.

EXTRA EXAMPLE

Prove or disprove that the quadrilateral determined by the points $R(-4, -1)$, $S(2, 2)$, $T(4, -1)$, and $U(-2, -4)$ is a parallelogram

slope of $\overline{RS}$ = slope of $\overline{TU} = \frac{1}{2}$

slope of $\overline{RU}$ = slope of $\overline{ST} = -\frac{3}{2}$

The slopes of opposite sides are equal, so opposite sides are parallel. So, quadrilateral *RSTU* is a parallelogram.

MATHEMATICAL PRACTICE

Highlighting the Standards

You can address Standard 3 (Construct viable arguments and critique the reasoning of others) as you teach this lesson. The standard states that mathematically proficient students should be able to "compare the effectiveness of two plausible arguments." To that end, you might have students write alternative proofs of the statement in the first example (by using the distance formula, for instance). Then, have students compare and critique the various proofs, not only from the point of view of valid reasoning, but also from the point of view of understandability and clarity.

Name_____ Class_____ Date_____

8-6

Coordinate Proofs Using Slope

COMMON CORE
CC.9-12.G.GPE.4

Essential question: *How can you use slope in coordinate proofs?*

You have already used the distance formula and the midpoint formula in coordinate proofs. As you will see, slope is useful in coordinate proofs whenever you need to show that lines are parallel or perpendicular.

1 EXAMPLE Proving a Quadrilateral Is a Parallelogram

Prove or disprove that the quadrilateral determined by the points $A(4, 4)$, $B(3, 1)$, $C(-2, -1)$, and $D(-1, 2)$ is a parallelogram.

A Plot the points on the coordinate plane at right.

Then draw quadrilateral *ABCD*.

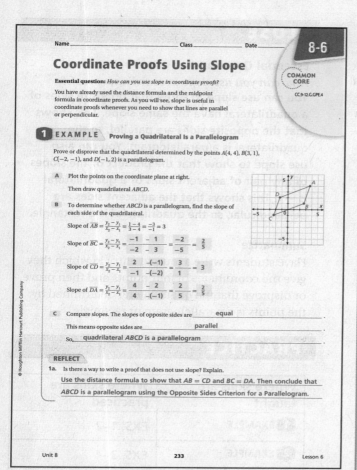

B To determine whether *ABCD* is a parallelogram, find the slope of each side of the quadrilateral.

Slope of $\overline{AB} = \frac{y_2 - y_1}{x_2 - x_1} = \frac{1 - 4}{3 - 4} = \frac{-3}{-1} = 3$

Slope of $\overline{BC} = \frac{y_2 - y_1}{x_2 - x_1} = \frac{-1 \; - \; 1}{-2 \; - \; 3} = \frac{-2}{-5} = \frac{2}{5}$

Slope of $\overline{CD} = \frac{y_2 - y_1}{x_2 - x_1} = \frac{2 \; -(-1)}{-1 \; -(-2)} = \frac{3}{1} = 3$

Slope of $\overline{DA} = \frac{y_2 - y_1}{x_2 - x_1} = \frac{4 \; - \; 2}{4 \; -(-1)} = \frac{2}{5} = \frac{2}{5}$

C Compare slopes. The slopes of opposite sides are ___equal___

This means opposite sides are ___parallel___

So, ___quadrilateral *ABCD* is a parallelogram___

REFLECT

1a. Is there a way to write a proof that does not use slope? Explain.

Use the distance formula to show that $AB = CD$ and $BC = DA$. Then conclude that

ABCD is a parallelogram using the Opposite Sides Criterion for a Parallelogram.

© Houghton Mifflin Harcourt Publishing Company

2 EXAMPLE Proving a Quadrilateral Is a Rectangle

Prove or disprove that the quadrilateral determined by the points $Q(2, -3)$, $R(-4, 0)$, $S(-2, 4)$, and $T(4, 1)$ is a rectangle.

A Plot the points on the coordinate plane at right.

Then draw quadrilateral *QRST*.

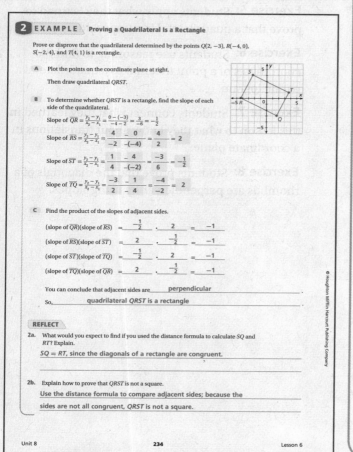

B To determine whether *QRST* is a rectangle, find the slope of each side of the quadrilateral.

Slope of $\overline{QR} = \frac{y_2 - y_1}{x_2 - x_1} = \frac{0 - (-3)}{-4 - 2} = \frac{3}{-6} = -\frac{1}{2}$

Slope of $\overline{RS} = \frac{y_2 - y_1}{x_2 - x_1} = \frac{4 \; - \; 0}{-2 \; -(-4)} = \frac{4}{2} = 2$

Slope of $\overline{ST} = \frac{y_2 - y_1}{x_2 - x_1} = \frac{1 \; - \; 4}{4 \; -(-2)} = \frac{-3}{6} = -\frac{1}{2}$

Slope of $\overline{TQ} = \frac{y_2 - y_1}{x_2 - x_1} = \frac{-3 \; - \; 1}{2 \; - \; 4} = \frac{-4}{-2} = 2$

C Find the product of the slopes of adjacent sides.

(slope of $\overline{QR}$)(slope of $\overline{RS}$) $= -\frac{1}{2} \cdot 2 = -1$

(slope of $\overline{RS}$)(slope of $\overline{ST}$) $= 2 \cdot -\frac{1}{2} = -1$

(slope of $\overline{ST}$)(slope of $\overline{TQ}$) $= -\frac{1}{2} \cdot 2 = -1$

(slope of $\overline{TQ}$)(slope of $\overline{QR}$) $= 2 \cdot -\frac{1}{2} = -1$

You can conclude that adjacent sides are ___perpendicular___

So, ___quadrilateral *QRST* is a rectangle___

REFLECT

2a. What would you expect to find if you used the distance formula to calculate *SQ* and *RT*? Explain.

$SQ = RT$, since the diagonals of a rectangle are congruent.

2b. Explain how to prove that *QRST* is not a square.

Use the distance formula to compare adjacent sides; because the

sides are not all congruent, *QRST* is not a square.

© Houghton Mifflin Harcourt Publishing Company

Questioning Strategies

- What must you show to prove that a quadrilateral is a rectangle? **Show that the quadrilateral has four right angles (i.e., that adjacent sides are perpendicular).**

- How can you show this? **Show that the product of the slopes of adjacent sides is −1.**

EXTRA EXAMPLE

Prove or disprove that the quadrilateral determined by the points $J(-4, -1)$, $K(-2, 5)$, $L(1, 4)$, and $M(-1, -2)$ is a rectangle.

slope of $\overline{JK}$ = slope of $\overline{LM}$ = 3

slope of $\overline{KL}$ = slope of $\overline{JM}$ = $-\frac{1}{3}$

The product of the slopes of adjacent sides is −1, so adjacent sides are perpendicular. So, quadrilateral *JKLM* is a rectangle.

Differentiated Instruction

Some students may have difficulty using the formula to calculate slopes. You might suggest that these students try a more visual approach. For example, to find the slope of $\overline{TQ}$, the rise and run can be determined from the graph, as shown below.

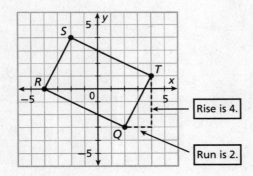

Essential Question

How can you use slope in coordinate proofs?
You can use slope to show that opposite sides of a quadrilateral have the same slope. This shows that the opposite sides are parallel, so the quadrilateral is a parallelogram. You can also use slope to show that the product of the slopes of any pair of adjacent sides of a quadrilateral is −1. This shows that the adjacent sides are perpendicular, so the quadrilateral is a rectangle.

Summarize

Have students write a journal entry in which they give the coordinates of four points and then prove or disprove that the quadrilateral determined by the points is a parallelogram or rectangle.

Where skills are taught	Where skills are practiced
1 EXAMPLE	EXS. 1–2
2 EXAMPLE	EXS. 3–4

Exercise 5: Students apply what they learned to prove that a quadrilateral is a trapezoid.

Exercise 6: Students use reasoning to find the coordinates of a point that makes a quadrilateral a parallelogram.

Exercise 7: Students connect what they learned in this lesson to what they know about translations in a coordinate plane.

Exercise 8: Students prove that the diagonals of a rhombus are perpendicular by using slopes.

PRACTICE

1. Prove or disprove that the quadrilateral determined by the points $J(-3, 1)$, $K(3, 3)$, $L(2, -1)$, and $M(-4, -3)$ is a parallelogram.

   Slope of $\overline{JK}$ = slope of $\overline{LM} = \frac{1}{3}$; slope of $\overline{MJ}$ = slope of $\overline{KL}$ = 4. Since the slopes of

   opposite sides are equal, opposite sides are parallel and quadrilateral $JKLM$ is a

   parallelogram.

2. Prove or disprove that the quadrilateral determined by the points $A(-2, 3)$, $B(5, 3)$, $C(3, -1)$, and $D(-3, -1)$ is a parallelogram.

   Slope of $\overline{AB}$ = slope of $\overline{CD}$ = 0; slope of $\overline{DA}$ = 4; slope of $\overline{BC}$ = 2. Since the slopes

   of one pair of opposite sides are not equal, these opposite sides are not parallel,

   and quadrilateral $ABCD$ is not a parallelogram.

3. Prove or disprove that the quadrilateral determined by the points $Q(-3, 4)$, $R(5, 2)$, $S(4, -1)$, and $T(-4, 1)$ is a rectangle.

   Slope of $\overline{TQ}$ = slope of $\overline{RS}$ = 3; slope of $\overline{QR}$ = slope of $\overline{ST} = -\frac{1}{4}$. The product of

   the slopes of adjacent sides is not −1, so adjacent sides are not perpendicular and

   quadrilateral $QRST$ is not a rectangle.

4. Prove or disprove that the quadrilateral determined by the points $W(1, 5)$, $X(4, 4)$, $Y(2, -2)$, and $Z(-1, -1)$ is a rectangle.

   Slope of $\overline{WX}$ = slope of $\overline{YZ} = -\frac{1}{3}$; slope of $\overline{XY}$ = slope of $\overline{ZW}$ = 3. The product

   of the slopes of adjacent sides is −1, so adjacent sides are perpendicular, and

   quadrilateral $WXYZ$ is a rectangle.

5. Prove or disprove that the quadrilateral determined by the points $D(-2, 3)$, $E(3, 4)$, $F(0, -2)$, and $G(-4, -1)$ is a trapezoid.

   Slope of $\overline{DE} = \frac{1}{5}$; slope of $\overline{EF}$ = 2; slope of $\overline{FG} = -\frac{1}{4}$; slope of $\overline{GD}$ = 2.

   Exactly one pair of opposite sides have the same slope, so these sides are

   parallel, and quadrilateral $DEFG$ is a trapezoid.

6. Consider points $L(3, -4)$, $M(1, -2)$, and $N(5, 2)$.

   a. Find the coordinates of point P so that the quadrilateral determined by points L, M, N, and P is a parallelogram. Is there more than one possibility? Explain.

   The coordinates of P may be (7, 0), (3, 4), or (−1, −8). These coordinates result

   in a parallelogram, because opposite sides have equal slopes.

   b. Are any of the parallelograms a rectangle? Why?

   When the coordinates of P are (7, 0), the quadrilateral is a rectangle, because

   the product of the slopes of adjacent sides is −1.

7. You are using a coordinate plane to create a quadrilateral. You start by drawing $\overline{MN}$, as shown.

   a. You decide to translate $\overline{MN}$ by the translation $(x, y) \rightarrow (x + 3, y + 2)$. What type of quadrilateral is $MM'N'N$? Why?

   Parallelogram; opposite sides of the quadrilateral have

   the same slope.

   b. Do you get the same type of quadrilateral for any translation of $\overline{MN}$ that results in a quadrilateral $MM'N'N$? Explain. (*Hint*: Find the coordinates of M' and N' under a general translation, $(x, y) \rightarrow (x + a, y + b)$. Then consider the slopes of the sides of quadrilateral $MM'N'N$.)

   The coordinates of M' are $M'(-2 + a, 2 + b)$ and the coordinates of N' are

   $N'(a, -4 + b)$. Slope of $\overline{MN}$ = slope of $\overline{M'N'}$ = −3; slope of $\overline{MM'}$ = slope of

   $\overline{NN'} = \frac{b}{a}$, assuming $a \neq 0$. If $a = 0$, $\overline{MM'}$ and $\overline{NN'}$ are vertical segments. So

   for all values of a and b, opposite sides have equal slopes and $MM'N'N$ is a

   parallelogram.

   c. You decide you want $MM'N'N$ to be a rectangle. What translations can you use? (*Hint*: What must be true about a and b?)

   Any translation $(x, y) \rightarrow (x + a, y + b)$ such that $a = 3b$ gives a rectangle.

8. Rhombus $OPQR$ has vertices $O(0, 0)$, $P(a, b)$, $Q(a + b, a + b)$, and $R(b, a)$. Prove the diagonals of the rhombus are perpendicular.

   The slope of one diagonal is $\frac{a + b}{a + b}$ = 1, and the slope of the other diagonal

   is $\frac{b - a}{a - b}$ = −1; because the product of 1 and −1 is −1, the diagonals of the

   rhombus are perpendicular.

Systems of Equations

Essential question: *How do you solve a system consisting of a linear equation in two variables and a quadratic equation in two variables?*

Standards for Mathematical Content

CC.9-12.A.REI.7 Solve a simple system consisting of a linear equation and a quadratic equation in two variables algebraically and graphically.

Prerequisites

The Equation of a Circle, Lesson 8-1

The Equation of a Parabola, Lesson 8-2

Solving Systems of Linear Equations, Algebra 1

Math Background

Students should already have some experience solving systems of equations that involve linear equations. In Algebra 1, students learned to solve such systems by graphing, by substitution, and by elimination. In this lesson, students extend these skills to systems that involve one linear equation and one quadratic equation. In general, such systems may have 0, 1, or 2 solutions, depending upon the number of intersection points of the graphs of the equations.

INTRODUCE

Remind students that they have already learned to solve systems of equations. Write the following simple system on the board:

$$\begin{cases} y = x + 1 \\ y = -x + 3 \end{cases}$$

Ask students to describe three different ways of solving the system. Students might mention graphing, substitution, and elimination. All of these methods result in a solution of (1, 2). Tell students that they will now see how some of these techniques can be used with systems that involve a linear equation and a quadratic equation.

TEACH

1 EXAMPLE

Questioning Strategies

• How do you graph $(x - 1)^2 + (y - 1)^2 = 16$? Locate the center, (1, 1). Then, use the radius, 4, to identify some points on the circle. Use a compass to complete the circle.

• How do you graph $y = x + 4$? The *y*-intercept is 4, so (0, 4) is on the line. Then use the slope, 1, to identify another point on the line. Use a straightedge to draw the line through the points.

EXTRA EXAMPLE

Solve the system of equations.

$$\begin{cases} (x + 1)^2 + (y - 1)^2 = 9 \\ y = x + 5 \end{cases}$$

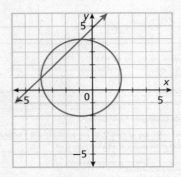

(−4, 1) and (−1, 4)

Highlighting the Standards

Standard 1 (Make sense of problems and persevere in solving them) emphasizes that students should continually ask themselves, "Does this make sense?" To that end, when students solve a system by graphing, remind them that they must check their answers to make sure they are solutions of each equation in the ordered pair.

Name_____ Class_____ Date_____

8-7

COMMON CORE
CC.9-12.A.REI.7

Systems of Equations

Essential question: *How do you solve a system consisting of a linear equation in two variables and a quadratic equation in two variables?*

Recall that you can solve a system of two equations in two unknowns by graphing both equations and finding the point(s) of intersection of the graphs. You can also solve a system using the algebraic methods of substitution or elimination. In this lesson, you will see how these techniques may be used with systems that include a quadratic equation.

1 EXAMPLE Solving a System by Graphing

Solve the system of equations. $\begin{cases} (x-1)^2 + (y-1)^2 = 16 \\ y = x + 4 \end{cases}$

A Graph the equations.

The equation $(x-1)^2 + (y-1)^2 = 16$ represents a circle with center __(1, 1)__ and radius __4__.

The equation $y = x + 4$ represents a line with slope __1__ and y-intercept __4__.

Use a compass and straightedge, and the above information, to help you graph the circle and the line.

B The solutions of $(x-1)^2 + (y-1)^2 = 16$ are exactly the points on the circle. The solutions of $y = x + 4$ are exactly the points on the line. The solutions of the system are points that lie on both the circle and the line. These are the points of intersection of the circle and the line.

So, the solutions of the system are ___(−3, 1) and (1, 5)___

REFLECT

1a. How can you check your solution?

Check that each ordered pair satisfies both equations.

1b. How many solutions are possible when a system of equations involves a circle and a line? Explain.

There are 0, 1, or 2 solutions, depending upon the number of points of intersection of the circle and the line.

2 EXAMPLE Solving a System Algebraically

Solve the system of equations. $\begin{cases} x^2 + y^2 = 13 \\ y = -5x \end{cases}$

A Use substitution to write an equation in one variable. The second equation is already solved for y, so substitute this expression for y into the first equation.

$x^2 + y^2 = 13$ Write the first equation.

$x^2 + (-5x)^2 = 13$ Substitute $-5x$ for y in the equation.

$x^2 + 25x^2 = 13$ Square the expression in parentheses.

$26x^2 = 13$ Combine like terms.

$x^2 = \frac{1}{2}$ Use the Division Property of Equality.

$x = \pm\sqrt{\frac{1}{2}}$ Take the square root of both sides.

$x = \pm\frac{\sqrt{2}}{2}$ Rationalize the denominator.

B Substitute each x-value into one of the original equations to find the corresponding y-values.

Substitute into the simpler equation, $y = -5x$.

When $x = \frac{\sqrt{2}}{2}$, $y = -\frac{5\sqrt{2}}{2}$.

When $x = -\frac{\sqrt{2}}{2}$, $y = \frac{5\sqrt{2}}{2}$.

So, the solutions of the system are $\left(\frac{\sqrt{2}}{2}, -\frac{5\sqrt{2}}{2}\right)$ and $\left(-\frac{\sqrt{2}}{2}, \frac{5\sqrt{2}}{2}\right)$.

REFLECT

2a. Is it possible to solve this system of equations by graphing? Explain.

No; it would not be easy to determine the exact points of intersection from the graph.

2b. Based on what you know about the graphs of the equations in this system, why does it make sense that there are two solutions?

The graphs are a circle centered at the origin and a straight line through the origin, so the graphs must have two points of intersection.

Questioning Strategies

- What does it mean to solve a system by substitution? You solve one equation for one variable. Then, you substitute the resulting expression in the other equation to get a new equation in one variable. Solving this equation gives the value of x or y. Substituting this value back into one of the original equations gives the value of the other variable.

EXTRA EXAMPLE

Solve the system of equations.

$$\begin{cases} x^2 + y^2 = 20 \\ y = 3x \end{cases}$$

$(\sqrt{2}, 3\sqrt{2})$ and $(-\sqrt{2}, -3\sqrt{2})$

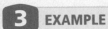

3 **EXAMPLE**

Questioning Strategies

- How is this system different from the one in the previous example? This system involves a line and a parabola rather than a line and a circle.

- Based on the solution, if you graphed the line and the parabola, what would you expect to see? The line and the parabola would intersect at one point, (4, 13).

EXTRA EXAMPLE

Solve the system of equations. $\begin{cases} y = -x^2 + 1 \\ y = 2x + 2 \end{cases}$
$(-1, 0)$

Teaching Strategies

You may wish to show students how they can solve the system in Example 3 by elimination. Subtracting the second equation from the first gives $0 = x^2 - 3 - 8x + 19$. Note that this is equivalent to the equation that results from substitution.

CLOSE

Essential Question

How do you solve a system consisting of a linear equation in two variables and a quadratic equation in two variables?

You can use graphing, in which case you graph the two equations and identify the coordinates of the points of intersection. You can also use substitution, in which case you solve one equation for one variable. Then, you substitute the resulting expression in the other equation to get a new equation in one variable. Solving this equation gives the value of x or y. Substituting this value back into one of the original equations gives the value of the other variable.

Summarize

Have students write a journal entry in which they explain how to solve a system of equations consisting of a linear equation in two variables and a quadratic equation in two variables.

PRACTICE

Where skills are taught	Where skills are practiced
1 EXAMPLE	EXS. 1–3
2 EXAMPLE	EXS. 4–6
3 EXAMPLE	EXS. 7–9

Exercise 10: Students critique another student's work.

3 EXAMPLE Solving a System Involving a Parabola

Solve the system of equations. $\begin{cases} y = x^2 - 3 \\ y = 8x - 19 \end{cases}$

A Use substitution to write an equation in one variable. Substitute the expression for y from the second equation into the first equation.

$y = x^2 - 3$	Write the first equation.
$\underline{8x - 19} = x^2 - 3$	Substitute $8x - 19$ for y in the equation.
$0 = \underline{x^2 - 3 - 8x + 19}$	Get 0 on one side of the equation.
$0 = \underline{x^2 - 8x + 16}$	Combine like terms.
$0 = \underline{(x - 4)^2}$	Factor.
$0 = \underline{|x - 4|}$	Take the square root of both sides.
$x = \underline{4}$	Solve for x.

B Substitute the x-value into one of the original equations to find the corresponding y-value.

Substitute into the equation $y = x^2 - 3$.

When $x = \underline{4}$, $y = \underline{13}$.

So, the solution of the system is $\underline{(4, 13)}$.

REFLECT

3a. In Step B, what would happen if you substituted the value of x in the other equation?

You would get the same result, $y = 13$.

3b. Verify that the slope of the line that contains $(0, -19)$ and $(4, 13)$ is 8.

$\frac{13 - (-19)}{4 - 0} = \frac{32}{4} = 8$

3c. Since there is only one solution of the system, what does this tell you about the line and the parabola that are represented by the equations?

They intersect at exactly one point, so the line is a tangent to the parabola.

3d. How many solutions are possible when a system of equations involves a parabola and a line? Explain.

There are 0, 1, or 2 solutions depending upon the number of points of intersection of the parabola and the line.

PRACTICE

Solve each system of equations by graphing.

1. $\begin{cases} (x - 2)^2 + y^2 = 4 \\ y = -x \end{cases}$

(0, 0); (2, −2)

2. $\begin{cases} (x + 1)^2 + (y - 1)^2 = 9 \\ y = x - 1 \end{cases}$

(−1, −2); (2, 1)

3. $\begin{cases} y = x^2 - 1 \\ y = -x + 1 \end{cases}$

(−2, 3); (1, 0)

Solve each system of equations algebraically.

4. $\begin{cases} x^2 + y^2 = 10 \\ y = -3x \end{cases}$

(1, −3); (−1, 3)

5. $\begin{cases} x^2 + y^2 = 25 \\ y = 7x \end{cases}$

$\left(\frac{\sqrt{2}}{2}, \frac{7\sqrt{2}}{2}\right)$; $\left(-\frac{\sqrt{2}}{2}, -\frac{7\sqrt{2}}{2}\right)$

6. $\begin{cases} x^2 + y^2 = 13 \\ y = -8x \end{cases}$

$\left(\frac{\sqrt{5}}{5}, -\frac{8\sqrt{5}}{5}\right)$; $\left(-\frac{\sqrt{5}}{5}, \frac{8\sqrt{5}}{5}\right)$

7. $\begin{cases} y = x^2 \\ y = -x + 2 \end{cases}$

(−2, 4); (1, 1)

8. $\begin{cases} y = x^2 + 2 \\ y = 4 \end{cases}$

(−√2, 4); (√2, 4)

9. $\begin{cases} y = -x^2 + 2 \\ y = x - 4 \end{cases}$

(−3, −7); (2, −2)

10. **Error Analysis** A student was asked to solve the system $\begin{cases} x^2 + y^2 = 9 \\ y = x \end{cases}$.
The student's solution is shown below. Critique the student's work. If there is an error, give the correct solution.

The graph of $x^2 + y^2 = 9$ is a circle centered at the origin with radius 3. The graph of $y = x$ is a straight line through the origin. The graphs intersect at (2, 2) and (−2, −2), so these are the solutions.

It is not possible to identify the points of intersection accurately from the graph.

The actual points of intersection are $\left(\frac{3\sqrt{2}}{2}, \frac{3\sqrt{2}}{2}\right)$ and $\left(-\frac{3\sqrt{2}}{2}, -\frac{3\sqrt{2}}{2}\right)$.

Notes

Standards	Item
CC.9-12.A.REI.7	5
CC.9-12.G.GPE.1	1, 2
CC.9-12.G.GPE.2	3
CC.9-12.G.GPE.4	9, 10
CC.9-12.G.GPE.5	4, 7, 8
CC.9-12.G.GPE.6	6

TEST PREP DOCTOR ⊕

Multiple Choice: Item 4

- Students who answered **F** may have incorrectly calculated the slope of line m.

- Students who answered **H** found the line that is perpendicular to line m and passes through point P rather than the line that is parallel to line m and that passes through point P.

- Students who answered **J** may have attempted to find the line that is perpendicular to line m and that passes through point P rather than the line that is parallel to line m and that passes through point P, or they may have incorrectly calculated the slope of line m.

Multiple Choice: Item 6

- Students who answered **F** may have found the correct percent of the run and the rise but added these values to the x- and y-coordinates of point M in the wrong order.

- Students who answered **H** found the point that partitions the segment in the ratio 1 to 3.

- Students who answered **J** found the correct percent of the run and the rise, but forgot to add these values to the x- and y-coordinates of point M.

Free Response: Item 8

- Students who wrote the equation $y = \frac{1}{3}x + \frac{14}{3}$ may have incorrectly found the slope of the line through $(2, 1)$ and $(0, -5)$ by finding the ratio of the run to the rise.

- Students who wrote the equation $y = -\frac{1}{3}x + \frac{16}{3}$ found the equation of the line through $(1, 5)$ that is perpendicular to the line that passes through $(2, 1)$ and $(0, -5)$.

- Students who wrote the equation $y = 3x + b$ for any value of b other than 2 may have had difficulty substituting the coordinates of the given point and simplifying to find b.

UNIT 8 TEST PREP

Name _____ Class _____ Date _____

MULTIPLE CHOICE

1. What is the center of the circle whose equation is $x^2 - 6x + y^2 + 6y = -9$?

(A) $(3, -3)$ **C.** $(-3, 3)$

B. $(3, 3)$ **D.** $(-3, -3)$

2. What is the equation of the circle with center $(4, -5)$ and radius 4?

F. $(x + 4)^2 + (y - 5)^2 = 4$

G. $(x - 4)^2 + (y + 5)^2 = 4$

H. $(x + 4)^2 + (y - 5)^2 = 16$

(J) $(x - 4)^2 + (y + 5)^2 = 16$

3. What is the equation of the parabola with focus $(0, -2)$ and directrix $y = 2$?

A. $y = \frac{1}{8}x^2$ **C.** $y = \frac{1}{16}x^2$

(B) $y = -\frac{1}{8}x^2$ **D.** $y = -\frac{1}{16}x^2$

4. What is the equation of the line parallel to line m that passes through point P?

F. $y = -2x + 3$ **H.** $y = -\frac{1}{2}x$

(G) $y = 2x - 5$ **J.** $y = \frac{1}{2}x - 2$

5. The ordered pair (x, y) is a solution of this system of equations.
$$\begin{cases} x^2 + y^2 = 10 \\ y = 7x \end{cases}$$

Which of the following could be the value of x?

A. $\frac{\sqrt{2}}{2}$ **C.** $\frac{\sqrt{5}}{2}$

(B) $\frac{\sqrt{3}}{5}$ **D.** $\frac{\sqrt{10}}{7}$

6. Which of the following points along the directed segment from M to N partitions the segment in the ratio 3 to 1?

F. $(-2.5, 6.25)$ **H.** $(-2.25, 1.5)$

(G) $(1.25, 2.5)$ **J.** $(5.25, 1.5)$

7. What is the equation of the line through the point $(3, 3)$ that is perpendicular to the line $y = -\frac{1}{2}x + 2$?

(A) $y = 2x - 3$ **C.** $y = -\frac{1}{2}x + \frac{9}{2}$

B. $y = -2x - 9$ **D.** $y = 2x + 3$

FREE RESPONSE

8. Find the equation of the line through the point $(1, 5)$ that is parallel to the line that passes through $(2, 1)$ and $(0, -5)$.

$y = 3x + 2$

9. Prove or disprove that the point $(2, \sqrt{5})$ lies on the circle that is centered at the origin and contains the point $(0, -3)$.

The radius of the circle is 3, so the equation of the circle is $x^2 + y^2 = 9$. Substituting the x- and y-coordinates of the given point into the equation shows that $(2, \sqrt{5})$ is a solution of the equation: $2^2 + (\sqrt{5})^2 = 4 + 5 = 9$. This means the point lies on the circle.

10. Prove or disprove that the quadrilateral determined by the points $A(-3, 1)$, $B(3, 3)$, $C(4, -1)$, and $D(-2, -3)$ is a rectangle.

Slope of $\overline{AB}$ = slope of $\overline{CD}$ = $\frac{1}{3}$

Slope of $\overline{BC}$ = slope of $\overline{DA}$ = -4

The product of the slopes of adjacent sides is not -1, so adjacent sides are not perpendicular and quadrilateral $ABCD$ is not a rectangle.

UNIT 9

Linear and Area Measurement

Unit Vocabulary

UNIT 9

Linear and Area Measurement

Unit Focus

In this unit, you will explore linear measurement, such as length and perimeter, as well as area. First you will learn how to use significant digits to report the results of calculations based on measurements. Then you will learn how to calculate perimeters and areas of figures on the coordinate plane. The remainder of the unit focuses on measuring circles and parts of circles, including arcs and sectors.

Unit at a Glance

COMMON CORE

Lesson		Standards for Mathematical Content
9-1	Precision and Significant Digits	CC.9-12.N.Q.3*
9-2	Perimeter and Area on the Coordinate Plane	CC.9-12.G.GPE.7*, CC.9-12.G.MG.1*, CC.9-12.G.MG.2*
9-3	Circumference	CC.9-12.G.GMD.1, CC.9-12.G.MG.1*
9-4	Arc Length and Radian Measure	CC.9-12.G.CO.1, CC.9-12.G.C.5
9-5	Area of Circles and Sectors	CC.9-12.G.C.5, CC.9-12.G.GMD.1
	Test Prep	

© Houghton Mifflin Harcourt Publishing Company

UNIT 9

Unit 9   243   Linear and Area Measurement

Unpacking the Common Core State Standards

Use the table to help you understand the Standards for Mathematical Content that are taught in this unit. Refer to the lessons listed after each standard for exploration and practice.

COMMON CORE — Standards for Mathematical Content	What It Means For You
CC.9-12.N.Q.3 Choose a level of accuracy appropriate to limitations on measurement when reporting quantities.* Lesson 9-1	You will learn about precision and learn how to use significant digits to report the results of calculations based on measurements.
CC.9-12.G.CO.1 Know precise definitions of angle, circle, perpendicular line, parallel line, and line segment, based on the undefined notions of point, line, distance along a line, and distance around a circular arc. Lesson 9-4	You have already used many undefined terms in this course. In this unit, you will be introduced to the undefined notion of arc length.
CC.9-12.G.C.5 Derive using similarity the fact that the length of the arc intercepted by an angle is proportional to the radius, and define the radian measure of the angle as the constant of proportionality; derive the formula for the area of a sector. Lessons 9-4, 9-5	Proportional reasoning plays a big role in this unit. You will see how to use proportional reasoning to find the area of a wedge-shaped part of a circle. You will also use proportional reasoning to learn about radians, which are another way to measure angles.
CC.9-12.G.GPE.7 Use coordinates to compute perimeters of polygons and areas of triangles and rectangles, e.g., using the distance formula.* Lesson 9-2	You have already worked with polygons on the coordinate plane. Now you will find perimeters and areas of such polygons.
CC.9-12.G.GMD.1 Give an informal argument for the formulas for the circumference of a circle, area of a circle, volume of a cylinder, pyramid, and cone. Lessons 9-3, 9-5	In this unit, you will develop formulas for the circumference of a circle and the area of a circle, using informal limit arguments that involve trigonometry and dissection.
CC.9-12.G.MG.1 Use geometric shapes, their measures, and their properties to describe objects (e.g., modeling a tree trunk or a human torso as a cylinder).* Lessons 9-2, 9-3	You will see how you can use mathematical concepts from this unit to model real-world objects and situations.
CC.9-12.G.MG.2 Apply concepts of density based on area and volume in modeling situations (e.g., persons per square mile, BTUs per cubic foot).* Lesson 9-2	You will learn about density and learn how to calculate population density.

© Houghton Mifflin Harcourt Publishing Company

Unpacking the Common Core State Standards

This page lists and explains the Standards for Mathematical Content that are addressed in this unit. For information about the Standards for Mathematical Practice, which are integrated throughout the text, see Teacher Edition pages x–xiii.

UNIT 9

Notes

_____

_____

_____

_____

_____

_____

_____

_____

_____

_____

9-1 Precision and Significant Digits

Essential question: *How do you use significant digits to report the results of calculations based on measurements?*

COMMON CORE Standards for Mathematical Content

CC.9-12.N.Q.3 Choose a level of accuracy appropriate to limitations on measurement when reporting quantities.*

Prerequisites
None

Math Background
In everyday situations, the terms *precision* and *accuracy* are often used interchangeably. Scientists and mathematicians assign special meanings to these terms. *Precision* is the level of detail an instrument can measure. *Accuracy* describes how close a measurement is to the actual or accepted value. A scale that gives the mass of an object to the nearest tenth of a milligram is a precise measurement tool, but the scale may or may not be accurate. For example, the scale might give the mass of a soil sample as 1732.4 mg. This is a relatively precise measurement, but if the actual mass of the sample is 2539.1 mg, the measurement is not very accurate.

INTRODUCE

Introduce the idea of precision. Explain to students that precision refers to the level of detail an instrument can measure. For example, a ruler that is marked in sixteenths of an inch allows you to make more precise measurements than a ruler that is only marked in eighths of an inch. Ask students to describe additional examples of measurement tools and have them identify the level of precision of each tool.

TEACH

1 EXPLORE

Materials: ruler

Questioning Strategies
- What does "measure to the nearest centimeter" mean? **You measure the object and round its length to the closest centimeter mark on the ruler.**
- What does "measure to the nearest tenth of a centimeter" mean? **You measure the object and round its length to the closest tenth of a centimeter mark on the ruler.**
- If an object's length, to the nearest tenth of a centimeter, is 9.4 cm, what can you say about the actual length of the object? **It is between 9.35 cm and 9.45 cm.**

Teaching Strategies
In Step B, students may have difficulty determining the range of possible values for the actual width and length of the book cover. Tell students that when you measure to the nearest centimeter, the actual length is within one-half centimeter (± 0.5 cm) of the measured length. When you measure to the nearest tenth of a centimeter, the actual length is within one-half of one tenth of a centimeter (± 0.05 cm) of the measured length.

MATHEMATICAL PRACTICE · Highlighting the Standards

Standard 6 (Attend to precision) includes the statement that mathematically proficient students "express answers with a degree of precision appropriate for the problem context." The Explore at the beginning of the lesson should help motivate the need for conventions about precision when reporting calculated measurements. The last example in the lesson gives students practice using significant digits to express answers to an appropriate degree of precision.

Name_____ Class_____ Date_____

Precision and Significant Digits

COMMON
CORE
CC.9-12.N.Q.3*

Essential question: *How do you use significant digits to report the results of calculations based on measurements?*

Precision is the level of detail an instrument can measure. For example, a ruler marked in millimeters is more precise than a ruler that is marked only in centimeters.

You can use precision to compare measurements. For example, a measurement of 25 inches is more precise than a measurement of 2 feet because an inch is a smaller unit than a foot. Similarly, 9.2 kg is more precise than 9 kg because a tenth of a kilogram is a smaller unit than a kilogram.

In the following activity, you will investigate how precision affects calculated measurements, such as area.

1 EXPLORE   Making Measurements to Calculate an Area

A Work with a partner. One of you should measure the width of a book cover to the nearest centimeter. Record the width below.   **Possible answers are shown.**

Width of book cover: 16 cm

The other person should measure the length of the book cover to the nearest tenth of a centimeter. Record the length below.

Length of book cover: 23.6 cm

B Determine the minimum and maximum possible values for the actual width and length of the book cover.

Example: When you measure an object to the nearest centimeter and get a measurement of 3 cm, the actual measurement is between 2.5 cm and 3.5 cm.

When measuring to the nearest centimeter, lengths in this range are rounded to 3 cm.

Minimum width: 15.5 cm   Maximum width: 16.5 cm

Minimum length: 23.55 cm   Maximum length: 23.65 cm

C Use the minimum width and minimum length to calculate the minimum possible area of the book cover. Then use the maximum width and maximum length to calculate the maximum possible area of the book cover.

Minimum area: 365.025 cm²   Maximum area: 390.225 cm²

REFLECT

1a. How does the precision of the linear measurements (width and length) affect the calculated measurement (area)?

The uncertainty in the linear measurements is compounded in the

calculated measurement, resulting in a wide range of possible areas.

In the preceding Explore, you may have discovered that there was a wide range of possible values for the actual area of the book cover. This raises the question of how a calculated measurement, like an area, should be reported. Significant digits offer one way to resolve this dilemma.

Significant digits are the digits in a measurement that carry meaning contributing to the precision of the measurement. The table gives rules for determining the number of significant digits in a measurement.

Rules for Determining Significant Digits			
Rule	Example	Significant Digits (Bold)	Number of Significant Digits
All nonzero digits	37.85	**37.85**	4
Zeros after the last nonzero digit and to the right of the decimal point	0.0070	0.00**70**	2
Zeros between significant digits	6500.0	**6500.0**	5

Note that zeros at the end of a whole number are usually not considered to be significant digits. For example, 4550 ft has 3 significant digits.

2 EXAMPLE   Determining the Number of Significant Digits

Determine the number of significant digits in each measurement.

A 840.09 m   **B** 36,000 mi   **C** 0.010 kg

A The digits 8, 4, and 9 are significant digits because _____ they are nonzero digits _____.

The zeros are significant digits because _____ they are between significant digits _____.

So, 840.09 m has ___5___ significant digits.

B The digits 3 and 6 are significant digits because _____ they are nonzero digits _____.

The zeros are not significant because _____ they are at the end of a whole number _____.

So, 36,000 mi has ___2___ significant digits.

Questioning Strategies

- If a measurement has non-zero digits on either end (for example, 840.09 m) can you conclude that all of the digits are significant digits? Explain. Yes; the non-zero digits are significant digits and any zeros between the significant digits are significant digits.

- If one measurement has more significant digits than another measurement, can you conclude that the measurement with more significant digits is the greater measurement? Explain. No; for example, 9.3 kg has 2 significant digits and 0.563 kg has 3 significant digits, but 9.3 kg is the greater measurement.

EXTRA EXAMPLE

Determine the number of significant digits in each measurement.

- **A.** 4.909 kg
  4 significant digits

- **B.** 0.050 m
  2 significant digits

- **C.** 657,000 mi
  3 significant digits

3 EXAMPLE

Questioning Strategies

- What operation do you use to find perimeter? addition

- What rule should you use when writing the perimeter? Round the sum to the same place as the last significant digit of the least precise measurement.

- What operation do you use to find area? multiplication

- What rule should you use when writing the area? The product must have the same number of significant digits as the measurement with the fewest significant digits.

EXTRA EXAMPLE

A student measures the width of a rectangular desk to the nearest centimeter and finds that the width is 43 cm. Another student measures the length of the desk to the nearest tenth of a centimeter and finds that the length is 86.3 cm. Use the correct number of significant digits to write the perimeter and area of the desk.

Perimeter: 259 cm; area: 3700 cm²

CLOSE

Essential Question

How do you use significant digits to report the results of calculations based on measurements?

If the calculation involves addition or subtraction, round the sum or difference to the same place as the last significant digit of the least precise measurement. If the calculation involves multiplication or division, the product or quotient must have the same number of significant digits as the measurement with the fewest significant digits.

Summarize

Have students write a journal entry in which they give the definition of the term *precision* in their own words. Then have students write a paragraph summarizing what they learned about significant digits.

PRACTICE

Where skills are taught	Where skills are practiced
① EXAMPLE	EX. 4
② EXAMPLE	EXS. 5–7
③ EXAMPLE	EXS. 8–10

Exercises 1–3: Students practice identifying the more precise measurement in a pair of measurements.

C The digit 1 is a significant digit because _____it is a nonzero digit_____.

The zero after the 1 is a significant digit because _it is after the last nonzero digit and to_

the right of the decimal point.

So, 0.010 kg has ____2____ significant digits.

REFLECT

2a. A student claimed that 0.045 m and 0.0045 m have the same number of significant digits. Do you agree or disagree? Why?

Agree; in each measurement only the 4 and 5 are significant digits,

so both measurements have 2 significant digits.

When you perform operations on measurements, use these rules for determining the number of significant digits you should report.

Rules for Significant Digits in Calculations	
Operations	**Rule**
Addition Subtraction	Round the sum or difference to the same place as the last significant digit of the least precise measurement.
Multiplication Division	The product or quotient must have the same number of significant digits as the measurement with the fewest significant digits.

3 EXAMPLE Calculating with Significant Digits

A student measures the width of a book cover to the nearest centimeter and finds that the width is 16 cm. Another student measures the length of the cover to the nearest tenth of a centimeter and finds that the length is 23.6 cm. Use the correct number of significant digits to write the perimeter and area of the cover.

A Find the perimeter: 16 cm + 23.6 cm + 16 cm + 23.6 cm = 79.2 cm

The least precise measurement is 16 cm. Its last significant digit is in the units place. Round the sum to the nearest whole number.

So, the perimeter is ___79 cm___.

B Find the area: 16 cm × 23.6 cm = 377.6 cm^2

The measurement with the fewest significant digits is 16 cm. It has 2 significant digits. Round the product to 2 significant digits.

So, the area is ___380 cm^2___

REFLECT

3a. Suppose the first student had measured the book cover to the nearest tenth of a centimeter and found that the width was 16.0 cm. Does this change how you would you report the perimeter and area? Explain.

Yes; now both measurements have 3 significant digits. Report the perimeter

as 79.2 cm and the area as 378 cm^2.

PRACTICE

Choose the more precise measurement in each pair.

1. 18 cm; 177 mm
   ____177 mm____

2. 3 yd; 10 ft
   ____10 ft____

3. 40.23 kg; 40.3 kg
   ____40.23 kg____

4. One student measures the length of a rectangular wall to the nearest meter and finds that the length is 5 m. Another student measures the height of the wall to the nearest tenth of a meter and finds that the height is 3.2 m. What are the minimum and maximum possible values for the area of the wall?

   minimum: 14.175 m^2; maximum: 17.875 m^2

Determine the number of significant digits in each measurement.

5. 12,080 ft
   4 significant digits

6. 0.8 mL
   1 significant digit

7. 1.0065 km
   5 significant digits

8. You measure a rectangular window to the nearest tenth of a centimeter and find that the length is 81.4 cm. A friend measures the width to the nearest centimeter and finds that the width is 38 cm. Use the correct number of significant digits to write the perimeter and area of the window.

   perimeter: 239 cm; area: 3100 cm^2

9. **Error Analysis** A student measured the length and width of a square rug to the nearest hundredth of a meter. He found that the length and width were 1.30 m. The student was asked to report the area using the correct number of significant digits and he wrote the area as 1.7 m^2. Explain the student's error.

   He should have used 3 significant digits and given the area as 1.69 m^2.

10. Measure the length and width of the rectangle to the nearest tenth of a centimeter. Then use the correct number of significant digits to write the perimeter and area of the rectangle.

    perimeter: 16.6 cm; 15 cm^2

Notes

Perimeter and Area on the Coordinate Plane

Essential question: *How do you find the perimeter and area of polygons on the coordinate plane?*

COMMON CORE **Standards for Mathematical Content**

CC.9-12.G.GPE.7 Use coordinates to compute perimeters of polygons and areas of triangles and rectangles, e.g., using the distance formula.*

CC.9-12.G.MG.1 Use geometric shapes, their measures, and their properties to describe objects (e.g., modeling a tree trunk or a human torso as a cylinder).*

CC.9-12.G.MG.2 Apply concepts of density based on area … in modeling situations (e.g., persons per square mile, …).*

Vocabulary
population density

Prerequisites
The Distance Formula, Lesson 1-2

Math Background
Students have already worked with perimeter and area in middle school and in Algebra 1. This lesson extends these concepts to the coordinate plane. Finding the perimeter of a polygon is an application of the distance formula. Finding the area of a polygon is based on dividing the polygon into simpler shapes for which it is easy to calculate the area, such as rectangles and triangles.

INTRODUCE

Remind students that the perimeter of a figure is the distance around the figure. In the case of a polygon, the perimeter is simply the sum of the lengths of the polygon's sides. You may wish to draw a polygon with vertical and horizontal sides on a coordinate plane and ask students to determine the perimeter. Explain that horizontal and vertical sides are easy to work with. For sides that are not horizontal or vertical, the distance formula is needed.

TEACH

1 EXAMPLE

Questioning Strategies
- Do you need to find all five side lengths or are there some shortcuts you can use? **You know that $BC = CD$ since $\overline{BC}$ and $\overline{CD}$ are reflection images of each other. This means you need to determine the length of only one of those segments.**

- At what point in the solution process should you round? **You should round at the end of the solution process.**

EXTRA EXAMPLE
Find the perimeter of the pentagon with vertices $J(0, 3)$, $K(3, 1)$, $L(0, -3)$, $M(-5, -3)$, and $N(-3, 1)$. Round to the nearest tenth. **21.7 units**

2 EXAMPLE

Questioning Strategies
- What state would you expect to have a low population density? Why? **Possible answer: Alaska. The population of the state is relatively small while the area of the state is quite large. This makes for a low ratio of population to area.**

- Suppose State A and State B have the same population, but State A has a greater area than State B. Which state has a greater population density? Why? **State B; the same number of people are living in a smaller area, so they are more densely packed.**

- Why is quadrilateral *ABCD* a trapezoid? **It has exactly one pair of opposite sides that are parallel.**

- What is another way to use a rectangle and a triangle to find the area of *ABCD*? **Draw a perpendicular from *C* that intersects the *x*-axis at *E*(0, 80). Rectangle *ABCE* has area $160 \cdot 80 = 12,800$ mi^2; subtract the area of $\triangle DEC$ ($\frac{1}{2} \cdot 40 \cdot 160 = 3200$ mi^2). This gives the area of the trapezoid (9600 mi^2).**

Perimeter and Area on the Coordinate Plane

COMMON CORE

CC.9-12.G.GPE.7*
CC.9-12.G.MG.1*
CC.9-12.G.MG.2*

Essential question: *How do you find the perimeter and area of polygons on the coordinate plane?*

Recall that the perimeter of a polygon is the sum of the lengths of the polygon's sides. You can use the distance formula to help you find perimeters of polygons in a coordinate plane.

1 EXAMPLE Finding a Perimeter

Find the perimeter of the pentagon with vertices $A(-4, 2)$, $B(-4, -2)$, $C(0, -3)$, $D(4, -2)$, and $E(2, 3)$. Round to the nearest tenth.

A Plot the points. Then use a straightedge to draw the pentagon that is determined by the points.

B Find the length of each side of the pentagon.

$\overline{AB}$ is vertical. You can find its length by counting units.

$AB = \underline{\quad 4 \quad}$ units

Use the distance formula to find the remaining side lengths.

$BC = \sqrt{(0 - (-4))^2 + (-3 - (-2))^2} = \sqrt{16 + 1} = \sqrt{17}$

$\overline{BC}$ and $\overline{CD}$ have the same length because

they are images of each other under a reflection across the y-axis.

$DE = \sqrt{(\underline{2} - \underline{4})^2 + (\underline{3} - \underline{(-2)})^2} = \sqrt{4 + 25} = \sqrt{29}$

$EA = \sqrt{(\underline{-4} - \underline{2})^2 + (\underline{2} - \underline{3})^2} = \sqrt{36 + 1} = \sqrt{37}$

C Find the sum of the side lengths.

$AB + BC + CD + DE + EA = \underline{4} + \underline{\sqrt{17}} + \underline{\sqrt{17}} + \underline{\sqrt{29}} + \underline{\sqrt{37}}$

Use a calculator to evaluate the expression. Then round to the nearest tenth.

So, the perimeter of $ABCDE$ is $\underline{23.7}$ units.

REFLECT

1a. Explain how you can find the perimeter of a rectangle to check that your answer is reasonable.

The perimeter is approximately equal to the perimeter of the rectangle with

vertices (−4, 2), (−4, −2), (4, −2), and (4, 2). This rectangle has a perimeter

of 24 units, so the answer is reasonable.

The *density* of an object is its mass per unit volume. For example, the density of gold is 19.3 g/cm³. This means each cubic centimeter of gold has a mass of 19.3 grams. You can also define density in other situations that involve area or volume. For example, the **population density** of a region is the population per unit area.

2 EXAMPLE Approximating a Population Density

Vermont has a population of 621,760. Its border can be modeled by the trapezoid with vertices $A(0, 0)$, $B(0, 160)$, $C(80, 160)$, and $D(40, 0)$, where each unit of the coordinate plane represents one mile. Find the approximate population density of Vermont. Round to the nearest tenth.

A Plot the points. Then use a straightedge to draw the trapezoid that is determined by the points.

B Find the area of the trapezoid. To do so, draw a perpendicular from D to $\overline{BC}$. This forms a rectangle and a triangle. The area of the trapezoid is the sum of the area of the rectangle and the area of the triangle.

Area of rectangle $= \ell \cdot w = \underline{160} \cdot \underline{40} = \underline{6400}$

Area of triangle $= \frac{1}{2}bh = \frac{1}{2} \cdot \underline{40} \cdot \underline{160} = \underline{3200}$

Area of trapezoid $= \underline{6400} + \underline{3200} = \underline{9600}$ mi²

C Find the population density.

Population density $= \frac{\text{population}}{\text{area}} = \frac{621{,}760}{9600} \approx \underline{64.77}$

Round to the nearest tenth.

So, the approximate population density of Vermont is $\underline{64.8}$ persons/mi².

Notes

EXTRA EXAMPLE

New Hampshire has a population of 1,324,575. Its border can be modeled by the trapezoid with vertices $R(0, 0)$, $S(70, 0)$, $T(70, 190)$, and $U(50, 190)$, where each unit of the coordinate plane represents one mile. Find the approximate population density of New Hampshire. Round to the nearest tenth.

154.9 persons/mi²

Avoid Common Errors

When calculating a population density, students may be confused about the order in which to form the ratio (i.e., population divided by area, or area divided by population). Tell students that the units of population density provide a clue. Because population density is expressed as persons per square mile, the ratio should be formed by dividing the population (the number of persons) by the area (the number of square miles).

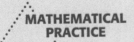

MATHEMATICAL PRACTICE   Highlighting the Standards

To address Standard 4 (Model with mathematics), discuss the modeling process that is used in the example on population density. In particular, ask students what assumptions they must make in order to use this mathematical model. Help students understand that the shape of the state of Vermont, which has some irregular boundaries formed by rivers, is assumed to be a perfect trapezoid. You may want to have students look at a map of the state and find the coordinates of a polygon that approximates the state's border even more closely.

Students should see that when developing a mathematical model, there is often a trade-off between a model that is a better "fit" (e.g., a more complex polygon) and one that is easy to work with (e.g., a trapezoid).

CLOSE

Essential Question

How do you find the perimeter and area of polygons on the coordinate plane?

To find the perimeter, use the distance formula to find the length of each side and then add the side lengths. To find the area, divide the polygon into rectangles and/or triangles, then add the areas of the rectangles and triangles.

Summarize

Have students write a journal entry in which they draw a polygon on a coordinate plane and then explain the steps for finding the polygon's perimeter and area.

PRACTICE

Where skills are taught	Where skills are practiced
1 EXAMPLE	EXS. 1–3
2 EXAMPLE	EXS. 4–5

REFLECT

2a. The actual area of Vermont is 9620 mi². Is your approximation of the population density an overestimate or underestimate? Why?

Overestimate; to find the exact population density, you divide by a greater value, so the population density decreases.

2b. Suppose the population of Vermont doubles in the next century. Would the population density change? If so, how?

Yes; the population density would also double.

PRACTICE

1. Find the perimeter of the hexagon with vertices $A(-5, 1)$, $B(0, 3)$, $C(5, 1)$, $D(4, -2)$, $E(0, -4)$, and $F(-2, -4)$. Round to the nearest tenth.

26.2 units

2. Find the perimeter of the hexagon with vertices $J(0, 5)$, $K(4, 3)$, $L(4, -1)$, $M(0, -4)$, $N(-4, -1)$, and $P(-4, 3)$. Round to the nearest tenth.

26.9 units

3. A plot of land is a pentagon with vertices $Q(-4, 4)$, $R(2, 4)$, $S(4, 1)$, $T(2, -4)$, and $U(-4, -4)$. Each unit of the coordinate grid represents one meter.

a. Fencing costs $24.75 per meter. What is the cost of placing a fence around the plot of land?

$717.52

b. Sod costs $1.85 per square meter. What is the cost of covering the plot of land with sod?

$103.60

4. Colorado has a population of 5,024,748. Its border can be modeled by the rectangle with vertices $A(-190, 0)$, $B(-190, 280)$, $C(190, 280)$, and $D(190, 0)$, where each unit of the coordinate plane represents one mile. Find the approximate population density of Colorado. Round to the nearest tenth.

47.2 persons/mi²

5. For the maximum grain yield, corn should be planted at a density of 38,000 plants per acre. A farmer has a field in the shape of a quadrilateral with vertices $J(0, 0)$, $K(0, 400)$, $L(500, 600)$, and $M(500, 0)$, where each unit of the coordinate plane represents one foot.

a. What is the area of the field to the nearest hundredth of an acre? (*Hint:* 1 acre equals 43,560 ft².)

5.74 acres

b. Approximately how many corn plants should be planted on the field for maximum grain yield? Round to the nearest ten thousand.

220,000

Circumference

9-3

Essential question: *How do you justify and use the formula for the circumference of a circle?*

COMMON CORE Standards for Mathematical Content

CC.9-12.G.GMD.1 Give an informal argument for the formula for the circumference of a circle....

CC.9-12.G.MG.1 Use geometric shapes, their measures, and their properties to describe objects (e.g., modeling a tree trunk or a human torso as a cylinder).*

Prerequisites

Using Congruence Criteria, Lesson 3-4
The Sine and Cosine Ratios, Lesson 6-2

Math Background

Students have already seen the formula for the circumference of a circle in earlier grades. In this lesson, they will explore a justification of the formula that is based on an informal limit argument. These types of arguments are of central importance in calculus. Although the term *limit* is not used here, and there is no attempt to give a rigorous explanation of the concept, the underlying idea should be accessible to students at this level, and it offers a preview of the mathematical thinking that students will do in future courses.

INTRODUCE

Begin by reminding students that π is a mathematical constant that is approximately equal to 3.14159. Tell students that π is irrational, which means it cannot be written as $\frac{a}{b}$ for any integers a and b. This also means its decimal form does not terminate and does not repeat. Explain to the class that they will be developing and justifying a formula for the circumference of a circle and that the constant π will play an important role in this investigation. (*Note:* In the Explore, students will need to recognize a sequence of numerical values that approach π.)

TEACH

1 EXPLORE

Materials: graphing calculator

Questioning Strategies

- How many sides does a regular n-gon have? How many angles does it have? **n sides and n angles**

- Why is $\overline{OA}$ congruent to $\overline{OB}$? **Both segments are radii, so they have the same length.**

- How can you use the expression you wrote for the perimeter of the n-gon to find the perimeter of the inscribed square when the circle's radius is 1? **In this case, $r = 1$ and $n = 4$, so the perimeter is $2nr \sin\left(\frac{180°}{n}\right) = 2 \cdot 4 \cdot 1 \cdot \sin 45° = 8 \cdot \frac{\sqrt{2}}{2} = 4\sqrt{2}$**

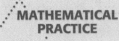

MATHEMATICAL PRACTICE

Highlighting the Standards

Standard 8 (Look for and express regularity in repeated reasoning) includes the statement that mathematically proficient students "maintain oversight of the process, while attending to details." This skill is essential in navigating the sophisticated argument of the Explore. The argument includes ideas about regular polygons, triangle congruence, trigonometry, and sequences. In order for students to be successful with this, they must continually check that their calculations are correct, since an error at any stage of the argument will ripple through the rest of their work. On the other hand, students must remember the overall goal of the argument so that they do not get lost in the details. Be sure students understand the plan for the argument before they begin the first step.

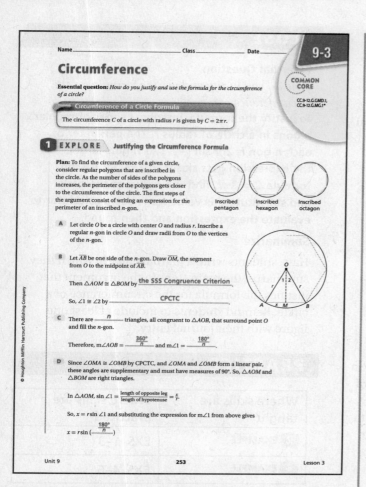

Name_____ Class_____ Date_____

Circumference

Essential question: *How do you justify and use the formula for the circumference of a circle?*

COMMON CORE
CC.9-12.G.GMD.1,
CC.9-12.G.MG.1*

Circumference of a Circle Formula

The circumference C of a circle with radius r is given by $C = 2\pi r$.

1 EXPLORE   Justifying the Circumference Formula

Plan: To find the circumference of a given circle, consider regular polygons that are inscribed in the circle. As the number of sides of the polygons increases, the perimeter of the polygons gets closer to the circumference of the circle. The first steps of the argument consist of writing an expression for the perimeter of an inscribed n-gon.

Inscribed pentagon   Inscribed hexagon   Inscribed octagon

A Let circle O be a circle with center O and radius r. Inscribe a regular n-gon in circle O and draw radii from O to the vertices of the n-gon.

B Let $\overline{AB}$ be one side of the n-gon. Draw $\overline{OM}$, the segment from O to the midpoint of $\overline{AB}$.

Then $\triangle AOM \cong \triangle BOM$ by __the SSS Congruence Criterion__

So, $\angle 1 \cong \angle 2$ by _____CPCTC_____.

C There are __n__ triangles, all congruent to $\triangle AOB$, that surround point O and fill the n-gon.

Therefore, $m\angle AOB = \dfrac{360°}{n}$ and $m\angle 1 = \dfrac{180°}{n}$.

D Since $\angle OMA \cong \angle OMB$ by CPCTC, and $\angle OMA$ and $\angle OMB$ form a linear pair, these angles are supplementary and must have measures of 90°. So, $\triangle AOM$ and $\triangle BOM$ are right triangles.

In $\triangle AOM$, $\sin \angle 1 = \dfrac{\text{length of opposite leg}}{\text{length of hypotenuse}} = \dfrac{x}{r}$.

So, $x = r \sin \angle 1$ and substituting the expression for $m\angle 1$ from above gives

$x = r \sin \left(\dfrac{180°}{n} \right)$

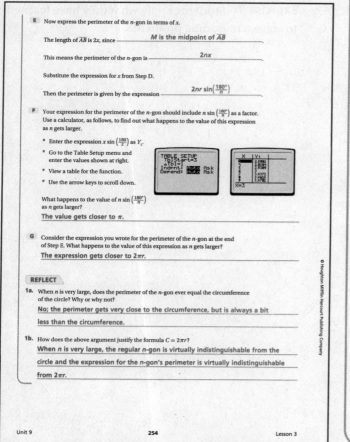

E Now express the perimeter of the n-gon in terms of x.

The length of $\overline{AB}$ is $2x$, since ___M is the midpoint of $\overline{AB}$___

This means the perimeter of the n-gon is ___$2nx$___.

Substitute the expression for x from Step D.

Then the perimeter is given by the expression ___$2nr \sin\left(\dfrac{180°}{n}\right)$___

F Your expression for the perimeter of the n-gon should include $n \sin \left(\dfrac{180°}{n} \right)$ as a factor. Use a calculator, as follows, to find out what happens to the value of this expression as n gets larger.

* Enter the expression $x \sin \left(\dfrac{180}{x} \right)$ as Y_1.
* Go to the Table Setup menu and enter the values shown at right.
* View a table for the function.
* Use the arrow keys to scroll down.

What happens to the value of $n \sin \left(\dfrac{180°}{n} \right)$ as n gets larger?

__The value gets closer to π.__

G Consider the expression you wrote for the perimeter of the n-gon at the end of Step E. What happens to the value of this expression as n gets larger?

__The expression gets closer to $2\pi r$.__

REFLECT

1a. When n is very large, does the perimeter of the n-gon ever equal the circumference of the circle? Why or why not?

__No; the perimeter gets very close to the circumference, but is always a bit__

__less than the circumference.__

1b. How does the above argument justify the formula $C = 2\pi r$?

__When n is very large, the regular n-gon is virtually indistinguishable from the__

__circle and the expression for the n-gon's perimeter is virtually indistinguishable__

__from $2\pi r$.__

Questioning Strategies

- How can you find the radius if you know the diameter? Divide the diameter by 2.

- At what point in the solution process should you round? You should round only as the final step of the solution.

EXTRA EXAMPLE

Find the circumference of circle Q. Round to the nearest tenth.

28.3 ft²

Avoid Common Errors

When students are given the diameter of a circle in a figure, they may sometimes make the mistake of using the given diameter as r in the formula $C = 2\pi r$. Remind students to pay close attention to whether they are given the radius or the diameter in a figure.

3 EXAMPLE

Questioning Strategies

- What assumption do you make in order to use this mathematical model? You assume that the tree's base is a perfect circle.

- What units will you use for the diameter? How do you know? Feet; the circumference is given in feet, so the diameter will also be measured in feet.

EXTRA EXAMPLE

The Mirny Diamond Mine in eastern Russia is one of the largest open mines in the world. The mine is approximately circular, with a circumference of 3.77 km. What is the approximate diameter of the mine? Round to the nearest tenth of a kilometer.
1.2 km

CLOSE

Essential Question

How do you justify and use the formula for the circumference of a circle?
To justify the formula, inscribe a series of regular n-gons in a circle of radius r. The perimeter of each n-gon is $2nr \sin\left(\frac{180°}{n}\right)$ As n gets larger, the expression gets closer to $2\pi r$. To use the formula $C = 2\pi r$, find the radius of the circle, and substitute this value for r. Use a calculator to evaluate the expression and then round.

Summarize

Have students write a journal entry in which they summarize the main steps in the argument that justifies the formula for the circumference of a circle. Remind students to include at least one figure with their journal entry.

PRACTICE

Where skills are taught	Where skills are practiced
2 EXAMPLE	EXS. 1–3
3 EXAMPLE	EXS. 4–6

Exercise 7: Students apply what they have learned to solve a reasoning problem.

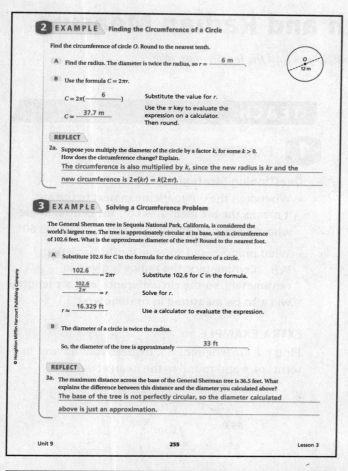

2 EXAMPLE Finding the Circumference of a Circle

Find the circumference of circle O. Round to the nearest tenth.

A Find the radius. The diameter is twice the radius, so $r =$ ___6 m___.

B Use the formula $C = 2\pi r$.

$C = 2\pi(\underline{\quad 6 \quad})$ Substitute the value for r.

$C \approx \underline{\quad 37.7 \text{ m} \quad}$ Use the π key to evaluate the expression on a calculator. Then round.

REFLECT

2a. Suppose you multiply the diameter of the circle by a factor k, for some $k > 0$. How does the circumference change? Explain.

The circumference is also multiplied by k, since the new radius is kr and the

new circumference is $2\pi(kr) = k(2\pi r)$.

3 EXAMPLE Solving a Circumference Problem

The General Sherman tree in Sequoia National Park, California, is considered the world's largest tree. The tree is approximately circular at its base, with a circumference of 102.6 feet. What is the approximate diameter of the tree? Round to the nearest foot.

A Substitute 102.6 for C in the formula for the circumference of a circle.

$\dfrac{102.6}{\quad} = 2\pi r$ Substitute 102.6 for C in the formula.

$\dfrac{102.6}{2\pi} = r$ Solve for r.

$r \approx \underline{\quad 16.329 \text{ ft} \quad}$ Use a calculator to evaluate the expression.

B The diameter of a circle is twice the radius.

So, the diameter of the tree is approximately ___33 ft___.

REFLECT

3a. The maximum distance across the base of the General Sherman tree is 36.5 feet. What explains the difference between this distance and the diameter you calculated above?

The base of the tree is not perfectly circular, so the diameter calculated

above is just an approximation.

PRACTICE

Find the circumference of each circle. Round to the nearest tenth.

1. [circle O, 9 cm]   56.5 cm

2. [circle C, 14.2 mm]   44.6 mm

3. [circle A, $\frac{4}{\pi}$ ft]   4 ft

4. The Parthenon is a Greek temple dating to approximately 445 BCE. The temple features 46 Doric columns, which are approximately cylindrical. The circumference of each column at the base is approximately 5.65 meters. What is the approximate diameter of each column? Round to the nearest tenth.

___1.8 m___

5. A circular track for a model train has a diameter of 8.5 feet. The train moves around the track at a constant speed of 0.7 ft/s.

a. To the nearest foot, how far does the train travel when it goes completely around the track 10 times?   ___267 ft___

b. To the nearest minute, how long does it take the train to go completely around the track 10 times?   ___6 min___

6. A standard bicycle wheel has a diameter of 26 inches. A student claims that during a one-mile bike ride the wheel makes more than 1000 complete revolutions. Do you agree or disagree? Explain. (*Hint:* 1 mile = 5280 feet)

Disagree; the total distance is 5280 × 12 = 63,360 inches and the number

of revolutions equals the total distance divided by the circumference,

which is $\frac{63,360}{26\pi} \approx 775.7$.

7. In the figure, $\overline{AB}$ is a diameter of circle C, D is the midpoint of $\overline{AC}$, and E is the midpoint of $\overline{AD}$. How does the circumference of circle E compare to the circumference of circle C? Explain.

The circumference of circle E is $\frac{1}{4}$ the circumference

of circle C because the radius of circle E is $\frac{1}{4}$ the

radius of circle C.

Notes

Arc Length and Radian Measure

Essential question: *How do you find the length of an arc?*

COMMON CORE Standards for Mathematical Content

CC.9-12.G.CO.1 Know ... the undefined notion of ... distance around a circular arc.

CC.9-12.G.C.5 Derive using similarity the fact that the length of the arc intercepted by an angle is proportional to the radius, and define the radian measure of the angle as the constant of proportionality ...

Vocabulary

arc length

radian measure

Prerequisites

Circumference, Lesson 9-3

Math Background

This is the first of two lessons in which students apply proportional reasoning to circles. In this lesson, students find arc lengths by considering the fraction of a full circle that is represented by a given arc. A similar process will be used in Lesson 9-5 when students find the area of a sector by considering the fraction of a full circle that is represented by a given sector. Be sure to alert students to the parallel reasoning in these two lessons.

INTRODUCE

Draw a circle on the board. Then plot two points on the circle and highlight the arc determined by the points. Ask students how they could find the length of the arc. If no one suggests it, you might describe placing a piece of string along the arc, cutting it to the correct length, straightening it out, and then measuring its length. Although this process would result in, at best, a rough estimate of the arc length, it may help students gain an intuitive sense of what is meant by arc length. Tell the class that they will see how to use proportional reasoning to calculate the length of an arc.

TEACH

1 EXAMPLE

Questioning Strategies

- What does the 60° mark mean next to the arc? It means the arc measures 60°; the central angle whose sides pass through *A* and *B* measures 60°.

- What units should you use for the arc length? Why? Centimeters; the radius is given in centimeters, so the circumference and arc length will also be measured in centimeters.

EXTRA EXAMPLE

Find the arc length of $\overset{\frown}{RS}$. Express your answer in terms of π and round to the nearest tenth.

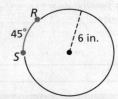

$\frac{3}{2}\pi$ in.; 4.7 in.

Teaching Strategies

This lesson includes the formula for the arc length *s* of an arc with measure *m*° and radius *r*. The formula, $s = \frac{m}{360} \cdot 2\pi r$, may seem complicated to some students and they may have difficulty remembering it. Explain that it is not necessary to memorize or use the formula. Instead, students can repeat the reasoning process that is used in the Explore. That is, students can find the circumference of the circle and then apply proportional reasoning to find the relevant arc length.

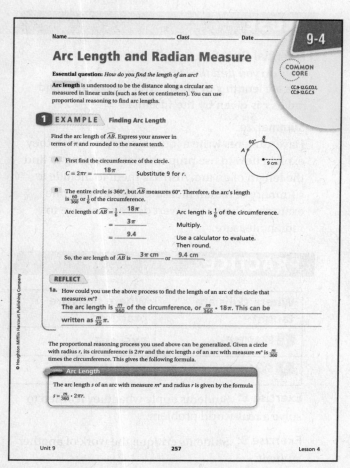

Name _____ **Class** _____ **Date** _____

Arc Length and Radian Measure

9-4

COMMON CORE

CC 9-12.G.CO.1,
CC 9-12.G.C.5

Essential question: *How do you find the length of an arc?*

Arc length is understood to be the distance along a circular arc measured in linear units (such as feet or centimeters). You can use proportional reasoning to find arc lengths.

1 EXAMPLE Finding Arc Length

Find the arc length of $\overset{\frown}{AB}$. Express your answer in terms of π and rounded to the nearest tenth.

A First find the circumference of the circle.

$C = 2\pi r = \underline{18\pi}$ Substitute 9 for r.

B The entire circle is 360°, but $\overset{\frown}{AB}$ measures 60°. Therefore, the arc's length is $\frac{60}{360}$ or $\frac{1}{6}$ of the circumference.

Arc length of $\overset{\frown}{AB} = \frac{1}{6} \cdot \underline{18\pi}$ Arc length is $\frac{1}{6}$ of the circumference.

$= \underline{3\pi}$ Multiply.

$= \underline{9.4}$ Use a calculator to evaluate. Then round.

So, the arc length of $\overset{\frown}{AB}$ is $\underline{3\pi}$ cm or $\underline{9.4}$ cm.

REFLECT

1a. How could you use the above process to find the length of an arc of the circle that measures $m°$?

The arc length is $\frac{m}{360}$ of the circumference, or $\frac{m}{360} \cdot 18\pi$. This can be written as $\frac{m}{20}\pi$.

The proportional reasoning process you used above can be generalized. Given a circle with radius r, its circumference is $2\pi r$ and the arc length s of an arc with measure $m°$ is $\frac{m}{360}$ times the circumference. This gives the following formula.

Arc Length

The arc length s of an arc with measure $m°$ and radius r is given by the formula
$s = \frac{m}{360} \cdot 2\pi r$.

© Houghton Mifflin Harcourt Publishing Company

Unit 9   257   Lesson 4

2 EXPLORE Investigating Arc Lengths in Concentric Circles

Consider a set of concentric circles with center O and radius 1, 2, 3, and so on. The central angle shown in the figure is a right angle and it cuts off arcs that measure 90°.

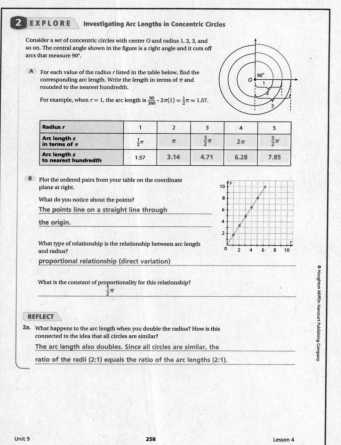

A For each value of the radius r listed in the table below, find the corresponding arc length. Write the length in terms of π and rounded to the nearest hundredth.

For example, when $r = 1$, the arc length is $\frac{90}{360} \cdot 2\pi(1) = \frac{1}{2}\pi \approx 1.57$.

Radius r	1	2	3	4	5
Arc length s in terms of π	$\frac{1}{2}\pi$	π	$\frac{3}{2}\pi$	2π	$\frac{5}{2}\pi$
Arc length s to nearest hundredth	1.57	3.14	4.71	6.28	7.85

B Plot the ordered pairs from your table on the coordinate plane at right.

What do you notice about the points?

The points line on a straight line through the origin.

What type of relationship is the relationship between arc length and radius?

proportional relationship (direct variation)

What is the constant of proportionality for this relationship?

$\frac{1}{2}\pi$

REFLECT

2a. What happens to the arc length when you double the radius? How is this connected to the idea that all circles are similar?

The arc length also doubles. Since all circles are similar, the ratio of the radii (2:1) equals the ratio of the arc lengths (2:1).

© Houghton Mifflin Harcourt Publishing Company

Unit 9   258   Lesson 4

Notes

MATHEMATICAL PRACTICE — Highlighting the Standards

Standard 8 (Look for and express regularity in repeated reasoning) explains that mathematically proficient students "look for both general methods and for shortcuts." The Explore and its follow-up discussion offer a perfect example of this. Any time students need to find an arc length, they can repeat the reasoning process used in the Explore. On the other hand, students should note the underlying process and understand how it can be generalized to give the formula for arc length.

Essential Question

How do you find the length of an arc?
The arc length s of an arc with measure $m°$ and radius r is given by the formula $s = \frac{m}{360} \cdot 2\pi r$.

Summarize

Have students write a journal entry in which they explain how to use proportional reasoning to find the length of an arc. Also ask them to include a summary of radian measure, with at least one example of how to convert degree measure to radian measure.

Where skills are taught	Where skills are practiced
1 EXAMPLE	EXS. 1–6
3 EXAMPLE	EX. 7

Exercise 8: Students apply what they learned to solve a real-world problem.

Exercise 9: Students critique the work of another student.

EXPLORE

Questioning Strategies

- What is the general equation of a proportional relationship? $y = ax$

- What is the name for the constant a in the equation? The constant a is the constant of proportionality.

- What are some characteristics of the graph of any proportional relationship? The graph is a straight line that passes through the origin.

EXAMPLE

Questioning Strategies

- How do you convert an angle's degree measure to radian measure? Substitute the angle's degree measure for m in the expression $\frac{m}{360} \cdot 2\pi$.

- You know that 360° is the degree measure that corresponds to a full circle. What radian measure corresponds to a full circle? 2π

- What degree measure and what radian measure correspond to a semi-circle? $180°; \pi$

EXTRA EXAMPLE

Convert each angle measure to radian measure.

A. 18° $\frac{\pi}{10}$ radians

B. 20° $\frac{\pi}{9}$ radians

As you discovered in the Explore, when the central angle is fixed at $m°$, the length of the arc cut off by the central angle is proportional to (or varies directly with) the radius. In fact, you can see that the formula for arc length is a proportional relationship when m is fixed.

$$s = \frac{m}{360} \cdot 2\pi r$$
constant of proportionality

The constant of proportionality for the proportional relationship is $\frac{m}{360} \cdot 2\pi$. This constant of proportionality is defined to be the **radian measure** of the angle.

3 EXAMPLE Converting to Radian Measure

Convert each angle measure to radian measure.

A 180°   **B** 60°

A To convert 180° to radian measure, let $m = 180$ in the expression $\frac{m}{360} \cdot 2\pi$.

$180° = \frac{\overset{180}{\cancel{180}}}{360} \cdot 2\pi$ radians   Substitute 180 for m.

$\quad\;\; = \pi$ radians   Simplify.

B To convert 60° to radian measure, let $m = 60$ in the expression $\frac{m}{360} \cdot 2\pi$.

$180° = \frac{\overset{60}{\cancel{60}}}{360} \cdot 2\pi$ radians   Substitute 180 for m.

$\quad\;\; = \frac{\pi}{3}$ radians   Simplify.

REFLECT

3a. Explain why the radian measure for an angle of $m°$ is sometimes defined as the length of the arc cut off on a circle of radius 1 by a central angle of $m°$.

By the arc length formula, the length of the arc cut off on a circle of

radius 1 by a central angle of $m°$ is $\frac{m}{360} \cdot 2\pi(1)$, and this is the radian

measure of the angle.

3b. Explain how to find the degree measure of an angle whose radian measure is $\frac{\pi}{4}$.

Solve $\frac{\pi}{4} = \frac{m}{360} \cdot 2\pi$. Dividing both sides by π and simplifying gives $\frac{1}{4} = \frac{m}{180}$

and multiplying both sides by 180 shows that $m = 45$, so the angle

measures 45°.

PRACTICE

Find the arc length of $\overset{\frown}{AB}$. Express your answer in terms of π and rounded to the nearest tenth.

1.

10π m or 31.4 m

2.

2π in. or 6.3 in.

3.

$\frac{67}{36}\pi$ cm or 5.8 cm

4.

4π ft or 12.6 ft

5.

$\frac{143}{18}\pi$ cm or 25.0 cm

6.

$\frac{34}{3}\pi$ in. or 35.6 in.

7. It is convenient to know the radian measure for benchmark angles such as 0°, 30°, 45°, and so on. Complete the table by finding the radian measure for each of the given benchmark angles.

Benchmark Angles									
Degree Measure	0°	30°	45°	60°	90°	120°	135°	150°	180°
Radian Measure	0	$\frac{\pi}{6}$	$\frac{\pi}{4}$	$\frac{\pi}{3}$	$\frac{\pi}{2}$	$\frac{2\pi}{3}$	$\frac{3\pi}{4}$	$\frac{5\pi}{6}$	π

8. The minute hand of a clock is 4 inches long. To the nearest tenth of an inch, how far does the tip of the minute hand travel as the time progresses from 12:00 to 12:25?

10.5 in.

9. Error Analysis A student was asked to find the arc length of $\overset{\frown}{PQ}$. The student's work is shown at right. Explain the student's error and give the correct arc length.

The student used the diameter instead of the

radius in the circumference formula. The correct

arc length is 2π m.

The entire circumference is $2\pi \cdot 16 = 32\pi$ and 45° is $\frac{1}{8}$ of the circle, so the arc length is $\frac{1}{8} \cdot 32\pi = 4\pi$ m.

Notes

Area of Circles and Sectors

Essential question: *How do you find the area of a circle and the area of a sector?*

COMMON **Standards for**
CORE **Mathematical Content**

CC.9-12.G.C.5 …derive the formula for the area of a sector.

CC.9-12.G.GMD.1 Give an informal argument for the formula for the … area of a circle, …

Vocabulary
sector

Prerequisites
Central Angles and Inscribed Angles, Lesson 7-1

Math Background
Students are likely to be familiar with the formula for the area of a circle from earlier grades, but they may not have seen a justification of the formula. In this lesson, student use a dissection argument to informally justify the formula. The argument is based on the idea of cutting a circle into wedges, rearranging the wedges to form a shape that is close to a shape for which the area is known (a parallelogram), and then considering what happens as the wedges get finer and finer. This type of argument is essential in calculus, so this lesson serves as a preview of the type of reasoning students will use in later mathematics courses.

INTRODUCE

Explain to students that the problem of finding the area of a circle has interested mathematicians since ancient times. In fact, Euclid's *Elements* (circa 300 BCE) contains a statement that is equivalent to the formula $A = \pi r^2$. Tell students that there are many ways to derive the formula for the area of a circle and that they will use a method that incorporates some ideas that they may study more deeply in a future calculus course.

TEACH

1 EXPLORE

Materials: compass, scissors

Questioning Strategies
- What is the formula for the area of a parallelogram? **$A = bh$, where b is the base and h is the height.**
- Suppose you folded the circle again and made 16 wedges instead of 8. How would the shape formed by these wedges compare to the shape formed in the Explore? **The shape would be an even closer approximation to a parallelogram.**

2 EXAMPLE

Questioning Strategies
- How does the area of sector *AOB* compare to the area of the complete circle? **The area of the sector is one-third of the area of the circle.**
- What are appropriate units for the area of the sector? Why? **Square millimeters; the radius is given in millimeters and areas are always expressed in square units.**

EXTRA EXAMPLE

Find the area of sector *GOH*. Express your answer in terms of π and rounded to the nearest tenth.

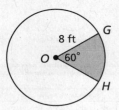

$\frac{32}{3}\pi$ ft^2; 33.5 ft^2

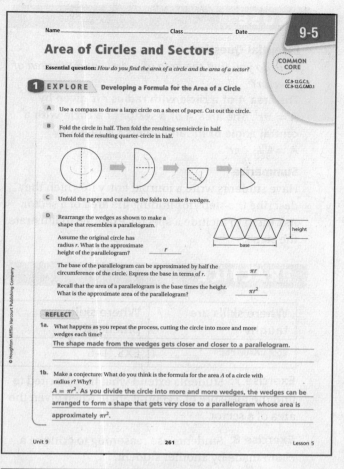

Name_____ Class_____ Date_____

9-5

COMMON CORE
CC.9-12.G.C.5,
CC.9-12.G.GMD.1

Area of Circles and Sectors

Essential question: *How do you find the area of a circle and the area of a sector?*

1 EXPLORE   Developing a Formula for the Area of a Circle

A Use a compass to draw a large circle on a sheet of paper. Cut out the circle.

B Fold the circle in half. Then fold the resulting semicircle in half. Then fold the resulting quarter-circle in half.

C Unfold the paper and cut along the folds to make 8 wedges.

D Rearrange the wedges as shown to make a shape that resembles a parallelogram.

Assume the original circle has radius r. What is the approximate height of the parallelogram? _____ r

The base of the parallelogram can be approximated by half the circumference of the circle. Express the base in terms of r. _____ πr

Recall that the area of a parallelogram is the base times the height. What is the approximate area of the parallelogram? _____ πr^2

REFLECT

1a. What happens as you repeat the process, cutting the circle into more and more wedges each time?

The shape made from the wedges gets closer and closer to a parallelogram.

1b. Make a conjecture: What do you think is the formula for the area A of a circle with radius r? Why?

$A = \pi r^2$. As you divide the circle into more and more wedges, the wedges can be arranged to form a shape that gets very close to a parallelogram whose area is approximately πr^2.

© Houghton Mifflin Harcourt Publishing Company

Unit 9   261   Lesson 5

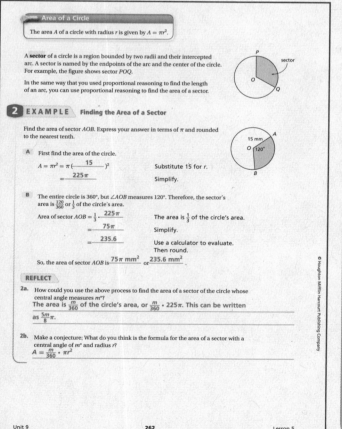

Area of a Circle

The area A of a circle with radius r is given by $A = \pi r^2$.

A **sector** of a circle is a region bounded by two radii and their intercepted arc. A sector is named by the endpoints of the arc and the center of the circle. For example, the figure shows sector *POQ*.

In the same way that you used proportional reasoning to find the length of an arc, you can use proportional reasoning to find the area of a sector.

2 EXAMPLE   Finding the Area of a Sector

Find the area of sector *AOB*. Express your answer in terms of π and rounded to the nearest tenth.

A First find the area of the circle.

$A = \pi r^2 = \pi (\underline{15})^2$ Substitute 15 for r.

$= \underline{225\pi}$ Simplify.

B The entire circle is 360°, but $\angle AOB$ measures 120°. Therefore, the sector's area is $\frac{120}{360}$ or $\frac{1}{3}$ of the circle's area.

Area of sector $AOB = \frac{1}{3} \cdot \underline{225\pi}$ The area is $\frac{1}{3}$ of the circle's area.

$= \underline{75\pi}$ Simplify.

$= \underline{235.6}$ Use a calculator to evaluate. Then round.

So, the area of sector AOB is $\underline{75\pi}$ mm² or $\underline{235.6}$ mm².

REFLECT

2a. How could you use the above process to find the area of a sector of the circle whose central angle measures m°?

The area is $\frac{m}{360}$ of the circle's area, or $\frac{m}{360} \cdot 225\pi$. This can be written as $\frac{5m}{8}\pi$.

2b. Make a conjecture: What do you think is the formula for the area of a sector with a central angle of m° and radius r?

$A = \frac{m}{360} \cdot \pi r^2$

© Houghton Mifflin Harcourt Publishing Company

Unit 9   262   Lesson 5

Differentiated Instruction

You may want to challenge students by having them derive the area formula for a circle by using a sequence of inscribed regular polygons. This is similar to the method used to develop the formula for the circumference of a circle in Lesson 9-3. In this case, the area of an inscribed n-gon is given by the expression $n \cdot r \sin\left(\frac{180°}{n}\right) \cdot r \cos\left(\frac{180°}{n}\right)$. Students can use the table feature of their calculator to show that as n gets larger, the expression $n \sin\left(\frac{180°}{n}\right) \cdot \cos\left(\frac{180°}{n}\right) \cdot$ gets closer to π. Thus, the expression for the area gets closer to πr^2.

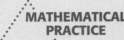

MATHEMATICAL PRACTICE Highlighting the Standards

Standard 6 (Attend to precision) states that mathematically proficient students are "careful about specifying units of measure." In this lesson, students should check their answers to make sure areas are always expressed in terms of square units, such as square inches or square meters.

Avoid Common Errors

If students are getting answers that are different from those in the text, check that they are using the π key on their calculator and then rounding as the final step of the solution. Students who enter 3.14 as an approximation of π will often get different results from students who use the π key and then round.

CLOSE

Essential Question

How do you find the area of a circle and the area of a sector?

The area A of a circle with radius r is given by $A = \pi r^2$. The area A of a sector of a circle with a central angle of $m°$ and radius r is given by $A = \frac{m}{360} \cdot \pi r^2$.

Summarize

Have students write a journal entry in which they describe the steps for finding the area of a sector. Ask them to include a specific example to illustrate the steps.

PRACTICE

Where skills are taught	Where skills are practiced
2 EXAMPLE	EXS. 1–6

Exercise 7: Students extend what they learned to find the measure of a central angle when given the area of a sector.

Exercise 8: Students use reasoning to critique a claim made by another student.

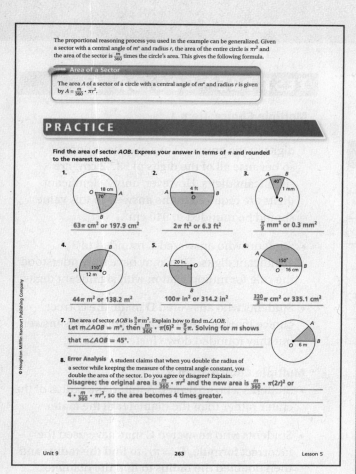

The proportional reasoning process you used in the example can be generalized. Given a sector with a central angle of $m°$ and radius r, the area of the entire circle is πr^2 and the area of the sector is $\frac{m}{360}$ times the circle's area. This gives the following formula.

Area of a Sector

The area A of a sector of a circle with a central angle of $m°$ and radius r is given by $A = \frac{m}{360} \cdot \pi r^2$.

PRACTICE

Find the area of sector AOB. Express your answer in terms of π and rounded to the nearest tenth.

1. [circle with O, 18 cm, 70°, A, B]

63π cm² or 197.9 cm²

2. [circle with 4 ft, A, O, B]

2π ft² or 6.3 ft²

3. [circle with A, B, 40°, 1 mm, O]

$\frac{\pi}{9}$ mm² or 0.3 mm²

4. [circle with B, A, 110°, 12 m, O]

44π m² or 138.2 m²

5. [circle with 20 in., A, O, B]

100π in² or 314.2 in²

6. [circle with A, 150°, 16 cm, O, B]

$\frac{320}{3}\pi$ cm² or 335.1 cm²

7. The area of sector AOB is $\frac{9}{2}\pi m^2$. Explain how to find m∠AOB.

Let m∠AOB = $m°$, then $\frac{m}{360} \cdot \pi(6)^2 = \frac{9}{2}\pi$. Solving for m shows that m∠AOB = 45°.

[circle with A, B, O, 6 m]

8. **Error Analysis** A student claims that when you double the radius of a sector while keeping the measure of the central angle constant, you double the area of the sector. Do you agree or disagree? Explain.

Disagree; the original area is $\frac{m}{360} \cdot \pi r^2$ and the new area is $\frac{m}{360} \cdot \pi(2r)^2$ or $4 \cdot \frac{m}{360} \cdot \pi r^2$, so the area becomes 4 times greater.

Notes

COMMON CORE CORRELATION

Standards	Item
CC.9-12.N.Q.3*	1, 3
CC.9-12.G.CO.1	4
CC.9-12.G.C.5	4, 6, 8
CC.9-12.G.GPE.7*	2, 9
CC.9-12.G.GMD.1	7
CC.9-12.G.MG.1*	5
CC.9-12.G.MG.2*	9

TEST PREP DOCTOR ⊕

Multiple Choice: Item 1

- Students who answered **B** included all of the digits in the answer. They may have done so because all of the digits of 937.2 cm^2 are significant digits. However, only 2 significant digits are required in the answer, so this value should be rounded to 940 cm^2.

- Students who answered **C** rounded to 3 significant digits. They may have misunderstood the rule for multiplication with significant digits.

- Students who answered **D** made the correct choice in using 2 significant digits in the answer, but they rounded down instead of up.

Multiple Choice: Item 5

- Students who answered **A** found the radius of the crater rather than the diameter of the crater.

- Students who answered **C** may have used the incorrect formula, $C = \pi r$, to find the radius and then doubled the radius to find the diameter.

- Students who answered **D** may have multiplied the circumference by π rather than dividing the circumference by π.

Free Response: Item 8

- Students who wrote the expression $\frac{m}{15} \pi$ may have found the circumference of the circle ($2\pi r$) rather than the area (πr^2).

- Students who wrote the expression $\frac{m}{30} \pi$ may have forgotten to square the value of r when calculating the area of the circle.

- Students who wrote the expression 144π may have forgotten to multiply the area of the circle by the fraction of the area represented by the sector, $\frac{m}{360}$.

Name _____ Class _____ Date _____

MULTIPLE CHOICE

1. A student measures the length of a rectangular poster to the nearest centimeter and finds that the length is 44 cm. Another student measures the poster's width to the nearest tenth of a centimeter and finds that the width is 21.3 cm. How should the students report the area of the poster using the correct number of significant digits?

(A) 940 cm²   **C.** 937 cm²

B. 937.2 cm²   **D.** 930 cm²

2. The figure shows a polygonal fence for part of a garden. Each unit of the coordinate plane represents one meter. What is the length of the fence to the nearest tenth of a meter?

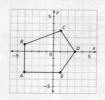

F. 16.1 m   **(H)** 21.6 m

G. 18.0 m   **J.** 31.0 m

3. A geologist reports the mass of a rock to 3 significant digits. Which of the following could be the mass of the rock?

A. 42.00 kg   **C.** 0.42 kg

(B) 4.20 kg   **D.** 0.042 kg

4. Using the figure below, Andrea discovers that the length of the arc intercepted by the 60° angle is proportional to the radius. What is the constant of proportionality for the relationship?

F. $\frac{\pi}{6}$ **H.** $\frac{1}{6}$

(G) $\frac{\pi}{3}$ **J.** $\frac{1}{3}$

5. Meteor Crater, near Flagstaff, Arizona, is an approximately circular crater, with a circumference of 2.32 miles. What is the diameter of the crater to the nearest hundredth of a mile?

A. 0.37 mi   **C.** 1.48 mi

(B) 0.74 mi   **D.** 7.29 mi

6. What is the radian measure of the angle whose degree measure is 20°?

F. $\frac{\pi}{20}$ **(H)** $\frac{\pi}{9}$

G. $\frac{\pi}{18}$ **J.** $\frac{2\pi}{9}$

© Houghton Mifflin Harcourt Publishing Company

FREE RESPONSE

7. In order to justify the formula for the circumference of a circle, you inscribe a regular n-gon in a circle of radius r, as shown in the figure.

You show that $\triangle AOM \cong \triangle BOM$ and conclude that $\angle 1 \cong \angle 2$ by CPCTC. Then you state that $m\angle AOB = \frac{360°}{n}$ and $m\angle 1 = \frac{180°}{n}$. Describe the main steps for finishing the justification of the circumference formula.

Show that $x = r\sin\left(\frac{180°}{n}\right)$, so that the

perimeter of n-gon is $2nr\sin\left(\frac{180°}{n}\right)$.

Use the table feature of a graphing

calculator to show that this expression

gets closer to $2\pi r$ as n gets larger.

_____

8. Write an expression in terms of m that you can use to find the area of sector AOB.

$\frac{2m}{5}\pi$

_____

9. The border of Utah can be modeled by the polygon with vertices $A(0, 0)$, $B(0, 350)$, $C(160, 350)$, $D(160, 280)$, $E(270, 280)$, and $F(270, 0)$. Each unit on the coordinate plane represents 1 mile.

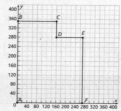

a. What is the approximate area of the state?

86,800 mi²

b. The population of Utah is 2,784,572. Explain how to find the state's population density. Round to the nearest tenth.

To find population density, find the

ratio of population to area.

Population density = $\frac{2,784,572}{86,800} \approx 32.1$

persons per square mile.

_____

_____

_____

_____

© Houghton Mifflin Harcourt Publishing Company

UNIT 10

Three-Dimensional Figures and Volume

Unit Vocabulary

cross section   (10-1)

oblique cylinder   (10-2)

Three-Dimensional Figures and Volume

Unit Focus

In this unit, you will turn your attention to three-dimensional figures. You will begin by exploring cross sections of three-dimensional figures and learn how to generate three-dimensional figures by rotating two-dimensional figures around a line. Then you will develop and justify volume formulas for a variety of solids. Finally, you will apply what you have learned to solve problems in which you must design a three-dimensional figure given one or more constraints.

Unit at a Glance

COMMON CORE

Lesson	Standards for Mathematical Content
10-1 Visualizing Three-Dimensional Figures	CC.9-12.G.GMD.4
10-2 Volume of Prisms and Cylinders	CC.9-12.G.GMD.1, CC.9-12.G.GMD.2(+), CC.9-12.G.GMD.3*, CC.9-12.G.MG.1*, CC.9-12.G.MG.2*
10-3 Volume of Pyramids	CC.9-12.G.GMD.1, CC.9-12.G.GMD.3*
10-4 Volume of Cones	CC.9-12.G.GMD.1, CC.9-12.G.GMD.3*
10-5 Volume of Spheres	CC.9-12.G.GMD.2(+), CC.9-12.G.GMD.3*, CC.9-12.G.MG.2*
10-6 Solving Design Problems	CC.9-12.G.GMD.3*, CC.9-12.G.MG.3*
Test Prep	

Unpacking the Common Core State Standards

Use the table to help you understand the Standards for Mathematical Content that are taught in this unit. Refer to the lessons listed after each standard for exploration and practice.

COMMON CORE Standards for Mathematical Content	What It Means For You
CC.9-12.G.GMD.1 **Give an informal argument for the formulas for the circumference of a circle, area of a circle, volume of a cylinder, pyramid, and cone.** Lessons 10-2, 10-3, 10-4	You may already be familiar with some of the formulas for volumes of three-dimensional figures, but now you will give logical arguments to justify the formulas.
CC.9-12.G.GMD.2(+) **Give an informal argument using Cavalieri's principle for the formulas for the volume of a sphere and other solid figures.** Lessons 10-2, 10-5	You will learn how to use Cavalieri's principle, which is a powerful tool for developing and justifying volume formulas.
CC.9-12.G.GMD.3 **Use volume formulas for cylinders, pyramids, cones, and spheres to solve problems.*** Lessons 10-2, 10-3, 10-4, 10-5, 10-6	Cylinders, pyramids, cones, and spheres occur in a wide range of real-world applications. You will learn how to use volume formulas to solve problems that involve these figures.
CC.9-12.G.GMD.4 **Identify the shapes of two-dimensional cross-sections of three-dimensional objects, and identify three-dimensional objects generated by rotations of two-dimensional objects.** Lesson 10-1	Visualization is an important element of working with three-dimensional figures. You will learn to visualize cross sections and rotations around a line in space.
CC.9-12.G.G.MG.1 **Use geometric shapes, their measures, and their properties to describe objects (e.g., modeling a tree trunk or a human torso as a cylinder).*** Lesson 10-2	You will see how you can model real-world objects with three-dimensional figures in order to solve problems.
CC.9-12.G.G.MG.2 **Apply concepts of density based on area and volume in modeling situations (e.g., persons per square mile, BTUs per cubic foot).*** Lessons 10-2, 10-5	You will do further work with density and learn how to measure the energy content of a fuel in terms of BTUs per unit of volume.
CC.9-12.G.G.MG.3 **Apply geometric methods to solve design problems (e.g., designing an object or structure to satisfy physical constraints or minimize cost; working with typographic grid systems based on ratios).*** Lesson 10-6	You will solve problems in which you are asked to design a three-dimensional figure that meets given conditions.

© Houghton Mifflin Harcourt Publishing Company

Unpacking the Common Core State Standards

This page lists and explains the Standards for Mathematical Content that are addressed in this unit. For information about the Standards for Mathematical Practice, which are integrated throughout the text, see Teacher Edition pages x–xiii.

Notes

Visualizing Three-Dimensional Figures

Essential question: *How do you identify cross sections of three-dimensional figures and how do you use rotations to generate three-dimensional figures?*

COMMON CORE **Standards for Mathematical Content**

CC.9-12.G.GMD.4 Identify the shapes of two-dimensional cross-sections of three-dimensional objects, and identify three-dimensional objects generated by rotations of two-dimensional objects.

Vocabulary

cross section

Prerequisites

Rotations, Lesson 2-6

Math Background

Until now, students have worked primarily with two-dimensional figures in this course. In Unit 10, the focus shifts to three-dimensional figures. Students have already explored three-dimensional figures in earlier grades, especially in the context of volume problems, but this unit offers an approach that is likely to be more deductive in nature than what students have seen before. Specifically, students will learn how to justify the essential volume formulas. This first lesson of the unit gives students experience in visualizing three-dimensional figures. It can also serve as an opportunity to review key vocabulary associated with such figures.

INTRODUCE

Remind students of some of the vocabulary related to three-dimensional figures. You may wish to sketch on the board figures like the ones below and work with students to label the parts of the figures.

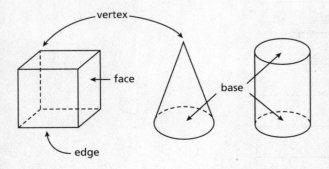

TEACH

1 EXAMPLE

Questioning Strategies

• What do the dashed lines represent in the figures? **The dashed lines are hidden lines.**

• How many bases does a cylinder have? What must be true about the bases? **Two; the bases must be congruent circles.**

EXTRA EXAMPLE

Describe each cross section.

A.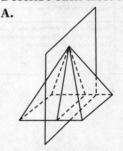

B.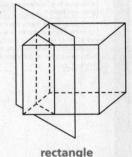

(isosceles) triangle   rectangle

Differentiated Instruction

Some students may have difficulty visualizing the cross sections in this lesson. Kinesthetic learners in particular might benefit from using clay to make small models of the relevant three-dimensional figures. Then, they can view cross sections by making straight slices through the figures with a plastic knife or with a taut piece of string or dental floss.

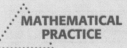

MATHEMATICAL PRACTICE **Highlighting the Standards**

To address Standard 7 (Look for and make use of structure), encourage students to use properties of three-dimensional figures to help them identify cross sections. For example, knowing that the faces of a rectangular prism meet at right angles can help students identify the figure that is formed by a plane that intersects the prism.

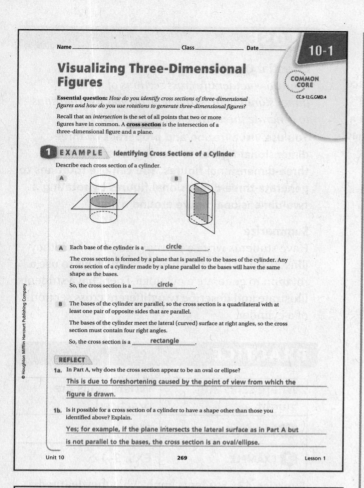

Name_____ Class_____ Date_____

10-1

COMMON CORE

CC.9-12.G.GMD.4

Visualizing Three-Dimensional Figures

Essential question: *How do you identify cross sections of three-dimensional figures and how do you use rotations to generate three-dimensional figures?*

Recall that an *intersection* is the set of all points that two or more figures have in common. A **cross section** is the intersection of a three-dimensional figure and a plane.

1 EXAMPLE Identifying Cross Sections of a Cylinder

Describe each cross section of a cylinder.

A

B

A Each base of the cylinder is a _____circle_____

The cross section is formed by a plane that is parallel to the bases of the cylinder. Any cross section of a cylinder made by a plane parallel to the bases will have the same shape as the bases.

So, the cross section is a _____circle_____.

B The bases of the cylinder are parallel, so the cross section is a quadrilateral with at least one pair of opposite sides that are parallel.

The bases of the cylinder meet the lateral (curved) surface at right angles, so the cross section must contain four right angles.

So, the cross section is a _____rectangle_____.

REFLECT

1a. In Part A, why does the cross section appear to be an oval or ellipse?

This is due to foreshortening caused by the point of view from which the figure is drawn.

1b. Is it possible for a cross section of a cylinder to have a shape other than those you identified above? Explain.

Yes; for example, if the plane intersects the lateral surface as in Part A but is not parallel to the bases, the cross section is an oval/ellipse.

Unit 10   269   Lesson 1

You have learned how to perform transformations in a plane. Transformations may also be carried out in three-dimensional space. In particular, you can rotate a two-dimensional figure around a line to generate a three-dimensional figure.

2 EXAMPLE Generating Three-Dimensional Figures

Sketch and describe the figure that is generated by each rotation in three-dimensional space.

A Rotate a right triangle around a line that contains one of its legs.

- Draw a right triangle and draw a line that contains one of its legs, as shown at right.
- To model the rotation of the triangle around the line, trace and cut out the triangle. Then tape the triangle to a piece of string so that one leg of the triangle is attached to the string. Hold both ends of the string and twirl it between your fingers to see the three-dimensional figure generated by the rotation. Sketch the figure at right.

Sketch of Two-Dimensional Figure and Line of Rotation	Sketch of Three-Dimensional Figure Generated by the Rotation

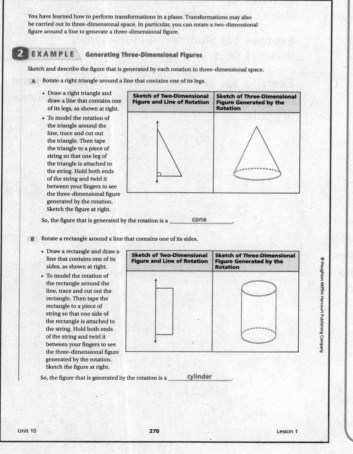

So, the figure that is generated by the rotation is a _____cone_____

B Rotate a rectangle around a line that contains one of its sides.

- Draw a rectangle and draw a line that contains one of its sides, as shown at right.
- To model the rotation of the rectangle around the line, trace and cut out the rectangle. Then tape the rectangle to a piece of string so that one side of the rectangle is attached to the string. Hold both ends of the string and twirl it between your fingers to see the three-dimensional figure generated by the rotation. Sketch the figure at right.

Sketch of Two-Dimensional Figure and Line of Rotation	Sketch of Three-Dimensional Figure Generated by the Rotation

So, the figure that is generated by the rotation is a _____cylinder_____.

Unit 10   270   Lesson 1

Questioning Strategies

- How do you think a rotation around a line in space is similar to a rotation around a point in a plane? **All points in space move around the line in such a way that their distance from the line is unchanged; points on the line of rotation are fixed.**

- In part A, what part of the cone is formed by the hypotenuse of the triangle? Explain. **As the hypotenuse is rotated around the line, it forms the lateral (curved) surface of the cone.**

EXTRA EXAMPLE

Sketch and describe the figure that is generated by each rotation in three-dimensional space.

A. Rotate a rectangle around one of the rectangle's lines of symmetry.

cylinder

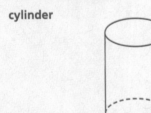

B. Rotate a circle around a line containing the circle's diameter.

sphere

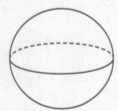

Differentiated Instruction

Challenge students by asking them to describe the three-dimensional figures that are formed by rotating figures in a coordinate plane. For example, you might have students describe the figure formed by rotating the part of the line $y = -x + 2$ that lies in quadrant I around the x-axis. Students should find that the figure is a cone with radius 2 and height 2.

CLOSE

Essential Question

How do you identify cross sections of three-dimensional figures and how do you use rotations to generate three-dimensional figures?

You use visualization and properties of three-dimensional figures to identify cross sections of three-dimensional figures. You can use rotations to generate three-dimensional figures by rotating a two-dimensional figure around a line.

Summarize

Have students write a journal entry in which they illustrate and describe two different ways to use a rotation to generate a cylinder. Then, have students illustrate and describe two different cross sections of a cylinder.

PRACTICE

Where skills are taught	Where skills are practiced
1 EXAMPLE	EXS. 1–8
2 EXAMPLE	EXS. 9–12

Exercise 13: Students apply what they learned about cross sections.

Exercise 14: Students critique another student's work.

Exercise 15: Students use visualization skills and reasoning to solve a problem about cross sections of a cube.

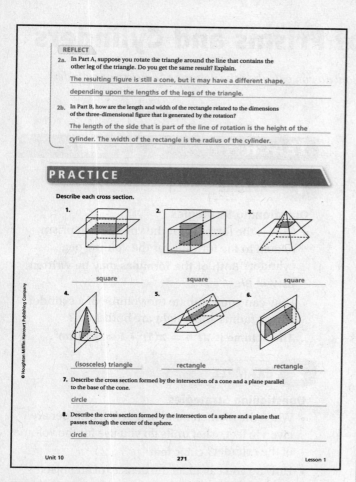

REFLECT

2a. In Part A, suppose you rotate the triangle around the line that contains the other leg of the triangle. Do you get the same result? Explain.

The resulting figure is still a cone, but it may have a different shape,

depending upon the lengths of the legs of the triangle.

2b. In Part B, how are the length and width of the rectangle related to the dimensions of the three-dimensional figure that is generated by the rotation?

The length of the side that is part of the line of rotation is the height of the

cylinder. The width of the rectangle is the radius of the cylinder.

PRACTICE

Describe each cross section.

1.

square

2.

square

3.

square

4.

(isosceles) triangle

5.

rectangle

6.

rectangle

7. Describe the cross section formed by the intersection of a cone and a plane parallel to the base of the cone.

circle

8. Describe the cross section formed by the intersection of a sphere and a plane that passes through the center of the sphere.

circle

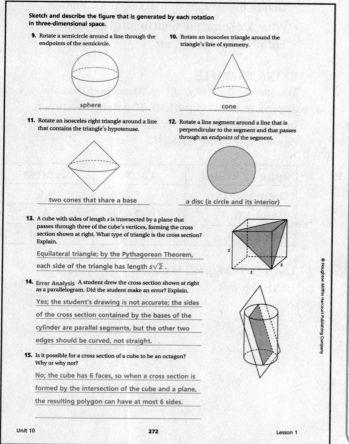

Sketch and describe the figure that is generated by each rotation in three-dimensional space.

9. Rotate a semicircle around a line through the endpoints of the semicircle.

sphere

10. Rotate an isosceles triangle around the triangle's line of symmetry.

cone

11. Rotate an isosceles right triangle around a line that contains the triangle's hypotenuse.

two cones that share a base

12. Rotate a line segment around a line that is perpendicular to the segment and that passes through an endpoint of the segment.

a disc (a circle and its interior)

13. A cube with sides of length *s* is intersected by a plane that passes through three of the cube's vertices, forming the cross section shown at right. What type of triangle is the cross section? Explain.

Equilateral triangle; by the Pythagorean Theorem,

each side of the triangle has length $s\sqrt{2}$.

14. **Error Analysis** A student drew the cross section shown at right as a parallelogram. Did the student make an error? Explain.

Yes; the student's drawing is not accurate; the sides

of the cross section contained by the bases of the

cylinder are parallel segments, but the other two

edges should be curved, not straight.

15. Is it possible for a cross section of a cube to be an octagon? Why or why not?

No; the cube has 6 faces, so when a cross section is

formed by the intersection of the cube and a plane,

the resulting polygon can have at most 6 sides.

Volume of Prisms and Cylinders

Essential question: *How do you calculate the volume of a prism or cylinder?*

COMMON CORE Standards for Mathematical Content

CC.9-12.G.GMD.1 Give an informal argument for the formula for the ... volume of a cylinder ....

CC.9-12.G.GMD.2(+) Give an informal argument using Cavalieri's principle for the formulas for the volume of ... other solid figures.

CC.9-12.G.GMD.3 Use volume formulas for cylinders ... to solve problems.*

CC.9-12.G.MG.1 Use geometric shapes, their measures, and their properties to describe objects (e.g., modeling a tree trunk or a human torso as a cylinder).*

CC.9-12.G.MG.2 Apply concepts of density based on area and volume in modeling situations (e.g., persons per square mile, BTUs per cubic foot).*

Vocabulary
oblique cylinder

Prerequisites
Visualizing Three-Dimensional Figures, Lesson 10-1

Math Background
This lesson introduces Cavalieri's principle, which is named after the Italian mathematician Bonaventura Cavalieri (1598–1647). The principle, which is taken here as a postulate, is one of the most useful ideas in geometry because it allows volume formulas to be extended from simple solids to more complex solids. Students will use Cavalieri's principle again in Lesson 10-5 to develop a formula for the volume of a sphere.

INTRODUCE

Begin by briefly reviewing the definitions of *prism* and *cylinder*. Be sure that students recognize the similarities in these three-dimensional figures and that they can identify the bases of a given prism or cylinder.

TEACH

1 EXPLORE

Questioning Strategies
- How is the formula for the volume of a prism related to the formula for the volume of a cylinder? **Both of the formulas may be written as $V = Bh$.**
- How can you estimate the volume of a cylinder whose radius and height are both 1 cm? **The volume is $\pi r^2 h = \pi(1)^2 \cdot 1 \approx 3.14 \text{ cm}^3$.**

2 EXAMPLE

Questioning Strategies
- When the diameter and height of a cylinder are given in feet, what units do you use for the volume of the cylinder? **cubic feet**
- How do you calculate the density of an object? **Divide the weight or mass by the volume.**
- What are some possible units of density? **kg/m^3, lb/ft^3, g/cm^3, etc.**

EXTRA EXAMPLE

You gather data about two wood logs that are approximately cylindrical. The data are shown in the table. Based on your data, which wood is denser, larch or cypress?

Type of Wood	Larch	Cypress
Diameter (m)	1	0.5
Height (m)	2	3
Mass (kg)	926.8	300.4

Larch ($\approx 590 \text{ kg/m}^3$) is denser than cypress ($\approx 510 \text{ kg/m}^3$).

Volume of Prisms and Cylinders

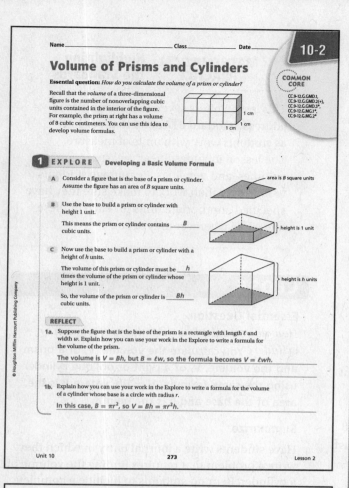

10-2

COMMON CORE

CC.9-12.G.GMD.1,
CC.9-12.G.GMD.2(+),
CC.9-12.G.GMD.3*,
CC.9-12.G.MG.1*,
CC.9-12.G.MG.2*

Essential question: *How do you calculate the volume of a prism or cylinder?*

Recall that the *volume* of a three-dimensional figure is the number of nonoverlapping cubic units contained in the interior of the figure. For example, the prism at right has a volume of 8 cubic centimeters. You can use this idea to develop volume formulas.

1 cm
1 cm
1 cm

1 EXPLORE   Developing a Basic Volume Formula

A Consider a figure that is the base of a prism or cylinder. Assume the figure has an area of *B* square units.

area is *B* square units

B Use the base to build a prism or cylinder with height 1 unit.

This means the prism or cylinder contains ___*B*___ cubic units.

height is 1 unit

C Now use the base to build a prism or cylinder with a height of *h* units.

The volume of this prism or cylinder must be ___*h*___ times the volume of the prism or cylinder whose height is 1 unit.

So, the volume of the prism or cylinder is ___*Bh*___ cubic units.

height is *h* units

REFLECT

1a. Suppose the figure that is the base of the prism is a rectangle with length ℓ and width *w*. Explain how you can use your work in the Explore to write a formula for the volume of the prism.

The volume is $V = Bh$, but $B = \ell w$, so the formula becomes $V = \ell wh$.

1b. Explain how you can use your work in the Explore to write a formula for the volume of a cylinder whose base is a circle with radius *r*.

In this case, $B = \pi r^2$, so $V = Bh = \pi r^2 h$.

Volume of a Cylinder

The volume *V* of a cylinder with base area *B* and height *h* is given by $V = Bh$ (or $V = \pi r^2 h$, where *r* is the radius of the base).

2 EXAMPLE   Comparing Densities

You gather data about two wood logs that are approximately cylindrical. Based on the data in the table, which wood is denser, Douglas fir or American redwood?

Type of Wood	Diameter (ft)	Height (ft)	Weight (lb)
Douglas fir	1	6	155.5
American redwood	3	4	791.7

A Find the volume of the Douglas fir log.

$V = \pi r^2 h$

$V = \pi(\ \underline{0.5}\ )^2 \cdot \underline{6}$ Substitute 0.5 for *r* and 6 for *h*.

$V \approx \underline{4.7}\ \text{ft}^3$ Use a calculator. Round to the nearest tenth.

B Find the volume of the American redwood log.

$V = \pi r^2 h$

$V = \pi(\ \underline{1.5}\ )^2 \cdot \underline{4}$ Substitute 1.5 for *r* and 4 for *h*.

$V \approx \underline{28.3}\ \text{ft}^3$ Use a calculator. Round to the nearest tenth.

C Calculate and compare densities.

The density of the wood is the ___weight___ per ___unit volume___.

Density of Douglas fir $= \dfrac{155.5}{4.7} \approx \underline{33}$ lb/ft³   Round to the nearest unit.

Density of American redwood $= \dfrac{791.7}{28.3} \approx \underline{28}$ lb/ft³   Round to the nearest unit.

So, ___Douglas fir___ is denser than ___American redwood___.

REFLECT

2a. Explain in your own words what your results tell you about the two types of wood.

Possible answer: Given blocks of wood with identical dimensions, a block of

Douglas fir is heavier than a block of American redwood.

Teaching Strategies

Kinesthetic learners can use a stack of pennies to understand Cavalieri's principle. Have students arrange the pennies to form a right cylinder and ask them to estimate the volume. Then, have students push the stack to form an oblique cylinder. Students should see that the volume of the stack does not change. This is supported by Cavalieri's principle because the cross-sectional area at each level (i.e., the area of the face of a penny) is unchanged when the stack is pushed to formed the oblique cylinder.

3 EXAMPLE

Questioning Strategies

- How is an oblique cylinder similar to a right cylinder? **The bases are circles. The bases are connected by a curved lateral surface. The same volume formula works for both types of cylinders.**
- How is an oblique cylinder different from a right cylinder? **In an oblique cylinder, the axis is not perpendicular to the bases.**
- When you solve $r^2 = 64$, how do you know $r = 8$ rather than -8? **The radius is a length, so it must be nonnegative.**

EXTRA EXAMPLE

The height of the cylinder shown here is half the diameter. What is the volume of the cylinder? Round to the nearest tenth.

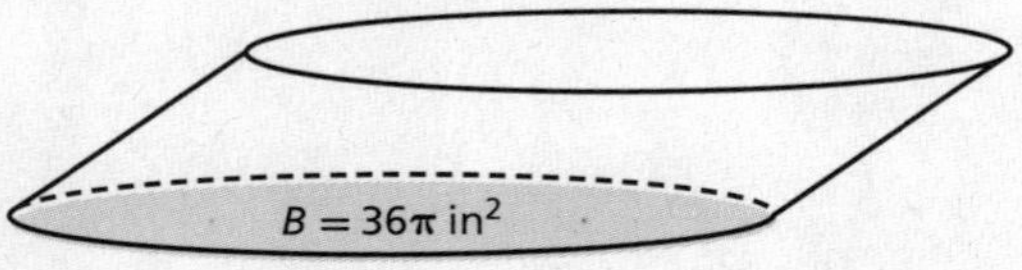

678.6 in.^{3}

MATHEMATICAL PRACTICE **Highlighting the Standards**

This lesson offers several opportunities to address Standard 6 (Attend to precision) as students work with units of measure. The lesson includes linear measures, areas, volumes, and densities. Encourage students to look over their work to make sure they have specified appropriate units for each of these measures wherever they occur.

CLOSE

Essential Question

How do you calculate the volume of a prism or cylinder? **You calculate the volume, V, of a prism and the volume, V, of a right or oblique cylinder using the same formula, $V = Bh$, where B is the area of the base and h is the height.**

Summarize

Have students write a journal entry in which they write a problem that requires finding the volume of a cylinder. Remind students to include a complete solution for the problem.

PRACTICE

Where skills are taught	Where skills are practiced
1 EXPLORE	EXS. 1–3
2 EXAMPLE	EX. 4
3 EXAMPLE	EX. 5

Exercise 6: Students apply what they have learned to critique another student's reasoning.

The axis of a cylinder is the segment whose endpoints are the centers of the bases. A right cylinder is a cylinder whose axis is perpendicular to the bases. An **oblique cylinder** is a cylinder whose axis is not perpendicular to the bases. Cavalieri's principle makes it possible to extend the formula for the volume of a cylinder to oblique cylinders.

You can think of any oblique cylinder as a right cylinder that has been "pushed over" so that the cross sections at every level have equal areas. By Cavalieri's principle, the volume of an oblique cylinder is equal to the volume of the associated right cylinder. This means the formula $V = Bh = \pi r^2 h$ works for any cylinder.

Cavalieri's Principle

If two solids have the same height and the same cross-sectional area at every level, then the two solids have the same volume.

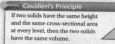

3 EXAMPLE Finding the Volume of an Oblique Cylinder

The height of the cylinder shown here is twice the radius. What is the volume of the cylinder? Round to the nearest tenth.

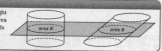

A Find the height of the cylinder. To do so, first find the radius of the cylinder.

Use the fact that the area of the base B is 64π cm².

$\pi r^2 = 64\pi$	The base is a circle, so $B = \pi r^2$.
$r^2 = \underline{64}$	Divide both sides by π.
$r = \underline{8}$ cm	Take the square root of both sides.

Since the height is twice the radius, the height is $\underline{16}$ cm.

B Find the volume of the cylinder.

$V = Bh$	The volume V of any cylinder is $V = Bh$.
$V = \underline{64\pi} \cdot \underline{16}$	Substitute.
$V \approx \underline{3217.0}$ cm³	Use a calulator. Round to the nearest tenth.

© Houghton Mifflin Harcourt Publishing Company

REFLECT

3a. A rectangular prism has the same height as the oblique cylinder in the example. The cross-sectional area at every level of the prism is 64π cm². Can you use Cavalieri's principle to make a conclusion about the volume of the prism? Why or why not?

Yes; since the heights are equal and the cross-sectional areas at every

level are equal, the prism has the same volume as the cylinder.

PRACTICE

Find the volume of each prism or cylinder. Round to the nearest tenth.

1.

164.6 mm³

2.

4.1 ft³

3.

229.4 m³

4. You gather data about two wood logs that are approximately cylindrical. The data are shown in the table. Based on your data, which wood is denser, aspen or juniper? Explain.

Type of Wood	Diameter (ft)	Height (ft)	Weight (lb)
Aspen	1.5	3	137.8
Juniper	2	5	549.8

Juniper; its density is approximately 35 lb/ft³, compared to a density of

approximately 26 lb/ft³ for aspen.

5. A vase in the shape of an oblique cylinder has the dimensions shown at right. How many liters of water does the vase hold? Round to the nearest tenth. (*Hint:* 1 liter = 1000 cm³)

1.5 liters

17 cm

14 cm

6. Error Analysis A student claims that the cylinder and cone at right have the same volume by Cavalieri's principle. Explain the student's error.

Cavalieri's principle does not apply; the cross-

sectional areas are not the same at every level.

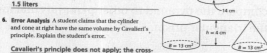

$h = 4$ cm

$B = 13$ cm²

$B = 13$ cm²

© Houghton Mifflin Harcourt Publishing Company

Volume of Pyramids

Essential question: *How do you calculate the volume of a pyramid?*

Standards for Mathematical Content

CC.9-12.G.GMD.1 Give an informal argument for the formula for the ... volume of a ... pyramid .... Use dissection arguments ....

CC.9-12.G.GMD.3 Use volume formulas for ... pyramids ... to solve problems.*

Prerequisites
Volume of Prisms and Cylinders, Lesson 10-2

Math Background
In this lesson, students develop and use a formula for the volume of a pyramid. There are several steps in the process of developing the formula, and you may want to outline these steps with students before beginning the lesson. In particular, students will first explore a key postulate about pyramids (pyramids that have equal base areas and equal heights have equal volumes). Then, students will find a volume formula for a "wedge pyramid." This is a pyramid in which the base is a triangle and a perpendicular segment from the pyramid's vertex to the base intersects the base at a vertex of the triangle. Finally, students will use an informal dissection argument to divide any pyramid into wedge pyramids. In this way, students will be able to extend their formula for wedge pyramids to general pyramids.

INTRODUCE

Remind students of the definition of *pyramid* and the associated vocabulary (lateral face, vertex, base). You may also want to review how to sketch a pyramid. Suggest that students start by drawing a polygonal base and plotting a point for the vertex. Then, students can draw straight lines from the vertex to each vertex of the polygonal base. Remind students to use dashed lines for edges that are hidden when the pyramid is viewed from the front.

TEACH

1 EXPLORE

Questioning Strategies

- Suppose $b = 4$ cm and $h = 1$ cm. What can you conclude about the triangles formed in Steps A and B of the Explore? **The area of the triangles is 2 cm².**

- Suppose you form a pyramid by choosing a point in plane R and connecting it to each vertex of the polygon. Then, you form a different pyramid in this way. What can you say about the heights of the pyramids? Why? **The heights are equal because in each case the height is the perpendicular distance between the plane of the base and plane R.**

2 EXPLORE

Questioning Strategies

- When you write the name of a pyramid as A-BCD, what information about the pyramid does the name give you? **The vertex of the pyramid is A; the base is $\triangle BCD$.**

- Given that A-BCD is a wedge pyramid as shown in the figure on the student page, what can you say about $\overline{AD}$ and $\overline{CD}$? **$\overline{AD}$ is perpendicular to $\overline{CD}$.**

- What is the height of the triangular prism in Step B of the Explore? Why? **AD or h; the height is the same as the height of pyramid A-BCD.**

Avoid Common Errors

In Step C of the Explore, some students may have difficulty visualizing the relationships among the three pyramids that make up the triangular prism. To help students with this part of the Explore, be sure they understand that pyramids A-CFE and C-EFA are the same pyramid. The pyramid is given different names at different times to emphasize a particular vertex and base. This makes it easier to compare the pyramid to other pyramids that form the triangular prism.

Name_____ Class_____ Date_____

Volume of Pyramids

Essential question: *How do you calculate the volume of a pyramid?*

Recall that a *pyramid* is a polyhedron formed by a polygonal base and triangular lateral faces that meet at a common point, called the vertex of the pyramid. The goal of this lesson is to develop a formula for volume of a pyramid.

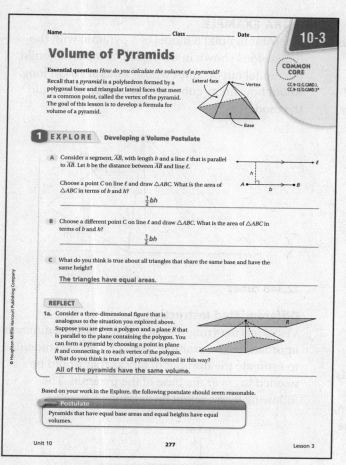

COMMON CORE
CC.9-12.G.GMD.1,
CC.9-12.G.GMD.3*

1 EXPLORE   Developing a Volume Postulate

A   Consider a segment, $\overline{AB}$, with length b and a line ℓ that is parallel to $\overline{AB}$. Let h be the distance between $\overline{AB}$ and line ℓ.

Choose a point C on line ℓ and draw $\triangle ABC$. What is the area of $\triangle ABC$ in terms of b and h?

_____$\frac{1}{2}bh$_____

B   Choose a different point C on line ℓ and draw $\triangle ABC$. What is the area of $\triangle ABC$ in terms of b and h?

_____$\frac{1}{2}bh$_____

C   What do you think is true about all triangles that share the same base and have the same height?

The triangles have equal areas.

REFLECT

1a.   Consider a three-dimensional figure that is analogous to the situation you explored above. Suppose you are given a polygon and a plane R that is parallel to the plane containing the polygon. You can form a pyramid by choosing a point in plane R and connecting it to each vertex of the polygon. What do you think is true of all pyramids formed in this way?

All of the pyramids have the same volume.

Based on your work in the Explore, the following postulate should seem reasonable.

Postulate

Pyramids that have equal base areas and equal heights have equal volumes.

In order to find a formula for the volume of any pyramid, you will first find a formula for the volume of a "wedge pyramid." A wedge pyramid is one in which the base is a triangle and a perpendicular segment from the pyramid's vertex to the base intersects the base at a vertex of the triangle. Pyramid A-BCD is a wedge pyramid.

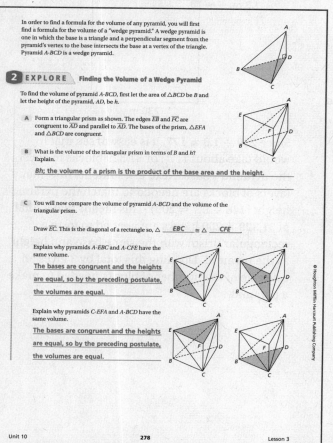

2 EXPLORE   Finding the Volume of a Wedge Pyramid

To find the volume of pyramid A-BCD, first let the area of $\triangle BCD$ be B and let the height of the pyramid, AD, be h.

A   Form a triangular prism as shown. The edges $\overline{EB}$ and $\overline{FC}$ are congruent to $\overline{AD}$ and parallel to $\overline{AD}$. The bases of the prism, $\triangle EFA$ and $\triangle BCD$, are congruent.

B   What is the volume of the triangular prism in terms of B and h? Explain.

Bh; the volume of a prism is the product of the base area and the height.

C   You will now compare the volume of pyramid A-BCD and the volume of the triangular prism.

Draw $\overline{EC}$. This is the diagonal of a rectangle so, $\triangle$ __EBC__ $\cong \triangle$ __CFE__

Explain why pyramids A-EBC and A-CFE have the same volume.

The bases are congruent and the heights are equal, so by the preceding postulate, the volumes are equal.

Explain why pyramids C-EFA and A-BCD have the same volume.

The bases are congruent and the heights are equal, so by the preceding postulate, the volumes are equal.

Teaching Strategies

If time permits, a hands-on activity can help students develop the formula for the volume of a pyramid from an inductive-reasoning perspective. Have students make nets for a square-based pyramid and a square-based prism that has the same height as the pyramid. Then, have students cut out, fold, and tape the nets to form the three-dimensional figures. Students can model the volume of the pyramid by filling it with uncooked rice, sand, or another granular material. Ask students to pour the rice from the pyramid into the prism as many times as necessary to see how the volumes of the figures are related. Students will discover that it takes three batches of rice from the pyramid to fill the prism. That is, the volume of the pyramid is one-third the volume of the associated prism.

 EXAMPLE

Questioning Strategies

- What are the main steps you will use to solve this problem? **First, find the volume of the pyramid. Then, find the volume of an average block. Then, divide the volume of the pyramid by the volume of an average block to estimate the number of blocks in the pyramid.**

- What units should you use for the volume of the pyramid? Why? **Use cubic meters since the lengths are given in meters.**

- The Great Pyramid has internal passageways and internal chambers. What might this tell you about your estimate of the number of blocks used to build the pyramid? Why? **The estimate may be an overestimate since fewer blocks would be needed.**

EXTRA EXAMPLE

You want to build a model of a pyramid with the dimensions shown in the figure. You plan to build the model out of cubes whose sides are 3 cm long. About how many cubes would you need to build the model?

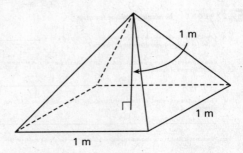

12,346 cubes

Differentiated Instruction

Visual learners might benefit from seeing a different approach to the example. Begin by asking students to estimate the number of blocks that would be needed to cover the base of the pyramid. The following figure might be helpful.

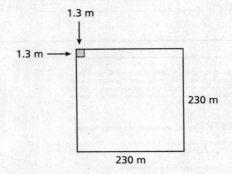

Since $230 \div 1.3 \approx 177$, it is easy to see that it would take about 177^2, or 31,329 blocks to cover the pyramid's base. Next, ask students how many layers of blocks are needed to match the pyramid's height ($146 \div 0.7 \approx 209$). This means that a total of $31,329 \times 209$ blocks are needed to form a rectangular prism with the same base and height as the pyramid. Dividing this total by 3 gives an estimate of the number of blocks needed to make a pyramid.

D You have shown that the three pyramids that form the triangular prism all have the same volume. Compare the volume of pyramid *A-BCD* and the volume of the triangular prism.

The volume of pyramid *A-BCD* is one-third the volume of the triangular prism.

E Write the volume of pyramid *A-BCD* in terms of *B* and *h*.
The volume of pyramid *A-BCD* is $\frac{1}{3}Bh$.

REFLECT

2a. Explain how you know that the three pyramids that form that triangular prism all have the same volume.

Pyramids *A-EBC* and *A-CFE* have the same volume and pyramids *C-EFA* and *A-BCD* have the same volume. But *A-CFE* and *C-EFA* are two names for the same pyramid, so by the Transitive Property of Equality, the pyramids all have the same volume.

In the Explore, you showed that the volume of any "wedge pyramid" is one-third the product of the base area and the height. Now consider a general pyramid. As shown in the figure, the pyramid can be partitioned into nonoverlapping wedge pyramids by drawing a perpendicular from the vertex to the base.

The volume *V* of the given pyramid is the sum of the volumes of the wedge pyramids.

That is, $V = \frac{1}{3}B_1h + \frac{1}{3}B_2h + \frac{1}{3}B_3h + \frac{1}{3}B_4h$.

Using the distributive property, this may be rewritten as $V = \frac{1}{3}h(B_1 + B_2 + B_3 + B_4)$.

Notice that $B_1 + B_2 + B_3 + B_4 = B$, where *B* is the base area of the given pyramid.

So, $V = \frac{1}{3}Bh$.

The above argument provides an informal justification for the following result.

> **Volume of a Pyramid**
> The volume *V* of a pyramid with base area *B* and height *h* is given by
> $V = \frac{1}{3}Bh$.

---

3 EXAMPLE   Solving a Volume Problem

The Great Pyramid in Giza, Egypt, is approximately a square pyramid with the dimensions shown. The pyramid is composed of stone blocks that are rectangular prisms. An average block has dimensions 1.3 m by 1.3 m by 0.7 m. Approximately how many stone blocks were used to build the pyramid? Round to the nearest hundred thousand.

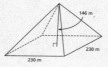

146 m
230 m
230 m

A Find the volume of the pyramid.

The area of the base *B* is the area of a square with sides of length 230 m.

So, $B = $ ___**52,900 m²**___

The volume *V* of the pyramid is $\frac{1}{3}Bh = \frac{1}{3} \cdot$ ___**52,900**___ $\cdot$ ___**146**___

So, $V = $ ___**2,574,466.6 m³**___

B Find the volume of an average block.

The volume of a rectangular prism is given by the formula ___$V = \ell wh$___

So, the volume *W* of an average block is ___**1.183 m³**___

C Find the approximate number of stone blocks in the pyramid.

To estimate the number of blocks in the pyramid, divide ___*V*___ by ___*W*___

So, the approximate number of blocks is ___**2,200,000**___

REFLECT

3a. What aspects of the model in this problem may lead to inaccuracies in your estimate?

___**Possible answer: The given dimensions of the pyramid and the blocks are**___
___**approximations; the blocks form not a true pyramid but rather a pyramid**___
___**consisting of many layers or "steps."**___

3b. Suppose you are told that the average height of a stone block is 0.69 m rather than 0.7 m. Would this increase or decrease your estimate of the total number of blocks in the pyramid? Explain.

___**Increase; this change would decrease *W*, so $\frac{V}{W}$ would increase.**___

Notes

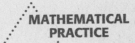

MATHEMATICAL PRACTICE

Highlighting the Standards

The process used in this lesson to develop the formula for the volume of a pyramid offers a connection to Standard 1 (Make sense of problems and persevere in solving them). The standard discusses "looking for entry points" and planning a "solution pathway." Explain to students that mathematicians use these strategies not only when solving specific problems but also when making generalizations and writing proofs.

For example, to find an entry point for developing the formula for the volume of a pyramid, a mathematician might start by asking what is already known. In this case, we already know the formula for the volume of a prism and cylinder. This suggests that it may be useful to somehow connect pyramids to prisms. Some initial efforts in this direction might show that it is awkward to relate a general pyramid to a prism but that a "wedge pyramid" can be related to a prism, as shown in the Explore.

This solution pathway illustrates how a new problem (finding the formula for the volume of a pyramid) may sometimes be related to a simpler problem that has already been solved (finding the formula for the volume of a prism). Encourage students to identify additional examples of this type of thinking as they continue to explore volume formulas.

CLOSE

Essential Question

How do you calculate the volume of a pyramid?

The volume, *V*, of a pyramid with base area *B* and height *h* is given by $V = \frac{1}{3}Bh$.

Summarize

Have students write a summary that describes the main steps they used to develop the formula for the volume of a pyramid.

PRACTICE

Where skills are taught	Where skills are practiced
3 EXAMPLE	EXS. 1–3, 5

Exercise 4: Students use visualization and reasoning to compare the volumes of solids.

Exercises 6 and 7: Students extend what they learned by solving problems that require ideas from earlier lessons or algebra skills.

PRACTICE

Find the volume of each pyramid. Round to the nearest tenth.

1.

4.9 cm
h
4.1 cm
6.2 cm

41.5 cm³

2.
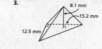
7 ft
h
7 ft
7 ft

114.3 ft³

3.
8.1 mm
15.2 mm
12.5 mm
h

256.5 mm³

4. As shown in the figure, polyhedron *ABCDEFGH* is a cube and *P* is any point on face *EFGH*. Compare the volume of pyramid *P-ABCD* and the volume of the cube.

   The volume of *P-ABCD* is $\frac{1}{3}$ the volume of the cube.

   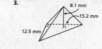
   H   G
   P
   E   F

   D   C
   A   B

5. A storage container for grain is in the shape of a square pyramid with the dimensions shown.

   a. What is the volume of the container in cubic centimeters?

      500,000 cm³

      1 m

      1.5 m

   b. Grain leaks from the container at a rate of 4 cm³ per second. Assuming the container starts completely full, about how many hours does it take until the container is empty?

      approximately 34.7 hours

6. A piece of pure silver in the shape of a rectangular pyramid with the dimensions shown at right has a mass of 19.7 grams. What is the density of silver? Round to the nearest tenth.

   10.5 g/cm³

   1.5 cm

   h   1.5 cm
   2.5 cm

7. A pyramid has a square base and a height of 5 ft. The volume of the pyramid is 60 ft³. Explain how to find the length of a side of the pyramid's base.

   Let *s* be the length of a side of the pyramid's base. Then the area of the base is s^2, and $\frac{1}{3}s^2(5) = 60$. Solving shows that $s = 6$ ft.

Volume of Cones

Essential question: *How do you calculate the volume of a cone?*

COMMON CORE **Standards for Mathematical Content**

CC.9-12.G.GMD.1 Given an informal argument for the formula for the ... volume of a ... cone.

CC.9-12.G.GMD.3 Use volume formulas for ... cones ... to solve problems.*

Prerequisites

Volume of Pyramids, Lesson 10-3

Math Background

The approach to finding a formula for the volume of a cone in this lesson is very similar to the approach to finding a formula for the circumference of a circle in Lesson 9-3. In Lesson 9-3, students used inscribed regular polygons and an informal limit argument to show that the circumference, C, of a circle with radius r is given by $C = 2\pi r$. In this lesson, students inscribe a sequence of pyramids in a given cone and use similar reasoning to show that the volume, V, of the cone is given by $V = \frac{1}{3}Bh$, where B is the base area and h is the cone's height. Note that the first few steps of the process are like those used in Lesson 9-3.

INTRODUCE

Review the process students used in Lesson 9-3 to develop a formula for the circumference of a circle. Then provide an overview of the similar process that will be used here.

- Given a cone, consider an inscribed pyramid with a base that is a regular polygon. Find an expression for the area of the base that is based on r (the radius of the cone) and n (the number of sides of the polygon).

- Find an expression for the volume of the inscribed pyramid.

- Use a calculator to find out what happens as n, the number of sides of the polygonal base, gets larger.

TEACH

1 EXPLORE

Questioning Strategies

- To develop a formula for the volume of a cone, why does it make sense to work with inscribed pyramids? **We already have a formula for the volume of a pyramid.**

- In general, what happens as the number of sides of the base of the inscribed pyramid gets larger? **The pyramid becomes a better fit for the cone; that is, the volume of the pyramid gets closer to the volume of the cone.**

- How is the area of the base of the pyramid related to the area of $\triangle AOB$? Why? **The area of the base of the pyramid is n times the area of $\triangle AOB$ since the base is composed of n triangles, all congruent to $\triangle AOB$.**

Teaching Strategies

In the Explore, students use their calculator's table feature to find out what happens to the expression

$$n \sin\left(\frac{180°}{n}\right) \cos\left(\frac{180°}{n}\right)$$

as n gets larger. You may also wish to have students investigate this question through graphing. Specifically, once students have entered the expression as Y_1, they can view the graph of the function and use the TRACE feature to see that as n gets larger, the y-values get closer to π. As shown below, students can also graph the function $Y_2 = \pi$ to support their findings. (The graph shown here has a viewing window of $3 \le x \le 20$ and $0 \le y \le 5$.)

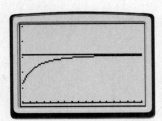

Name_____ Class_____ Date_____

Volume of Cones

Essential question: *How do you calculate the volume of a cone?*

Recall that a *cone* is a three-dimensional figure with a circular base and a curved lateral surface that connects the base to a point called the vertex. You can use the formula for the volume of a pyramid to develop a formula for the volume of a cone.

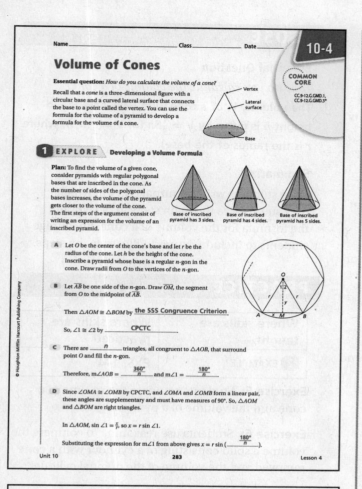

Vertex
Lateral surface
Base

1 EXPLORE Developing a Volume Formula

Plan: To find the volume of a given cone, consider pyramids with regular polygonal bases that are inscribed in the cone. As the number of sides of the polygonal bases increases, the volume of the pyramid gets closer to the volume of the cone. The first steps of the argument consist of writing an expression for the volume of an inscribed pyramid.

Base of inscribed pyramid has 3 sides.   Base of inscribed pyramid has 4 sides.   Base of inscribed pyramid has 5 sides.

A Let O be the center of the cone's base and let r be the radius of the cone. Let h be the height of the cone. Inscribe a pyramid whose base is a regular n-gon in the cone. Draw radii from O to the vertices of the n-gon.

B Let $\overline{AB}$ be one side of the n-gon. Draw $\overline{OM}$, the segment from O to the midpoint of $\overline{AB}$.

Then $\triangle AOM \cong \triangle BOM$ by ___the SSS Congruence Criterion___

So, $\angle 1 \cong \angle 2$ by _____CPCTC_____

C There are ___n___ triangles, all congruent to $\triangle AOB$, that surround point O and fill the n-gon.

Therefore, m$\angle AOB = $ ___$\frac{360°}{n}$___ and m$\angle 1 = $ ___$\frac{180°}{n}$___

D Since $\angle OMA \cong \angle OMB$ by CPCTC, and $\angle OMA$ and $\angle OMB$ form a linear pair, these angles are supplementary and must have measures of 90°. So, $\triangle AOM$ and $\triangle BOM$ are right triangles.

In $\triangle AOM$, $\sin \angle 1 = \frac{x}{r}$, so $x = r \sin \angle 1$.

Substituting the expression for m$\angle 1$ from above gives $x = r \sin \left(\dfrac{180°}{n} \right)$.

E In $\triangle AOM$, $\cos \angle 1 = \frac{y}{r}$, so $y = r \cos \angle 1$.

Substituting the expression for m$\angle 1$ from above gives $y = r \cos \left(\dfrac{180°}{n} \right)$.

F To write an expression for the area of the base of the pyramid, first write an expression for the area of $\triangle AOB$.

Area($\triangle AOB$) $= \frac{1}{2} \cdot$ base $\cdot$ height $= \frac{1}{2} \cdot 2x \cdot y = xy$

Substituting the expressions for x and y from above gives the following.

Area ($\triangle AOB$) $=$ ___$r \sin \left(\frac{180°}{n} \right) r \cos \left(\frac{180°}{n} \right)$___

The base of the pyramid is composed of n triangles that are congruent to $\triangle AOB$, so the area of the base of the pyramid is given by the following.

Area (base of pyramid) $=$ ___$nr \sin \left(\frac{180°}{n} \right) r \cos \left(\frac{180°}{n} \right)$___

The volume of the pyramid is $\frac{1}{3} \cdot$ base $\cdot$ height, which may be written as

Volume (pyramid) $=$ ___$\frac{1}{3} hn \, r^2 \sin \left(\frac{180°}{n} \right) \cos \left(\frac{180°}{n} \right)$___

G Your expression for the pyramid's volume should include the expression

$$n \sin \left(\frac{180°}{n} \right) \cos \left(\frac{180°}{n} \right)$$

as a factor. Use a calculator, as follows, to find out what happens to the value of this expression as n gets larger and larger.

* Enter the expression
  $x \sin \left(\frac{180}{X} \right) \cos \left(\frac{180}{X} \right)$ as Y_1.
* Go to the Table Setup menu and enter the values shown at right.
* View a table for the function.
* Use the arrow keys to scroll down.

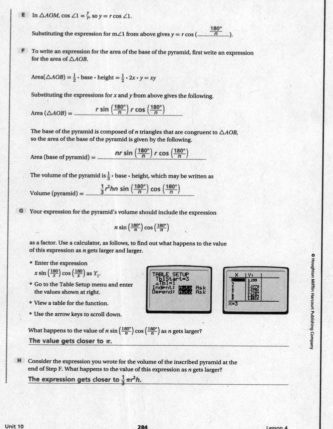

What happens to the value of $n \sin \left(\frac{180°}{n} \right) \cos \left(\frac{180°}{n} \right)$ as n gets larger?
___The value gets closer to π.___

H Consider the expression you wrote for the volume of the inscribed pyramid at the end of Step F. What happens to the value of this expression as n gets larger?
___The expression gets closer to $\frac{1}{3} \pi r^2 h$.___

Questioning Strategies

- Can you find the volume of the cone using only the given dimensions? Why or why not? **No; the formula requires the height of the cone, which is not given.**

- Once you know the volume of the cone, what do you need to do? How can you do this? **Convert the volume to fluid ounces using the fact that 1 in.^{3} is approximately 0.554 fl oz. (That is, multiply the volume in cubic inches by the factor 0.554 to convert to fluid ounces.)**

- Does the paper cone hold a cup of water? Why or why not? **No; a cup is 8 fl oz, but the volume of the cone is only 5.8 fl oz.**

EXTRA EXAMPLE

A conical paper cup has the dimensions shown. How many liters of liquid does the cup hold? Round to the nearest tenth. (*Hint:* 1 cm$^3 \approx 0.001$ L)

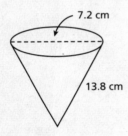

7.2 cm

13.8 cm

0.2 L

MATHEMATICAL PRACTICE **Highlighting the Standards**

To address Standard 1 (Make sense of problems and persevere in solving them), ask students whether their answer to the example seems reasonable. Help students recognize that a volume of 5.8 fl oz is a bit less than a cup (8 fl oz) and that this is a sensible volume for a cone with the given dimensions. Also, ask students to give examples of answers that might have raised a red flag and prompted them to double check their calculations.

CLOSE

Essential Question

How do you calculate the volume of a cone?

The volume, *V*, of a cone with base area *B* and height *h* is given by $V = \frac{1}{3}Bh$ (or $V = \frac{1}{3}\pi r^2 h$, where *r* is the radius of the base).

Summarize

Have students write a journal entry in which they summarize the main steps in developing the formula for the volume of a cone. Encourage students to include figures to illustrate the steps.

PRACTICE

Where skills are taught	Where skills are practiced
2 EXAMPLE	EXS. 1–4

Exercise 5: Students compare the volume of a cone and the volume of a pyramid.

Exercise 6: Students use reasoning to compare the volume a solid consisting of a cylinder with a cone removed and the volume of the original cylinder.

REFLECT

1a. How is the formula for the volume of a cone, which you derived above, similar to the formula for the volume of a pyramid?

Since πr^2 is the area of the base, the formula can be written as $V = \frac{1}{3}Bh$,

which is the same as the formula for the volume of a pyramid.

The argument in the Explore provides a justification for the following result.

> **Volume of a Cone**
>
> The volume V of a cone with base area B and height h is given by $V = \frac{1}{3}Bh$
> (or $V = \frac{1}{3}\pi r^2 h$, where r is the radius of the base).

2 EXAMPLE Solving a Volume Problem

A conical paper cup has the dimensions shown. How many fluid ounces of liquid does the cup hold? Round to the nearest tenth. (*Hint:* 1 in.³ ≈ 0.554 fl oz.)

A Find the radius and height of the cone.

The radius r is half the diameter, so $r = \underline{1.375 \text{ in.}}$

To find the height h of the cone, use the Pythagorean Theorem.

$h^2 + r^2 = 5.5^2$ Pythagorean Theorem

$h^2 + (\underline{1.375})^2 = 5.5^2$ Substitute the value of r.

$h^2 = \underline{28.359375}$ Solve for h^2.

$h \approx \underline{5.325}$ in.   Solve for h. Round to the nearest thousandth.

B Find the volume of the cone to the nearest hundredth.

$V = \frac{1}{3}\pi r^2 h = \frac{1}{3}\pi \cdot (\underline{1.375})^2 \cdot (\underline{5.325}) \approx \underline{10.54} \text{ in.}^3$

C Convert the volume to fluid ounces.

$\underline{10.54}$ in.³ ≈ $\underline{10.54} \cdot 0.554$ fl oz ≈ $\underline{5.8}$ fl oz

So, the cup holds approximately $\underline{5.8}$ fluid ounces.

© Houghton Mifflin Harcourt Publishing Company

REFLECT

2a. A cylindrical cup has the same diameter and height as the conical cup. How can you find the number of fluid ounces that the cylindrical cup holds?

Multiply the conical cup's volume in fluid ounces by 3.

PRACTICE

Find the volume of each cone. Round to the nearest tenth.

1.
1.9 mm
4.2 mm

15.9 mm³

2.
6.3 ft
5.9 ft

50.7 ft³

3.
22 cm
20 cm

1759.3 cm³

4. The figure shows a water tank that consists of a cylinder and cone. How many gallons of water does the tank hold? Round to the nearest gallon. (*Hint:* 1 ft³ ≈ 7.48 gal.)

9952 gal

6 ft
10 ft
8 ft

5. Popcorn is available in two cups: a square pyramid or a cone, as shown. The price of each cup of popcorn is the same. Which cup is the better deal? Explain.

The pyramid is the better deal because you

get a greater volume of popcorn (960 cm³

versus 754 cm³) for the same price.

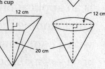
12 cm
12 cm
20 cm

6. A sculptor removes a cone from a cylindrical block of wood so that the vertex of the cone is the center of the cylinder's base, as shown. Explain how the volume of the remaining solid compares with the volume of the original cylindrical block of wood.

The solid has $\frac{2}{3}$ the volume of the cylinder since the

cone that is removed has $\frac{1}{3}$ the volume of the cylinder.

© Houghton Mifflin Harcourt Publishing Company

Volume of Spheres

Essential question: *How do you calculate the volume of a sphere?*

○ **COMMON** Standards for
○ **CORE** **Mathematical Content**

CC.9-12.G.GMD.2(+) Give an informal argument using Cavalieri's principle for the formula for the volume of a sphere ....

CC.9-12.G.GMD.3 Use volume formulas for ... spheres to solve problems.*

CC.9-12.G.MG.2 Apply concepts of density based on area and volume in modeling situations (e.g., ... BTUs per cubic foot).*

Prerequisites

Volume of Prisms and Cylinders, Lesson 10-2

Volume of Cones, Lesson 10-4

Math Background

The steps used in this lesson to develop a formula for the volume of a sphere offer a surprising application of Cavalieri's principle. It is surprising because the argument is based on showing that two seemingly unrelated solids have the same volume. The solids—a hemisphere and a cylinder from which a cone has been removed—are shown to have the same cross-sectional area at every level and therefore must have the same volume.

The formula for the volume, V, of a sphere with radius r is $V = \frac{4}{3}\pi r^3$. A bit of algebra shows that the volume of a sphere is equal to $\frac{2}{3}$ the volume of its circumscribed cylinder. This result, which has been known since ancient times, was of such importance to the Greek mathematician Archimedes that he requested that a drawing of a sphere and cylinder be placed on his tomb.

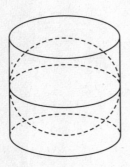

INTRODUCE

Review the definition of *sphere* and discuss the related terms *hemisphere* and *great circle*. Explain to students that when a plane intersects a sphere, the cross section that is formed is either a single point or a circle. In the case where the plane passes through the center of the sphere, the cross section is a great circle. Tell students that a great circle is sometimes called an equator.

TEACH

1 **EXPLORE**

Questioning Strategies

• What is the height of the hemisphere? What is the height of the cylinder from which a cone has been removed? **Both have height r.**

• What do you need to show to use Cavalieri's principle? **Show that the figures have the same cross-sectional area at every level.**

• What does Cavalieri's principle allow you to conclude? **The two figures have the same volume.**

⋰ **MATHEMATICAL** **Highlighting**
  PRACTICE **the Standards**

The argument in the Explore offers opportunities to focus on Standard 7 (Look for and make use of structure). For example, showing that the two figures have equal cross-sectional areas at every level requires recognizing that $\pi(r^2 - x^2) = \pi r^2 - \pi x^2$. This is an application of the distributive property. Later, finding the volume of the cylinder with a cone removed results in the expression $\pi r^2 h - \frac{1}{3}\pi r^2 h$. Students should be able to view this as a difference of two expressions. However, they should also be able to see that it has the form $a - \frac{1}{3}a$, which makes it possible to combine like terms.

Name_____ Class_____ Date_____

Volume of Spheres

10-5

COMMON CORE
CC.9-12.G.GMD.2(+),
CC.9-12.G.GMD.3*,
CC.9-12.G.MG.2*

Essential question: *How do you calculate the volume of a sphere?*

Recall that a *sphere* is the set of points in space that are a fixed distance from a point called the *center* of the sphere. The intersection of a sphere and a plane that contains the center of the sphere is a *great circle*. A great circle divides a sphere into two congruent halves that are called *hemispheres*.

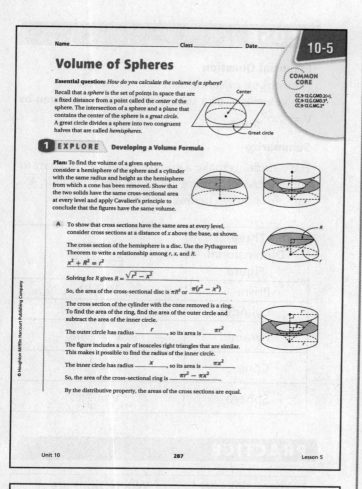

Center

Great circle

1 EXPLORE Developing a Volume Formula

Plan: To find the volume of a given sphere, consider a hemisphere of the sphere and a cylinder with the same radius and height as the hemisphere from which a cone has been removed. Show that the two solids have the same cross-sectional area at every level and apply Cavalieri's principle to conclude that the figures have the same volume.

A To show that cross sections have the same area at every level, consider cross sections at a distance of *x* above the base, as shown.

The cross section of the hemisphere is a disc. Use the Pythagorean Theorem to write a relationship among *r*, *x*, and *R*.

$$x^2 + R^2 = r^2$$

Solving for *R* gives $R = \sqrt{r^2 - x^2}$

So, the area of the cross-sectional disc is πR^2 or $\underline{\pi(r^2 - x^2)}$

The cross section of the cylinder with the cone removed is a ring. To find the area of the ring, find the area of the outer circle and subtract the area of the inner circle.

The outer circle has radius ___*r*___, so its area is $\underline{\pi r^2}$

The figure includes a pair of isosceles right triangles that are similar. This makes it possible to find the radius of the inner circle.

The inner circle has radius ___*x*___, so its area is $\underline{\pi x^2}$

So, the area of the cross-sectional ring is $\underline{\pi r^2 - \pi x^2}$

By the distributive property, the areas of the cross sections are equal.

B By Cavalieri's principle, the hemisphere has the same volume as the cylinder with the cone removed.

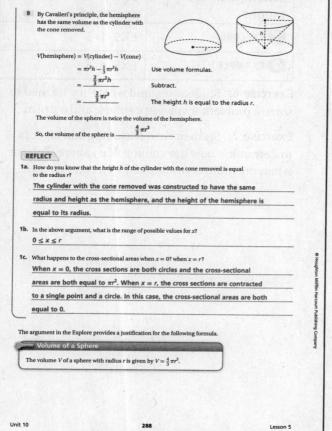

$V(\text{hemisphere}) = V(\text{cylinder}) - V(\text{cone})$

$\qquad = \pi r^2 h - \frac{1}{3}\pi r^2 h$ 　　Use volume formulas.

$\qquad = \underline{\frac{2}{3}\pi r^2 h}$ 　　Subtract.

$\qquad = \underline{\frac{2}{3}\pi r^3}$ 　　The height *h* is equal to the radius *r*.

The volume of the sphere is twice the volume of the hemisphere.

So, the volume of the sphere is $\underline{\frac{4}{3}\pi r^3}$

REFLECT

1a. How do you know that the height *h* of the cylinder with the cone removed is equal to the radius *r*?

The cylinder with the cone removed was constructed to have the same radius and height as the hemisphere, and the height of the hemisphere is equal to its radius.

1b. In the above argument, what is the range of possible values for *x*?

$0 \le x \le r$

1c. What happens to the cross-sectional areas when *x* = 0? when *x* = *r*?

When *x* = 0, the cross sections are both circles and the cross-sectional areas are both equal to πr^2. When *x* = *r*, the cross sections are contracted to a single point and a circle. In this case, the cross-sectional areas are both equal to 0.

The argument in the Explore provides a justification for the following formula.

Volume of a Sphere

The volume *V* of a sphere with radius *r* is given by $V = \frac{4}{3}\pi r^3$.

CLOSE

Questioning Strategies

- The gas tank provides 275,321 BTU. How can you interpret this measurement? **This is the amount of energy required to increase the temperature of 275,321 pounds of water by one degree Fahrenheit.**

- What dimension or dimensions do you need to know to find the volume of the sphere? **You only need to know the radius.**

EXTRA EXAMPLE

A spherical gas tank has the dimensions shown. When filled with propane, it provides 4506.2 BTU. How many BTUs does one cubic foot of propane yield? Round to the nearest BTU.

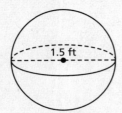

1.5 ft

2550 BTU

Avoid Common Errors

Students may not be sure whether they need to divide 275,321 by $\frac{256}{3}\pi$ or vice-versa. Explain that 275,321 BTU corresponds to a volume of $\frac{256}{3}\pi$ ft^3 of natural gas. This may be written as follows.

$$275{,}321 \text{ BTU} \leftrightarrow \frac{256}{3}\pi \text{ ft}^3$$

You are interested in the number of BTUs that correspond to 1 ft^3 of natural gas. You can get 1 ft^3 on the right side of the correspondence by dividing both sides by $\frac{256}{3}\pi$. That is, divide 275,321 by $\frac{256}{3}\pi$.

Essential Question

How do you calculate the volume of a sphere?
The volume, *V*, of a sphere with radius *r* is given by $V = \frac{4}{3}\pi r^3$.

Summarize

Have students make a graphic organizer or chart to summarize the volume formulas from this unit. A sample is shown below.

Three-Dimensional Figure	Volume Formula
Prism	$V = Bh$
Cylinder	$V = Bh$
Pyramid	$V = \frac{1}{3}Bh$
Cone	$V = \frac{1}{3}Bh$
Sphere	$V = \frac{4}{3}\pi^3$

PRACTICE

Where skills are taught	Where skills are practiced
1 EXPLORE	EXS. 1–3
2 EXAMPLE	EXS. 4–5

Exercise 6: Students extend what they learned to solve a problem involving a sphere and a prism.

Exercise 7: Students use reasoning and algebra to determine how the volume of a sphere changes when the radius is multiplied by a constant.

A British thermal unit (BTU) is a unit of energy. It is approximately the amount of energy needed to increase the temperature of one pound of water by one degree Fahrenheit. As you will see in the following example, the energy content of a fuel may be measured in BTUs per unit of volume.

2 EXAMPLE Solving a Volume Problem

A spherical gas tank has the dimensions shown. When filled with natural gas, it provides 275,321 BTU. How many BTUs does one cubic foot of natural gas yield? Round to the nearest BTU.

8 ft

A Find the volume of the sphere.

The diameter is 8 feet, so the radius r is ___4 ft.___

$V = \frac{4}{3}\pi r^3$ Use the volume formula for a sphere.

$V = \frac{4}{3}\pi (4)^3$ Substitute for r.

$V = \frac{256}{3}\pi \ ft^3$ Simplify. Leave the answer in terms of π.

B Find the number of BTUs contained in one cubic foot of natural gas.

Since there are 275,321 BTU in $\frac{256}{3}\pi$ ft³ of natural gas, divide

___275,321___ by $\frac{256}{3}\pi$ to find the number of BTUs in 1 ft³.

Use a calculator to divide. Round to the nearest whole number.

So, one cubic foot of natural gas yields about ___1027___ BTU.

REFLECT

2a. How many pounds of water can be heated from 59°F to 60°F by one cubic foot of natural gas? Explain.

___1027 pounds; each BTU of natural gas can increase the temperature of one___

___pound of water by one degree Fahrenheit.___

2b. How many pounds of water can be heated from 70°F to 83°F by one cubic foot of natural gas? Explain.

___79 pounds; for each pound of water, it takes 13 BTU of natural gas to___

___increase the temperature by 13°F, and 1027 ÷ 13 = 79.___

PRACTICE

Find the volume of each sphere. Round to the nearest tenth.

1.

3.7 in.

___212.2 in³___

2.

11 ft

___696.9 ft³___

3.

Circumference of great circle is 14π cm.

___1436.8 cm³___

4. One gallon of propane yields approximately 91,500 BTU. About how many BTUs does the spherical storage tank at right provide? Round to the nearest million BTUs. (*Hint:* 1 ft³ ≈ 7.48 gal.)

5 ft

___358,000,000 BTU___

5. **Error Analysis** A student solved the following problem as shown below. Explain the student's error and give the correct answer to the problem.

A spherical gasoline tank has a radius of 0.5 ft. When filled, the tank provides 446,483 BTU. How many BTUs does one gallon of gasoline yield? Round to the nearest thousand BTUs and use the fact that 1 ft³ ≈ 7.48 gal.

> The volume of the tank is $\frac{4}{3}\pi r^3 = \frac{4}{3}\pi(0.5)^3$ ft³. Multiplying by 7.48 shows that this is approximately 3.92 gal. So the number of BTUs in one gallon of gasoline is approximately 446,483 × 3.92 ≈ 1,750,000 BTU.

___The student should have divided the total number of___

___BTUs by 3.92; the correct answer is 114,000 BTU.___

6. The aquarium shown at right is a rectangular prism that is filled with water. You drop a spherical ball with a diameter of 6 inches into the aquarium. The ball sinks, causing water to spill from the tank. How much water is left in the tank? Express your answer to the nearest cubic inch and nearest gallon. (*Hint:* 1 in.³ ≈ 0.00433 gal)

12 in.
12 in.
20 in.

___2767 in.³; 12 gal___

7. How does the volume of a sphere change when you multiply its radius by a factor k, where $k > 0$? Explain.

___The volume is multiplied by k^3, since the new volume is___

$\frac{4}{3}\pi(kr)^3 = \frac{4}{3}\pi k^3 r^3 = k^3 \cdot \frac{4}{3}\pi r^3$, which is k^3 times the

___original volume.___

Solving Design Problems

Essential question: *How do you use geometry to solve design problems?*

COMMON CORE **Standards for Mathematical Content**

CC.9-12.G.GMD.3 Use volume formulas for cylinders, pyramids, cones, and spheres to solve problems.*

CC.9-12.G.MG.3 Apply geometric methods to solve design problems (e.g., designing an object or structure to satisfy physical constraints or minimize cost ...).*

Prerequisites

Volume of Prisms and Cylinders, Lesson 10-2

Volume of Pyramids, Lesson 10-3

Volume of Cones, Lesson 10-4

Volume of Spheres, Lesson 10-5

Math Background

Optimization problems are a common application in many calculus courses. For example, students may be asked to determine the cylinder with the maximum volume given a specific surface area or to determine the rectangular prism with minimum surface area given a specific volume. Students solve such problems in calculus by writing an equation for the quantity to be optimized and finding the derivative. This lesson gives students a preview of some of these ideas. Although no calculus is used, the lesson serves as an informal introduction to the types of design problems students will encounter in later courses.

INTRODUCE

Explain that a design problem is one in which you must design an object that satisfies some given conditions. You may want to give students a simple example, such as the following: Design a rectangular picture frame that has the maximum area, given that the frame's perimeter is 24 inches. Students can suggest different lengths and widths that give a perimeter of 24 inches and then calculate the corresponding area. The following table shows some possibilities.

Length (in.)	Width (in.)	Area (in.^{2})
8	4	32
7	5	35
6	6	36
5	7	35

From the table, the greatest possible area appears to be 36 in.^{2} This can be verified using algebra and a graphing calculator.

TEACH

 EXAMPLE

Questioning Strategies

• What are the given conditions or "constraints" in this problem? **The candle must be a cylinder, it must have a volume of 100 cm^3, and the height must be equal to the diameter.**

• To check your answer, what must be true about the height and radius that you find? **The height must be twice the radius; they must result in a cylinder with a volume of approximately 100 cm^3.**

EXTRA EXAMPLE

You want to make a sculpture in the shape of a square-based pyramid using exactly 300 cm^3 of clay. You want the side length of the base to be equal to the pyramid's height. What dimensions should the sculpture have?
The side lengths and height should be approximately 9.65 cm.

Technology

In this example, students use their calculator to solve $2\pi r^3 = 100$ by graphing $y = 2\pi r^3$ and $y = 100$ and finding the point of intersection of the graphs. Students can also solve the equation by writing it as $r^3 = \frac{100}{2\pi}$. To solve for r, take the cube root of both sides. Students can then use their calculator to evaluate $\sqrt[3]{\frac{100}{2\pi}}$ by entering the expression as $(100 / (2\pi))\wedge(1/3)$.

Name_____ Class_____ Date_____

10-6

COMMON CORE

CC.9-12.G.GMD.3*,
CC.9-12.G.MG.3*

Solving Design Problems

Essential question: *How do you use geometry to solve design problems?*

A design problem is one is which you must design an object that satisfies given conditions or minimizes cost. Volume formulas from this unit are often helpful in solving such problems.

1 EXAMPLE Determining Dimensions Given a Volume

You want to make a cylindrical candle using exactly 100 cm³ of wax. You want the candle's height to be equal to its diameter. What radius and height should the candle have?

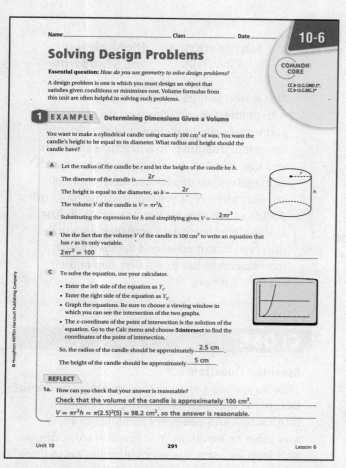

A Let the radius of the candle be r and let the height of the candle be h.

The diameter of the candle is ___2r___.

The height is equal to the diameter, so $h =$ ___2r___.

The volume V of the candle is $V = \pi r^2 h$.

Substituting the expression for h and simplifying gives $V =$ ___$2\pi r^3$___.

B Use the fact that the volume V of the candle is 100 cm³ to write an equation that has r as its only variable.

___$2\pi r^3 = 100$___

C To solve the equation, use your calculator.

• Enter the left side of the equation as Y_1.

• Enter the right side of the equation as Y_2.

• Graph the equations. Be sure to choose a viewing window in which you can see the intersection of the two graphs.

• The x-coordinate of the point of intersection is the solution of the equation. Go to the Calc menu and choose **5:intersect** to find the coordinates of the point of intersection.

So, the radius of the candle should be approximately ___2.5 cm___.

The height of the candle should be approximately ___5 cm___.

REFLECT

1a. How can you check that your answer is reasonable?

Check that the volume of the candle is approximately 100 cm³.

$V = \pi r^2 h = \pi(2.5)^2(5) \approx 98.2$ cm², so the answer is reasonable.

2 EXAMPLE Designing a Box with Maximum Volume

You want to build a storage box from a piece of plywood that is 4 feet by 8 feet. You must use 6 pieces (for the top, bottom, and sides of the box) and you must make cuts that are parallel and perpendicular to the edges of the plywood. Describe three possible designs. What do you think is the maximum possible volume for the box?

A Consider Design 1 at right. The top, bottom, front, and back of the box are congruent rectangles. The ends are squares. The gray piece is waste.

From the figure, $4x =$ ___4___, so $x =$ ___1___ ft

and $8 - x =$ ___7___ ft.

$V =$ ___7___ · ___1___ · ___1___ = ___7___ ft³

Design 1

B Consider Design 2 at right. The top, bottom, front, and back of the box are congruent rectangles. The ends are squares. The gray piece is waste.

From the figure, $5x =$ ___8___, so $x =$ ___1.6___ ft.

$V =$ ___4___ · ___1.6___ · ___1.6___ = ___10.24___ ft³

Design 2

C Consider Design 3 at right. The top, bottom, front, and back of the box are congruent rectangles. The ends are squares. There is no waste.

From the figure, $2x =$ ___4___, so $x =$ ___2___ ft

and $\frac{8-x}{2} =$ ___3___ ft.

$V =$ ___3___ · ___2___ · ___2___ = ___12___ ft³

Design 3

D Based on these designs, the maximum possible volume appears to be ___12 ft³___.

REFLECT

2a. Is it possible to make a box all of whose sides are not squares? If so, give the dimensions of the box and find its volume.

Yes; possible answer: a box with dimensions 2 ft, $\frac{4}{3}$ ft, and 4 ft can be made with

no waste. Its volume is about 10.66 ft³.

2b. Is it possible to say what the maximum volume of the box is based on your work above? Why or why not?

No; although 12 ft³ is the greatest volume among the three designs,

there might be a design that results in a greater volume.

Questioning Strategies

- What are the given conditions or "constraints" in this problem? The box is built from wood that is 4 feet by 8 feet, you can only cut the wood into 6 pieces, and all cuts must be parallel and perpendicular to the edges.

EXTRA EXAMPLE

You want to build a box from a piece of wood that is 6 feet by 6 feet. You must use 6 pieces (for the top, bottom, and sides of the box) and you must make cuts that are parallel and perpendicular to the edges of the wood. Describe three possible designs. What do you think is the maximum possible volume for the box?

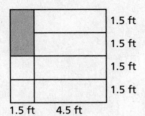

1.5 ft
1.5 ft
1.5 ft
1.5 ft

1.5 ft   4.5 ft $V = 10.125 \text{ ft}^3$

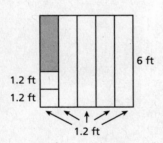

6 ft

1.2 ft
1.2 ft

1.2 ft $V = 8.64 \text{ ft}^3$

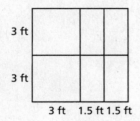

3 ft

3 ft

3 ft   1.5 ft 1.5 ft $V = 13.5 \text{ ft}^3$

Based on these designs, the maximum possible volume appears to be 13.5 ft³.

This lesson addresses Standard 4 (Model with mathematics). The standard states that mathematically proficient students "identify important quantities in a practical situation and map their relationships using tools such as diagrams." In this lesson, students must not only identify important information, but decide which information to work with first. Ask students to explain how they prioritized the given information and decided which information to use in the first step of their solution process.

CLOSE

Essential Question

How do you use geometry to solve design problems? Determine dimensions by using the given information and geometry formulas to write and solve an equation. You can also solve design problems by using the given information to draw and label one or more diagrams that meet the required conditions.

Summarize

Have students write a journal entry in which they explain what a design problem is and give an example of how they solved such a problem.

PRACTICE

Where skills are taught	Where skills are practiced
1 EXAMPLE	EX. 1
2 EXAMPLE	EXS. 2–3

PRACTICE

1. You have 500 cm³ of clay and want to make a sculpture in the shape of a cone. You want the height of the cone to be 3 times the cone's radius and you want to use all the clay. What radius and height should the sculpture have?

$r \approx 5.42$ cm; $h \approx 16.26$ cm

2. You want to build a box in the shape of a rectangular prism. The box must have a volume of 420 in.³ As shown in the figure, the ends of the box must be squares. In order to minimize the cost, you want to use the least possible amount of material. Follow these steps to determine the dimensions you should use for the box.

a. Let the ends of the box be x in. by x in. and let the length of the box be ℓ in. The amount of material M needed to make the box is its surface area. Write an expression for M by adding the areas of the six faces.

$M = 2x^2 + 4x\ell$

b. Write an equation for the volume of the box and then solve it for ℓ.

$x^2\ell = 420$; $\ell = \dfrac{420}{x^2}$

c. Substitute the expression for ℓ in the expression for M from part (a).

$M = 2x^2 + \dfrac{1680}{x}$

d. To find the value of x that minimizes M, enter the expression for M as Y_1 in your calculator. Graph the function in a suitable viewing window. Go to the Calc menu and choose **3: minimum** to find the value of x that minimizes M. Use your equation from part (b) to find the corresponding value of ℓ. What dimensions should you use for the box?

The box should be a cube where each side has length ≈ 7.49 in.

3. You have a flexible piece of sheet metal that measures 4 feet by 8 feet. You want to build a cylinder by cutting out two circles for the bases and a rectangular piece that can be bent to form the lateral surface.

a. Let r be the radius of the cylinder. From the figure, there are two constraints on r: $4r \leq 4$ (based on the width of the metal) and $2r + 2\pi r \leq 8$ (based on the length of the metal). What is the greatest value of r that satisfies both constraints?

$r = \dfrac{4}{1 + 2\pi} \approx 0.966$

b. What is the approximate volume of the cylinder with this radius?

11.7 ft³

© Houghton Mifflin Harcourt Publishing Company

COMMON CORE CORRELATION

Standard	Items
CC.9-12.G.GMD.1	7
CC.9-12.G.GMD.2(+)	9
CC.9-12.G.GMD.3*	3, 4, 5, 6, 8
CC.9-12.G.GMD.4	1, 2
CC.9-12.G.MG.1*	3
CC.9-12.G.MG.2*	3, 8
CC.9-12.G.MG.3*	6

TEST PREP DOCTOR ⊕

Multiple Choice: Item 4

- Students who answered **G** may have found the area of the base of the pyramid.

- Students who answered **H** may have forgotten the factor of $\frac{1}{3}$ in the formula for the volume of a pyramid. These students may also have found the volume of the cube.

- Students who answered **J** may have tried to use the formula $V = \frac{1}{3}\pi r^2 h$ to find the volume of the pyramid.

Multiple Choice: Item 5

- Students who answered **A** may have forgotten to multiply by the height when finding the volume of the cone, or they may have multiplied the volume of the cone by 0.0034 to convert to fluid ounces.

- Students who answered **C** may have forgotten the factor of $\frac{1}{3}$ in the formula for the volume of a cone.

- Students who answered **D** may have used 8 cm as the radius of the cone rather than 4 cm.

Free Response: Item 8

- Students who answered 10,595 BTU may have used an incorrect formula for the volume of a sphere ($V = \frac{4}{3}\pi r^2$ rather than $V = \frac{4}{3}\pi r^3$).

- Students who answered 4347 BTU may have forgotten the factor of $\frac{4}{3}$ in the formula for the volume of a sphere.

- Students who answered 67,405,417 BTU may have multiplied the volume of the sphere by 468,766 BTU rather than divided 468,766 BTU by the volume of the sphere.

UNIT 10 TEST PREP

Name _____ Class _____ Date _____

MULTIPLE CHOICE

1. The figure shows a rectangular prism that is intersected by a plane parallel to a face of the prism. Which is the most precise description of the cross section?

  A. parallelogram   **C.** trapezoid
  B. rectangle   **D.** triangle

2. In the figure, $\overline{BA} \cong \overline{BC}$. You rotate $\angle ABC$ around a line that bisects the angle. What figure is generated by this rotation in three-dimensional space?

  F. cone   **H.** pyramid
  G. cylinder   **J.** sphere

3. A wood log is approximately cylindrical with the dimensions shown below. The log weighs 206.8 pounds. What is the density of the wood, to the nearest whole number?

  A. 7 lb/ft³   **C.** 20 lb/ft³
  B. 8 lb/ft³   **D.** 26 lb/ft³

4. A wire frame in the shape of the cube is used to support a pyramid-shaped basket, as shown. The vertex of the pyramid lies in the same plane as a face of the cube. To the nearest tenth, what is the volume of the pyramid-shaped basket?

  F. 0.7 ft³   **H.** 2.2 ft³
  G. 1.7 ft³   **J.** 2.3 ft³

5. A food manufacturer sells yogurt in cone-shaped cups with the dimensions shown. To the nearest tenth, how many fluid ounces of yogurt does the cup hold?
(*Hint:* 1 cm³ ≈ 0.034 fl oz)

  A. 0.6 fl oz   **C.** 17.1 fl oz
  B. 5.7 fl oz   **D.** 22.8 fl oz

6. You want to design a cylindrical container for oatmeal that has a volume of 90 in.³ You also want the height of the container to be 3.5 times the radius. To the nearest tenth, what should the radius of the container be?

  F. 2.0 in.   **H.** 3.0 in.
  G. 2.9 in.   **J.** 3.1 in.

© Houghton Mifflin Harcourt Publishing Company

FREE RESPONSE

7. In order to develop and justify the formula for the volume of a cone, you begin with a given cone that has radius r and height h. You consider pyramids with regular polygonal bases that are inscribed in the cone.

You show that when the inscribed pyramid has a base that is a regular n-gon, the volume of the pyramid is given by the following expression.

$$\frac{1}{3}r^2 h n \sin\left(\frac{180°}{n}\right) \cos\left(\frac{180°}{n}\right)$$

Describe the remaining steps of the argument.

The expression includes the factor

$n \sin\left(\frac{180°}{n}\right) \cos\left(\frac{180°}{n}\right)$. Using a

graphing calculator, you can see that

as n gets larger, this expression gets

closer to π. Therefore, the expression

for the volume of the inscribed

pyramid gets closer to $\frac{1}{3}\pi r^2 h$, which is

the formula for the volume of a cone.

8. A spherical gas tank has the dimensions shown. When filled with butane, it provides 468,766 BTU. How many BTUs does one cubic foot of butane yield? Round to the nearest BTU.

3260 BTU

9. To find the volume of a sphere of radius r, you consider a hemisphere of the sphere and a cylinder with the same radius and height as the hemisphere from which a cone has been removed. You show that the solids have the same cross-sectional area at every level. Explain how to use the solids to derive the formula for the volume of a sphere.

By Cavalieri's principle, the

hemisphere has the same volume as

the cylinder with the cone removed.

This volume is $\pi r^2 h - \frac{1}{3}\pi r^2 h$ or $\frac{2}{3}\pi r^2$

h. But $h = r$, so the volume is $\frac{2}{3}\pi r^3$.

The volume of the sphere is twice the

volume of the hemisphere, or $\frac{4}{3}\pi r^3$.

© Houghton Mifflin Harcourt Publishing Company

UNIT 11

Probability

Unit Vocabulary

combination	(11-4)
complement	(11-1)
conditional probability	(11-6)
dependent events	(11-8)
element	(11-1)
empty set	(11-1)
factorial	(11-3)
independent events	(11-7)
intersection	(11-1)
mutually exclusive events	(11-5)
overlapping events	(11-5)
permutation	(11-3)
set	(11-1)
subset	(11-1)
theoretical probability	(11-1)
union	(11-1)
universal set	(11-1)

UNIT 11

UNIT 11

Probability

Unit Focus

Probability theory is the branch of mathematics concerned with situations involving chance. You will learn how to use set theory to help you calculate basic probabilities and will investigate the role of permutations and combinations in probability. You will also learn how to determine the probability of mutually exclusive events, overlapping events, independent events, and dependent events. Along the way, you will perform simulations and learn how to use probability to make and analyze decisions.

Unit at a Glance

COMMON CORE

Lesson	Standards for Mathematical Content
11-1 Probability and Set Theory	CC.9-12.S.CP.1*
11-2 Random Sampling and Probability	CC.9-12.S.MD.6(+)*
11-3 Permutations and Probability	CC.9-12.S.CP.9(+)*
11-4 Combinations and Probability	CC.9-12.S.CP.9(+)*
11-5 Mutually Exclusive and Overlapping Events	CC.9-12.S.CP.7*
11-6 Conditional Probability	CC.9-12.S.CP.3*, CC.9-12.S.CP.4*, CC.9-12.S.CP.5*, CC.9-12.S.CP.6*
11-7 Independent Events	CC.9-12.S.CP.2*, CC.9-12.S.CP.3*, CC.9-12.S.CP.4*, CC.9-12.S.CP.5*
11-8 Dependent Events	CC.9-12.S.CP.8(+)*
11-9 Making Fair Decisions	CC.9-12.S.MD.6(+)*
11-10 Analyzing Decisions	CC.9-12.S.CP.4*, CC.9-12.S.MD.7(+)*
Test Prep	

UNIT 11

Unit 11 297 Probability

This page lists and explains the Standards for Mathematical Content that are addressed in this unit. For information about the Standards for Mathematical Practice, which are integrated throughout the text, see Teacher Edition pages x–xiii.

Unpacking the Common Core State Standards

Use the table to help you understand the Standards for Mathematical Content that are taught in this unit. Refer to the lessons listed after each standard for exploration and practice.

UNIT 11

COMMON CORE Standards for Mathematical Content	What It Means For You
CC.9-12.S.CP.1 Describe events as subsets of a sample space (the set of outcomes) using characteristics (or categories) of the outcomes, or as unions, intersections, or complements of other events ("or," "and," "not").* Lesson 11-1	You will see that set notation and vocabulary is useful for calculating simple probabilities.
CC.9-12.S.CP.2 Understand that two events A and B are independent if the probability of A and B occurring together is the product of their probabilities, and use this characterization to determine if they are independent.* Lesson 11-7	Two events are independent if the occurrence of one event does not affect the occurrence of the other. You will learn how to determine whether two events are independent.
CC.9-12.S.CP.3 Understand the conditional probability of A given B as $P(A$ and $B)/P(B)$, and interpret independence of A and B as saying that the conditional probability of A given B is the same as the probability of A, and the conditional probability of B given A is the same as the probability of B.* Lessons 11-6, 11-7	You will find the probability of an event given that another event has already occurred.
CC.9-12.S.CP.4 Construct and interpret two-way frequency tables of data when two categories are associated with each object being classified. Use the two-way table as a sample space to decide if events are independent and to approximate conditional probabilities.* Lessons 11-6, 11-7, 11-10	A two-way table is a useful tool for working with probabilities. You will make and interpret two-way tables.
CC.9-12.S.CP.5 Recognize and explain the concepts of conditional probability and independence in everyday language and everyday situations.* Lessons 11-6, 11-7	You will see how to use ideas from probability to help you understand a variety of real-world situations.
CC.9-12.S.CP.6 Find the conditional probability of A given B as the fraction of B's outcomes that also belong to A, and interpret the answer in terms of the model.* Lesson 11-6	You will find the probability of an event given that another event has already occurred and you will explain the meaning of your answer.
CC.9-12.S.CP.7 Apply the Addition Rule, $P(A$ or $B) = P(A) + P(B) - P(A$ and $B)$, and interpret the answer in terms of the model.* Lesson 11-5	You will learn to use a rule to find the probability of events consisting of more than one outcome.

© Houghton Mifflin Harcourt Publishing Company

Notes

_____

_____

_____

_____

_____

_____

_____

_____

_____

_____

_____

UNIT 11

UNIT 11

COMMON CORE Standards for Mathematical Content	What It Means For You
CC.9-12.S.CP.8(+) Apply the general Multiplication Rule in a uniform probability model, $P(A \text{ and } B) = P(A) P(B \mid A) = P(B) P(A \mid B)$, and interpret the answer in terms of the model.* Lesson 11-8	You will learn to use a rule to find the probability of events when the outcome of one event affects the probability of the other event.
CC.9-12.S.CP.9(+) Use permutations and combinations to compute probabilities of compound events and solve problems.* Lessons 11-3, 11-4	Permutations and combinations will be helpful when you count the number of outcomes in a probability experiment.
CC.9-12.S.MD.6(+) Use probabilities to make fair decisions (e.g., drawing by lots, using a random number generator).* Lessons 11-2, 11-9	You will explore the connection between probability and decision making.
CC.9-12.S.MD.7(+) Analyze decisions and strategies using probability concepts (e.g., product testing, medical testing, pulling a hockey goalie at the end of a game).* Lesson 11-10	As you will see, ideas from probability can help you decide if a decision is good or bad.

Notes

_____

_____

_____

_____

_____

_____

_____

_____

_____

Notes

_____

_____

_____

_____

_____

_____

_____

_____

_____

_____

_____

_____

_____

_____

_____

_____

_____

_____

_____

_____

_____

_____

_____

_____

Probability and Set Theory

Essential question: *How can you use set theory to help you calculate theoretical probabilities?*

COMMON **Standards for**
CORE **Mathematical Content**

CC.9-12.S.CP.1 Describe events as subsets of a sample space (the set of outcomes) using characteristics (or categories) of the outcomes, or as unions, intersections, or complements of other events ("or," "and," "not").*

Vocabulary
set

element

empty set

universal set

subset

intersection

union

complement

theoretical probability

Prerequisites
none

Math Background
Students are likely to be familiar with basic probability concepts, and they may have seen set notation and terminology in earlier grades. However, they may not have explored the connections between these ideas. In this lesson, students use set theory to build a definition of the theoretical probability of an event. The notation of set theory will also be useful in later lessons when students consider the probability of compound events.

INTRODUCE

Define *set*. Ask students to give examples of sets from everyday life. For example, students might mention the set of all states of the United States or the set of all teachers at your school. Be sure students understand that a set may be specified in different ways. For the purposes of this unit, most sets can be specified by a written description (for example, the set of all odd numbers less than 8) or by a list that shows all elements of the set (for example, {1, 3, 5, 7}).

TEACH

1 ENGAGE

Questioning Strategies
- If S is the set of prime numbers less than 10 and T is the set of even numbers less than 10, what is $S \cup T$? What is $S \cap T$? $S \cup T = \{2, 3, 4, 5, 6, 7, 8\}$; $S \cap T = \{2\}$
- Give an example of a set that is a subset of set S. **Possible answer: {2, 3}**
- Suppose the universal set U is the set of whole numbers less than 10. What is the complement of set S? **{0, 1, 4, 6, 8, 9}**

2 EXAMPLE

Questioning Strategies
- When you roll a number cube, what are the possible outcomes? **1, 2, 3, 4, 5, 6**
- How does $P(A)$ compare with $P(B)$? Why does this make sense? $P(A) = P(B) = \frac{1}{2}$; **both events are equally likely, and this makes sense since both events contain 3 outcomes.**
- Is it possible for the probability of an event to be 0? If so, give an example. **Yes; the probability of rolling a 7 is 0.**

EXTRA EXAMPLE
You spin a spinner with 8 equal sections that are numbered 1 through 8. Event A is the spinner landing on an odd number. Event B is the spinner landing on 8. Calculate each of the following probabilities.

A. $P(A)$ $\frac{1}{2}$

B. $P(A \cup B)$ $\frac{5}{8}$

C. $P(A \cap B)$ **0**

D. $P(A^c)$ $\frac{1}{2}$

Name_____ Class_____ Date_____

Probability and Set Theory

Essential question: *How can you use set theory to help you calculate theoretical probabilities?*

COMMON
CORE

CC.9-12.S.CP.1*

1 ENGAGE Introducing the Vocabulary of Sets

You will see that set theory is useful in calculating probabilities. A **set** is a well-defined collection of distinct objects. Each object in a set is called an **element** of the set. A set may be specified by writing its elements in braces. For example, the set *S* of prime numbers less than 10 may be written as $S = \{2, 3, 5, 7\}$.

The number of elements in a set *S* may be written as $n(S)$. For the set *S* of prime numbers less than 10, $n(S) = 4$.

The set with no elements is the **empty set** and is denoted by ∅ or { }. The set of all elements under consideration is the **universal set** and is denoted by *U*. The following terms describe how sets are related to each other.

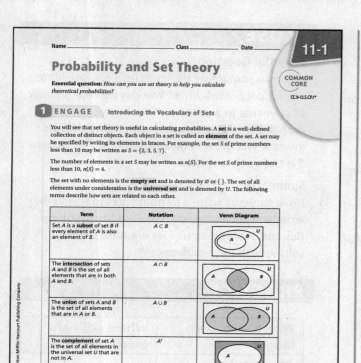

Term	Notation	Venn Diagram
Set *A* is a **subset** of set *B* if every element of *A* is also an element of *B*.	$A \subset B$	
The **intersection** of sets *A* and *B* is the set of all elements that are in both *A* and *B*.	$A \cap B$	
The **union** of sets *A* and *B* is the set of all elements that are in *A* or *B*.	$A \cup B$	
The **complement** of set *A* is the set of all elements in the universal set *U* that are not in *A*.	A^c	

REFLECT

1a. For any set *A*, what is $A \cap \varnothing$? Explain.

$A \cap \varnothing = \varnothing$ since $A \cap \varnothing$ is the intersection of *A* and ∅ and there are no elements in both *A* and ∅.

Recall that a *probability experiment* is an activity involving chance. Each repetition of the experiment is a *trial* and each possible result is an *outcome*. The *sample space* of an experiment is the set of all possible outcomes. An *event* is a set of outcomes.

When all outcomes of an experiment are equally likely, the **theoretical probability** that an event *A* will occur is given by $P(A) = \frac{n(A)}{n(S)}$, where *S* is the sample space.

2 EXAMPLE Calculating Theoretical Probabilities

You roll a number cube. Event *A* is rolling an even number. Event *B* is rolling a prime number. Calculate each of the following probabilities.

A $P(A)$ B $P(A \cup B)$ C $P(A \cap B)$ D $P(A^c)$

A $P(A)$ is the probability of rolling an even number. To calculate $P(A)$, first identify the sample space *S*.

$S = $ ___{1, 2, 3, 4, 5, 6}___ , so $n(S) = $ __6__ .

$A = $ ___{2, 4, 6}___ , so $n(A) = $ __3__ .

So, $P(A) = \frac{n(A)}{n(S)} = \frac{3}{6} = \frac{1}{2}$.

B $P(A \cup B)$ is the probability of rolling an even number *or* a prime number.

$A \cup B = $ ___{2, 3, 4, 5, 6}___ , so $n(A \cup B) = $ __5__ .

So, $P(A \cup B) = \frac{n(A \cup B)}{n(S)} = \frac{5}{6}$.

C $P(A \cap B)$ is the probability of rolling an even number *and* a prime number.

$A \cap B = $ ___{2}___ , so $n(A \cap B) = $ __1__ .

So, $P(A \cap B) = \frac{n(A \cap B)}{n(S)} = \frac{1}{6}$.

D $P(A^c)$ is the probability of rolling a number that is *not* even.

$A^c = $ ___{1, 3, 5}___ , so $n(A^c) = $ __3__ .

So, $P(A^c) = \frac{n(A^c)}{n(S)} = \frac{3}{6} = \frac{1}{2}$.

REFLECT

2a. Explain what $P(S)$ represents and then calculate this probability. Do you think this result is true in general? Explain.

$P(S)$ is the probability of rolling any number in the sample space (1, 2, 3, 4, 5, or 6).

$P(S) = 1$. This is true in general since $P(S) = \frac{n(S)}{n(S)} = 1$.

© Houghton Mifflin Harcourt Publishing Company

Questioning Strategies

- What is the sample space in this problem? **It is all possible pairs of numbers that you can roll on two number cubes.**

- Aside from the table shown on the student page, what is another way you could find all outcomes in the sample space? **Make a tree diagram or an organized list.**

- Based on your results, how likely is it that you will not roll doubles? Explain. **It is quite likely that you will not roll doubles, since the probability of this event is close to 1.**

EXTRA EXAMPLE

You roll a blue number cube and white number cube at the same time. What is the probability that the sum of the numbers that you roll is not 2? $\frac{35}{36}$

Avoid Common Errors

Some students may state that the sample space for this experiment consists of 21 outcomes because they may not distinguish between outcomes like 3-5 and 5-3. Point out to students that the number cubes have different colors, so the outcome 3-5 means rolling a 3 on the blue cube and a 5 on the white cube, whereas 5-3 means rolling a 5 on the blue cube and a 3 on the white cube. This should help students understand that the sample space actually consists of 36 distinct outcomes.

MATHEMATICAL PRACTICE | **Highlighting the Standards**

To address Standard 2 (Reason abstractly and quantitatively), be sure to ask students to move back and forth between the decontextualized calculations that are involved in solving a probability problem and the contextualized interpretation of the results. That is, when students calculate that an event has a probability of 0.9, be sure they understand what this means in the context of the original problem. In particular, students should realize that an event with such a probability is very likely to occur.

CLOSE

Essential Question

How can you use set theory to help you calculate theoretical probabilities? **You can use the number of elements in a set to define theoretical probability: the theoretical probability that an event A will occur is given by $P(A) = \frac{n(A)}{n(S)}$, where S is the sample space.**

Summarize

Have students write a journal entry in which they write and solve their own probability problems. Remind students to use set notation in their solutions to the problems.

PRACTICE

Where skills are taught	Where skills are practiced
2 EXAMPLE	EXS. 1–7
3 EXAMPLE	EXS. 8–9

Exercise 10: Students use reasoning to critique another student's work.

You may have noticed in the example that $P(A) + P(A^c) = 1$. To see why this is true in general, note that an event and its complement represent all outcomes in the sample space, so $n(A) + n(A^c) = n(S)$.

$$P(A) + P(A^c) = \frac{n(A)}{n(S)} + \frac{n(A^c)}{n(S)} \qquad \text{Definition of theoretical probability}$$

$$= \frac{n(A) + n(A^c)}{n(S)} \qquad \text{Add.}$$

$$= \frac{n(S)}{n(S)} = 1 \qquad n(A) + n(A^c) = n(S)$$

You can write this relationship as $P(A) = 1 - P(A^c)$ and use it to help you find probabilities when it is more convenient to calculate the probability of the complement of an event.

Probabilities of an Event and Its Complement

The probability of an event and the probability of its complement have a sum of 1. So, the probability of an event is one minus the probability of its complement. Also, the probability of the complement of an event is one minus the probability of the event.

$$P(A) + P(A^c) = 1$$
$$P(A) = 1 - P(A^c)$$
$$P(A^c) = 1 - P(A)$$

3 EXAMPLE Using the Complement of an Event

You roll a blue number cube and white number cube at the same time. What is the probability that you do not roll doubles?

A Let A be the event that you do not roll doubles. Then A^c is the event that you do roll doubles.

Complete the table at right to show all outcomes in the sample space.

Circle the outcomes in A^c (rolling doubles).

	White Number Cube					
Blue Number Cube		**1**	**2**	**3**	**4**	**5**	**6**
1	1-1	1-2	1-3	1-4	1-5	1-6
2	2-1	2-2	2-3	2-4	2-5	2-6
3	3-1	3-2	3-3	3-4	3-5	3-6
4	4-1	4-2	4-3	4-4	4-5	4-6
5	5-1	5-2	5-3	5-4	5-5	5-6
6	6-1	6-2	6-3	6-4	6-5	6-6

B Find the probability of rolling doubles.

$$P(A^c) = \frac{n(A^c)}{n(S)} = \frac{6}{36} = \frac{1}{6}$$

C Find the probability that you do not roll doubles.

$$P(A) = 1 - P(A^c) = 1 - \frac{1}{6} = \frac{5}{6}$$

REFLECT

3a. Describe a different way you could have calculated the probability that you do not roll doubles.

Use the table to count the number of outcomes in event A. Since $n(A) = 30$,

$$P(A) = \frac{n(A)}{n(S)} = \frac{30}{36} = \frac{5}{6}.$$

PRACTICE

You have a set of 10 cards numbered 1 to 10. You choose a card at random. Event A is choosing a number less than 7. Event B is choosing an odd number. Calculate each of the following probabilities.

1. $P(A)$
$\frac{3}{5}$

2. $P(B)$
$\frac{1}{2}$

3. $P(A \cup B)$
$\frac{4}{5}$

4. $P(A \cap B)$
$\frac{3}{10}$

5. $P(A^c)$
$\frac{2}{5}$

6. $P(B^c)$
$\frac{1}{2}$

7. A bag contains 5 red marbles and 10 blue marbles. You choose a marble without looking. Event A is choosing a red marble. Event B is choosing a blue marble. What is $P(A \cap B)$? Explain.

0; $A \cap B = \varnothing$ since a marble cannot be both red and blue.

8. A standard deck of cards has 13 cards (2, 3, 4, 5, 6, 7, 8, 9, 10, jack, queen, king, ace) in each of 4 suits (hearts, clubs, diamonds, spades). You choose a card from a deck at random. What is the probability that you do not choose an ace? Explain.

$\frac{12}{13}$; there are 4 aces in the 52-card deck, so $P(\text{ace}) = \frac{4}{52} = \frac{1}{13}$.

This means $P(\text{not ace}) = 1 - \frac{1}{13} = \frac{12}{13}$.

9. You choose a card from a standard deck of cards at random. What is the probability that you do not choose a club? Explain.

$\frac{3}{4}$; there are 13 clubs in the 52-card deck, so $P(\text{club}) = \frac{13}{52} = \frac{1}{4}$.

This means $P(\text{not club}) = 1 - \frac{1}{4} = \frac{3}{4}$.

10. Error Analysis A bag contains white tiles, black tiles, and gray tiles. $P(W)$, the probability of choosing a tile at random and choosing a white tile, is $\frac{1}{4}$. A student claims that the probability of choosing a black tile, $P(B)$, is $\frac{3}{4}$ since $P(B) = 1 - P(W) = 1 - \frac{1}{4} = \frac{3}{4}$. Do you agree? Explain.

No; choosing a black tile is not the complement of choosing a white tile since the bag also contains gray tiles. It is not possible to calculate $P(B)$ from the given information.

© Houghton Mifflin Harcourt Publishing Company

Notes

Random Sampling and Probability

Essential question: How can you use probabilities to help you make fair decisions?

COMMON CORE Standards for Mathematical Content

CC.9-12.S.MD.6(+) Use probabilities to make fair decisions (e.g., drawing by lots, using a random number generator).*

Prerequisites
Probability and Set Theory, Lesson 11-1

Math Background
Standards CC.9-12.S.MD.6(+) and CC.9-12.S.MD.7(+) are concerned with using probability to make and analyze decisions. Lessons 11-2, 11-9, and 11-10 address these decision-making standards. In this lesson, students work with a single overarching investigation to explore the connections among random samples, convenience samples, fairness, and probability.

INTRODUCE

Begin by reviewing random samples and convenience samples. To do so, ask students how you could choose 5 students from the class using a random sample. Students might suggest putting the names of all students in a hat and choosing 5 names without looking. Ask students what makes the sample a random sample and be sure students understand that a key characteristic of a random sample is that each member of the population has an equal probability of being chosen.

Next, ask students how you might choose 5 students from the class using a convenience sample. Students might suggest choosing the first 5 students in the first row of desks or the 5 students who sit closest to the teacher. Be sure students understand that a key characteristic of a convenience sample is that the members of the sample are easy to choose.

Explain to students that they will now explore connections among random samples, convenience samples, and probability and learn how these ideas can help them make fair decisions.

TEACH

1 ENGAGE

Questioning Strategies
- Look at the square in the center of the 5-by-5 grid on the student page. What information is contained in this square? **The resident is resident number 13. This resident prefers that the money be used for a senior center. There is a 20% chance that the resident is at the movie theater when the survey is conducted.**
- Which resident is most likely to be at the movie theater when the survey is conducted? Why? **Resident number 25; his or her probability of being at the movie theater is 90%, which is greater than every other resident's probability.**

2 EXPLORE

Materials: calculator

Questioning Strategies
- When you use your calculator and choose the random integer function, why do you enter "(1,25)" after the name of the function? **This ensures that the random integer is greater than or equal to 1 and less than or equal to 25.**
- Does every student in your class get the same result for the percent of residents who favor the teen center? Why or why not? **No; the results are based on a random sample that is chosen through a random-number generator. Each student is likely to get a different set of numbers and a different percent of residents who favor the teen center.**

11-2

Random Sampling and Probability

COMMON CORE

CC.9-12.S.MD.6(+)*

Essential question: *How can you use probabilites to help you make fair decisions?*

1 ENGAGE   Introducing a Decision-Making Problem

A small town has 25 residents. The state has given the town money that must be used for something that benefits the community. The town's mayor has decided that the money will be used to build a teen center or a senior center.

In order to make a decision about the type of community center to build, the mayor plans to survey a subset of town residents. There are two survey methods: a random sample and a convenience sample. The convenience sample will be conducted by surveying town residents at a local movie theater.

In the table below, each resident of the town is identified by a number from 1 to 25. The table shows each resident's preference: T for the teen center, S for the senior center. The table also gives the probability that each resident is at the movie theater when the convenience-sample survey is conducted.

1	2	3	4	5
S	S	T	S	T
0.2	0.3	0.8	0.1	0.8
6	**7**	**8**	**9**	**10**
T	S	T	S	S
0.7	0.2	0.8	0.1	0.3
11	**12**	**13**	**14**	**15**
S	T	S	S	S
0.1	0.7	0.2	0.2	0.4
16	**17**	**18**	**19**	**20**
T	S	S	S	T
0.6	0.7	0.1	0.1	0.6
21	**22**	**23**	**24**	**25**
S	S	S	S	T
0.3	0.2	0.3	0.1	0.9

REFLECT

1a. Based on the data in the table, what percent of all residents favor the teen center? the senior center?

Teen center: 32%; senior center: 68%

1b. If it were possible for the mayor to survey every resident, what decision do you think the mayor would make? Why?

Senior center; this is the choice of more than $\frac{2}{3}$ of the town's residents.

2 EXPLORE   Using a Random Sample

Suppose the mayor of the town is not able to survey every resident, so the mayor decides to survey a random sample of 10 residents.

A   You can use your calculator to simulate the process of choosing and surveying a random sample of residents.

- Go to the MATH menu.
- Use the right arrow key to access the PRB menu.
- Use the down arrow key to select **5:randInt(** .
- Use "randInt(1,25)" as shown at the right.
- Each time you press Enter, the calculator will return a random integer from 1 to 25.

`randInt(1,25)` 13

Generate 10 random integers in this way. For each integer, note the corresponding preference (T or S) of that resident of the town. (If a number is selected more than once, ignore the duplicates and choose a new number.) This ensures that no resident is surveyed more than once.) Record your results in the table.   Sample results are shown.

Resident Number	13	4	19	17	24	6	23	11	3	16
Preference (T or S)	S	S	S	S	S	T	S	S	T	T

B   Based on the random sample, what percent of residents favor the teen center? the senior center?

Sample answer: Teen center: 30%; senior center: 70%

REFLECT

2a. What is the probability that any resident is chosen to be part of the random sample? Explain.

$\frac{1}{25}$; there are 25 possible outcomes of the random-number

generator and all are equally likely.

2b. What decision do you think the mayor would make based on the random sample? Why?

Senior center; this appears to be the choice of a majority of residents.

2c. Compare your results with those of other students. In general, how well do the results of the random sample predict the preferences of the town as a whole?

The random sample closely matches the preferences of the town as a whole.

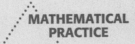

MATHEMATICAL PRACTICE Highlighting the Standards

To address Standard 5 (Use appropriate tools strategically), ask students about the advantages and disadvantages of using a calculator to generate random numbers. For example, students might suggest that the calculator is easy to use and can be counted on to return numbers that are truly random. On the other hand, the calculator may repeat numbers. This inconvenience would not arise if students generated the random numbers by choosing numbered slips of paper from a bag without replacing the slips of paper after they are chosen.

 3 EXPLORE

Materials: small slips of paper, bag

Questioning Strategies

- How do you represent Resident 13 in this simulation? Why? **There should be 2 slips of paper with the number 13 since this resident has a 0.2 probability of being at the movie theater.**

- Which resident is represented by the greatest number of slips of paper? Why does this make sense? **Resident 25; this resident has the greatest probability of being at the theater, so he or she should have the greatest chance of being picked for the survey.**

- Which sampling method does a better job of representing the wishes of the town as a whole? Why? **The random sample; since every resident has an equal probability of being chosen for the sample, this method does a better job of representing the wishes of the town as a whole.**

Avoid Common Errors

Some students may replace a slip of paper in the bag once it has been chosen. Remind students that once someone has been selected for the survey, he or she should not be surveyed again. For this reason, once a slip of paper is chosen, it should be put aside and any future draws of that resident's number should be ignored.

CLOSE

Essential Question

How can you use probabilities to help you make fair decisions? You can use probabilities to help you choose a random sample from a population. The results of surveying a random sample are likely to be representative of the population as a whole.

Summarize

Have students write a journal entry in which they summarize the main steps of this investigation. Ask them to include a discussion of how probability helped them conduct the random sample and the convenience sample.

3 EXPLORE   Using a Convenience Sample

The mayor of the town decides to use a convenience sample by surveying the first 10 residents of the town to leave a local movie theater.

A You can use slips of paper to simulate the process of choosing and surveying this convenience sample.

- For each resident, prepare 1 to 10 small slips of paper with the resident's number on them. The number of slips of paper is determined by the probability that the resident is at the movie theater when the survey is conducted. For example, Resident 1 has a 0.2 probability of being at the theater, so prepare 2 slips of paper with the number 1; Resident 2 has a 0.3 probability of being at the theater, so prepare 3 slips of paper with the number 2; and so on.

- Place all of the slips of paper in a bag and mix them well.

- Choose slips of paper one at a time without looking.

Choose 10 residents in this way. For each resident, note the corresponding preference (T or S) using the table on the first page of the lesson. (If a resident is selected more than once, ignore the duplicates and choose a new number from the bag. This ensures that no resident is surveyed more than once.) Record your results in the table.

Sample results are shown.

Resident Number	8	5	14	25	12	7	20	9	23	16
Preference (T or S)	T	T	S	T	T	S	T	S	S	T

B Based on the convenience sample, what percent of residents favor the teen center? the senior center?

Sample answer: Teen center: 60%; senior center: 40%

REFLECT

3a. Why do some residents of the town have more slips of paper representing them than other residents? How does this connect to the way the convenience sample is conducted?

Residents who have a greater probability of being at the movie theater
when the survey is conducted have more slips of paper representing them.
This simulates the fact that they are more likely to be chosen for the
convenience sample.

3b. What decision do you think the mayor would make based on the convenience sample? Why?

Teen center; this appears to be the choice of a majority of residents.

3c. Compare your results with those of other students. In general, how well do the results of the convenience sample predict the preferences of the town as a whole?

The convenience sample does not do a good job of predicting the preferences
of the town as a whole.

3d. Which sampling method is more likely to lead to fair decision-making? Explain.

The random sample gives results that are more likely to be representative of the
whole population, so it is more likely to lead to fair decisions.

3e. What factors might explain why the results of the convenience sample are different from the results of the random sample?

There may be a greater proportion of young people at the movie theater
than in the general population and young people might be more likely to favor
building a teen center.

3f. When you conduct the random-sample simulation is it possible that you might choose 10 residents who all favor the senior center? Is this result possible when you conduct the convenience-sample simulation? In which simulation do you think this result is more likely?

This result is possible (but unlikely) in both simulations. It is more likely to happen
in the random-sample simulation, since the convenience-sample simulation is
weighted toward residents who prefer the teen center.

3g. What are some limitations or drawbacks of the simulations?

The convenience-sample simulation depends on knowing the probability that each
resident is at the movie theater; the simulation method would be impractical to
carry out with a larger population.

3h. In a town of 25 residents, it is likely that the mayor could actually survey all the residents, instead of using a random sample or convenience sample. What are some reasons that sampling might be used in situations involving populations that are much larger than 25?

It may be difficult to survey all members of a population; it may be too expensive,
too time-consuming, or too impractical to attempt to reach every member of a
very large population.

Permutations and Probability

Essential question: *What are permutations and how can you use them to calculate probabilities?*

COMMON CORE Standards for Mathematical Content

CC.9-12.S.CP.9(+) Use permutations ... to compute probabilities of compound events and solve problems.*

Vocabulary
permutation

factorial

Prerequisites
Probability and Set Theory, Lesson 11-1

Math Background
A compound event is an event that consists of more than one outcome. To find the probability of a compound event, find the ratio of the number of outcomes in the event to the number of outcomes in the sample space. Counting the number of outcomes in the event and in the sample space can often be the most challenging part of calculating a probability. Permutations and combinations are two tools for counting outcomes.

INTRODUCE

Define *permutation*. Work with students to list all permutations of the numbers 1, 2, and 3. You may want to construct a tree diagram as shown below. The diagram shows that there are 6 different permutations of the numbers.

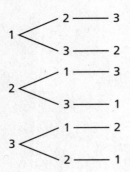

TEACH

1 EXAMPLE

Questioning Strategies

• Suppose the club needs to choose only a president. In how many different ways can the position be filled in this case? **7**

• Suppose the club needs to choose only a president and a vice-president. In how many different ways can the positions be filled in this case? Why? **42; once you choose a president, you have 6 remaining candidates for vice-president.**

• Why is this situation an example of a permutation? **The order in which you fill the positions is important.**

EXTRA EXAMPLE

There are 6 different flavors of frozen yogurt. A cafeteria offers 1 flavor per day. The manager of the cafeteria wants to choose 4 different flavors to serve on Monday, Tuesday, Wednesday, and Thursday. In how many different ways can the manager choose the flavors and assign them to days of the week? **360**

MATHEMATICAL PRACTICE

Highlighting the Standards

The process of developing a formula for permutations is a good opportunity to address Standard 8 (Look for and express regularity in repeated reasoning). Have students calculate the number of permutations in various situations "by hand"; that is, by reasoning about the situation and using multiplication, as in the first example. Then ask students what patterns they notice. A common element of every solution should be the product of a string of descending, consecutive integers. Once students have been introduced to factorial notation, the formula for the number of permutations of *n* objects taken *r* at a time should seem natural.

Permutations and Probability

COMMON CORE

CC.9-12.S.CP.9(+)*

Essential question: *What are permutations and how can you use them to calculate probabilities?*

A **permutation** is a selection of a group of objects in which order is important. For example, there are 6 permutations of the letters A, B, and C.

ABC	ACB
BAC	BCA
CAB	CBA

1 EXAMPLE Finding Permutations

The members of a club want to choose a president, a vice-president, and a treasurer. Seven members of the club are eligible to fill these positions. In how many different ways can the positions be filled?

A Consider the number of ways each position can be filled.

There are ___7___ different ways the position of president can be filled.

Once the president has been chosen, there are ___6___ different ways the position of vice-president can be filled.

Once the president and vice-president have been chosen, there are ___5___ different ways the position of treasurer can be filled.

B Multiply to find the total number of different ways the positions can be filled.

President	Vice-President	Treasurer

___7___ × ___6___ × ___5___ = ___210___ permutations

So, there are ___210___ different ways that the positions can be filled.

REFLECT

1a. Suppose the club members also want to choose a secretary from the group of 7 eligible members. In how many different ways can the four positions (president, vice-president, treasurer, secretary) be filled? Explain.

840; there are 7 × 6 × 5 × 4 = 840 permutations

1b. Suppose 8 members of the club are eligible to fill the original three positions (president, vice-president, treasurer). In how many different ways can the positions be filled? Explain.

336; there are 8 × 7 × 6 = 336 permutations

The process you used in the example can be generalized to give a formula for permutations. To do so, it is helpful to use factorials. For a positive integer n, n **factorial**, written $n!$, is defined as follows.

$$n! = n \cdot (n-1) \cdot (n-2) \cdot \ldots \cdot 3 \cdot 2 \cdot 1$$

That is, $n!$ is the product of n and all the positive integers less than n. Note that 0! is defined to be 1.

In the example, the number of permutations of 7 objects taken 3 at a time is

$$7 \cdot 6 \cdot 5 = \frac{7 \cdot 6 \cdot 5 \cdot 4 \cdot 3 \cdot 2 \cdot 1}{4 \cdot 3 \cdot 2 \cdot 1} = \frac{7!}{4!} = \frac{7!}{(7-3)!}.$$

This can be generalized as follows.

Permutations

The number of permutations of n objects taken r at a time is given by

$$_nP_r = \frac{n!}{(n-r)!}.$$

2 EXAMPLE Using Permutations to Calculate a Probability

Every student at your school is assigned a four-digit code, such as 6953, to access the computer system. In each code, no digit is repeated. What is the probability that you are assigned a code with the digits 1, 2, 3, and 4 in any order?

A Let S be the sample space. Find $n(S)$.

The sample space consists of all permutations of 4 digits taken from the 10 digits 0 through 9.

$$n(S) = {}_{10}P_4 = \frac{10!}{(10-4)!} = \frac{10!}{6!} = \frac{10 \cdot 9 \cdot 8 \cdot 7 \cdot 6 \cdot 5 \cdot 4 \cdot 3 \cdot 2 \cdot 1}{6 \cdot 5 \cdot 4 \cdot 3 \cdot 2 \cdot 1} = \underline{5040}$$

B Let A be the event that your code has the digits 1, 2, 3, and 4. Find $n(A)$.

The event consists of all permutations of 4 digits chosen from the 4 digits 1 through 4.

$$n(A) = {}_4P_4 = \frac{4!}{(4-4)!} = \frac{4!}{0!} = \frac{4 \cdot 3 \cdot 2 \cdot 1}{1} = \underline{24}$$

C Find $P(A)$.

$$P(A) = \frac{n(A)}{n(S)} = \frac{24}{5040} = \frac{1}{210}$$

So, the probability that your code has the digits 1, 2, 3, and 4 is $\frac{1}{210}$.

Questioning Strategies

- What are some examples of four-digit codes in the sample space? **Possible answers: 7421, 9605, 7534**

- Is the code 4878 in the sample space? Why or why not? **No; no digit may be repeated in a code.**

- What are some examples of four-digit codes in event *A*? **Possible answers: 1234, 2314, 4231**

- Is the code 4215 in event *A*? Why or why not? **No; codes in event *A* consist of the digits 1, 2, 3, and 4 in any order.**

EXTRA EXAMPLE

To buy concert tickets at a Web site, you must first type a random code consisting of 5 letters, such as JQBKN. (This prevents computer programs from purchasing the tickets.) In each code, no letter is repeated. When you buy concert tickets at the Web site, what is the probability that your code will consist of the letters A, E, I, O, and U in any order? $\frac{1}{65,780}$

Technology

You may want to have students use their calculators to check their work. In fact, graphing calculators have a built-in function that calculates permutations. For example, to find $_{10}P_4$, first enter 10. Then press MATH and use the arrow keys to choose the PRB menu. Select **2:nPr** and press ENTER. Now enter 4 and then press ENTER to see that $_{10}P_4 = 5040$.

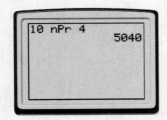

CLOSE

Essential Question

What are permutations and how can you use them to calculate probabilities?

A permutation is a selection of a group of objects in which order is important. You can use permutations to find the number of outcomes in a sample space and/or the number of outcomes in an event.

Summarize

Have students make a graphic organizer to summarize what they know about permutations. A sample is shown below.

Definition	Example
A permutation is a selection of a group of objects in which order is important.	Permutations of A, B, and C: ABC ACB BAC BCA CAB CBA

Permutations

Formula	Factorials
$_{n}P_r = \dfrac{n!}{(n-r)!}$	*n* factorial (*n*!) is the product of *n* and all the positive integers less than *n*. 0! is 1.

PRACTICE

Where skills are taught	Where skills are practiced
1 EXAMPLE	EXS. 1–4
2 EXAMPLE	EXS. 5–6

Exercise 7: Students apply what they learned to critique another student's work.

REFLECT

2a. What is the probability that you are assigned the code 1234? Explain.

$\frac{1}{5040}$; in this case $n(A) = 1$, so $P(A) = \frac{n(A)}{n(S)} = \frac{1}{5040}$.

PRACTICE

1. An MP3 player has a playlist with 12 songs. You select the shuffle option for the playlist. In how many different orders can the songs be played?

479,001,600

2. There are 10 runners in a race. Medals are awarded for 1st, 2nd, and 3rd place. In how many different ways can the medals be awarded?

720

3. There are 9 players on a baseball team. In how many ways can the coach choose players for first base, second base, third base, and shortstop?

3024

4. You have 15 photographs of your school. In how many different ways can you arrange 6 of them in a line for the cover of the school yearbook?

3,603,600

5. A bag contains 9 tiles, each with a different number from 1 to 9. You choose a tile, put it aside, choose a second tile, put it aside, and then choose a third tile. What is the probability that you choose tiles with the numbers 1, 2, and 3 in that order?

$\frac{1}{362,880}$

6. There are 11 students on a committee. To decide which 3 of these students will attend a conference, 3 names are chosen at random by pulling names one at a time from a hat. What is the probability that Sarah, Jamal, and Mai are chosen in any order?

$\frac{1}{165}$

7. Error Analysis A student solved the problem at right. The student's work is shown. Did the student make an error? If so, explain the error and provide the correct answer.

The student made an error; $n(A)$

should be 1 since the tiles must

appear in the order B-E-A-D. The

correct probability is $\frac{1}{360}$.

A bag contains 6 tiles with the letters A, B, C, D, E, and F. You choose 4 tiles one at a time without looking and line up the tiles as you choose them. What is the probability that your tiles spell BEAD?

Let S be the sample space and let A be the event that the tiles spell BEAD.

$n(S) = {}_6P_4 = \frac{6!}{(6-4)!} = \frac{6!}{2!} = 360$

$n(A) = {}_4P_4 = \frac{4!}{(4-4)!} = \frac{4!}{0!} = 4! = 24$

So, $P(A) = \frac{n(A)}{n(S)} = \frac{24}{360} = \frac{1}{15}$.

11-4   Combinations and Probability

Essential question: *What are combinations and how can you use them to calculate probabilities?*

COMMON Standards for
CORE   Mathematical Content

CC.9-12.S.CP.9(+) Use ... combinations to compute probabilities of compound events and solve problems.*

Vocabulary
combination

Prerequisites
Probability and Set Theory, Lesson 11-1
Permutations and Probability, Lesson 11-3

Math Background
In Lesson 11-3, students learned how to find the number of permutations of n objects taken r at a time. They also learned how to use permutations to count the number of outcomes in a sample space and/or in an event. In this lesson, the process will be repeated with combinations.

INTRODUCE

Define *combination*. Work with students to list all combinations of 3 numbers taken from the numbers 1, 2, 3, 4, and 5. As you work with students, emphasize that the key to finding all combinations while avoiding duplicates is to list the combinations in an organized way. The following list shows one way to do this:

1, 2, 3
1, 2, 4
1, 2, 5
1, 3, 4
1, 3, 5
1, 4, 5
2, 3, 4
2, 3, 5
2, 4, 5
3, 4, 5

The list shows that there are 10 different ways to choose 3 numbers from the set of 5 numbers when order does not matter. Explain to students that this lesson will introduce more efficient techniques for counting combinations.

TEACH

1   EXAMPLE

Questioning Strategies
- Give some examples of possible combinations. **Possible answers: beets-potatoes-carrots, beets-salad-rice, broccoli-salad-carrots, etc.**
- Once you find the number of ways to choose 3 side dishes when order does matter, why do you then divide by $_3P_3$? **When order matters, each side dish is counted $_3P_3 = 6$ times, so you must divide by 6 to count each combination just once.**

EXTRA EXAMPLE
A winner on a game show gets to choose 4 prize boxes from a set of 10 prize boxes. In how many different ways can the contestant choose 4 prize boxes? **210**

Teaching Strategies
You may wish to show students a different way of solving the problem in the first example. There are 8 choices for the first side dish, 7 choices for the second side dish, and 6 choices for the third side dish. This is $8 \times 7 \times 6 = 336$ possibilities. However, each combination is counted $3! = 6$ times, so the number of combinations is $336 \div 6 = 56$.

MATHEMATICAL   **Highlighting the**
PRACTICE   **Standards**

To address Standard 7 (Look for and make use of structure) ask students to explain how the formula for the number of combinations of n objects taken r at a time is related to the formula for the number of permutations of n objects taken r at a time. Students should see that the number of permutations divided by $r!$ is equal to the number of combinations.

Name_____ Class_____ Date_____

11-4

COMMON CORE
CC.9-12.S.CP.9(+)*

Combinations and Probability

Essential question: *What are combinations and how can you use them to calculate probabilities?*

A **combination** is a grouping of objects in which order does not matter. For example, when you choose 3 letters from the letters A, B, C, and D, there are 4 different combinations.

ABC   ABD   ACD   BCD

1 EXAMPLE   Finding Combinations

A restaurant offers 8 side dishes. When you order an entree, you can choose 3 of the side dishes. In how many ways can you choose 3 side dishes?

Side Dishes	
Beets	Rice
Potatoes	Broccoli
Carrots	Cole slaw
Salad	Apple sauce

A First find the number of ways to choose 3 sides dishes when order does matter. This is the number of permutations of 8 objects taken 3 at a time.

$$_8P_3 = \frac{8!}{(8-3)!} = \frac{8!}{5!} = \frac{8 \cdot 7 \cdot 6 \cdot \cancel{5} \cdot \cancel{4} \cdot \cancel{3} \cdot \cancel{2} \cdot \cancel{1}}{\cancel{5} \cdot \cancel{4} \cdot \cancel{3} \cdot \cancel{2} \cdot \cancel{1}} = \underline{336}$$

B In this problem, order does not matter, since choosing beets, carrots, and rice is the same as choosing rice, beets, and carrots.

Divide the result from Step A by $_3P_3$, which is the number of ways the 3 side dishes can be ordered.

$$_3P_3 = \frac{3!}{(3-3)!} = \frac{3!}{0!} = \underline{6}$$

So, the number of ways you can choose 3 side dishes is $\frac{336}{6} = \underline{56}$

REFLECT

1a. Suppose the restaurant offers a special on Mondays that allows you to choose 4 side dishes. In how many ways can you choose the side dishes?

_____ 70 _____

1b. In general, are there more ways or fewer ways to select objects when order does not matter? Why?

Fewer; when order does not matter, multiple selections are counted as the same

combination.

Unit 11   313   Lesson 4

The process you used in the example can be generalized to give a formula for combinations. In order to find $_8C_3$, the number of combinations of 8 objects taken 3 at a time, you first found the number of permutations of 8 objects taken 3 at a time, then you divided by 3! That is,

$$_8C_3 = \frac{8!}{(8-3)!} \div 3! \text{ or } \frac{8!}{3!(8-3)!}.$$

This can be generalized as follows.

Combinations

The number of combinations of *n* objects taken *r* at a time is given by

$$_nC_r = \frac{n!}{r!(n-r)!}.$$

2 EXAMPLE   Using Combinations to Calculate a Probability

There are 5 boys and 6 girls in a school play. The director randomly chooses 3 of the students to meet with a costume designer. What is the probability that the director chooses all boys?

A Let *S* be the sample space. Find *n(S)*.

The sample space consists of all combinations of 3 students taken from the group of 11 students.

$$n(S) = {}_{11}C_3 = \frac{11!}{3!(11-3)!} = \frac{11!}{3! \cdot 8!} = \frac{11 \cdot 10 \cdot 9 \cdot \cancel{8} \cdot \cancel{7} \cdot \cancel{6} \cdot \cancel{5} \cdot \cancel{4} \cdot \cancel{3} \cdot \cancel{2} \cdot \cancel{1}}{3 \cdot 2 \cdot 1 \cdot \cancel{8} \cdot \cancel{7} \cdot \cancel{6} \cdot \cancel{5} \cdot \cancel{4} \cdot \cancel{3} \cdot \cancel{2} \cdot \cancel{1}} = \underline{165}$$

B Let *A* be the event that the director chooses all boys. Find *n(A)*.

Suppose the 11 students are $B_1, B_2, B_3, B_4, B_5, G_1, G_2, G_3, G_4, G_5, G_6$, where the *B*s represent boys and the *G*s represent girls.

The combinations in event *A* are combinations like $B_2B_4B_5$ and $B_1B_3B_4$. That is, event *A* consists of all combinations of 3 boys taken from the set of 5 boys.

So, $n(A) = {}_5C_3 = \frac{5!}{3!(5-3)!} = \frac{5!}{3! \cdot 2!} = \frac{5 \cdot 4 \cdot \cancel{3} \cdot \cancel{2} \cdot \cancel{1}}{\cancel{3} \cdot \cancel{2} \cdot \cancel{1} \cdot 2 \cdot 1} = \underline{10}$

C Find *P(A)*.

$$P(A) = \frac{n(A)}{n(S)} = \frac{10}{165} = \underline{\frac{2}{33}}$$

So, the probability that the director chooses all boys is $\underline{\frac{2}{33}}$

Unit 11   314   Lesson 4

© Houghton Mifflin Harcourt Publishing Company

Questioning Strategies

- Does this problem involve permutations or combinations? Why? Combinations; the order in which the students are chosen does not matter.

- Based on your answer, is the director likely to choose all boys? Explain. No; this is not likely, since the probability is only $\frac{2}{33}$.

EXTRA EXAMPLE

A box contains 4 bottles of orange juice and 5 bottles of grapefruit juice. You randomly choose 3 of the bottles to serve at a school breakfast. What is the probability that you choose 3 bottles of grapefruit juice? $\frac{5}{42}$

Teaching Strategies

You might want to revisit the second example once students have learned about the probability of dependent events in Lesson 11-7. At that point, students will have another way to solve the problem. Specifically, the probability of choosing 3 boys is the probability that the first student is a boy times the probability that the second student is a boy given that the first student was a boy times the probability that the third student is a boy given that the first two students were boys. This probability is $\frac{5}{11} \cdot \frac{4}{10} \cdot \frac{3}{9} = \frac{2}{33}$.

CLOSE

Essential Question

What are combinations and how can you use them to calculate probabilities? A combination is a grouping of objects in which order does not matter. You can use combinations to find the number of outcomes in a sample space and/or the number of outcomes in an event.

Summarize

Have students make a graphic organizer to summarize what they know about combinations. A sample is shown below.

Definition	Example
A combination is a grouping of objects in which order does not matter.	Combinations of 2 letters from A, B, C, and D: AB AC AD BC BD CD

Combinations

Formula	Factorials
$_nC_r = \dfrac{n!}{r!(n-r)!}$	n factorial ($n!$) is the product of n and all the positive integers less than n. 0! is 1.

PRACTICE

Where skills are taught	Where skills are practiced
1 EXAMPLE	EXS. 1–2
2 EXAMPLE	EXS. 3–6

Exercises 7–8: Students use reasoning to state a generalization about combinations.

REFLECT

2a. Is the director more likely to choose all boys or all girls? Why?

All girls; $_6C_3 = 20$, so $P(\text{all girls}) = \frac{20}{165} = \frac{4}{33}$, which is greater than the probability

of choosing all boys, $\frac{2}{33}$.

PRACTICE

1. A cat has a litter of 6 kittens. You plan to adopt 2 of the kittens. In how many ways can you choose 2 of the kittens from the litter?

15

2. An amusement park has 11 roller coasters. In how many ways can you choose 4 of the roller coasters to ride during your visit to the park?

330

3. A school has 5 Spanish teachers and 4 French teachers. The school's principal randomly chooses 2 of the teachers to attend a conference. What is the probability that the principal chooses 2 Spanish teachers?

$\frac{5}{18}$

4. There are 6 fiction books and 8 nonfiction books on a reading list. Your teacher randomly assigns you 4 books to read over the summer. What is the probability that you are assigned all nonfiction books?

$\frac{10}{143}$

5. A bag contains 26 tiles, each with a different letter of the alphabet written on it. You choose 3 tiles from the bag without looking. What is the probability that you choose the tiles containing the letters A, B, and C?

$\frac{1}{2600}$

6. You are randomly assigned a password consisting of 6 different characters chosen from the digits 0 to 9 and the letters A to Z. As a percent, what is the probability that you are assigned a password consisting of only letters?

$\approx 11.8\%$

7. Calculate $_{10}C_6$ and $_{10}C_4$.

a. What do you notice about these values? Explain why this makes sense.

$_{10}C_6 = {}_{10}C_4 = 210$; it makes sense that these values are equal because every

combination of 6 objects that are selected has a corresponding combination

of 4 objects that are not selected.

b. Use your observations to help you state a generalization about combinations.

In general, $_nC_r = {}_nC_{n-r}$.

8. Use the formula for combinations to make a generalization about $_nC_n$. Explain why this makes sense.

Using the formula for combinations and the fact that $0! = 1$, $_nC_n = \frac{n!}{n!(n-n)!} =$

$\frac{n!}{n!(0!)} = \frac{n!}{n!} = 1$; this makes sense because there is only 1 combination of n objects

taken n at a time.

Mutually Exclusive and Overlapping Events

Essential question: *How do you find the probability of mutually exclusive events and overlapping events?*

COMMON CORE **Standards for Mathematical Content**

CC.9-12.S.CP.7 Apply the Addition Rule, $P(A \text{ or } B) = P(A) + P(B) - P(A \text{ and } B)$, and interpret the answer in terms of the model.*

Vocabulary

mutually exclusive events

overlapping events

Prerequisites

Probability and Set Theory, Lesson 11-1

Math Background

Mutually exclusive events have no outcomes in common. Thus, mutually exclusive events cannot both occur on the same trial of an experiment. Overlapping or inclusive events have one or more outcomes in common. For overlapping events A and B, $P(A \text{ or } B) = P(A) + P(B) - P(A \text{ and } B)$. In the case that A and B are mutually exclusive events, $P(A \text{ and } B) = 0$, so the rule takes on the simpler form $P(A \text{ or } B) = P(A) + P(B)$.

INTRODUCE

Define *mutually exclusive events*. Give students an example of mutually exclusive events. For example, when you roll a standard number cube, rolling a number less than 3 and rolling a 6 are mutually exclusive events because the events have no outcomes in common. Ask students to give additional examples of mutually exclusive events based on rolling a number cube.

TEACH

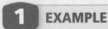

Questioning Strategies

• Why are events A and B mutually exclusive events? **They have no outcomes in common.**

• How is this reflected in the Venn diagram? **The ovals representing the events do not intersect.**

EXTRA EXAMPLE

You choose a card at random from a standard deck of playing cards. What is the probability that you choose a queen or the 7 of diamonds? $\frac{5}{52}$

2 EXAMPLE

Questioning Strategies

• Why are events A and B overlapping? **They have some outcomes in common.**

• How is this reflected in the Venn diagram? **The ovals representing the events intersect.**

• If A and B are overlapping events, what can you say about $A \cap B$? **$A \cap B$ is not the empty set.**

EXTRA EXAMPLE

You have a set of 20 cards that are numbered 1–20. You shuffle the cards and choose one at random. What is the probability that you choose an even number or a number greater than 15? $\frac{3}{5}$

> MATHEMATICAL PRACTICE **Highlighting the Standards**
>
> According to Standard 1 (Make sense of problems and persevere in solving them), mathematically proficient students continually ask themselves, "Does this make sense?" This lesson provides an especially good opportunity for this type of reflective thinking. Whenever students calculate a probability they should ask themselves whether the probability seems reasonable. For instance, in the second example, students find that the probability, of rolling an even number or a number greater than 7 on a dodecahedral number cube is $\frac{2}{3}$. This seems reasonable since more than half of the outcomes in the sample space are in at least one of these events.

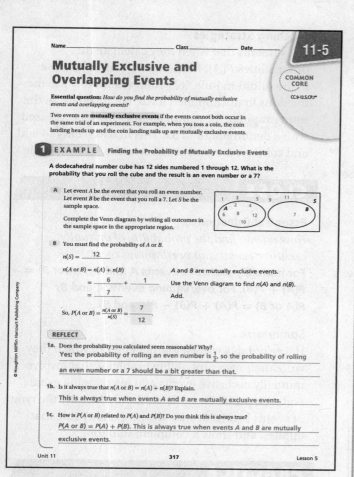

Name _____ Class _____ Date _____

Mutually Exclusive and Overlapping Events

11-5

COMMON CORE

CC.9-12.S.CP.7*

Essential question: *How do you find the probability of mutually exclusive events and overlapping events?*

Two events are **mutually exclusive events** if the events cannot both occur in the same trial of an experiment. For example, when you toss a coin, the coin landing heads up and the coin landing tails up are mutually exclusive events.

1 EXAMPLE Finding the Probability of Mutually Exclusive Events

A dodecahedral number cube has 12 sides numbered 1 through 12. What is the probability that you roll the cube and the result is an even number or a 7?

A Let event *A* be the event that you roll an even number. Let event *B* be the event that you roll a 7. Let *S* be the sample space.

Complete the Venn diagram by writing all outcomes in the sample space in the appropriate region.

B You must find the probability of *A* or *B*.

$n(S) = \underline{\quad 12 \quad}$

$n(A \text{ or } B) = n(A) + n(B)$ *A* and *B* are mutually exclusive events.

$\qquad = \underline{\quad 6 \quad} + \underline{\quad 1 \quad}$ Use the Venn diagram to find $n(A)$ and $n(B)$.

$\qquad = \underline{\quad 7 \quad}$ Add.

So, $P(A \text{ or } B) = \frac{n(A \text{ or } B)}{n(S)} = \underline{\frac{7}{12}}$.

REFLECT

1a. Does the probability you calculated seem reasonable? Why?

Yes; the probability of rolling an even number is $\frac{1}{2}$, so the probability of rolling

an even number or a 7 should be a bit greater than that.

1b. Is it always true that $n(A \text{ or } B) = n(A) + n(B)$? Explain.

This is always true when events *A* and *B* are mutually exclusive events.

1c. How is $P(A \text{ or } B)$ related to $P(A)$ and $P(B)$? Do you think this is always true?

$P(A \text{ or } B) = P(A) + P(B)$. This is always true when events *A* and *B* are mutually

exclusive events.

Unit 11   317   Lesson 5

© Houghton Mifflin Harcourt Publishing Company

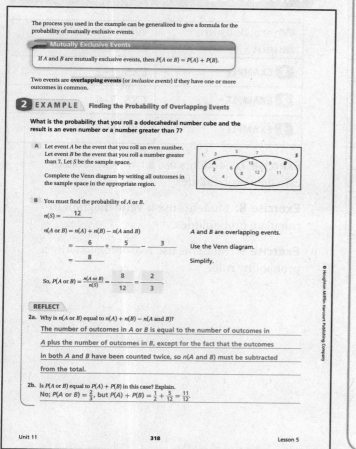

The process you used in the example can be generalized to give a formula for the probability of mutually exclusive events.

Mutually Exclusive Events

If *A* and *B* are mutually exclusive events, then $P(A \text{ or } B) = P(A) + P(B)$.

Two events are **overlapping events** (or *inclusive events*) if they have one or more outcomes in common.

2 EXAMPLE Finding the Probability of Overlapping Events

What is the probability that you roll a dodecahedral number cube and the result is an even number or a number greater than 7?

A Let event *A* be the event that you roll an even number. Let event *B* be the event that you roll a number greater than 7. Let *S* be the sample space.

Complete the Venn diagram by writing all outcomes in the sample space in the appropriate region.

B You must find the probability of *A* or *B*.

$n(S) = \underline{\quad 12 \quad}$

$n(A \text{ or } B) = n(A) + n(B) - n(A \text{ and } B)$ *A* and *B* are overlapping events.

$\qquad = \underline{\quad 6 \quad} + \underline{\quad 5 \quad} - \underline{\quad 3 \quad}$ Use the Venn diagram.

$\qquad = \underline{\quad 8 \quad}$ Simplify.

So, $P(A \text{ or } B) = \frac{n(A \text{ or } B)}{n(S)} = \frac{8}{12} = \frac{2}{3}$.

REFLECT

2a. Why is $n(A \text{ or } B)$ equal to $n(A) + n(B) - n(A \text{ and } B)$?

The number of outcomes in *A* or *B* is equal to the number of outcomes in

A plus the number of outcomes in *B*, except for the fact that the outcomes

in both *A* and *B* have been counted twice, so $n(A \text{ and } B)$ must be subtracted

from the total.

2b. Is $P(A \text{ or } B)$ equal to $P(A) + P(B)$ in this case? Explain.

No; $P(A \text{ or } B) = \frac{2}{3}$, but $P(A) + P(B) = \frac{1}{2} + \frac{5}{12} = \frac{11}{12}$.

Unit 11   318   Lesson 5

© Houghton Mifflin Harcourt Publishing Company

Unit 11   **318**   Lesson 5

Questioning Strategies

• How are the cards in a standard deck organized?
There are 13 cards (ace, 2, 3, 4, 5, 6, 7, 8, 9, 10,
jack, queen, king), each in 4 suits (hearts, clubs,
diamonds, spades), for a total of 52 cards.

• What card or cards does $A \cap B$ represent? Why?
$A \cap B$ is the king of hearts since the card must be
both a king and a heart.

EXTRA EXAMPLE

You have a set of 26 cards with the letters A
through Z. You shuffle the cards and choose one
at random. What is the probability that you choose
a card with a consonant or a letter in the word
PROBABILITY? $\frac{12}{13}$

Differentiated Instruction

Some students may find it easier to solve the
problem in the third example by making a chart
that shows all of the cards in a deck of cards and
then highlighting the cards in events A and B.

A ♥	A ♣	A ♦	A ♠
2 ♥	2 ♣	2 ♦	2 ♠
3 ♥	3 ♣	3 ♦	3 ♠
4 ♥	4 ♣	4 ♦	4 ♠
5 ♥	5 ♣	5 ♦	5 ♠
6 ♥	6 ♣	6 ♦	6 ♠
7 ♥	7 ♣	7 ♦	7 ♠
8 ♥	8 ♣	8 ♦	8 ♠
9 ♥	9 ♣	9 ♦	9 ♠
10 ♥	10 ♣	10 ♦	10 ♠
J ♥	J ♣	J ♦	J ♠
Q ♥	Q ♣	Q ♦	Q ♠
K ♥	K ♣	K ♦	K ♠

Teaching Strategies

Tell students that when they calculate the
probabilities $P(A)$, $P(B)$, and $P(A \text{ and } B)$ for use
in the Addition Rule, it is often easiest to leave the
fractions in unsimplified form. For instance, in the
third example, these probabilities are all expressed
with a denominator of 52. This makes it easy to add
and subtract the probabilities in the Addition Rule.

CLOSE

Essential Question

*How do you find the probability of mutually
exclusive events and overlapping events?*
For mutually exclusive events A and B, $P(A \text{ or } B) =$
$P(A) + P(B)$. For overlapping events A and B,
$P(A \text{ or } B) = P(A) + P(B) - P(A \text{ and } B)$.

Summarize

Have students write a journal entry in which they
write their own probability problems that involve
mutually exclusive events and overlapping events.
For each problem, students should identify the type
of events involved, state the probability rule that
applies, and show a complete solution.

PRACTICE

Where skills are taught	Where skills are practiced
1 EXAMPLE	EXS. 1–2
2 EXAMPLE	EXS. 3–4
3 EXAMPLE	EXS. 5–6

Exercise 7: Students use a two-way table to
calculate probabilities.

Exercise 8: Students use a Venn diagram to
calculate probabilities.

Exercise 9: Students use reasoning to write a
probability rule.

In the previous example you saw that for overlapping events A and B, $n(A \cup B) = n(A) + n(B) - n(A \cap B)$. You can convert these counts to probabilities by dividing each term by $n(S)$ as shown below.

$$\frac{n(A \cup B)}{n(S)} = \frac{n(A)}{n(S)} + \frac{n(B)}{n(S)} - \frac{n(A \cap B)}{n(S)}$$

Rewriting each term as a probability results in the following rule.

Addition Rule

$P(A \text{ or } B) = P(A) + P(B) - P(A \text{ and } B)$

Notice that when A and B are mutually exclusive events, $P(A \text{ and } B) = 0$, and the rule becomes the simpler rule for mutually exclusive events on the previous page.

3 EXAMPLE Using the Addition Rule

You shuffle a standard deck of playing cards and choose a card at random. What is the probability that you choose a king or a heart?

A Let event A be the event that you choose a king. Let event B be the event that you choose a heart. Let S be the sample space.

There are 52 cards in the deck, so $n(S) =$ ___52___

There are 4 kings in the deck, so $n(A) =$ ___4___ and $P(A) =$ ___$\frac{4}{52}$___.

There are 13 hearts in the deck, so $n(B) =$ ___13___ and $P(B) =$ ___$\frac{13}{52}$___.

There is one king of hearts in the deck, so $P(A \text{ and } B) =$ ___$\frac{1}{52}$___.

B Use the Addition Rule.

$P(A \text{ or } B) = P(A) + P(B) - P(A \text{ and } B)$

$= \frac{4}{52} + \frac{13}{52} - \frac{1}{52}$ Substitute.

$= \frac{16}{52}$ or $\frac{4}{13}$ Simplify.

So, the probability of choosing a king or a heart is $\frac{4}{13}$.

REFLECT

3a. What does the answer tell you about the likelihood of choosing a king or a heart from the deck?

The probability is about 31%, so the outcome is not very likely (it will occur about 31% of the time).

PRACTICE

1. A bag contains 3 blue marbles, 5 red marbles, and 4 green marbles. You choose a marble without looking. What is the probability that you choose a red marble or a green marble? $\frac{3}{4}$

2. An icosahedral number cube has 20 sides numbered 1 through 20. What is the probability that you roll the cube and the result is a number that is less than 4 or greater than 11? $\frac{3}{5}$

3. A bag contains 26 tiles, each with a different letter of the alphabet written on it. You choose a tile without looking. What is the probability that you choose a vowel or a letter in the word GEOMETRY? $\frac{5}{13}$

4. You roll two number cubes at the same time. Each cube has sides numbered 1 through 6. What is the probability that the sum of the numbers rolled is even or greater than 9? $\frac{5}{9}$

5. You shuffle a standard deck of playing cards and choose a card at random. What is the probability that you choose a face card (jack, queen, or king) or a club? $\frac{11}{26}$

6. You have a set of 25 cards numbered 1 through 25. You shuffle the cards and choose a card at random. What is the probability that you choose a multiple of 3 or a multiple of 4? $\frac{12}{25}$

7. The two-way table provides data on the students at a high school. You randomly choose a student at the school. Find each probability.

	Freshman	Sophomore	Junior	Senior	TOTAL
Boy	98	104	100	94	396
Girl	102	106	96	108	412
TOTAL	200	210	196	202	808

a. The student is a senior. $\frac{1}{4}$

b. The student is a girl. $\frac{103}{202}$

c. The student is a senior and a girl. $\frac{27}{202}$

d. The student is a senior or a girl. $\frac{253}{404}$

8. A survey of the 1108 employees at a software company finds that 621 employees take a bus to work and 445 employees take a train to work. Some employees take both a bus and a train, and 312 employees take only a train. To the nearest percent, what is the probability that a randomly-chosen employee takes a bus or a train to work? (*Hint:* Make a Venn diagram.)   84%

9. Suppose A and B are complementary events. Explain how you can rewrite the Addition Rule in a simpler form for this case.

Because $P(A \text{ and } B) = 0$ for complementary events, $P(A \text{ or } B) = P(A) + P(B) = 1$.

© Houghton Mifflin Harcourt Publishing Company

11-6

Conditional Probability

Essential question: *How do you calculate a conditional probability?*

COMMON CORE **Standards for Mathematical Content**

CC.9-12.S.CP.3 Understand the conditional probability of *A* given *B* as *P*(*A* and *B*)/*P*(*B*) ....*

CC.9-12.S.CP.4 Construct and interpret two-way frequency tables of data when two categories are associated with each object being classified. Use the two-way table ... to approximate conditional probabilities.*

CC.9-12.S.CP.5 Recognize and explain the concept of conditional probability ... in everyday language and everyday situations.*

CC.9-12.S.CP.6 Find the conditional probability of *A* given *B* as the fraction of *B*'s outcomes that also belong to *A*, and interpret the answer in terms of the model.*

Vocabulary

conditional probability

Prerequisites

Probability and Set Theory, Lesson 11-1

Math Background

This is the first of three related lessons that cover the concepts of conditional probability, independent events, and dependent events. Many texts begin by defining independent and dependent events. Conditional probability is introduced along the way as a tool for calculating the probability of dependent events. The approach in this text rearranges the sequence to begin with a deeper treatment of conditional probability. This has the advantage of establishing conditional probability as a powerful idea in its own right, one that can be used in a number of applications beyond the probability of dependent events. Also, this approach gives students many opportunities to work with two-way tables, which can be used to make sense of a wide range of probability and statistics problems.

INTRODUCE

Define *conditional probability*. Give students a simple example. For instance, when you roll a number cube, the probability that you roll a 6 is $\frac{1}{6}$. The conditional probability that you roll a 6 given that you roll a number greater than 4 is $\frac{1}{2}$ since this condition effectively restricts the sample space to {5, 6}.

TEACH

1 EXAMPLE

Questioning Strategies

• What percent of the participants in the study were given the medicine? **60%**

• How many participants in the study did not get a headache? **73**

• Was a participant who got a headache more likely to have taken the medicine or not? **The participant was more likely to have not taken the medicine.**

EXTRA EXAMPLE

The manager of a produce stand wants to find out whether there is a connection between people who buy fresh vegetables and people who buy eggs. The manager collects data on 200 randomly chosen shoppers, as shown in the two-way table.

	Bought Vegetables	No Vegetables	TOTAL
Eggs	56	20	76
No Eggs	49	75	124
TOTAL	105	95	200

A. To the nearest percent, what is the probability that a shopper who bought eggs also bought vegetables? **74%**

B. To the nearest percent, what is the probability that a shopper who bought vegetables also bought eggs? **53%**

Name_____ Class_____ Date_____

11-6

COMMON
CORE
CC-9-12.S.CP.3*,
CC-9-12.S.CP.4*,
CC-9-12.S.CP.5*,
CC-9-12.S.CP.6*

Conditional Probability

Essential question: *How do you calculate a conditional probability?*

The probability that event *B* occurs given that event *A* has already occurred is called the **conditional probability** of *B* given *A* and is written $P(B \mid A)$.

1 EXAMPLE   Finding Conditional Probabilities

One hundred people who frequently get migraine headaches were chosen to participate in a study of a new anti-headache medicine. Some of the particpants were given the medicine; others were not. After one week, the participants were asked if they got a headache during the week. The two-way table summarizes the results.

	Took Medicine	No Medicine	TOTAL
Headache	12	15	27
No Headache	48	25	73
TOTAL	60	40	100

A To the nearest percent, what is the probability that a participant who took the medicine did not get a headache?

Let event *A* be the event that a participant took the medicine. Let event *B* be the event that a participant did not get a headache.

To find the probability that a participant who took the medicine did not get a headache, you must find $P(B \mid A)$. You are only concerned with participants who took the medicine, so look at the data in the "Took Medicine" column.

There were ___60___ participants who took the medicine.

Of these participants, ___48___ participants did not get a headache.

So, $P(B \mid A) = \dfrac{48}{60} = $ ___80%___

B To the nearest percent, what is the probability that a participant who did not get a headache took the medicine?

To find the probability that a participant who did not get a headache took the medicine, you must find $P(A \mid B)$. You are only concerned with participants who did not get a headache, so look at the data in the "No headache" row.

There were ___73___ participants who did not get a headache.

Of these participants, ___48___ participants took the medicine.

So, $P(A \mid B) = \dfrac{48}{73} \approx$ ___66%___

© Houghton Mifflin Harcourt Publishing Company

REFLECT

1a. In general, do you think $P(B \mid A) = P(A \mid B)$? Why or why not?

No; these conditional probabilities are not equal in the example.

1b. How can you use set notation to represent the event that a participant took the medicine and did not get a headache? Is the probability that a participant took the medicine and did not get a headache equal to either of the conditional probabilities you calculated in the example?

This is represented by $A \cap B$; $P(A \cap B) = \dfrac{48}{100} = 48\%$; this probability is not

equal to $P(B \mid A)$ or $P(A \mid B)$.

2 EXPLORE   Developing a Formula for Conditional Probability

You can generalize your work from the previous example to develop a formula for finding conditional probabilities.

A Recall how you calculated $P(B \mid A)$, the probability that a participant who took the medicine did not get a headache.

You found that $P(B \mid A) = \dfrac{48}{60}$.

Use the table shown here to help you write this quotient in terms of events *A* and *B*.

		Event A		
		Took Medicine	No Medicine	TOTAL
	Headache	12	15	27
Event B	No Headache	$48 = n(A \cap B)$	25	$73 = n(B)$
	TOTAL	$60 = n(A)$	40	100

$P(B \mid A) = \dfrac{n(A \cap B)}{n(A)}$

B Now divide the numerator and denominator of the quotient by $n(S)$, the number of outcomes in the sample space. This converts the counts to probabilities.

$P(B \mid A) = \dfrac{n(A \cap B) \big/ n(S)}{n(A) \big/ n(S)} = \dfrac{P(A \cap B)}{P(A)}$

REFLECT

2a. Write a formula for $P(A \mid B)$ in terms of $n(A \cap B)$ and $n(B)$.
$P(A \mid B) = \dfrac{n(A \cap B)}{n(B)}$

2b. Write a formula for $P(A \mid B)$ in terms of $P(A \cap B)$ and $P(B)$.
$P(A \mid B) = \dfrac{P(A \cap B)}{P(B)}$

© Houghton Mifflin Harcourt Publishing Company

MATHEMATICAL PRACTICE — Highlighting the Standards

Standard 4 (Model with mathematics) includes the statement that mathematically proficient students are able to map relationships among important quantities using tools like two-way tables. Furthermore, "they can analyze those relationships mathematically to draw conclusions." This lesson offers many opportunities for such analyses. After the first example, ask students what conclusions they can draw about the effectiveness of the headache medicine. The data in the two-way table and the conditional probabilities indicate that the medicine is at least somewhat effective in preventing headaches.

2 EXPLORE

Questioning Strategies

• What does $A \cap B$ represent? **participants who took the medicine and did not get a headache**

• How many participants are in $A \cap B$? How do you know? **48; this is the number in the cell corresponding to "Took Medicine" and "No Headache."**

• What is $n(S)$? Why? **100;100 people participated in the study.**

Teaching Strategies

English language learners may have difficulty with conditional probability because so much depends upon understanding that "What is the probability that a participant who took the medicine did not get a headache?" and "What is the probability that a participant who did not get a headache took the medicine?" are different questions. When working with such statements, you may want to prompt students to underline the words that correspond to the event that is assumed to have already occurred.

3 EXAMPLE

Questioning Strategies

• In this situation, which event can be considered to have already occurred? **the event that the card is red**

• What are the red cards in a deck of cards? **The red cards are the 13 hearts and the 13 diamonds.**

EXTRA EXAMPLE

In a standard deck of playing cards, find the probability that a face card is a king. $\frac{1}{3}$

CLOSE

Essential Question

How do you calculate a conditional probability?
You can calculate a conditional probability from a two-way table. You can also use the formula
$P(B \mid A) = \frac{P(A \cap B)}{P(A)}$.

Summarize

Have students write a journal entry in which they explain conditional probability in their own words. Also, ask students to give an example of how to use the formula for conditional probability.

PRACTICE

Where skills are taught	Where skills are practiced
1 EXAMPLE	EXS. 1–2
3 EXAMPLE	EXS. 3–9

You may have discovered the following formula for conditional probability.

> **Conditional Probability**
>
> The conditional probability of B given A (the probability that event B occurs given that event A occurs) is given by the following formula:
>
> $$P(B \mid A) = \frac{P(A \cap B)}{P(A)}$$

3 EXAMPLE Using the Conditional Probability Formula

In a standard deck of playing cards, find the probability that a red card is a queen.

A   Let event Q be the event that a card is a queen. Let event R be the event that a card is red. You are asked to find $P(Q \mid R)$. First find $P(R \cap Q)$ and $P(R)$.

$R \cap Q$ represents cards that are both red and a queen; that is, red queens.

There are ____2____ red queens in the deck of 52 cards, so $P(R \cap Q) = \frac{2}{52}$

There are ___26___ red cards in the deck, so $P(R) = \frac{26}{52}$

B   Use the formula for conditional probability.

$P(Q \mid R) = \dfrac{P(Q \cap R)}{P(R)} = \dfrac{\frac{2}{52}}{\frac{26}{52}}$ Substitute probabilities from above.

$= \dfrac{2}{26}$ Multiply numerator and denominator by 52.

$= \dfrac{1}{13}$ Simplify.

So, the probability that a red card is a queen is $\frac{1}{13}$

REFLECT

3a. How can you interpret the probability you calculated above?

If you choose a red card at random, it is very unlikely that it will be a queen
(it will be a queen about 8% of the time).

3b. Is the probability that a red card is a queen equal to the probability that a queen is red? Explain.

No; $P(R \mid Q) = \frac{1}{2}$, whereas $P(Q \mid R) = \frac{1}{13}$.

PRACTICE

1. In order to study the connection between the amount of sleep a student gets and his or her school performance, data was collected about 120 students. The two-way table shows the number of students who passed and failed an exam and the number of students who got more or less than 6 hours of sleep the night before.

	Passed Exam	Failed Exam	TOTAL
Less than 6 hours of sleep	12	10	22
More than 6 hours of sleep	90	8	98
TOTAL	102	18	120

a. To the nearest percent, what is the probability that a student who failed the exam got less than 6 hours of sleep? __56%__

b. To the nearest percent, what is the probability that a student who got less than 6 hours of sleep failed the exam? __45%__

c. To the nearest percent, what is the probability that a student got less than 6 hours of sleep and failed the exam? __8%__

2. A botanist studied the effect of a new fertilizer by choosing 100 orchids and giving 70% of these plants the fertilizer. Of the plants that got the fertilizer, 40% produced flowers within a month. Of the plants that did not get the fertilizer, 10% produced flowers within a month. Find each probability to the nearest percent. (*Hint:* Construct a two-way table.)

a. Find the probability that a plant that produced flowers got the fertilizer. __90%__

b. Find the probability that a plant that got the fertilizer produced flowers. __40%__

3. At a school fair, a box contains 24 yellow balls and 76 red balls. One-fourth of the balls of each color are labeled "Win a prize." Find each probability as a percent.

a. Find the probability that a ball labeled "Win a prize" is yellow. __24%__

b. Find the probability that a ball labeled "Win a prize" is red. __76%__

c. Find the probability that a ball is labeled "Win a prize" and is red. __19%__

d. Find the probability that a yellow ball is labeled "Win a prize." __25%__

In Exercises 4–9, consider a standard deck of playing cards and the following events: *A*: the card is an ace; *B*: the card is black; *C*: the card is a club. Find each probability as a fraction.

4. $P(A \mid B)$ $\frac{1}{13}$

5. $P(B \mid A)$ $\frac{1}{2}$

6. $P(A \mid C)$ $\frac{1}{13}$

7. $P(C \mid A)$ $\frac{1}{4}$

8. $P(B \mid C)$ 1

9. $P(C \mid B)$ $\frac{1}{2}$

Notes

Independent Events

Essential question: *How do you determine if two events are independent events?*

COMMON Standards for
CORE Mathematical Content

CC.9-12.S.CP.2 Understand that two events *A* and *B* are independent if the probability of *A* and *B* occurring together is the product of their probabilities, and use this characterization to determine if they are independent.*

CC.9-12.S.CP.3 … interpret independence of *A* and *B* as saying that the conditional probability of *A* given *B* is the same as the probability of *A*, and the conditional probability of *B* given *A* is the same as the probability of *B*.*

CC.9-12.S.CP.4 Construct and interpret two-way frequency tables of data when two categories are associated with each object being classified. Use the two-way table as a sample space to decide if events are independent ….*

CC.9-12.S.CP.5 Recognize and explain the concept of … independence in everyday language and everyday situations.*

Vocabulary
independent events

Prerequisites
Probability and Set Theory, Lesson 11-1
Conditional Probability, Lesson 11-6

Math Background
In this lesson, students learn two different ways to identify independent events. For two events *A* and *B*, if $P(A) = P(A \mid B)$, then the events are independent. Also, if $P(A \text{ and } B) = P(A) \cdot P(B)$, then the events are independent.

INTRODUCE

Define *independent events*. Ask students to suggest examples of independent events. Be sure to discuss examples from everyday life, such as the event that it is cloudy tomorrow and the event that there is a math test tomorrow. The events are independent since the occurrence of one event does not affect the occurrence of the other.

TEACH

1 EXAMPLE

Questioning Strategies
- What percent of all flights are late? Where do you find this information? **10%; look at the bottom row of the table.**
- What percent of all domestic flights are late? Where do you find this information? **10%; look at the "Domestic Flight" row of the table.**
- What percent of all international flights are late? Where do you find this information? **10%; Look at the "International Flight" row of the table.**

EXTRA EXAMPLE
A doctor collects data on 120 randomly-chosen patients. The data are shown in the two-way table. Is taking vitamins independent of exercising regularly? Why or why not?

	Takes Vitamins	No Vitamins	TOTAL
Exercises Regularly	28	48	76
Does Not Exercise	12	32	44
TOTAL	40	80	120

No; the events are not independent because $P(\text{exercise})$ does not equal $P(\text{exercise}\mid\text{vitamins})$.

MATHEMATICAL PRACTICE **Highlighting the Standards**

Standard 6 (Attend to precision) states that mathematically proficient students "try to use clear definitions in discussion with others." Have students communicate their results from this lesson orally and in writing. Ask them to check that they are using terms correctly. In particular, be sure students understand that the word *independent* has a specific meaning in probability theory that may be different from its meaning in everyday conversation.

Name_____ Class_____ Date_____

11-7

COMMON CORE

CC.9-12.S.CP.2*
CC.9-12.S.CP.3*
CC.9-12.S.CP.4*
CC.9-12.S.CP.5*

Independent Events

Essential question: *How do you determine if two events are independent events?*

Two events are **independent events** if the occurrence of one event does not affect the occurrence of the other event. For example, rolling a 1 on a number cube and choosing an ace at random from a deck of cards are independent events.

If two events A and B are independent events, then the fact that event B has occurred does not affect the probability of event A. In other words, for independent events A and B, $P(A) = P(A \mid B)$. You can use this as a criterion to determine whether two events are independent.

1 EXAMPLE Determining If Events are Independent

An airport employee collects data on 180 random flights that arrive at the airport. The data is shown in the two-way table. Is a late arrival independent of the flight being an international flight? Why or why not?

	Late Arrival	On Time	TOTAL
Domestic Flight	12	108	120
International Flight	6	54	60
TOTAL	18	162	180

A Let event A be the event that a flight arrives late. Let event B be the event that a flight is an international flight.

To find $P(A)$, first note that there is a total of ___180___ flights.

Of these flights, there is a total of ___18___ late flights.

So, $P(A) = \dfrac{18}{180} = $ ___10%___ .

To find $P(A \mid B)$, first note that there is a total of ___60___ international flights.

Of these flights, there is a total of ___6___ late flights.

So, $P(A \mid B) = \dfrac{6}{60} = $ ___10%___ .

B Compare $P(A)$ and $P(A \mid B)$.

So, a late arrival is independent of the flight being an international flight because

$P(A) = P(A \mid B)$, which means that events A and B are independent events.

REFLECT

1a. In the example, you compared $P(A)$ and $P(A \mid B)$. Suppose you compare $P(B)$ and $P(B \mid A)$. What do you find? What does this tell you?

$P(B) = P(B \mid A) = 33.3\%$; this also shows A and B are independent events.

© Houghton Mifflin Harcourt Publishing Company

You can use a tree diagram to help you understand the formula for the probability of independent events. For example, consider tossing a coin two times. The outcome of one toss does not affect the outcome of the other toss, so the events are independent.

The tree diagram shows that the probability of the coin landing heads up on both tosses is $\frac{1}{4}$ because this is 1 of 4 equally-likely outcomes at the end of Toss 2. This probability is simply the product of the probabilities of the coin landing heads up on each individual toss: $\frac{1}{2} \cdot \frac{1}{2} = \frac{1}{4}$.

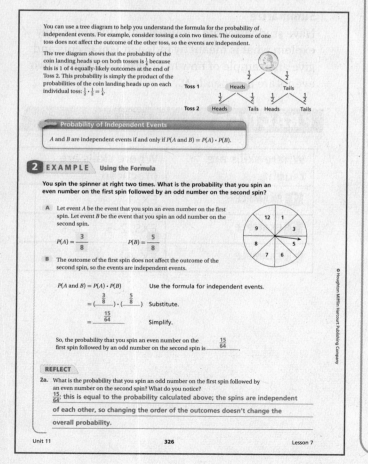

Probability of Independent Events

A and B are independent events if and only if $P(A \text{ and } B) = P(A) \cdot P(B)$.

2 EXAMPLE Using the Formula

You spin the spinner at right two times. What is the probability that you spin an even number on the first spin followed by an odd number on the second spin?

A Let event A be the event that you spin an even number on the first spin. Let event B be the event that you spin an odd number on the second spin.

$P(A) = \dfrac{3}{8}$ $P(B) = \dfrac{5}{8}$

B The outcome of the first spin does not affect the outcome of the second spin, so the events are independent events.

$P(A \text{ and } B) = P(A) \cdot P(B)$ Use the formula for independent events.

$= \left(\dfrac{3}{8}\right) \cdot \left(\dfrac{5}{8}\right)$ Substitute.

$= \dfrac{15}{64}$ Simplify.

So, the probability that you spin an even number on the first spin followed by an odd number on the second spin is ___$\frac{15}{64}$___ .

REFLECT

2a. What is the probability that you spin an odd number on the first spin followed by an even number on the second spin? What do you notice?

$\frac{15}{64}$; this is equal to the probability calculated above; the spins are independent of each other, so changing the order of the outcomes doesn't change the overall probability.

© Houghton Mifflin Harcourt Publishing Company

Questioning Strategies

- What is the sample space for each spin? {1, 3, 5, 6, 7, 8, 9, 12}

- On any given spin, are you more likely to spin an even number or an odd number? Why? Odd; 5 of the 8 numbers on the spinner are odd.

- Why are the events in this problem independent events? The outcome of the first spin does not affect the outcome of the second spin.

EXTRA EXAMPLE

A number cube has the numbers 3, 5, 6, 8, 10, and 12 on its faces. You roll the number cube twice. What is the probability that you roll an odd number on both rolls? $\frac{1}{9}$

Avoid Common Errors

Students sometimes confuse independent events and mutually exclusive events. This may lead students to add the probabilities of event A and event B in the second example. If students do add the probabilities, they will find that $P(A) + P(B) = 1$, which would mean that $A \cap B$ is a certainty. This result, which does not make sense in the context of the problem, should alert students that they may have made an error.

3 EXAMPLE

Questioning Strategies

- Which column or row of the table do you look at to calculate $P(A)$? the bottom row of the table

- Which column or row of the table do you look at to calculate $P(B)$? the right- most column of the table

EXTRA EXAMPLE

The two-way table shows the data from the first extra example. Show that a patient taking vitamins and a patient exercising regularly are not independent events.

	Takes Vitamins	No Vitamins	TOTAL
Exercises Regularly	28	48	76
Does Not Exercise	12	32	44
TOTAL	40	80	120

$P(\text{exercise}) = \frac{19}{30}$; $P(\text{vitamins}) = \frac{1}{3}$; $P(\text{exercise and vitamins}) = \frac{7}{30}$; since the product of $P(\text{exercise})$ and $P(\text{vitamins})$ does not equal $P(\text{exercise and vitamins})$, the events are not independent events.

CLOSE

Essential Question

How do you determine if two events are independent events?
Show that $P(A) = P(A \mid B)$ or that $P(A \text{ and } B) = P(A) \cdot P(B)$.

Summarize

Have students write a journal entry in which they explain what is meant by independent events and give an example of how to determine whether two events are independent.

PRACTICE

Where skills are taught	Where skills are practiced
1 EXAMPLE	EX. 1
2 EXAMPLE	EXS. 2–5
3 EXAMPLE	EX. 6

The formula for the probability of independent events gives you another way to determine whether two events are independent. That is, two events A and B are independent events if $P(A \text{ and } B) = P(A) \cdot P(B)$.

3 EXAMPLE Showing that Events are Independent

The two-way table shows the data from the first example. Show that a flight arriving on time and a flight being a domestic flight are independent events.

	Late Arrival	On Time	TOTAL
Domestic Flight	12	108	120
International Flight	6	54	60
TOTAL	18	162	180

A   Let event A be the event that a flight arrives on time. Let event B be the event that a flight is a domestic flight.

To find $P(A)$, $P(B)$, and $P(A \text{ and } B)$ note that there is a total of ___180___ flights.

There is a total of ___162___ on-time flights.

So, $P(A) = \dfrac{162}{180} = \dfrac{9}{10}$.

There is a total of ___120___ domestic flights.

So, $P(B) = \dfrac{120}{180} = \dfrac{2}{3}$.

There is a total of ___108___ on-time domestic flights.

So, $P(A \text{ and } B) = \dfrac{108}{180} = \dfrac{3}{5}$.

B   Compare $P(A \text{ and } B)$ and $P(A) \cdot P(B)$.

$P(A) \cdot P(B) = (\dfrac{9}{10}) \cdot (\dfrac{2}{3}) = \dfrac{3}{5}$

So, the events are independent events because

$P(A \text{ and } B) = P(A) \cdot P(B)$.

REFLECT

3a. Describe a different way you can show that a flight arriving on time and a flight being a domestic flight are independent events.

Let events A and B be as in the example and show that $P(A) = P(A \mid B)$.

Unit 11 327 Lesson 7

PRACTICE

1. A farmer wants to know if an insecticide is effective in preventing small insects called aphids from living on tomato plants. The farmer checks 80 plants. The data is shown in the two-way table. Is having aphids independent of being sprayed with the insecticide? Why or why not?

	Has Aphids	No Aphids	TOTAL
Was sprayed with insecticide	12	40	52
Was not sprayed with insecticide	14	14	28
TOTAL	26	54	80

No; $P(\text{aphids}) = \dfrac{26}{80} = 32.5\%$ and $P(\text{aphids} \mid \text{insecticide}) = \dfrac{12}{52} \approx 23\%$; since these

probabilities are not equal, the events are not independent.

You spin a spinner with 8 equal sections numbered 1 through 8 and you roll a number cube with sides numbered 1 through 6. Find the probability of each of the following. Write the probabilities as fractions.

2. The spinner lands on 1 and you roll a 5. $\dfrac{1}{48}$

3. The spinner lands on an even number and you roll an even number. $\dfrac{1}{4}$

4. The spinner lands on a prime number and you roll a number greater than 4. $\dfrac{1}{6}$

5. The sum of the number on which the spinner lands and the number you roll is 14. $\dfrac{1}{48}$

6. A student wants to know if right-handed people are more or less likely to play a musical instrument than left-handed people. The student collects data from 250 people, as shown in the two-way table. Show that being right handed and playing a musical instrument are independent events.

	Right Handed	Left Handed	TOTAL
Plays a musical instrument	44	6	50
Does not play a musical instrument	176	24	200
TOTAL	220	30	250

$P(\text{right}) = \dfrac{220}{250} = \dfrac{22}{25}$; $P(\text{plays}) = \dfrac{50}{250} = \dfrac{1}{5}$; $P(\text{right and plays}) = \dfrac{44}{250} = \dfrac{22}{125}$;

since $P(\text{right}) \cdot P(\text{plays}) = P(\text{right and plays})$, the events are independent.

© Houghton Mifflin Harcourt Publishing Company

Dependent Events

Essential question: *How do you find the probability of dependent events?*

COMMON Standards for
CORE Mathematical Content

CC.9-12.S.CP.8(+) Apply the general Multiplication Rule in a uniform probability model,
$P(A \text{ and } B) = P(A)\,P(B \mid A) = P(B)\,P(A \mid B)$, and interpret the answer in terms of the model.*

Vocabulary

dependent events

Prerequisites

Probability and Set Theory, Lesson 11-1
Conditional Probability, Lesson 11-6
Independent Events, Lesson 11-7

Math Background

This is the last of three closely related lessons. In Lesson 11-6, students were introduced to conditional probability. In Lesson 11-7, students learned to identify independent events and calculate the probability of independent events. In this lesson, students use what they have learned about conditional probability to develop the Multiplication Rule. This rule can be used to find the probability of dependent events.

INTRODUCE

Define *dependent events*. To illustrate the difference between independent events and dependent events, discuss two different ways of choosing two colored marbles from a bag: 1) with replacement and 2) without replacement.

When you choose with replacement, you select the first marble, note its color, and put the marble back in the bag before choosing the second marble. In this case, the two selections are independent events. The sample space for the two events is the same.

When you choose without replacement, you select the first marble, put it aside, and then choose the second marble. In this case, the two selections are dependent events because the marble you choose first changes the sample space for your second selection.

TEACH

1 ENGAGE

Questioning Strategies

- Suppose the first marble you choose is blue. What happens to the sample space for your second pick? **The sample space changes; it consists of 1 blue marble and 2 black marbles.**

- Suppose you replace the first marble you pick. Are the events dependent events in this case? Why or why not? **No; if you replace the first marble, the events are independent because the result of the first pick does not affect the sample space for the second pick.**

2 EXAMPLE

Questioning Strategies

- Why are these events dependent events? **The tile you choose for your first pick changes the sample space for your second pick. That is, the occurrence of event A affects the probability of event B.**

- How many consonants and vowels are in the bag? **3 consonants, 2 vowels**

EXTRA EXAMPLE

You choose a marble at random from the bag shown here. You put the marble aside and then choose another marble. Find the probability that you choose a gray marble followed by a blue marble. $\frac{4}{15}$

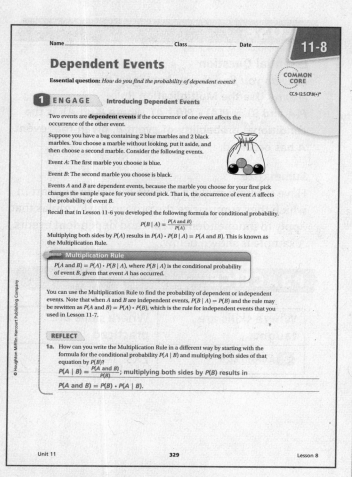

Dependent Events

Essential question: *How do you find the probability of dependent events?*

COMMON CORE
CC.9-12.S.CP.8(+)*

1 ENGAGE   Introducing Dependent Events

Two events are **dependent events** if the occurrence of one event affects the occurrence of the other event.

Suppose you have a bag containing 2 blue marbles and 2 black marbles. You choose a marble without looking, put it aside, and then choose a second marble. Consider the following events.

Event *A*: The first marble you choose is blue.

Event *B*: The second marble you choose is black.

Events *A* and *B* are dependent events, because the marble you choose for your first pick changes the sample space for your second pick. That is, the occurrence of event *A* affects the probability of event *B*.

Recall that in Lesson 11-6 you developed the following formula for conditional probability.

$$P(B \mid A) = \frac{P(A \text{ and } B)}{P(A)}$$

Multiplying both sides by $P(A)$ results in $P(A) \cdot P(B \mid A) = P(A \text{ and } B)$. This is known as the Multiplication Rule.

> **Multiplication Rule**
>
> $P(A \text{ and } B) = P(A) \cdot P(B \mid A)$, where $P(B \mid A)$ is the conditional probability of event *B*, given that event *A* has occurred.

You can use the Multiplication Rule to find the probability of dependent or independent events. Note that when *A* and *B* are independent events, $P(B \mid A) = P(B)$ and the rule may be rewritten as $P(A \text{ and } B) = P(A) \cdot P(B)$, which is the rule for independent events that you used in Lesson 11-7.

REFLECT

1a. How can you write the Multiplication Rule in a different way by starting with the formula for the conditional probability $P(A \mid B)$ and multiplying both sides of that equation by $P(B)$?

$P(A \mid B) = \frac{P(A \text{ and } B)}{P(B)}$; multiplying both sides by $P(B)$ results in

$P(A \text{ and } B) = P(B) \cdot P(A \mid B).$

2 EXAMPLE   Finding the Probability of Dependent Events

There are 5 tiles with the letters A, B, C, D, and E in a bag. You choose a tile without looking, put it aside, and then choose another tile. Find the probability that you choose a consonant followed by a vowel.

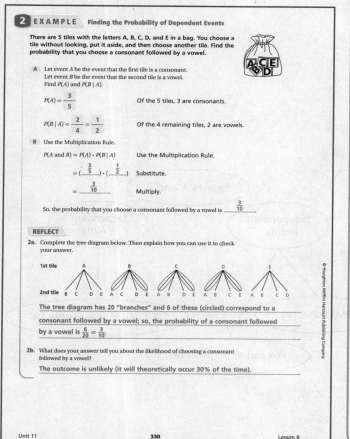

A   Let event *A* be the event that the first tile is a consonant.
Let event *B* be the event that the second tile is a vowel.
Find $P(A)$ and $P(B \mid A)$.

$P(A) = \dfrac{3}{5}$ Of the 5 tiles, 3 are consonants.

$P(B \mid A) = \dfrac{2}{4} = \dfrac{1}{2}$ Of the 4 remaining tiles, 2 are vowels.

B   Use the Multiplication Rule.

$P(A \text{ and } B) = P(A) \cdot P(B \mid A)$ Use the Multiplication Rule.

$= \left(\dfrac{3}{5}\right) \cdot \left(\dfrac{1}{2}\right)$ Substitute.

$= \dfrac{3}{10}$ Multiply.

So, the probability that you choose a consonant followed by a vowel is $\dfrac{3}{10}$.

REFLECT

2a. Complete the tree diagram below. Then explain how you can use it to check your answer.

1st tile   A   B   C   D   E

2nd tile   B C   D E   A C   E A   B D   E A   B C   E A   B C   D

The tree diagram has 20 "branches" and 6 of these (circled) correspond to a

consonant followed by a vowel; so, the probability of a consonant followed

by a vowel is $\frac{6}{20} = \frac{3}{10}$.

2b. What does your answer tell you about the likelihood of choosing a consonant followed by a vowel?

The outcome is unlikely (it will theoretically occur 30% of the time).

Teaching Strategies

The student page shows two different ways to determine the probability in the example: 1) by using the formula for the Multiplication Rule and 2) by making a tree diagram. You may also wish to tell students that they can determine the probability by thinking about permutations. The number of outcomes in the sample space is $_5P_2 = 20$. The number of favorable outcomes (that is, outcomes consisting of a consonant followed by a vowel) is $3 \cdot 2 = 6$, since there are 3 consonants and 2 vowels in the bag. Thus, the required probability is $\frac{6}{20}$, or $\frac{3}{10}$.

⋰ **MATHEMATICAL PRACTICE** **Highlighting the Standards**

Standard 1 (Make sense of problems and persevere in solving them) discusses the need for students to plan a "solution pathway" when they are confronted with a new problem. The example in this lesson can serve as an illustration to students that a single problem may have many correct solution pathways. As described in the above Teaching Strategy note, students can find the required probability by using a formula, by making a tree diagram, or by using permutations. Students could also make an organized list of all outcomes. If possible, take some time to discuss the pros and cons of the various methods so that students will feel more confident in choosing a solution pathway the next time they see a similar problem.

CLOSE

Essential Question

How do you find the probability of dependent events? Use the Multiplication Rule: $P(A \text{ and } B) = P(A) \cdot P(B \mid A)$, where $P(B \mid A)$ is the conditional probability of event B, given that event A has occurred.

Summarize

Have students make a graphic organizer or chart in which they summarize the probability formulas that apply to independent events and dependent events. A sample is shown below.

PRACTICE

Where skills are taught	Where skills are practiced
② EXAMPLE	EXS. 1–6

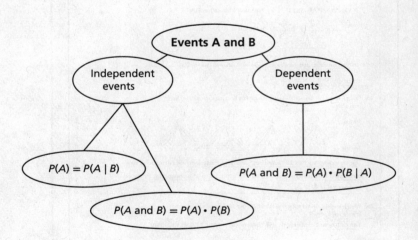

PRACTICE

1. A basket contains 6 bottles of apple juice and 8 bottles of grape juice. You choose a bottle without looking, put it aside, and then choose another bottle. What is the probability that you choose a bottle of apple juice followed by a bottle of grape juice?

$$\frac{6}{14} \cdot \frac{8}{13} = \frac{24}{91}$$

2. You have a set of ten cards that are numbered 1 through 10. You shuffle the cards and choose a card at random. You put the card aside and choose another card. What is the probability that you choose an even number followed by an odd number?

$$\frac{5}{10} \cdot \frac{5}{9} = \frac{5}{18}$$

3. A bag contains 3 red marbles and 5 green marbles. You choose a marble without looking, put it aside, and then choose another marble.

   a. What is the probability that you choose two red marbles? $\frac{3}{28}$

   b. Is the probability different if you replace the first marble before choosing the second marble? Explain.

   Yes; in this case the events are independent, so the probability is $\frac{3}{8} \cdot \frac{3}{8} = \frac{9}{64}$.

4. There are 12 boys and 14 girls in Ms. Garcia's class. She chooses a student at random to solve a geometry problem at the board. Then she chooses another student at random to check the first student's work. Is she more likely to choose a boy followed by a girl, a girl followed by a boy, or are these both equally likely? Explain.

   Equally likely; the probability of a boy followed by a girl is $\frac{12}{26} \cdot \frac{14}{25} = \frac{84}{325}$; the probability of a girl followed by a boy is $\frac{14}{26} \cdot \frac{12}{25} = \frac{84}{325}$.

5. You roll a blue number cube and a red number cube at the same time. You are interested in the probability that you roll a 2 on the blue cube and that the sum of the numbers shown on the cubes is 7.

   a. Are these dependent events or independent events? Explain.

   Dependent; rolling a 2 on the blue cube affects the probability that the sum of the numbers rolled is 7.

   b. What is the probability? $\frac{1}{36}$

6. A bag contains 4 blue marbles and 4 red marbles. You choose a marble without looking, put it aside, and then choose another marble. Is there a greater than or less than 50% chance that you choose two marbles with different colors? Explain.

   Greater than 50%; the probability of choosing blue then red is $\frac{4}{8} \cdot \frac{4}{7}$; the probability of choosing red then blue is $\frac{4}{8} \cdot \frac{4}{7}$; the sum of these probabilities is $\frac{4}{7}$, which is greater than 50%.

Making Fair Decisions

Essential question: *How can you use probability to help you make fair decisions?*

COMMON CORE **Standards for Mathematical Content**

CC.9-12.S.MD.6(+) Use probabilities to make fair decisions (e.g., drawing by lots, using a random number generator).*

Prerequisites
Probability and Set Theory, Lesson 11-1

Math Background
Students have already considered the connection between probability and fair decision-making in Lesson 11-2. In this lesson, they investigate the connection between these ideas from a somewhat different perspective. The scenario presented in this lesson is based on the famous "Problem of Points," which was originally investigated by the French mathematicians Blaise Pascal and Pierre de Fermat in 1654.

INTRODUCE

Remind students that they have already seen an example of the role probability can play in making fair decisions. In Lesson 11-2, students used probability to help them simulate choosing a random sample and a convenience sample. Explain that in this lesson, students will use probability to determine how a game prize should be divided between two competitors.

TEACH

 ENGAGE

Questioning Strategies
- At the start, does one student have a greater chance of winning than the other? Explain. **No; both students have an equal chance of winning since the game depends solely upon chance and since each student has an equal chance of winning each coin toss.**
- What is the greatest number of coin tosses that might be needed to play the game from start to finish? **39**

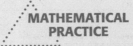 **EXPLORE**

Questioning Strategies
- How can you make an organized list of all possible results of 4 coin tosses? **First, assume there are no tails among the 4 tosses; then, assume there is 1 tail among the 4 tosses and put it in each of the possible positions; then, assume there are 2 tails; and so on.**
- How many different outcomes of 4 coin tosses are there? **16**

⋮ MATHEMATICAL PRACTICE   **Highlighting the Standards**

To address Standard 5 (Use appropriate tools strategically) you might have students think about how they can use their calculators to simulate the remainder of the game between Lee and Rory. Students can use the calculator's random-number generator to simulate flipping a coin (1 = heads, 2 = tails), keep track of their results, and pool their findings with those of other students. Over the course of many trials, students should find that their simulations lead to a win for Lee about $\frac{11}{16}$ of the time and a win for Rory about $\frac{5}{16}$ of the time.

CLOSE

Essential Question
How can you use probability to help you make fair decisions? **You can use probability to help determine how a game prize should be divided between two equally-skilled players when the game is interrupted before someone has won.**

Summarize
Have students write a journal entry in which they summarize the Problem of Points and explain how probability is used to solve the problem.

Name _____ Class _____ Date _____

Making Fair Decisions

Essential question: *How can you use probability to help you make fair decisions?*

Probability theory arose from a need to make decisions fairly. In fact, the decision-making situation that you will investigate in this lesson is based on a famous problem that was studied by the French mathematicians Blaise Pascal and Pierre de Fermat in the 17th century. Their work on the problem launched the branch of mathematics now known as probability.

COMMON
CORE
CC.9-12.S.MD.6(+)*

1 ENGAGE   Introducing the Problem of Points

Two students, Lee and Rory, find a box containing 100 baseball cards. To determine who should get the cards, they decide to play a game with the rules shown at right.

As Lee and Rory are playing the game they get interrupted and are unable to continue. When they are interrupted, Lee has 18 points and Rory has 17 points.

How should the 100 baseball cards be divided between the students given that the game was interrupted at this moment? This is known as the "Problem of Points."

> **Game Rules**
> • One of the students repeatedly tosses a coin.
> • When the coin lands heads up, Lee gets a point.
> • When the coin lands tails up, Rory gets a point.
> • The first student to reach 20 points wins the game and gets the baseball cards.

REFLECT

1a. Which student has a greater probability of winning the game if it were to continue until someone reaches 20 points? Why?

Lee has a greater probability of winning since Lee needs only 2 more points, while Rory still needs 3.

1b. If the students divide the baseball cards between themselves, which student do you think should get a greater number of cards? Why?

Lee should get a greater number of cards, because Lee had a greater number of points when the game was interrupted.

1c. Describe one way you might divide the baseball cards between Lee and Rory.

Possible answer: Since a total of 35 points were scored, Lee should get $\frac{18}{35}$ of the cards (i.e., 51 cards) and Rory should get $\frac{17}{35}$ of the cards (i.e., 49 cards).

© Houghton Mifflin Harcourt Publishing Company

Unit 11   333   Lesson 9

You may have decided that it would be fair to divide the baseball cards in proportion to the number of points each student scored, as summarized at right.

However, this solution doesn't work well if the game is interrupted very early. If Rory won the first point and ended the game, it would not be fair to give Rory all the cards just because Rory had 1 point and Lee had 0 points.

The following solution is the one proposed by Blaise Pascal and Pierre de Fermat.

> **One Method of Dividing the Cards**
> • A total of 17 + 18 = 35 points were scored.
> • Lee scored 18 points, so Lee gets $\frac{18}{35}$ of the cards.
> • Rory scored 17 points, so Rory gets $\frac{17}{35}$ of the cards.

2 EXPLORE   Solving the Problem of Points

Consider the different ways the game might have continued if it had not been interrupted.

A What is the maximum number of coin tosses that would have been needed for someone to win the game? ____4____

B Make an organized list to show all possible results of these coin tosses. The list has been started below. Look for patterns to help you complete the list.
(H = heads; T = Tails)

0T, 4H	1T, 3H	2T, 2H	3T, 1H	4T, 0H
HHHH	THHH	TTHH	TTTH	TTTT
	HTHH	THTH	TTHT	
	HHTH	THHT	THTT	
	HHHT	HTTH	HTTT	
		HTHT		
		HHTT		

C Circle the above outcomes in which Lee wins the game.

In how many outcomes would Lee win? ____11____

In how many outcomes would Rory win? ____5____

D What is the probability that Lee would have won had the game continued? $\frac{11}{16}$

What is the probability that Rory would have won had the game continued? $\frac{5}{16}$

REFLECT

2a. Based on your work in the Explore, what do you think is a fair way to divide the baseball cards?

Lee should get $\frac{11}{16}$ of the cards (i.e., 69 cards) and Rory should get $\frac{5}{16}$ of the cards (i.e., 31 cards).

© Houghton Mifflin Harcourt Publishing Company

Unit 11   334   Lesson 9

11-10 Analyzing Decisions

Essential question: *How can you use probability to help you analyze decisions?*

COMMON CORE Standards for Mathematical Content

CC.9-12.S.CP.4 Construct and interpret two-way frequency tables of data when two categories are associated with each object being classified .... *

CC.9-12.S.MD.7(+) Analyze decisions and strategies using probability concepts (e.g., product testing, medical testing ...).*

Prerequisites

Probability and Set Theory, Lesson 11-1

Mutually Exclusive and Overlapping Events, Lesson 11-5

Conditional Probability, Lesson 11-6

Independent Events, Lesson 11-7

Dependent Events, Lesson 11-8

Math Background

At the heart of this lesson is Bayes's Theorem, a probability formula named after the English mathematician Thomas Bayes (1702–1761). The theorem is useful when you want to "reverse" a conditional probability. For example, you might know the probability that someone who has tuberculosis tests positive for the disease, but you may want to know the probability that someone who tests positive actually has tuberculosis. Bayes's Theorem is generally the appropriate tool for calculating this probability. Note that the theorem can appear daunting when presented as a formula. However, any problem that can be solved by the formula can also be solved by constructing a two-way table. Because this latter method may seem more intuitive, it is the method used in the first example of the lesson.

INTRODUCE

Explain to students that they will learn how to use probability to analyze a decision. Point out that many ideas from this unit will come together in this lesson, including two-way tables, conditional probability, and complementary events.

TEACH

1 EXAMPLE

Questioning Strategies

- You start by assuming a population of 1,000,000. Does this choice affect the solution of the problem? Why or why not? **No; you can use any population because this does not affect the relevant percents and probabilities.**

- How can you check that you have filled in the two-way table correctly? **The sum of the values in the "Total" column should be 1,000,000; the sum of the values in the "Total" row should be 1,000,000.**

EXTRA EXAMPLE

You want to hand out coupons for a local restaurant to students who live off campus at a rural college. You know that 1% of the students live off campus and that 98% of the students who live off campus ride a bike. Also, 92% of the students who live on campus do not have a bike. You decide to give a coupon to any student you see who is riding a bike. Is this a good decision? Why or why not? **No; the probability that a student who is riding a bike lives off campus is only 11%.**

Teaching Strategies

The results of the first example are likely to seem unintuitive and surprising to students. To help them understand why there is only a 33.2% probability that someone who tests positive for the virus actually has the virus, point out that the vast majority of the population (99.5%) does not have the virus. Even though false positives only occur 1% of the time for this group of people, these positive results greatly outweigh the relatively smaller number of true positives for people who actually have the virus.

Name_____ Class_____ Date_____

Analyzing Decisions

Essential question: *How can you use probability to help you analyze decisions?*

You can use a two-way table and what you know about probability to help you evaluate decisions.

COMMON
CORE

CC.9-12.S.CP.4*,
CC.9-12.S.MD.7(+)*

1 EXAMPLE Analyzing a Decision

A test for a virus correctly identifies someone who has the virus (by returning a positive result) 99% of the time. The test correctly identifies someone who does not have the virus (by returning a negative result) 99% of the time. It is known that 0.5% of the population has the virus. A doctor decides to treat anyone who tests positive for the virus. Is this a good decision?

A In order to analyze the decision, you need to know the probability that someone who tests positive actually has the virus.

Make a two-way table. Begin by assuming a large overall population of 1,000,000. This value appears in the cell at the lower right, as shown.

- Use the fact that 0.5% of the population has the virus to complete the rightmost column.
- Use the fact that the test correctly identifies someone who has the virus 99% of the time to complete the "Has the virus" row.
- Use the fact that the test correctly identifies someone who does not have the virus 99% of the time to complete the "Does not have the virus" row.
- Finally, complete the bottom row of the table by finding totals.
- Check your work by verifying that the numbers in the bottom row have a sum of 1,000,000.

	Tests Positive	Tests Negative	TOTAL
Has the virus	4,950	50	5,000
Does not have the virus	9,950	985,050	995,000
TOTAL	14,900	985,100	1,000,000

B Use the table to find the the probability that someone who tests positive actually has the virus.

There is a total of ___14,900___ people who test positive.

Of these people, ___4,950___ people actually have the virus.

So, the probability that some who tests positive has the virus is ___33.2%___ .

REFLECT

1a. Do you think the doctor made a good decision in treating everyone who tests positive for the virus? Why or why not?

Possible answer: No; there is only a 33.2% probability that someone who tests

positive actually has the virus.

The method that you used in the example can be generalized. The generalization is known as Bayes's Theorem.

Bayes's Theorem

Given two events A and B with $P(B) \neq 0$, $P(A \mid B) = \dfrac{P(B \mid A) \cdot P(A)}{P(B)}$.

The following example shows how you can use Bayes's Theorem to help you analyze a decision.

2 EXAMPLE Using Bayes's Theorem

The principal of a school plans a school picnic for June 2. A few days before the event, the weather forecast predicts rain for June 2, so the principal decides to cancel the picnic. Consider the following information.

- In the school's town, the probability that it rains on any day in June is 3%.
- When it rains, the forecast correctly predicts rain 90% of the time.
- When it does not rain, the forecast incorrectly predicts rain 5% of the time.

Do you think the principal made a good decision? Why or why not?

A Let event A be the event that it rains on a day in June. Let event B be the event that the forecast predicts rain. To evaluate the decision to cancel the picnic, you want to know $P(A \mid B)$, the probability that it rains given that the forecast predicts rain.

In order use Bayes's Theorem to calculate $P(A \mid B)$, you must find $P(B \mid A)$, $P(A)$, and $P(B)$. For convenience, find these probabilities as decimals.

$P(B \mid A)$ is the probability of a prediction of rain given that it actually rains. This value is provided in the given information.

$P(B \mid A) =$ ___0.9___

$P(A)$ is the probability of rain on any day in June. This value is also provided in the given information.

$P(A) =$ ___0.03___

$P(B)$ is the probability of a prediction of rain. This value is not provided in the given information. In order to calculate $P(B)$, make a tree diagram, as shown on the following page.

2 EXAMPLE

Questioning Strategies

- What conditional probability do you need to know to evaluate the principal's decision? **You need to know the probability that it rains given a forecast of rain.**

- How can you find the missing probabilities on the right side of the tree diagram? **Use the fact that the sum of the probabilities of complementary events is 1, as well as the given information that the forecast predicts rain 5% of the time when it does not rain.**

EXTRA EXAMPLE

A veterinarian knows that 1.5% of all dogs have a particular condition. According to a recent study, 91% of dogs that have the condition also have patches of missing fur. Also, 3% of dogs that do not have the condition have patches of missing fur. The veterinarian sees a dog which has patches of missing fur and decides to treat the dog for the condition. Is this a good decision? Why or why not? **No; the probability that a dog which has patches of missing fur has the condition is only 31.6%.**

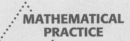

MATHEMATICAL PRACTICE **Highlighting the Standards**

Standard 4 (Model with mathematics) discusses the need for students to interpret mathematical results in the context of the situation. This lesson offers many opportunities for students to practice this skill. When students use Bayes's Theorem to find a conditional probability, the specific value they find for the probability is less important than understanding what this value means. In the problems presented in this lesson, interpreting the mathematical result is the essential step in determining whether a good decision was made.

CLOSE

Essential Question

How can you use probability to help you analyze decisions? **You can use a two-way table and/or Bayes's Theorem to use given information to calculate a conditional probability. Then, you can use the conditional probability to evaluate a decision that may have been made based on the given information.**

Summarize

Have students write a journal entry in which they compare two methods of analyzing a decision: 1) making a two-way table and 2) using Bayes's Theorem. Prompt students to describe the pros and cons of each method.

PRACTICE

Where skills are taught	Where skills are practiced
1 EXAMPLE	EXS. 1, 3
2 EXAMPLE	EX. 2

Exercise 4: Students use reasoning and algebra to justify the formula in Bayes's Theorem.

B Make a tree diagram to find $P(B)$. The values on the "branches" show the probability of the associated event. Complete the right side of the tree diagram by writing the correct probabilities. Remember that the probabilities of events that are complements must add up to 1.

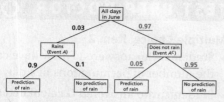

All days in June

0.03   0.97

Rains (Event A)   Does not rain (Event A^c)

0.9   0.1   0.05   0.95

Prediction of rain   No prediction of rain   Prediction of rain   No prediction of rain

$P(B)$ is the probability that there is a prediction of rain when it actually rains plus the probability that there is a prediction of rain when it does not rain.

$P(B) = P(A) \cdot P(B|A) + P(A^c) \cdot P(B|A^c)$

$= 0.03 \cdot 0.9 + \underline{0.97} \cdot \underline{0.05}$ Substitute values from the tree diagram.

$= \underline{0.0755}$ Simplify.

C Use Bayes's Theorem to find $P(A|B)$.

$P(A|B) = \frac{P(B|A) \cdot P(A)}{P(B)}$ Use Bayes's Theorem.

$= \frac{\underline{0.9} \cdot \underline{0.03}}{0.0755}$ Substitute.

$\approx \underline{0.358}$ Simplify. Round to the nearest thousandth.

So, as a percent, the probability that it rains given that the forecast predicts rain is approximately $\underline{35.8\%}$.

REFLECT

2a. Do you think the principal made a good decision when canceling the picnic? Why or why not?

No; the probability that it actually rains on June 2 given a forecast of rain

is only 35.8%

2b. What would $P(A)$, the probability that it rains on any day in June, have to be for the value of $P(A|B)$ to be greater than 50%? Explain.

$P(A)$ would have to be greater than about 5.26% for $P(A|B)$ to exceed 50%;

let $P(A) = x$ and $P(B) = 0.5$, then solve $0.5 = \frac{0.9 \cdot x}{x \cdot 0.9 + (1-x) \cdot 0.05}$.

Unit 11   337   Lesson 10

PRACTICE

1. It is known that 2% of the population has a certain allergy. A test correctly identifies people who have the allergy 98% of the time. The test correctly identifies people who do not have the allergy 94% of the time. A doctor decides that anyone who tests positive for the allergy should begin taking anti-allergy medication. Do you think this a good decision? Why or why not?

No; there is only a 25% probability that someone who tests positive actually

has the allergy.

2. Company X supplies 20% of the MP3 players to an electronics store and Company Y supplies the remainder. The manager of the store knows that 80% of the MP3 players in the last shipment from Company X were defective, while only 5% of the MP3 players from Company Y were defective. The manager chooses an MP3 player at random and finds that it is defective. The manager decides that the MP3 player must have come from Company X. Do you think this is a good decision? Why or why not?

Yes; there is an 80% probability that the defective MP3 player came from

Company X.

3. You can solve Example 2 using a two-way table. Consider a population of 10,000 randomly chosen June days. Complete the table. Then explain how to find the probability that it rains given that the forecast predicts rain.

	Rains	Does not rain	TOTAL
Prediction of rain	270	485	755
No prediction of rain	30	9215	9245
TOTAL	300	9700	10,000

Using the "Prediction of rain" row, the probability that it rains given that the

forecast predicts rain is $\frac{270}{755} \approx 35.8\%$.

4. Explain how to derive Bayes's Theorem using the Multiplication Rule.
(*Hint:* The Multiplication Rule can be written as $P(A \text{ and } B) = P(B) \cdot P(A|B)$ or as $P(A \text{ and } B) = P(A) \cdot P(B|A)$.)

Setting the right sides of the two versions of the Multiplication Rule equal to

each other yields $P(B) \cdot P(A|B) = P(A) \cdot P(B|A)$. Dividing both sides by $P(B)$ gives

Bayes's Theorem.

Unit 11   338   Lesson 10

© Houghton Mifflin Harcourt Publishing Company

Notes

UNIT 11 TEST PREP

COMMON CORE CORRELATION

Standard	Items
CC.9-12.S.CP.1*	1
CC.9-12.S.CP.2*	8
CC.9-12.S.CP.3*	9
CC.9-12.S.CP.4*	5
CC.9-12.S.CP.5*	5
CC.9-12.S.CP.6*	6
CC.9-12.S.CP.7*	4
CC.9-12.S.CP.8(+)*	7
CC.9-12.S.CP.9(+)*	2, 3
CC.9-12.S.MD.6(+)*	11
CC.9-12.S.MD.7(+)*	10

TEST PREP DOCTOR ✚

Multiple Choice: Item 2
- Students who answered **F** may have calculated the number of permutations of 4 players.
- Students who answered **G** calculated the number of combinations of 9 players taken 4 at a time, rather than the number of permutations.
- Students who answered **H** may have simply multiplied the values that are given in the problem ($9 \cdot 4 \cdot 5 = 180$).

Multiple Choice: Item 6
- Students who answered **F** may have found the probability that a visitor to the movie theater purchases a snack and pays for a discount admission.
- Students who answered **G** may have found the probability that a visitor to the movie theater pays for a discount admission given that they purchase a snack.
- Students who answered **J** may have found the probability that a visitor to the movie theater pays for a regular admission given that they purchase a snack.

Free Response: Item 11
- Students who answered that Naomi should get 47 fruit chews and Kayla should get 33 fruit chews may have divided the prize proportionally according to the number of points already won by each player. This does not take into account the number of points needed to win the game, so it is not a fair way to divide the prize.
- Students who answered that Naomi should get 60 fruit chews and Kayla should get 20 fruit chews may have tried to use the solution method in Lesson 11-9, but may have incorrectly determined that there are only 4 possible ways the game could have been played to its conclusion:

  T T H (Naomi wins)
  T H T (Naomi wins)
  H T T (Naomi wins)
  T T T (Kayla wins)

Name _____ Class _____ Date _____

MULTIPLE CHOICE

1. You spin a spinner with 10 equal sections that are numbered 1 through 10. Event A is rolling an odd number. Event B is rolling a number greater than 5. What is $P(A \cap B)$?

   A. $\frac{1}{8}$ C. $\frac{1}{2}$

   B. $\frac{1}{5}$ D. $\frac{4}{5}$

2. There are 9 players on a basketball team. For a team photo, 4 of the players are seated on a row of chairs and 5 players stand behind them. In how many different ways can 4 players be arranged on the row of chairs?

   F. 24   H. 180

   G. 126   J. 3024

3. There are 5 peaches and 4 nectarines in a bowl. You randomly choose 2 pieces of fruit to pack in your lunch. What is the probability that you choose 2 peaches?

   A. $\frac{5}{36}$ C. $\frac{2}{5}$

   B. $\frac{5}{18}$ D. $\frac{5}{9}$

4. You shuffle the cards shown below and choose one at random. What is the probability that you choose a gray card or an even number?

1	2	4	5	7	9
10	11	13	16	18	19

   F. $\frac{1}{10}$ H. $\frac{5}{6}$

   G. $\frac{35}{144}$ J. 1

The two-way table provides data about 240 randomly chosen people who visit a movie theater. Use the table for Items 5 and 6.

	Discount Admission	Regular Admission	TOTAL
Purchases a snack	24	72	96
Purchases no snack	36	108	144
TOTAL	60	180	240

5. Consider the following events.

   Event A: Pays for a regular admission.
   Event B: Purchases a snack.

   Which is the best description of the two events?

   A. complementary events

   B. dependent events

   C. independent events

   D. mutually exclusive events

6. What is the probability that a visitor to the movie theater purchases a snack given that the visitor pays for a discount admission?

   F. 0.1   H. 0.4

   G. 0.25   J. 0.75

7. A bag contains 8 yellow marbles and 4 blue marbles. You choose a marble, put it aside, and then choose another marble. What is the probability that you choose two yellow marbles?

   A. $\frac{7}{18}$ C. $\frac{4}{9}$

   B. $\frac{14}{33}$ D. $\frac{2}{3}$

8. Events A and B are independent events. Which of the following must be true?

   F. $P(A \text{ and } B) = P(A) \cdot P(B)$

   G. $P(A \text{ and } B) = P(A) + P(B)$

   H. $P(A) = P(B)$

   J. $P(B \mid A) = P(A \mid B)$

9. Which expression can you use to calculate the conditional probability of event A given that event B has occurred?

   A. $P(A) + P(B) - P(A \text{ and } B)$

   B. $P(B) \cdot P(A \mid B)$

   C. $\frac{P(A \text{ and } B)}{P(B)}$

   D. $\frac{P(A)}{P(B)}$

FREE RESPONSE

10. It is known that 1% of all mice in a laboratory have a genetic mutation. A test for the mutation correctly identifies mice that have the mutation 98% of the time. The test correctly identifies mice that do not have the mutation 96% of the time. A lab assistant tests a mouse and finds that the mouse tests positive for the mutation. The lab assistant decides that the mouse must have the mutation. Is this a good decision? Explain.

    No; there is only a 19.8% probability that a mouse that tests positive for the mutation actually has the mutation.

11. Two students, Naomi and Kayla, play a game using the rules shown below. The winner of the game gets a box of 80 fruit chews.

    Game Rules
    - One student repeatedly tosses a coin.
    - When the coin lands heads up, Naomi gets a point.
    - When the coin lands tails up, Kayla gets a point.
    - The first student to reach 8 points wins the game and gets the fruit chews.

    The game gets interrupted when Naomi has 7 points and Kayla has 5 points. How should the 80 fruit chews be divided between the students given that the game was interrupted at this moment? Explain why your answer provides a fair way to divide the fruit chews.

    Naomi should get $\frac{7}{8}$ of the fruit chews (i.e., 70 fruit chews) and Kayla should get $\frac{1}{8}$ of the fruit chews (i.e., 10 fruit chews). The game would end in at most three additional coin tosses. There are 8 possible outcomes of these tosses: 7 result in a win for Naomi, while 1 results in a win for Kayla.

Formula Reference

Postulates, Theorems, and Formulas

Lesson	Postulates, Theorems, and Formulas
1-2	**The Distance Formula** The distance between two points (x_1, y_1) and (x_2, y_2) in the coordinate plane is $\sqrt{(x_2 - x_1)^2 + (y_2 - y_1)^2}$.
1-3	**The Midpoint Formula** The midpoint M of $\overline{AB}$ with endpoints $A(x_1, y_1)$ and $B(x_2, y_2)$ is given by $M\left(\frac{x_1 + x_2}{2}, \frac{y_1 + y_2}{2}\right)$.
1-6	**Properties of Equality** Addition Property of Equality: If $a = b$, then $a + c = b + c$. Subtraction Property of Equality: If $a = b$, then $a - c = b - c$. Multiplication Property of Equality: If $a = b$, then $ac = bc$. Division Property of Equality: If $a = b$ and $c \neq 0$, then $\frac{a}{c} = \frac{b}{c}$. Reflexive Property of Equality: $a = a$ Symmetric Property of Equality: If $a = b$, then $b = a$. Transitive Property of Equality: If $a = b$ and $b = c$, then $a = c$. Substitution Property of Equality: If $a = b$, then b can be substituted for a in any expression.
1-6	**Segment Addition Postulate** If B is between A and C, then $AB + BC = AC$.
1-6	**Common Segments Theorem** If A, B, C, and D are collinear, as shown in the figure, with $AB = CD$, then $AC = BD$.
1-6	**Angle Addition Postulate** If D is in the interior of $\angle ABC$, then $m\angle ABD + m\angle DBC = m\angle ABC$.
1-6	**Linear Pair Theorem** If two angles form a linear pair, then they are supplementary.
1-6	**Vertical Angles Theorem** If two angles are vertical angles, then they have equal measures.
1-7	**Same-Side Interior Angles Postulate** If two parallel lines are cut by a transversal, then the pairs of same-side interior angles are supplementary.
1-7	**Alternate Interior Angles Theorem** If two parallel lines are cut by a transversal, then the pairs of alternate interior angles have the same measure.
1-7	**Corresponding Angles Theorem** If two parallel lines are cut by a transversal, then the pairs of corresponding angles have the same measure.
1-7	**Converse of the Same-Side Interior Angles Postulate** If two lines are cut by a transversal so that a pair of same-side interior angles are supplementary, then the lines are parallel.
1-7	**Converse of the Alternate Interior Angles Theorem** If two lines are cut by a transversal so that a pair of alternate interior angles have the same measure, then the lines are parallel.
1-7	**Converse of the Corresponding Angles Theorem** If two lines are cut by a transversal so that a pair of corresponding angles have the same measure, then the lines are parallel.

Lesson	Postulates, Theorems, and Formulas
1-7	**Equal-Measure Linear Pair Theorem** If two intersecting lines form a linear pair of angles with equal measures, then the lines are perpendicular.
2-1	**Properties of Rigid Motions (Isometries)** Rigid motions preserve distance, angle measure, betweenness, and collinearity. If a figure is determined by certain points, then its image under a rigid motion is determined by the images of those points.
2-3	**Angle Bisection Theorem** If a line bisects an angle, then each side of the angle is the image of the other under a reflection across the line.
2-3	**Converse of the Angle Bisection Theorem** If each side of an angle is the image of the other under a reflection across a line, then the line bisects the angle.
2-3	**Reflected Points on an Angle Theorem** If two points of an angle are located the same distance from the vertex but on different sides of the angle, then the points are images of each other under a reflection across the line that bisects the angle.
2-4	**Perpendicular Bisector Theorem** If a point is on the perpendicular bisector of a segment, then it is equidistant from the endpoints of the segment.
2-4	**Converse of the Perpendicular Bisector Theorem** If a point is equidistant from the endpoints of a segment, then it lies on the perpendicular bisector of the segment.
3-1	**Properties of Congruence** Reflexive Property of Congruence: $\overline{AB} \cong \overline{AB}$ Symmetric Property of Congruence: If $\overline{AB} \cong \overline{CD}$, then $\overline{CD} \cong \overline{AB}$. Transitive Property of Congruence: If $\overline{AB} \cong \overline{CD}$ and $\overline{CD} \cong \overline{EF}$, then $\overline{AB} \cong \overline{EF}$.
3-2	**Corresponding Parts of Congruent Triangles are Congruent Theorem (CPCTC)** If two triangles are congruent, then corresponding sides are congruent and corresponding angles are congruent.
3-3	**SSS Congruence Criterion** If three sides of one triangle are congruent to three sides of another triangle, then the triangles are congruent.
3-3	**SAS Congruence Criterion** If two sides and the included angle of one triangle are congruent to two sides and the included angle of another triangle, then the triangles are congruent.
3-3	**ASA Congruence Criterion** If two angles and the included side of one triangle are congruent to two angles and the included side of another triangle, then the triangles are congruent.
3-5	**Triangle Sum Theorem** The sum of the angle measures in a triangle is 180°.
3-5	**Parallel Postulate** Through a point P not on a line ℓ, there is exactly one line parallel to ℓ.
3-5	**Exterior Angle Theorem** The measure of an exterior angle of a triangle is equal to the sum of the measures of its remote interior angles.
3-5	**Quadrilateral Sum Theorem** The sum of the angle measures in a quadrilateral is 360°.
3-6	**Isosceles Triangle Theorem** The base angles of an isosceles triangle are congruent.

Lesson	Postulates, Theorems, and Formulas
3-6	**AAS Congruence Criterion** If two angles and a non-included side of one triangle are congruent to two angles and the corresponding non-included side of another triangle, then the triangles are congruent.
3-6	**Converse of the Isosceles Triangle Theorem** If two angles of a triangle are congruent, then the sides opposite them are congruent.
3-8	**Midsegment Theorem** A midsegment of a triangle is parallel to the third side of the triangle and is half as long as the third side.
3-9	**Concurrency of Medians Theorem** The medians of a triangle are concurrent.
4-2	**Theorem** If a quadrilateral is a parallelogram, then opposite sides are congruent.
4-2	**Theorem** If a quadrilateral is a parallelogram, then opposite angles are congruent.
4-3	**Theorem** If a quadrilateral is a parallelogram, then the diagonals bisect each other.
4-4	**Opposite Sides Criterion for a Parallelogram** If both pairs of opposite sides of a quadrilateral are congruent, then the quadrilateral is a parallelogram.
4-4	**Opposite Angles Criterion for a Parallelogram** If both pairs of opposite angles of a quadrilateral are congruent, then the quadrilateral is a parallelogram.
4-4	**Bisecting Diagonals Criterion for a Parallelogram** If the diagonals of a quadrilateral bisect each other, then the quadrilateral is a parallelogram.
4-5	**Rectangle Theorem** A rectangle is a parallelogram with congruent diagonals.
4-5	**Properties of Rhombuses** If a quadrilateral is a rhombus, then the quadrilateral is a parallelogram, the diagonals are perpendicular, and each diagonal bisects a pair of opposite angles.
5-1	**Properties of Dilations** • Dilations preserve angle measure. • Dilations preserve betweenness. • Dilations preserve collinearity. • A dilation maps a line not passing through the center of dilation to a parallel line and leaves a line passing through the center unchanged. • The dilation of a line segment is longer or shorter in the ratio given by the scale factor.
5-3	**Theorem** All circles are similar.
5-4	**AA Similarity Criterion** If two angles of one triangle are congruent to two angles of another triangle, then the triangles are similar.
5-4	**SAS Similarity Criterion** If two sides of one triangle are proportional to two sides of another triangle and their included angles are congruent, then the triangles are similar.
5-6	**Triangle Proportionality Theorem** If a line parallel to one side of a triangle intersects the other two sides, then it divides those sides proportionally.
5-6	**Converse of the Triangle Proportionality Theorem** If a line divides two sides of a triangle proportionally, then it is parallel to the third side.

Lesson	Postulates, Theorems, and Formulas
5-7	**Pythagorean Theorem** In a right triangle, the sum of the squares of the lengths of the legs is equal to the square of the length of the hypotenuse.
6-5	**Area of a Triangle** The area A of $\triangle ABC$ is given by $A = \frac{1}{2} ab \sin C$.
6-6	**Law of Sines** For $\triangle ABC$, $\frac{\sin A}{a} = \frac{\sin B}{b} = \frac{\sin C}{c}$.
6-7	**Law of Cosines** For $\triangle ABC$, $a^2 = b^2 + c^2 - 2bc \cos A$, $b^2 = a^2 + c^2 - 2ac \cos B$, and $c^2 = a^2 + b^2 - 2ab \cos C$.
7-1	**Arc Addition Postulate** The measure of an arc formed by two adjacent arcs is the sum of the measures of the two arcs.
7-1	**Inscribed Angle Theorem** The measure of an inscribed angle is half the measure of its intercepted arc.
7-1	**Theorem** The endpoints of a diameter lie on an inscribed angle if and only if the inscribed angle is a right angle.
7-4	**Inscribed Quadrilateral Theorem** If a quadrilateral is inscribed in a circle, then its opposite angles are supplementary.
7-4	**Converse of the Inscribed Quadrilateral Theorem** If the opposite angles of a quadrilateral are supplementary, then the quadrilateral can be inscribed in a circle.
7-5	**Tangent-Radius Theorem** If a line is tangent to a circle, then it is perpendicular to the radius drawn to the point of tangency.
7-5	**Converse of the Tangent-Radius Theorem** If a line is perpendicular to a radius of a circle at a point on the circle, then the line is a tangent to the circle.
7-5	**Circumscribed Angle Theorem** A circumscribed angle of a circle and its associated central angle are supplementary.
8-1	**Equation of a Circle** The equation of a circle with center (h, k) and radius r is $(x - h)^2 + (y - k)^2 = r^2$.
8-2	**Equation of a Parabola** The equation of the parabola with focus $(0, p)$ and directrix $y = -p$ is $y = \frac{1}{4p} x^2$.
8-4	**Slope Criterion for Parallel Lines** Two non-vertical lines are parallel if and only if they have the same slope.
8-5	**Slope Criterion for Perpendicular Lines** Two non-vertical lines are perpendicular if and only if the product of their slopes is -1.
9-3	**Circumference of a Circle** The circumference C of a circle with radius r is given by $C = 2\pi r$.
9-4	**Arc Length** The arc length s of an arc with measure $m°$ and radius r is given by the formula $s = \frac{m}{360} \cdot 2\pi r$.
9-5	**Area of a Circle** The area A of a circle with radius r is given by $A = \pi r^2$.

Lesson	Postulates, Theorems, and Formulas
9-5	**Area of a Sector** The area A of a sector of a circle with a central angle of $m°$ and radius r is given by $A = \frac{m}{360} \cdot \pi r^2$.
10-2	**Volume of a Cylinder** The volume V of a cylinder with base area B and height h is given by $V = Bh$ (or $V = \pi r^2 h$, where r is the radius of a base).
10-2	**Cavalieri's Principle** If two solids have the same height and the same cross-sectional area at every level, then the two solids have the same volume.
10-3	**Postulate** Pyramids that have equal base areas and equal heights have equal volumes.
10-3	**Volume of a Pyramid** The volume V of a pyramid with base area B and height h is given by $V = \frac{1}{3} Bh$.
10-4	**Volume of a Cone** The volume V of a cone with base area B and height h is given by $V = \frac{1}{3} Bh$ (or $V = \frac{1}{3} \pi r^2 h$, where r is the radius of the base).
10-5	**Volume of a Sphere** The volume V of a sphere with radius r is given by $V = \frac{4}{3} \pi r^3$.
11-1	**Probabilities of an Event and Its Complement** The probability of an event and the probability of its complement have a sum of 1. So, the probability of an event is one minus the probability of its complement. Also, the probability of the complement of an event is one minus the probability of the event.
11-3	**Permutations** The number of permutations of n objects taken r at a time is given by $_nP_r = \frac{n!}{(n-r)!}$.
11-4	**Combinations** The number of combinations of n objects taken r at a time is given by $_nC_r = \frac{n!}{r!(n-r)!}$.
11-5	**Mutually Exclusive Events** If A and B are mutually exclusive events, then $P(A \text{ or } B) = P(A) + P(B)$.
11-5	**Addition Rule** $P(A \text{ or } B) = P(A) + P(B) - P(A \text{ and } B)$.
11-6	**Conditional Probability** The conditional probability of B given A (the probability that event B occurs given that event A occurs) is given by the formula $P(B|A) = \frac{P(A \text{ and } B)}{P(A)}$.
11-7	**Probability of Independent Events** A and B are independent events if and only if $P(A \text{ and } B) = P(A) \cdot P(B)$.
11-8	**Multiplication Rule** $P(A \text{ and } B) = P(A) \cdot P(B|A)$, where $P(B|A)$ is the conditional probability of event B, given that event A has occurred.
11-10	**Bayes's Theorem** Given two events A and B with $P(B) \neq 0$, $P(A|B) = \frac{P(B|A) \cdot P(A)}{P(B)}$.

Correlation of *On Core Mathematics* to the Common Core State Standards

Standards	Algebra 1	Geometry	Algebra 2
Number and Quantity			
The Real Number System			
CC.9-12.N.RN.1 Explain how the definition of the meaning of rational exponents follows from extending the properties of integer exponents to those values, allowing for a notation for radicals in terms of rational exponents.			Lesson 1-2
CC.9-12.N.RN.2 Rewrite expressions involving radicals and rational exponents using the properties of exponents.			Lesson 1-2
CC.9-12.N.RN.3 Explain why the sum or product of two rational numbers is rational; that the sum of a rational number and an irrational number is irrational; and that the product of a nonzero rational number and an irrational number is irrational.			Lesson 1-1
Quantities			
CC.9-12.N.Q.1 Use units as a way to understand problems and to guide the solution of multi-step problems; choose and interpret units consistently in formulas; choose and interpret the scale and the origin in graphs and data displays.*	Lessons 1-1, 1-2, 1-3, 1-5, 1-6, 2-3, 2-8, 3-6, 4-2, 4-3, 7-6		Lesson 2-6
CC.9-12.N.Q.2 Define appropriate quantities for the purpose of descriptive modeling.*	Lessons 1-3, 1-4, 2-3, 2-8, 3-6, 7-6		
CC.9-12.N.Q.3 Choose a level of accuracy appropriate to limitations on measurement when reporting quantities.*		**Lesson 9-1**	
The Complex Number System			
CC.9-12.N.CN.1 Know there is a complex number i such that $i^2 = -1$, and every complex number has the form $a + bi$ with a and b real.			Lesson 1-3
CC.9-12.N.CN.2 Use the relation $i^2 = -1$ and the commutative, associative, and distributive properties to add, subtract, and multiply complex numbers.			Lesson 1-3
CC.9-12.N.CN.3(+) Find the conjugate of a complex number; use conjugates to find moduli and quotients of complex numbers.			Lesson 1-4

(+) Advanced   * = Also a Modeling Standard

Standards	Algebra 1	Geometry	Algebra 2
CC.9-12.N.CN.7 Solve quadratic equations with real coefficients that have complex solutions.			Lesson 1-5
CC.9-12.N.CN.9(+) Know the Fundamental Theorem of Algebra; show that it is true for quadratic polynomials.			Lesson 3-10
Algebra			
Seeing Structure in Expressions			
CC.9-12.A.SSE.1 Interpret expressions that represent a quantity in terms of its context.* **a.** Interpret parts of an expression, such as terms, factors, and coefficients. **b.** Interpret complicated expressions by viewing one or more of their parts as a single entity.	Lessons 1-1, 1-2, 1-3, 2-8		Lessons 2-6, 3-5, 3-11, 4-4, 4-5, 9-4, 9-5
CC.9-12.A.SSE.2 Use the structure of an expression to identify ways to rewrite it.	Lessons 1-2, 1-3, 2-1, 2-2, 8-1		Lessons 3-9, 3-10
CC.9-12.A.SSE.3 Choose and produce an equivalent form of an expression to reveal and explain properties of the quantity represented by the expression. **a.** Factor a quadratic expression to reveal the zeros of the function it defines. **b.** Complete the square in a quadratic expression to reveal the maximum or minimum value of the function it defines. **c.** Use the properties of exponents to transform expressions for exponential functions.	Lessons 8-2, 8-3, 8-10		Lessons 2-4, 2-5, 6-4, 6-6
CC.9-12.A.SSE.4 Derive the formula for the sum of a finite geometric series (when the common ratio is not 1), and use the formula to solve problems.			Lessons 9-4, 9-5
Arithmetic with Polynomials and Rational Expressions			
CC.9-12.A.APR.1 Understand that polynomials form a system analogous to the integers, namely, they are closed under the operations of addition, subtraction, and multiplication; add, subtract, and multiply polynomials.	Lessons 4-6, 8-1		Lessons 3-5, 3-6, 3-7, 3-8
CC.9-12.A.APR.2 Know and apply the Remainder Theorem: For a polynomial $p(x)$ and a number a, the remainder on division by $x - a$ is $p(a)$, so $p(a) = 0$ if and only if $(x - a)$ is a factor of $p(x)$.			Lesson 3-8
CC.9-12.A.APR.3 Identify zeros of polynomials when suitable factorizations are available, and use the zeros to construct a rough graph of the function defined by the polynomial.			Lesson 3-9
CC.9-12.A.APR.4 Prove polynomial identities and use them to describe numerical relationships.			Lesson 3-6

(+) Advanced   * = Also a Modeling Standard

Standards	Algebra 1	Geometry	Algebra 2
CC.9-12.A.APR.5(+) Know and apply the Binomial Theorem for the expansion of $(x + y)^n$ in powers of x and y for a positive integer n, where x and y are any numbers, with coefficients determined for example by Pascal's Triangle. (The Binomial Theorem can be proved by mathematical induction or by a combinatorial argument.)			Lesson 3-7
CC.9-12.A.APR.6 Rewrite simple rational expressions in different forms; write $a(x)/b(x)$ in the form $q(x) + r(x)/b(x)$, where $a(x)$, $b(x)$, $q(x)$, and $r(x)$ are polynomials with the degree of $r(x)$ less than the degree of $b(x)$, using inspection, long division, or, for the more complicated examples, a computer algebra system.			Lesson 4-3
CC.9-12.A.APR.7(+) Understand that rational expressions form a system analogous to the rational numbers, closed under addition, subtraction, multiplication, and division by a nonzero rational expression; add, subtract, multiply, and divide rational expressions.			Lessons 4-4, 4-5
Creating Equations			
CC.9-12.A.CED.1 Create equations and inequalities in one variable and use them to solve problems.*	Lessons 1-4, 2-3, 5-5, 6-5, 7-4, 7-5, 8-3, 8-7		Lessons 3-11, 4-6, 6-7, 7-4
CC.9-12.A.CED.2 Create equations in two or more variables to represent relationships between quantities; graph equations on coordinate axes with labels and scales.*	Lessons 2-3, 2-5, 2-8, 3-6, 4-2, 4-3, 4-5, 4-6, 5-1, 5-5, 5-6, 5-8, 6-1, 6-2, 6-3, 6-4, 6-5, 6-6, 7-1, 7-2, 7-3, 7-4, 7-6, 8-9, 8-10		Lessons 2-3, 2-4, 2-5, 2-6, 3-9, 3-11, 4-1, 4-2, 4-3, 4-7, 5-1, 5-2, 5-3, 5-5, 5-6, 6-2, 6-3, 6-4, 6-5, 6-6, 7-5, 8-9
CC.9-12.A.CED.3 Represent constraints by equations or inequalities, and by systems of equations and/or inequalities, and interpret solutions as viable or nonviable options in a modeling context.*	Lessons 1-4, 2-3, 2-8, 3-6		Lessons 2-6, 3-11, 9-5
CC.9-12.A.CED.4 Rearrange formulas to highlight a quantity of interest, using the same reasoning as in solving equations.*	Lesson 2-5		Lesson 7-5
Reasoning with Equations and Inequalities			
CC.9-12.A.REI.1. Explain each step in solving a simple equation as following from the equality of numbers asserted at the previous step, starting from the assumption that the original equation has a solution. Construct a viable argument to justify a solution method.	Lessons 2-1, 2-2, 2-4		
CC.9-12.A.REI.2 Solve simple rational and radical equations in one variable, and give examples showing how extraneous solutions may arise.			Lessons 4-6, 5-7
CC.9-12.A.REI.3 Solve linear equations and inequalities in one variable, including equations with coefficients represented by letters.	Lessons 2-1, 2-2, 2-3, 2-4		

(+) Advanced   * = Also a Modeling Standard

Standards	Algebra 1	Geometry	Algebra 2
CC.9-12.A.REI.4 Solve quadratic equations in one variable. **a.** Use the method of completing the square to transform any quadratic equation in x into an equation of the form $(x - p)^2 = q$ that has the same solutions. Derive the quadratic formula from this form. **b.** Solve quadratic equations by inspection (e.g., for $x^2 = 49$), taking square roots, completing the square, the quadratic formula and factoring, as appropriate to the initial form of the equation. Recognize when the quadratic formula gives complex solutions and write them as $a \pm bi$ for real numbers a and b.	Lessons 7-5, 8-2, 8-3, 8-4, 8-5, 8-6, 8-7, 8-9, 8-10		Lesson 1-5
CC.9-12.A.REI.5 Prove that, given a system of two equations in two variables, replacing one equation by the sum of that equation and a multiple of the other produces a system with the same solutions.	Lesson 3-4		
CC.9-12.A.REI.6 Solve systems of linear equations exactly and approximately (e.g., with graphs), focusing on pairs of linear equations in two variables.	Lessons 3-1, 3-2, 3-3, 3-4, 3-6		
CC.9-12.A.REI.7 Solve a simple system consisting of a linear equation and a quadratic equation in two variables algebraically and graphically.	Lesson 8-9	**Lesson 8-7**	
CC.9-12.A.REI.10 Understand that the graph of an equation in two variables is the set of all its solutions plotted in the coordinate plane, often forming a curve (which could be a line).	Lessons 2-6, 2-7		
CC.9-12.A.REI.11 Explain why the x-coordinates of the points where the graphs of the equations $y = f(x)$ and $y = g(x)$ intersect are the solutions of the equation $f(x) = g(x)$; find the solutions approximately, e.g., using technology to graph the functions, make tables of values, or find successive approximations. Include cases where $f(x)$ and/or $g(x)$ are linear, polynomial, rational, absolute value, exponential, and logarithmic functions.*	Lessons 4-5, 5-5, 5-8, 6-5, 7-4		Lessons 4-6, 5-7, 6-7, 7-4
CC.9-12.A.REI.12 Graph the solutions to a linear inequality in two variables as a half-plane (excluding the boundary in the case of a strict inequality), and graph the solution set to a system of linear inequalities in two variables as the intersection of the corresponding half-planes.	Lessons 2-6, 2-7, 3-5, 3-6		
Functions			
Interpreting Functions			
CC.9-12.F.IF.1 Understand that a function from one set (called the domain) to another set (called the range) assigns to each element of the domain exactly one element of the range. If f is a function and x is an element of its domain, then $f(x)$ denotes the output of f corresponding to the input x. The graph of f is the graph of the equation $y = f(x)$.	Lessons 1-5, 1-6, 4-2, 4-7, 5-2		Lesson 8-3

(+) Advanced   * = Also a Modeling Standard

Standards	Algebra 1	Geometry	Algebra 2
CC.9-12.F.IF.2 Use function notation, evaluate functions for inputs in their domains, and interpret statements that use function notation in terms of a context.	Lessons 1-5, 1-6, 4-1, 4-2, 4-7, 5-1, 6-1, 6-2, 6-3, 6-4, 6-6, 7-1, 7-2, 7-3, 7-6, 8-10		Lessons 2-1, 2-2, 2-3, 2-4, 2-5, 2-6, 3-4, 4-1, 4-2, 4-3, 4-7, 5-1, 5-2, 5-3, 5-5, 5-6, 6-1, 6-2, 6-3, 6-4, 6-5, 7-1, 7-5, 8-9, 9-1
CC.9-12.F.IF.3 Recognize that sequences are functions, sometimes defined recursively, whose domain is a subset of the integers.	Lessons 4-1, 5-1		Lesson 9-1
CC.9-12.F.IF.4 For a function that models a relationship between two quantities, interpret key features of graphs and tables in terms of the quantities, and sketch graphs showing key features given a verbal description of the relationship.*	Lessons 4-3, 4-4, 4-5, 5-3, 5-4, 6-1, 6-6, 7-1, 7-2, 7-3, 7-6, 8-8, 8-9, 8-10		Lessons 2-6, 3-11, 4-1, 4-2, 4-3, 4-7, 5-5, 5-6, 6-2, 6-3, 6-6, 7-5, 8-9
CC.9-12.F.IF.5 Relate the domain of a function to its graph and, where applicable, to the quantitative relationship it describes.*	Lessons 1-5, 1-6, 4-1, 4-2, 5-1, 5-2, 5-8, 6-1, 6-6, 7-1, 8-8		Lessons 2-6, 3-11
CC.9-12.F.IF.6 Calculate and interpret the average rate of change of a function (presented symbolically or as a table) over a specified interval. Estimate the rate of change from a graph.*	Lessons 4-3, 4-5, 8-10		Lessons 2-6
CC.9-12.F.IF.7 Graph functions expressed symbolically and show key features of the graph, by hand in simple cases and using technology for more complicated cases.* **a.** Graph linear and quadratic functions and show intercepts, maxima, and minima. **b.** Graph square root, cube root, and piecewise-defined functions, including step functions and absolute value functions. **c.** Graph polynomial functions, identifying zeros when suitable factorizations are available, and showing end behavior. **d.** (+) Graph rational functions, identifying zeros and asymptotes when suitable factorizations are available, and showing end behavior. **e.** Graph exponential and logarithmic functions, showing intercepts and end behavior, and trigonometric functions, showing period, midline, and amplitude.	Lessons 4-1, 4-3, 4-5, 5-1, 5-2, 5-3, 5-8, 6-1, 6-2, 6-3, 6-4, 6-6, 7-1, 7-2, 7-3, 8-8		Lessons 2-1, 2-2, 2-3, 2-4, 2-5, 2-6, 3-1, 3-2, 3-3, 3-4, 3-9, 3-11, 4-1, 4-2, 4-3, 4-7, 5-1, 5-2, 5-3, 5-4, 5-5, 5-6, 6-1, 6-2, 6-3, 6-4, 6-5, 6-6, 6-7, 7-1, 7-2, 8-5, 8-6, 8-7, 8-8, 8-9
CC.9-12.F.IF.8 Write a function defined by an expression in different but equivalent forms to reveal and explain different properties of the function. **a.** Use the process of factoring and completing the square in a quadratic function to show zeros, extreme values, and symmetry of the graph, and interpret these in terms of a context. **b.** Use the properties of exponents to interpret expressions for exponential functions.	Lessons 8-2, 8-3, 8-8, 8-10		Lessons 2-4, 2-5, 6-4, 6-6
CC.9-12.F.IF.9 Compare properties of two functions each represented in a different way (algebraically, graphically, numerically in tables, or by verbal descriptions).	Lessons 4-2, 8-10		Lesson 4-7

(+) Advanced   * = Also a Modeling Standard

Standards	Algebra 1	Geometry	Algebra 2
Building Functions			
CC.9-12.F.BF.1 Write a function that describes a relationship between two quantities.* a. Determine an explicit expression, a recursive process, or steps for calculation from a context. b. Combine standard function types using arithmetic operations. c. (+) Compose functions.	Lessons 1-6, 2-3, 2-8, 4-5, 4-6, 4-9, 5-5, 5-6, 5-8, 6-1, 6-2, 6-3, 6-4, 6-6, 7-1, 7-2, 7-3, 7-6, 8-3, 8-8, 8-10		Lessons 2-6, 3-5, 3-11, 4-1, 4-2, 4-3, 4-4, 4-5, 4-7, 5-5, 5-6, 6-2, 6-3, 6-4, 6-6, 7-5, 8-9, 9-1, 9-2, 9-3
CC.9-12.F.BF.2 Write arithmetic and geometric sequences both recursively and with an explicit formula, use them to model situations, and translate between the two forms.*	Lesson 4-1		Lessons 9-2, 9-3
CC.9-12.F.BF.3 Identify the effect on the graph of replacing $f(x)$ by $f(x) + k$, $kf(x)$, $f(kx)$, and $f(x + k)$ for specific values of k (both positive and negative); find the value of k given the graphs. Experiment with cases and illustrate an explanation of the effects on the graph using technology.	Lessons 4-4, 5-4, 6-2, 6-3, 6-4, 7-1, 7-2, 7-3		Lessons 2-1, 2-2, 2-3, 3-1, 3-2, 3-3, 4-1, 4-2, 5-4, 6-2, 6-3, 6-4, 6-5, 7-2, 8-7, 8-8, 8-9
CC.9-12.F.BF.4 Find inverse functions. a. Solve an equation of the form $f(x) = c$ for a simple function f that has an inverse and write an expression for the inverse. b. (+) Verify by composition that one function is the inverse of another. c. (+) Read values of an inverse function from a graph or a table, given that the function has an inverse. d. (+) Produce an invertible function from a non-invertible function by restricting the domain.	Lesson 4-7		Lessons 5-1, 5-2, 5-3, 5-5, 5-6
CC.9-12.F.BF.5(+) Understand the inverse relationship between exponents and logarithms and use this relationship to solve problems involving logarithms and exponents.			Lessons 7-1, 7-3
Linear, Quadratic, and Exponential Models			
CC.9-12.F.LE.1 Distinguish between situations that can be modeled with linear functions and with exponential functions.* a. Prove that linear functions grow by equal differences over equal intervals, and that exponential functions grow by equal factors over equal intervals. b. Recognize situations in which one quantity changes at a constant rate per unit interval relative to another. c. Recognize situations in which a quantity grows or decays by a constant percent rate per unit interval relative to another.	Lessons 5-2, 5-3, 5-6, 5-7, 5-8		
CC.9-12.F.LE.2 Construct linear and exponential functions, including arithmetic and geometric sequences, given a graph, a description of a relationship, or two input-output pairs (include reading these from a table).*	Lessons 4-5, 4-6, 5-1, 5-2, 5-3, 5-5, 5-8		Lessons 6-2, 6-3, 6-4, 6-5, 9-2, 9-3

(+) Advanced   * = Also a Modeling Standard

Standards	Algebra 1	Geometry	Algebra 2
CC.9-12.F.LE.3 Observe using graphs and tables that a quantity increasing exponentially eventually exceeds a quantity increasing linearly, quadratically, or (more generally) as a polynomial function.*	Lesson 5-7		Lessons 6-1, 6-6
CC.9-12.F.LE.4 For exponential models, express as a logarithm the solution to $ab^{ct} = d$ where a, c, and d are numbers and the base b is 2, 10, or e; evaluate the logarithm using technology.*			Lesson 7-4
CC.9-12.F.LE.5 Interpret the parameters in a linear or exponential function in terms of a context.*	Lessons 4-4, 4-5, 4-6, 4-9, 4-10, 5-2, 5-3, 5-6, 5-8		Lessons 6-4, 6-5
Trigonometric Functions			
CC.9-12.F.TF.1 Understand radian measure of an angle as the length of the arc on the unit circle subtended by the angle.			Lesson 8-2
CC.9-12.F.TF.2 Explain how the unit circle in the coordinate plane enables the extension of trigonometric functions to all real numbers, interpreted as radian measures of angles traversed counterclockwise around the unit circle.			Lesson 8-3
CC.9-12.F.TF.3(+) Use special triangles to determine geometrically the values of sine, cosine, tangent for $\pi/3$, $\pi/4$ and $\pi/6$, and use the unit circle to express the values of sine, cosines, and tangent for x, $\pi + x$, and $2\pi - x$ in terms of their values for x, where x is any real number.			Lesson 8-3
CC.9-12.F.TF.4(+) Use the unit circle to explain symmetry (odd and even) and periodicity of trigonometric functions.			Lessons 8-5, 8-6
CC.9-12.F.TF.5 Choose trigonometric functions to model periodic phenomena with specified amplitude, frequency, and midline.*			Lesson 8-9
CC.9-12.F.TF.8 Prove the Pythagorean identity $\sin^2(\theta) + \cos^2(\theta) = 1$ and use it to calculate trigonometric ratios.			Lesson 8-4
Geometry			
Congruence			
CC.9-12.G.CO.1 Know precise definitions of angle, circle, perpendicular line, parallel line, and line segment, based on the undefined notions of point, line, distance along a line, and distance around a circular arc.		Lessons 1-1, 1-4, 1-5, 9-4	
CC.9-12.G.CO.2 Represent transformations in the plane using, e.g., transparencies and geometry software; describe transformations as functions that take points in the plane as inputs and give other points as outputs. Compare transformations that preserve distance and angle to those that do not (e.g., translation versus horizontal stretch).		Lessons 2-1, 2-2, 2-3, 2-4, 2-5, 2-6, 5-1, 5-2	

(+) Advanced   * = Also a Modeling Standard

Standards	Algebra 1	Geometry	Algebra 2
CC.9-12.G.CO.3 Given a rectangle, parallelogram, trapezoid, or regular polygon, describe the rotations and reflections that carry it onto itself.		Lesson 4-1	
CC.9-12.G.CO.4 Develop definitions of rotations, reflections, and translations in terms of angles, circles, perpendicular lines, parallel lines, and line segments.		Lessons 2-2, 2-5, 2-6	
CC.9-12.G.CO.5 Given a geometric figure and a rotation, reflection, or translation, draw the transformed figure using, e.g., graph paper, tracing paper, or geometry software. Specify a sequence of transformations that will carry a given figure onto another.		Lessons 2-2, 2-5, 2-6, 3-1	
CC.9-12.G.CO.6 Use geometric descriptions of rigid motions to transform figures and to predict the effect of a given rigid motion on a given figure; given two figures, use the definition of congruence in terms of rigid motions to decide if they are congruent.		Lessons 2-2, 2-5, 2-6, 3-1	
CC.9-12.G.CO.7 Use the definition of congruence in terms of rigid motions to show that two triangles are congruent if and only if corresponding pairs of sides and corresponding pairs of angles are congruent.		Lessons 3-2, 3-3	
CC.9-12.G.CO.8 Explain how the criteria for triangle congruence (ASA, SAS, and SSS) follow from the definition of congruence in terms of rigid motions.		Lesson 3-3	
CC.9-12.G.CO.9 Prove geometric theorems about lines and angles.		Lessons 1-6, 1-7, 2-3, 2-4	
CC.9-12.G.CO.10 Prove theorems about triangles.		Lessons 3-5, 3-6, 3-7, 3-8, 3-9	
CC.9-12.G.CO.11 Prove theorems about parallelograms.		Lessons 4-2, 4-3, 4-4, 4-5	
CC.9-12.G.CO.12 Make formal geometric constructions with a variety of tools and methods (compass and straightedge, string, reflective devices, paper folding, dynamic geometry software, etc.).		Lessons 1-1, 1-4, 1-5	
CC.9-12.G.CO.13 Construct an equilateral triangle, a square, and a regular hexagon inscribed in a circle.		Lesson 7-3	
Similarity, Right Triangles, and Trigonometry			
CC.9-12.G.SRT.1 Verify experimentally the properties of dilations given by a center and a scale factor: **a.** A dilation takes a line not passing through the center of the dilation to a parallel line, and leaves a line passing through the center unchanged. **b.** The dilation of a line segment is longer or shorter in the ratio given by the scale factor.		Lesson 5-1	

(+) Advanced   * = Also a Modeling Standard

Standards	Algebra 1	Geometry	Algebra 2
CC.9-12.G.SRT.2 Given two figures, use the definition of similarity in terms of similarity transformations to decide if they are similar; explain using similarity transformations the meaning of similarity for triangles as the equality of all corresponding angles and the proportionality of all corresponding pairs of sides.		Lessons 5-3, 5-4	
CC.9-12.G.SRT.3 Use the properties of similarity transformations to establish the AA criterion for two triangles to be similar.		Lesson 5-4	
CC.9-12.G.SRT.4 Prove theorems about triangles.		Lessons 5-6, 5-7	
CC.9-12.G.SRT.5 Use congruence and similarity criteria for triangles to solve problems and prove relationships in geometric figures.		Lessons 3-4, 4-2, 4-3, 4-4, 4-5, 5-5, 5-6, 5-7	
CC.9-12.G.SRT.6 Understand that by similarity, side ratios in right triangles are properties of the angles in the triangle, leading to definitions of trigonometric ratios for acute angles.		Lessons 6-1, 6-2, 6-3	
CC.9-12.G.SRT.7 Explain and use the relationship between the sine and cosine of complementary angles.		Lessons 6-2, 6-3	
CC.9-12.G.SRT.8 Use trigonometric ratios and the Pythagorean Theorem to solve right triangles in applied problems.		Lesson 6-4	
CC.9-12.G.SRT.9(+) Derive the formula $A = 1/2\ ab \sin(C)$ for the area of a triangle by drawing an auxiliary line from a vertex perpendicular to the opposite side.		Lesson 6-5	
CC.9-12.G.SRT.10(+) Prove the Laws of Sines and Cosines and use them to solve problems.		Lessons 6-6, 6-7	
CC.9-12.G.SRT.11(+) Understand and apply the Law of Sines and the Law of Cosines to find unknown measurements in right and non-right triangles (e.g., surveying problems, resultant forces).		Lessons 6-6, 6-7	
Circles			
CC.9-12.G.C.1 Prove that all circles are similar.		Lesson 5-3	
CC.9-12.G.C.2 Identify and describe relationships among inscribed angles, radii, and chords.		Lessons 7-1, 7-5	
CC.9-12.G.C.3 Construct the inscribed and circumscribed circles of a triangle, and prove properties of angles for a quadrilateral inscribed in a circle.		Lessons 7-2, 7-4, 7-6	
CC.9-12.G.C.4(+) Construct a tangent line from a point outside a given circle to the circle.		Lesson 7-5	

(+) Advanced   * = Also a Modeling Standard

Standards	Algebra 1	Geometry	Algebra 2
CC.9-12.G.C.5 Derive using similarity the fact that the length of the arc intercepted by an angle is proportional to the radius, and define the radian measure of the angle as the constant of proportionality; derive the formula for the area of a sector.		**Lessons 9-4, 9-5**	Lesson 8-1
Expressing Geometric Properties with Equations			
CC.9-12.G.GPE.1 Derive the equation of a circle of given center and radius using the Pythagorean Theorem; complete the square to find the center and radius of a circle given by an equation.		**Lesson 8-1**	
CC.9-12.G.GPE.2 Derive the equation of a parabola given a focus and directrix.		**Lesson 8-2**	
CC.9-12.G.GPE.4 Use coordinates to prove simple geometric theorems algebraically.		**Lessons 1-2, 1-3, 3-7, 3-8, 3-9, 8-1, 8-6**	
CC.9-12.G.GPE.5 Prove the slope criteria for parallel and perpendicular lines and use them to solve geometric problems (e.g., find the equation of line parallel or perpendicular to a given line that passes through a given point).		**Lessons 8-4, 8-5**	
CC.9-12.G.GPE.6 Find the point on a directed line segment between two given points that partitions the segment in a given ratio.		**Lesson 8-3**	
CC.9-12.G.GPE.7 Use coordinates to compute perimeters of polygons and areas of triangles and rectangles, e.g., using the distance formula.*		**Lesson 9-2**	
Geometric Measurement and Dimension			
CC.9-12.G.GMD.1 Give an informal argument for the formulas for the circumference of a circle, area of a circle, volume of a cylinder, pyramid, and cone.		**Lessons 9-3, 9-5, 10-2, 10-3, 10-4**	
CC.9-12.G.GMD.2(+) Give an informal argument using Cavalieri's principle for the formulas for the volume of a sphere and other solid figures.		**Lessons 10-2, 10-5**	
CC.9-12.G.GMD.3 Use volume formulas for cylinders, pyramids, cones, and spheres to solve problems.*		**Lessons 10-2, 10-3, 10-4, 10-5, 10-6**	
CC.9-12.G.GMD.4 Identify the shapes of two-dimensional cross-sections of three-dimensional objects, and identify three-dimensional objects generated by rotations of two-dimensional objects.		**Lesson 10-1**	

(+) Advanced   * = Also a Modeling Standard

Standards	Algebra 1	Geometry	Algebra 2
Modeling with Geometry			
CC.9-12.G.MG.1 Use geometric shapes, their measures, and their properties to describe objects (e.g., modeling a tree trunk or a human torso as a cylinder).*		Lessons 9-2, 9-3, 10-2	
CC.9-12.G.MG.2 Apply concepts of density based on area and volume in modeling situations (e.g., persons per square mile, BTUs per cubic foot).*		Lessons 9-2, 10-2, 10-5	
CC.9-12.G.MG.3 Apply geometric methods to solve design problems (e.g., designing an object or structure to satisfy physical constraints or minimize cost; working with typographic grid systems based on ratios).*		Lessons 5-5, 10-6	
Statistics and Probability			
Interpreting Categorical and Quantitative Data			
CC.9-12.S.ID.1 Represent data with plots on the real number line (dot plots, histograms, and box plots).*	Lessons 9-2, 9-3, 9-4		Lessons 10-2, 10-3
CC.9-12.S.ID.2 Use statistics appropriate to the shape of the data distribution to compare center (median, mean) and spread (interquartile range, standard deviation) of two or more different data sets.*	Lessons 9-1, 9-2, 9-3, 9-4		
CC.9-12.S.ID.3 Interpret differences in shape, center, and spread in the context of the data sets, accounting for possible effects of extreme data points (outliers).*	Lesson 9-2		Lesson 10-2
CC.9-12.S.ID.4 Use the mean and standard deviation of a data set to fit it to a normal distribution and to estimate population percentages. Recognize that there are data sets for which such a procedure is not appropriate. Use calculators, spreadsheets, and tables to estimate areas under the normal curve.*			Lesson 10-4
CC.9-12.S.ID.5 Summarize categorical data for two categories in two-way frequency tables. Interpret relative frequencies in the context of the data (including joint, marginal, and conditional relative frequencies). Recognize possible associations and trends in the data.*	Lesson 9-5		
CC.9-12.S.ID.6 Represent data on two quantitative variables on a scatter plot, and describe how the variables are related.* a. Fit a function to the data; use functions fitted to data to solve problems in the context of the data. b. Informally assess the fit of a function by plotting and analyzing residuals. c. Fit a linear function for a scatter plot that suggests a linear association.	Lessons 4-9, 4-10, 5-6, 5-8		Lessons 5-5, 5-6, 6-6

(+) Advanced   * = Also a Modeling Standard

Standards	Algebra 1	Geometry	Algebra 2
CC.9-12.S.ID.7 Interpret the slope (rate of change) and the intercept (constant term) of a linear model in the context of the data.*	Lessons 4-9, 4-10		
CC.9-12.S.ID.8 Compute (using technology) and interpret the correlation coefficient of a linear fit.*	Lessons 4-8, 4-10		
CC.9-12.S.ID.9 Distinguish between correlation and causation.*	Lesson 4-8		
Making Inferences and Justifying Conclusions			
CC.9-12.S.IC.1 Understand statistics as a process for making inferences about population parameters based on a random sample from that population.*			Lesson 10-1
CC.9-12.S.IC.2 Decide if a specified model is consistent with results from a given data-generating process, e.g., using simulation.*			Lesson 10-3
CC.9-12.S.IC.3 Recognize the purposes of and differences among sample surveys, experiments, and observational studies; explain how randomization relates to each.*			Lesson 10-7
CC.9-12.S.IC.4 Use data from a sample survey to estimate a population mean or proportion; develop a margin of error through the use of simulation models for random sampling.*			Lessons 10-5, 10-6
CC.9-12.S.IC.5 Use data from a randomized experiment to compare two treatments; use simulations to decide if differences between parameters are significant.*			Lesson 10-8
CC.9-12.S.IC.6 Evaluate reports based on data.*	Lesson 4-8		Lesson 10-7
Conditional Probability and the Rules of Probability			
CC.9-12.S.CP.1 Describe events as subsets of a sample space (the set of outcomes) using characteristics (or categories) of the outcomes, or as unions, intersections, or complements of other events ("or," "and," "not").*		**Lesson 11-1**	
CC.9-12.S.CP.2 Understand that two events A and B are independent if the probability of A and B occurring together is the product of their probabilities, and use this characterization to determine if they are independent.*		**Lesson 11-7**	
CC.9-12.S.CP.3 Understand the conditional probability of A given B as $P(A$ and $B)/P(B)$, and interpret independence of A and B as saying that the conditional probability of A given B is the same as the probability of A, and the conditional probability of B given A is the same as the probability of B.*		**Lessons 11-6, 11-7**	

(+) Advanced   * = Also a Modeling Standard

Standards	Algebra 1	Geometry	Algebra 2
CC.9-12.S.CP.4 Construct and interpret two-way frequency tables of data when two categories are associated with each object being classified. Use the two-way table as a sample space to decide if events are independent and to approximate conditional probabilities.*		**Lessons 11-6, 11-7, 11-10**	
CC.9-12.S.CP.5 Recognize and explain the concepts of conditional probability and independence in everyday language and everyday situations.*		**Lessons 11-6, 11-7**	
CC.9-12.S.CP.6 Find the conditional probability of A given B as the fraction of B's outcomes that also belong to A, and interpret the answer in terms of the model.*		**Lesson 11-6**	
CC.9-12.S.CP.7 Apply the Addition Rule, $P(A \text{ or } B) = P(A) + P(B) - P(A \text{ and } B)$, and interpret the answer in terms of the model.*		**Lesson 11-5**	
CC.9-12.S.CP.8(+) Apply the general Multiplication Rule in a uniform probability model, $P(A \text{ and } B) = P(A)P(B|A) = P(B)P(A|B)$, and interpret the answer in terms of the model.*		**Lesson 11-8**	
CC.9-12.S.CP.9(+) Use permutations and combinations to compute probabilities of compound events and solve problems.*		**Lessons 11-3, 11-4**	
Using Probability to Make Decisions			
CC.9-12.S.MD.6(+) Use probabilities to make fair decisions (e.g., drawing by lots, using a random number generator).*		**Lessons 11-2, 11-9**	
CC.9-12.S.MD.7(+) Analyze decisions and strategies using probability concepts (e.g., product testing, medical testing, pulling a hockey goalie at the end of a game).*		**Lesson 11-10**	

(+) Advanced   * = Also a Modeling Standard